CHILD PSYCHOLOGY TODAY

CHILD PSYCHOLOGY TODAY

Elizabeth Hall

Advisory Editors: Michael E. Lamb   Marion Perlmutter
                       University of Utah   *University of Minnesota*

RANDOM HOUSE
NEW YORK

First Edition
98765432
Copyright © 1982   by Random House, Inc.

Library of Congress Cataloging in Publication Data

Hall, Elizabeth, 1929-
     Child psychology today.

     Includes index.
     1. Child psychology.   I. Lamb, Michael E., 1953-   II. Perlmutter, Marion.   III. Title.
BF721.H2175   155.4   81-15848
ISBN 0-394-32568-0   AACR2

Design: Levavi & Levavi

Cover Painting—"Child Wearing Red Scarf" by Édouard Vuillard. National Gallery of Art, Washington. Ailsa Mellon Bruce Collection.

Manufactured in the United States of America

Preface

Developmental psychologists are divided about how to teach developmental psychology. Some focus on the whole person, looking simultaneously at all aspects of development, progressing from birth onward. They prefer to use a book with a chronological organization. Others think it is more important to focus on processes, exploring a single domain over the life span before taking up another developmental process. As a result, these instructors prefer a book with a topical organization. Both approaches have their merits, but no single book can satisfy both groups.

One of the most popular texts is *Developmental Psychology Today*. It is widely respected as a well-researched and well-written book on life-span development, but it takes a chronological approach. Thus, many instructors who cover development on a topic-by-topic basis have been forced to rearrange the book in order to use it. Such a procedure can present problems, and many of these instructors have expressed the wish for a research-based, topic-oriented text that would hold their students' interest. In response to this need, we decided to prepare a topical version of *Developmental Psychology Today*.

As the book took shape, however, it became more than simply a reorganization of *Developmental Psychology Today*. Although it retains that text's firm basis in research and its readability, *Child Psychology Today* has additional strengths — strengths that derive from the expertise of our special consultants on the project, Dr. Marion Perlmutter and Dr. Michael Lamb, who understood the different kind of coverage required by a topical text.

Although the book is a collaborative effort, each consultant has primary responsibility for different sections. Marion Perlmutter is an associate professor of psychology at the University of Minnesota's Institute of Child Development and a recipient of a 1981 American Psychological Association's Boyd McCandless Young Scientist Award. She edited *Children's Memory*, in the *New Directions in Child Development* series. In shaping the coverage on cognitive development, Perlmutter contributed heavily to the chapter on brain development (Chapter 7), the language unit (Chapters 8 and 9), the unit on cognition (Chapters 10, 11, 12, and 13), and the chapter on social cognition (Chapter 19), as well as collaborating on the presentation of theory (Chapter 2). Her research with infants and young children has helped to change developmental psychology's approach to memory by showing that youngsters' recall is organized and that in their daily lives infants demonstrate recall capabilities that escape laboratory inspection.

Michael Lamb, who is professor of psychology and research professor of pediatrics at the University of Utah, has received both a 1976 American Psychological Association Young Psychologist Award and the 1978 Boyd Mc-Candless Young Scientist Award for Contributions to Developmental Psychology from APA's Division on Developmental Psychology. He is the editor of *The Role of the Father in Child Development*, of *Social and Personality Development*, and of *Nontraditional Families: Parenting and Childrearing*, as well as co-editor of *Infant Social Cognition: Theoretical and Empirical Considerations*. In shaping the sections on personality and social development, Lamb contributed to the introductory unit (Chapters 1, 2, and 3), the neonatal unit (Chapters 4 and 5), the chapter on physical development (Chapter 6), the unit on social and personality development (Chapters 14, 15, 16, and 17), and the chapter on moral development (Chapter 18). Lamb's studies of the role and influence of the father helped break the limited focus of developmental psychology on the mother-infant dyad.

Building on the content of *Developmental Psychology Today*, Perlmutter and Lamb added new aspects to its coverage of development through adolescence. As instructors who use the topical approach realize, a presentation of the content of development within a topical framework allows us to keep in sight the long-term, continuous processes that are the heart of developmental psychology, thereby making the early basis of later development clear. The discussion of personality development in infancy, for example (Chapter 14), attempts to show how infancy relates to later development rather than

treating infancy as a stage of life. The treatment delves into the important influences on the infant and shows *why* they are important. It looks at the way later personality emerges from infancy.

We found that arranging the story of development in a topical manner has other advantages. When a single topic is followed from infancy through adolescence, similarities as well as differences can be discussed without producing a redundant coverage. In addition, by placing the primary focus on aspects of development instead of on agencies of influence (such as the school), our account becomes more coherent and even less redundant.

The topical approach also permitted us to explore each topic more deeply, focusing on theory. And with an increased concentration on theory, findings can be discussed in the context of their implications so that the *whys* of development become clearer. Despite the book's emphasis on theory, the text is written with the assumption that students have no prior acquaintance with psychology. Theory, findings, and interpretations are explained clearly so that students at all levels can understand them.

In treating theory, we have provided a fairly eclectic account, considering a number of theories and showing how each is useful and how each can explain certain aspects of development. This book presents the organismic, psychodynamic, and learning theories that have dominated the field of developmental psychology, but it discusses other approaches as well. Ethology, with its emphasis on our common heritage as members of the human species is presented and given special emphasis in the discussion of attachment. The coverage of cognitive development adds to the customary consideration of Piagetian views, including a thorough discussion of information-processing and its application to all cognitive processes: perception, attention, memory, and thought. Finally, development is approached from the position of dialectical psychology, a view that is rarely mentioned in introductory texts despite the fact that much developmental research has been influenced by it.

The book's dominant theme is interaction. Throughout the text, interaction is stressed on two levels: first, the interplay of cognitive development, heredity, and experience; and second, the interaction between the growing child and other people. Always the stress is on the point that influence continually runs two ways: the child affects parents, siblings, and peers at the same time that these people affect the child. In Chapter 18, for example, research is presented that shows how a child's actions can evoke the kind of discipline a parent uses.

Indeed, throughout the book the emphasis is on research. As students follow the development of each topic area, they are introduced to research that supports the facts presented or the conclusions drawn. They learn not only what researchers in child development know about child development but how they have come to know it.

This book differs from other topical texts in developmental psychology in the topics selected for chapter-length consideration:

- An entire chapter on brain development (Chapter 7) discusses traditional views of brain development in the light of new, contradictory research and presents a rigorous treatment of the research in hemispheric specialization.

- Allocating a full chapter to intelligence (Chapter 13) permits a discussion that goes beyond the traditional psychometric perspective to explore biological, cognitive, and information-processing views of intelligence. In addition to the expected discussion of what IQ tests can and cannot do, there is an explanation of the links between IQ and school success, success in life, and creativity—and *why* the link appears when it does. There is also a lengthy treatment of the way heredity, health, nutrition, and environment interact to affect both intelligence and IQ scores.

- A chapter on sex-role development (Chapter 17) allows us to place sex-roles within the context of the life span, showing how their influence alternately tightens and loosens.

- A chapter on social cognition (Chapter 19) attempts to show how understanding of others and of society grows naturally out of self-concept and the separation of self and world.

- By devoting two chapters instead of one to language (Chapters 8 and 9), we have been able to present new trends in the study and theory of language development without slighting the coverage of syntax and phonology. We have provided a full account of the increased emphasis on the role of meaning in children's speech and of research in pragmatics, which reveals the intimate connection between language acquisition and social interaction.

- Consistent with this book's emphasis on process, aspects of abnormal development are considered in the context of topical areas. Brain development provides a framework for the discussion of hyperactivity and developmental dyslexia; peer relationships a framework for the discussion of social isolation; moral development a framework for the discussion of empathy in emotionally disturbed children; physical development a framework for the discussion of Sudden Infant Death Syndrome; perception a framework for the discussion of blind and deaf children; family influence a framework for the discussion of child abuse; and attachment, for Down's syndrome.

Covering the development of both sexes in the face of a sexist language can be a problem. We have chosen to eliminate English's emphasis on the male by using plural subjects as often as possible and at other times have resorted to the admittedly ungraceful "his or her," "girl or boy" approach. A further, less obvious but we hope more telling, strike against sexism has been the retention of a practice begun by *Developmental Psychology Today* of giving the full names of researchers whenever experiments are discussed in detail. This is done neither to flatter the investigators mentioned nor to add to the names students must remember, but to point out—without making an issue of it—that men have no monopoly on the field of developmental psychology and that much of the important research has come from women.

Elizabeth Hall

ACKNOWLEDGMENTS

That this book ever rolled off the press is due in great part to the skill and effort of the editorial staff members at Random House. Many have played a role: Virginia Hoitsma, the editor who first approached the three of us to collaborate on the project; Judith Kromm, the editor whose careful readings led to many helpful suggestions; Anna Marie Muskelly, the editor who meticulously supervised the copy-editing and production processes; Evelyn Katrak, a most capable copy editor; and Lynn Goldberg, in-house photo editor.

The final manuscript of this book was enormously improved by suggestions from a number of academic reviewers, including Harriett Amster, University of Texas, Arlington; Frank R. Ascione, Utah State University, Logan; Marvin W. Daehler, University of Massachusetts, Amherst; Philip S. Dale, University of Washington, Seattle; Michael S. Gazzaniga, Department of Neurology, Division of Cognitive Neuroscience, The New York Hospital Cornell Medical Center; Mark T. Greenberg, University of Washington, Seattle; David T. Hakes, University of Texas, Austin; Sharon Herzberger, Trinity College, Hartford; Dr. Stan A. Kuczaj, Southern Methodist University; Kathleen A. Lawler, University of Tennessee, Knoxville; Marigold Linton, University of Utah, Salt Lake City; Robert B. McCall, Senior Scientist and Science Writer, Boystown; Dennis Molfese, Southern Illinois University, Carbondale; Victoria Molfese, Southern Illinois University, Carbondale; Nora Newcombe, Temple University; Lila Tabor, University of North Dakota, Grand Forks; and Thomas Trabasso, The University of Chicago.

And very special thanks to Scott, whose cup of patience never ran dry.

E.H.

Contents

CHILD
PSYCHOLOGY
TODAY

PART 1

The Meaning of Development

Babies grow into adult human beings. But a person watching a baby boy gazing intently at his fist cannot possibly predict whether the adult that infant becomes will be honest or dishonest, rash or careful, confident or insecure. Developmental psychologists attempt to describe how the baby develops into an adult and to explain why he develops into one kind of adult and not another. Heredity, culture, and personal experience all play a part in that development, and different psychologists have explained their influences in different ways. When you have finished Part 1, you will begin to see that no one approach can answer every question and that there is more than one path to the study of human development.

The Concept of Development

Only two hundred years ago people did not know that a human being developed from a fertilized cell. Most biologists believed that a preformed infant existed in either the mother's egg or the father's sperm. Those who contended the infant was in the egg said that the sperm simply stimulated the baby's growth. Those who argued that the infant was in the sperm maintained that the mother's role was to serve as an incubator. It was not until the middle of the eighteenth century that any scientist suggested that each human being began as a cluster of cells, and it was another fifty years before the theory was verified by the microscopic discovery of the mammalian egg cell. Today we can describe the development of the fertilized egg into a baby and the baby's development into an adult. But despite centuries of effort, we cannot say precisely how two babies, born within minutes of each other in the same hospital, become such radically different people.

Developmental psychologists, whose aim is to understand the processes involved in changes over the life span, are attempting to solve the puzzle. They have come to realize that human development is the result of a complex interaction among multiple influences. The interaction begins at conception and continues until the end of life. Investigators are beginning to understand how biological and cultural determinants interact to produce development and to realize that these forces are neither haphazard nor static, but are organized and continually changing.

Although development takes place at all ages, we shall limit our exploration to that portion of the life span from conception to adolescence.

This is a period of rapid development, and changes can be measured in a relatively short period. Psychologists who study the developing child explore the ways in which children's physical growth and intellectual and social behavior change over time, and they seek to understand how growth and behavior relate to each other. In this first part of the book, we shall examine the entire field of developmental psychology in order to provide a context for the study of development during childhood and adolescence.

In this chapter, we shall see how the concept of childhood emerged as a separate stage of life and how the social and economic structure of a society shapes the way its members view the life span. We shall discover that developmental psychology has disparate origins in nineteenth-century baby biographies, in evolutionary views of development, in mental testing, and in experimental psychology, child-guidance clinics, and institutes for child study, where long-term studies of individuals began. We shall learn that development is an orderly, usually increasing, and ever more complex change in a consistent direction; and that developmental psychology draws on different disciplines, different types of information, and different levels of explanation to describe that change. We shall discover that research-based statements explaining average development may not always predict the behavior of some individuals. In addition, we shall find that developmental psychology explores questions that bear directly on the lives of every one of us. Finally, we shall become familiar with the method of approaching child development that is followed in all the future discussions in this book.

HISTORICAL BACKGROUND

In the Middle Ages, childhood as we know it did not exist. According to Philippe Ariès 1962), there was a period of infancy, which lasted until a child was about seven years old. From that time on, however, people we would consider children were simply assimilated into the adult world. The art and social documents of the Middle Ages show children and adults mingling together in one unified community, wearing the same clothes and performing the same functions. Society made no distinction among them on the basis of age or phase of psychological development.

Today we take the periods of childhood, adolescence, adulthood, and late adulthood for granted, and we divide development into phases that are marked by *social* events: the beginning of meaningful speech (the end of infancy and the start of childhood, at about the age of two); the assumption of adult roles in employment, marriage, and reproduction (the end of adolescence and the start of adulthood, in the early twenties for many people); the loss of roles involved in retirement from work (the onset of late adulthood, generally in the sixties or early seventies). Other markers we attach to the life span are *biological:* birth (the end of the prenatal period and the start of infancy) and reproductive maturity at puberty (the end of childhood and the start of adolescence). We are not consistent in our choice of markers; nor are the markers we use to divide up the life span by any means universal. Other contemporary societies divide life into three periods—such as infancy, childhood, and adulthood—or only two—infancy and adulthood (Mead, 1968).

The way in which people in a society view the life span depends largely on that society's social and economic system. If the preparation for adult roles is gradual and continuous from early childhood and if the necessary technology can be acquired by apprenticeship, then adulthood is likely to begin shortly after a person reaches reproductive maturity. On the other hand, if full participation in the economic system depends on years of technical education, a period of adolescence is likely to be recognized. But that recognition cannot take place if the society cannot afford to support the additional stage.

Toward the end of the life span, when their participation in the economic system becomes less active, older adults may be forced to retire from their jobs, creating a period that some call "old age." This loss of social and economic roles can drastically change the experience of later adulthood.

The Emergence of Childhood

It was only in the seventeenth and eighteenth centuries that the concept of childhood as a separate stage of life evolved. A new and sentimental view of childhood sprang up, along with new theories of education that were concerned with promoting children's moral and intellectual development, protecting them from the evils and corruptions of adult society, and preserving their real or imagined childhood virtues.

From historical evidence, it seems clear that childhood became a separate stage of life in Europe and North America only when large numbers of people entered the middle class, the amount of leisure time increased, and the rate of infant mortality decreased. As the middle class prospered, there was less need for their children to work in order to ensure the family's economic survival. The lowered rate of childhood mortality meant that more children would live to reach puberty; therefore, parents were less fearful of losing a child to disease. And the new mercantile capitalism required that a larger portion of the citizenry be literate and fluent with numbers; thus more children had to go to school.

Ariès' analysis of the emerging concept of childhood has had far-reaching implications for understanding the relationship between historical change and psychological development. Ariès has spoken explicitly about the changing concepts of childhood; but historically the experience of childhood has changed as well. According to Lloyd DeMause (1974), infanticide was common during antiquity; the usual victims were babies with birth defects, girl babies,

and illegitimate babies. The practice continued, and during the Middle Ages many of the children who were permitted to live, died before the age of six, victims of disease, neglect, or child abuse.

In many European societies, family life as we know it hardly existed before the eighteenth century. Among all but the poorest families, children spent the first few years away from their parents, living with wet-nurses. As late as 1780, only 1,400 of the 21,000 children born in Paris remained with their own parents (DeMause, 1974). Children returned home from the wet-nurse some time between the ages of two and five, only to be apprenticed out or put

By the seventeenth century, the concept of childhood had begun to emerge. Although little girls still dressed like miniature women, little boys wore a long robe that distinguished them from adults. (Peter Paul Rubens, "Deborah Kip, Wife of Sir Balthasar Gerbier and Her Children." Courtesy, The National Gallery of Art, Andrew W. Mellon Fund, 1971)

to work by the time they were seven. Parents and masters often treated children with what we would consider a shocking lack of tenderness, protectiveness, attention, and care. Child abuse was widespread, even casual, and most advice on child rearing recommended severe beatings as the way to inculcate discipline. Parents seem to have invested little emotional energy in their children; children were not regarded as very important.

The experience of childhood has been strongly affected by society's need for schooled workers. During the Middle Ages, the minimal schooling required to become a priest or clerk was received in ungraded schools, where children, adolescents, and adults learned together. As the concept of childhood began to emerge, schools came to be graded by age, and both the average length of schooling and the number of children who received formal education increased. This meant that an ever larger proportion of those between the ages of six and fourteen were segregated into schools. Such segregation sheltered children from the demands of adult work. They found new freedom to play and to experiment, and had systematic opportunities to develop new interpersonal and technical skills.

In Western industrialized societies, the segregation of childhood is now virtually complete, but only in this century has it finally been extended to the working and lower classes. The mark of this full institutionalization of childhood is universal primary education. It has taken four centuries for us to move from an era in which childhood was unrecognized to an era in which we take it completely for granted and protect it with an array of legal, social, and educational institutions.

The Emergence of Adolescence

The concept of adolescence is of more recent origin—although adolescence as a stage of psychological growth existed before society formulated the concept. In previous centuries, many men and women passed through what would now be recognized as an adolescent experience. But it was only after childhood had been marked off from adulthood that adolescence could be interposed between them as the period between reproductive maturity and the assumption of adult responsibilities. In early Western societies, therefore, biological maturation largely went unmarked. When children were considered neither innocent nor importantly different from adults, the fact of puberty constituted neither a fall from innocence nor a change in status, and it had little special meaning.

The official emergence of adolescence was made possible by social, economic, and historical changes. Increasing industrialization freed most young people from the requirements of farm and factory labor. Indeed, rising standards of economic productivity made the adolescent, especially the uneducated adolescent, almost impossible to employ. New attitudes toward adolescence were expressed in laws that made full-time employment before the age of sixteen or eighteen illegal. Growing affluence provided most families and the larger society with the wealth needed to support these economically unproductive adolescents in school. All these changes have happened, on a mass scale, almost within living memory; most of our child labor laws were passed only in this century.

Today society sanctions and supports adolescence, buttressing it with education, familial, institutional, and economic resources. These new resources, coupled with other changes in society, have protected an ever larger proportion of young people from adult responsibilities and have given them the possibility of continuing psychological growth during the years from thirteen to eighteen.

However, such generalizations overlook certain pockets of poverty in the society. Among migratory farm laborers, for example, financial considerations force children and adolescents to work, in defiance of the law. And in the inner cities there is a large pool of young people whose

top—For centuries, children and adolescents worked as hard as adults. Not until this century were adolescents like this girl freed from the drudgery of factory labor and given the opportunity for continuing psychological growth. (Lewis W. Hine/National Archives)

bottom—An affluent society can afford to support a phase of adolescence, in which adult responsibilities are postponed in favor of a period of psychological growth. (© Stephen Shames 1980/Woodfin Camp & Assoc.)

parents lack the resources to keep them in school. These adolescents, whose youth and lack of education make them unemployable, have no income, nothing to fill their time, and limited prospects for the future.

Adulthood

Adulthood has always been recognized as the normal phase of human existence. Traditionally, since it has been seen as the goal of development, it has been the yardstick by which other stages of life have been measured.

But our concept of adulthood has itself changed. Instead of regarding the person on the threshold of adulthood as having completed the course of human development, we now see the adult as a person who continues to develop. If the development goes on successfully, the person becomes mature. The mature adult makes commitments, takes on responsibilities, can relate intimately to another person, is productive, and can devote him- or herself to the welfare of others. Maturity also includes an awareness and realistic acceptance of the changes in life during the passage from young to middle adulthood. And it is during the middle years that people must cope with the realization that life will end.

The Emergence of Late Adulthood

Until this century, most people died before they reached their seventies. Today, ten out of every hundred Americans is more than sixty-five years old; and once that marker is reached, a man can expect to live to seventy-nine, a woman to eighty-three. In some societies older adults are regarded as wise, experienced advisers. In the United States, however, many younger adults view older people as irrelevant. Because older adults acquired their experiences during an era that no longer exists, the young regard them as

outdated. And perhaps they also see them as an uncomfortable reminder of their own fate. Thus older adults, like children and adolescents, are sometimes encouraged to segregate themselves into special institutions and communities that keep them out of view and out of the minds of the younger members of society. Such segregation results in many problems for the old and many losses for the young.

However, the experience of later adulthood has changed greatly. In past centuries, old age started early in life; before the eighteenth century, a person of fifty or sixty was regarded as doddering (Ariès, 1962). The concept of "old age"—in which a person looks different and acts differently from the rest of society, becoming frail, invalided, and even senile—does not describe today's older adult. Most older adults now remain healthy, alert, and economically self-sufficient. The radical change has led researchers in the field of adult development to call such people "young-old," reserving the term "old-old" for the less than 15 percent of men and women over sixty-five who fit the stereotype of late adulthood (E. Hall, 1980).

THE EMERGENCE OF DEVELOPMENTAL PSYCHOLOGY

Developmental psychology, as the description and explanation of age-related changes in behavior over the life span, has only recently emerged as a separate branch of general psychology. Its origins go back to the turn of the century and to the development of various ways of studying the child. Later, after World War II, a spurt of studies on the problems connected with aging led to a concentration on the latter part of the life cycle. Finally, as the original subjects in studies that followed children over the years grew up, researchers became interested in the processes of adult development (Charles, 1970). Although most developmental psychol-

The experience of later adulthood has changed radically, and today many "young-old" people in their sixties and seventies—and beyond—are healthy, alert, and economically self-sufficient. (© Sherry Suris)

ogists focus on small sections of the life span, taken together their work is beginning to give us a clearer picture of the determinants and processes of development from birth to death.

One early influence on the study of child development came from the diaries kept by a number of ardent parents during the nineteenth century. Although these baby biographies were not objective or scientific descriptions, psychologists found them useful in describing sequences of development and differences among babies in the way they attained the various developmental milestones.

Another early influence came from the work of G. Stanley Hall, who established child and adolescent development as fields of study. Hall viewed development as being primarily determined by genetic and biological factors until adolescence, believing that from conception to birth, each developing individual passed through the evolutionary history of the species and that from birth to adolescence, each person repeated the social evolution of the species. This led him to suggest that efforts to curb the natural unruliness of children would be ineffectual until they were about twelve, when after allowing "the fundamental traits of savagery their fling," society could modify and control children's character (G. Hall, 1904). Hall supported his theories on human development by collecting information through questionnaires, and in 1904 he published an enormously influential two-volume work on adolescence.

Interest in developmental questions increased sharply when child-guidance and psychological clinics began to be founded early in the twentieth century (Sears, 1975). Such clinics represented popular acceptance of the idea that children should be helped with their emotional and intellectual problems in order to enable them to lead constructive lives. This movement also influenced the focus of developmental studies, because it shifted attention from the general development of the species that was Hall's concern to the interests of the individual child (Charles, 1970).

The mental-testing movement, which was pioneered by Lewis Terman, one of Hall's students, also influenced the study of development. Terman studied one thousand children, ranging in age from three to eighteen, and provided standards for mental development during childhood and adolescence. By testing the same children over a period of years, psychologists could study the patterns of mental development.

As educators became convinced that both the content of schooling and the ways in which children are taught must take into account the nature of the growing child, they demanded research that would establish the nature of the child's interests and capabilities (Charles, 1970). This demand led to an increase in experimental studies of children, giving rise to educational psychology, which under the influence of E. L.

Thorndike (1913) stressed the way that learning affects children's natural tendencies.

The influence of Thorndike, together with the early writings of J. B. Watson (1913), convinced both researchers and the general public that the scientific study and explanation of behavior was within grasp (Charles, 1970). Like Thorndike, Watson believed in the primacy of learning, and his research focused on the process of *conditioning*, a form of learning in which a person comes to respond in a specific manner to a specific object, action, or situation. As a result of public confidence, a number of child-development research centers were established at major universities across the country. These institutes were set up to carry out research, to teach, and to disseminate information on child development. They investigated all aspects of children's development and welfare, and their shared goal was to acquire a comprehensive understanding of development that could be used to help children and those who care for them. Many of these institutes are still active.

At some of these research centers, studies of behavior over the life span were begun. At the University of California, for example, babies born in 1928 and 1929 were enrolled in a study of physical and intellectual development that still continues. At Fels Research Institute in Ohio, each year since 1929 another small group of infants has been added to a long-term study of intellectual and personality development. And at Stanford University, 1,500 gifted California children identified by intelligence testing have been followed since 1921, with investigators studying all phases of their development.

Although major research had been done on the psychological aspects of aging as early as 1928, it was not until after World War II that the study of aging caught the interest of many psychologists. In 1943, a committee on social adjustment in old age was formed at the University of Chicago; and during the postwar period, centers to study the effects of aging and the developmental tasks faced by older people were established at universities in many states.

Research on the latter half of the life cycle expanded so much that James Birren (1961) has reported that more research was published in the decade of the 1950s than during the previous 115 years.

In the past twenty-five years, there has been a decided shift in the emphasis of developmental psychologists. They have moved from describing what people do at specific periods in life to emphasizing how circumstances affect what they do at different periods and what kind of sequence takes place in development. Along with this shift has come an increased interest in the intellectual aspects of development and a greater appreciation of differences among individuals.

STUDYING HUMAN DEVELOPMENT

When students enroll in a course on developmental psychology, they may first want to know *when* children develop certain skills and abilities. They may want a description of *what* behavior is typical of children at various ages. Most students think of developmental psychology as a source of data about average development. When should children know their colors? When does the adolescent growth spurt begin? What differences are there in the IQ scores of children from different ethnic and socioeconomic backgrounds? These expectations are not wrong; developmental psychology does answer many questions about the sequence and timing of human development. But more interesting than descriptive questions are questions that ask how and why development occurs as it does. Why do most children know primary color names by kindergarten? (Why not earlier or later?) Why does the adolescent growth spurt begin and then end so regularly? Why do children differ in IQ scores? And so forth.

Questions about the hows and whys of development give us a sound basis for explaining changes in human behavior across the life span.

In order to understand the way human beings change, we first must gather accurate and detailed descriptions of those changes. On the basis of these descriptions, we can attempt to explain the changes. If our observations and explanations are accurate enough, the theories we develop will allow us to predict behavior. And once prediction is probable, a certain degree of control becomes possible.

Describing Human Development

Human development is reflected in behavioral change. A *behavior* is an observable act that can be described or measured reliably; and *reliability* means that two or more observations of the same act will yield the same information. Behavior can be measured in many ways — sometimes simply by watching, at other times by using instruments of various kinds, such as questionnaires, films of children's interactions, or devices that record heart rates. The behavior that is seen, heard, or measured serves as a window through which psychologists can analyze children's or adults' underlying competencies, motives, and emotions. Since studying all possible human behavior is obviously impossible, and selecting any behavior at random has little purpose, psychologists select for detailed study behavior that is important for theoretical or practical reasons.

THE NATURE OF DEVELOPMENT Normal infants grow first into children and then into adults, and this progression implies several characteristics about developmental change: (1) it is orderly, (2) it is directional, (3) it is to a large extent cumulative, and (4) it is characterized by increasing differentiation and complexity of organization.

The changes in behavior over the life span are neither accidental nor random. There is an orderly sequence to behavioral development,

whether we talk about language acquisition, social play, or moral judgment. Each kind of behavior can be described in a series of developmental steps, and before any behavior — whether pertaining to thought processes, language, perception, social interaction, or personality — can be explained, it is necessary to specify the exact nature of its sequence.

For example, the sequence of language acquisition is orderly, directional, and predictable. When children first use words, around eleven to fourteen months of age, they typically use one word at a time. Later, at about twenty-one to twenty-four months, they begin to put two or three words together. By three to three and a half years, most children use complex sentences and can tell brief stories. But no child begins by speaking in sentences and then develops to a one-word phase.

The same sort of orderly, predictable development occurs in social play. Nine-month-olds hardly notice each other, whereas preschool children generally play together and enjoy each other's actions. By the early school years, most children interact in games that have specific rules and that require each child to play a role. The sequence is the same for all children.

Sequences of development often proceed from simple, global behaviors to increasingly complex but integrated sets of behaviors. For example, the moral judgments of young children are often based on global concepts of "right" and "wrong." Their ideas of rightness and wrongness depend more on the outcome of an act than on the intentions of the actor. A child of four or five may feel that a boy who breaks a cookie jar in the act of stealing a cookie is no worse than another who breaks the jar while reaching for a cookie his mother told him to get. In both cases the boy broke the cookie jar. But most older children and adults would separate the two cases and base their moral judgments on the boys' intentions. Older children can also differentiate shades of wrongdoing. Many adolescents and adults base specific moral judgments on complex ideals they have abstracted from experience in concrete situations. The development of moral judgment closely parallels other changes in children's thinking, which becomes more hypothetical from childhood to maturity.

TYPES OF KNOWLEDGE
Most developmental psychologists gather four types of information: Type 1—on behavior at different ages; Type 2—on behavioral change as people grow older; Type 3—on environmental events that influence behavior; and Type 4—on variations among individuals in their development. These four kinds of information make up most of the knowledge in developmental psychology.

The following descriptions of sucking patterns show how information of all four types may be gathered on a single topic. Lewis Lipsitt (1967a) and Arnold Sameroff (1968) have discovered that all normal newborns show the same components of sucking, which they combine in a rhythmic alternation of bursts and rests (Type 1 information). Additional descriptions of sucking in one-month-olds indicate the changes that occur with increasing maturity and experience (Type 2 information). Investigations of the effect of rewards on rates of sucking demonstrate that newborns will alter their sucking patterns to get sweetened water (Type 3 information). Finally, there are studies showing that individual babies have distinctive patterns of sucking, which, when recorded, identify them at least as well as their footprints; that is, the individual baby's sucking pattern is a kind of signature (Type 4 information). For example, all normal babies suck in bursts interrupted by rests, but individual babies have different numbers of sucks per burst and shorter or longer rests between them. The four types of knowledge are complementary, and each is valuable in its own way. No explanation of any behavior would be complete unless it took them all into account, for one type of information can affect the others. Experiences with sweetened water (Type 3), for example, might affect both the way a baby's sucking pattern changed with age

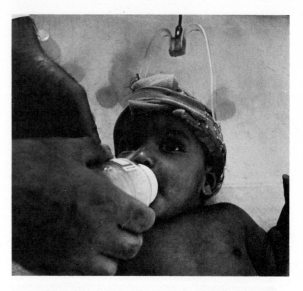

The sucking patterns of newborns show the four types of information used by developmental psychologists to explain behavior: the description of a specific behavior; its changes with age; its changes in response to the environment; and individual differences in its development. (Jason Lauré)

(Type 2) and the infant's signature pattern (Type 4).

Explaining Human Development

Studying developmental psychology provides new ways of looking at the development of human behavior. It is easy to view lower organisms with detachment, for their behavior is removed from anything we have experienced. It is more difficult to look at the behavior of a child in a similarly objective fashion. But a major message of developmental psychology is that human behavior has its antecedents and its consequences, that there is a regularity and a degree of lawfulness in development. With appropriate analysis and objective study, we can discover why certain types of behavior occur and how conditions may influence later behavior. Such explanations, which take the form of theories, must be careful to adopt an appropriate level of explanation, drawing on other disciplines when necessary and allowing for individual variations in behavior.

USE OF THEORY To explain how and why behavior develops, psychologists have constructed sets of logically related statements about the nature of development called *theories*. A theoretical statement is usually abstract and does not refer directly to what is observed. For example, Erik Erikson's (1963) theory of psychosocial development stipulates that the growing child faces a crisis at each stage of development, a crisis whose resolution will affect the way the child approaches the next stage. Erikson claims that young children around the ages of two to four need to develop *autonomy*, a feeling of self-control and self-determination. We cannot observe autonomy directly, but if Erikson is correct about the young child's need to direct his or her own behavior, we should see behavioral evidence, such as the two-year-old's emphatic "No" to parental requests, the verbal response "Me do it" to proffered help, the temper tantrums that sometimes occur when a child's goals are thwarted, and so forth. Erikson's theoretical statement about autonomy predicts such behavior.

Theories should lead to testable hypotheses or predictions about observable behavior. If the statements of a theory successfully predict a great deal of human behavior, then we say that the theory is a useful explanation of human development. Thus far, no theory has satisfactorily covered all aspects of human development. Instead, theories tend to be restricted to some part of development, such as social behavior, intellectual development, or language acquisition.

Like the rest of psychology, developmental psychology uses scientific methods and procedures to study human behavior. Researchers emphasize the testing of hypotheses derived from theories, using methods that other investigators can apply. If the studies are useful, they will lead to results that others can repeat and confirm. Simply describing the actions of children and adolescents does not adequately explain their behavior.

CONTRIBUTIONS OF OTHER DISCIPLINES Developmental psychologists depend on information about the individual's biological history and maturation, about the organization of his or her society, and about the influences of the culture — information that comes from other disciplines: biology, sociology, and anthropology. Such information is required to explain behavior because psychologists see the developing person as a changing system that integrates biological factors and experience. The kinds of experiences individuals have in growing up depend largely on the kind of family and society they live in (for example, how many brothers and sisters they have, how punitive their parents are, how the society divides people by age, what kinds of institutions exist) and on cultural values that distinguish right from wrong, good from bad. What individuals learn in the sociocultural context depends both on their readiness to learn and on the availability of materials and ideas. Additionally in the case of children, maturational level has a profound influence on what they notice in the world around them.

This interplay of information can be seen in the child's acquisition of language. The ability to learn a language is one of humankind's evolved characteristics. All normal members of the species learn to speak. But developmentalists know that children are not able to talk until they have attained a certain level of neurological development; no six-month-old child speaks in sentences (biological information). Nevertheless, a child living in a relatively unstimulating, unresponsive environment begins to speak later than a child reared in a more stimulating en vironment (sociological information). In the first case, the six-month-old child is not biologically ready to speak; in the second, the older child's world does not offer adequate speech models from which to learn. Nevertheless, all normal children in every society learn to speak the language of their cultural group at approximately the same age (anthropological information).

As the foregoing example shows, biologists have emphasized the importance of humanity's evolutionary history and provided detailed descriptions of embryological and later physical development, giving us models for understanding all development. The complex interaction of genetic and environmental influences across the life span, and from the level of the single cell to that of the whole organism, has made psychologists aware of the need to consider genetic and biological influences on human development. A child's temperament, height, or intelligence may show the influences of genes or of such physical factors as hormones, nutrition, or disease.

Sociologists and cultural anthropologists have emphasized the importance of understanding development within a sociocultural context. A child is always a member of a human group: a family, a neighborhood group, a school class, and so forth. This setting, whether the immediate circumstances or their longer-range memberships in various groups, influences most of children's behavior. As shown in the historical perspective on childhood and adolescence, the ways in which a culture interprets the life span can have profound influences on the expectations that others have for a person's behavior at different times in life.

LEVELS OF EXPLANATION Human development is determined by interaction among all levels of influence: psychological, biological, sociological, and anthropological. Adequate explanations of development demand that all be taken into consideration, but at specified times certain aspects of development may be more heavily affected by one level of influence than another.

Suppose that psychologists are trying to explain sex differences in aggression. A study emphasizing biological factors might indicate that male hormones explain why eight-year-old boys act more aggressively than girls. Such research would be criticized because it reduces the causes of complex behavior to a single explanation, relying on a single biological factor. The concentration of male hormones may contribute (greatly or little) to sex differences in behavior, but by itself, it cannot explain most observed differences. Many factors that do not involve hormones—such as different parental responses to boys and girls, different rewards for appropriate sex-role behavior, and so forth—may also play important roles in making boys more aggressive than girls. To explain observed differences in aggression, we must consider the effects of hormones along with other prenatal and postnatal differences in environment. In this example, hormones are only one component in the behavioral system; whether they are an important influence can be determined by research that varies hormones and rearing conditions separately (Money and Ehrhardt, 1972). But if one is attempting to explain sex differences in behavior among newborns in a hospital nursery, hormones might be expected to play a larger role—although not to the exclusion of the infants' prenatal environments and the circumstances of their deliveries. In the case of newborns, a biological level of explanation may help psychologists to look at an aspect of development in a new way. But focusing on any one influence—or even a pair of influences—can cause them to lose sight of the context in which all children live their lives. When drawing on findings from other fields, it is always essential to integrate the information into the picture of human development at the level at which behavior is influenced.

INDIVIDUAL VARIATION A major concern of developmental psychology is to understand the process that accounts for individual differences in behavior. Most research leads to general statements summarizing what was found to be true for the largest number of subjects or for the "average" subject in an experiment. But some children or adults in almost every experiment behave or develop in a way that is different from that of the majority. For example, William Rohwer's (1971) study of children's learning showed that categorically organized lists are easier to remember than randomly organized lists. That is, the list "car, boat, plane; chair, table, bed" is easier to remember than the list "car, bed, table; plane, chair, boat." Most elementary-school children will look at the first list and think "three things to ride in, three pieces of furniture," which helps them recall the individual items. Some children, however, do not use categories to help them remember and thus recall as few items from the first list as from the second.

Developmental psychologists acknowledge that the results shown for most people do not apply to all individuals. Thus one can say that elementary-school children are likely to use categories to help them remember lists, even if all children do not use that strategy. But individual differences are not simply annoyances that obscure the orderly, predictable behavior of a group. Differences may be the result of some inborn predisposition or of certain environmental influences or of a combination of the two effects, and learning the reason for their appearance can help us further understand the way development proceeds.

Studying individual variations in behavior may also provide clues about the many possible ways of behaving in the same situation. Children who learn to read successfully in the first grade seem to do so in a variety of ways. Choosing a single method to teach reading to less successful readers has been nearly impossible because no one method has been successful with all children who have reading problems. Studies indicate that some children learn more quickly with a phonic approach, whereas others learn best

At first glance, a group of similarly clad human beings look identical, but closer inspection reveals wide differences—a demonstration that their heritage is unique as well as common to the species and a warning that research findings that describe most people do not apply to everyone. (© Michael Weisbrot & Family)

using a sight, or look-say, method (Chall, 1967). Individual differences in aptitudes for reading are only one example of normal variation.

The fact of individual differences in almost all behavior does not keep developmental psychologists from testing general hypotheses about development or from making general statements about their results. Although individual exceptions exist, such general statements are useful in practical as well as theoretical ways.

Ethical Considerations

When studying human behavior, researchers often set up experiments or intervene in people's lives in some way. Without such research, we would know little about human development and would be unable to test theories or to develop effective means of intervening when development goes awry. But experiments are just as much an environmental experience as are incidents in daily life. Suppose a researcher wants to learn about the effects of repeated failure upon children's self-concepts. If children are subjected to situations in which they fail because of the researcher's manipulations, they are suffering the same consequences as a child who encounters failure in the world.

In the past few years, researchers in all fields have become increasingly aware that such research can lead to invasions of privacy and sometimes to social, physical, and psychological risks. As a result, they now take steps to ensure that their research has no harmful consequences. An investigator who subjected children to failure would, after gathering the data, place the children in situations that guaranteed success so that the experiment would not leave any child feeling helpless or incompetent.

Today, any proposed study must pass a number of tests that ensure adherence to the protective regulations formulated by the federal government and major scientific and professional organizations. According to the ethical standards formulated by the American Psychological Association (1972), for example, researchers must obtain the informed consent of individuals who serve as subjects. People must be free to participate or not, as they see fit. And all must be protected from harmful psychological or physical stress. Should the procedures used in a study lead to undesirable consequences for any participant, the researcher is expected to detect and correct them.

The study must be carried out in an atmosphere of openness and honesty. The investigator is expected to tell the participants about all aspects of the research that might affect their readiness to take part, and to answer all their questions so they can understand the consequences of their participation. When the study is complete, the investigator is required to tell the participants about the purpose and uses of the research and to clarify any misconceptions

that may have arisen. Information about participants remains confidential and anonymous.

Adherence to high ethical standards is especially important in the case of children and adolescents. They are not likely to be fully informed about their civil and human rights and are less able to take action to protect themselves. In research with babies, for example, the parent must give full consent; and when children are studied, informed consent must be obtained from both child and parent. When necessary, the informed consent of those who serve in a parentlike role (e.g., teacher, principal) must be obtained.

Given the subtleties involved in ethical decisions, no guidelines can cover every possible case. Therefore, most institutions that engage in or sponsor research have established ethics advisory committees to evaluate proposed research and to monitor studies once they are under way. The job of such a committee is to make sure that the rights of each participant are safeguarded. In spite of all these efforts to protect the well-being of subjects, unethical practices do occur, and ethical research sometimes has unforeseen consequences. Ignorance, faulty thinking, or mixed motives can distress or harm people who participate in studies. By establishing standards, researchers hope to protect participants while still making possible the discovery of new knowledge about human beings.

ISSUES IN DEVELOPMENTAL PSYCHOLOGY

The fascination of finding out how babies learn to speak fluently or how small boys and girls develop their concepts of appropriate male and female behavior is rewarding in itself. But discovering how and why human beings develop in certain characteristic ways also has a practical importance. A knowledge of the way the very young acquire language may provide clues that lead to more efficient ways of helping children with educational problems. And understanding how children develop their notions of male and female behavior can help prevent the growth of limiting and often destructive sexual stereotypes.

Information from developmental psychology bears directly on many of the basic problems that face society. As more and more mothers of babies work outside the home, for example, the question of day care takes on social and political significance. We know, for example, that excellent day care does not harm most children (Belsky and Steinberg, 1978). The development of young children in such day care is as normal, on the average, as the development of children at home with their mothers; and it may be, as Craig Ramey and Frances Campbell (1977) found, that educational day care keeps young children from suffering the drop in IQ scores that is so prevalent among children from disadvantaged homes. But we also know that some day-care placements are not good and that some children are more upset than others about being separated from their mothers. And we may also suspect that disadvantaged children will show pronounced benefits only when the day-care center provides an enriched environment such as that provided by the center Ramey and Campbell studied. Developmental research in this case has political as well as practical implications.

Similarly, the issue of busing has caused emotions to run high in many communities, and the question is often stated in terms that pit the ideal of integration against that of the neighborhood school. As a result, people tend to react to the issue in terms of their adherence to one or other of these ideals, and the interests of the children suffer. When Aline Mahan and Thomas Mahan (1970) studied children who changed schools to conform with an integration policy, they found that primary-age black children who were sent to white schools in the suburbs did much better on IQ tests and assessments of academic achievement than did their counterparts who stayed behind in city schools. But

black children in the intermediate grades fared better if they stayed in the city. Such a finding indicates that we have much to learn about the effects of integration. Psychologists are still exploring what busing does to children—how it affects their acquisition of basic skills, their self-concept and self-esteem, and the way they feel about other ethnic and socioeconomic groups.

Another current issue is the effect of television on children. The friends of television have pointed out that it introduces children to a wider world, increasing their knowledge and teaching them academic skills. But critics have charged that television viewing increases violence and apathy, stifles children's imaginations, and leads them to choose unhealthy diets. In an attempt to explore this last indictment, Charles Atkin, Byron Reeves, and John Hocking (1979) examined children's responses to food advertising. They found that very young children develop a personal bond with the fantasy figures that populate the Saturday morning commercials. Children trust Ronald McDonald, Fred Flintstone, and Cap'n Crunch, and believe that they tell the truth about their fries, shakes, and sugared cereals. Most young children believe that the commercial characters know whether the children eat their products, and nearly half of the five- to seven-year-olds believe their fantasy friends would feel bad if the young viewers ate competing products. On a more ominous note, nearly a third believe the characters would be angry. We cannot, of course, alter public policy on the strength of a single study, but as results from experiment after experiment pile up, it will become possible for parents, government planners, and network executives to make informed decisions about children's programs.

There is hardly an issue that involves children that is not under study by developmental psychologists. Information generated by their research is useful to students, parents, teachers, pediatricians, social workers, government planners, and others who need to understand how people's development can be enhanced or improved, how best to plan programs for children and the adults who care for them, and how to increase everyone's chances for optimum development. Parents face problems in the management and rearing of their own children. Teachers are confronted with difficulties in instructing their students. Pediatricians are aware of the relationship of behavior to physical problems in their young patients. Social workers must make decisions that affect the future success of children in families under their charge. Government planners need to know what kinds of programs will best serve young children in day care, children in compensatory education classes, teen-agers in work-study programs, and so forth. Although many questions about human development cannot yet be answered, there is enough sound information and incisive theory to provide possibilities for understanding and influencing the development of human behavior.

APPROACHES TO DEVELOPMENTAL PSYCHOLOGY

Developmental psychology can be explored in different ways. In the *chronological approach*, all aspects of the child's growth are studied simultaneously, progressing from infancy through adolescence. In the *topical approach*, a single process—such as intellectual development—is explored from birth through adolescence before another domain of development is considered.

Sometimes the choice of approaches is clear. If the parents of a newborn baby girl wanted to discover what to expect as their infant grew from a tiny organism that only cries, eats, sleeps, and wets to a competent woman who will make her way in the world and perhaps produce grandchildren for them to spoil, they would adopt the chronological approach. After discovering the present capabilities of their baby, they would look ahead, hoping to learn what

she might do in her first year—how rapidly she would grow, how she would become attached to them, how her memory and knowledge of the world would develop, how she would begin the mastery of language. Probably not until their baby was toddling around the house would they be concerned about the development of a three- or four- or five-year-old. And it would be several more years before the social and intellectual development of a ten-year-old held the slightest interest for them.

When studying developmental psychology, we could follow their example. After learning all there is to know about infancy, we could move on to early childhood, then to middle childhood, and finally to adolescence. This chronological approach would allow us to keep in mind the fact that children are developing in many ways at the same time. But unlike the parents, we could also look at specific processes of development, studying first the physical, then the intellectual, then the social development of children. This approach would allow us to follow a single process as it unfolds. Choosing intellectual development, for example, we could observe how the infant gains knowledge of the world, how the meanings that are founded in sensations and motor activities gradually become the symbolic and logical understanding of the child and culminate in the adolescent's ability to construct abstract systems.

Each way of studying child development has advantages and drawbacks. If we adopt the chronological approach, we may have trouble maintaining a sense of the way the child's intellectual processes develop from birth to adolescence. On the other hand, if we adopt the topical approach, we may tend to forget that no process develops independently, but that each area of development influences the others. The IQ scores and language facility of a three-year-old girl, for example, are affected by the responsiveness of her parents and how involved they are with their child, by the availability of toys, and by the predictability and regularity of the child's own home environment.

Since understanding development is easiest when the focus is on its processes, this book follows the topical approach, breaking down development into biological, linguistic, intellectual, and social areas. In order to overcome the inevitable separation that accompanies the topical approach, reminders of the way various processes interact are scattered throughout the book's discussions, and in the last unit an attempt is made to reweave the threads of development into a sturdy fabric.

SUMMARY

1. Psychologists generally divide the life span after birth into infancy, childhood, adolescence, and adulthood. The concept of a separate childhood emerged with the rise of the middle class; adolescence, with growing industrialization; and late adulthood, with increased life expectancy.

2. The field of developmental psychology has disparate origins in the general field of psychology. Nineteenth-century baby biographies, evolutionary views of development, the foundation of child-guidance clinics, the mental-testing movement, the demand of educators for research on children, experimental psychology, and the foundation of institutes for child study all played important roles. Interest expanded beyond childhood as the subjects in long-term developmental studies grew up and researchers continued to follow their development.

3. Developmental psychology attempts to describe, to explain, and to predict changes in human behavior across the life span. It holds that development from infancy to adulthood involves orderly change that is directional, is largely cumulative, and involves increasing complexity and organization.

4. Developmental psychologists construct theories of human behavior using information from psychology as well as from biology, sociology, and anthropology. They are careful to use an appropriate level to explain a given behavior.

5. When studying human behavior, researchers take steps to protect the people in their study. Experiments must have the informed, free consent of participants and an honest, open atmosphere; and information concerning subjects must be kept confidential and anonymous.

6. Information from developmental psychology bears directly on social and political issues. Judicious use of research results can help individuals and government agencies make informed decisions about problems and programs concerning children.

7. There are two major ways of studying developmental psychology: the chronological approach, in which all aspects of the child's growth are studied simultaneously, progressing from infancy through adolescence, and the topical approach, in which a single process is explored from birth through adolescence before another domain of development is considered. Each approach has its advantages and drawbacks.

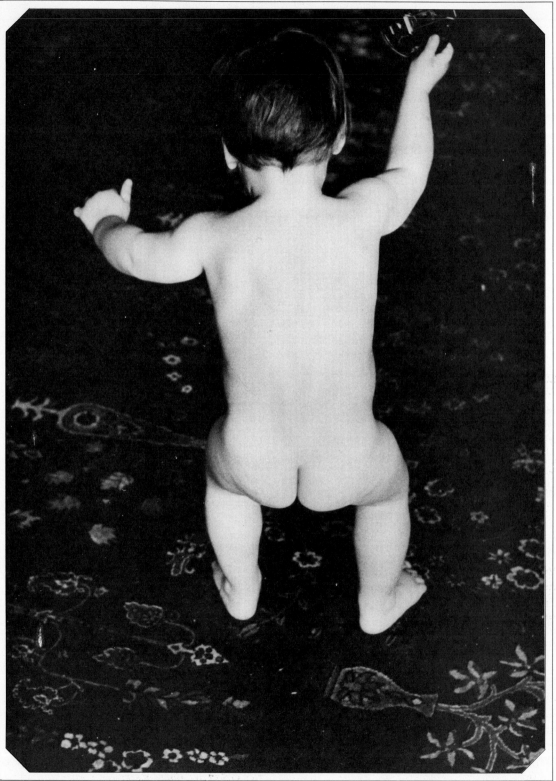

CHAPTER TWO

Theories of Development

A dvising parents on child-rearing, one psychologist might warn, "Never tell a disobedient child, 'I'm disappointed in you.' Assure children that you disapprove of their behavior but still love them." Hearing this, another psychologist might say, "Nonsense. What we call conscience cannot develop unless there is fear. Withdrawal of love is a most effective discipline." Both psychologists could point to theoretical principles that support their statements, and each advice may be correct in some situations and not in others.

Like the rest of us, scientific observers and theorists make assumptions, often unstated, about the nature of human development. In developmental psychology, these assumptions frequently focus on the existence of inborn differences among people, on how much human behavior can change in response to the environment, on the role of human beings in their own development, on the existence of natural good or evil in humanity, and on the relationship of child to adult behavior.

Throughout history, assumptions about human nature have fluctuated, and the prevailing notions have tended to influence the way people reared their children. As long ago as the third century B.C., Plato stressed that there were innate differences in aptitude among human beings and that these individual differences should be recognized and used in child rearing and education. His pupil Aristotle, in turn, proposed that although people were the same at birth (because the human mind was a *tabula rasa*, or blank slate), there were also individual differences in natural inclinations and talents, and he suggested that education and training should be designed to fit these differences.

During medieval times, human beings were considered to be sinful and corrupt by nature. Harsh, primitive training designed to correct people's supposedly depraved nature was common.

By the seventeenth century, a different view had emerged. Human beings were thought to be born innocent and then corrupted by society. Childhood came to be distinguished from adulthood, and moral education – the way to train children to be trustworthy, disciplined, and rational human beings – was stressed.

In the latter part of the seventeenth century, John Locke (1690), a British philosopher, proposed a different view. He stressed that all human beings are born equal in terms of inborn or native propensities. At birth, however, the human mind is a blank slate (as Aristotle had proposed), and ideas, concepts, and other human qualities are instilled as a result of training or experience.

Almost a century later, Jean Jacques Rousseau (1762), a French philosopher, reacting to the prevalent idea that human beings are inherently wicked, revived the view that human beings are born peaceful and compassionate, only to be turned from their good nature by an evil society. Their inborn propensities needed only to be allowed expression and given minimal guidance in order to bring about healthy and acceptable development.

In this chapter, we shall examine the way in which various views of human beings have influenced theories of human development. We shall explore five types of developmental theories and learn the assumptions that theories within each type share. We shall investigate theories that assume the environment is all-powerful, theories that spring from Sigmund Freud's insights into human motivation, theories that consider the evolutionary heritage of the human species to be a powerful force, theories that see the biological organism as the active creator of reality, and theories that place that organism within the framework of dialectical philosophy. Finally, we shall see that although no one group of theories can explain the development of all human behavior, each can make a useful contribution.

Modern theories of development combine assumptions about human nature in various ways to explain different aspects of development. They fall into five broad, but sometimes overlapping, categories, which we shall call mechanistic theories, psychodynamic theories, adaptation theories, organismic theories, and dialectical theories. Each set of theories is based on different assumptions about human beings, and each generates testable hypotheses about the development of behavior.

Some of these theories, especially some mechanistic theories, see development as continuous, with the child gradually developing new understandings through a combination of maturation and experience but never making sudden jumps to new levels of functioning. The child grows as does a plant, from seedling to mature form, without showing sudden changes in form.

Psychodynamic, organismic, and dialectical theories agree that human development is continuous but see great discontinuities in the process as well. They point to the existence of radically different stages, in which the child thinks or feels about the world in such a changed manner that his or her behavior shows an accompanying qualitative change. Organismic theories, for example, see abrupt changes in the structure of a child's thought from one stage to the next. The change is so marked, it is as if a caterpillar had just become a butterfly.

Stage theories are useful because they give organization to development, making it easier to think about the process. But stage theories cannot be applied rigidly; we cannot place every child neatly into one of the stages. When children are classified as to their stage of intellectual development, for example, many children turn out to be in transition from one stage to another, exhibiting some characteristics of the lower stage and some belonging to the higher stage of thought. Indeed, in some areas of understanding the process of transition may take years (Flavell, 1977).

Whether development is continuous or discontinuous—or both—theories of all kinds, each with its own view of development, continue to flourish. They have managed to exist simultaneously largely because they concentrate on different developmental processes, so that they rarely come into contact with one another.

MECHANISTIC THEORIES

The machine is the basic metaphor in the mechanistic world view, both for the universe and for human beings. Some years ago, the switchboard was a favorite model of the human mind; today, many psychologists prefer the computer. In this view, which goes back to John Locke's proposal that the infant mind is a blank slate, the child is passive. He or she receives stimulation from the environment but imposes no selectivity, so that the child's perceptions are true copies of the real world, which exists independently of the perceiver—a position called *naïve realism*. All causes are external, and the child acts in response to these external forces. Thus, if we had complete knowledge of the child's past history and present condition, we could—theoretically—predict how the child would act in any situation (Overton and Reese, 1973). Actually, no psychologist who adheres to the mechanistic view expects to be able to predict a person's every act because there is no way to discover every event in the person's history.

During development, thought and behavior change as a result of accumulated knowledge and experience. The child becomes more competent, but this competence is the result of increased knowledge; there is no accompanying change in the structure of the child's mind.

Development is gradual and continuous, and since there are no changes in mental processes or structures, any designation of "stages" in development is simply a convenient way to divide the life span in order to analyze the complex relationships involved in the child's passage to adulthood (Bijou, 1976).

Learning theories, which include reinforcement theory and social-learning theories, represent the major mechanistic view of development; but the information-processing perspective, which relies on a computer model of the mind, shares some of its assumptions.

Behavior-Learning Theories

Learning theorists see the human being as an organism that has learned to behave in uniquely human ways. The newborn baby is regarded as a malleable recipient of environmental stimulation. Most of what babies become is a matter of what they have experienced or learned, and learning begins even before birth. Although the idea that human beings learn or acquire much that characterizes them has been advanced by thinkers as diverse as Aristotle and Locke, formal learning theories date back only as far as the early part of this century and the establishment of behaviorism.

John B. Watson (1913, 1924), a founder of the behavioral school of psychology, believed that psychologists should limit themselves to the study of behavior—what people do or say—and forget the study of consciousness—what people feel or think. Watson studied behavior by examining the relationship between stimulus and response, defining a *stimulus* as anything within the body or in the world outside that evokes a response, and a *response* as anything a person does or says. Watson was so convinced of the power of experience that he once offered to take a group of infants and produce any kind of adult his critics specified. Although he became less certain about such sweeping early claims, his work left an indelible mark on American psychology. It was interpreted to mean that human behavior could be molded in almost limitless ways, and that human beings could be improved in any desired direction.

CONDITIONING Watson explained his observations of learning in human beings by adopting the language of Ivan Pavlov (1927), whose research into the workings of the dog's digestive system had led to his development of the principle of *conditioning*, a process in which a person comes to respond in the same way to a particular stimulus each time he or she encounters it. During Pavlov's research, he noticed that as soon as a spoonful of meat powder was placed into a dog's mouth, saliva began to flow, starting the digestive process. It was not long, however, before the dog began to salivate the instant it caught sight of the man who fed it. Pavlov then discovered that by starting a metronome each time he fed a dog, he could establish the same kind of response, so that the sound of the metronome would make the dog drool.

In the case of the dog, salivation on contact with food was an *unconditioned reflex,* that is, a response that a person or animal naturally produces before any learning takes place, such as blinking the eye when a puff of air strikes the eyeball. The dog's salivation at the sight of the keeper or later at the sound of the metronome was a *conditioned reflex,* or a response in which a neutral stimulus (the metronome) is transformed by association with an unconditioned stimulus (meat powder), so that it becomes a conditioned stimulus and brings forth the same response that once followed only the unconditioned stimulus.

The conditioning described by Pavlov is called *classical conditioning*, and it disregards the consequences of a person's response, concentrating instead on the association of one stimulus with another. This troubled B. F. Skinner (1979), a young psychologist at Harvard in the 1930s who had come under the influence first of Watson and then of Pavlov, and who firmly believed that any person's behavior at any time can be explained by his or her genetic endowment, past history, and the present situation (Hall, 1972). Skinner (1938) agreed that classical conditioning explained some behavior, but he maintained that the rats in his studies that pressed levers to get food were demonstrating another kind of learning, which he called *operant conditioning.* In operant conditioning, a person's or animal's responses are strengthened or changed as a result of the rewards or punishments that follow those actions.

In this basic kind of learning, the frequency of a response changes with reinforcement, and a *reinforcer* is anything that makes it more likely that a person will repeat a response. A *positive reinforcer* comes after a person acts; it can be concrete, such as money or toys or candy, or it can be intangible, such as affection, praise, attention, or the intrinsic satisfaction that comes when a person completes a difficult task. A *negative reinforcer* relieves an unpleasant situation, also making a person more likely to repeat a response. For example, rats that learn to press a lever to stop an electric shock have responded to negative reinforcement, just as has a person who learns to reach for aspirin when a headache starts or to lie to get out of an uncomfortable situation.

Punishment can also affect learning, and people who are punished, whether by physical pain, harsh words, fines, the withdrawal of affection, or being put in isolation, tend to stop responding in the way that brought about the punishment. Responses that are not reinforced decrease in frequency or may even be *extinguished,* or eliminated. Responses that are punished appear to be extinguished, but sometimes they are only suppressed; once the punishing stimulus is gone, the response may reappear.

Because Skinner placed such great importance on the consequences of an organism's actions, theories of development that are based on his approach are sometimes called *reinforcement theory.* Although reinforcement can be used to explain a wide range of behavior, from how the child acquires language and forms concepts to why the artist paints pictures—and why other people want to look at them (Skinner, 1972), its acceptance by learning theorists did not mean that classical conditioning had been rejected. The process continues to be used as an explanation for the establishment of emotional responses. For example, a year-old baby often begins to cry at the sight of a pediatrician who has been associated with painful injections. A child who has been bitten by a dog may come to fear the yard in which the attack occurred. A child may even generalize fear. Thus the infant who has been given injections by a pediatrician may come to fear all people in white coats or all rooms that look like doctors' offices. And the child bitten by a dog may come to fear all four-legged creatures.

Skinner never set forth a theory of child development based on his findings, but other psychologists have undertaken the translation. Sidney Bijou and Donald Baer (1961, 1965), who have used his approach, see the developing child as an "interrelated cluster of responses and stimuli." Because the child and the environment are interacting continuously, they suggest, the child's development consists of progressive changes in the ways of interaction, changes that are the result of opportunities and circumstances. These changes serve as the basis for their division of the life span into three stages. The first part of life is the *universal* stage, which begins before birth and lasts until about eighteen months, when a child begins to talk. The stage is universal because children in every society appear to develop similarly during this period. At this time the child, although learning rapidly, is less responsive to the environment than he or she will be later, when biological maturation plays a less powerful role in development.

The second, or *basic* stage begins when a child starts to talk and lasts until the child enters school. The ability to talk obviously changes the way a child interacts with others. When a child starts school, the school environment is so

different from the home that ways of interacting shift again, perhaps dramatically, and the child enters the *societal* stage of development, which occupies the rest of the life span.

Developmental psychologists who wish to use operant techniques search for the relationships that exist between responses and stimuli (including reinforcers). They also concentrate on how the timing of reinforcement changes the frequency of responses. These timetables for reinforcing behavior are called *schedules of reinforcement*. A child at first may be reinforced for each correct response, but once the behavior is established, such a schedule is not necessary. Numerous studies have shown that responses can be maintained just as effectively by reinforcing children for their first response after a specified time has passed or by reinforcing them only after they have responded a certain number of times. These schedules of reinforcement have counterparts in daily life: some children must do their chores every day but get an allowance only once each week; other children get paid after they have completed a certain number of chores.

Another important procedure in operant learning concerns the development of new behavior. By rewarding *successive approximations*, or behavior that resembles more and more closely the final desired response, it is possible to shape behavior. Using this technique, some experimenters have taught pigeons to play Ping-Pong and to guide missiles (Skinner, 1960); others have taught various intellectual, social, and language skills to children and adults (Semb, 1972).

SOCIAL LEARNING Social-learning theory grew out of earlier behavior-learning views. Its proponents consider earlier views too narrow and inflexible. They believe that operant and classical conditioning account for only part of behavior and development, and they stress that many kinds of behavior are learned simply by observation. Seeing or hearing someone else

Social-learning theorists believe that development cannot be understood without the concept of imitation and point to the increasing resemblance of children's behavior to that of the adult models they see around them. (© Susan Shapiro)

act in a certain way can be a more effective form of learning than reinforcement for both children and adults.

Thus the concept of imitation plays a key role in most social-learning accounts of human development. Studies and casual observation demonstrate the increasing resemblance of children's social behavior to that of adult models such as parents or teachers. Some researchers have discovered that if a child is rewarded for imitating a model, the child will tend to imitate the model on later occasions even if not rewarded (Bandura, 1969b). And if the child sees that the model is rewarded for his or her ac-

tions, the child will tend to copy the rewarded behavior.

Interpretations of the role and importance of imitation have grown. In one of the first analyses, Neal Miller and John Dollard (1941) proposed that nurturance from parents becomes the motivating force for a child's imitations. That is, as parents satisfy the child's needs for food, warmth, and affection, the parents become associated with the satisfaction of those needs and take on reinforcing properties themselves. Because the parents' behavior has become reinforcing, the child imitates them to reward him- or herself. Jerome Kagan (1958) and John Whiting (1960) added to the picture, pointing out that parents also have more power and control more possessions than the child does, and that the child envies their status and therefore copies both parents in the hope that the imitations will bring to the child their influence and status.

In the past few years, social-learning theory has gradually shifted in a more radical direction. The work of Albert Bandura and his colleagues is representative of this shift, and Bandura (1977) has restated many aspects of human learning and motivation in terms of *cognition*, or all the processes of sensing, perceiving, remembering, using symbols, and thinking that we use to gain knowledge about the world. According to Bandura, cognitive processes play a central role in regulating what children attend to, how they describe or think about what they see, and whether they repeat it to themselves and lodge it in memory. Short-lived daily experiences can have lasting effects because they are retained in memory. Learning from a model consequently is not simply a matter of imitation. As children and adults watch others, they form concepts about possible behavior that will later guide their own actions. As they then observe their actions and the consequences, they can change their concepts and act in a different way.

Children tend to copy complete patterns of behavior from models instead of slowly acquiring bits of a pattern in response to reinforce-

Courtesy Dr. Albert Bandura

Albert Bandura (1925–   )

Albert Bandura received his doctorate in clinical psychology from Iowa State University in 1952; after completing a postdoctoral internship, he accepted a position at Stanford University, where he is professor of psychology. His research and writing on personality and social development reflect his background in clinical psychology and his strong interest in child development. Over the past few years, his theories have had a major influence on the thought of developmental psychologists.

Early in his career, Bandura became dissatisfied with the gaps that existed between the concepts of clinical psychology and those of general psychology. He also believed that behavior-learning views, including social learning, were too narrow to account for socialization and the development of behavior.

To overcome the deficiencies, Bandura developed a broad, integrated sociobehavioral approach to human behavior. According to his view, direct experience is not the only teacher; human beings learn from infancy by simply observing what other people do and noticing what happens to them. Other symbolic models are provided by way of television, books, or magazines, and such models may teach unacceptable as well as acceptable behavior. Bandura emphasizes the importance of distinguishing between learning and performance. He stresses that although people learn to do many things, they are most likely to do the things that they or others consider acceptable or rewarding.

Bandura's work stresses the links between cognitive processes, learning, and performance. Thus, cognitive skills, information, and rules strongly affect what an individual does. And because people can think about what happened to them or what may happen to them, their behavior cannot be manipulated simply by reinforcement. Bandura sees people as freer to choose and to make changes in their lives than did the original behavior-learning theorists.

ment. Exposure to a model can have one of three effects: (1) the child can learn a completely new pattern of behavior (trying out a new disco step); (2) the child can inhibit the performance of already learned behavior (ceasing to ride a bicycle on a busy street after seeing another child punished for it) or can indulge in previously learned behavior that has been forbidden (jumping a bicycle off a ramp after watching another child do so); or (3) the child can behave in previously learned ways that are recalled from memory by the model (playing a game that had been lying on the shelf but that the child just saw advertised on television) (Bandura and Walters, 1963). Not all children who watch a model later imitate the model's behavior. Children may observe a model and acquire the ability to copy the behavior they have just seen yet not perform it. Not all children, for example, who watch a television program filled with fistfights later go out and punch the first person who disagrees with them. They may never engage in a violent fight. But placed in a situation in which that behavior seems an appropriate response, say when a bully backs them into a corner in the schoolyard, they may indeed call upon the behavior they witnessed weeks or months ago.

In this new view, stimuli are no longer seen as purely external physical events that control behavior; instead they are signals—information that helps people decide what to do. The person's interpretation of a stimulus, not the stimulus itself, regulates behavior.

Cognitive social-learning theorists, as proponents of this stance are sometimes called, stress that people process and synthesize information from their experiences over long periods of time; consequently, they are not bound by what takes place in the immediate situation. On the basis of their past experiences, they decide what behavior may be effective. As human beings develop, they construct and reconstruct expectations about future events. They learn to estimate the possible positive and negative consequences of various actions, and accordingly set their own standards of behavior, which they use to evaluate their performance, to reward their actions, and to provide their motivation.

Unlike other behavior-learning theorists, cognitive social-learning theorists give human thought and knowledge central importance in explaining the development of human behavior. They see children as approaching, exploring, and dealing with things that they perceive are within their abilities. Children tend to avoid things that seem stressful or beyond their capabilities. Because other people become sources of information in this process, through their actions and words, they play a primary role in the development of children.

Information-Processing Perspective

During the 1950s, the development of computers gave psychologists a new way of looking at the human mind; human beings could be seen as information-gathering, information-processing systems. This approach was spurred by A. M. Turing (1950), who proposed that if a person communicating with a computer could not say whether the responses were generated by the machine or by a human being, we would have to admit that machines could think. And if machines could think, we would have duplicated the human ability to manipulate information. Although no computer has yet been developed that can fool a person indefinitely, the possibility excited psychologists, many of whom believed that the decision-making powers of the human mind could not be explained by theories of reinforcement. They began to translate human cognitive processes into the computer model.

Computers and the human mind do have a lot in common: both take information from the outside world, encode it, combine it with other information, store it, retrieve it, and pass it out again to the world in a decoded form. As Earl Hunt (1971) describes it, we each have a slow, subtle computer in our heads, surrounded by a number of high-capacity, parallel-input transmission lines. Regarding human thought as slow may conflict with our experience, but in comparison with a computer, the human mind is sluggish. (See Table 2-1.) Retrieving information from long-term memory requires from 180 microseconds to a full second, and getting information that already is in working memory takes 25 microseconds (Estes, 1980). But a computer can deliver information in a single microsecond.

Human beings see much but think about only some of it, because our inner computer is protected by a buffer system that screens sensation and presents orderly data to the system. Our computer consists of *hardware*, the basic storage system itself, and *software*, the programs, or sets of instructions, we use for coding, analyzing, and retrieving information and for making decisions. We have, for example, one program for multiplying numbers, another for driving a car. Although both system and programs develop, most research indicates that the major develop-

Table 2-1 THE HUMAN COMPUTER

	Human Memory	Computer Memory
Preferred method of storage	Time-oriented	List-oriented
Retention of information	Graded	All-or-none
Efficiency (bits of information per second)	Low	High
Capacity	Dependent on experience	Independent of experience
Retrieval		
Relative to context	Strongly dependent	Independent
Relative to previous retrievals	Dependent	Independent
Purpose	General purpose; open set of functions	Special or general purpose; closed set of functions

This comparison of human and computer memories shows that the computer's speed and precision is offset by the adaptability and general-purpose capability of human memory. (Reprinted with permission of American Scientist 68 [1980], W. K. Estes. "Is Human Memory Obsolete?")

ments take place in cognitive software. There is little evidence of significant changes in cognitive hardware after the first couple of years of life.

Hunt and other cognitive psychologists have tried to simulate human thought processes by reducing mental operations to computer operations. Some psychologists have gone so far as to write programs for the computer that simulate complex cognitive functioning. For example, Herbert Simon (1970) assumes that children, faced with a problem, attack it with a program similar to a computer program. His own General Problem Solver program supposes that children — if they are not born with the ability — very early develop certain memory skills: the capacity to store symbols in lists and to bring

into consciousness the item stored next to any item already in consciousness. As children grow, they become adept at manipulating items and groups of items within the memory system. A child who reaches this stage of cognitive development has attained the ability to generate hypotheses and use formal logic. Simon points out that, although his model can simulate the problem-solving thought of a child at a particular stage of development, it cannot account for the child's transition from one stage to another. Nor can his approach handle emotion and its effect on the child's thought processes.

David Klahr and J. G. Wallace (1976) have built upon Simon's theory, producing programs that simulate the way children handle several mental tasks. They have, for example, developed a program that describes the way children think when trying to decide whether a lump of clay that is squeezed into a ball contains the same amount of clay as a lump of the same size that is stretched into a long, narrow shape. Klahr and Wallace's programs have gone partway toward handling the transition of children's thinking from one stage to another.

But not all psychologists who believe children's minds resemble computers work on such a technical level. Many developmental psychologists simply use the computer as a metaphor and study thinking by looking at one or more of the processes that comprise it. A psychologist may study perception (information reception and coding), memory (information storage and retrieval), hypothesis testing (thinking), or evaluation (children's ability to assess their own thinking) (Ault, 1977). For example, studies (Hagen and Huntsman, 1971) have indicated that an eleven-year-old retarded child with a mental age of eight memorizes about as efficiently as does a nonretarded eight-year-old. With training, retarded children show some improvement on specific memory tasks. This has been interpreted as indicating the possibility that the cognitive hardware of mildly retarded children may be intact and that the deficits may be confined to their cognitive software, in this case the techniques they use to commit material to memory (Campione and Brown, 1977).

PSYCHODYNAMIC THEORIES

Psychodynamic theories view human behavior as resulting from the interplay of active (dynamic) mental and biological forces with the environment. Although some theories regard the forces as benign, others see them as irrational forces that must be controlled by socialization. Most psychodynamic theorists, therefore, discuss and analyze human development in terms of confrontations between the growing individual and the social world. They stress that the individual must accommodate to the demands of society while gratifying basic human drives. Most also emphasize that children gradually develop a sense of self, an identity against which to judge their own behavior.

Psychodynamic theories have centered on the development of emotion and personality. The concern has been to understand and explain the development of both rational and irrational feelings and behavior. To some extent, all psychodynamic theories describe human development in terms of early experiences that may influence later behavior.

Since Sigmund Freud developed the first psychodynamic theory, other psychodynamic theorists have constructed their own accounts of personality development. But because the other theories are either modifications of Freud's thought or reactions to it, this discussion is limited to Freud's views and those of Erik Erikson—a modifier of Freud's views whose theory has been widely used by developmental psychologists.

Freud's Theory

Sigmund Freud (1905) is the father of psychodynamic theories and the founder of psychoanal-ysis, a type of psychotherapy that attempts to give a patient insight into his or her unconscious conflicts. His theories of personality and development grew out of the insights that came from working with his patients.

As Freud saw it, from earliest infancy human beings are motivated by irrational urges toward pleasure, urges that are an expression of the *libido*, or "life force," that propels us all. Rational behavior develops out of conflict between social demands and the young child's instincts, which are *sublimated* (altered in socially acceptable ways) in the course of the child's adaptation to the environment.

Freud's theory of personality described three conflicting aspects of human personality: the id, the ego, and the superego. In the *id* reside all of the unconscious impulses, or drives. The newborn baby is pure id. The *superego* is the conscience, which develops in early childhood as a child internalizes parental values and standards of conduct. The *ego* guides actual behavior and mediates the perpetual conflict between what the individual wants to do (the province of the id) and what the individual must or must not do (the province of the superego).

According to Freud, development proceeds through a series of stages in which instinctual impulses are expressed through various pleasure centers of the body. His theory of development describes human development as a series of sexual conflicts that a child must resolve in order to become a mature, well-adjusted adult. Unless the growing child successfully navigates each stage, Freud believed, he or she will become *fixated* at that stage; that is, the child's emotional growth will be stunted, and as an adult he or she will have an immature personality in which the characteristic traits of that stage predominate. This series of stages Freud labeled oral, anal, phallic, latency, and genital.

The first year of the child's life Freud designated the *oral stage*, because the lips and mouth are the focus of sensual pleasure. A baby busily sucking away at pacifier or thumb, breast or bottle, may not be hungry but simply enjoying

(Photo by Edmund Engelman, from Berggasse 19)

Sigmund Freud (1856–1939)

Sigmund Freud's theories reflect his training in the biological sciences and his clinical experience. He specialized in physiology, received his M.D. degree in Vienna in 1881, and began lecturing and doing research in neuropathology. A grant enabled him to go to Paris and study under the famous neurologist Jean Martin Charcot, who was using hypnosis to treat hysteria.

Later, as Freud treated his patients, he developed the therapeutic methods of free association and dream interpretation. He found that his adult neurotic patients had repressed their memories of early childhood emotional experiences, which generally involved sex, aggression, or jealousy. Because these experiences were unpleasant, Freud proposed that they became lost to awareness because they were pushed into an unreachable area of the mind, the unconscious.

In his theory of psychosexual development, he interpreted what he learned from treating his patients in the light of embryology and physics. He proposed that the emergence of psychosexual stages was primarily determined by maturation and that mental life followed the law of conservation of energy, which states that energy cannot be created or destroyed, only transformed. People's mental and emotional lives, he believed, show a comparable transformation of psychic energy (libido) from one stage to the next. This energy motivates people's thinking, their perceptions, and their memories, and it remains constant even though it becomes associated with different regions of the body during development.

the pleasurable feelings that arise when the mouth is stimulated. Although during the first few months babies lack the coordination to pick up an object and deliberately insert it into their mouths, whatever brushes cheek or lips goes in. Babies actively seek oral stimulation.

At about their first birthdays, babies enter Freud's second stage of psychosexual development, the *anal stage*. During this period, which lasts until they are about three, pleasurable feelings center around the rectum. The delights of oral stimulation do not fade completely away, but children now enjoy both expelling feces and retaining them. Toilet training may be-

come a battle, in which children learn to use their libidinal pleasures as a weapon against their parents.

The third, and in Freudian theory highly critical, period spans the years from three to five or six. During this *phallic stage*, the genitals become the focus, and children learn to derive pleasure from fondling them. Boys are said to fear castration and girls to be filled with penis envy. Boys are said to fall in love with their mothers (Oedipus complex) and girls with their fathers (Electra complex). Powerless to push the other parent out of the way, both girls and boys resolve this conflict by identifying with the parent of the same sex, boys assuming their fathers' masculine characteristics and girls the feminine characteristics of their mothers.

After the stormy phallic period, Freud believed, sexual feelings become less important in children. From about six until they reach puberty, children are in the *latency period*. Tenderness predominates over sexual feelings, and children learn to feel shame and guilt. With the mastery of Oedipal and Electra conflicts, they have developed a superego. During the latency period, they also discover moral and esthetic interests.

The final period of psychosexual development, the *genital stage*, emerges with puberty. Among children who have successfully navigated all the earlier stages, primary sensual pleasure transfers to mature sexual relationships with members of the opposite sex.

Once Freud's theories found their way into academic and popular thinking, the field of human development changed. His theory was the first to consider the way biological, psychic, and environmental influences affect personality development and the first to realize that all children have sexual urges. Freud's direct influence is clearest in John Bowlby's (1969) influential theory of attachment, which is based in part on Freud's belief that rupturing the tie between a child and his or her mother during the early years can have harmful psychological consequences. Indirectly, Freud's influence is so pervasive that some of his insights—such as his focus on early experiences and on the role played by a child's identification with the parent in the development of conscience—are used even by many researchers who reject his formal theory of development.

Erikson's Psychosocial Theory

Erik Erikson (1963), one modifier of Freud's analytic theory, has developed an elaborate stage theory that is unusual because it describes emotional development across the life span. His theory is called *psychosocial* because it focuses on the individual's interactions with society, instead of on sexual conflicts as does Freud's theory.

According to Erikson, personality develops in steps determined by the human organism's readiness to move toward, to be aware of, and to interact with a widening social world—a

Freud's Psychosexual Stages	Erikson's Psychosocial Stages	Possible Outcomes
Oral	Oral/Sensory	Basic Trust vs. Mistrust
Anal	Muscular/Anal	Autonomy vs. Shame
Phallic	Locomotor/Genital	Initiative vs. Guilt
Latency	Latency	Industry vs. Inferiority
Genital	Puberty and Adolescence	Identity vs. Role Confusion
	Young Adulthood	Intimacy vs. Isolation
	Adulthood	Generativity vs. Stagnation
	Maturity	Ego Integrity vs. Despair

Figure 2.1 PSYCHODYNAMIC STAGES OF DEVELOPMENT Erikson's first five stages of development roughly correspond to Freud's five stages, but Erikson has elaborated on Freud's theory, adding three stages, each with its own developmental task.

Olive R. Pierce/Black Star

Erik Erikson (1902–   )

Erik Erikson was born in Germany of Danish parents. He was graduated from art school and went to Florence, Italy, intending to become an art teacher. In Vienna, where he had gone to teach children of American families, he met Freud and other analysts, and soon entered psychoanalytic training.

When Hitler came to power in Germany,

Erikson emigrated to America. He held a series of positions in child-guidance clinics and major universities while maintaining a private practice. During an appointment at Harvard University, Erikson developed an interest in anthropology and studied the Sioux and Yurok Indians. During a subsequent appointment at the University of California, Berkeley, he studied adolescents, using a technique in which the way young people played with dolls revealed their unconscious thoughts and feelings.

Erikson is one of the few theorists to describe emotional development across the life span. In his theory, personality develops through eight stages, from infancy to the final stage of life. As a person interacts with a widening social world, he or she moves from a universe of self and mother to an image of humankind. Each stage has its own conflict to be resolved, and the failure to resolve any of these conflicts can lead to psychological disorders. Erikson's psychodynamic theory is important because, unlike Freud, he believes neuroses can develop at any stage during life and that they are not necessarily the result of problems in infancy or early childhood.

world that begins with a dim image of mother and ends with an image of humankind. Erikson saw development as the progressive resolution of conflicts between a person's needs and the demands of society. At each of eight stages, conflicts must be resolved, at least partially, before progress can be made on the problems of the next stage. Failure to resolve problems at any stage can result in lasting psychological disorders. (See Figure 2.1.)

FROM TRUST TO INDUSTRY In the first stage, babies need to develop a relationship in

which they can get what they require from a person who is ready to provide it—almost always a mother. Constant, reliable care promotes the baby's sense of *trust*, enabling the infant to learn to tolerate frustrations and to delay immediate gratification. If a baby's needs are not consistently met, he or she can develop a sense of mistrust and will react to frustration with anxiety and upset.

After infants begin to walk and to exercise some self-direction, they run into social restraints. During this second stage, they increasingly demand to control their own behavior ("Me do it!"), but because they have little judg-

According to Erik Erikson, a sense of trust, which most babies get from the parental relationship, lies at the basis of later abilities to tolerate frustration and to postpone pleasure. (© Suzanne Szasz)

The toddler's task is to develop a sense of autonomy, and Erikson regards this as crucial if the child is not to be ridden with shame or doubt. (© Michael Weisbrot & Family)

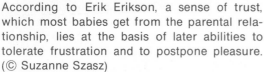

ment about their capabilities, they need to be protected from excesses while being granted *autonomy* in matters they can handle. It is particularly important at this stage, Erikson suggests, that parents not shame a child into feeling that he or she is incompetent. Shame can be a devastating experience for anyone, and it is particularly difficult for young children who are struggling for autonomy and who are not yet sure that they can develop competent self-regulation.

After children gain a relatively secure sense of autonomy, they enter the third stage of development and are ready to take the initiative in planning their activities. As Erikson sees it, *initiative* adds to autonomy the quality of undertaking a task for the sake of being active and on the move. In the preceding stage, self-will often inspired acts of defiance. In this stage, children

are ready for positive, constructive activities under their own initiative. The potential problem at this period is guilt; a child may come to feel that his or her intrusiveness and activity have evil consequences. This is the period of sexual attraction to the opposite-sex parent, and as a child resolves this hopeless attraction, he or she identifies with the same-sex parent and develops a conscience. Harsh parental responses to a child's initiatives and sexual overtures can lead to an overdeveloped conscience that may always plague the person with guilt.

Once children come to terms with their families by identifying with the same-sex parent, they enter the fourth stage and are ready to move into the larger world. About this time in our culture, children go to school. Before children can become adults, they must become workers, learning to gain recognition by pro-

The preschooler's task, according to Erikson, is to develop initiative, so that activities are planned and undertaken out of pure enjoyment. (© Christine A. Pullo 1981)

The schoolchild, who is in Erikson's fourth stage, develops a sense of industry, learning the pleasure that comes when diligence and attention lead to the successful completion of a project. (© Suzanne Szasz)

ducing things *(industry)*, so at this stage they want to learn the technical skills that characterize adults. The potential problem in this period lies in a sense of inadequacy and inferiority, which can develop if children are not praised for their accomplishments. In Erikson's theory, this is a decisive stage in the child's preparation to assume effective adult roles.

FROM IDENTITY TO EGO INTEGRITY

In the fifth stage, adolescents question all their previous solutions to problems of trust, autonomy, initiative, and industry. Rapid body growth and genital maturity create a physiological revolution within them at the time that they face adult life. According to Erikson, adolescents search for continuity and sameness within themselves—a sense of *identity*—and in

their search they must refight the battles of earlier years, usually casting their parents in the role of adversaries. The potential problem at this period is that adolescents' identities will fail to become consistent and that they will be unable to develop a sense of who they are as people, as sexual beings, as adult workers, as potential parents. If this role confusion lasts into adulthood, they may never be able to make consistent decisions about who they are and where they are going in life.

Young adults, emerging from the search for identity, are eager and willing to fuse their own identities with those of others. In terms of Erikson's sixth stage, they are ready for *intimacy* —for relationships with others in which they are strong enough to make sacrifices for another's welfare without losing themselves in another's identity. It is at this point that true sexual love can emerge. The potential problem at this period is isolation from others—a failure to commit oneself to loving relationships because of fear or a need to compete.

Generativity characterizes the seventh stage and refers to the adult's concern with establishing and guiding the next generation. According to Erikson, productivity in work and creativity in one's life are important concepts in this period. The possible dangers of this period are self-absorption and a sense of stagnation, a sense of going nowhere, doing nothing important.

In Erikson's theory, the final stage of the life cycle should result in a sense of wholeness, of purposes accomplished and a life well lived. The potential problem in the final stage is regret and despair over wasted chances and unfortunate choices. A person in this stage who feels despair fears death in an ironic way that those with *ego integrity* do not. The despairing person, while expressing disgust with life, continues to yearn for another chance. The person with ego integrity accepts death as the end of a meaningful trip.

Translating Freud Into Learning Theory

Although learning theory and psychoanalysis generally keep to their own sides of the street, an attempt has been made by John Dollard and Neal Miller (1950), two social-learning theorists, to translate Freudian theory into the language of learning theorists. Dollard and Miller proposed that the two theories are complementary. Where Freud talks about pleasure, they speak of reinforcement. Although their insistence on learning does not lend itself to the idea of a psyche divided into ego, id, and superego, they have little disagreement with Freud's belief in the existence of basic human drives, which they regard as strong stimuli.

They are comfortable with Freud's stages of psychosexual development and with his prin-

ciple that a child's basic attitudes are formed in the early years. But instead of focusing on specific sites of libidinous pleasure, they concentrate on the child's typical experiences during these periods: the stimuli the child encounters, the responses made, the habits built up. They see disturbances not in terms of fixation but as learning that occurs in situations of conflict between drives and social pressures. For them, toilet training is important not because of the child's sensual pleasures but because it represents the child's first encounter with the culture's insistence on order and cleanliness. Similarly, Dollard and Miller see the identification that is established during the phallic period not as the child's way of overcoming incestuous desires but as the simple imitation of a powerful parent that is followed by reinforcement.

ADAPTATION THEORIES

Adaptation theories suggest that human behavior is the product of our evolutionary history. Human beings have evolved to behave in specifically human ways. Just as our internal organs and external limbs have evolved to certain forms, so our behavior has characteristic patterns, which develop in interaction with the environment. The force behind this way of looking at development comes from *ethology*, which is the scientific study of animal behavior in evolutionary terms. Ethologists rely on rigorous observations of natural behavior and on studies carried out in natural settings—practices that have been increasingly adopted by developmental psychologists, including those who may not have been influenced by the stress on evolutionary significance.

In the view of adaptation theorists, the human species (like every other species) has evolved in environmental contexts that are as important to understand as the nature of humanity itself. The necessity for human beings to be in harmony with their environment leads ethologists of human behavior to look at development as adaptation. They see social behavior as related to group cohesion, to the competition for mates, to survival of the young, and so forth. Intelligence is a prime mechanism for adaptation; during the course of human evolution, those individuals who solved problems related to their own survival were more likely to leave offspring for the next generation.

Human behavior is, therefore, best understood by looking at the way it enables babies, children, or adults to survive and flourish in an environment like that in which our species evolved. For this reason, newborn infants, whose behavior is relatively little influenced by culture, human groups that live in conditions like those of our early ancestors, and apes and other primates are favorite subjects for developmental psychologists who have been influenced by ethology.

Researchers who wonder about infancy among our forebears often look at the !Kung San, a much-studied band of hunter-gatherers, who live a nomadic life in Africa's Kalahari desert under conditions much like those of our early ancestors. Observations of the !Kung San, says Melvin Konner (1977), indicate that in an environment like the one in which humanity evolved, a sensitive, immediately responsive mother is a regular part of child rearing. !Kung San babies spend most of their first year or two in close human contact, either on their mothers' laps or carried in a sling on their hips. The babies have continual access to the breast and nurse frequently. When they cry or fuss, their mothers' response is immediate, and the babies' whims are indulged. Yet when these indulged babies are two to five years old, they do not hang on to their mothers as observers from our own society might expect. Far from being spoiled or dependent, they show considerable independence, interacting less with their mothers and more with other children than English children of the same age.

Such observations indicate that human beings have evolved with close ties between mother and infant, and such seems to be the case. The bond between mother and infant is regarded by adaptation theorists as part of a behavioral system that evolved to protect the developing organism. Because human infants are helpless for so long, their survival depends upon protection from mature members of the species, and the attachment of babies to their caregivers generally keeps the pair in close physical proximity (Bowlby, 1969). As will become clear in later chapters, although attachment is expressed in varying ways in different cultures, bonding between infant and caregiver has been present in every society studied.

Given the need of human infants for protection, we might expect that some sort of mechanism had evolved to ensure the establishment of the bond, and adaptation theorists point to the existence of two such devices: the baby's smile and the baby's "cuteness." These qualities are considered *releasing stimuli*, or events that regularly evoke certain behavior in all members of a

The baby's smile and cuteness may act as releasing stimuli, which evoke joy in adults, thereby establishing the bond that ensures infant survival. (© Harvey Stein)

species. Such stimuli help explain regularities in mating patterns, aggression, appeasement, and other typical behavior. In the case of the human infant's survival, the smile evokes a feeling of joy in the caregiver, an observation made long ago by Charles Darwin (1872). Studies of blind and deaf-blind infants have found that the babies smile in response to voice or touch, so it appears that the smile is as "natural" as walking, a part of our evolutionary heritage (Freedman, 1974). Blind babies have no model, hence their smiles cannot have been learned from watching the caregiver.

Cuteness may also be regarded as a releasing stimulus for human caregiving, a response that evolved because it improves the chance of adequate infant care and survival (Lorenz, 1942–1943). In every culture, most human beings respond to cuteness in babies and baby animals by wanting to pick them up and cuddle them. In species other than humanity, the baby forms elicit caregiving from adult animals, whereas adult forms do not. Babies and young animals are cute because they have relatively large heads, particularly foreheads, and foreshortened facial features. The toy industry takes advantage of this and makes cute dolls with very small features embedded in large heads and small bodies.

In tracing development through childhood, psychologists have speculated on the evolutionary value of the long period of immaturity in the human species and suggested that evolution has guaranteed that during these years children will want to learn the skills required by adults, ensuring the species' survival. Babies and children yearn to explore and to learn, and they learn easily. In play, they practice skills without suffering adult consequences—as when they play house or doctor or soldier. According to Jerome Bruner (1972), language, playfulness, curiosity, and the need to master the environment appear to be evolved characteristics that make human development what it is.

Adaptation theorists have had other insights on human development from their observations

The infant who endlessly explores the environment is exhibiting the playfulness, curiosity, and need for mastery that adaptation theorists see as evolved characteristics that guarantee human survival. (© Michael Weisbrot & Family)

of similarities in the social behavior of human beings and their nearest primate relatives. Some investigators have pointed out that children's play groups have "dominance hierarchies" much like troops of macaques or chimpanzees. Children climb the dominance ladder by means of physical attack, threats, or struggles over objects. Even among preschool play groups, most children know to which rung of the ladder each child belongs (Strayer and Strayer, 1976). Usually, the children agree on who is "toughest," who is "smartest," and so forth, and the roles of leader and follower are solidly established.

Studies of the way dominance is established and maintained among young children throw light on power relations in groups and on individual responses to those relations. As Janet Strayer (1977) found in a study of several preschool groups, the most aggressive child in a group is rarely the child at the top of the dominance hierarchy, and the child who winds up as the scapegoat is one who does not keep on the appropriate rung. Scapegoats are neither extremely aggressive nor extremely submissive;

they either do not understand the group's structure, or else they know it and deliberately violate it. As we shall see in Chapter 16, getting along in the peer group is an important part of the development of social competence.

ORGANISMIC THEORIES

Like adaptation theories, organismic theories view human development from an evolutionary perspective; but organismic theories make no attempt to interpret development in terms of its evolutionary function. Instead, they look at the human infant as evolved to develop in certain ways along a path determined by the interaction of genetic maturation and experience.

The biological organism is the metaphor that dominates the view of organismic theorists (Reese and Overton, 1970). The individual is seen as a spontaneously active organism, and because some activity is not a response to external events, it is theoretically impossible ever to predict all of a person's acts.

Constructionism is the hallmark of the organismic view. Unlike learning theorists, who espouse the concept of naïve realism, organismic theorists assert that the world cannot be known objectively; instead knowledge of it is actively constructed by the child. Change is not simply cumulative. As the child develops, his or her mind undergoes a series of reorganizations, each one moving the child into a higher stage of psychological functioning. In the organismic view, we can never understand a child's behavior apart from its purpose. Breaking up behavior into bits and studying it apart from its context, therefore, serves no purpose.

Organismic theories developed in Europe early in this century, and two of the foremost theorists were Heinz Werner (1948, 1957) and Jean Piaget (1952b, 1970b), who shared common influences. Both were affected by evolutionary theory and trained in the biological and natural sciences. This training led them to emphasize the adaptive functions of behavior in maintaining an equilibrium between the individual and the environment. Both emphasized that change in behavior and functioning result from the interaction of maturation and experience.

Werner and Piaget viewed cognition as a biological system. The function and characteristics of thought were like those of respiration or digestion — taking in, modifying, and using whatever elements were needed.

From birth, human beings actively engage and use their environment, and as time passes they gradually construct their own understanding of the world. At first, babies are *egocentric*. They make no distinction between themselves and the external world, or among feeling, thought, and the external world. As they develop, children gradually acquire *perspective*, a sense of themselves as people who are separate from the world, and develop objectively based concepts about the world that they share with others.

Werner and Piaget studied development at an everyday level, intervening in common situations and studying the effects of their experimental manipulations on a child's behavior. This approach was consistent with their belief that fragmenting natural patterns of behavior, as when memory is investigated by requiring children to memorize lists of words, leads to a limited understanding of development.

Piaget's Theory

Piaget's theory has had more influence in recent years than other organismic theories. It gives meaningful continuity to the development of human understanding, and it has strongly influenced research in the fields of perceptual and intellectual development. Piaget called his approach *genetic epistemology*. Epistemology is the study of knowledge — how we know what we know. The term "genetic" here means developmental. Piaget's theory covers the development of intelligence (ways of knowing).

For Piaget, knowledge came from action. Using *schemes*, or patterns of action, babies act

Yves de Braine/Black Star

Jean Piaget (1896–1980)

Jean Piaget was born and reared in Switzerland. As a boy he was a keen observer of animal behavior, and when he was only fifteen, published a paper on shells in a scientific journal. He came by his interest in knowledge and knowing (epistemology) as a result of studying philosophy and logic. Whereas most American psychologists have been influenced by the evolutionary theories of Charles Darwin, Piaget was influenced by the creative evolution of Henri Bergson, who saw a divine agency instead of chance as the force behind evolution.

After receiving his doctorate in biological science at the University of Lausanne in 1918,

he became interested in psychology. In order to pursue his interest in abnormal psychology, he went to Paris and, while studying at the Sorbonne, secured a position in Alfred Binet's laboratory. During his work there, he began to pay more attention to children's wrong answers than to their right ones, realizing that the wrong answers provided invaluable clues to the nature of their thinking.

Piaget's interest in children's mental processes shifted and deepened when, in 1929, he began observing his own children. As he kept detailed records of their behavior, he worked at tracing the origins of children's thought to their behavior as babies. Later, he became interested in the thought of adolescents. Piaget's primary method was to present problems in a standardized way to children of different ages. He then asked each child to explain his or her answers and probed these explanations with a series of carefully phrased questions.

Soon after completing his work in Paris, Piaget accepted an appointment as director of research at the Jean Jacques Rousseau Institute in Geneva. Thereafter he lived in Geneva, conducting research and writing on cognitive development as professor of experimental psychology and genetic epistemology at the University of Geneva.

on objects around them—they feel, turn, bang, or mouth them. Their knowledge of those objects grows neither from the objects themselves nor from the babies themselves, but from the interaction of the two, as the babies *assimilate*, or incorporate, new knowledge into their existing schemes and *accommodate*, or modify, their schemes to acquire knowledge that does not fit them. As a result of this process, children pass through a series of developmental stages as they mature, each stage representing an advance in their thinking, a qualitatively different way of understanding the world in which they live.

SCHEMES In Piagetian terms, a child's understanding of the world arises from the coordination of actions and the interrelationships of those actions with objects in the environment. The infant, in other words, is a *constructionist*. The baby constructs reality from the relationships of actions and objects, not simply from actions alone nor from the perceptual qualities of objects alone. For example, infants can throw a ball and roll it; they can apply those same actions to an orange. They learn that both objects roll (are round) but that when thrown, the ball bounces and the orange goes "thud." From their ordinary and simple actions on objects, infants come to know the effects of their actions and the properties of objects. They also learn to coordinate their actions—they cannot simultaneously throw and roll the same object. These schemes, such as grasping or throwing, are the infant's forms of thought.

Older children and adults still think in the same kind of action patterns when they drive a car or play a piano or type a letter; but they also have internalized schemes derived from earlier concrete experiences, so that they can manipulate objects mentally, classifying them and understanding their relationships. They need not literally try out the solution to every problem. Mental arithmetic replaces the physical act of counting; logical sequences of thought, such as "If . . . then" statements, replace the younger child's concrete manipulations of cause-effect relations.

For example, most adults have come to understand the principle of gravity: when released from an elevated position, objects fall. But a ten-month-old baby explores gravity by dropping bits of dinner from the highchair tray and watching intently as each piece hits the floor. (The baby also discovers that cups fall, spoons fall, cookies fall.) A baby's scheme of dropping objects in space soon becomes coordinated with many objects, so that he or she no longer creates the same mess again and again. And since dropping food is antithetical to eating it, a hungry baby comes to recognize that eating and dropping the same object are not compatible schemes.

ASSIMILATION AND ACCOMMODATION In Piaget's theory, children's thinking develops through the processes of assimilation and accommodation. For example, a baby can bang a large variety of objects, incorporating new knowledge through an existing "banging" scheme, assimilating to the scheme whether

In Piaget's view, to obtain the toy this baby first tries a familiar grasping scheme (assimilation) and then alters it with new knowledge (accommodation) to get the toy through the bars. (George S. Zimbel/Monkmeyer Press)

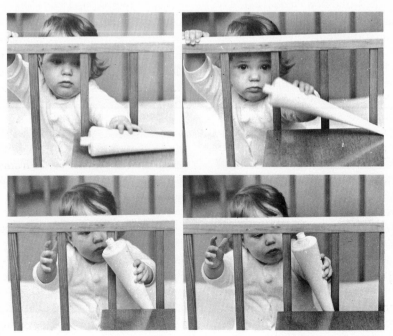

"banging" is a primary attribute of each object. But if the baby has always picked up rigid objects and now reaches for a soft one, the same grasping scheme will not effectively hold the toy, so the baby must accommodate the grasping scheme, altering it to fit the qualities of the new object if banging is to be successful.

The processes of assimilation and accommodation work together in complementary fashion. To assimilate is to use what we already know how to do in order to do something new; to accommodate is to acquire a new way of doing something. Both processes continue to function throughout the life span. For example, in the United States we are being asked to convert our thinking to the metric system. In essence, we are being asked to restructure our existing schemes (accommodation). After we have learned the metric units of weight, volume, and linear measure, we will have to assimilate much of what we knew under the old scheme to the new one. Does one wear a sweater outdoors at 30°C? (No.) Is 80 kilometers per hour too fast a speed to drive on a freeway? (Probably not.) Is $3.50 per kilogram too much to pay for pork chops? (No.) In other words, the new knowledge will have to be acquired by applying what we have already learned in a different way under other schemes.

At any given time, the developing person can make only limited changes in his or her cognitive structures. There must always be some continuity. Over the life span, the balance, or equilibrium, between assimilation and accommodation changes in the direction of greater balance. *Equilibration*, the most general developmental principle in Piaget's theory, states that the organism always tends toward biological and psychological balance and that development is a progressive approximation to an ideal state of equilibrium that it never fully achieves. A child's equilibrium at any one stage may be upset by external events, such as new information he or she cannot readily assimilate, or by internal processes that bring the child to a new "readiness" to accommodate. In both cases, the child's previous temporary equilibrium is upset, and development advances to a new, higher level of organization.

STAGES According to Piaget, intellectual development goes through a series of stages, and the organization of behavior is qualitatively different at each stage. The two essential points of Piaget's stage theory are: (1) stages emerge in a constant order of succession, and (2) neither heredity nor environment independently explains the progressive development of mental structures. Piaget proposed three major stages of intellectual development: a *sensorimotor* period, a period of *representational* thought, and a *formal operational* period.

The sensorimotor period begins at birth and extends until the child is eighteen months to two years old. Piaget subdivided this period into six substages. The first covers the newborn period, when the baby's actions are primarily based on reflexes and are rigid and inflexible. Inflexible as these innate actions are, they can be affected by experience. A baby learns to regulate sucking, for example, and will suck more slowly for sweetened than for unsweetened water. During these first few weeks of life, primitive reflexes tend to disappear and the adaptive reflexes, such as vocalizing, grasping and sucking, stabilize and become more efficient.

The hallmark of the second sensorimotor substage, which occupies the next two or three months, is the *primary circular reaction*. A circular reaction is any behavior—whether grasping, sucking, looking, or vocalizing—that the baby tends to repeat again and again because of the stimulation provided by it. Now babies intentionally look and listen to the sights and sounds of the world. They are beginning to coordinate their senses and will, for example, use their eyes to direct their grasp.

In the third substage, which lasts until they are seven or eight months old, babies rely on *secondary circular reactions*. Their repetitive acts—shaking a rattle or banging a cup on the highchair tray — are learned, reinforced by the effects of their actions. Their action schemes are often meant to prolong events that interest them. Sensorimotor coordination is improving, and babies are more proficient at grasping objects that attract them.

During the fourth substage, which often occupies the rest of the first year, babies coordinate their secondary circular reactions and develop adaptive schemes, which they apply with intent to the world around them. They are busily engaged in solving problems and instead of simply prolonging interesting events, will use them to obtain some goal. Although the concept is not complete, babies now show some awareness that objects continue to exist when out of sight. If a baby sees someone put a cloth or pillow over a toy, he or she will look for and find the toy.

The fifth substage occupies up to half of the second year of life. Babies' schemes have become *tertiary circular reactions,* which are intelligent, systematic adaptations to specific situations. Faced with a problem, they will set about solving it with a process of trial and error, If someone hides a toy, the infant will look for it wherever he or she has seen it hidden — an advance over the last substage when, if the baby saw a cloth placed over a toy and a pillow placed on top of the cloth, the infant gave up the search. But babies still do not suspect that someone might surreptitiously move the toy; they will also stop searching if the toy is not just where they saw someone hide it.

The last substage of the sensorimotor period, which can extend through the last half of the second year, marks a significant advance. Now babies form mental representations of their own actions and of events in the world around them. They do not have to imitate an adult's actions immediately but can store the representation and imitate the person the next day. The idea that hidden objects continue to exist is fully developed. When looking for a hidden toy, babies will search in all the places it might have been placed. And when solving a problem, they no

longer have to rely on trial and error; they have internalized schemes, solving problems in their heads and then applying the solutions. They are ready to move out of infancy and into the preoperational period.

Piaget divided the period of representational thought into the *preoperational* and *concrete operational* stages. The preoperational stage covers the preschool years and can last until a child is seven or eight. Although children at this stage can certainly form mental representations, those representations do not, for Piaget, qualify as mental operations because such children do not understand certain logical rules. For example, although they know that seven chocolate drops and five caramels are all candy, they will stoutly maintain that there are more chocolates than candy. Children's representations at this stage also fail on another count: they are not integrated. Because of these failures, children harbor some beliefs that adults might find amusing — such as the belief that everything in the world, including stones and rivers, was made by some person; or that their bicycles are alive. They also believe that putting a mask on an animal or person truly transforms that person. During this preoperational period, a good part of children's language is not meant for communication but is addressed to themselves. When they think, they think out loud. They are also egocentric, according to Piaget, and believe that everyone sees the world exactly as they do. All in all, although this is an exciting period of cognitive development, when measured against the formal logical thought that Piaget saw as the goal of development, the thought of the preoperational child falls short on every count.

During the concrete operational period, which lasts until a child is about eleven or twelve, children do indeed attain logical thought, but their schemes apply only to concrete objects. They now understand logical operations, including reversible transformations. They know that a string of beads that is stretched out straight is no longer than it was when it lay in a curve. They also know that when they have

Courtesy International
Universities Press

Heinz Werner (1890–1964)

Heinz Werner was interested in formulating a comprehensive theory of cognitive development. He adopted principles and concepts from embryology, biology, and other natural sciences and applied them to mental development. Werner considered learning views of development wrong, because he believed development was much more than a gradual and continuous process of acquiring bits of behavior.

Because he was interested in explaining mental life, his approach was broad, eclectic, and comparative. He wanted his theory to explain the course of cognitive development over the life span and to account for differences in thought among species, among cultures, and among abnormal groups.

He stressed that the development of human beings shows both change and stability. People go through an ordered sequence of stages, which are characterized by different organizations of cognitive structure and functioning. Each stage involves both adaptive change and organizational stability. Adaptive change means that with maturation there is a progressive development of specific, separate ways of doing and seeing things, and that these more advanced ways take precedence over early, simple forms. Organizational stability means that, even though changes occur, a person retains an essential and basic organization.

Werner showed that even as infants, human beings are organized and have some degree of competence, and this inborn organization is the basis for adaptive behavior and learning. Although movement, vision, thinking, and so on, are always organized, they undergo progressive changes in a patterned order.

seven chocolate drops and five caramels, they have more candy than chocolate drops. They can reason about the solid, concrete objects in the world around them. Their language is now intended for communication, because they now think silently. And they have put aside all the childish beliefs that adults find so charming.

The stage of formal operational thought is the culmination of cognitive development. It can appear when a child is about eleven years old, although many children do not enter this stage until they are adolescents. Children can now use abstract reasoning and are capable of adopting artificial premises they know to be untrue. It is this ability to be flexible and to reason in the absence of observed fact—to use hypothetical or propositional schemes ("if . . . then" statements)—that marks the adult manner of thought.

Werner's Theory

Like Piaget, Heinz Werner emphasized the interacting roles of genetic maturation and environmental experience. He believed that psychological development resembles the development of the embryo; that is, all normal children pass through the same milestones of development in the same order. Yet Werner never set forth a general system of development, identifying each stage and its characteristics as did Piaget.

The major theme of Werner's developmental theory is the *orthogenetic principle* (Werner, 1948), for Werner tried to establish the principles of correct (ortho) development (genetic) in both physical and psychological growth. He saw the child as moving from a global, undifferentiated state to one of high differentiation and integration. Responses and skills are increasingly organized into hierarchies, a trend Werner called *hierarchic integration.* This is easy to see in the physical area, where the baby develops hierarchic patterns of movement that bring each separate motor capability into the service of others in a highly organized way. When a baby first learns to drink from a cup, for example, he combines and integrates a series of simple skills. First a little boy must be able to sit up and fix his eyes on the cup. Then he must be able to use visual information to reach out, find the cup, grasp it, and hold it upright. He must then combine visual information with kinesthetic information about the position of his head and mouth, arms and hands, in order to bring the cup to his mouth, tilt it at the correct angle, stop tilting it before it spills, and swallow. When the little boy drinks from a cup, he combines and integrates all these skills so smoothly that his mother never considers the number of simple abilities that are involved.

As babies become able to integrate perception and thought into hierarchies, they learn to distinguish parts from the whole, see relationships, and understand the difference between relevant and irrelevant qualities. They understand, for example, that Mother is still the same person, even though she has cut her hair and put a blonde rinse on it. Gradually, the higher mental functions come to control the lower ones. Children use language to direct their behavior. By the time they are seven, they understand that the dreams they once thought arose from an external source originate within them and are private. They become less bound by the immediate situation and increasingly able to plan and

to tolerate delay. Instead of interpreting the world entirely in terms of their own needs, children begin to appreciate the needs and goals of others.

Although Werner has not been the dominant figure Piaget has become, his concept of differentiation and hierarchic integration has been incorporated into general theories of child development, his research in the field of perception has stimulated a good deal of theory and research, and his students have made significant advances in the field of child development.

DIALECTICAL THEORIES

Dissatisfaction with both mechanistic and organismic approaches to child development has given rise to yet another way of looking at the developing child: dialectical psychology. With its roots in the philosophy of Hegel and Karl Marx, this kind of psychology sees development as a dialectical process. In a *dialectic*, each idea is seen as a thesis that interacts with its antithesis, or opposite, to form a synthesis on a new level. The synthesis becomes a new thesis that again interacts with its antithesis to form a new synthesis, and so on. In the dialectical view, human development proceeds in the same way; in each individual stage of development, a person interacts with society to reach a new level of functioning.

Although psychologists with differing theoretical views agree that the aim of developmental psychology is to understand the changing individual in the changing world, dialectical psychologists believe that this concept receives mostly lip service. That is, most psychologists fail to consider how historical-social changes affect behavior and its development. They seem to believe that if they can understand behavior as it was in 1900, they understand it as it is in the 1980s. In the dialectical view, however, knowledge is social; it is created by society and transmitted to the individual. Dialectical psychologists have suggested that major cultural changes, such as television and computers, can have an enormous impact on the nature of thought and its development.

The discomfort of dialectical psychologists with mechanistic psychology was summed up by Robert Wozniak (1975), who said that behavioral psychologists do not study change; instead, they analyze development into its elements and then recombine them into the whole, assuming that if they understand the elements and the way they are combined, they will understand development. Organismic psychologists come closer to the dialectical view, for they see development as arising out of the child's active operations on the environment. But the dialectic is incomplete. For Piaget, said Klaus Riegel (1975a), the environment appeared to be an assemblage of things without activity or history; social interaction received little consideration in his theory. In addition, Piaget focused on equilibrium, overemphasizing stability at the expense of change.

The dialectical view first became prominent when Soviet psychologists were searching for an approach to psychology that would fit comfortably within the Marxist framework. In recent years, American psychologists have re-evaluated the methods of Soviet psychology, and many have come to regard dialectics as a helpful tool instead of as a dogmatic straitjacket.

Vygotsky's View

Shortly after the Russian Revolution, Lev S. Vygotsky became a leading Soviet psychologist. Society, he believed, was essential to human development. Instead of regarding intellectual development as primarily the result of maturation, he saw children as active organizers who used the tools and language of culture in a continual interaction with the social world, thereby changing both the world and themselves.

Everything that distinguishes the child's mind from that of a chimpanzee comes from the culture, he believed, and every facet of development begins between the child and another person. Vygotsky included voluntary attention, logical memory, the foundation of concepts, and language in his list of developmental facets. He saw each process as appearing twice in a child's development—first shared between the child and an adult (an interpersonal process) and then reappearing inside the child (an intrapersonal process) (Vygotsky, 1978). As the child reconstructs a process internally, he or she moves through an upward spiral of development and increasingly is able to control his or her behavior. Development is neither an accumulation of small changes in behavior nor a single upward line but a dialectical process. In each succeeding stage, the developing person creates new responses and carries them out in new ways under the influence of different psychological processes.

Because of his emphasis on the role of society in development, Vygotsky was especially interested in language. He saw language as the primary means used by society to affect a child's development and as the only way abstract thought could be transmitted. In addition, he believed that once a child developed the ability to think in words, the nature of development changed radically (Vygotsky, 1962).

At each stage, Vygotsky believed, the child is always more capable than testing shows, and he urged educators to exploit this fact. Tests measure a child's developmental level, but there is also a zone of *proximal development*, which is the distance between the level at which a child can solve problems alone and the level at which the child can solve problems with adult guidance or with more capable peers. This zone can be extended by play and by learning, and its width varies among children. For example, one eight-year-old may, with cooperation, be able to solve problems designed for twelve-year-olds; another, with similar cooperation, may only be able to solve problems designed for nine-year-olds.

Vygotsky's influence has been strongest

Lev Semanovich Vygotsky (1896–1934)

Lev S. Vygotsky, who was born in Russia, was a contemporary of Piaget and Werner. He was graduated from Moscow University in 1917 and until 1923 taught both literature and psychology in Gomel. In 1924, just after Soviet psychology had officially adopted "reactology"—an approach to psychology that depended upon behavioral reactions in a Marxist framework (Cole and Scribner, 1978), Vygotsky returned to Moscow to work at the Institute of Psychology. His views did not coincide with either of the major European approaches to psychology, which were either introspective or behavioristic (as was reactology). Nor did he find the Gestalt psychologists' attempts to study behavior and experience as wholes a satisfactory solution.

Vygotsky believed that psychologists should study processes and the way they change, for as people respond to a situation, they alter it. One of his complaints about Piaget's theory was that the Swiss psychologist did not give enough weight to the influence of the environment on the developing child. Vygotsky believed that the internalization of social and cultural activities was the key to human development and that it distinguished human beings from animals.

Vygotsky's primary interests were thought, language, memory, and play. Toward the end of his life, he worked on the problems of education. But Vygotsky was also trained as a physician and advocated the combination of neurology and physiology with the experimental study of thought processes and their development. Just before his death from tuberculosis in 1934, he had been asked to head the department of psychology in the All-Union Institute of Experimental Medicine.

Vygotsky died at thirty-eight, but his influence on Soviet psychology continued through his students, who hold major positions throughout the Soviet Union. For years after his death, Vygotsky's views were disregarded in this country; but in 1962, *Thought and Language* was translated and his ideas entered the American psychological community. With each passing year, his notions about the relation of thought and language, the natures and uses of play, and the concept of proximal development have received more attention. In 1978, his essays, *Mind in Society*, were translated and published.

among psychologists who are interested in comparing the way thought develops in various cultures and among psychologists who study the development of play and language.

American Dialectical Psychology

Among American psychologists, Klaus Riegel (1976) has been the most enthusiastic proponent of dialectical psychology. He saw this approach as concerned with the way children, adults, and groups recognize challenges and ask questions.

He was opposed to a child-centered developmental psychology, for he believed that development and change were constant companions of life. Like Vygotsky, Riegel believed that all psychology is developmental psychology. Studying the thought of a single child is the study of inner dialectics; studying the child in relation to others is the study of outer dialectics. Ideally, Riegel believed, both should be studied together.

Development, according to Riegel, progresses simultaneously along several dimensions: biological, sociological, psychological, and physical (Riegel, 1975b). These dimensions are interdependent but not always coordinated. When one dimension is out of phase with the rest, a developmental crisis occurs. Once the dimensions are again synchronized, the child makes a developmental leap. Without such crises, there would be no change—in either the individual or society.

The existence of these crises and contradictions led Riegel (1975a) to propose the addition of a fifth and final stage to Piaget's stages of cognitive development: the stage of dialectical operations. In this stage, a person does not require equilibrium but can accept contradictions as the basis of all thought. Such a person realizes that contradiction is both essential and constructive, and does not regard a crisis as a catastrophe.

Many psychologists who do not consider themselves dialectical psychologists conduct research that meets the requirements of dialectical psychology. Piaget's exploration of the way children wrestle with problems requiring formal operations—for example, determining what factors affect the speed of a pendulum (Inhelder and Piaget, 1958)—is a study of inner dialectics. And Jerome Bruner's (1978) observation of prelinguistic games and dialogues between mother and child, is a study of outer dialectics.

THEORIES IN PERSPECTIVE

Although the groups of theories presented in this chapter may appear to have little in common, they are largely complementary. All suggest that human growth and development is regular, and all assume that most behavior is potentially predictable. But they often attend to different behavior (even if they give it the same label, such as "learning"), and they often explain different aspects of the developmental process.

When different theories look at the same process, they often talk about it in different ways. The relationship between baby and caregiver, called attachment, for example, is regarded by psychoanalytic theorists as an outgrowth of the caregiver satisfying the infant's

need to suck that characterizes the oral period. Learning theorists see attachment as the result of conditioning; the primary caregiver both satisfies the infant's basic needs and provides interesting and satisfying stimulation. And ethological theories view attachment as an evolved response that increases the likelihood of the infant's—and therefore the species'—survival.

On the other hand, the various viewpoints appear to be converging, and they may one day approach a common theoretical framework. All have a common concern with identifying the processes involved in human growth and development. And they share the goal of synthesizing observations and experimental findings to explain how and why behavior originates and develops. In recent years, as we have seen, social-learning theorists have begun to modify early, narrow positions and to use insights from cognitive theories to expand their explanations of human behavior and development. Other theorists have attempted to reconcile information-processing views with organismic theories No matter which theory a developmental psychologist espouses, his or her explanations necessarily involve an exploration and documentation of multiple, interacting causes, as the next chapter makes clear.

SUMMARY

1. Theories of human development are based on different assumptions about human nature. These assumptions focus on inborn differences among people, environmental influences, the role of human beings in their own development, the natural goodness or evil of humanity, and the relationship of child to adult behavior.

2. Behavior-learning theories view human behavior as primarily the result of experience. There are two major types of learning: classical conditioning and operant conditioning. Social-learning theories add to conditioning the role of

observational learning and, in recent years, have expanded their view to include the role of human thought in development.

3. Psychodynamic theories see human behavior as motivated by various internal and external forces. For Freud, the unconscious forces of the id are tempered and sublimated by the ego and the superego, and the child moves through a series of psychosexual stages, each characterized by the way psychic energy is expressed. For Erikson, personality develops according to steps determined by the organism's readiness to interact with the world, and the series of stages are called psychosocial because interaction with society is the dominant factor.

4. Adaptation theories see human behavior from an evolutionary perspective, describing its development in terms of its effect on human survival. Both the viewpoints and the methods of adaptation theorists come from the field of ethology.

5. Organismic theories also see human development in evolutionary terms, stressing the interaction between the person and the environment. They see the development of behavior as progressing by stages. In Piaget's theory, the child assimilates and accommodates new knowledge, thus approaching an equilibrium between internal schemes and the outside world. Intellectually, the child progresses through the sensorimotor, the representational, and the formal operational stages. In Werner's theory, the child moves from a global, undifferentiated state to one of high differentiation and integration, in which responses and skills are organized into hierarchies.

6. Dialectical theories have much in common with organismic theories, but they stress the social nature of knowledge. All knowledge is created by society and transmitted to the individual; therefore, major cultural changes can have profound impacts on the nature and development of human thought.

C H A P T E R   T H R E E

Determinants of Development

If a boy who is arrested for stealing a car has a brother with a prison record, people often say, "He's just like his brother. Criminality runs in the family." But the boy was slow to talk and has always done poorly in school, has a quick temper and often gets into fights with his peers, his father cannot keep a job, and his family lives in a poverty area. Had any of these influences—intelligence, temperament, peer relations, father's continual unemployment, brother's example, or socioeconomic environment—been different, the boy might not have taken the car. Although finding a single cause for a developmental effect is attractive and easy, the relationship is invariably complicated. Few aspects of development or behavior can be understood by examining only one cause.

Developmentalists are aware that both genetic and environmental determinants are responsible for the changes that occur in the developing person. *Genes*, the microscopic elements that carry the blueprints of heredity, combine with the *environment*, the physical and social conditions that surround the child, to produce development. Nearly every aspect of children's lives, including their concept of themselves, their scores on intelligence tests, their height, and the time at which they become sexually mature, are affected by both kinds of influence.

In this chapter, we shall explore some of the different influences on human behavior and the ways that developmental psychologists set about studying them. We shall see that heredity and environment always work together to shape behavior and that maturation plays an important part in the process. Genetic research with animals, we shall find, helps us to understand the unfolding of heredity in human beings, and another good way to look at human heredity is to compare related and unrelated people. We shall look at environments and observe how they influence the developing person. Next, we shall examine instances of interaction among various determinants, stressing the intertwining of genetic, physical, and social determinants in every aspect of development. Finally, we shall discuss the ways in which developmental psychologists investigate determinants of development, finding that each type of study has its particular strengths and weaknesses, and that none is superior in all situations.

GENETIC DETERMINANTS

Our heredity is of two kinds: the general inheritance of our species that makes us into that peculiar primate *Homo sapiens*, and our specific inheritance from our parents, grandparents, and great-grandparents that makes each of us visibly and temperamentally different from other members of our species. Both inheritances are carried within our body cells, and in Chapter 4 we shall discuss in detail the ways in which genes transmit this hereditary information. Genes begin working on us at the moment of conception and continue their work until we die. They determine whether a child will be a boy or a girl; they determine the specific color of a person's eyes as well as the general fact that each member of the species has two and that those eyes can perceive various wavelengths of light; and they determine a person's susceptibility to certain types of diseases, such as diabetes.

Although the importance of genetic determinants is established, discovering specific genetic influences on behavior and development is a difficult task. Ethics forbids researchers to manipulate a human being's genetic structure. Nor is it ethical to select two people, ask them

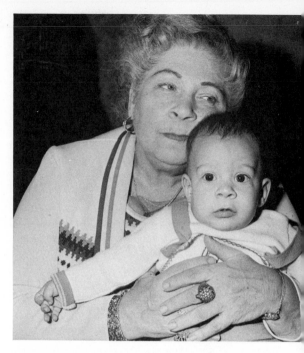

This infant's resemblance to his grandmother demonstrates the transmission of specific genetic information that is not part of the general inheritance which accompanies membership in the human species. (© Michael Weisbrot & Family)

to mate and produce children, and subject their offspring to one environment or another in order to determine the kinds of behavior that might be attributed to genetic differences. How, then, do we know about the contribution of genetics to human behavior?

Genetic Studies With Animals

Most of our knowledge has come from research on lower animals, in which nearly ideal genetic research can be performed. Such studies can suggest general principles that alert us to possible genetic influences on human behavior. By breeding genetically related animals, for example, researchers have discovered that genes go beyond dictating an animal's physical structure and play a role in its temperament and behavior. After testing rats on their ability to learn the path through a maze, R. C. Tryon (1940) interbred those rats that learned quickly. By repeating this process with the offspring, generation after generation, he developed a group of rats that were almost "purebred" for superior performance in mazes. And by interbreeding rats who had trouble finding their way through a maze, he developed another group that had enormous difficulty in learning the path. His research indicates that genes do indeed affect a rat's ability in maze learning. Similar studies have shown that genetic differences can also affect aggressiveness, hoarding, exploratory behavior, sex drive, alcohol preference, and a variety of other traits (McClearn, 1970).

Since different strains of animals do not always respond to the same experience with the same kind of behavior, we know that it is impossible to predict the precise outcome of a particular learning experience on any animal or human being unless we know its genetic make-up—knowledge that is lacking outside the animal research laboratory.

Daniel Freedman's (1958) experiments on the connection between indulging or disciplining a young puppy and its later self-control provide an example of the effects of genes on experience. Freedman selected dogs from four different breeds: Basenji, Shetland sheepdog, wirehaired fox terrier, and beagle. The caretakers indulged some of the dogs from each breed between the third and eighth weeks of their lives by encouraging them to play, to be aggressive, and to engage in rough-and-tumble activities. In contrast, the caretakers disciplined other dogs from each breed by restraining them, teaching them to sit, stay, come on command, and so forth. After this training, each dog was tested. When it was hungry, its caretaker took it into a room containing a bowl of meat. For three minutes the caretaker prevented the animal from eating by hitting it on the rump with a rolled newspaper and shouting "No!" every time the dog approached the food. Then the handler left the room and the experimenter recorded the length of time that elapsed before the dog ate the meat.

Some theories of development might lead to the conclusion that an overindulged dog will not be able to inhibit its impulse to eat in such a test. But the results of eight days of testing indicate that such a prediction is not valid for dogs. In two breeds, the terriers and the beagles, the indulged animals waited longer before approaching the food than did their disciplined companions. Neither the indulged nor the disciplined Shetlands ever ate the food; but all the Basenjis dug right into the meal. Had Freedman studied only terriers and beagles, he would have assumed that environment determined self-control; had he studied only Shetlands and Basenjis, he would have assumed that genes determine it. But by using four breeds, he discovered that gene-environment interaction must always be considered, even in areas where our first assumption is that the environment is the overriding factor.

Momentary environmental circumstances may also affect the way that genetically influenced behavior is expressed or whether it appears at all. In many cases, hereditary behavior patterns appear only in the presence of a releasing stimulus. For example, Niko Tinbergen (1951) has observed that the male stickleback fish will attack a strange male stickleback only if the intruder is ready to mate, a condition revealed by a red belly. The fight that ensues looks natural and flexible, but the fish protecting its territory merely imitates the fighting characteristics of the intruder. If the intruder bites, the defender bites back; if it threatens, the defender threatens, and so on. The intruder's red belly releases the defender's attack, and each fighting thrust of the intruder releases a response that is identical to the stimulus. The result is an adaptive, natural, and flexible behavioral pattern, but its components are fixed patterns released by the specific stimuli of the intruder. Thus genetic behavior requires the appropriate environmental stimuli in order for it to appear. Although human behavior is unlikely to be influenced by fixed patterns of action, some of our behavior that appears spontaneous may have genetic components. One such example is human caregiving, which, as we noted in Chapter 2, appears to be released by a baby's "cuteness."

We know, then, that genes may play a role in temperament and behavior, that their influence may extend to areas where we do not expect to find it, that it is impossible to predict the outcome of experience without knowing a person's genetic make-up, and that particular environmental circumstances are sometimes required for the appearance of genetically influenced behavior. Using such principles, researchers in *genetics*, the scientific study of the effects of heredity, have explored the role of genes in human development.

Human Genetics

Researchers ask two questions about the role of genes in human development: "How" and "How much?" The question "How?" refers to the ways in which heredity interacts with the environment to produce development in all human beings. For example, how do genes combine with environmental factors, such as nutrition, to produce growth. Answers to the question "How?" come from studies of people in general. The question "How much?" refers to the sources of differences among individuals. How much of the differences in height among people in a developmental psychology class are due to each student's different heredity (genetic effects) as distinguished from nutritional differences while the students were growing up (environmental effects)? Answers to the question "How much?" come from studies of the ways that people differ in their individual development. "How?" and "How much?" are both important questions.

With our present knowledge, we cannot say *how* genes affect behavior. Many genes contribute to the development of most behavioral characteristics. We know, for example, that 150 independent genes can cause different forms of mental retardation and that at least several hundred more genes are required to develop a normal human brain. But we do not know the ways in which these hundreds of genes act together to produce a normal brain or normal intelligence.

The timing of growth and aging and the sequence of development are, we know, related to gene action. Genes are "turned on" at some but not other points in development. The "turned-on" genes are active in producing substances within the body that create new structures, regulate their functions, or maintain their state. It appears that aging is also under the control of genes and may be related to gradual deteriorations in the genetic code (Jarvik and Cohen, 1973).

Whereas specifying how heredity interacts with environment to affect growth and development in the human species is extremely difficult, questions that ask *how much* genes affect the development of differences among individuals are easier to answer. Although no one has yet been able to isolate a single gene that accounts for a substantial amount of the differences in normal behavior among people (Freedman, 1974), we do have conclusive answers for some abnormal physical traits caused by single genes, as we shall describe in Chapter 4. In the case of such traits as height, we can get some idea of genetic influences by comparing the trait among related and unrelated people. The more closely people are related and the more similar the trait, the more likely it is that genetic factors have influenced the trait. (See Figure 3.1.) Physical appearance is obviously influenced by genetic differences, because genetically related people resemble one another more than do unrelated people.

Yet even if two people have the same genes for a particular trait, it may not show itself in the same way. The genetic make-up of each person has a unique range of possible responses, called the *reaction range*, whose realization depends upon the particular environment he or she encounters. This reaction range limits the ways each of us can respond to specific environmental conditions—whether good or bad. In the case of height: good nutrition will make all of

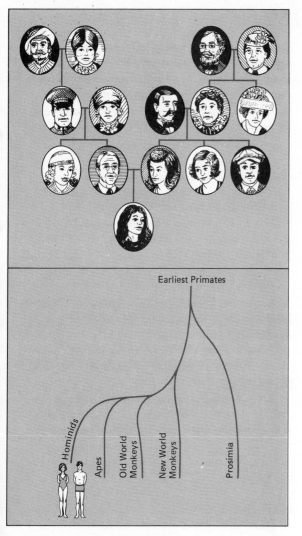

Figure 3.1 *(top)* The family tree of one human being. This tree traces the ancestry of a single individual and covers a time span of a little more than a hundred years. Inheritance on this scale accounts for the biological determination of certain characteristics that distinguish one individual from another.

(bottom) The evolution of *Homo sapiens*. This tree traces the ancestry of an entire species and covers a time span of tens of millions of years. Inheritance on this scale accounts for the biological determination of characteristics that all human beings have in common. (After Washburn and Moore, 1974)

us taller than poor nutrition will, but given the same nutrition, some of us will be taller than others because of our genetic inheritance. The development of intellectual skills also has a reaction range: a stimulating environment will not make Albert Einsteins or Leonardo da Vincis of us all, nor will moderately deprived circumstances make us mentally retarded. In other words, genes do not specify a particular height or intelligence for anyone; they specify a range for development that depends on environmental factors. Thus the physical height and the level of intellectual development we ultimately achieve depend on both genetic and environmental factors.

Heritability

We know that the individuals in any group have different genetic compositions as well as different life experiences. But how much of the variability in height or intellectual ability is associated with differences in their genetic make-up rather than with differences in their lives? The relative contribution of genetics to any trait in a given group is called the *heritability* of the trait. But heritability is only an estimate based on the number of cases in the particular group; it may or may not represent the heritability of that trait in the general population.

Because heritability depends on the specific characteristics of the sample, the heritability for a given trait may change from one year to the next, especially if the factors that produce that trait change. Years ago, for example, the heritability for tuberculosis was quite high. At that time, the bacillus for TB was widespread and nearly every individual came into contact with it. Since all were exposed to the disease (same environment for this factor), whether one actually developed TB depended primarily on one's inborn biochemical susceptibility to that bacillus. In contrast, the TB bacillus is now present only in the most unsanitary circumstances, and many people who have a biochemical susceptibility to TB never come in contact with the bacillus. Thus the major determinant of whether one succumbs to TB is now exposure to the bacillus, not inborn susceptibility. Consequently, the heritability for TB is now quite low.

The cause of TB is the same today as it always was: the invasion of the TB bacillus in an individual with a biochemical susceptibility to that bacillus. But the heritability for TB has changed because getting the disease is now more closely associated with where one lives than with genetic predisposition. Therefore, the fact that a trait has a high heritability does not mean that genes cause it; nor does a low heritability mean that appearance of the trait is caused by environmental circumstances.

ENVIRONMENTAL DETERMINANTS

There is an old expression that genes set limits on development while environments determine what actually develops. This is not true. As we have seen, by responding to given environments in unique ways, genes help to determine the actual level of development. Environments are equally implicated in setting limits on development—by providing only certain opportunities and stimuli for a person to develop a particular characteristic or behavior. In an optimum environment, genetic factors are given full expression, unhindered by environmental constraints.

Even the most genetically oriented theorist would agree that environmental determinants play a powerful role in the development of the growing child. But the term "environment," which encompasses every influence, both physical and social, is too broad to have much scientific usefulness. It is always necessary to specify which features of any environment affect any particular behavior. To explain why some children achieve low scores on intelligence tests, for example, some environmentalists merely point to the obvious disparities between advantaged and disadvantaged homes, schools, and neigh-

borhoods, claiming that (somehow) all the noticeable differences determine differences in test scores. However, there are various ways of defining the environment and of explaining how individual experience influences development. All such ways can be sometimes useful and sometimes inappropriate, depending on the behavior that we are trying to explain.

Physical Factors

It is obvious that all organisms must have sufficient air, water, food, and light to maintain life. Without these, there is biological deterioration and even death. What is not so obvious is the extent to which other features of the physical environment affect the course of development. For example, the environment of the mother's uterus is critical to the survival and development of the fetus, which requires an efficient exchange of oxygen and nutrients and the elimination of wastes. If the maternal environment is deficient in nutrients such as calcium or protein, the infant's development will be stunted. Or the maternal environment may be crowded: short mothers have small and premature babies more often than tall mothers do, and twins are often so crowded that they are born prematurely. As Chapter 4 explains, the maternal physical environment has other important effects on fetal development.

Once out of the uterus, children live in a physical environment that wraps them in a metaphorical rather than a literal capsule. The physical features of their world—both natural and man-made—limit and determine their development. Life in a nomad's tent and life in a city apartment have different effects on a growing child. The physical context of any child's life offers some kinds of experiences and limits others.

Think, for example, of a young, inner-city boy who wants to swing. His parent must take him down fifteen floors in the elevator, then walk him four blocks through automobile traffic,

The physical aspects of the environment have potent effects on the growing child; each of these environments offers some experiences to children and denies them others. (© Michael Weisbrot & Family; © Beryl Goldberg; © Suzanne Szasz)

crowds of pedestrians, noise, and a whirring visual kaleidoscope to a park. In contrast, the suburban child merely walks out into the backyard and climbs onto the swing.

Just how potent the physical context can be is illustrated by a study of the effects of loud noise on children's development. Sheldon Cohen, David Glass, and Jerome E. Singer (1973) studied children who lived in a thirty-two-story apartment building located over a noisy expressway in Manhattan. As one went from the lower to the higher floors of the building, the noise level dropped. Cohen and his associates found that children who had lived at least four years on the lower, noisier floors were less able to tell the differences between subtle but contrastive speech sounds, such as "gear-beer" or "cope-coke," than children who lived on the higher, quieter floors. They also found that children who lived on the lower floors read less well than those on the higher floors. Both auditory discrimination and reading ability correlated highly with the noise levels in the apartments and the length of time the children had lived there. Although other factors may have been involved in the children's ability to hear or read well, the study seems to show that the physical environment can affect physical and mental abilities in a multitude of ways. The physical environment comprises more than a child's home or the wider world he or she walks through. It includes the internal environment as well, with its changing body chemistry, which is continually altered by the intake of food or medication. A boy who has been diagnosed as hyperactive and who therefore takes a stimulant drug four times a day reacts to experiences in a changed way and, as we shall see in Chapter 7, may not recall, when off the drug, what he learned under its influence. Hunger, thirst, pain, the presence of harmful bacteria or viruses, the malfunctioning of a gland or organ, can all affect the way a child responds to events, and serious disturbances of the internal environment can have lasting effects.

Social Factors

The social environment includes all those effects that people have on one another—in families, in peer groups, and in neighborhoods. It also encompasses the influences of social institutions, such as schools; cultural and subcultural values, attitudes, and beliefs; and the media, such as newspapers and television. As children grow and develop, their social involvement with their environment increases, and as we shall see throughout this book, the nature of their social experience has an impact on the total developmental process.

THE FAMILY Most children grow up in the context of a family—father, mother, perhaps brothers and sisters. The family is generally the first social unit with which a child comes in contact, and it has been shown to influence many aspects of behavioral development: sex roles, self-concepts, and interpersonal and intellectual skills. For example, the presence of a father has been shown to be important in the early years of a boy's life if he is to develop a traditional masculine role (Hetherington and Deur, 1972). Girls, too, seem to need their fathers, especially during the early years of life. Research with lower-class and lower-middle-class girls indicates that girls may acquire from their fathers the social skills needed to interact with the opposite sex (Hetherington, 1972).

The age and sex of siblings also help determine sex-role development. Boys with older sisters show a weaker preference for the traditional masculine sex role than boys with older brothers or boys who lack older siblings (H. Koch, 1966; Sutton-Smith and Rosenberg, 1970). Girls with older brothers behave in more traditionally masculine ways than do girls with older sisters or no older siblings. Because older siblings tend to act like parents toward younger children in the family, especially if there is a large age difference, it is not surprising to find

The effects of family size and birth order seem to come about because parents pay less attention to any one child when there are many, and to later-born children in general (Belmont and Marolla, 1973). The dilution of parental attention may also be responsible for the lower intelligence test scores of twins as compared to those of single children. When there are twins to care for, the amount or quality of attention that parents can give seems to diminish.

PEERS Peers affect behavior from early school age throughout the life span. When children go to nursery school, kindergarten, or first grade, they move partly out of the family world into the environment of the peer group. The peer group usually has its own values and rules of behavior, which may differ radically from those of the family.

In middle childhood and adolescence, the peer group provides an important testing ground for becoming a person. Because one cannot go through life being "Mama's boy" or "Daddy's girl," one has to establish other identifications and goals. Adolescent peers are decidedly important in the development of a sense of identity (Erikson, 1968). Because peers share the problems of establishing independence and identity, they provide positive support in the often painful process of becoming an adult.

Whether a child lives in a one- or two-parent family, has many siblings or none, will influence all aspects of development, from self-concept to intellectual skills. (© Barbara Alper 1981)

that older siblings appear to affect the sex-role development of younger children.

Families also provide a context for intellectual development. The opportunities that are available to children and the way that the parents respond to their curiosity affect what the children learn and how rapidly they learn it. If there are many children in the family, their intellectual skills tend to be less well developed than those of children in smaller families. Birth order also has an effect: first-born children and those early in birth rank tend to have higher scores on intelligence tests than children born later.

THE NEIGHBORHOOD Over the years it has been found that many features of a neighborhood influence its structure and function, affecting the development and behavior of the people who live there. In close-knit, active neighborhoods, children use the sidewalks to get acquainted, to meet their friends, and to play. Such neighborhoods provide a setting that encourages contacts. But if street traffic is dense and rapid, the sidewalks cannot be used as social areas and the neighborhood is less likely to be friendly. Similarly, unless the space near or

In a neighborhood that encourages contacts, residents are likely to use the sidewalks as meeting places and to make friends within the area. (© Harvey Stein 1979)

around buildings is open to view and hence "defensible" (capable of supervision), people will not use it for play, recreation, or socializing.

In addition, the ethnic flavor, socioeconomic level, and age range of the inhabitants can radically affect the growing child. School-age children who live near a college, for example, are likely to have fewer playmates their own age than children who live farther from the campus. Similarly, for a young child life in an area predominantly inhabited by retired people will be very different from life in an area inhabited by young families.

Although neighborhoods tend to shape the development and activity of residents, residents also shape the activity of neighborhoods. If, for example, a major change occurs in the ethnic background, age, interests, or life style of neighborhood residents, major changes in neighborhood events or projects are likely to follow.

THE SCHOOL Schools socialize children in many of the same ways that families and peer groups do. They influence social skills, psychological growth, and children's feelings about the rules and regulations of society. When children enter school, they face new demands—demands that they support their peers, reduce their pleasure, find satisfaction in the completion of tasks, and become industrious (Gump, 1978). Such requirements may have an important influence on their feelings of competence and on the way they regard themselves and others.

In addition, the school staff sets standards of conduct and values that may not be the same as those of the children's families and friends. Notable problems have arisen when the school represents an alien middle-class white world in the middle of a culturally different neighborhood. In large cities, ethnic groups have demanded more control over what their children are taught in school, because they believe that the established curriculum (and perhaps the staff) is irrelevant to their particular needs and values. In other places, fears that the curriculum's inclusion of certain subjects—such as sex education or evolution—threatens cherished values has led parents to demand similar control. In such circumstances, the influence of school may be different from its effect in communities that are content with the staff and curriculum and believe that success in school is a necessary prelude to success in life.

THE MEDIA All media affect behavior—for good or for bad. But the most pervasive medium in today's society is television, and it is virtually impossible for a child to grow up without being exposed to heavy doses of it. Surveys indicate that 99 percent of all families with children own television sets, and most children spend from one-fifth to one-third of their waking hours before the flickering screen (Murray and Kippax, 1979).

The effects on children of aggressive television shows is an area of heated debate in our society, and in Chapter 18 we will explore the controversy in some depth. In general, watching violence on television does not seem to trigger aggressive behavior in most children; but some violence-prone youngsters appear to be influenced toward more aggression by watching aggressive models (Bandura, 1973).

Nonviolent programming aimed at enhancing children's learning experiences has also come under fire. Educational television programs such as "Sesame Street" and "The Electric Company," which are designed to teach number and letter skills and reading to disadvantaged children who would have difficulty acquiring these skills at school, have demonstrated success in teaching the skills to children who watch them (Lesser, 1974). But middle-class children also watch these programs, and they seem to benefit

By the time these children start school, they will have had six years of exposure to television, so that they will begin their academic careers with a very different background from that of six-year-olds of 1930, when preschool influence was largely limited to the family and neighborhood. (© Camilla Smith)

as much as the children for whom the programs were designed. As a result, the widespread watching of educational television maintains the greater literacy of advantaged children over disadvantaged children.

CULTURE It is easy to forget that what seems true or natural to an American may seem false or unnatural to people in other cultures, and vice versa. People raised in Baghdad or Botswana or Bolivia, for example, are very different from those raised in Boston. The influence of culture begins the moment a child is born, and it shapes much of human behavior—from the way people dress and relate to others to the way they think and solve problems and the things they believe and value. Even appropriate male and female behavior varies widely among cultures.

In some cultures, mothers and fathers have

As children partake of cultural traditions, such as the practice of gathering the generations for a Christmas feast, they are also absorbing the values and attitudes of the culture. (© Joel Gordon 1979)

little to do with the rearing of their children; cultural practices and beliefs are passed on by others, such as brothers or sisters, or older un-related children or adults who have been given the child-rearing function.

Also, within cultures are subcultural varia-tions related to ethnic background, social class, and economic status—all of which influence how a person develops. For example, in the United States, ethnic and social-class differences often predict an individual's wealth, education, and intelligence test scores (Hess, 1970). Thus children in middle- or upper-class families are more likely to feel that they have the chance and ability to shape their own futures. On the other hand, lower-class children and adolescents may be wiser than middle- or upper-class children in

other respects and better able to survive should they suddenly be cast on their own resources.

INTERACTION OF DETERMINANTS

All the influences we have discussed are power-ful, but none of them works in isolation. Genetic, physical, and social factors are intertwined in every aspect of development. In an *ecological* approach to development, Urie Bronfenbrenner (1979) has highlighted this continually changing process. He proposes that descriptions of de-velopmental influence must include the active, growing child, the child's changing physical and social settings, the relationship among those settings, and the way the entire process is af-fected by the society in which the settings are embedded. When reading about the influence of schools (or peers or parents or genes) on a child's development, we should recall that all of the other factors are simultaneously making a sig-nificant impact on the child.

Heredity-Environment Interaction

Although genes are always implicated in behavior, inasmuch as a child's behavior is made possible by his or her membership in the human species, researchers are searching for more specific influence. By looking at examples of physical growth, intelligence, and personality, we can get a glimpse of the way that nature and nurture interact.

PHYSICAL GROWTH   The interaction of genes and environment is especially clear in the case of a child's growth. Two children of the same genetic make-up will not be precisely the same size unless their environments are alike. J. M. Tanner (1978) reports the case of twin boys, each with identical genetic make-up, who were separated at birth. One boy was brought up in a normal manner, the other lived with cruel people who neglected him, failed to give him proper food, and often shut him in the dark for long periods. As adults, the first twin was three inches taller than the second and a good many pounds heavier. The twins' common inheritance showed in their shapes; the neglected twin's body was a scaled-down replica of the larger twin. Such extreme examples are rare, but as we shall see in Chapter 6, children who grow up in environments where good food is scarce and disease rampant, and where they and their parents live under some sort of stress, will be shorter on the average than children who grow up in enriched, middle-class homes.

INTELLIGENCE   Measures of intelligence show the interaction of genes and environment. The more closely two people are related, the more closely their scores on intelligence tests correspond, suggesting some sort of genetic influence on the scores. However, genetic make-up is not the primary determinant of a person's intellectual ability. As relatedness between individuals increases, so does the similarity of the environment in which they live. Brothers and sisters share half their genes. They also share some of their environment. But because they are born at different times and because each is subjected to some unique experiences, their environments are not identical. Identical twins (twins developed from a single female egg cell) have identical genetic make-ups, so the often-demonstrated correspondence in their test scores has been taken to argue for a strong genetic component in the scores. But because identical twins look alike, parents are apt to treat them alike, so that we might equally claim that two people will make similar scores on intelligence tests if their environments are similar. Research indicates that a genetic component in intelligence cannot be dismissed. When the scores of adopted children are compared with the scores of their biological parents and with the parents who reared them, the children's scores bear a closer resemblance to the scores of their biological parents than to those of their rearing parents (Honzik, 1957; Scarr-Salapatek, 1975; Skodak and Skeels, 1949). As we shall see in Chapter 13, the various influences on intelligence are a matter of strenuous debate.

PERSONALITY   Some evidence exists for the presence of a nature-nurture interaction on personality. A relation between genetic factors and adolescents' interests and attitudes turned up when Sandra Scarr and Richard Weinberg (1978) studied a number of adopted children. On a test of vocational interests, biologically related parents and children, and blood brothers and sisters, resembled one another much more closely than the adopted adolescents resembled either their adoptive parents or their adoptive siblings. The adolescents had been adopted in the first weeks or months of their lives and had spent fifteen to twenty years in the same stable family. The closest scores were made by biologically related siblings; and there was no resemblance between the scores of husbands and wives—two findings one would expect if vocational interests show some hereditary influence. On a test of political and social attitudes, similar relationships showed between the scores of biologically related family members—and failed to show between those related only by adoption. Although these tests turned up a possible genetic influence in an unexpected place, the concept of reaction range helps explain it. The study looked only at children in comfortable middle- or upper-middle-class families, the kind of favorable environment that permits genetic background to play a larger role than it does in less benevolent circumstances where genetic influence is expressed at the lower end of the reaction range.

Physical-Social Interaction

Not all interaction is primarily a matter of genes and environment. There is also interaction between physical and social factors.

SOCIALIZATION The presence of particular objects in the environment can affect social behavior, at least among preschool children. Peter K. Smith (1974) found that when little play equipment was available, children shared their toys and apparatus and tended to form large play groups. On the other hand, when many toys and equipment were available, children tended to keep the toys to themselves, playing either in small groups or alone. Even the kind of equipment affected the children's behavior. Some were given only apparatus—such as chairs, tables, and a ladder—to play with, while others were given only toys—such as puzzles, dress-up clothes, tea sets, and blocks. The children who had only apparatus to play with increased their verbal and physical contacts, played more in cooperative groups, smiled and laughed more, and devised new and creative uses for the apparatus. It seems that when the environment has few resources, children can cooperate and invent creative ways to use the available material.

BIRTH ACCIDENTS Complications of pregnancy and delivery sometimes result in a very sick baby, one we would expect to be permanently damaged. Studies of birth complications indicate, however, that the effect of a good environment often overcomes early hazards. In a longitudinal study of babies who were deprived of oxygen during labor and delivery, noticeable impairments were found during the first few days of life. The finding is not surprising, because the expectation is that depriving the brain of oxygen leads to impaired intellectual functioning. When these babies were three years old, they scored lower than normal children on all tests of cognitive functioning. But by the time they were seven years old, there were no significant differences between children who had been starved for oxygen and children who had had no problems at birth (Sameroff, 1978).

A similar pattern emerges with regard to the accident of prematurity. Premature babies run a much greater than normal risk of mental retardation, and among year-old babies prematurity is associated with intellectual impairment. By the time children reach school age, however, the relationship has disappeared among middle-class babies, but it remains among lower-class babies (Kopp and Parmalee, 1979). It may be, as Arnold Sameroff (1978) suggests, that parents in impoverished environments are often unable to provide the greater amount of care that such babies require.

STUDYING DETERMINANTS

Discovering just what factors affect any particular aspect of development is like solving an intricate puzzle. Suppose we are interested in the relationship between children's play and the establishment of sex roles—that is, the culturally prescribed pattern of behavior for each gender. How would we go about discovering the connection? Jan Carpenter and Aletha Huston-

Stein (1980) chose *naturalistic observation* to tease out the relationship. They watched nursery-school children at play, noting the kind of activity (dolls, blocks, swings, play dough, etc.) children chose, when they complied with a teacher's suggestion, when they made novel use of play material, and how often the teacher guided or commented on a child's play. Many studies had shown that young children tend to play with toys designed for their own gender and that such play probably strengthened sex roles, but Carpenter and Huston-Stein believed that it was not the sex-role-related aspects of the toys but the structure that was responsible. For example, playing house is a highly structured activity, because children fit their play into structures provided by others. But sand box play is low in structure, for there are no guidelines; children provide their own structure. Sure enough, they found that girls spent more time than boys in play that was highly structured, either by teachers' comments or by models at home whom they could imitate, and that boys spent more time in low-structure play, play that teachers generally ignored and that could not be patterned after the behavior of adults in the home. Further, the degree of compliance or originality in play bore a relation not to the children's gender but to the degree of structure in their play activities. Boys playing in highly structured situations tended to be compliant; girls playing in low-structured situations tended to find novel uses for toys. The investigators concluded that the degree of structure of their typical activities teaches boys and girls different skills, and that through such activities girls learn to be passive and boys to be aggressive and independent.

Carpenter and Huston-Stein could have sought their answers in other ways. For example, they might have interviewed the children and teachers; or they might have introduced some element into the nursery-school play situation and watched the children's responses; or they might have brought the children to a laboratory, where they had placed carefully selected toys, arranged so that children would have to respond in particular ways.

Distinctions among the methods for collecting information on human development center on how much *control* the investigator has over (1) the selection of subjects for study, (2) the specific experience the researcher wants to study, and (3) the possible responses subjects can give to that experience. At one extreme is the simple, naturalistic observation chosen by Carpenter and Huston-Stein, in which the children behaved naturally in their own environment without any interference from the investigators. At the other extreme is the *experiment*, which allows the investigator to control all three aspects of the study. Carpenter and Huston-Stein apparently felt that the advantages of watching children at natural play outweighed the advantages of having carefully selected subjects playing in a tightly controlled situation. Between the two extremes are *clinical studies* and numerous types of *field studies*, where some but not other types of control are possible.

No single study in psychology—or any science for that matter—ever answers all relevant questions. A soundly designed and executed study can, at best, confirm or contradict our subjective judgment that a previous conclusion is correct. The best studies are objective, clear, reliable, and replicable. As noted in Chapter 1, the final test is replication. A scientific finding becomes established when the same results are obtained in several investigations (the more, the better) conducted by different researchers in different places but using the same basic methods.

Sampling

The reliability of a study's results often depends upon the nature of the *sample:* the subjects of the study. If an investigator examines the development of concepts among children in a Kansas City suburb, for example, the results may show not what is typical for children in general but only how concepts develop in middle-class American children. And if the investigator has limited his study to children in his own neighborhood, the results may not even be typical of middle-class American children. Similarly, the findings of a study about preschool development conducted at a private nursery school would not be equally valid for children who live in the inner city or in rural Appalachia.

Sex, age, ethnic background, and socioeconomic level are some of the factors that can bias the results of a study. In order to make sure that sex does not bias a study, for example, investigators either make sure they study an equal number of boys and girls or else study only girls or only boys, limiting their findings to one gender. Today, most researchers who study boys and girls together look at the responses of each gender separately and indicate in their reports whether major differences appeared that are related to gender.

Cross-Sectional and Longitudinal Designs

Any study, no matter what its type, can study people once and then get out of their lives; or it can follow the same people over months or years, repeatedly observing or interviewing them, or subjecting them to various experiments. Each method has its own strengths and weaknesses.

CROSS-SECTIONAL DESIGN Much of the information we have concerning development comes from studies that compare different age groups, called cross-sectional studies. Such studies are common because they are relatively inexpensive and can be done quickly. Researchers generally assume that the differences found among such groups are the result of developmental change.

Often this is true. But if the samples of people at various ages are not selected carefully, the cross-sectional design has two major flaws:

the different age groups may be affected by experiences peculiar to their cohorts (age-group members); and the age-group changes may not represent the specific patterns of change for the individuals in the group. For example, a cross-sectional study of the decline of intelligence test scores in later life might show a curve like that in Figure 3.2. The scores appear to decline with increasing age. Remember, however, that people studied at age eighty in 1975 were born in 1895, whereas those studied at age twenty in 1975 were born in 1955. Much happened to our cultural and social environment in the time between those two groups of cohorts, and sociocultural influences affect the development and maintenance of intellectual skills. In fact, there is good evidence that, as a nation, each new generation scores higher on intelligence tests— presumably because longer education and mass communications expose more people to the information required to score well on such tests (Baltes and Schaie, 1974). Younger cohorts score higher on the tests than older cohorts did at the same age. Thus what appears to be a dramatic decline in scores over age is in part an effect of the lower scores for older groups throughout their lives. Cross-sectional studies cannot detect cohort changes.

However, not all cross-sectional studies are flawed by cohort effects. If differences appear between close age groups—such as three- and four-year-olds, or even six- and ten-year-olds— it is less likely that cohort effects are responsible, because the sociocultural environment generally changes slowly. With close age groups, it is more likely that differences are due to development.

Cross-sectional groups may not show the actual pattern of individual change, especially in the case of a developmental shift that occurs rapidly. At puberty, the growth of any one individual accelerates and decelerates rapidly, but because individuals begin and end their growth at different times, graphs of group averages will show a smooth curve for the entire cohort. Thus cross-sectional data alone would not reveal the pubescent growth spurt.

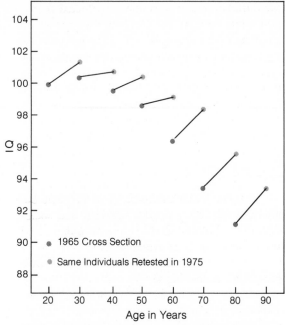

Figure 3.2 Hypothetical example illustrating apparent changes with age in IQ scores. The dots representing average scores of people at different ages tested in a cross-sectional study show a downward trend in IQ score with age. The dots representing average scores of these same samples of people tested again ten years later as part of a longitudinal study show a similar downward trend in IQ score with age, but each age group also shows an increase in the average score. (Adapted from Nesselroade, Schaie, and Baltes, 1972)

LONGITUDINAL DESIGN In contrast to cross-sectional studies, *longitudinal* studies follow the same subjects over time. The same people can be compared with themselves at ages twenty and eighty. One such study, begun in the 1920s by Lewis Terman, followed 1,500 gifted California schoolchildren, reporting from time to time on how these extremely intelligent people developed and coped with life's problems. They were checked most recently in 1972, when the average age of the "children" was sixty-two (Sears, 1977).

Longitudinal studies may seem to be the answer to design flaws, but they have their own problems. Longitudinal studies are expensive and time-consuming. Exploring developmental processes by this method requires years, demanding a major commitment by both the researcher and the people under study. In addition, people tend to move or to become weary of being studied, and some die; so that over the years many subjects are lost. A more serious problem is the fact that studying the same people repeatedly over many years may affect their development, and their behavior may be distorted by the continual testing. Finally, long-term changes in their behavior may be a response to sociocultural shifts as well as evidence of developmental change. Examples of some recent shifts in the sociocultural environment are the changes wrought by the civil rights movement, the investigation of space, the resignation of a President, the dawning realization of an energy shortage, and the widespread acceptance of computers. Such life-span shifts in the environment may have profound effects on some aspects of people's development.

FINDING A MIDDLE GROUND Neither cross-sectional nor longitudinal studies alone can provide the basic data for developmental studies. Because of this, K. Warner Schaie (1965) has proposed that the two designs be combined to provide controls over the biases in each design. He suggests that researchers sample subjects cross-sectionally and then follow them longitudinally until the samples overlap in age. For example, initial samples drawn at ages two, four, six, and eight can be followed for two years — until the two-year-olds are four, the four-year-olds are six, and so forth. And a final cross-sectional sample can be drawn at age ten to compare to the longitudinal eight-year-olds, who would then be ten. (See Figure 3.3.) The effects of repeated testing, if any, will appear as differences between, for example, the starting scores for four-year-olds and the ending scores for the two-year-olds at age four. If the whole design is repeated some years later, cohort effects will appear; important shifts in the socio-cultural environment will be revealed by higher or lower scores at all ages than the scores in the first study.

The advantage of combining the two designs becomes clear when we look at people's heights. Height measurements of a cross-sectional sample seem to indicate that people grow until middle adolescence and then begin to shrink. This "shrinkage" is due to cohort effects: people born a number of years ago are shorter on the average than people born more recently, and they were always shorter. A longitudinal study of people now in their seventies would show that they grew until late adolescence and then maintained their heights until late adulthood, when they may actually have shrunk a bit. A comparative longitudinal study of a younger cohort would find them reaching maximum growth at an earlier age; because of better nutrition, they are both taller and earlier-maturing than older cohorts. When studying height, it is necessary to separate developmental changes from long-term changes in the sociocultural environment. When studying other factors, it would also be important to separate developmental change from the effects of repeated measurements.

Types of Studies

The type of study selected by researchers depends upon the process being studied. Sometimes the disadvantages of a particular type make that design impractical for the process under investigation. Ethical considerations might eliminate an ideal study because of the psychological harm the situation could inflict upon the subjects. Each type of study has its own place in the investigation of development.

EXPERIMENTATION   An experiment gives the investigator the greatest amount of control over the situation, which can be contrived to eliminate influences that might be present in natural settings. The subjects of the experiment can be chosen to reflect the group that embodies the process under study (newborns, adolescents,

Figure 3.3 A research design that combines cross-sectional and longitudinal research. First, samples of children at each of four ages (two, four, six, and eight) are selected and studied. Two years later the same samples of children are studied again, and another sample of ten-year-olds is included. Using both methods on the same group of children offsets the weaknesses inherent in each type of study.

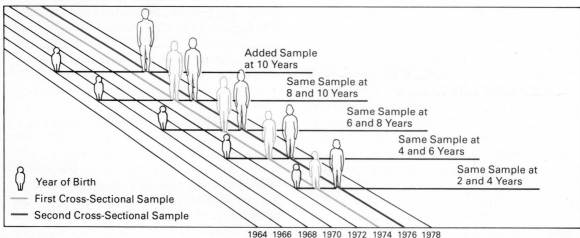

Added Sample
at 10 Years

Same Sample at
8 and 10 Years

Same Sample at
6 and 8 Years

Same Sample at
4 and 6 Years

Same Sample at
2 and 4 Years

Year of Birth

First Cross-Sectional Sample

Second Cross-Sectional Sample

1964 1966 1968 1970 1972 1974 1976 1978
Year

children of working mothers, children in bilingual homes, and so forth). Researchers examine the effect of selected factors or events on a child's behavior. These factors are called *variables*, and in an experiment, the researcher controls and manipulates the variable under study. The variable that is selected or changed in some way by the investigator is called an *independent variable*. The factor that changes as a result of the independent variable's introduction is called a *dependent variable*. For example, if we wanted to measure the effect of hunger on a baby's attention, we would test the baby just before the next feeding was due. In this experiment, the independent variable would be the length of time since the last feeding; the dependent variable would be the length of time the hungry baby watched a display. If we then compared this time with the length of time the baby watched a display when *not* hungry, we would know something about the effects of hunger on attention.

Studying behavior through the experimental method has been used successfully in thousands of psychological studies. In a typical experiment, Arthur Jensen and William Rohwer (1965) designed a study to show developmental changes in children's learning. Their subjects were children from kindergarten through the twelfth grade. One at a time, the children saw pairs of pictures of common objects. Half of the children at each age level were asked to name each picture, and the other half were asked to construct a sentence that related each pair of pictures. Afterward, all the children were shown the pairs of pictures and asked to learn the members of each pair well enough so that when one picture was shown, they could recall the other. From the second grade on, the children who had constructed sentences learned the material much faster. In this experiment, naming the picture or constructing a sentence were the independent variables; the length of time the children required to learn the pairs was the dependent variable. In addition to showing developmental changes in learning, Jensen and Rohwer's experiment illustrated the powerful effects of re-

lating objects in a meaningful manner. It is doubtful if this information could have been discovered so efficiently or convincingly had the researchers relied on a less controlled method of study.

Despite their advantages, experimental studies are not perfect. Because such studies are often conducted in laboratories, the subjects of the experiment may not respond to the situation as they would in a familiar setting. At one time, for example, it was widely believed that when they were about eight months old, all babies developed a fear of strangers. Later it was discovered that although babies might indeed be afraid of strangers in the unfamiliar surroundings of a laboratory, most babies showed much less fear when encountering a stranger in their own homes (Tracy, Lamb, and Ainsworth, 1976). In this case, the variable the researchers were changing in order to study infants' reactions (the stranger) had less influence on their subjects than the variable that remained constant (the laboratory itself). Unless investigators take seriously the systematic effect that surroundings have on children's responses, their experiments will demonstrate less about development than they believe.

The second pitfall in experimental studies comes from the rigid control that is also their virtue. Because the researcher designs the experiment so that he or she can control as many variables as possible, the situation may have no counterpart in the child's world. Therefore the results, although valid within the confines of the experiment, may be typical only of situations children never encounter in the world and thus bear little resemblance to their natural behavior.

Experimental studies often use animals because researchers can manipulate their subjects' environments in ways that are neither desired nor tolerated with human beings, and the knowledge derived can sometimes be applied to children. For example, raising baby monkeys in isolation has increased our understanding of the human baby's crucial need for close contact with a caregiver.

We cannot transfer the findings of animal research directly to the social development of children. However, social behavior among primates — including human beings — often seems to serve similar functions, just as the very different wings of butterflies and bats enable both to fly. Monkeys that had spent the first six months of their lives in total isolation and developed extremely abnormal behavior were rehabilitated by young monkey "therapists" — by the companionship of a monkey much younger than themselves (Suomi and Harlow, 1972); but isolated monkeys that were placed with peers or adult monkeys failed to show the same improvement. These studies show that early experiences of severe deprivation can be partially overcome, and they therefore hold out hope for human children who have been severely deprived — such as children who are occasionally discovered after having been shut away for years in prisonlike rooms by abusive parents.

Research with monkeys has also shown us something about the effect of fathers on the development of young children. Stephen Suomi (1977) housed monkey families in cages that confined the parents to the family home but allowed the offspring to travel freely from cage to cage. Monkey fathers played with both their sons and their daughters and with visiting young males; but they refused to play with visiting females. They were more hostile toward visiting monkeys of both sexes than toward their own offspring, and they showed least hostility toward their own daughters. The net effect of the fathers' behavior was to encourage the visits of male infants and to curtail the visits of female infants. If adult males in the wild behave in a similar fashion, their actions would encourage males to be independent and free-ranging and girls to stay near their mothers, thereby establishing the nucleus for a stable social group. Suomi's findings may throw light on the work of researchers who are seeking to discover whether human fathers play a more important role in social development than traditional mother-oriented infant research has indicated.

NATURALISTIC OBSERVATION Human behavior is most appropriately studied by careful observation in natural settings, because people are more likely to behave naturally under these conditions. It was for this reason that Carpenter and Huston-Stein chose the method for exploring the connection between play and sex roles. In naturalistic observation, however, the investigator has less control than in any other method. Every variable is uncontrolled. Carpenter and Huston-Stein had no control over the socioeconomic level, ethnic group, or gender of children enrolled in the nursery school; nor could they control the toys that were available or the way the teachers interacted with the children or the children with each other.

The critical aspect of naturalistic observation is having explicit rules for categorizing and recording what the observer sees, so that the observations of two watchers will be comparable. If you have ever gone to a movie with several friends and disagreed afterward about the film's quality, plot, or motivation, you can appreciate the necessity of having observers in a research study see things the same way and record them in a like manner. If such a study is well conducted, valuable information can be gained about the everyday effect of environmental variables on human behavior.

James Johnson, Joan Ershler, and Coleen Bell (1980) used naturalistic observation to investigate the effects of different nursery-school programs on free play. They watched each child in two different programs twenty times over an eleven-week period, for one minute at a time. Observers scored play on both its social and cognitive aspects and noted when the observed child was not playing but watching others or simply doing nothing. Before they began their study, the investigators had clear definitions of the variables they were concerned with. They agreed on how long children had to play for the activity to be considered an episode and how each type of play was to be defined. In this case, the investigators found no difference in the social play of the two groups but a large difference in the children's cognitive play, indicating that a nursery school's program may indeed influence the way young children play.

The great advantage of naturalistic observation is, of course, its direct application to life. Its disadvantages lie in the lack of control. Variables investigators do not even consider can affect the results. One uncontrolled variable that may plague an observational study is the effect of the watching psychologist on the child's behavior. Children may behave differently if they know they are being observed. When children are studied in a laboratory, psychologists can watch through a one-way mirror; but outside the laboratory, it often becomes a matter of trying to be inconspicuous or of becoming so familiar to the children that one's presence is ignored.

FIELD STUDY Field studies also take place in natural social settings, but they differ from naturalistic observations in that the investigator introduces some factor into the natural situation that changes it. Field studies are not true experiments because the researcher can control only some aspects of the situation; but they are often more closely controlled than either observational or clinical studies.

In one field study, designed to explore the way group membership affects behavior, middle-class boys at a summer camp unwittingly participated in an elaborate situation (Sherif et al., 1961). The boys, who were placed in two groups, came to camp in separate buses and played, hiked, swam, and shared cabins only with members of their own group. After the boys had settled into the camp routine, psychologists pitted one group against the other, setting up tugs-of-war and baseball and football games. Soon the competition turned the groups into two warring tribes. They called each other names and raided each other's cabins. Fistfights broke out. Then the psychologists introduced two factors to change camp life. First, they cut the pipeline that brought water into the camp, so

that all the boys had to work together to repair it. Next, they ran a truck loaded with food for an overnight hike into a ditch, so the boys had to pull together on a tow rope to get the vehicle back on the road. Cooperation dissolved the enmity between the two groups and the boys gradually became friends.

Few field studies are this complicated or this lengthy. For example, a researcher might simply introduce a highly unusual object into a play yard or have one child pretend to be in distress, then retire to observe how the children reacted to the strange sight or the unhappy child. Such control over the independent variable allows investigators to study important phenomena that cannot be brought into the laboratory, yet with more control than naturalistic observation permits. Except for this added control, however, field studies have the same advantages and disadvantages as naturalistic observation. The investigator may not have complete control over the experiences of the subjects or their reactions. Also, investigators generally cannot assign subjects randomly to one group or another. In order to obtain comparable results they must, therefore, be aware of ways in which comparison groups differ. And because they can never prove that all the differences between comparison groups have been identified, the results of field studies are often less certain than those of true experiments.

CLINICAL STUDY Clinical study often consists of in-depth interviews and observation. It may be controlled in a way that is not always possible in a field study: the same methods can be applied in a standardized way to each subject, or the psychologist can vary the approach with each subject. When a clinical study is designed with appropriate controls, it can yield interesting and important data. For example, a wealth of information on child rearing during infancy and the preschool years came from lengthy interviews with nearly four hundred middle- and working-class mothers in New

England. Robert Sears, Eleanor Maccoby, and Harry Levin (1957) studied how parents rear children, what effects different kinds of training have on youngsters, and what leads a mother to use one method rather than another. All mothers responded at length to seventy-two identical questions, but interviewers were free to probe deeply into any of the topics discussed.

The procedures for a controlled study must be clearly and precisely defined; the investigator can improvise only in such matters as introducing the subject to the clinical situation or maintaining the subject's cooperation. Unless these actions are explicitly stated and controlled, they may bias the results of a study. For example, in his earlier studies, Jean Piaget (1952b) talked freely with a child, asking whatever questions seemed necessary to reveal the child's concepts and thinking processes. Piaget was critical of standardized tests, but he later realized that differences in the way the questions were presented could affect his results. He chose an intermediate method, using a more standardized procedure in his later studies. By presenting the same questions to all children, Piaget gained a stronger basis for suggesting that the differences in children's responses at different ages are the result of actual changes in their cognitive activity.

Interpreting the Results

Once investigators have obtained their results, they must interpret them. Various statistical measures have been devised for the purpose, and one commonly used tool is *correlation*. Correlation is a numerical expression of how closely two sets of measurements correspond. A correlation of .00 represents no direct relationship at all. For example, in the New England study of child rearing, the correlation between which parent established child-rearing policies and the family's general adjustment level was .00. This number implies that knowing which parent set policy tells nothing about the adjustment of the family. If the correlation were +1.00, then the

correspondence between the two measures would be perfect. In this case, knowing that the father set policy would indicate that family life is invariably harmonious. If the correlation were −1.00, then knowing that the father set policy would indicate that family life is never harmonious.

In psychological research, correlations are rarely exactly .00 or +1.00 or −1.00. They generally fall at various places in between. The larger the correlation, the more closely two measures correspond and the better one measure can predict the other. In the New England child-rearing study, for example, warmth on the part of the mother correlated +.34 with the amount of affectionate interaction with her baby and +.37 with a tendency to use reasoning in disciplining her child; but the correlation between maternal warmth and how highly she valued school achievement in her child was nonexistent (−.01). So we can say that a warm mother tends to be affectionate with her baby and to use reason as a disciplinary tool, but that she may or may not value school achievement. Although there was no correlation between which parent set child-rearing policies and the level of family harmony, the correlation between conflict over policies and level of family adjustment was −.60, indicating that when parents do not agree, the family is rarely a harmonious one.

Correlations tell us what sorts of behavior go together, and the higher the positive correlation, the more confidently we can predict that one will be accompanied by the other. The higher the negative correlation, the more confident we can be that the two will not appear together. But correlation tells us nothing about causation. We do not know, for example, whether disagreement over discipline leads to an unhappy home or whether an unhappy home results in parents being unable to agree on discipline. In fact, both the unhappy home and the disagreement may be caused by a third factor we know nothing about.

A second frequently encountered measure is that of *probability* (p), which indicates the likelihood that experimental findings are simply the result of chance. Probability is expressed in decimals, and a figure of .10 means that there is one chance in ten that the findings are meaningless; .50 means that the probability of a chance finding is one in two. When a researcher reports "significant" findings, it generally means the chances are not greater than one in twenty that they are the result of chance ($p = .05$). In the New England study, 35 percent of the cold mothers had children with feeding problems, but only 11 percent of the exceptionally warm mothers had children with feeding problems. The probability that the link between coldness in a mother and feeding problems in her child was the result of chance was one in a hundred ($p = .01$)—a figure that researchers would feel warranted some attention. If researchers can get the measure of probability down to .001 (one chance in a thousand), they feel fairly certain of their results.

SUMMARY

1. Human development is the result of multiple interacting causes operating through heredity (nature) and through environment (nurture). Questions arise over "how" and "how much" each contributes to development.

2. In studying the role of heredity, researchers have concentrated on animal genetics. Such studies help establish general principles and provide important information on the effects of genetic and genetic-environment interactions. They cannot, however, provide specific details about the way these interactions affect human development. Some insight into the way that genetic differences affect human beings has been gained by studying individuals of various degrees of relatedness. The concept of reaction range, which refers to the limits set by genetic conditions on an individual's possible behavior, is important in understanding the effects of genetic factors on human beings.

3. The term "heritability" refers to the relative contribution of genetics to a trait or behavior. It is at best an estimate, and it varies with who is studied and when. Heritability does not indicate that either genes or environment "causes" a trait. Instead, its appearance is a function of both genetic and environmental determinants.

4. Environmental determinants of human development include physical and social factors. Physical factors include those ecological features that maintain life—air, water, food, and light—the interior environment of the body, and every feature of the surrounding world, whether natural or man-made.

5. No determinant ever works in isolation. Genetic, physical, and social factors are implicated in every aspect of development. Physical growth, intelligence, personality, socialization, and hazards of birth all show the interaction of determinants.

6. Each method of studying the determinants of development has its own advantages and disadvantages, and each permits a different degree of control over who is studied, the circumstances, and the behavior that can occur. They also vary in how closely they resemble life situations. In both respects, naturalistic observation falls at one extreme (low in control, high in correspondence to life) and experimentation at the other (high in control, low in correspondence to life), with field and clinical studies in between.

7. Studies may use either a cross-sectional design, in which different age groups are compared, or a longitudinal design, in which the same people are followed for months or years. The reliability of a study may be assessed in terms of correlation (how closely one measure corresponds with another) or probability (an estimate of the likelihood that the findings are simply the result of chance).

P A R T 2

The Beginning of
Life

A newborn baby is both an end and a beginning. The forty weeks of growth within the mother's body suddenly ends with birth. No other developmental period will ever end so dramatically in so short a time. Birth represents separation and deprivation as well as independence and the necessity for self-reliance. No longer are babies able to rely on the resources of a mother's body; now their own physical, mental, and social capacities must develop. By the moment of birth, much that will distinguish children for the rest of their lives already has happened. A baby's heredity, fully determined at conception, has had its initial expression in the infant's physical form. An active, inquiring, responsive infant enters the world equipped with a growing body and rapidly expanding motor, sensory, and mental capacities. This part of the book describes the baby's development within the uterus and traces the first four weeks of independent life.

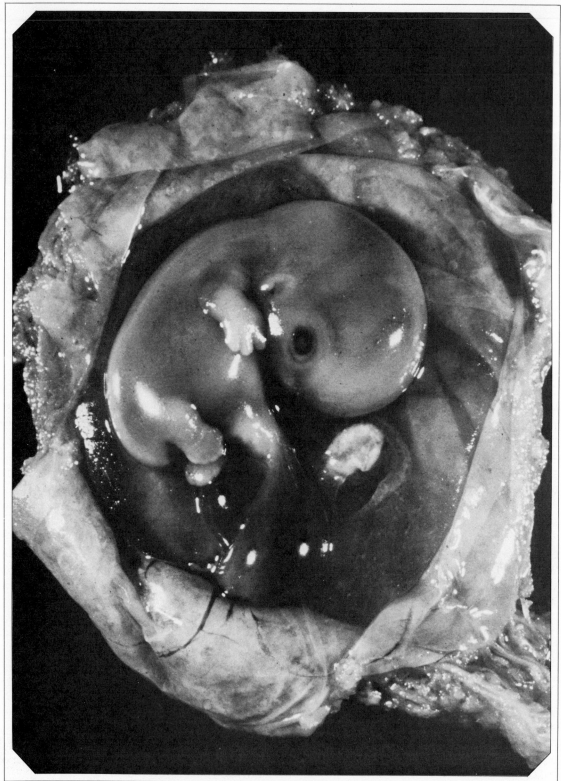

Prenatal Development

Human development cannot be understood without examining the prenatal period. More growth and development take place during these thirty-eight weeks than in any comparable segment of life. The structures and functions that develop within the womb provide the basis of the new human being's body and behavior for the rest of life. Each baby has a unique inheritance, a genetic blueprint that specifies certain physical, mental, and personal characteristics. But the blueprint does not specify exactly how the new individual will look, function, or behave. From the moment of conception, environment interacts with heredity, affecting the way the blueprint is translated into flesh. During the prenatal period, the primary environmental influences are biological: nutrients, oxygen, waste disposal, exposure to drugs, disease, or environmental contaminants. But there are psychological influences as well: a mother's emotional condition during pregnancy can influence the baby developing within her.

In this chapter we shall follow the development of the fertilized egg into a healthy, normal baby who is ready for independent life outside the mother's womb. We shall study the transmission of traits from parent to child, a subject that was introduced in Chapter 3. And the behavior and capabilities of the growing fetus and the problems that can arise in the course of its development will be spelled out. We shall also look at the link between the mother and her unborn child and discover the importance of maternal health, diet, habits, and emotions. Finally, we shall discuss the detection of fetal abnormalities and the role of genetic counseling in alerting prospective parents to possible defects in their unborn child.

HOW HEREDITY WORKS

The traits and dispositions that parents transmit to their offspring are coded in twenty-three pairs of *chromosomes,* which are present in every cell of the body. The chromosomes are composed of beadlike strings of *genes,* microscopic entities containing the instructions that guide the development of physical traits and behavioral dispositions. Whatever we pass on to our offspring is contained in approximately 250,000 genes composed principally of *deoxyribonucleic acid* (DNA), a complex chemical code that guides the development of bones and eyes, brain and fingernails, and disposes the offspring toward certain behavioral patterns. All of that information is contained in a fertilized cell smaller than the period that follows this sentence.

The Production of Gametes

Most cells of the human body contain twenty-three pairs of chromosomes, direct copies of the original twenty-three pairs with which each person begins life. There is one major exception to this rule: the *gametes* (the sperm cell, or *spermatozoon,* of the father and the egg cell, or *ovum,* of the mother) that will eventually unite to produce a new human being each have twenty-three single chromosomes instead of twenty-three pairs. The difference arises because when gametes form they divide in a different way. When other body cells divide (a process called *mitosis*), the chromosomes duplicate themselves and then divide to form two daughter cells, each with a full complement of forty-six chromosomes (twenty-three pairs). But when gametes divide (a process called *meiosis*), the chromosomes duplicate themselves, then the members of each pair gravitate to opposite ends of the cell, which splits into two cells, each containing twenty-three single chromosomes. These cells then duplicate themselves and divide again, so that each original gamete produces four daughter cells containing twenty-three single chromosomes. At conception, when a sperm unites with

Figure 4.1 (*A*) The production of sex cells. Certain cells in the ovaries of the mother and in the testes of the father divide twice in a special pattern of cell division called meiosis to produce gametes—ova and sperm—that have only half the number of chromosomes of the parent cells. The chromosomes occur in the parent cells in pairs, and each chromosome is itself a double strand. For simplicity, only two of the twenty-three pairs of human chromosomes are shown here. In meiosis, first the members of each pair split up (*First Division*), and then the chromosomes themselves split in half (*Second Division*). They regenerate their missing halves in a subsequent step (*next line*). The union of the gametes in conception results in a zygote that has the full number of chromosomes, half from the mother and half from the father.

(*B*) Transmission of alleles in the inheritance of PKU. In this diagram only a single pair of chromosomes is represented. These chromosomes bear the alleles *N* and *p*. Both parents have both forms of the gene, and therefore they produce gametes with chromosomes bearing either the *N* or the *p* gene in equal numbers. Depending on which gametes happen to unite in conception, the new cell may have the alleles *NN, Np, pN,* or *pp*. Because *p* is a recessive gene, only babies with *pp* will have PKU.

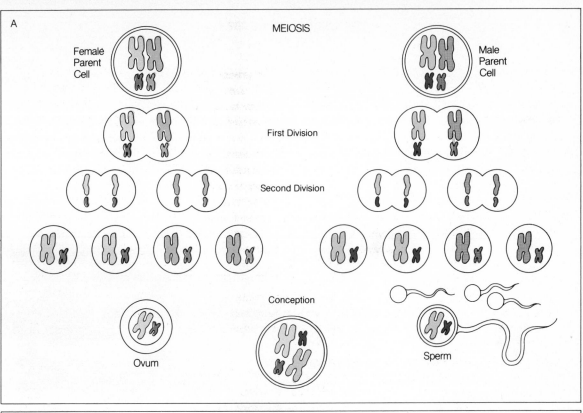

A

MEIOSIS

Female Parent Cell

Male Parent Cell

First Division

Second Division

Conception

Ovum

Sperm

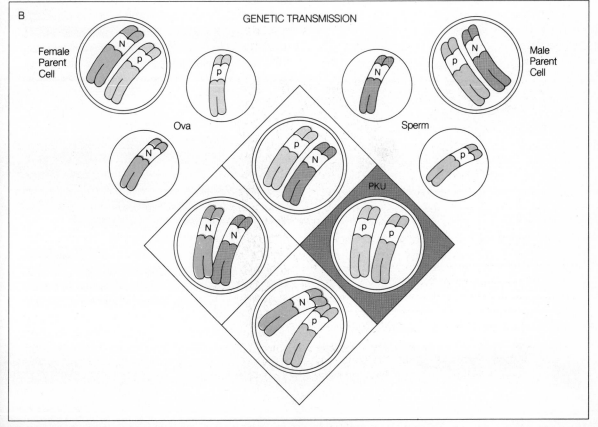

B

GENETIC TRANSMISSION

Female Parent Cell

Male Parent Cell

Ova

Sperm

PKU

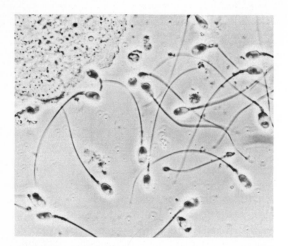

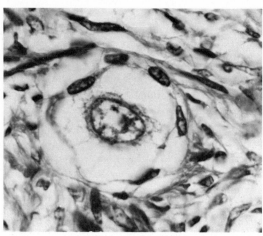

Swimming motions of the tail propel human spermatozoa (highly magnified) toward their meeting with the ovum; the chromosomes that can provide one-half of a new individual's genetic inheritance are located in the head.

The other half of a potential genetic inheritance is in the ovum (magnified); in order to produce a new individual both gametes must travel fast enough to meet in the Fallopian tube while they are still alive. (Manfred Kage/Peter Arnold, Inc.; Martin M. Rotker/Taurus Photos)

an egg, the result is a single cell having twenty-three pairs of chromosomes. Figure 4.1A illustrates meiosis in two pairs of chromosomes.

Genetic Transmission

Children sometimes resemble their parents in certain physical characteristics and sometimes do not. For example, a mother and father may both have brown hair, but one of their three children may be blond. How are physical characteristics passed on from parent to child?

Although hair color is a common and easily observed characteristic, its transmission is complicated, because hair color is determined by more than one gene. It is simpler to explain genetic transmission by examining a characteristic that depends on a single gene, such as *phenylketonuria*, or PKU, an inherited inability to metabolize phenylalanine, a component of some foods. If this metabolic abnormality is left untreated, the afflicted child will have fair skin and hair, a small head in proportion to body size, eczema, agitated and restless behavior, a stiff gait, and moderate to severe mental retardation.

In order to understand how PKU occurs, let N symbolize the gene corresponding to normal metabolic ability and p represent the gene for PKU. The related genes, N and p, are called *alleles*. Now look at Figure 4.1B, which illustrates the alleles in only one pair of chromosomes. The parent cells in the figure contain the alleles of interest, labeled N and p. In this example, the mother's and father's cells have a gene for both N and p. When the parent cells divide to form gametes, half of the father's sperm cells and half of the mother's ova will contain a gene for PKU (p) and half will contain a gene for the normal metabolic condition (N). During conception, one of four possible combinations of these gametes will result. Depending on which male gamete unites with which female gamete, the new baby will have a genetic inheritance of NN, Np (which is the same as pN), or pp; these are shown in Figure 4.1B. If the selection process were perfectly random, one-fourth of the offspring of these parents would have the combination NN, one-fourth would have pp, and one-half would have Np.

But which of these offspring will be normal children, and which will show symptoms of PKU? In this example, the *NN* baby will be normal, and the *pp* baby will have PKU. These offspring are *homozygous*, which means that their cells have matching genes for this characteristic. But an *Np* baby is *heterozygous*, meaning that his cells have different genes for the same trait. Are these *Np* babies normal, or do they have PKU?

The answer depends on which gene is *dominant* and which is *recessive*. A dominant gene is one whose corresponding trait appears in the individual even when that gene is paired with a different gene for the trait. The paired gene whose corresponding trait fails to appear is recessive. In the case of PKU, the normal gene is dominant over the recessive PKU gene, and therefore *Np* individuals will be normal.

Notice that there is not a perfect one-to-one correspondence between the genes a person carries and the traits that appear. This lack of correspondence illustrates the difference between *genotype* and *phenotype*. The genotype is the specific combination of alleles that characterize one's genetic make-up, whereas the phenotype is the nature of the trait as it appears in the individual. The genes that produce PKU can combine to form three genotypes: *NN*, *Np*, *pp*. But there are only two phenotypes: normal and PKU. The genotypes *NN* and *Np* both produce the normal phenotype because *N* is dominant over *p*. There are, therefore, some differences between what we actually look like and how we behave (phenotype) and our genetic make-up (genotype).

For a variety of reasons, genetic transmission is rarely as simple as it is in the case of PKU. First, most traits, especially behavioral ones, are *polygenic*, which means that several genes have an equal and cumulative effect in producing the trait. Or, in other cases, some genes in the combination have more influence than others on the phenotype. Second, dominance is not always all-or-none. That is, there appear to be gradations of dominance, so that one allele for a trait is not totally dominant. The result may be some-

what of an "average" of two extremes. Third, one allele may not express itself unless an allele of quite a different characteristic is also present. For example, although cataracts are caused by a single dominant gene, another gene determines the form the cataracts will take (Stern, 1960). Consequently, it is possible for a person to carry a dominant gene that does not affect his or her phenotype.

The example of PKU as a genetically transmitted trait reminds us of another important point about genetic transmission. Since a highly restricted diet can prevent most of PKU's effects, it indicates that the expression of genetic traits is affected by the environment.

PRENATAL GROWTH

At the moment of conception, the spermatozoon from the father unites with the ovum of the mother in one of the *Fallopian tubes*, the passages leading from the ovaries to the uterus. The ovum is the largest cell in the human body, and it can sometimes be seen without a microscope. Eggs mature in the female's ovaries, and one egg is released approximately every twenty-eight days during a woman's fertile years. The freed egg, which probably can be fertilized for less than twenty-four hours, travels down the Fallopian tube toward the uterus (see Figure 4.2).

As soon as sperm and egg unite, development begins, and it then progresses at a rapid rate. In approximately thirty-eight weeks, the organism grows from one tiny cell to a newborn baby. The total *gestation period* usually lasts about 266 days (thirty-eight weeks). Since most women do not know the precise date of conception, physicians commonly calculate fetal age from the beginning of the mother's last menstrual period, resulting in a gestation period of 280 days (forty weeks, or nine calendar months). However, we shall adopt the more accurate thirty-eight week gestation period in discussions of prenatal life.

The course of prenatal development falls into

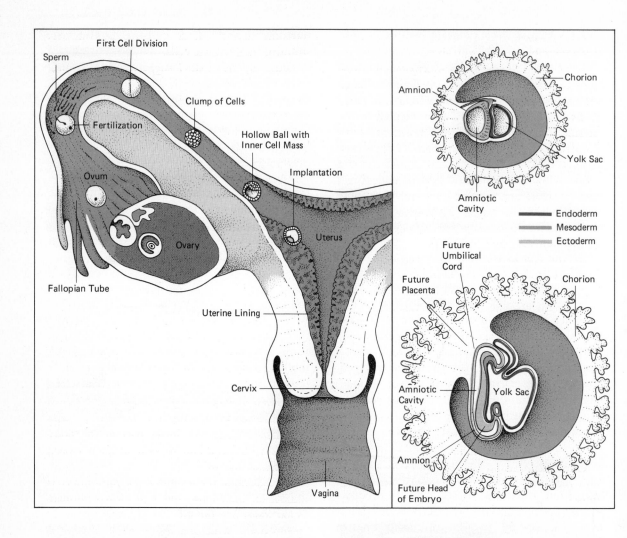

Figure 4.2 The early development of the human embryo. Fertilization occurs at the upper end of the Fallopian tube. By the time the fertilized ovum reaches the uterus, it has already divided many times. Within seven or eight days, it is securely implanted in the uterine wall, where the process of prenatal development continues.

after, from approximately eight weeks after conception to birth, the developing organism is called a *fetus*.

The Germinal Period

Almost immediately after fertilization, the egg begins the process of cell division that will eventually produce a human body made up of many billions of cells. Although the cells of an adult are highly differentiated according to their location and function in the body (for example, nerve cells are quite different in form and func-

roughly three periods. During the first two weeks after conception, called the *germinal period*, the fertilized egg is primarily engaged in cell division. In the next six weeks, the *embryonic period*, the organism begins to take shape, and its various organ systems begin to form. There-

tion from muscle cells), the cells at this point in development are all identical.

The fertilized ovum takes approximately three days to progress through the Fallopian tube to the uterus, where it floats freely for another four or five days before becoming implanted in the uterine wall, which maternal hormones have prepared for the developing egg. The network of tiny roots that anchor the organism to the uterus will grow into the *placenta*, a pliable structure of tissue and blood vessels that transmits nourishment and wastes between mother and fetus. At two weeks its primitive beginnings can be distinguished by microscope.

By the end of the first two weeks, the cells have multiplied greatly in number and have begun to differentiate. An outer membrane and an inner membrane form a sac that surrounds and protects the developing organism. Three primary layers of cells have formed: the *ectoderm*, which is the source of cells composing the skin, sense organs, and nervous system; the *mesoderm*, from which the muscular, circulatory, and skeletal systems will develop; and the *endoderm*, which will give rise to the lining of the intestinal tract and to related organs such as the liver, pancreas, and thyroid.

One phenomenon that needs explanation is how these cells become differentiated into nerve, muscle, fat, and blood. Some scientists have speculated that newly produced cells are essentially neutral, or undifferentiated. Somehow, these neutral cells are attracted to locations that need them, and then by some means, probably chemical, they are altered to serve the purpose required at that location.

The process may proceed in the same manner as a wound heals. For example, when skin is cut, neutral cells are sent to the wound, where they are transformed into specialized skin cells by chemicals apparently released by layers of tissue immediately below the skin. If the wound is not too deep, the cell differentiation is almost perfect, and there is no scar. However, if the cut is deep enough to destroy the layers that produce the differentiating chemicals, the body's repair job is incomplete, and a scar forms. It is possible that the fetus develops by similarly transforming neutral cells.

Other scientists have suggested that the process of cell differentiation is under the joint control of mother and organism. It may be that both the mother's genes and the genes that are active early in the division of the fertilized egg reprogram the genes of embryonic cells, determining their proper sites and functions (Kolata 1979).

The Embryonic Period

Four weeks after conception, the organism, now called an *embryo*, is about one-fifth of an inch long, 10,000 times larger than the original fertilized egg. In addition, its heart is pumping blood through microscopic veins and arteries, and there are a rudimentary brain, kidneys, liver, and digestive tract, and indentations that will eventually become jaws, eyes, and ears.

Organs along the central axis of the body develop first; the extremities develop later. Thus in the early weeks an embryo is literally all head and heart. Later, the lower part of the body begins to enlarge and to assume its newborn proportion and size.

By the end of the seventh week, the embryo is almost an inch long, and it is clearly human. What looks like the gill slits of a fish are really rudimentary structures in the neck and lower face. What seems to be a primitive tail eventually becomes the tip of the baby's spine; the tail reaches its maximum length at about six weeks and then slowly recedes. The head is now clearly distinct from the rounded, skin-covered body and accounts for about half the embryo's total size. The eyes have come forward from the sides of the head and eyelids have begun to form. The face clearly contains ears, nose, lips, tongue, and even the buds of teeth. The knobs that will be arms and legs grow, and in a matter of weeks, they differentiate into hands and feet and then into fingers and toes. The *umbilical cord*, containing two arteries and one vein, has formed at the bottom of the tiny abdomen to connect embryo and placenta. Through the vessels in this flexible cord nourishment passes to the embryo and waste is taken from it.

In this early period, the brain sends out impulses that coordinate the functioning of other organ systems. The heart beats sturdily, the stomach produces some digestive juices, the liver manufactures blood cells, and the kidneys purify the blood. Testes or ovaries can be distinguished, and the endocrine system has begun to produce hormones. All these organisms are in a primitive form, and it will be several months before they can be considered fully functional (Pritchard and McDonald, 1976).

The Fetal Period

Approximately eight weeks past conception, when bone cells begin to develop, the organism is known as a *fetus*. Within twelve weeks it has begun to stretch out of its C-like posture, and the head is more erect. The limbs are nicely molded, and folds for fingernails and toenails are present. An external inspection could readily determine the sex of the fetus. The lips have separated from the jaws, crude teeth are apparent, the nasal passages have formed, the lungs have acquired their definitive shape, and the brain has attained its general structure; the eyes are organized, and the retina has become layered. The liver secretes bile, and the bone marrow has begun to produce blood. At this time, the fetus weighs about an ounce and is approximately three inches long.

By sixteen weeks, the fetus is approximately six to seven inches long and weighs about four ounces. Until now, its head has been enormous in relation to the rest of its body, but by sixteen weeks the lower part of the body has grown until the head is only about one-fourth of the total body size. The sixteen-week-old fetus looks like a miniature baby. Its face looks "human," hair may appear on the head, bones can be distinguished throughout the body, and the sense organs approximate their final appearance. All

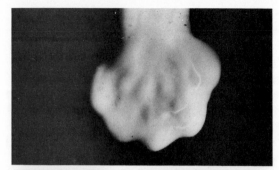

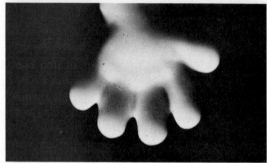

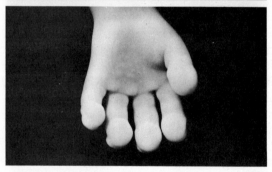

In the fifth week, hands are a "molding plate" with finger ridges. In the sixth week, finger buds form. In the seventh and eighth weeks, the fingers, thumbs, and fingerprints form, and the touch pads are prominent. (Courtesy Carnegie Institution of Washington)

major internal organs have attained their typical shape and plan.

Nevertheless, the fetus could not survive if it were delivered at this point because it lacks the ability to breathe. A necessary component in this process is the liquid *surfactin*, which enables the lungs to transmit oxygen from the air to the blood. Around the age of twenty-three weeks, the fetus begins to produce surfactin, but if it is born at this time, it often cannot maintain the important liquid at the necessary levels and may develop *respiratory distress syndrome* and die. By about thirty-five weeks (sometimes earlier), the fetus develops a new system for maintaining surfactin, and this new method will allow it to live outside the uterus (Gluck and Kulovich, 1973).

Generally speaking, 175 days (twenty-five weeks, or just under six months) is regarded as the minimum possible age at which a fetus can survive. Babies born as early as 175 days after conception have lived, although it is only in recent years that such immature infants have survived. Fetuses born after 252 days (thirty-six weeks) are considered to be of normal term, although unusual circumstances may still make special care necessary for the first few days or weeks of life.

During the final period of prenatal development, at a time when the fetus could survive on its own, its organs step up their activity, and its heart rate becomes quite rapid. Fat forms over its entire body smoothing out the wrinkled skin and rounding out contours. The fetus usually gains about half a pound a week during the last eight or nine weeks in the uterus. After its thirty-eight weeks in the uterus, the average full-term baby at birth is about twenty inches long and weighs a little more than seven pounds, although weight may vary from less than five to more than twelve pounds (see Figure 4.3 for average weight gain of *mothers* during pregnancy), and length may vary from less than seventeen to more than twenty-two inches.

BRAIN DEVELOPMENT

The *central nervous system* (brain and spinal cord) is of special interest to developmental psychologists because it is the brain that processes information, makes decisions, solves problems, and directs behavior. Its development is both intricate and extremely fast. It starts as a cluster of cells. As these cells continue to differentiate and multiply, they form a tubelike structure, which bends over at one end as it develops. This end eventually becomes the brain. By the end of the first four weeks of life, the embryo has a spinal cord and a recognizable brain with two lobes; by the sixteenth week the brain's major structures and shape resemble those of an adult. By this time, the *cortex*—a mantle of neural cells covering the cerebral hemispheres—has grown back over the lower parts of the brain.

The lower parts of the brain are primarily responsible for sustaining life, the coordination of reflexes, and other primitive behavior, but their development is not sufficient to maintain life outside the womb much before twenty-eight weeks. By thirty-two to thirty-six weeks, the areas of the cortex governing motor and sensory behavior are reasonably mature, as are parts of the primary hearing areas. But at birth, the remaining and larger mass of the cortex is still very immature.

During the prenatal period, two major events mark cell growth in the brain (Dobbing and Smart, 1974). The first is the development of all the neural cells, or *neurons*, that make up the adult brain. Many more neurons are formed than the brain actually needs, and those that do not make contact with other cells die during the developmental stage (Cowan, 1979). Neurobiologists estimate that the average adult brain has 100 billion neurons (Hubel, 1979). Research indicates that these cells begin to develop when the fetus is about ten weeks old and that all 100 billion may be developed by about sixteen to twenty weeks. The second major event involves the continuing growth of these neurons and the growth of *glial cells*, which seem to play an essential role in the nourishment of neurons and in the development around each neuron of a sheath of *myelin*, a fatty substance that keeps nerve impulses channeled along the neural fibers and reduces the random spread of impulses from one fiber to another. This development begins

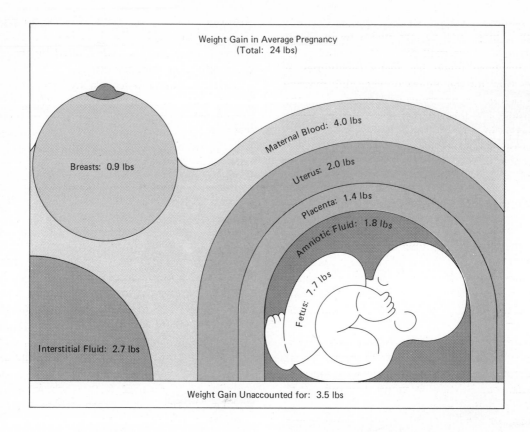

Weight Gain in Average Pregnancy
(Total: 24 lbs)

Maternal Blood: 4.0 lbs

Breasts: 0.9 lbs

Uterus: 2.0 lbs

Placenta: 1.4 lbs

Amniotic Fluid: 1.8 lbs

Fetus: 7.7 lbs

Interstitial Fluid: 2.7 lbs

Weight Gain Unaccounted for: 3.5 lbs

Figure 4.3 Of the twenty-four pounds recommended as the weight gain during a normal pregnancy, only about three and a half pounds is stored as fat and protein. This extra weight acts as a buffer against the stresses of the postnatal period. (Source: From Newton and Modahl, "Pregnancy, The Closest Human Relationship," *Human Nature,* March 1978, p. 47.)

at about twenty weeks and accelerates until the fetus is about twenty-eight to thirty-two weeks old. The glial cells continue to multiply until about the second year after birth, and myelination also continues for several years after birth. Indeed, in parts of the forebrain and in the reticular formation—an area of the brain that helps maintain attention and consciousness—myelination continues until adolescence (Tan-

ner, 1978). As neurons move from the depth of the developing brain, where they are formed, to their final position, they appear to migrate along a path charted by special glial cells whose excessively long fibers extend to the outer surface of the brain (Cowan, 1979).

Despite its full complement of neurons, the fetal brain remains immature in other respects. For one thing, the adult cortex is composed of nine types of neurons arranged in six different layers. Not all these cells reach a mature form in the fetal cortex, nor are the cells distributed in the neat, layered arrangement of the mature cortex. Further, according to best estimates, each neuron in the adult brain has about ten thousand connections with other cells, whereas connections among cells in the fetal brain are, in comparison, sparse, and the fibers that extend from the neurons are short and stumpy; as the cells mature, many will be retracted (Cowan, 1979). Although, as we shall see in the next chapter, the newborn infant has many capabilities, it takes time for the almost unbelievably massive and rich interconnections to develop among the neurons. The formation of nerve circuits seems to occur in a precise order and according to a rigid timetable (Hirsch and Jacobson, 1975).

PRENATAL BEHAVIOR

Movement, the major behavior that characterizes the fetus, begins long before the fetal neurons have developed. Mothers often report feeling movement when the fetus is approximately sixteen weeks old; but the muscles of the fetus are in fact capable of movement at about eight weeks.

Developmental psychologists are interested in how early the fetus responds to stimuli, what kinds of responses it makes, and what kinds of spontaneous behavior it shows. It is difficult to study prenatal behavior, but some years ago Davenport Hooker (1952) studied embryos and fetuses delivered by Caesarean section that were too immature to survive. His research shows that by twelve weeks after conception, the fetus can kick its legs, turn its feet, close its fingers, bend its wrists, turn its head, squint, frown, open and close its mouth, stick out its tongue, and respond to touch.

By twenty-three weeks the fetus shows a great deal of spontaneous activity, as many pregnant women report. It sleeps and wakes as a newborn does, but unlike the newborn infant, it also becomes sluggish at times, perhaps because its rapid growth results in a reduced oxygen supply (Humphrey, 1970). The fetus also has a favorite position for naps. By twenty-four weeks, it can cry, open and close its eyes, and look up, down, and sideways (Hooker, 1952). By this time it has also developed a grasp reflex and will soon be strong enough to support its weight

with one hand. It may hiccup. During the final eight or nine weeks, the fetus is quite active, although its actions become limited by the increasingly snug fit of the uterus.

Behavioral development in the prenatal organism corresponds to the development of its nervous system and of the muscles of its body. The earliest responses found in embryos appear at about five and a half weeks after conception (Humphrey, 1970). Stroking the area of the mouth with a fine hair causes the embryo to respond in a general manner, moving its upper trunk and neck. By nine weeks, the fetus will bend its fingers when the palm of its hand is touched and either curl or straighten its toes in response to a touch on the sole of the foot. By eleven weeks, the fetus can swallow. As the organism develops, more and more of its body becomes sensitive to stimulation, and the response eventually narrows to the area stimulated. Thus, when the mouth is touched, only reflexes about the mouth appear. Within the last few months before birth, the fetus behaves essentially as it does at birth, with grasping, sucking, kicking, and other typical infant reflexes.

Such behavior is all either spontaneous or a reaction to immediate stimulation. It appears, however, that the fetus can learn as well, depending on what the researcher wants to teach it. Lester Sontag made a loud noise near a pregnant woman's abdomen. At first the sound produced a large change in fetal heart rate, but after Sontag repeatedly made the noise near the woman's abdomen on successive days, the fetus no longer responded. Apparently, it had adapted to the sound—it had "learned" it in a sense (Sontag and Newbery, 1940). David Spelt (1948) showed that a twenty-eight-week-old fetus that responds to very loud noises can also learn to respond to the neutral stimulus of a vibrator applied to the maternal abdomen. Neither of these observations has ever been repeated, although both suggest that a fetus is capable of a rudimentary kind of learning, or remembering.

BIRTH

Near the end of pregnancy, the fetus normally lies head down in the uterus, which resembles a large sack opening into the vagina through the cervix. The exact mechanisms that begin labor are not well understood. They may involve changes in hormone levels in both mother and fetus. On the mother's side, her pituitary gland releases the hormone, *oxytocin*, her uterus stretches, the relationship of other hormones within her uterus changes, and her body releases a substance that causes the uterus to contract. When the fetus is ready to be born, its adrenal gland produces cortisol and its pituitary produces oxytocin. Although some researchers believe that the production of fetal oxytocin is the signal that begins birth, they have yet to establish the direct transfer of the hormone through the placenta (Kumaresan *et al.*, 1975).

Labor and Delivery

Labor, or the birth process, progresses in three stages. For first-born infants, labor often lasts thirteen to fifteen hours, although its actual length varies greatly from mother to mother and is markedly less for later-born children.

In the first stage of labor, which lasts until the cervix is completely dilated, the upper portion of the uterus contracts at regular and progressively shorter intervals. During this period, the lower part of the uterus thins out and the cervix dilates to permit the fetus to pass through the birth canal.

In the second stage of labor, which lasts until the fetus is born, the mother's abdominal muscles also contract in a bearing-down motion. Unless drugs deaden sensations, she usually pushes hard to get the baby out. During this period, the fetus passes head first through the birth canal and emerges from the mother's body, a process that lasts approximately eighty minutes in the birth of a first baby.

After the birth, the physician cleans the baby's nose and mouth with a suction apparatus to make breathing easier and to prevent mucus, blood, or the baby's own waste products from entering the lungs. Then the umbilical cord is tied and cut.

In the final stage of labor, uterine contractions expel the *afterbirth* — the placenta, its membranes, and the rest of the umbilical cord. This process lasts approximately five to twenty minutes, and the afterbirth is immediately examined by the physician to determine whether it is complete and normal.

Not all deliveries proceed in this normal fashion. In a breech delivery, the baby's buttocks appear first, then the legs, and finally the head. Such deliveries can be dangerous because the baby may suffocate before the head emerges. Some babies must be delivered surgically, by Caesarean section, because the mother's pelvis is too small to permit her baby to pass through.

The newborn baby is assessed for appearance (color), heart rate, reflex irritability, activity, muscle tone, and respiratory effort to determine whether further medical help is needed. A much-used and practical scoring system for assessing these attributes is known as the *Apgar score* (Apgar and James, 1962). Each of the characteristics is rated 0, 1, or 2 (2 being best), and these scores are added together to obtain the baby's Apgar score, which may vary from 0 to 10. Another widely used measure is the Brazelton Neonatal Behavioral Assessment Scale (Brazelton, 1973), which consists of approximately thirty tests that score the baby on twenty reflexes and twenty-seven kinds of behavior, including alertness, cuddliness, motor maturity, and responses to stress and to environmental stimuli. The Brazelton scale was originally developed to provide a way of documenting differences in temperament among newborns, with the hope of predicting how those differences might affect the relationship between baby and caregiver (Als *et al.*, 1979). It is more complicated than the Apgar and is not routinely administered, but it enables researchers to measure behavior that previously could not be assessed

Shall We Have a Boy or a Girl?

Prospective parents may one day be able to load the dice of gender selection by timing intercourse in relation to the woman's menstrual cycle. When Susan Harlap (1979) studied 3,658 live births among Orthodox Jewish women, she discovered that among women who resumed intercourse on the probable date of their ovulation or one day later, those with regular cycles produced approximately an equal number of boy and girl babies, but women with irregular cycles produced more girls. Women who resumed intercourse a day or two before ovulation gave birth to a slight preponderance of boys. But of the babies born to women who waited until two days after ovulation to resume sexual relations, more than 65 percent were boys. Among the last group, women whose menstrual cycles were regular showed an even stronger trend: more than 67 percent of their babies were boys.

Harlap's work confirms earlier studies (e.g., Guerrero, 1975) that showed similar results; but many of the women in the earlier studies either suffered from subfertility or had been using periodic abstinence as a contraceptive. In Harlap's study the ritual laws served as a natural control over the circumstances of conception.

The Talmudic rules regarding sexual relations are strict. Intercourse is forbidden during menstruation and for an additional seven days. On the seventh day, the woman undergoes a ritual bath and the couple resumes sexual relations that night.

Harlap calculated the day of ovulation by subtracting 14 days from the expected onset of the next menstruation (which never took place because the women were pregnant), the dates she selected may therefore be erroneous in some cases. But, as she points out, such errors are unlikely to have biased the data consistently in the same direction.

Harlap cautions couples against deliberate delay should they decide to try for a boy. Fertilization late in the menstrual cycle may mean that the ovum is "overripe," a condition that is thought to be possibly linked with congenital malformations. Until that question has been settled, she suggests that couples not attempt to apply her findings to their own family planning.

SEX PROPORTION ACCORDING TO CYCLE DAY OF RESUMING INTERCOURSE IN WOMEN WITH REGULAR AND IRREGULAR CYCLES*

Cycle Day of Resuming Intercourse†	Regular Cycles		Irregular Cycles		Total	
	No. of Births	% Male	No. of Births	% Male	No. of Births	% Male
−2	1419	53.9	254	50.0	1673	53.3
−1	567	54.3	315	51.4	882	53.3
0	453	50.1	192	47.4	645	49.3
+1	225	52.9	88	43.2	313	50.2
+2	102	67.6	43	60.5	145	65.5
Total	2766	53.8	892	49.8	3658	52.8

* $\chi_9^2 = 19.061$, $P < 0.025$ † Day of ovulation = 0.

Reprinted by permission of *The New England Journal of Medicine*, 3, p. 1446, 1979.

until babies were older. For example, the scale has been used to investigate such varied aspects of infancy as cross-cultural differences in the behavior of newborns, the effects on the newborn of maternal medication during delivery, and the condition of babies who are born prematurely or who suffer respiratory distress.

Methods of Childbirth

For a good many years, American obstetrical practices were generally accepted by women and physicians alike as the best possible care for both mothers and babies. But in recent years, a growing number of parents and medical personnel have seriously questioned the procedures in many American hospitals. In most of them, labor was regarded as difficult and painful, drugs were routinely given, and episiotomies (surgical incisions to enlarge the vaginal orifice) and forceps were used to speed the birth process.

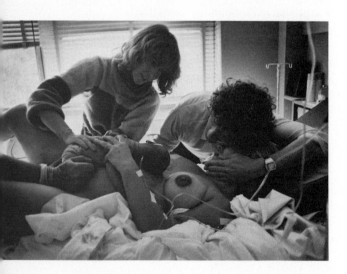

Before the umbilical cord was cut, this baby was placed on the mother's abdomen. Since the baby was born by Leboyer's method, the next experience was immersion in warm water to simulate uterine conditions, thereby easing the transition to a new environment. (© Irene Barki 1979/Woodfin Camp & Assoc.)

Anthropologists have reported that childbirth varies dramatically around the world. In cultures that regard birth as fearful and something that should be hidden, women often have prolonged and difficult labors. On the other hand, in cultures that regard birth as an open, easy process, women generally have short, uncomplicated labors (Mead and Newton, 1967).

Grantly Dick-Read (1944), a British physician who had noticed that some of his patients found childbirth a relatively peaceful, painless experience, believed that fear generated a tension that produced pain among most women. His urging of what he called "natural childbirth" met with some success, and his techniques, combined with the more recently introduced Lamaze method, have brought about changes in the way many obstetricians handle childbirth. In the Lamaze method, women learn to substitute new responses for learned responses of pain, and by concentrating on breathing, try to inhibit painful sensations (Chabon, 1966).

The rising popularity of the Lamaze method has gradually led many American hospitals to change their procedures. The medical profession has come to realize that all family members benefit from sharing the experience of childbirth and has urged a more homelike hospital atmosphere, where older children can be with their mothers during the early stage of labor. In a joint position statement, the branches of the medical profession involved in childbirth have advocated the use of a birthing room for normal deliveries (Interprofessional Task Force, 1978). This combination labor and delivery room, where the father remains with the mother, is decorated like a bedroom instead of a hospital room, and the bed allows the mother to give birth in a semisitting position. A crib for the baby is in the room, and both breast-feeding and handling of the new baby are encouraged. In most cities where birthing rooms are not available, a husband is now permitted to accompany his wife into the delivery room, where he can offer her emotional support and can participate in the birth process. Further, some of the routine hospital procedures—from automatic medication to episiotomy—that tend to make birth an abnormal and unpleasant experience, have been eliminated for normal deliveries in a number of hospitals.

Frederick Leboyer (1975), a French obstetrician, has taken the psychological approach to childbirth a step further. He focuses on the emotions and sensations of the baby, urging peace and quiet, dim lights, delay in severing the umbilical cord, body contact for newborns, and an immediate bath in warm water that approximates the conditions within the womb. Leboyer contrasts the traditional picture of a screaming newborn held upside down by its ankles with the smiling, bright-eyed, contented infants delivered by his method. Although Leboyer's proposals seem strange to American physicians, many of the practices he advocates are routine in the Netherlands (Newton, 1975).

DEVELOPMENTAL AND BIRTH COMPLICATIONS

Most pregnancies follow a normal course of development, and most babies are normal and healthy. On occasion, however, a genetic abnormality or an environmental factor, such as prenatal exposure to drugs or radiation, affects the developing fetus. Some of the resulting defects are minor, some respond to medical or surgical intervention, and others are so serious that they threaten the life of the baby.

No matter what the source of developmental or birth complications, their effects can range far wider than the physical malformations, the reduced birth weights, or the mental retardation that results. They may change the reactions of parents during the first few hours after delivery, when the critical emotional bond between them and their offspring is forming, so that the emotional tone of their relationship is never quite the same as it would have been had their baby been completely normal. The parents may be less loving or even reject their child. Or they may, over time, smother the child with attention or be so overprotective that he or she finds it difficult to develop a sense of competence or independence. Thus developmental complications are yet another strand in the intricate web of child development.

Chromosomal Abnormalities

Approximately one out of every hundred babies born has some sort of chromosomal abnormality, caused when cell division in the gamete goes wrong. During meiosis, a pair of chromosomes may fail to separate, so that one of the gametes has one chromosome too many and the other lacks a chromosome. Such cells, if they develop, produce individuals with an abnormal number of chromosomes in all their cells. Any abnormalities caused by such cell division are irreversible, and their consequences are often serious.

Sometimes the error in cell division is found in the sex chromosomes. Normal female gametes carry a female sex chromosome (X) and normal male gametes carry either a female sex chromosome or a male sex chromosome (Y). When the gametes unite in the fertilized egg, either a female (XX—an X chromosome from each gamete) or a male (XY—an X chromosome from the female gamete and a Y chromosome from the male gamete) is produced. Errors in the division of sex chromosomes may produce only a slight abnormality—as when a baby boy is born with an extra male sex chromosome (XYY)—and be apparent only upon microscopic examination. Such babies, with one female and two male sex chromosomes, grow to be taller than average men. Claims that such boys are extremely aggressive and violent have not been substantiated (Witkin *et al.*, 1976). When a baby boy is born with an extra female sex chromosome (XXY—two female and one male sex chromosomes), he will have *Klinefelter's syndrome*. The boy will be sterile, will have a hippy, rounded body, will tend to develop breasts, and may be somewhat retarded.

Girls born with a missing female sex chromosome (XO—one female and no male sex chromosomes) suffer from *Turner's syndrome*. These girls tend to have short stature, a webbing or shortening of the neck, a broad-bridged nose, low-set ears, and short, chubby fingers. They generally lack secondary sex characteristics and have mild to moderate mental retardation.

The extra chromosome is not always a sex chromosome. Each of the twenty-three pairs of chromosomes has been numbered by researchers. If the fertilized egg has an extra Chromosome 21 (three instead of two), the egg will develop into a baby who suffers from *Down's syndrome* (formerly called mongolism). These children tend to be short and stocky. They have a broad nose bridge; a large, protruding tongue; an open mouth; square-shaped ears; a broad, short neck with extra, loose skin over the nape; and large folds of skin above the eyes that give the child an "Oriental" appearance. Such children frequently have congenital heart disease and other problems, and often do not live past the teens. They have moderate to severe mental retardation, although the extent of retardation varies considerably from case to case.

Down's syndrome is caused in one of two ways. In one case, it arises when extra material from Chromosome 21 becomes attached to another chromosome. This process is extremely rare and the tendency is inherited. The other cause of Down's syndrome arises when an error in cell division produces an offspring with an extra Chromosome 21, a genetic make-up unlike that of either parent. This tendency is not inherited.

It was always assumed that the extra chromosome came from faulty cell division within the egg. But today it is possible to stain and compare chromosomes. When such comparisons have been made, about one-fourth of the cases of Down's syndrome have been traced to faulty cell division within the sperm (Holmes, 1978). The presumption that a defective egg was al-

ways responsible may be due to the fact that the likelihood of producing children with Down's syndrome through an error in cell division increases as a mother ages. Some studies show that the risk of producing a child with Down's syndrome is only about 1 in 2,500 for mothers less than twenty years old, 1 in 1,900 for mothers thirty to thirty-four years old, but 1 in 50 for forty-five-year-old mothers (Frias, 1975). However, older mothers are likely to be married to older men, and older men sometimes produce faulty sperm. Other abnormalities also occur more frequently in children born to older parents, which is the reason most geneticists encourage couples to have their children before the mother reaches forty.

Genetic Diseases

Sometimes mutations in single genes produce new alleles that are transmitted to future generations. Some of these mutations lead to defects in body proteins that cause errors in metabolism, as is the case with PKU. Most mutations are caused by recessive genes, which must be paired with a similar gene to have a visible effect on the developing baby. Some, like PKU, are treatable; others are not.

In *Tay-Sachs disease*, the baby lacks Hex A, an enzyme that is required for the metabolism of certain fatty substances. Consequently, these substances accumulate throughout the body, including the brain, with lethal results. Such babies have convulsions, become blind or paralyzed or both, and undergo mental degeneration. They invariably die before they are seven years old.

Each year more than one hundred babies are born in the United States with Tay-Sachs disease, an affliction confined almost entirely to people whose Jewish ancestry can be traced back to an area in Eastern Europe between Russia and Poland. Since Tay-Sachs is caused by a recessive allele, many people who show no symptoms are carriers of the disease. And since carriers have a level of Hex A far below that of

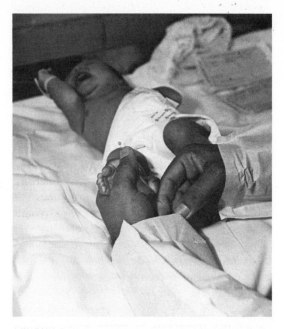

Blood drawn from this neonate's heel will be tested for PKU, a genetically transmitted disease that can have serious consequences. (© Laurence Frank 1981)

the general population, a blood test can identify them. Only if both parents are carriers will the child be born with the disease.

In *sickle-cell anemia*, a genetic flaw affects the production of hemoglobin, a substance in red blood cells that combines with and releases oxygen. People with sickle-cell anemia have sickle-shaped blood cells that can clog the circulatory system, causing pain and tissue damage. Since these abnormal cells are rapidly destroyed by the spleen, the sufferer may develop severe anemia. Other destructive effects of the disease are rheumatism, pneumonia, kidney failure, and enlargement of the spleen. People with sickle-cell anemia often die before they are forty years old.

Sickle-cell anemia is largely confined to blacks; about 1 percent of American blacks have the disease, and another 8 percent carry a single allele. Since the gene is not recessive but *codominant*, a person must have two alleles to develop anemia; but among those with a single allele, 50 percent of the red blood cells are affected. Although such people do not develop anemia, should they go to very high altitudes, half their blood cells will sickle and they will become seriously ill. In tropical countries, however, such people are at an advantage, for possession of the allele protects them against malaria. Since people with sickle-cell anemia often live long enough to have children and since the gene protects against malaria, it tends to perpetuate itself. Indeed, although the possession of both alleles may be fatal, possession of a single allele confers a selective advantage in tropical areas where malaria is prevalent, since it represents a life-saving adaptation. A blood test can reveal the presence of the allele.

Prenatal Environmental Hazards

A fertilized egg that has a normal genetic make-up still faces many possible hazards before the course of pregnancy is completed. Although the environment within the uterus is usually stable, it is not proof against influences that can alter or kill the developing organism. At one time it was believed that the placental membranes, which filter all substances that pass between mother and fetus, acted as a barrier to any disease, drug, or antibody that might harm the fetus. Research and experience have destroyed this confidence, and a growing list of substances are now known to penetrate the barrier.

Even when fetal exposure to a destructive influence, called a *teratogen*, is known, there is no way to predict the precise influence the factor will have upon the developing organism. Timing is apparently a crucial factor in determining whether an environmental influence will produce an abnormality in the developing fetus. If some destructive agent is introduced at the time an organ is forming (see Figure 4.4), that organ may never develop properly; however,

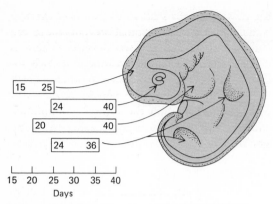

```
15    25
      24        40
  20            40
      24    36
```

```
15  20  25  30  35  40
         Days
```

Figure 4.4 Organs are most susceptible to a teratogen when they are forming. For example, the eyes are most vulnerable between the twenty-fourth and the fortieth days after conception, as the drawing of a human embryo indicates. (From H. Tuchmann-Duplessis, *Drug Effects on the Fetus.* Reproduced with the permission of the publishers, ADIS Press, Sydney, Australia.)

the agent may have less serious effects—or no effect at all—on organs already formed or those not yet ready to make their appearance. Most of the basic organ systems develop in the first third, or *trimester*, of pregnancy, so maternal health problems are likely to have a greater impact on the fetus at this time than later.

In addition to timing, dosage may determine the destructiveness of a teratogen. Low levels of some substances, such as lead or mercury or radiation or alcohol, may have little or no effect on the fetus. Heavy dosages may lead to gross malformations.

Nevertheless, the same extent of exposure to a teratogen at the same point in development can affect two fetuses differently. The genetic susceptibility of the fetus and the mother's physical condition are factors that can limit or exaggerate the likelihood of fetal malformation (Tuchmann-Duplessis, 1975).

DISEASE A number of viruses, including mumps, influenza, and polio, pass through the placental barrier and may affect the fetus. One of the most common culprits is rubella (German measles). If a pregnant woman contracts rubella during the first trimester, her baby may be born blind, deaf, brain-damaged, or with heart defects. Not all babies born to mothers who have suffered from rubella are abnormal, but the earlier in the pregnancy the mother contracts the disease, the more likely it is that her baby will be affected. A study by Richard Michaels and Gilbert Mellin (1960) indicates that 47 percent of the babies born to mothers who had rubella during the first month of pregnancy were abnormal, whereas 22 percent of the babies whose mothers had the disease in the second month, and 7 percent of those whose mothers had it in the third month were seriously affected.

Venereal diseases, such as syphilis, gonorrhea, and herpes simplex, can also seriously affect the fetus. In the case of *syphilis*, if a pregnant woman is in only the first or second stage of the disease, with symptoms of canker sore, rash, or fever, and if she receives treatment, her baby is likely to be born without ill effects. But if she remains untreated or if she is in a more advanced stage of the disease, the fetus may be deformed or die. If it survives, it is likely to be born prematurely and to have congenital syphilis, with all its debilitating consequences.

As the fetus moves down the birth canal, it can come into contact with *gonococcus*, the bacterium that produces gonorrhea. A number of years ago, many babies became blind when their eyes were infected during the birth process. Because many women have gonorrhea without showing any symptoms, it has become common practice to place drops of silver nitrate or penicillin in the eyes of all newborn babies. The practice has almost wiped out this kind of blindness.

The prospects are less hopeful for a *herpes simplex* infection, which represents a real danger for a fetus that picks up the virus in the birth canal. Since the incubation period for this virus is from four to twenty-one days, infected babies may not show any symptoms until after they go home from the hospital, when skin lesions may alert the mother. Up to half of the babies born to mothers with a genital herpes infection contract the disease, and only about half of them survive it (Babson *et al.*, 1980).

Rh FACTOR Human blood comes in many types. Most are not compatible, which is why a doctor who administers a transfusion always makes sure that a person receives blood that matches his or her own. Generally, no serious incompatibility exists between a mother and her baby, because blood types are transmitted according to the genetic principles discussed earlier. However, in about 1 in 200 births, there is a crucial difference in the *Rh factor*—the blood antigens that stimulate antibody production—of mother and baby.

This occurs when the mother is Rh negative and the father is Rh positive, and their child is born with the dominant Rh-positive factor. Unless the mother has previously received a transfusion of Rh-positive blood, there will usually be no problem when their first baby is born. The mother's and baby's blood circulations are kept separate by the placental barrier, so that only slight mixing occurs during pregnancy, although the mingling of blood is increased at birth, when the membranes of the placenta are ruptured. However, if this couple has another baby and that baby is also Rh positive, there is a chance— a less than 10 percent chance—that the baby may suffer serious complications. In such cases, the mother's immune system produces antibodies that cross the placenta, enter the baby's circulatory system, and begin destroying its developing red blood cells, causing it to become anemic and oxygen- and nutrition-deficient. Sometimes the baby with this condition, which is called *erythroblastosis*, is stillborn. If it survives, such a baby may become mentally retarded or have cerebral palsy.

At one time, it was necessary to monitor the Rh-negative mother's blood throughout pregnancy and, if she began to show signs of incompatibility, be prepared to exchange completely the newborn baby's blood by means of massive transfusions, a treatment that prevents the severe jaundice these babies often develop. There is now a relatively simple treatment for Rh incompatibility. The Rh-negative mother is given an injection soon after the delivery of each Rh-positive child, stopping the formation of immune substances in her blood and making her body safe for the development of her next Rh-positive baby (Freda *et al.*, 1975).

Should the injection have been omitted, the presence of erythroblastosis can be detected by amniocentesis, a procedure discussed in the section on genetic counseling. In such cases, blood compatible with that of the mother can be transfused into the umbilical vein of the fetus, which generally results in the delivery of a living but probably very sick baby, who usually recovers.

NUTRITIONAL DEFICIENCIES Almost all vitamins, minerals, and nutrients are transported to the fetus through the placenta. The fetus stores none of these necessary substances against the time of its independent existence except iron. Consequently, the nutritional state of the mother, especially during the first trimester, appears to be important for normal development.

Severely deficient maternal diets are associated with increased rates of abnormality (Robinson and Robinson, 1965). Diets deficient in calcium, phosphorus, and vitamins B, C, and D are associated with an increase in malformed fetuses. During the German occupation of the Netherlands in the 1940s, when food became extremely scarce, the rate of stillbirths and premature births increased among Dutch women, and the birth weight and birth length of their babies decreased. After the war, when food again became plentiful, these rates returned to normal (C. Smith, 1947). Additional data supporting the importance of adequate prenatal nutrition for fetal development come from depressed areas of the United States and from other countries where individuals customarily exist on relatively poor diets. In these regions, dietary supplements (both protein and calories) have led to improved maternal health, higher infant birth weight, and reduced levels of disease and death among infants (Pitkin, 1976).

It is less clear from findings on maternal nutrition how serious and widespread the effects of minor deficiencies in the mother's diet are on the developing fetus. There are, however, many indications that maternal and fetal well-being may be affected also by minor nutritional deficiencies.

DRUGS AND SMOKING A golden rule of obstetric practice has been to advise women to take as little medication during pregnancy as possible. Even aspirin has become suspect, and some researchers believe it can lengthen pregnancy and lead to bleeding in the newborn infant. The thalidomide tragedies of the 1960s, when many mothers who took the sedative thalidomide during the early weeks of pregnancy produced babies with grossly deformed arms and legs, vividly illustrates the consequences that heedless drug taking can have. Another example involves a drug given to maintain a pregnancy. Diethylstilbestrol (DES), a synthetic hormone that was widely prescribed during the 1950s, has been associated with vaginal cancer in women whose mothers received the drug. And prednisone, a drug prescribed for infertility, for the subsequent maintenance of pregnancy, and for such unrelated conditions as asthma or arthritis, has been associated with significantly reduced birth weights in full-term babies (Reinisch et al., 1979).

Heroin use creates an added problem. The newborn infant of a heroin or methadone user must often go through withdrawal, because both drugs pass through the placental barrier. Withdrawal symptoms usually appear about twenty-four hours after birth, and the baby may have tremors, vomiting, diarrhea, rapid breathing, high temperatures, and convulsions. In addition, almost half of these babies have low birth weights.

The seriousness of alcohol's effects on the fetus became apparent several years ago when a small group of pediatricians in the United States and Europe noticed that babies born to alcoholic mothers often suffered from what has become known as *fetal alcohol syndrome*. Studies in many countries have shown that a baby born to an alcoholic mother may have a low birth weight, an odd, conical-shaped head, and characteristic facial features and may be mentally retarded. Occasionally these infants have cleft palates, heart murmurs, hernias, kidney damage, and eye or skeletal defects (Streissguth et al., 1980). But a mother need not be an alcoholic for her baby to be affected. Infants born to heavy social drinkers may have low birth weights, abnormal heart rates, and low Apgar scores, and may suck weakly and perform poorly on tests of newborn behavior. Heavy drinkers also have about three times as many stillbirths as light drinkers. Not all these effects may be the result of alcohol by itself, because heavy drinkers often smoke, use both prescription and nonprescription drugs, and eat unwisely. As yet, no adverse effects have been found among women who take less than two drinks each day, but animal research indicates that even moderate dosages of alcohol may cause malformation (Chernoff, 1977).

Cigarette smoking can also affect the fetus. Cigarette smoking by pregnant women who normally do not smoke produces an increase in fetal heart rate. Nicotine, tar, and carbon monoxide appear to be the noxious influences, and smoking appears to reduce the capacity of the blood to carry oxygen. Heavy smokers tend to miscarry more often than nonsmokers, to have smaller, lighter babies, and to have significantly more low birth weight babies (Babson et al., 1980). In fact, a study of 17,000 births in Britain showed that smoking during the second half of pregnancy increased the rate of infant mortality by 30 percent and lowered the average birth weight of all babies by nearly eight ounces (Butler, 1974). When these children were seven years old, regardless of their social class, they were shorter than their peers, and lagged behind them in reading ability and social adjustment by a small but significant amount.

The fetus faces a final hazard in the delivery room. Since a number of studies (e.g., Bowes *et al.*, 1970; Alexandrowicz and Alexandrowicz, 1974; Brackbill, 1979) have found that pain-relieving drugs given to women in labor can produce lingering effects on babies' behavior, some physicians have become increasingly reluctant to administer them. As Yvonne Brackbill (1979) has pointed out, the systems and organs most susceptible to drugs or most needed to clear drugs from the baby's system are also the most immature at birth. Her review of more than thirty studies revealed that in twenty of the studies drugs had substantial effects on a baby's behavior, in nine there were significant but less substantial effects, and in only two did the effects seem negligible. In most studies, the drugged babies performed poorly on standard tests of infant behavior as compared with babies whose mothers received no drugs.

In one of the studies that showed negligible results, Frances Horowitz and her colleagues (1977) found that medication during labor produced little effect on babies in Israel and Uruguay. The investigators point out that most American mothers who receive drugs—at least those in a group of Kansas births they studied—are more heavily sedated than women in Israel and Uruguay. Their data indicate that light dosage of pain-relieving medication has little effect on babies' behavior. However, Horowitz and her colleagues suggest that genetic and biological differences among the three groups, as well as the attitudes of women toward drugs, could magnify or diminish the effects of medication on their babies. The apathy of drugged babies can have a long-term effect on their relationships with their primary caregivers, as we shall see in Chapter 5.

EMOTIONAL CONDITION It is not far-fetched to suspect that a pregnant woman who is under considerable emotional stress is likely to find that her emotions have affected her newborn baby in some way. Stress causes chemical changes in the body, which can lead to gastric ulcers, high blood pressure, migraine headaches, cardiovascular disease, and neck pain (Selye, 1976), and women under emotional stress have more difficult pregnancies and deliveries than other women.

Some scientific investigations have suggested that a mother's emotional state can indeed influence her offspring. A number of researchers have demonstrated that stressful experiences in human and rat mothers during pregnancy affect the activity level, birth weight, heart rate, motor development, and emotionality of their offspring (Joffe, 1965; Thompson, 1957). Among women studied by Lester Sontag (1966), sudden grief, fear, or anxiety invariably caused violent activity on the part of their fetuses. In one case, when a woman's husband threatened to kill her, her fetus kicked so violently that she was in pain. Subsequent recordings showed a tenfold increase in activity over the levels at previous weekly checks. After these babies were born, they were irritable and hyperactive, and some had severe feeding problems.

Prematurity

Many of the environmental hazards discussed in the previous section can lead to premature birth, a term whose meaning has changed over the years. At one time "premature" simply referred to the baby that was born before *term*, a gestational age of thirty-eight weeks from conception. This definition proved to be inadequate, because some early babies were of normal weight and health, while some babies born late had serious weight deficiencies and reduced abilities to survive. As a result, prematurity came to be defined in terms of birth weight. Newborn babies who weighed less than 2,500 grams (about 5½ pounds) at birth, regardless of their gestational age, were simply labeled "low birth weight" and considered premature. This criterion also proved to be inadequate, because some newborns who weigh less than five and a half pounds – including those who are less than full term – may be completely normal.

Some babies are simply born small. Consider, for example, the cases of two babies whose birth weight is only two pounds. The first was born substantially before term, and the young gestational age explains the small size. Given proper premature infant care, the baby will probably show an accelerated "catch-up growth" once the weight of five pounds is reached. (Catch-up growth is discussed in greater detail in Chapter 6.) By three years of age this child may be of average height and weight. In contrast, the second baby has spent the full thirty-eight weeks in the uterus but is underweight for gestational age, that is, small-for-gestational age (SGA). In this case, it is likely that some aspect of development has gone awry and has inhibited fetal growth. This baby is likely to have physical problems. Whatever circumstance kept him or her from gaining weight also seems to inhibit catch-up growth. An SGA infant generally remains somewhat shorter and lighter in weight than one would otherwise expect (Cruise, 1973).

Babies who are born before they have completed thirty-three weeks in the uterus and those who weigh less than 2,000 grams (about 4 pounds 7 ounces) are considered high-risk infants (Babson et al., 1980). If they are to survive, they need special care – and even then about 10 percent of them will not live. These babies receive intensive care in modern nurseries, where blood pressure, temperature, respiration, and heart rate can be continually monitored and where they can receive intravenous feedings of water and milk. These babies face additional hazards of development and lag behind normal babies in mental and motor skills. Although most catch up with other babies by the time they are four years old, about 15 percent of those who weigh less than 1,500 grams (3 pounds 5 ounces) at birth suffer some kind of intellectual impairment (Kopp and Parmalee, 1979).

PREVENTING DEVELOPMENTAL DEFECTS

Some prospective parents who know of malformed children, mental retardation, or life-threatening diseases among their relatives are hesitant to produce children for fear their baby will be defective. Advances in prenatal diagnosis and the emergence of genetic counseling have made it possible for many of these people to have children without fear.

Diagnosing Abnormalities

Gross abnormalities of development can now be discovered by using ultrasound to look at the developing fetus. In an ultrasound examination, sound is bounced off the fetus and the echoes are transformed into thousands of dots that appear on a screen. The dots form a picture, called a *sonogram*, that shows details of fetus, *amniotic fluid* (the liquid in which the fetus floats), and placenta. Sonograms can find visible abnormalities, resolve confusion over the age of the fetus, and discover such conditions as a placenta that blocks the birth canal or the presence of more than one fetus.

Ultrasound is often used as a guide in performing another procedure that detects abnormalities. In this procedure, called *amniocentesis*, the physician inserts a hollow needle through the maternal abdomen and draws out a sample of amniotic fluid. The fetus sheds cells into this fluid, and if the fetal cells in the sample are grown in a culture, technicians can perform chromosomal analyses that will detect such abnormalities as Down's syndrome, Turner's syndrome, Tay-Sachs disease, sickle-cell anemia, and others. In addition, the chemical composition of the fluid frequently provides clues to other diseases and reveals whether the fetus can produce enough surfactin to avoid respiratory distress when it is born. Tests can also detect the blood group and sex of the fetus. When this procedure is used, it should be done between the fourteenth and sixteenth weeks after conception, when enough cells are present in the fluid to make diagnosis possible. The procedure carries a slight risk for the fetus, however, so it is not used routinely.

Genetic Counseling

As more ways are developed to detect abnormalities, genetic counseling takes on increased importance. The role of the genetic counselor is twofold: to provide information about the probability of fetal malformation before children are conceived, and to discuss the use of diagnostic techniques and explain the implications of test results with parents who have already conceived.

In the first role, the genetic counselor discusses probabilities. Couples who fear that they may carry a genetic disease can be tested, and often they can be reassured that their fears are groundless. For example, the Hex A level of their blood reveals whether the prospective parents are carriers of Tay-Sachs disease; if neither or only one of the couple is a carrier, the counselor can assure them that their child will not have the disease. If both are carriers, the counselor can explain the probabilities (25 percent) that their child will be born with Tay-Sachs. The couple must then decide whether to go ahead with their plans to have a child. In the case of PKU, if both are carriers and the couple — knowing that there is a 75 percent probability that their child will be normal — decide to take the chance, the mother can be put on a diet that is low in phenylalanine before she conceives, thereby limiting any damage to the fetus.

With parents who have already conceived, the counselor explains the results of sonograms and amniocentesis. When the tests show a normal fetus — and most tests do, since the chances of normality are much greater than the chances of abnormality, even when both parents are car-

This mother is undergoing a sonogram; on a screen she can see the fetus growing within her, a picture formed when reflected sound is transformed into thousands of dots. (Michael Weisbrot & Family)

riers of a disease — the parents can look forward to the birth confidently, free from the worry and uncertainty that used to accompany such pregnancies. If the fetus proves to be abnormal, the counselor can discuss the extent of the possible damage and the kind of care the child will require, so that parents can decide whether to go ahead with the pregnancy or to terminate it. Many parents decide to go ahead and, forewarned that their baby will have Down's syndrome or sickle-cell anemia, are better able to handle the extra care the child will require and to establish emotional bonds with the baby without the hindrance of the sudden painful shock that used to accompany such discoveries.

One day, perhaps, the genetic counselor will be able to advise carriers how to have healthy children. As researchers learn more about DNA and how to splice genes, it might become possible to remove defective genes from an ovum, for example, then replant it in the mother's uterus. But that day remains years in the future.

TERMINATED PREGNANCIES

Sometimes pregnancies are terminated, and the developing organism is expelled or removed from the uterus. If this happens spontaneously and without deliberate interference on the part of the mother or a physician, it is called a *miscarriage*, or *spontaneous abortion*, when the fetus is less than twenty weeks old and a *premature delivery* if the fetus is older. It has long been thought that miscarriages are nature's way of eliminating an abnormal fetus and that such an event, although sad, should be viewed as a blessing. Science supports this notion. Examinations of spontaneously aborted fetuses indicate that from 30 to 50 percent of all miscarried fetuses have chromosomal abnormalities. Some researchers believe that 95 percent of the embryos and fetuses with such abnormalities miscarry (Babson *et al.*, 1980).

There is evidence that male fetuses are spontaneously aborted more often than female fetuses. Although it is difficult to make such estimates, it is believed that approximately 130 to 150 males are conceived for every 100 females, but that only about 106 males are born for every 100 females (Beatty and Gluecksohn-Waelsch, 1972). Consequently, it would appear that the prenatal death rate is higher for males than for females, a proposition that squares with the fact that following birth, females resist infection better, survive the infancy period more often, and live longer than males do (Fryer and Ashford, 1972).

Not all terminations are spontaneous. Since the United States Supreme Court upheld the right of abortion, legal *induced abortions* have been more frequent. Physicians prefer to abort a fetus before it is twelve weeks old, because abortion is then relatively simple. The procedure involves the use of suction to remove the embryo or fetus together with the uterine lining that sloughs off during a normal menstrual period. From twelve to twenty weeks, an abortion usually requires injecting a substance into the amniotic fluid surrounding the fetus so as to make the uterus contract. This is a more difficult procedure and carries a greater risk to the mother. After twenty weeks, induced abortion is not advisable because there is a chance of delivering a baby who has a remote possibility of surviving.

The decision to have an abortion, especially when the life or health of the mother is in no danger, presents complicated legal, psychological, social, and moral problems. From society's point of view, one important question is whether a fetus has a right to be born, and if so, at what point in development this right begins. Another important question is whether a woman has the right to determine how many children she will bear and when she will bear them. These issues are the focus of passionate debate and personal conflict.

BECOMING A SEPARATE PERSON

In spite of all the possible complications of the prenatal period set forth in this chapter, most babies come into the world as normal individuals. As each baby emerges from the dark of the uterus, the most intimate human relationship ends. Within the womb, the child is dependent on the mother for the automatic satisfaction of every need; with birth, the child begins the process of learning to satisfy his or her own needs.

What happens during the prenatal period can affect the way the child will go about that process, and it can influence the entire course of the child's development. A fetus that experiences severe malnutrition, that has a genetic abnormality, or whose mother smokes heavily or drinks excessive amounts of alcohol will live in a different world from the fetus with normal genetic make-up whose prenatal existence was free from any of the environmental hazards the uterus can present. Compared to a normal baby, a baby who is deformed, sick, or thrust into the world prematurely will find that people react to him or her in altered ways. For example, the experience of spending the first several weeks of life in an intensive care nursery, separated from parents, can hamper the formation of affectional bonds between baby and caregivers. The sluggishness of a heavily sedated baby or the hyperactivity of a baby whose mother has been under severe emotional stress can alter the infant-parent relationship in subtle but sometimes important ways.

At birth, babies start life as separate individuals with all the advantages or disadvantages prenatal life has bestowed upon them. In the next chapter, we shall look at the beginnings of independent life—the world of the newborn child.

SUMMARY

1. Human development begins when the father's sperm cell, or spermatozoon, unites with the mother's egg, or ovum. These gametes each have twenty-three single chromosomes. Chromosomes are made up of genes, which transmit traits and predispositions from parents to offspring.

2. The complex process of genetic combination determines the offspring's genotype, the unique combination of genes that he or she carries. The phenotype, or expression in physical appearance or behavioral predisposition, is often different from the genotype because some genes are dominant and some are recessive. The inherited metabolic abnormality called PKU appears when two recessive genes for the trait are paired; in all other cases the dominant normal gene masks the gene for PKU.

3. During a thirty-eight-week gestation period, the organism rapidly progresses from a fertilized egg engaged in cell division (germinal period) to an embryo with organ systems beginning to take shape (embryonic period) to a fetus that in-

creasingly resembles a human being (fetal period).

4. The central nervous system starts as a cluster of cells and develops rapidly; by twenty weeks all the neurons that make up the adult brain have formed. Behavioral development corresponds to development of the nervous system and muscles. At twelve weeks the fetus has developed many responses, and by twenty-eight weeks, a rudimentary capacity for learning. Twenty-five weeks is the minimum age at which a fetus can possibly survive outside the womb.

5. Birth begins with labor, in which strong uterine contractions push the infant and the afterbirth through the birth canal. The physician then evaluates the baby's appearance and functioning. The experience of childbirth varies dramatically around the world; the popularity of natural methods of childbirth has led to changes in the way American hospitals manage birth.

6. Complications occasionally occur in prenatal development and birth. Abnormalities in cell division can result in a missing or extra chromosome, which creates such physical abnormalities as Down's syndrome; genetically linked metabolic errors can result in such disorders as Tay-Sachs disease or sickle-cell anemia.

7. The uterine environment—which is affected by disease, nutrition, drugs, and emotional stress—can also complicate prenatal development, depending on the timing and amount (dosage) of the hazard, fetal predisposition, and maternal health. Drugs administered during labor can also affect the fetus.

8. Ultrasound and amniocentesis can detect many fetal abnormalities, and genetic counseling can advise couples as to the likelihood of abnormalities and their meaning for the baby. Most genetically abnormal embryos and fetuses miscarry, and more males than females are spontaneously aborted. Legal induced abortion is a focus of continuing controversy.

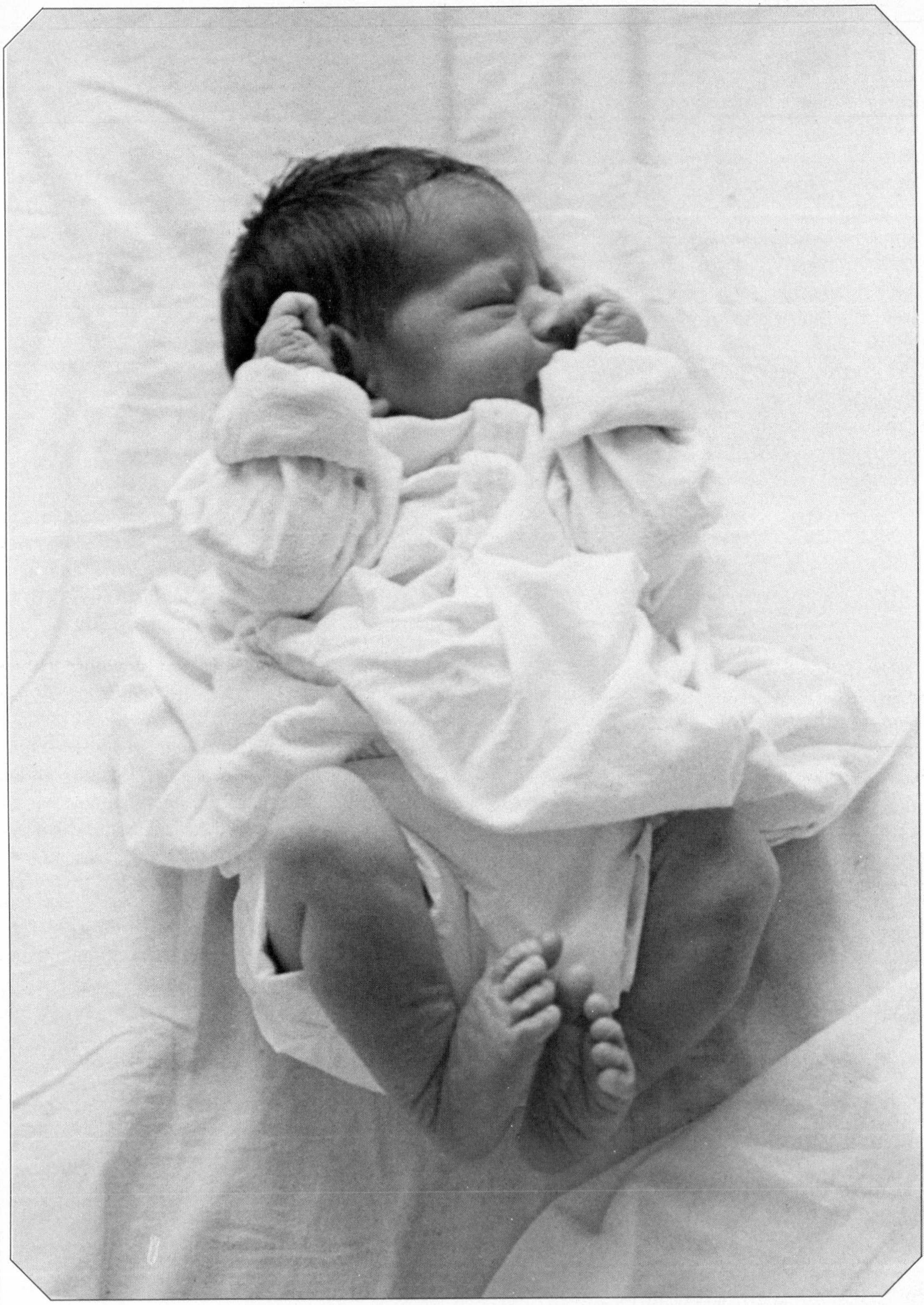

(© Lilo Raymond 1981/Woodfin Camp & Assoc.)

The World of the Newborn

Only a few decades ago, newborn babies were considered to be helpless creatures with extremely limited sensory capacities who comprehended almost nothing of the chaotic world around them. Indeed, at one time the newborn infant was compared to a "decerebrate frog" and described as a "reflex being of a lower type." Nothing could be farther from the picture of the newborn infant as painted by today's developmental psychologists. Newborn infants can see and hear and smell; they can cry and feed and move their limbs. But they can do even more. Instead of being helpless creatures who are assailed by a barrage of meaningless stimuli, they are seen as active, searching, dynamic organisms who create much of their own experience. Newborns are now regarded as organisms constructed to acquire knowledge, and it is generally agreed that the acquisition begins almost immediately.

In this chapter, we shall discover that although newborn babies spend most of their time asleep, their bodies are remarkably prepared for life outside the womb, and that many of their basic functions and rhythms—such as sleeping and waking, hunger and thirst, sucking, elimination, and body temperature—follow rhythmic biological schedules. Various studies will be described that demonstrate the possession of a set of reflexes—many of which are lost in a few weeks—that help newborns accomplish the tasks of feeding and coping with this strange environment. Looking at the newborn's sense organs, we shall find that most of them are functional, or soon will be, and that the baby uses them in an active and selective search of the environment. As we shall discover, newborn infants are capable of learning, and each possesses the rudiments of a unique personality and temperament. Finally, we shall see how the way newborns look and listen or the way they quiet when upset may provide the basis for and key to their differing social development, which begins in their relations with their parents.

The technical term for a newborn baby is *neonate*, a word derived from Greek and Latin terms, meaning newly born. Although some would limit the neonatal period to the first week of life and others would limit it to the first two weeks, most researchers agree that we can refer to a baby as a neonate until the end of his or her first month of independent life (Pratt, 1954).

BIRTH: THE NEWBORN

To most of us, the thought of a little baby brings to mind images of a warm, roly-poly, cuddly, cooing bundle of softness and joy. Although this characterization will be apt in a few weeks, the sight of the newborn baby sometimes disappoints, if it does not shock, parents. Although most parents soon come to regard their own babies as beautiful, outsiders often disagree. One of America's earliest child psychologists, G. Stanley Hall (1891), described the neonate as arriving with a "monotonous and dismal cry, with its red, shriveled, parboiled skin . . . , squinting, cross eyed, pot bellied, and bow legged." Others have likened the physical appearance of the newborn to that of a defeated prize fighter—swollen eyelids, puffy, bluish-red

skin, a broad flat nose, ears matted back at weird angles, and so forth. Considering the wet, cramped quarters of the uterus and the violent thrusting necessary for delivery, we should not regard this ragged appearance as surprising.

At the moment of birth, a newborn emerges blotched with maternal blood and covered with a white, greasy substance called *vernix*, which has facilitated passage through the birth canal. The baby's puffy, wrinkled appearance derives in part from the presence of fluid and small pads of fat under the skin. Some newborns have fine hair, called *lanugo*, over parts of their body. When the baby emerges, the lanugo appears pasted to the skin by the greasy vernix, but after the baby is cleaned and dried, he or she may look quite furry for a few weeks until the lanugo disappears.

A newborn baby often looks somewhat battered. For example, the head may be oddly shaped—sometimes peaked rather than rounded —because the "bones" of the skull are not yet hard and consist of overlapping pieces of cartilage. This condition allows the head to compress, permitting passage through the mother's pelvis. As a result, the head is lumpy: hard in some places and soft in others. The soft areas at the crown of the head, which lack cartilage, pulsate up and down as blood is pumped about the brain. At the other end of the body, the legs are bowed and the feet cocked at a strange angle —a result of the legs having been tucked around the baby in the cramped quarters of the uterus.

Newborn babies look odd, and they often sound strange as well. In the uterus, they were suspended in liquid, and they arrive with nasal and oral passages filled with amniotic fluid and mucus. In Western hospitals, the physician cleans these passages with a suction bulb as soon as the baby's head has emerged from the uterus so that a newborn does not inhale this liquid into the lungs with the first gasping breath. Sometimes a little remains, however, and bursts of rapid gasps, chokes, gags, coughs, and pauses can make the baby sound like a badly operating steam engine.

After the umbilical cord has been tied and cut,

a nurse drops silver nitrate or penicillin into the newborn's eyes to prevent infection, makes simple tests for certain diseases, and then swaddles the infant and allows him or her to sleep.

Although newborns occasionally jerk or cough up mucus, their first sleep is usually quite deep. They are difficult to arouse, and even a loud sound may fail to elicit any obvious response. During this sleep, their bodies are preparing to function on their own. In the uterus, the placenta linked the fetal circulatory, digestive, temperature regulation, and excretory systems with those of the mother; but now the infant's own physiological equipment must take over these necessary functions.

While these systems are being balanced and tuned, a baby frequently does not eat. Stores of fat and fluid will tide the neonate over until the first meal, which may take place within several hours of birth or may not occur for several days. As a result of this delay in feeding, most neonates lose weight during the first few days of life.

BASIC FUNCTIONS AND RHYTHMS

Newborns are not thrust into the world without some mechanisms to keep their body systems in balance. A certain pattern or rhythm characterizes many of these basic body functions.

Temperature

The human being is a warm-blooded animal, which means that the body maintains its temperature within a certain range. In the newborn, temperature regulation is important because the functions performed by most cells and organs are governed by enzymes that can act only within a narrow range of temperature. If the baby's temperature is much lower than the optimum, several body functions might slow to dangerous levels. For example, the metabolic

rate might decline so much that the infant dies. If body temperature is too high, the baby's physiological activity might be too rapid, triggering a mechanism that tends to shut down enzyme activity. Moreover, when newborns are too hot, they tend to breathe more rapidly, their blood becomes too acid, and several other biochemical and physiological systems are thrown out of balance. Consequently, the baby must maintain a relatively constant temperature.

When adults become overheated, their metabolism slows and their blood vessels dilate so that more blood can go to the body surface, where heat is dissipated into the air; they sweat and lose heat through evaporation, and they pant and release heat by exhalation. Conversely, when adults are too cold, they conserve heat by shunting blood away from the surface of the body, where it would cool, and they may move around or shiver, thus generating heat.

The newborn baby, in contrast, has a problem. In proportion to body weight, the newborn has more surface area exposed to cool air and less insulating fat than an adult. Together these factors mean that a newborn loses heat almost four times as fast as does an adult (Brück, 1961). The newborn rapidly develops mechanisms to cope with this problem. Within fifteen minutes of birth, babies — whether premature or full-term — respond to cold by constricting surface blood vessels and increasing their heat production. Two or three hours later, the newborn baby's metabolic response to cold is nearly as good as that of the adult, relative to the baby's body weight if not to body surface area. The problem is not that the newborn lacks the equipment to regulate body temperature but that the task is so great.

The efficiency of the newborn's temperature control is quickly put to the test in its first encounters in the hospital environment. The uterus generally remains at a constant 98.6°F., but the gaseous environment that greets the newborn is invariably colder: rarely over 80°F. and sometimes as low as 60°F. Because babies are born wet and are sometimes bathed, they lose considerable heat through evaporation and exposure of their skin to cool air. In fact, the drop in temperature may be so steep and rapid that the baby would have to produce twice as much heat energy per unit of body weight as the adult does in order to offset these conditions (Adamsons, 1966). Although many hospitals try to minimize this shock, life in the uterus still is considerably warmer than life in the delivery room or hospital nursery, and newborns need to be able to regulate their temperature to handle the transition. This is one reason that very small neonates often require a stay in an incubator.

Sleep

Newborn infants sleep a lot—approximately sixteen out of each twenty-four hours. Unfortunately for parents, most newborns package this sleep into seven or eight naps per day, with their longest single sleep averaging about four and a half hours. Consequently, newborns are roughly on a four-hour sleep/wake cycle, sleeping a little less than three hours in each four. By six weeks, however, their naps have become longer, and they take only two to four of them each day. Even newborns sleep a little more at night than during the day, and by approximately twenty-eight weeks, most babies sleep through the night without waking even once.

In addition to differences in the amount and phases of sleep, the quality of the newborn's sleep is also different from that of the adult. Recently scientists have studied certain body activities that occur during sleep in both adults and babies. There are two general kinds of sleep, distinguished principally by whether *rapid eye movement* (REM) occurs. During REM, or *active*, sleep, eye movements are accompanied by more rapid and changeable respiration, less muscular activity, and a more even pattern of brain waves. In Figure 5.1, the tube around the baby's stomach expands and contracts with each breath, the electrodes on the chest detect heart rate, and the stabilimeter that the baby lies on detects body movements. In addition, electrodes

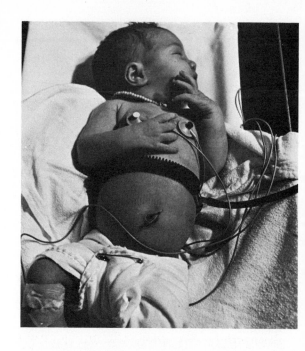

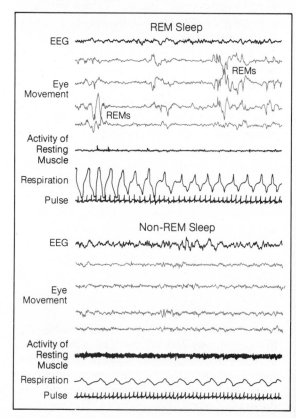

REM Sleep

EEG

Eye Movement — REMs / REMs

Activity of Resting Muscle

Respiration

Pulse

Non-REM Sleep

EEG

Eye Movement

Activity of Resting Muscle

Respiration

Pulse

placed near the eyes detect eye movements, and other electrodes placed on the head record brain waves on an electroencephalograph (EEG). The minute electrical changes that accompany muscular movements are amplified and written by a polygraph on a continuously flowing sheet of paper.

Newborns spend almost half of their sixteen hours of sleep in REM sleep. Not until children are almost five years old does this proportion drop to approximately 20 percent, which is the adult average. The amount of non-REM, or *quiet*, sleep changes little over the childhood years, indicating that much of the newborn's extra sleep is composed of REM sleep.

What do the rapid eye movements of REM sleep signify? Adults wakened during REM sleep often report that they have been dreaming. Consequently, some people have supposed that newborn babies (and perhaps pet dogs) dream during REM sleep. Physiologically, the REM sleep of neonates is nearly identical to that of dreaming adults, but it is unlikely that a newborn baby experiences anything like the integrated series of clear images that most adults do, especially when the limited visual capability and experience of the newborn is considered. The neurological activity of REM sleep apparently serves a physiological purpose, because most adults whose REM sleep is interrupted become nervous, anxious, and have

Figure 5.1 *(top)* This baby is in a stabilimeter crib, which measures the muscular activity. The belt around the abdomen measures respiration, and the electrodes on the chest produce electrocardiographic records. When electroencephalographic recordings are made, electrodes are placed at the outer corners of the eyes. Although cumbersome, the apparatus is not uncomfortable for the baby. *(bottom)* Recordings showing the differences between thirty seconds of REM sleep and non-REM sleep in a newborn. Besides the heightened eye activity during REM sleep, note the absence of muscle activity, the rapid respiratory rate, and changing respiratory amplitude. (Photograph by Jason Lauré; chart after Roffwarg, Dement, and Fisher, 1967)

trouble concentrating (Dement, 1960), and they make up for the loss of REM sleep by showing a higher percentage of it in subsequent sleep periods. Some scientists have suggested that the brain requires periodic neural activity, either from external or internal sources, and that REM sleep signifies self-generated activity in the absence of any external stimulus (Roffwarg, Muzio, and Dement, 1966). Others suggest that REM sleep reflects either a high metabolic rate or neural immaturity (Berg and Berg, 1979). Because newborns sleep so much and have less opportunity to respond to events in the world around them, they may require more of this neurological self-stimulation. In one study, neonates who spent a good deal of their waking time looking attentively at stimuli afterward showed a temporary decrease in REM sleep (Boismier, 1977). Premature babies show even higher percentages of REM sleep than do full-term infants. It is possible that such activity is necessary before birth if neurological development is to occur. Therefore, the first function of REM sleep may be to act as an internal stimulus to neurological development; later it will carry the visual patterns and integrated experiences that constitute the dreams of older children and adults (Roffwarg, Muzio and Dement, 1966).

An infant's physiological state fluctuates regularly. During the eight hours when babies are not asleep, they may be drowsy, alert, fussy, or crying. Obviously, a sleepy, fussy, or wailing baby is likely to be uncooperative and show little interest in tests devised to explore his or her capabilities. For that reason, most studies are performed when babies are alert—a state limited to about 11 percent of the first week outside the uterus (Wolff, 1963). But by the time babies are four weeks old, they are alert about 21 percent of the time.

Feeding

The newborn's sleep/wake cycle is closely tied to the need for nourishment. The typical neonate sleeps, wakes up hungry, eats, remains quietly alert for a short time, becomes drowsy, and then falls back to sleep. When unrestricted breast-feeding is practiced, in which babies are given the breast whenever they cry or fuss, they are likely to eat ten or more times a day during the first few weeks (Newton, 1979).

Books advising parents often suggest a four-hour feeding schedule. The four-hour schedule may have emerged from a study in 1900 of three newborns who were fed a barium-milk solution and then x-rayed periodically after they had swallowed it. The study showed that within four hours the stomach had emptied (Frank, 1966). Some years ago it was common practice to feed young babies on a strict schedule regardless of whether they appeared to be hungry. Parents even waked sleeping babies to feed them. If left to choose their own schedules, a practice called *self-demand feeding*, only about a fourth of them would adopt a four-hour regimen. C. Anderson Aldrich and Edith Hewitt (1947) studied one hundred babies who were allowed to establish their own feeding schedules during the first twelve months of life. At every age, different babies demanded different numbers of meals. For example, during the first month of life, 60 percent of the babies ate every three hours, 26 percent ate every four hours, and approximately 10 percent demanded a feeding every two hours. Most newborns begin by putting themselves on a three-hour schedule and reach three meals a day by the time they are ten months old. Although all babies show some rhythm in their feeding patterns and all require progressively fewer daily feedings as they get older, there are marked differences among babies in the frequency of their meals. Because of studies like this, parents are now encouraged to feed their babies whenever they are hungry, while working toward fewer and fewer feedings as their babies grow.

Sucking

Being able to suck effectively is the foundation of feeding and therefore of survival. Conse-

quently, it is one behavior that the newborn must perform competently and precisely, and it has been studied in great detail.

The young baby sucks rhythmically, in bursts separated by pauses. On the average, a baby puts together approximately five to twenty-four sucks in a single burst, sucking at a rate of approximately one to two and a half times each second, and then takes a brief rest. Although a baby's hunger, age, health, and level of arousal influence the pattern of sucking, individual babies also have their own characteristic patterns of sucking. Whether particular sucking patterns are innate is unknown, because sucking at birth is affected by drugs that pass through the placenta during labor. Several days later, when these drugs have worn off, sucking patterns may already have been affected by the behavior of the mother (Crook, 1979).

The neonate's feeding performance is often a little ragged during the first few days of life, but a baby quickly develops a fairly smooth coordination between sucking, swallowing, and breathing. The fact that a newborn can swallow almost three times faster than an adult, and can suck at the same time that he or she takes in air, aids in the accomplishment of this feat.

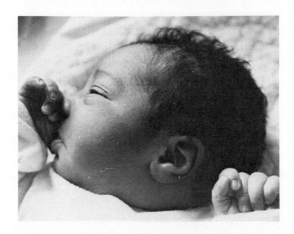

Within a few days, newborns have coordinated sucking, swallowing, and breathing into a smooth and efficient system, but each baby has his or her own characteristic pattern. (© Camilla Smith)

Adults who sucked in a liquid and breathed at the same time would probably choke. Babies can manage simultaneous sucking and breathing because they extract milk from the nipple by pressing the nipple against the roof of the mouth instead of by inhalation.

REFLEXES

The reflexes of the newborn attracted the attention of neurophysiologists and pediatricians quite early, and their studies have provided us with an extensive catalog of reflexive behavior. The newborn comes equipped with a set of reflexes that are elicited by specific stimuli. Some are adaptive and may help the new baby avoid danger. For example, babies close their eyes to bright light and twist their bodies or move their limbs away from sources of pain. Others appear to be vestiges of the past, left over from our nonhuman ancestors. Still others are simple manifestations of neurological circuitry in the baby that later will come under voluntary command or will be integrated in more useful patterns of behavior. Most of these reflexes disappear within a few weeks or months, primarily as the result of neurological development, especially in the cortex of the brain (Minkowski, 1967). When these reflexes fail to drop away, it may be a sign of abnormal neurological development.

The Rooting Reflex

All newborns have a *rooting reflex*—a tendency to turn the head and mouth in the direction of any object that gently stimulates the corner of the mouth. Babies are most likely to show this at about a week or two of age when they are quietly awake with their eyes open, especially if they are somewhat hungry. If one strokes the corner of the baby's mouth with an index finger, moving sideways from the mouth toward the cheek, the baby may move tongue, mouth, or whole head toward the stimulated side. At

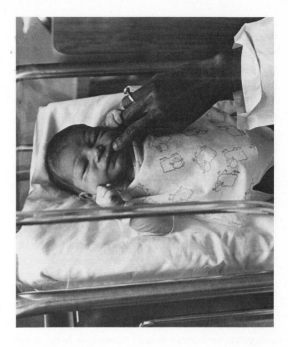

The rooting reflex is produced when the corner of the mouth is stimulated; the newborn responds by moving tongue, mouth, or head toward the source of stimulation. (© Lawrence Frank 1981)

first this reflex appears even when the cheek is stroked a long way from the mouth. As the baby gets older, the reflex will appear only when the stimulation is at the mouth, and only the baby's mouth will respond. The rooting reflex generally disappears at three to four months. This reflex has obvious adaptive significance because it helps a baby to place the nipple in the mouth. Babies sometimes learn to suck their thumbs while rooting, when a thumb and mouth accidentally make contact.

Grasping and the Moro Reflex

A baby in the first weeks of life has a strong grasping reflex. If one places a one-week-old baby on his or her back and places a finger in the infant's hand, the baby is likely to grasp that finger sturdily. Sometimes a grasping newborn can literally hang by one hand. Although the reflex becomes stronger during the first month, it then begins to fade, disappearing at three or four months.

Ernst Moro (1918) first described the *Moro reflex*, which consists of a thrusting out of the arms in an embracelike movement when the baby suddenly loses support for the neck and head. It is easily seen after the first week when the baby is alert, with eyes open or barely closed. It can be elicited by holding a baby with one hand under the head and the other in the small of the back and then abruptly lowering one's hands, especially the hand holding the head. A second way to obtain the Moro reflex is to lay a baby on his or her back, with the head facing straight up, and then slap the mattress behind the head with enough force to jerk the head and neck slightly. Typically, the arms shoot out and upward and the baby's hands curl slightly as if preparing to grab something. In fact, if one places a finger in the baby's hand and has somebody else provides the stimulus for the Moro, one can feel the baby suddenly

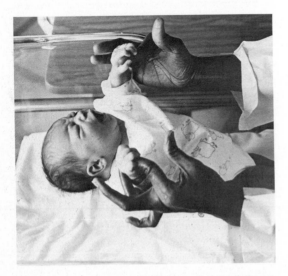

Newborns display the grasping reflex by tightening their fingers around anything placed in their hands. (© Lawrence Frank 1981)

tighten his or her grip. The Moro reflex decreases as the baby gets older; it is difficult to elicit after the baby is three months old, and it is almost always gone by five or six months.

The meaning and purpose of the grasping and Moro reflexes are not clear. It has been suggested that this behavior is an inheritance from our animal ancestors. Because monkeys carry their young on their backs or stomachs, a loss of support is less likely to produce a fall if the youngster reaches out and grasps its mother's fur or skin (Prechtl, 1965).

Walking Movements

A one- or two-week-old baby shows behavior that resembles the movements required in walking. One of these is a *stepping* motion that can be elicited by holding a baby under the arms while gently lowering the infant to a surface until the feet touch and both knees bend. If the baby is slowly bounced up and down, he or she may straighten out both legs at the knees and hips as if to stand. Then if the infant is moved forward, he or she may make stepping movements as if walking, although the baby can neither support his or her own weight nor maintain balance.

The second walking motion, a *placing* response, is simply the baby's propensity to lift the feet onto a surface. If held up and moved toward a surface until the top part of a foot touches the edge, the baby is likely to lift up the foot and place it on the surface.

Such behavior has relatively little practical utility in itself, because the one- or two-week-old baby possesses neither the strength nor the balance either to walk or to step. However, the two reflexes appear to indicate a certain inborn neurological organization that forms the basis for later standing and walking. These reflexes tend to disappear between the third and fourth month, probably because the baby's cortex has developed to a point where it inhibits them. When stepping movements next appear, they

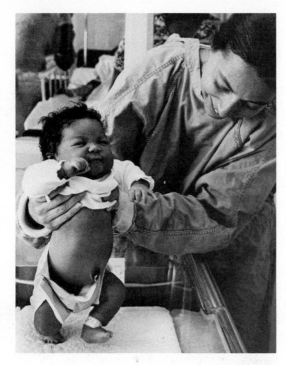

The stepping motion appears when a baby is lowered until the feet touch a surface; the baby responds by making walking movements. (© Camilla Smith)

will be voluntary acts from a baby who is getting ready to rise up and walk.

SENSORY CAPABILITIES

Some years ago, many people believed that the newborn baby could not sense the physical energies in the environment. It was held that the baby could not see clearly, could not smell or taste, and could feel only pain, cold, and hunger. However, research has established that neonates' senses, although not as precise as those of adults, do inform them about their surroundings. Since the ability to learn, to think, and to become a social being depends upon our perceptions of the world, the newborn's sensory capabilities are important. If we know what

newborns can see, hear, smell, and taste, we can discover which events in the environment might influence them.

Vision

If children or adults hold one finger a few inches from the nose and another at arm's length, they can quickly alternate their focus from one to the other, an ability called *visual accommodation*. The newborn does not possess this capability but instead operates like a fixed-focus camera: only objects that are about nine inches from the eye are in focus. Focal distance varies from baby to baby, ranging from seven to fifteen inches. By the age of six weeks, the baby's ability to accommodate appears to improve markedly, but infants are not as skilled as adults until they are approximately four months old (Haynes, White, and Held, 1965). The staggering limit this places on the young baby's visual experience becomes apparent if one focuses on a finger, held about nine inches from the nose, and then attempts to concentrate on other objects in the room. This limited focus is one mechanism that minimizes the confusion in a baby's world; the limitation sharply reduces the amount of distinctive visual stimulation that gets through. The newborn's peripheral vision is also quite limited. Whereas an adult's field of vision covers 180 degrees, the newborn's is only 60 degrees, shutting out two-thirds of the available stimulation and further minimizing possible confusion.

When adults look at an object, they focus both eyes on it. Each eye sees a slightly different image, and by a mechanism called *convergence*, the two images come together until only a single object appears. If one holds a finger at arm's length, focuses on it, and then moves it toward the tip of the nose, one can feel the muscles of the eyes perform this function. The newborn does not possess this ability until the age of about seven or eight weeks. If, therefore, two objects are held nine inches in front of the baby's face, it is possible that the infant's right eye will look at the right object and the left eye at the left object (Wickelgren, 1967).

Because the newborn's eyes are not usually directed toward precisely the same point, the baby often looks wall-eyed (a condition known as *strabismus*) for the first month or so. Given their limited muscular ability, newborns are lucky if they move both eyes in the same direction half the time, let alone keep both trained on the same object. Even without convergence, however, newborns have some sense of depth perception (Yonas and Pick, 1975). Using only one eye, a newborn can tell whether an object appears to have moved nearer or farther by relying on the cues of changing size and clarity. Thus when a relatively small and blurred image that is projected on the eye becomes larger and clearer, the baby detects and responds to the implied difference in depth.

Seeing objects clearly and resolving their detail—an ability called visual *acuity*—is possible only within a very small range for the newborn. And if a newborn's acuity was such that he or she could see equally well at all distances, then the week-old baby would have approximately 20/200 vision. In terms of adult standards, this means that at a distance of twenty feet from an object, the newborn would see it only about as well as adults do at a distance of 200 feet— an acuity that constitutes legal blindness. Vision improves rapidly, however, and by six months, babies can see as clearly as the average adult.

For almost a century, scientists have been trying to determine whether newborn babies can see color. Babies easily tell the difference between objects that differ in brightness, but it is extremely difficult to separate brightness and hue in such a way as to test newborns for color vision (Maurer, 1975). On the basis of physiological evidence, it appears that the color-sensitive cells in the eyes of newborns are few in number and barely developed in structure. This suggests that for at least the first several weeks or so of life the newborn is likely to be colorblind.

Hearing

There is no question that newborn babies hear. Their ears operate four months before they are born; the basic neurology that enables them to discriminate between different tones and intensities is probably ready two months before birth; and approximately one month before birth they are prepared to direct their attention toward a sound. At first, the sounds reaching a neonate may be somewhat dampened, because for the first few days of life the middle-ear passages are filled with amniotic fluid. However, all normal newborns can hear, and some can hear very well. Most newborns will turn their heads in the direction of a shaking rattle (Muir and Field, 1979), and one study suggests that the faintest sound that a baby can detect is about as soft as the faintest sound heard by the average adult (Eisenberg, 1970). Although the newborn can hear a sound, as opposed to no sound, babies have difficulty in discriminating one sound from another. For example, the average newborn can only detect the difference between tones of 200 and 1,000 cycles per second—which is roughly comparable to the difference between a foghorn and a clarinet (Leventhal and Lipsitt, 1964). On the other hand, some exceptional infants have responded to tones that differ as little as 60 cycles per second, which is roughly equivalent to one step on a musical scale (Bridger, 1961).

Taste

Like many of the newborn's other abilities, the sensitivity to taste is much more highly developed than was believed only a few years ago. When drops of various concentrated solutions are placed on their tongues, newborn babies respond with facial expressions much like those of adults. Jacob Steiner (1979) tested 175 full-term babies and found that an extremely sweet liquid brought forth smiles, followed by an eager licking and sucking. When they tasted a sour solution, most babies pursed their lips, wrinkled their noses, and blinked their eyes. When a bitter fluid was dripped into their mouths, the babies stuck out their tongues and spat. (See Figure 5.2.) Some even tried to vomit. Yet when Steiner placed distilled water on their tongues, the babies simply swallowed, showing no expression at all. A group of twenty premature infants, given plain water and a sour solution, responded just as the full-term infants had done.

Within several weeks after birth, a baby's taste sensitivity becomes more acute (Johnson and Salisbury, 1975). For example, when fed solutions of salt water, sterile water, artificial milk, or breast milk, a baby is likely to show a distinctly different pattern of sucking, swallowing, and breathing for each solution. Newborns also alter sucking patterns when the solution is sweet. Charles Crook and Lewis Lipsitt (1976) found that babies suck more slowly and their heart rate increases as solutions get sweeter. These results appear contradictory, because we might expect a baby to suck more vigorously when given a solution that tastes good. Crook and Lipsitt resolve this paradox by suggesting that because babies savor the taste of the sweeter solutions, they slow down to enjoy them, and that pleasurable excitement causes their hearts to speed up.

Smell

Newborns definitely react to strong odors. Babies less than twelve hours old responded in

Figure 5.2 Although it was once believed that newborn infants were unable to tell the difference between lemon juice and sugar, research has shown that they respond to strong tastes much as adults do. The facial expressions of the neonate resemble those of an adult who has just tasted similar solutions, and the accompanying table shows how widespread such reactions were among a group of 175 babies, whose ages ranged from several hours to a week old.

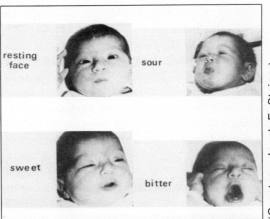

(Courtesy, Jacob E. Steiner)

NEWBORN RESPONSES TO STRONG TASTES

Response	Percentage Responding	
	Less than 20 hours old (N=75)	Three to seven days old (N=100)
Sweets		
Retraction of mouth angle	81	87
Satisfied smile	77	73
Eager sucking and licking of upper lip	99	97
Sour		
Pursed lips	100	98
Wrinkled nose	77	73
Repeated blinking	89	70
Increased salivation	81	65
Flushing	76	64
Bitter		
"Arch-like" lips with depressed mouth angles	97	96
Protruding tongue	79	81
Salivation and spitting	76	87
Expression of "anger" & dislike	79	86
Vomiting	45	52

(*Source:* Adapted from Jacob E. Steiner, "Facial Expressions of the Neonate Infant Indicating the Hedonics of Food-related Chemical Stimuli," in *The Genesis of Sweet Preference,* by James M. Weiffenbach (ed.), National Institute of Dental Research, DHEW Publication No. (NIH) 77-1068, U. S. Department of Health, Education and Welfare, 1977.)

a recognizable manner to synthetic odors of various foods (Steiner, 1979). When a cotton swab saturated with the odor of rotten eggs or concentrated shrimp was waved beneath their noses, the infants reacted as babies in Steiner's previous experiment had responded to bitter tastes. To the aroma of butter, bananas, vanilla, chocolate, strawberry, and honey, the babies responded with expressions of enjoyment and satisfaction.

In earlier experiments, newborns quickly turned away from the smell of ammonia or vinegar (Engen and Lipsitt, 1965). Within two or three days, newborns also recognize a strong odor they have smelled before. When first presented with the odor of anise oil, for example, a baby's activity increases and his or her heart rate and breathing pattern change. If the odor continues, the baby gradually stops responding to it. At this point, if a new odor, such as phenyl alcohol, reaches the baby's nose, the infant again becomes more active, and shows a changed heart rate and breathing pattern.

The keenness of the newborn's sense of smell was further suggested by the research of Aidan Macfarlane (1977) at Oxford University. He had noticed that when placed next to the mother's breast, a typical newborn turns his or her face toward it before seeing it or touching the nipple. Macfarlane wondered if this was because the baby could smell the milk beginning to drip from the nipple. To test this notion, he performed two simple experiments. First, he collected breast pads that mothers had used to absorb the small amount of milk that leaks between feedings. For the first experiment, he placed the mother's breast pad on one side of a baby's head and a clean pad on the other side next to the cheek. Because many babies prefer one side or the other, usually the right, care was taken to alternate the pads' placement. Babies spent more time with their heads turned toward their own mothers' milk-scented pads than toward the clean pads. But the babies' noses were sharper than Macfarlane had expected. In the second experiment, he substituted a milk-scented pad from another mother for the clean pad and compared the reactions. He found that babies turned their heads toward both pads for about the same amount of time during the first two days; but by the time they were six to ten days old, they turned most of the time toward their own mothers' pads.

PERCEPTION AND ATTENTION

Because a newborn is not a passive recipient of whatever stimulation the environment presents, he or she pays attention to some stimuli and ignores others, actively selecting aspects of the world to notice and learn about. As Marshall Haith (1980) puts it, the neonate is biologically prepared to seek information and able to adapt to the consequences of information acquired in the search.

Visual Attention

As we have seen, the visual system is active at birth, and stimulation such as that found in contours and contrasts causes neurons to fire in the visual cortex of the brain. It appears probable, says Haith, that a single organizing principle underlies visual attention in the neonate: looking at objects in the world in order to maintain the firing of those cells at a high rate. Although babies are certainly not aware that this is their biological goal, the resulting activation of cells maintains established neural pathways and sets up new ones. Haith believes that this principle can explain the effect of illumination and contrast on the infant's visual system as well as neonatal visual search strategies.

When alert babies are in the light, they generally open their eyes, but objects that are too dim or too bright will not attract their gaze. Maurice Hershenson (1964) found that a baby who is two or three days old will look longer at objects of moderate brightness than at those that are either extremely bright or very dim, a discovery that confirms the experiences of parents that newborns shut their eyes and turn away from bright sunlight. Placed in the dark, these same babies open their eyes wide, as if straining to see, a technique that increases the chances of detecting visual stimulation, thereby increasing neural firing (Haith, 1980).

PATTERN AND CONTRAST A great deal of research has been devoted to a baby's attention to pattern. As early as 1944, Fritz Stirnimann found that babies only a day old would look longer at a patterned surface than at a plain one. In the first modern experiments on a baby's attention, Robert Fantz (1965) used a "looking chamber" with babies as young as two days old. Fantz placed the baby in a drawerlike carriage and slid the carriage into the looking chamber, where stimuli were placed directly above the infant. Using this procedure, he found that newborns look more at patterns than at homogeneous gray stimuli, a practice that would increase stimulation of cells in the visual cortex.

Certain aspects of a pattern are more likely than others to attract an infant's gaze. By recording babies' eye movements, Philip Salapatek and William Kessen (1966) found that newborns do not devote an equal amount of attention to all parts of a figure. Shown a triangle, they concentrate their gaze on a corner and perhaps on the sides forming that corner. Here at the edges, black and white contrast is highest, providing peak stimulation, as shown in Figure 5.3 (p. 118). The gaze of these newborns was anything but random, however; once they found a point of contrast, they were not likely to search the figure for another.

SEARCH STRATEGY AND MOVEMENT Babies respond early to movement. A five-day-old newborn who is sucking on a pacifier will stop this rhythmical sucking if a light moves across the visual field (Haith, 1966). Despite the fact that their right and left eyes do not always look at the same thing, newborns briefly pursue a slowly moving object with a smooth eye movement; but the movement soon becomes jerky (Kremenitzer et al., 1979). Not until babies are about three to six weeks old does their visual pursuit become coordinated and smooth. If the movement is not too rapid, newborns are more attracted to a moving object than to a stationary one.

Not all objects move, and when stimulation is stationary, newborns use some simple strategies to govern their visual searches. When in the dark, they tend to scan the environment systematically in a horizontal rather than vertical direction, scanning rhythmically at the rate of approximately two scans per second (about the same as their sucking rhythm). This sort of search, says Haith (1980), maximizes the baby's chance of finding subtle shadows, edges, or any lit areas.

If light is available, the baby uses a different strategy, searching for edges with broad, jerky sweeps of the visual field. Once an edge is found, the baby stops the broad sweeps and stays in the region of the edge, as did the babies who looked at the triangles in the earlier study. Because their scanning strategy is mostly horizontal, babies are more likely to encounter a vertical edge than a horizontal one (Kessen, Haith, and Salapatek, 1970).

These patterns of search indicate that babies plan their looking patterns; small eye movements that cross edges are determined *before* the eye moves, and the size of the eye movement is not affected by the actual crossing of the edge. Such findings indicate that instead of being merely a reflexive organism that is captured by stimuli, the neonate has an organized information-gathering system, constructed to acquire knowledge (Haith, 1980).

Auditory Attention

It is difficult to discover whether neonates are as selective listeners to sounds as they are selec-

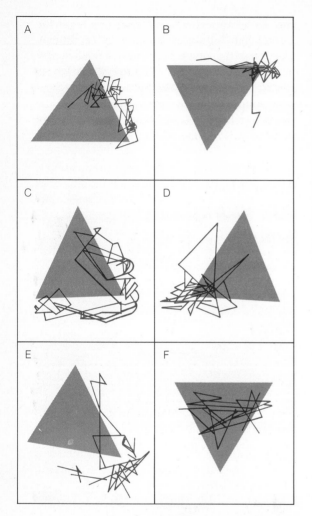

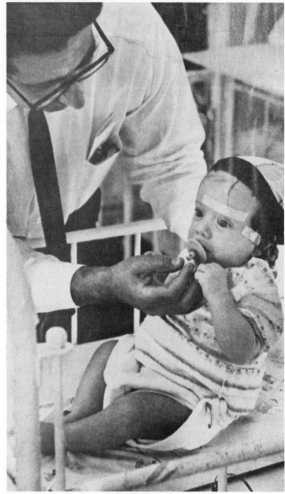

Figure 5.3 In this perception experiment, new-born babies were shown a large black triangle on a white field. *(left)* Infrared marker lights were placed behind the triangle and reflected in the baby's pupil, permitting the baby's eye movements to be traced and photographed. *(right)* Besides showing that the infants looked more toward the corners of the triangle, the six tracings illustrate the wide variation in patterns of scanning that occurs among babies. (Photograph courtesy Dr. William Kessen; data from Salapatek and Kessen, 1966)

tive viewers of sights. By observing where a baby's eyes are turned, researchers find it relatively easy to determine when babies look at something or on what part of an object they focus. It is much harder to tell whether infants listen and even more problematical to tell what aspect of an auditory stimulus they listen to. However, some information has been gained by monitoring the heart rates, respiratory rates, brain waves, and sucking patterns of babies who are exposed to various sounds.

Babies do respond differently to sounds of contrasting frequencies or pitch. Low tones tend to quiet an upset baby, whereas high frequencies are likely to distress the infant and may even produce a kind of freezing reaction (Eisenberg et al., 1964). Some scientists have called attention to the parallel between the newborn's response to these sounds and the tendency among adults to use sounds of different frequencies to convey feelings of distress or calm. For example, the acoustical properties of musical instruments, alarm systems, and even some words that describe reactions to certain events use high frequencies to alert and to convey excitement or disturbance and low frequencies to communicate relative calm (Eisenberg, 1970).

There is some indication that newborns are especially responsive to sounds in the frequency of the human voice (200 to 500 cycles per second) and to sounds of moderate length, approximately five to fifteen seconds in duration (Eisenberg, 1970). In one study, three-day-old babies clearly showed a preference for their own mothers' voices over those of strange women (De-Casper and Fifer, 1980), and in Chapter 9 we will see how this response to the human voice plays a role in the development of language.

A neonate's response to a sound is also affected by illumination. Newborns who are in a dim room open their eyes to mild noises, as if they are trying to investigate the sounds (Kearsley, 1973). But babies in a bright room shut their eyes when they hear a noise; if their eyes are already shut, they will clamp the lids, shutting them even more tightly, perhaps in a defensive reaction.

As these examples of visual and auditory attention make clear, the newborn's perceptual world is less confusing than psychologists once thought. The sensory systems of newborns function, but their ability to detect stimuli or to discriminate among them is seriously limited, and a considerable amount of the visual environment simply is not accessible. Although some babies are quite good at discriminating between one kind of sound and another, many sounds that adults would detect as different are perceived by the average newborn as being the

same. Finally, neonates are selective as to the stimuli that attract their attention or increase their responses; they tune some things in and tune other things out. As a result, the newborn neither detects nor pays attention to much of what adults perceive. The newborn's perceptual world is probably simpler and more orderly than we might guess.

ADAPTING TO THE WORLD

Given that babies have many ways of sensing events in the outside world and certain coordinated patterns of behavior for meeting situations that might arise, what are the mechanisms by which they adapt to the environment? How does the newborn come to know more about the world?

The neonate can learn — at least some things under some circumstances. For example, newborns learn to integrate sucking and breathing into an efficient feeding process, and they can learn to modify this behavior to fit the circumstances. In addition, they can form crude memories, remembering certain stimuli for several seconds.

Memory

The newborn baby spends most of the time asleep, fussing and crying, or feeding. In fact, the average newborn is quietly alert for less than thirty minutes in every four hours. Is it possible that babies who are alert for such short periods can become familiar with the mobiles and other objects that parents put in their cribs? Can they form memories of these toys, retain the memories, and recognize an old mobile or detect the strangeness of a new one?

Steven Friedman explored this possibility with babies from one to four days old (Friedman, 1972; Friedman, Bruno, and Vietze, 1974).

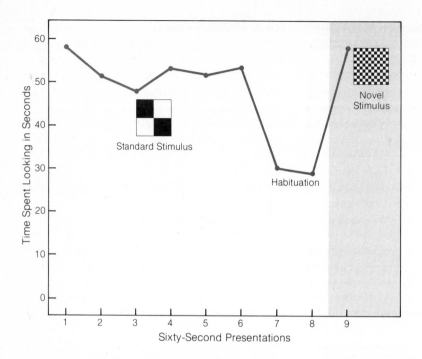

Figure 5.4 One newborn's response to familiar and unfamiliar checkerboard stimuli. After seven sixty-second exposures to the standard (familiar) stimulus, the baby became habituated. When the baby was then exposed to a novel (unfamiliar) stimulus on the ninth presentation, however, the infant immediately looked at it for an extended time. (After Friedman, 1972)

One of the checkerboards pictured in Figure 5.4 was shown to babies for sixty seconds at a time. The babies saw the checkerboard again and again until on two of its successive appearances, the baby looked a total of eight seconds less than he or she had looked at the board on the first two occasions. When this happened, an infant had *habituated*. The process of habituation is roughly analogous to becoming bored, and it implies that the baby has learned and remembered something about the stimulus. Such a decline in looking after repeated exposure may signify that the baby remembers the stimulus. On the other hand, the baby may simply be tired or fussy and not remember it at all. To find out whether a baby was showing memory or fatigue, Friedman changed the stimulus on a later test. If the baby looked longer at the new stimulus than at the last appearance of the checkerboard, the baby must have formed a memory that signaled the new stimulus was different. One neonate's pattern of looking under such a procedure is shown in Figure 5.4. Notice that during the familiarization phase, this neonate looked for about the same length of time again and again until suddenly the looking time dropped sharply on two successive occasions. When Friedman then introduced a new stimulus, the baby looked a long time (almost the entire sixty seconds), indicating that the neonate detected the new stimulus as being different from an earlier memory, and that fatigue had not been responsible for the earlier drop in looking time.

Given the stimuli used in this study, it was possible to find out whether newborns look longer at a new stimulus that is radically different from the familiar stimulus than at one that is only slightly different. The results suggest that the length of time the babies looked at the novel stimulus depended on how great the difference was. Apparently, newborns perform a crude perceptual analysis of the difference between the new stimulus and their memory of the old familiar one.

On the basis of such research, we can conclude that newborns can form a memory of a stimulus, retain that memory for five to ten seconds, retrieve the memory, and make some kind of analysis of the relationship between the memory and a new stimulus.

Conditions for Learning

It is clear that human newborns can learn. Just how much they actually do learn in their natural surroundings, however, is another question. We have seen that newborns have certain limitations; their environment may not satisfy the stringent conditions necessary before they are able to sense, perceive, attend, and learn.

One requirement of the learning situation is *timing*. Experimental studies have shown that there can be almost no delay of reward for the newborn; the baby who does not receive reinforcement (such as sweetened water, a smile, a sound, a touch) within one second is unlikely to learn (Millar, 1972). Another requirement is *repetition;* a stimulus must be presented over and over again with only short delays between each presentation in order for the young baby to form a memory of it (Lewis, 1969). As a baby grows older, however, learning proceeds in spite of delays between the infant's response and the reward or between the presentation of one stimulus and another.

Although scientists can construct a situation that satisfies the newborn's requirement for close timing, the baby's natural environment does not always meet that rigid standard. The delay between a baby's actions and their effects on people and objects nearby will often be longer than a second, making learning unlikely. Even when the condition of timing is met, the condition of repetition may not be. For example, a push of the hand may immediately remove a blanket that has fallen across the baby's face, but the opportunity to repeat that action may not quickly recur. In a sense, then, there may be a period of "natural deprivation" (J. S. Watson, 1966), in which the baby is capable of learning but in which environmental conditions provide no opportunity to learn.

Other studies have discovered additional limits on the young baby's ability to learn (Fitzgerald and Brackbill, 1976). For example, even among very young babies, there are individual differences in the ability to learn. Some newborns can learn tasks that are difficult or impossible for other babies of the same age. It also matters whether the response to be learned is one that the baby performs voluntarily or one that normally appears as an involuntary response. Learning to perform a naturally involuntary response in the absence of the stimulus that naturally evokes it—such as the blink of an eye at the sound of a buzzer—may be extremely difficult, whereas learning to perform a voluntary response—such as turning toward the buzzer—may be relatively easy. That is, babies learn responses that are operantly conditioned faster and more efficiently than they learn classically conditioned responses.

PERSONALITY AND SOCIAL RELATIONS

It is difficult to talk about the personality of a newborn. Adults think of personality in terms of verbal, cognitive, and emotional behavior displayed in a social context, and it is difficult for newborns to express their personalities in this way. However, newborn babies do differ in their behavior, and they can, and do, engage in primitive social relations.

Temperament

Temperamental differences among babies can be identified in the first few days of life, and newborn predispositions that may be important to a child's personality have been identified and described by Alexander Thomas and his colleagues (1963). These researchers decided that the intimate knowledge mothers gain in the constant care of their babies would be a source of meaningful data. Using carefully formulated interviews, they conducted an extensive study that disclosed four major behavioral characteristics that seem important for personality: activity level; approach-withdrawal behavior, as seen in the baby's characteristic first reaction to any new stimulus; responsiveness, or the amount of stimulation required to evoke a visible or audible response; and general mood, such as friendly, unfriendly, joyful, or angry.

Of course, personality is more complex than these simple categories imply. A child's personality is a developing and evolving set of tendencies to behave in various ways. Nevertheless, it is easy to see how the general tone of social interaction within the family could be influenced by a baby's consistent behavioral characteristics. Temperamental differences that correspond to three of the four characteristics identified by Thomas' group have appeared in other studies.

Indeed, an important early study by Margaret Fries (1954), in which she carefully observed the amount and vigor of neonate *activity*, led her to classify newborns into three activity types: the active, the moderately active, and the quiet. Some newborns are more active than others; they frequently thrash about with their arms and legs, and later bang toys and shake rattles with considerable gusto. Other babies are more placid, moving slowly and with less exaggeration. Mothers are sometimes aware of this kind of difference before their babies are born. Some fetuses kick and move about more than others, and there is some relationship between such fetal kicking and differences in behavior among

children for at least two years (C. E. Walters, 1965).

Newborns also differ in mood, an aspect of temperament that has been described as *irritability*. Some cry a lot; others do not. Certain babies are restless sleepers and tend to have fits of irritability during sleep or wakefulness. There is evidence that irritable or fitful sleepers may have different personalities as young children from babies who do not show such restless sleep (Thomas, Chess, and Birch, 1970).

Newborn babies also differ in *responsiveness*. Some babies are cuddlers. They are soft and snuggly and seem to enjoy being cuddled, kissed, and rolled about in their parents' arms. In contrast, other babies resist such affectionate play by stiffening their bodies when they are handled (Schaffer, 1971). It is easy to understand how such a rudimentary social response might have a substantial impact on parents who have been looking forward to hugging and kissing their newborn and then find themselves the parents of a noncuddler. They may falsely infer that their baby dislikes them or that they are inadequate parents, forming negative attitudes that can color the way they subsequently interact with their child.

A baby's level of responsiveness may not always be an inborn predisposition; sometimes it is simply an accident of birth or development. As noted in the last chapter, drugs administered during labor affect a baby's behavior (Brackbill, 1979). A baby born to a heavily sedated mother may be drowsy, sluggish, and slow to respond to her overtures. A malnourished baby also tends to be apathetic and sluggish. As Herbert Birch (1968) has pointed out, a baby's rate of development is affected by the mother's responses to his or her actions, which in turn stimulate the baby. If babies are sluggish and apathetic, their mothers' responsiveness may diminish, setting an unfortunate pattern for their relationship. English babies studied by Martin Richards (1975) showed such a pattern of development. The painkilling drug (Penthilorfan) administered to their mothers during labor passed

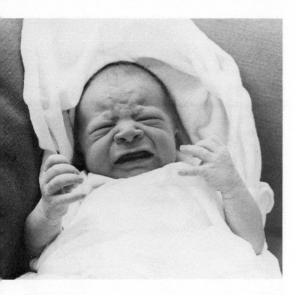

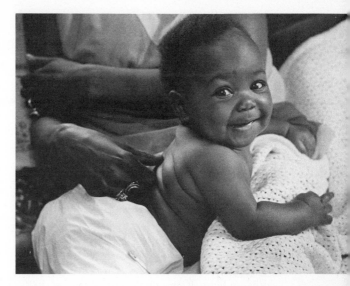

Temperamental differences in babies appear at birth; some are irritable and cry a lot, some are extremely responsive and enjoy being cuddled, some resist affection, some are extremely active, and some are placid and slow-moving. (© Michael Weisbrot & Family; © Suzanne Szasz)

through the placenta. In the first week after birth, these drugged babies were sleepy and unresponsive, and their mothers had to work to keep them awake and sucking at feeding time. A year later, the babies engaged in more self-stimulation (such as thumb-sucking) and were less involved in social interchanges with their mothers than babies who had never been drugged.

Medication at delivery also affected the subsequent relationship between Australian babies and their mothers studied by Ann Murray and her colleagues (1981). Epidural anesthesia, which blocks sensation in the legs and abdomen but leaves the mother alert, was the principal drug used in these deliveries. In the first day of life, the babies showed clear signs of being drugged. A month later, when they were again tested by researchers, the drug effects had vanished. But the mothers of the drugged babies were less responsive to their babies, fed them less often, and

were less affectionate with them than were mothers in the control group who had had no anesthesia. The mothers themselves found the medicated babies difficult to care for, and their ratings of their babies at one month were similar to the ratings the researchers had made just after the infants were born.

Parents often interpret the smallest behavior as revealing their new baby's personality, and by the time an infant is two weeks old, a mother may develop a style of relating to her baby as well as an opinion of his or her personality (Osofsky and Connors, 1979). Murray and her colleagues speculate in their study that the unresponsive state of the drugged babies shortly after birth shaped the mothers' expectations and behavior, setting the tone for the future mother-infant relationship.

Social Relations

Social relations in the newborn are primitive by adult standards; yet as we have seen, they exist. Whenever there is communication between individuals, there is a social relation, and newborns and their parents certainly carry on a rudimentary sort of nonverbal communication.

Historically, the way in which a newborn was fed was thought to have major consequences for both the child's developing social relations and his or her personality. Such ideas stemmed from Freudian theory, which placed great emphasis on the possible impact of events early in the child's life. Because the newborn spends most of his or her waking hours feeding, it made good sense to assume that social relations begin in the feeding situation. The design of the human body ensures that nursing neonate and mother are placed in a situation that facilitates communication. A newborn being breast-fed for the first time is cradled in the mother's arms with his or her face about nine inches from hers—the distance at which the baby's eyes can most easily focus.

Research by Kenneth Kaye and Anne Wells (1980) indicates that the feeding period may contain the seeds of turn-taking, a skill that is essential to language and social development. Mothers, whether breast- or bottle-feeding, tend either to jiggle the nipple in the baby's mouth or to stroke the baby about the mouth whenever sucking stops. But the baby does not resume sucking until the mother stops these actions. It appears that the infant's normal sucking pattern of bursts and pauses fits naturally into the turn-taking of human dialogue, and that a mother uses her child's natural feeding rhythm as a basis for early social communication.

Without realizing they are doing it, parents also tend to structure their interactions to fit their babies' capacities. According to Hanuš and Mechthild Papoušek (1978), analyses of films and video recordings reveal that mothers use the position of their babies' hands, small tests of muscle tone (such as touching the infant's chin), and eye contact as cues to the type and amount of stimulation they give their babies, thereby tailoring their own behavior to the baby's state.

Perhaps the most obvious method that the newborn uses to communicate with the social environment is crying. Crying appears to be a wired-in, autonomous activity. If earphones are

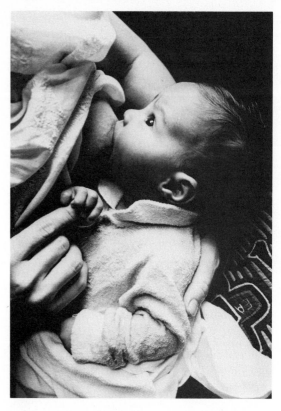

Social relations begin in the feeding situation, and a baby's natural feeding rhythm can be the basis for early social communication. (© Joel Gordon 1974)

placed on the crying newborn's head and sounds are played, the crying pattern shows no interruption, even though such competing stimulation would disrupt the speech of an adult (P. Wolff, 1967). Despite its automatic nature, a baby's cry is a signal of distress, saying, "Help me"; and the appeal is often successful. Although babies may not yet realize why their cries are followed by dry diapers and warm milk, they are communicating effectively, influencing the people around them.

Even quite young babies display different cries, depending upon whether the crying is stimulated by hunger, pain, or anger. Each of these three basic cries can be distinguished by

Starting Off on the Wrong Cry

Each year many children are abused by their parents; some of them suffer permanent damage and some even die. Frequently, only a single child in a family is abused. A number of investigators suspect that the seeds of child abuse are often sown in the first few weeks of a child's life, and recent studies support those suspicions.

In England, A. M. Lynch (1975) discovered that the abused children he studied were more likely than their brothers or sisters to have spent their first few days or weeks of life in special-care nurseries. Babies who need special care are likely to be premature or to have suffered some kind of complication during birth.

Philip Zeskind and Barry Lester (1978), noting that babies with neurological disorders have characteristic, high-pitched cries, wondered if babies who have experienced stressful births showed similar abnormalities. Indeed, they discovered distinct differences between the cries of normal babies and those of full-term, full birth weight babies whose births had involved obstetrical complications (at-risk babies). These differences were noticeable to adults who had had no previous experience with babies. Both parents and "naïve" adults found the cries of at-risk babies more grating, aversive, and indicating illness than the cries of normal babies.

Ann Frodi and her colleagues (1978b) found similar patterns of difference in adults' reactions to the cries of normal and premature babies. These investigators took the study a step further than other researchers have done. They showed parents videotapes of a normal baby paired with normal cries, a premature baby paired with premature cries, a normal baby paired with premature cries, and a premature baby paired with normal cries. Fathers and mothers both responded to the wailing of a premature baby with increased skin conductance, faster heartbeat, and higher blood pressure than they showed when listening to the cries of a normal baby. Such a pattern of arousal is associated with anger and aversion. The parents indicated that they were more irritated, annoyed, and disturbed by the premature baby's cry. Both fathers and mothers said that, given a choice, they would prefer to interact with the normal baby.

If the cries of at-risk babies, including those born small-for-gestational-age, are especially unpleasant, then—as these investigators speculate—the infants may become unpleasant objects to their parents, making them targets for abuse. Such conditioning may explain the results of a study by Ann Frodi and Michael Lamb (1980), in which admitted child abusers responded with anger and physiological arousal to both crying and smiling babies. Apparently, child abusers have come to find *any* sort of social overture from an infant unpleasant.

But the quality of the cry is not a sufficient explanation for abuse. If, as ethologists (Lorenz, 1942–1943) have suggested, human beings have evolved so that the "cute" look of the normal baby releases an adult's predisposition to care for the helpless young, then the appearance of premature infants would also make them less attractive to most people than full-term babies. In addition, the fact that premature babies develop on a timetable geared to their gestaïonal as opposed to their actual birth dates means that premature babies with aversive cries are slow to smile at their parents. Time spent in special-care nurseries is also time spent away from parents. As we shall see in later chapters on personality, some investigators have speculated that early, prolonged separation of baby and caregiver can seriously impair the nature of the infant-parent relationship.

Child abuse, like any other problem, cannot be traced to a single cause. As the discussion in Chapter 15 will show, certain environments are more likely than others to evoke child abuse. Nevertheless, when other factors make abuse more probable, it is the premature infant, with its aversive cry, who runs an increased risk of being the abused child.

the pattern of pauses between bursts of crying, by the duration of the cry, and by its tonal characteristics (P. Wolff, 1967).

Are differences in crying detectable by parents or only by scientists armed with complex technical instruments? Complex instruments are superfluous, it seems. If a mother hears tape recordings of the cries of her own baby and the cries of four other babies, all responding to a slight pinprick on the foot, the mother readily picks out the cry of her own baby even when her infant is only a few weeks old (Lind, 1971). A mother's response to the hunger cry of her baby involves more than just making a mental note of the fact that her child is hungry. If she is breast-feeding her baby, she responds physiologically: an increased flow of blood and milk raises the surface heat of her breasts (Lind, 1971). Many a lactating mother can relate occasions when her baby has given a hunger cry and she has discovered milk gushing from her breasts in response.

Crying is an effective means of communication because it evokes a range of physiological and emotional responses in parents—fathers as well as mothers. As Ann Frodi and her colleagues (1978a) discovered, there is no detectable difference in the general physiological reactions of mothers and fathers to a crying baby: blood pressure rises and skin conductance increases. This arousal is accompanied by feelings of annoyance, irritation, and distress. So when a parent picks up a wailing baby, it is apparently as much to stop the aversive sound as to relieve the baby's distress.

Sometimes parents let their babies "cry out" their distress, and the lack of response also tells the baby something. Whether a mother picks up and feeds her crying newborn or lets the baby cry may depend on the context of the cry. Among the English mothers Judith Bernal (1972) studied, unless three hours had passed since the last feeding, most left their babies to cry, perhaps communicating to the baby the news that crying has little effect.

Almost from the moment of birth, a baby responds emotionally to the crying of other infants. In a study by Marvin Simner (1971), two- to three-day-old babies started to cry much more frequently when they heard another newborn crying than when they heard nonhuman sounds of equal range and volume. These findings are corroborated by people who work in hospital nurseries; they note that when one baby starts to cry, other babies in the nursery soon join in. Abraham Sagi and Martin Hoffman (1976) have confirmed this contagion of crying, and they suggest that it may be an inborn, early precursor to later forms of human empathy.

But not every baby in a hospital nursery will join the crying throng. As we have seen throughout this chapter, from the first moment of independent life, babies are different. They differ in their need for sleep, for food, for stimulation. Some learn quickly, some learn slowly. Some want to be cuddled, others do not like to be held. Some are placid, others are fussy. With such a wide span of individual differences at birth, it is no wonder that—given the additional influence of widely differing environments—no two children or adults are alike. From the time that babies draw their first breath, the differences among them become more and more pronounced—and the process continues throughout life. Yet despite these wide human differences, there are common themes in human development—similar tasks and challenges that each child will meet in his or her own way.

SUMMARY

1. The newborn quickly develops functional patterns or rhythms: body temperature becomes regulated; sleep, composed of both REM and non-REM patterns, evolves into a four-hour sleep/wake cycle for many newborns; and feeding, if left to the newborn's self-demand, occurs every three to four hours for most.

2. From birth, the newborn is equipped with reflexive behavior that may be elicited by specific stimuli. These reflexes include the rooting reflex, the grasping reflex, the Moro reflex, and stepping and placing responses. When these reflexes fail to drop away after several months, it may be a sign of abnormal neurological development.

3. The sensory capabilities of newborns keep them in touch with their environment. Although they may be color-blind during this period, they become capable of accommodation, or focus; of convergence, or seeing an image with both eyes; and of acuity, or seeing detail. Their auditory sense allows newborns to discriminate loudness and pitch, and their senses of taste and smell become increasingly acute.

4. Newborns actively select visual and auditory stimuli, gathering information from the environment. Their patterns of visual attention and search appear aimed at increasing stimulation in the visual cortex, and in that quest, they attend to movement, pattern, and contrast.

5. In adapting to the world, the neonate forms short-term memories of certain stimuli and then compares new stimuli to them. Such learning appears to depend on the timing of reward and the repetition of the stimulus.

6. Newborn babies differ in temperament, and their predispositions to activity, irritability, and responsiveness to affection influence the tone of their social relationships. The sluggishness of babies born to heavily sedated mothers may have a negative influence on the developing relationship between mother and infant. Feeding and the responses of others to their cries offer the neonate the first chances for social interaction.

PART 3

Physical Development

Physical growth and maturation have wide psychological and social consequences. The world of an infant who can do nothing without assistance is very different from the world of the competent child. As the baby's chubby body becomes straight and slim, motions that were awkward and tentative become sophisticated, smooth probes into the workings of the world. Situations of "I can't" increasingly become opportunities for "I can," and the child's world widens. The rapidly maturing brain allows the child to understand the results of explorations and to apply the lessons from one experience to new challenges and opportunities. Finally, the major physical changes of adolescence, which turn the child into an adult man or woman, further alter the psychological and social consequences of almost every event in the child's life.

CHAPTER SIX

Elements of Physical Growth

Rob, who is four, can turn a somersault with ease, his head tucked and his back rounded. Mark, who just turned six, cannot execute this simple maneuver, and when he sees Rob turning triumphant somersaults in the yard next door, he often feels jealous of the younger boy's skill and some anger at his own lack of physical ability. But children are not all alike, and although most learn to somersault proficiently when they are five, some learn the skill much earlier than the average child and others much later.

Marked structural differences develop among children soon after conception, and their individual environments tend to accentuate some of these differences. If Rob becomes fascinated with gymnastics, with practice he may develop into a champion, perhaps someday reaching the Olympics. But no matter how hard Mark tries, no matter how many hours he devotes to gymnastics, he will never make the Olympic team.

Growth is the result of a series of interactions between an organism and its environment. During this process, babies become larger, the structure and function of their bodies become increasingly complex, and they approach ever more closely their adult size, organic structure, and body build. The rate of physical change is greater in infancy than at any other time after birth.

Psychologists study physical changes to gain

insight into the relationship between inherited factors and the child's environment, hoping to identify the conditions that lower a child's efficiency or hinder normal development. Once such interactions are understood, there is some possibility of controlling unwanted deviations from normal patterns of growth.

In this chapter, we shall follow a baby's physical development through childhood and adolescence. Basing our discussion on some basic principles that govern all physical growth, we shall outline the ways in which psychologists summarize growth. Because each baby's combined environment and heredity are unique, we shall consider the ways in which physical development may differ from one child to the next, noticing that diet, illness, socioeconomic status, and emotional stress can affect physical growth. A look at the development of motor skills will show us the part played by practice and instruction in their acquisition and refinement. We shall explore the differences between boys and girls in motor and physical growth, and conclude by discussing historical trends toward an earlier onset of puberty.

DIRECTIONS OF GROWTH

The systematic study of any phenomenon, whether it be growth or gravity, usually begins with a description of the way that phenomenon ordinarily occurs. Thus the systematic study of physical development requires the observation of large numbers of infants and children over a considerable period of time. From such observations, scientists have formulated some basic principles of growth and outlined the general development of the average infant and child.

At the most general level of description, three basic principles underlie the growth and development of all body systems. These are cephalocaudal development, proximodistal development, and differentiation and hierarchic integration.

Cephalocaudal Development

The word "cephalocaudal" comes from the Greek word for "head" and the Latin word for "tail," and cephalocaudal development refers to the literal direction of the body's physical growth. It is reflected in the order in which parts of the body become larger and in the order in which functions and structures become more complex. Physical growth progresses from head to foot; a baby's head develops and grows before the torso, arms, and legs. This pattern of growing seems to reflect the fact that the most rapid embryological development occurs in or near those cells destined to be parts of the brain and nervous system (Debakan, 1959).

At birth, a baby's head is nearer to its adult size than any other portion of the body. From

Babies first gain control over their head and neck muscles, learning to hold up their heads long before they can sit. (© Suzanne Szasz)

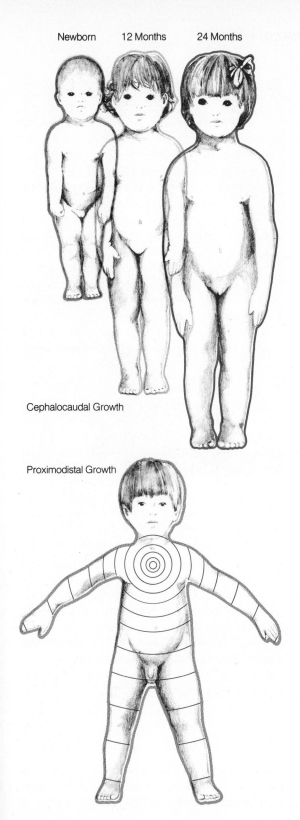

Newborn　　12 Months　　24 Months

Cephalocaudal Growth

Proximodistal Growth

Figure 6.1 Physical growth and motor abilities develop in two directions simultaneously: from top to bottom (cephalocaudal) and from center to periphery (proximodistal).

birth to adulthood, a person's head doubles in size. In contrast, the trunk trebles, the arms and hands quadruple, and the legs and feet grow fivefold. Much of the increase in height that takes place in childhood is an increase in the length of the lower limbs. As a child grows, the head contributes proportionately less to total body length, shrinking from one-quarter of the total at birth to one-twelfth at maturity (Bayley, 1956). These changes in body proportions are shown in Figure 6.1.

Movement and motor ability also become more controlled and complex in a progression from head to toe. Babies first gain control over the muscles of the head and neck, then the arms and abdomen, and finally the legs. Thus babies learn to hold up their heads before they learn to sit; they learn to sit before they learn to walk; and long before they can walk or run steadily, they can make complicated, controlled movements of their arms and fingers, picking up even tiny specks of lint.

Proximodistal Development

Physical growth and motor development proceed also in a *proximodistal* direction. That is, growth and function progress from the center of the body toward the periphery. Babies learn to control the movements of their shoulders before they can direct their arms or fingers. In general, control over movement travels down a baby's arm as he or she becomes increasingly sophisticated in attempts to reach for and grasp an object.

During the first few weeks of life, a baby reaches for an object that comes into view but does not grasp it because the infant lacks control over hand and finger muscles. This reaching reflex does not represent learned control, and it disappears at the end of the neonatal period. Not until a baby is about twenty weeks old does he or she make crude attempts to grab an object, using both hands. Then within a month, the infant develops a one-handed reach, usually managing to brush the object. In another four weeks, the baby is able to flex the whole hand while reaching and, somewhat later, to poke at the object with an index finger. Finally, at about forty weeks, mature grasping appears, and the baby can oppose thumb and forefinger when trying to grab a toy. In the same manner, babies gain control over their upper legs before they can control the lower leg, foot, or toes.

Differentiation and Integration

The third principle of growth involves differentiation and integration. *Differentiation* means that infants' abilities become increasingly distinct and specific. They gain mastery of movement after movement. For example, when a baby is only a month old, the infant reacts to a shoe that is too tight with the whole body—wiggling, thrashing, crying, and generally creating a ruckus. As the baby grows older, movements became more specific, so that the response to a tight shoe is to thrash about with only the offending foot. Eventually the child learns to make specific and highly complex responses. The sensory stimulation that has traveled from the foot to the brain is now interpreted, and this interpretation takes the form of language, so that the child might say, for example, "Foot hurt."

Complex responses require the infant to combine and integrate many lesser skills. As noted in Chapter 2, Heinz Werner (1948) used the term *hierarchic integration* to describe this trend toward combining simple, differentiated skills into more complex skills. For example, after a baby has mastered the use of the arms as levers, the muscles of the abdomen as lifters of the upper body, and the neck muscles to gain con-

As babies develop, they combine simple motor skills into complex integrated patterns: coordinating fingers, hands, arms, eyes, head, body, legs, and feet in order to explore the satisfying possibilities of a metal pan. (© Suzanne Szasz)

trol of the head, he or she develops hierarchic patterns of movement that bring each separate motor capability into the service of the others in a highly organized way. Thus, after each of these various simpler movements has been developed, the baby is able to put them all together and soon can sit up.

NORMS

The principles we have just discussed describe growth and development at a general level. Psychologists interested in the normal course of development have compiled detailed, specific descriptions of individual events in the growth process. A number of investigators (Bayley, 1956; Cattell, 1940; Gesell, 1925; Griffiths, 1954; Lenneberg, 1967) have analyzed the sequence in which physical characteristics and motor, language, and social skills emerge. Their investigations have resulted in *norms*, or typical patterns that describe the way in which important attributes and skills develop and the approximate ages at which they appear.

These norms allow us to summarize patterns of infant motor development (Figure 6.2). During the first year of life, the baby shows extensive growth changes. Body length increases more than one-third and weight almost triples. During the first two years, a child's head grows more slowly than the trunk and limbs, so that body

Figure 6.2 Some of the major milestones in motor development that occur over the first two years of life. Each dot indicates the approximate average age of occurrence. Individual infants may demonstrate these skills somewhat earlier or later than the average indicated. (After Lenneberg, 1967, and Bayley, 1969)

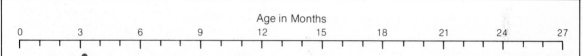

Age in Months

Supports head when in prone position; hands mostly open; no grasp reflex

Shakes and stares at rattle placed in hands; head self-supported

Sits with props

Sits using hands for support; bears weight when held in standing position; reaches with one hand; grasps, but with no thumb opposition, and releases object when given another

Stands holding on; grasps with thumb opposition; picks up small object with thumb and fingertips

Creeps efficiently; takes side steps, holding on; pulls to standing position

Walks alone or when held by one hand; seats self on floor

Walks sideways and backwards; walks upstairs and downstairs with help; throws ball

Grasp and release fully developed; sits on child's chair with fair aim; has difficulty building tower of three blocks

Runs, but falls in sudden turns; quickly sits then stands; walks up and down stairs with little or no help

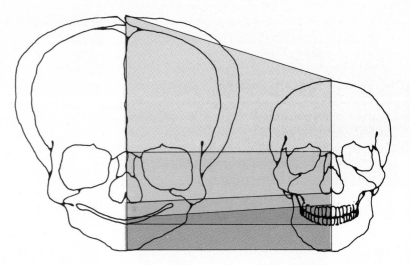

proportions become more adultlike. In addition, the facial skeleton becomes relatively larger, so that a child's cranium is no longer so out of proportion with the face (see Figure 6.3).

Growth in early childhood is not as dramatic as it is during infancy. The velocity, or rate, of growth—in both height and weight—decelerates markedly during infancy and, about the time a child is three or four, settles into a steady rate. Figure 6.4, which charts the average child's annual height increase, shows a velocity curve that flattens and remains about the same until just before the child enters puberty (Falkner, 1966). At that time, the plateau period of childhood growth ends and the adolescent growth spurt begins. Adolescence is virtually the only time in a person's life that this curve accelerates. Once the adolescent reaches the maximum point of growth velocity (in the case of stature, "peak height velocity"), deceleration again occurs until the annual growth increment is zero and growth ceases.

Using Norms

When using norms to study child development, we need to understand that they are based on simple mathematical calculations that reflect average growth tendencies. They do not explain growth or development, they merely describe it,

Figure 6.3 Changes in skull and facial proportions with growth. The skull outlined at the left is that of a newborn, whereas the skull at the right is that of a mature adult. (Adapted from Jackson, 1923)

indicating what is most likely to appear in the development of children at various ages.

Norms can be useful in describing how most infants develop. They can help in the assessment of environmental change on behavior—such as the effect of separating children from their mothers—or they can be useful in studying cross-cultural and subcultural variations. They have been used to examine the effects of institutionalization, of gender, and of birth order on a child's development. They have been helpful in studies of prematurity and of early pathology (Kessen, Haith, and Salapatek, 1970).

The value of norms as a diagnostic tool for the individual child is, however, limited; because in every aspect of growth, normal children vary widely on each side of a norm. This range within which growth is still considered normal shows clearly in a study Howard Meredith (1963) conducted among Iowa males. At the age of eighteen, the lightest boy in his study weighed no more than the heaviest boy had weighed when he was eight. The boy who was lightest at age eight weighed about the same as the heaviest boy had at age two.

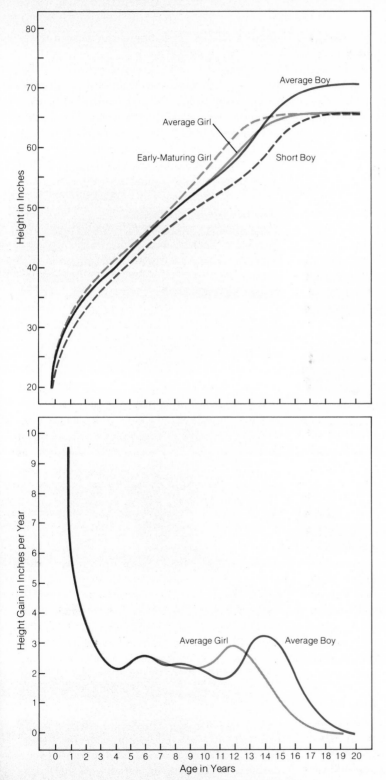

Figure 6.4 Sample growth curves for children. (*top*) The growth curves of an early-maturing girl and a short boy are compared to similar curves depicting the rates of growth for an average boy and girl. (*bottom*) Averaged and smoothed curves for boys and girls show inches gained in height per year. After the initial growth spurt of infancy, the rate of growth (velocity) first declines and then remains relatively stable until puberty. (Adapted from Bayley, 1956)

The age at which normal children master motor skills also shows great variability. Some normal children never crawl or creep at all but go directly from sitting to standing and taking their first steps. The normal range for the onset of walking is itself large—from as early as eight months to as late as twenty months.

Individual Rates of Growth

There are great individual differences in the velocity of growth, and some normal children mature much more slowly or more quickly than the mythical average child described by norms. The distance a child has progressed toward physiological maturity can be measured by the rate at which teeth erupt and bones approach mature shape and position, or by the time at which puberty occurs. Researchers have found that maturation rates seem to be related to body build. The child who is broadly built, large, and strong is likely to be a fast grower; whereas a slender, long-legged but small and lightly muscled child is likely to grow more slowly (Bayley, 1956).

It may well be that in some areas, individual development that does not match the norm has distinct advantages. As we shall see in Chapter 17, male children who become sexually mature earlier than their age-mates may experience some psychological and social benefits. In a number of ways, boys who reach puberty early appear to be better adjusted than late-maturing boys (Mussen and Jones, 1957).

One possible solution to the confusion created by great differences in growth is to assess an individual's growth only in relation to his or her own growth curve. For example, data taken on a child over long periods of time allow us to make a statement about that child's growth relative to him- or herself. This means that we take the child's status at a particular time (for example, height, weight, the closure of bones in the hand) and use it as the standard against which to compare his or her status at other times. Such individual growth rates can be compared to relevant norms in order to find indica-

tions of relative precocity or slowness in tempo of growth.

Although growth curves are relatively stable, severe dietary deficiencies and stress can affect them, temporarily slowing growth. When the condition responsible for the retarded growth is eliminated, a child often goes through a period of *"catch-up" growth*. This temporary deviation from the child's normal growth curve and the subsequent return results from the *canalization* of growth. (See Figure 6.5.) According to J. M. Tanner (1978) growth curves of individual children are genetically determined and self-stabilizing. Illness or malnutrition may temporarily deflect a child's growth from this natural curve, as a stream can be temporarily deflected from its normal course by an obstruc-

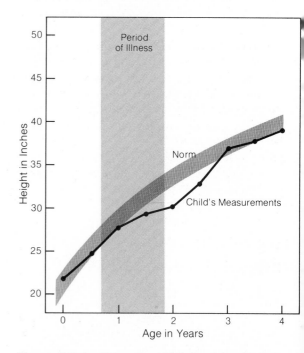

Figure 6.5 An illness in which food intake was greatly reduced for approximately one year affected the growth of a young child. When the illness ended and food intake was restored to normal levels, the child caught up with his own time pattern in approximately two years, providing an example of canalization. (Adapted from Prader, Tanner, and von Harnack, 1963)

tion, but once the environment becomes normal, the child catches up.

Newborn babies show catch-up growth in both weight and height. From birth to six months or so, smaller babies gain more weight than larger ones (Tanner, 1978). This explains the fact that small women often bear babies who become large adults. Such newborn catch-up growth is usually completed by the end of the third year. Because most babies have caught up by that time, if we know the height and weight of a three-year-old, our chances of predicting the child's approximate weight and height as an adult are quite good.

Because genetic influence plays such a large part in determining growth curves, it is always important to compare children with their parents and older siblings before comparing them with the norm for the population. This is especially necessary when a child appears to diverge greatly from the norm. According to Tanner (1978), by averaging the heights of both parents, it is possible to predict a seventeen-centimeter (6.7 inch) height range for each sex within which 97 percent of a specific couple's children will fall. Using such procedures, growth charts have been developed that can reveal whether a child's growth curve is normal and, for children between the ages of two and nine years, can closely predict adult height.

ENVIRONMENTAL INFLUENCES ON GROWTH

A variety of environmental factors, including diet, general health, stress, and socioeconomic determinants, can either support normal growth and development or impede it. Exactly how or why environmental factors influence growth during early childhood is uncertain. The internal mechanism that regulates growth includes hormones and chemical factors; their production and composition may be affected by nutrition, illness, and stress (Tanner, 1978).

Diet

Dietary deficiencies are a common cause of abnormal growth curves during infancy. In Chapter 4 we saw the effect of extreme dietary deficiency on the developing fetus. The importance of diet in growth and development continues after the baby is born. In general malnutrition, children simply do not get enough food to eat; their diets lack calories as well as protein, vitamins, and minerals. This near starvation sometimes occurs in developing countries (Waterlow and Payne, 1975). As the number of calories available to a young child drops dangerously near the level required for maintenance and growth, the child becomes sluggish and ceases to play or to explore the environment. When calorie intake drops below the minimum level, growth ceases.

Records of infants who have been exposed to wartime famine show delayed growth during periods of malnutrition (Tanner, 1978). Georg Wolff's (1935) study of Berlin children during World War I demonstrated that malnutrition at age five retards the development of height and weight. Once these children had a normal diet, however, they began to overcome the adverse effects and by adolescence had caught up with their well-fed contemporaries. Studies of war children in Russia, Spain, France, Belgium, and Japan have shown the same general results as those in Berlin (Acheson, 1960).

If the episode of malnutrition is neither too severe nor too long, children can usually overcome the effects of acute malnourishment with periods of catch-up growth. However, a child who is chronically undernourished will suffer permanent effects. Such children generally grow to be smaller adults than they would have been had they eaten an adequate diet.

The probable effects of severe malnutrition on the human nervous system have been discussed by Neville Scrimshaw and John Gordon (1968). They point out that although head circumference shows no relationship to intelligence among normal children, it is a reasonably good indicator of brain size. They then cite the reports

Malnourished children, like those in this family whose only home is the pavement in an Indian city, not only grow slowly but may also become apathetic and show little interest in the environment. (© Jehangir Gazdar 1981/Woodfin Camp & Assoc.)

of researchers in Mexico, Guatemala, Peru, Uganda, and other developing countries, which show that children who have had severely deficient diets from birth show smaller head circumference than children of the same ethnic group who have always been well-fed.

Such speculation is supported by findings that severe malnutrition in laboratory animals, especially when the animals are very young, stunts brain growth. John Dobbing (1968) and others have shown that young pigs that suffer severe malnutrition during their first year of life never catch up with normal animals in brain development. Even after two and a half years of normal

feeding, such animals show structural changes in their nervous systems, with certain cortical neurons, brain enzymes, and the cerebellum (a portion of the brain that controls muscular coordination) especially affected. The possible effects of severe malnutrition on human cognitive functioning will be discussed in Chapter 13.

Deficiencies of various nutrients can affect growth in different ways. Protein deficiency has widespread effects. If one group of average babies has a protein-deficient diet and the other eats protein-rich food, the deficient babies will grow to be shorter and less muscular, on the average, than the well-fed babies. If the two groups are compared to the norms of growth, it is apparent that the deficient babies are behind in development, while the well-fed babies are growing according to the average.

Severe, prolonged protein deficiency can lead to *kwashiorkor*, a serious, often fatal, disease found among infants in developing countries whose diets consist largely of breast milk after they are a year old (Scrimshaw, 1969; Waterlow, 1973). The symptoms of this disease include scaly skin, profound apathy, diarrhea, swollen limbs and abdomen, and liver degeneration. According to studies reported by Heinz Eichenwald and Peggy Crooke Fry (1969), when infants who are suffering from kwashiorkor eat adequate protein, they begin to grow rapidly but never catch up with normal children of their own age. This finding underlines the importance of diet as a central environmental determinant of normal physical growth.

Deficiencies of other nutrients can have specific effects. For example, calcium is crucial to the replacement of cartilage in the infant's skeleton with bone. A deficiency of vitamin D during infancy and childhood interferes with the metabolism of calcium and leads to a condition known as *rickets*, which is characterized by softening and bending of the bones, especially those that bear body weight. The condition is sometimes accompanied by cramps and muscle spasms.

Dietary excesses can also upset normal growth patterns by making a child *obese*, or excessively fat. A number of researchers (e.g., Bronstein et al., 1942; Bruch, 1957) have found that obesity in children most often results from overfeeding; malfunctioning glands are rarely responsible. In affluent Western nations, excessive feeding is common, and too much of even the healthiest food produces overweight children who may become unhappy and socially maladjusted. And overweight children generally become fat adults. Some studies (e.g., Dwyer and Mayer, 1973) have suggested that overnutrition in infancy (often caused by a mother determined to have a large, healthy baby) may lead to a multiplication of extra-large fat cells. Fat cells have tiny nucleii in comparison with muscle cells, but each cell can expand to an enormous size with stored fat. Once formed, fat cells never disappear, so that a baby with extra fat cells would be susceptible to obesity and might easily become a fat child. Others have suggested that when babies become fat from overfeeding, the extra fat does not create new cells but instead fills already present but minute cells until they can be seen (Tanner, 1978). The danger of obesity does not end when a child grows past infancy. Parents can also make their children obese by forcing food on a two- or three-year-old whose growth rate has settled into the childhood plateau, the period of relatively stable growth between infancy and puberty.

Illness

A child who escapes serious illness will show a more regular and satisfactory growth curve than one who is ill for any length of time, because severe illness tends to slow certain aspects of growth. Short illnesses have little effect, especially the communicable diseases common among children from two to six. Although a child's growth rate may slow slightly during an extended bout with illness, catch-up growth normally compensates for such slowing. Roy Acheson (1960) found that one year of severe, confining illness resulted in a height loss of only about one-fourth of an inch. When perma-

nent underdevelopment results, it is not merely from the effect of the sickness but because a serious and protracted illness costs the child the periods of reasonably steady growth needed for adequate development.

Socioeconomic Status

Setbacks to growth are most common among children of the lower socioeconomic classes, where inadequate nutrition can have less dramatic but more insidious effects than severe malnutrition. Low energy levels produce sluggish children whose interest is hard to arouse. Undernourished children are also more vulnerable to infections, especially to diseases of the eyes, skin, and respiratory and gastrointestinal tracts. Because these children are unlikely to have regular medical care, they may suffer from additional nagging ailments, including badly decayed teeth.

The basis of these observations is the 1965 National Child Development Survey conducted in England, comparing all children born during a single week in 1958 (Tanner, 1978). This survey indicated that the more skilled the father's occupation, the more rapidly the children grew. Growth differences between the children of fathers in highly skilled and less skilled occupations became steadily larger with age among children between the ages of two and four and a half. Studies conducted in Scotland (E. Scott, Illsby, and Thomson, 1956) support the results of the English survey, as do studies conducted in the United States (Hamill, Johnston, and Lemeshow, 1972).

Children of higher socioeconomic backgrounds tend to be larger at all ages. Part of the difference in stature among socioeconomic groups is probably a result of the fact that children of the wealthier classes generally have faster growth rates, reaching puberty earlier. As the more slowly developing children mature, however, they do not make up all of the height difference, which results in a socioeconomic difference in adult height.

Crib Death—
The Silent Killer

Every year, thousands of babies die in their sleep from apparently unknown causes. Crib death, called sudden infant death syndrome (SIDS) by investigators, kills about 10,000 babies each year in the United States (Steinschneider, 1975). Most babies who succumb to SIDS are between two and four months old, although babies older than six months are also occasionally victims. The pattern of death is familiar. Parents put to bed an apparently healthy baby, one who may have a slight runny nose or minor sign of nasal congestion. When they go to check on the infant, they find their child has died quietly during sleep.

Investigators are not sure what causes SIDS, and at least seventy-three different hypotheses have been proposed to account for the affliction (Beckwith, 1973). Victims of SIDS come from every country and every socioeconomic level, although deaths are more frequent among families of low socioeconomic status. Babies who die from SIDS generally have low birth weights; more males than females succumb; more blacks and American Indians than whites. The ethnic link to SIDS may be primarily socioeconomic because of the higher incidence of low birth weight among the first two groups, as well as the greater number of infections spread by overcrowding and poor health conditions

(Steinschneider, 1975). Death from SIDS tends to recur in the same family, leading to the suspicion of some genetic predisposition. The rate among the general population is 3 in 1,000, but the rate among siblings of SIDS victims is from 11 to 22 per thousand (Froggatt et al., 1971).

Alfred Steinschneider (1975) believes that *sleep apnea,* or a temporary halt in breathing during sleep, is the primary cause of SIDS. Although physicians once thought that prolonged bouts of sleep apnea were confined to the first two or three weeks of a premature infant's life, Steinschneider has discovered widespread evidence of such episodes in older babies and believes they are common among infants who die of SIDS. By studying sleeping babies attached to instruments that record body functions, Steinschneider has found that periods of prolonged apnea tend to occur during REM sleep (which was discussed in the last chapter) and that they are often accompanied by slowed heart rates. He also found that the lower a baby's birth weight, the more likely the infant is to stop breathing periodically during sleep.

Most babies have increased heart rates during the first few weeks of life, which may explain why SIDS is rare among infants less than two months old. Since heart rates become progressively slower during long periods of sleep, Steinschneider points out that the longer the sleep period, the greater the possibility of apnea at a time when the heart is beating slowly. He notes that the highest

Differences in nutrition and the availability of medical care may be only partially responsible for these socioeconomic differences. Some researchers have suggested that class differences in habits of sleep, exercise, and general home life may contribute to the effect. For whatever reason, children from poor homes suffer more illnesses, are more vulnerable to accidents and

disasters, and undergo more physical trauma than do middle-class children (R. Hess, 1970).

Meager resources and large families may combine to diminish the quality of material care, leading to retarded growth rates. When English researchers rated the "efficiency" of mothers (a measure that included how organized a mother seemed to be at meeting her child's basic needs),

incidence of SIDS occurs at the age when the length of the baby's longest sleep period is rapidly increasing (Parmalee, Wenner, and Schulz, 1964).

Steinschneider (1975) has been working with infants who have had recurrent, prolonged episodes of sleep apnea but have recovered. When these babies are admitted to the hospital, the apneic episodes decrease markedly; when they go home, the episodes increase. Steinschneider suggests that the noisier hospital environment may keep babies from falling into the prolonged deep sleep, with its accompanying slowed heart rate, that precedes a bout of apnea—especially since parents report that the episodes rarely occur during naptimes, when the house is especially noisy.

Many babies who succumb to SIDS have slight head colds, which has led some investigators to propose that a slight nasal obstruction during sleep sets off the apnea (Shaw, 1970; 1974). A profile of the baby who is unlikely to be able to clear the obstruction appeared when Lewis Lipsitt, William Sturner, and Patrick Burke (1979) studied all cases of SIDS among a group of 4,000 infants who had been part of a Brown University project. When the fifteen babies who died were compared with a control group of fifteen other babies from the study, it became clear that the SIDS victims were different. Their mothers were likely to have been anemic; the SIDS babies had lower Apgar scores at birth, taking five minutes to reach the scores the control babies showed at one minute after birth; the SIDS babies were lower in birth weight, were shorter, had severe respiratory problems and signs of jaundice, and spent more days in the hospital than the control group.

As in other areas of development, the apparent physical affliction interacts with experience. Lipsitt (1979) suggests that a learning disorder is implicated in these deaths. The unconditioned, defensive reflexes that babies use to clear their air passages may be weak in SIDS infants. Unless these reflexes work properly during the neonatal period, babies will not learn to clear obstructions by the time the reflexes drop away. Because the babies are weaker and not as visually alert, and engage their environment less, they may have fewer opportunities to learn the voluntary responses that would later save their lives. Other findings support this proposal. Babies who later died from SIDS have been found to react poorly just after birth to tests of defensive reflexes in which cotton is placed over the nostrils and cellophane over the nose and mouth (Anderson and Rosenblith, 1971).

The goal of investigators is to locate babies who are at risk for SIDS. Steinschneider has been focusing on babies who have recovered from at least one bout of apnea. Lipsitt's group has been trying to locate them at birth, hoping that identifying these babies will make possible effective early care that might protect them from SIDS during that critical first year.

they found that the more efficient the mother, the taller her children (Acheson, 1960). When inefficiency was combined with poor socioeconomic conditions, the effect on growth was striking. In these same studies, birth order also correlated with height. First-born children tended to be taller than later-born children. The height advantage could be, at least in part, a result of the first-born's temporary status as an only child who receives the full attention of both parents.

Only one study has found no correlation between size and social status. Gunilla Lindgren (1976), who surveyed all urban schoolchildren in Sweden, found no relation between father's occupation and children's height at any age between seven and seventeen years. Tanner (1978), who adds that there is no longer any correlation between parental occupation and the height of Swedish military conscripts, suggests that a lack of discrepancy in children's growth on the basis of father's occupation might be a good measure of the classlessness of a society.

Stress

Growth can also be retarded by severe emotional stress, apparently through its effect on hormonal secretions. Although a number of hormones have important roles in the regulation of growth, the growth hormone (GH) itself is one of the most interesting. At one time, children who lacked GH became midgets — perfectly proportioned adults about fifty-one inches tall. Today, such children receive injections of GH taken from human pituitary glands, which stimulate catch-up growth, enabling them to attain a height within the normal range. According to Tanner (1978), GH levels rise in the blood only a few times each day — about an hour or so after children go to sleep, after they have exercised, and when they are anxious. GH stimulates the liver to produce somatomedin, a hormone that acts on the growing cartilage cells at the end of bones, and probably on the muscle cells as well. A single dose of GH keeps somatomedin blood levels high for at least twenty-four hours.

Some children react to severe psychological stress not by increasing the amount of GH but by switching off its production. They simply fail to grow, just as do children whose bodies do not produce the hormone. Their skeletal structure is immature, with the bones exhibiting the shape and relation of those of a much younger child. This condition, called "psychosocial dwarfism," is associated with severe emotional distress in young children from homes in which family members are emotionally detached and there are no emotional bonds between parent and child (Powell, Brasel, and Blizzard, 1967; L. Gardner, 1972). If such children are removed from their disturbed environments, they show rapid catch-up growth.

Stress that is not quite so severe may sharply reduce the secretion of GH. For example, Elsie Widdowson (1951) found that children in an orphanage under the regime of a punitive and unfair teacher grew more slowly than orphanage children whose diet had 20 percent fewer calories but whose environment was less stressful. In some boarding schools, boys have been known to grow more slowly during the school term than when they were home for the holidays (Tanner, 1978). But it takes severe psychological or physical stress to affect a child's growth; the everyday stresses and illnesses of a child's life have little impact.

DEVELOPMENT OF MOTOR ABILITIES

Some motor skills appear to develop in simple, orderly fashion, whereas others are complex and show little consistency in their development. Even simple sequences depend on an intricate interplay between maturational changes and experience.

Maturation and Experience

Maturation means simply an organism's progression toward physiological maturity. But when psychologists refer to maturation in relation to experience, they are stressing the effect on behavior of such factors as genes, hormones, nutrition, and metabolism, as opposed to the effect of learning. In other words, we are once again facing the nature-nurture question.

Certain motor skills appear to have a developmental sequence in which early, more primitive coordinations disappear and then reappear later in more advanced forms. Although the causes of this sequence are not known, it is possible that they are connected with maturation, in this case, with developmental changes in brain and nervous system organization. Depending on the skill involved, the change can be influenced by stimulation, that is, learning. If, for example, babies are given practice in the stepping reflex for about ten minutes each day from two weeks until they are eight weeks old, they are likely to walk a bit earlier than the average baby (Zelazo, Zelazo, and Kolb, 1972).

Yet studies of infants in different cultures indicate that in spite of widely different opportunities to practice the skill, children walk at roughly the same time in all cultures. For example, Hopi Indian infants spend their first year bound to cradleboards; nevertheless, they walk at about the same time as do infants in other cultures who have had more practice in muscular coordination (Dennis and Dennis, 1940). Records from five of Europe's largest urban centers show that despite different child-rearing methods, most infants in the five cities take their first steps within a few months of one another (see Figure 6.6, p. 146).

Another way to study the relative contributions of maturation and experience is that of *co-twin control*, in which the experimenter gives one of a pair of twins some experiences believed to be important in learning a skill and withholds or delays those same experiences for the other twin. In Myrtle McGraw's (1935, 1939) classic co-twin control study, one twin received practice in crawling and standing and the other was kept from all opportunities. Despite the difference in their experience, both twins crawled and walked at the same age.

Deliberately restricting a child's movement has been used as a means of evaluating the roles of maturation and experience. For example, Wayne Dennis (1941) left a pair of female twins on their backs from birth to nine months, never allowing them to sit or to stand. Yet the sitting and standing of both twins emerged fully developed, with little or no practice. It should be noted that except for the experimental restriction, both girls had a fairly normal environment.

When the environment is both socially and physically impoverished, the development of

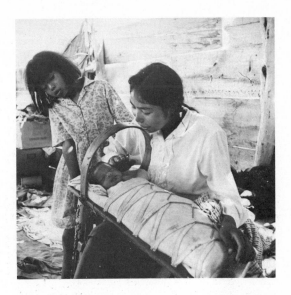

Children walk at about the same time in all cultures; this Hopi baby, who will spend most of the first year strapped to a restricting cradleboard, will walk at about the same time as a baby whose limbs have never been confined. (© Michal Heron 1980/Woodfin Camp & Assoc.)

motor skills may lag severely. In a series of studies conducted in institutions with such environments, Dennis and his associates (Dennis, 1960; Dennis and Najarian, 1957; Dennis and Sayegh, 1965) found that children who were neither attended to by adults nor surrounded by a stimulating environment showed retarded motor development from the time they were two months old. In one study, Dennis and Yvonne Sayegh (1965) worked with infants in The Creche, a foundling home in Lebanon. In that institution, infants spent most of their first year lying on their backs in cribs. Some of the infants who were more than one year old could not sit up. Infants in the experimental group were propped into a sitting position and allowed to play with such simple attractive objects as fresh flowers, pieces of colored sponge, and colored plastic disks strung on a chain, for as little as an hour each day. This seemingly small amount

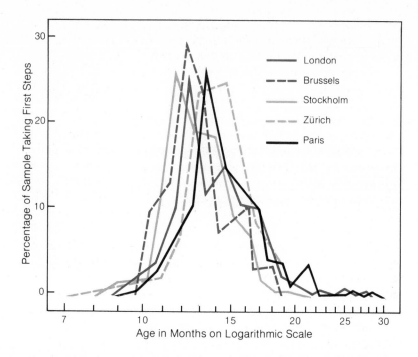

Figure 6.6 Ages in months at which infants in several cities took their first steps. (Adapted from Hindley *et al.*, 1966)

of stimulation caused the babies' developmental age to jump dramatically.

In a related study, Burton White and Richard Held (1966) investigated the effect of enriched stimulation on the development of grasping. They concluded that appropriate extra stimulation could accelerate the baby's acquisition of grasping. However, more detailed studies have suggested (B. White, 1967, 1971) that stimulation must be appropriate to both the age of a baby and his or her abilities. Too much stimulation, for example, may be irritating or confusing, at least temporarily, and fail to accelerate the development of the baby's motor skills.

It seems clear from such studies that even though a child's motor development may require only normal freedom for spontaneous activity, some environments promote development and others retard it.

Skill Development

Maturation of muscles and bones plays a large part in the emergence of such skills as running,

jumping, and skipping; but the opportunity to practice and the encouragement of others help to guarantee the smooth, speedy, confident mastery and refinement of such abilities. To master a particular motor skill, a child must pass through several stages of proficiency.

M. V. Gutteridge (1939), after studying more than 2,000 preschool children, constructed a scale of motor-skill development, which is reproduced in Table 6.1 and can be used to measure the specific skills of any child. The Gutteridge scale describes four general phases of motor development, within which are varying degrees of skill. The first ten degrees of skill mark the progressive acquisition of the ability; the final four degrees (A–D) measure the elaboration and use of the ability after the child has achieved competence.

There are, of course, large individual differences in the ages at which various children are able to do different things, as well as differences in the degree of their skill and coordination in each activity. For simple movement patterns, says Caroline Sinclair (1973), instruction and coaching are not necessary. All a child needs is time, space, equipment, and encouragement.

More complicated motor skills require formal instruction and special equipment. These include such sports as swimming, skating, skiing, tennis, and so forth. Many children are exposed to these skills during early childhood, and such early exposure and practice appear to give children an advantage in their performance. In McGraw's (1935) co-twin study, for example, although one twin seemed to gain little from training in such skills as walking and stair-climbing, early training in swimming had some advantages. Researchers began training one twin to swim at eight months, and when he was seventeen months old, he could swim up to fifteen feet without help while his twin could not swim at all. McGraw also had success in teaching the same twin diving and skating. Other studies have demonstrated that observation and verbal instruction increase a child's skill at throwing and catching, and of course, fine motor skills such as writing and drawing improve with instruction.

SEX DIFFERENCES

Even before birth, girls and boys grow at different rates. By the time they are halfway through the fetal period, girls' skeletal development is three weeks ahead of boys'; and by the time they are born, girls have outstripped boys by four to six weeks in skeletal maturity, although not in size (Tanner, 1978). Some organ systems also are more developed in newborn girls, which may help explain why more newborn girls than boys survive.

Prepubertal Differences

Baby girls have proportionately more fat and less muscle tissue and water than boys (Falkner, 1966). This difference exists throughout life. Young girls lose their fatty infant tissue at a far slower rate than do their male contemporaries (Stolz and Stolz, 1951).

Table 6.1 GUTTERIDGE SCALE OF MOTOR SKILLS

Phase	Scale	Degree of Motor Skill
No attempt made	1	Withdraws or retreats when opportunity is given
	2	Makes no approach or attempt but does not withdraw
Skill in process of formation	3	Attempts activity but seeks help or support
	4	Tries even when not helped or supported but is inept
	5	Is progressing but still uses unnecessary movements
	6	Is practicing basic movements
	7	In process of refining movements
Basic movements achieved	8	Coordinates movements
	9	Performs easily with display of satisfaction
	10	Shows evidence of accuracy, poise, and grace
Skillful execution with variations in use	A	Tests skill by adding difficulties or taking chances
	B	Combines activity with other skill or skills
	C	Speeds, races, or competes with self or others
	D	Uses skill in larger projects such as dramatic play

(*Source:* Adapted from M. V. Gutteridge, "A Study of Motor Achievement of Young Children," *Archives of Psychology* (1939), No. 244.)

Walking and running depend primarily upon the maturation of bones and muscles, but encouragement and practice foster smooth, self-confident mastery of the skills. (© Joel Gordon 1979)

Boys grow faster than girls during the first few months of life, but girls outstrip boys from seven months until they are four years old. Between four and puberty, there are no apparent differences in the velocity of growth, and differences in appearance are slight. Body proportions in both sexes are similar: straight and flat. Girls, however, remain ahead of boys in maturation. Until adolescence, the skeletal maturity (but not size) of boys is only 80 percent that of girls the same age (Tanner, Whitehouse, and Healy, 1962). And girls reach sexual maturity about two years sooner than boys.

According to an old rule, children reach half their adult height by the end of their second year. However, differences discovered in the growth patterns of boys and girls make this old rule unreliable for girls. Since girls grow up faster than boys, they reach the halfway mark sooner: at about eighteen months (Acheson, 1966; Tanner, 1978). The old rule remains fairly reliable for boys, however.

Growth regulation is more efficient in girls than in boys. Girls catch up after a period of arrested growth more quickly than boys do, and placed under the same adverse circumstances, whether poor nutrition or exposure to atomic radiation, the growth of boys slows down more (Tanner, 1978).

Until they are four, girls have a slight advantage in the development of motor skills. Around the age of three, boys become more proficient than girls at tasks that require strength, such as throwing (Sinclair, 1973), and after age six, boys gain in strength more quickly than girls. By age seven, girls demonstrate about 10 percent less muscular strength than boys. Louis Govatos (1959) tested ten-year-old children and found no sex differences on tasks as diverse as jumping, reaching, the standing broadjump, the twenty-five-yard dash, or throwing a ball for accuracy. But boys were more proficient than girls in tasks that require superior strength in the arms and legs, such as soccer-style kicking or throwing a ball for distance.

Sex-related differences are also evident in brain development and function, a topic we shall discuss in Chapter 7, and in some involuntary physical functions as well (see Figure 6.7). In a measure of *vital capacity* (lung capacity), girls, when asked to inhale as much air as they could and then to expel it, demonstrated 7 percent less vital capacity than boys (Sherman, 1973). Vital capacity can be an important factor in tasks that require sustained energy output. However, females exhibit lower *basal metabolism* rates than males; that is, they require less energy while resting to maintain the same amount of body tissue. Boys develop larger hearts and lungs than girls. In addition, boys have a lower heart rate than girls (Hutt, 1972).

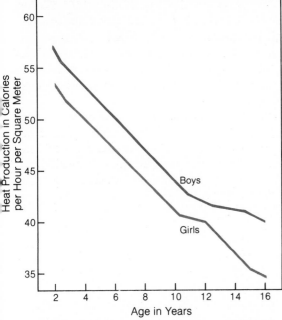

Figure 6.7 As this graph shows, the basal metabolic rate of boys is higher than that of girls, indicating that boys convert food and oxygen to various forms of energy faster than girls do. The difference is slight throughout childhood but increases somewhat during adolescence. (Adapted from Lewis, Duval, and Iliff, 1943)

During early childhood, motor abilities and physical growth play an important part in the developing self-image of both boys and girls. When children are asked what they like and do not like about themselves, physical characteristics, appearance, and motor abilities play an important part in their answers (Jersild, 1952). As discussions of personality development in Chapter 16 will show, the "social hierarchies," or patterns of dominance and submission, among boys rest more often on who is bigger, faster, and tougher than girls' hierarchies do. Children's social hierarchies, of course, also reflect their parents' values, and studies of sex-role behavior clearly show that adults value strength and athletic abilities more in males than in females (Sherman, 1973).

Sexual Maturation

Adolescence begins as a biological phenomenon, with sexual maturation as its central theme. Long before emotional considerations and social conflicts become important in the course of adolescent growth, hormonal changes begin to affect the body. The main biological event of adolescence is *puberty*, which is characterized by the attainment of biological sexual maturity During puberty, the reproductive glands begin to release sperm and ova. These glands are the *testes* in boys and the *ovaries* in girls. With the release of sperm or ova, the individual is, for the first time, capable of reproduction.

Both boys and girls produce male hormones (*androgens*) as well as female hormones (*estrogens*) in relatively equal amounts throughout their childhood. Hormones help to regulate growth at all stages, but it is only when a child reaches puberty that the hypothalamus of the brain signals the pituitary gland to begin the hormonal production found in adult men and women. The pituitary gland stimulates other endocrine glands, the adrenals, ovaries, and testes (shown in Figure 6.8), to secrete hormones directly into the bloodstream, creating a balance that includes more androgens in boys and more estrogens in girls. These hormonal changes lead directly to the physical developments that emerge during puberty (Tanner, 1962).

During puberty, the ovaries and testes produce enough hormones to cause accelerated growth of the genitals and the appearance of *secondary sex characteristics*, which differentiate the genders but have no direct reproductive function. In girls, a cyclic secretion of estrogens anticipates the rhythm of the menstrual cycle well before *menarche* — the first incidence of menstruation — which is an obvious milestone in puberty (Meredith, 1967).

The female adolescent growth spurt typically begins at around age ten, peaks at twelve and continues until about fifteen, although puberty varies so widely that its onset can occur at any time between the ages of eight and thirteen

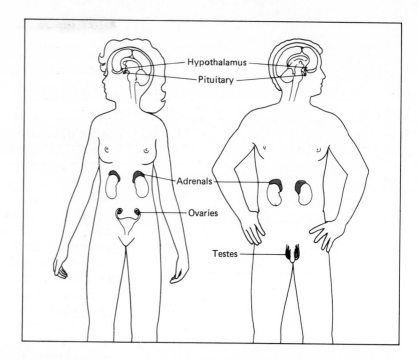

(Tanner, 1962). The appearance of secondary sex characteristics signals the onset of puberty in girls. The "breast bud" develops (Tanner, 1962), and pigmented pubic hair appears. Breast enlargement begins some time around the middle of the tenth year and continues for approximately three years until full size is reached. The entire breast enlarges and changes in its shape and appearance. At the same time, a girl's voice lowers somewhat and her vagina and uterus begin to mature.

In boys, the adolescent growth spurt generally occurs about two years later than in girls and peaks at about the age of fourteen. The onset of puberty typically occurs at about twelve among boys, and as is the case for girls, puberty includes more than one event. The appearance of live spermatozoa in the urine marks the onset of puberty, but because this event can be detected only by clinical tests, more observable changes are generally used. These changes include accelerated growth of the testes and scrotum, the pubertal height spurt, and nocturnal emissions. Secondary sex characteristics in boys include

Figure 6.8 The endocrine system, showing only the major glands involved in pubertal changes. The hypothalamus (a part of the brain with neural and endocrine functions) signals the pituitary gland, which in turn stimulates hormonal secretions from other endocrine glands, resulting in many of the changes typifying adolescent physical and pubertal development.

pubic hair, a deepened voice that results from an enlarged larynx and lengthened vocal cords, and the appearance of facial hair.

Although boys begin the pubertal growth spurt later than girls, their growth spurt lasts about three or four years longer than that of girls (see Figure 6.9). For this reason, girls between the ages of twelve and fifteen tend to be taller than boys; but the boys catch up as they enter puberty and end their growth spurt significantly taller, on the average, than girls.

Both sexes experience a growth characteristic called *asynchrony*. Asynchrony refers to the fact that different body parts mature at different

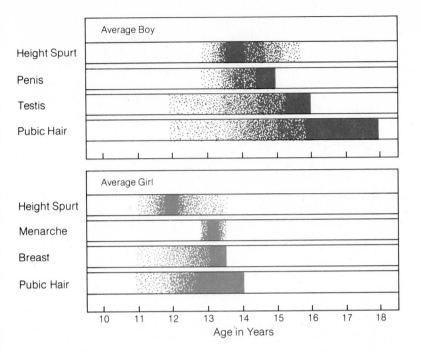

Average Boy

Height Spurt	
Penis	
Testis	
Pubic Hair	

Average Girl

Height Spurt	
Menarche	
Breast	
Pubic Hair	

10   11   12   13   14   15   16   17   18
Age in Years

Figure 6.9 The pubertal development of an average boy and girl. Shaded areas represent the range of years during which such development usually occurs, with the darker shading indicating the period of most rapid growth or change. Although individual growth and change patterns may vary widely from these norms, girls generally start and end such development earlier than boys. (Adapted from Tanner, 1962)

rates. This means that at any given time during adolescence, certain body parts may be disproportionately large or small in relation to the rest of the body. This disproportion becomes most pronounced with puberty (Dwyer and Mayer, 1968–1969). For example, some girls complain that their hands and feet are too big, and boys may object that their jaws are too prominent or their noses too large. As growth progresses, body proportions become more harmonious; a girl gradually takes on the figure of a mature woman, while a boy develops the physique of a man.

SIZE AND MATURATIONAL TRENDS

Where records have been kept, they have indicated a trend toward earlier onset of puberty over the past century or more. In 1840, the average girl's first menstruation occurred at the age of seventeen (see Figure 6.10); each decade since, menarche has tended to occur about four months earlier. In 1960 the average age of menarche in the United States was about thirteen; by 1970 the average age had dropped to slightly less than thirteen (Muuss, 1970).

Data concerning the onset of puberty in boys are not as complete as those for girls, but there has also been a trend toward earlier sexual maturity among males, at least since the beginning of this century. In addition to maturing earlier sexually, boys and girls today are taller and heavier before, during, and at the end of adolescence than they were some generations ago. Howard Meredith (1963) points out that in 1955

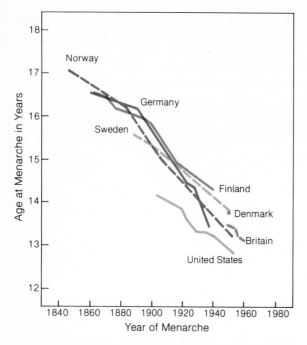

Figure 6.10 Over the last century, the average age of menarche (onset of menstruation) has declined in the United States and in various European countries. (After Tanner, 1962)

the average American boy was five and a quarter inches taller than a boy of the same age in 1870. Over the same period, the average weight for fifteen-year-old boys increased by thirty-three pounds.

Both sexes now reach their final adult height at an earlier age than they did a century ago. The average boy now reaches his adult height at eighteen instead of between twenty-three and twenty-five, as he would have in 1880. Similarly, the average girl now reaches her full height at about sixteen instead of at eighteen or nineteen.

Such changes are not unique to the United States; many countries around the world report similar trends. The difference in height between the average British factory worker in 1830 and his contemporary counterpart, for example, is much greater than the present height difference between slum children in underdeveloped countries and affluent children in Western industrialized societies (Tanner, 1978). The trend

toward taller adults also shows up in their feet; the size of the average American foot has been increasing about half an inch each generation (Muuss, 1970), which means that the average shoe size is increasing one size per generation.

These trends have resulted from the interplay of environmental and genetic factors, in which better nutrition and sanitation and freedom from disease have allowed human stature to approach the maximum of its reaction range—a concept discussed in Chapter 3. If the trend were a purely linear progression, we would have to assume that in the Middle Ages females could not bear children before they were about twenty-five and that in a few centuries they will be able to do so before they are eight. A linear trend would also mean that adults in the future would be giants. None of these assumptions, of course, is accurate or biologically sensible. First, size and maturation trends form an undulating curve over time. Second, although adults are today getting larger and larger, they are also maturing earlier and earlier, hence their growth ends at an earlier age. Finally, there are signs that the trend toward earlier menarche has stopped among the upper socioeconomic classes in Norway, the United States, and the United Kingdom. In the two latter countries, the trend toward greater height also seems to have stopped among the upper social classes.

Since a person's diet plays a crucial role in development and maturation, children from upper- and middle-class backgrounds become taller and heavier and reach puberty earlier than their lower-class peers do. Another factor is the increased availability and sophistication of medical care. Today's children experience fewer severely debilitating diseases, and modern procedures prevent many diseases from exerting a negative influence. Finally, since some of the genes governing height seem to be dominant, the height of a child born to a union of a tall and a short parent would tend to be not halfway between their relative heights but a little to the tall side (Tanner, 1978). Modern mobility has affected the breeding patterns of many populations, making it easier to marry outside the community and allowing such an effect to operate more freely.

Various other factors also influence the onset of puberty within any given generation. For example, geographic and climatic variations affect the average age of menarche. A girl living at sea level is likely to have her first menstrual period several months before a girl of the same age living at a much higher altitude. In spite of traditional beliefs and a few early studies, it also appears that girls who live in hot, humid climates are likely to reach menarche later than girls who live in cooler climates.

The three-year decrease in the average age of the onset of puberty mentioned at the beginning of this section represents a radical change in the timetable of development over the past 130 years. Childhood is shortened, and the social demands and urges associated with sexual maturity occur sooner. As yet, the social and cultural climate has not adjusted to the trend toward earlier sexual maturation, and today's adolescent is still sometimes treated as an overgrown child.

SUMMARY

1. From the systematic study of physical development, scientists have formulated three basic principles that underlie the growth and development of all body systems: (1) cephalocaudal development, which means that growth progresses from the head downward; (2) proximodistal development, which means that growth progresses from the center to the periphery; and (3) the principle of differentiation and integration, which refers to the increasing specificity and complexity of growth and skills.

2. Psychologists have compiled descriptive summaries of important attributes and skills, called norms, which indicate average tendencies for a large number of children. Despite the nearly universal sequences of development described by norms, individual children may differ greatly from them. Once a temporary cause of growth retardation is removed, children go through a period of catch-up growth; the sequence is attributed to canalization of growth.

3. A variety of environmental influences can either promote or impede a child's physical growth. These influences include diet, general health, and the type and quality of maternal care. In addition, severe emotional stress can switch off the production of growth hormones.

4. Using several different methods of study, psychologists have learned that only minimal normal practice may be necessary for the development of most skills, although encouragement and some formal instruction in more complicated skills may be required if the child is to become proficient in them.

5. During early childhood, physical growth and developmental differences between the sexes are relatively slight: the average boy is a little taller than the average girl, but girls are more advanced in some areas of motor development. Differences between the sexes have also been found in vital capacity and metabolic rate.

6. The physical and maturational changes that indicate increased hormone production are dramatically reflected in the adolescent growth spurt. Among the signs most often used to mark the attainment of sexual maturity are the first incidence of menstruation in girls and the appearance of pubic hair, nocturnal emissions, and enlarging sex organs in boys.

7. Size and maturational trends over the decades indicate an earlier onset of puberty, increases in size and weight, and the earlier attainment of final adult height than was once the case. Improved nutrition, more sophisticated medical care, genetic effects, and climatic differences are among the environmental factors that appear to explain these changes across and variations within generations.

The Developing Human Brain

Watch a two-year-old boy walk down a flight of stairs. He must integrate a host of sensory information and motor skills in order to move himself safely from the landing on the second floor to the hall below. Both visual information and kinesthetic feedback guide the way he places his feet, changes his posture, and shifts his weight as he makes his way down the steps. Not many months ago he could not have managed the job, but now the primary motor and sensory areas of his cortex have matured, and he has taken a giant step toward independence.

The development of the human brain is important to the study of human development because the brain is the seat of consciousness and of behavior. If we can understand how thought and behavior depend on the intricate connections and chemistry of the brain, we will have advanced our understanding of human limitations and possibilities. But even a thorough understanding of the brain will leave our understanding of the mind incomplete; for the mind is more than a collection of nerve cells and chemicals, just as a book is more than specks of black ink on paper.

In our explorations of the brain, we shall follow the cortical development that enables a toddler to descend safely from the second floor to the hall of his home and, when he gets there, to run to the kitchen and tell his mother that he wants a glass of milk and a cookie. We shall begin by taking a look at the evolution of the human brain and the physiological differences between animal and human brains. Next we shall discuss the chemicals that pass messages along in the brain and the electrical activity that results when that message is transmitted. We shall find that each hemisphere has its own tasks and that when the band of fibers that connects them is severed, it is almost as if two minds were living in a single body. From the time they are born, babies show signs of specialized function in each hemisphere, and among the consequences of this specialization are handedness and different cognitive abilities in boys and girls. We shall note that the mature brain is more resilient than was once thought. Finally, we shall look at two common childhood problems that have been associated with brain functioning: developmental dyslexia and hyperactivity.

EVOLUTION OF THE BRAIN

The human brain is an intricate tissue composed of about a hundred billion highly specialized cells that pass electrical and chemical signals across perhaps a hundred trillion *synapses*, or spaces between the cells (Hubel, 1979). This mass of tissue, which weighs about three pounds when fully mature, has evolved from far simpler structures. As human beings evolved, both body and brain got larger; but the increase in the size of the brain was far greater than might be predicted from the increase in body size. It was the development of this extra brain tissue that allowed intelligence to develop (Jerison, 1973). (Although a woman's brain weighs less than a man's brain, it is fully as large in proportion to body size.)

As brains evolved, few structures disappeared. Instead, as new ones developed, the old structures shrank in relative size and became less im-

portant (Rose, 1973). The maintenance of old structures deep within the human brain has led Paul MacLean (1970) to propose that human beings have a "triune brain," that is, a brain made up of three interconnected units that function in a coordinated fashion. The first to evolve, a reptilian brain, includes the brainstem and cerebellum. It maintains consciousness and alertness, and is responsible for such automatic functions as breathing, digestion, and metabolism. The second, or paleomammalian brain, includes the limbic system, thalamus, and hippocampus. This brain contains the "old cortex," and it plays a major part in emotions, scent, taste, and sexual behavior. Here we find control over such behavior as eating, fighting, drinking, and self-defense (Fishbein, 1976). The third brain, or neocortex, makes up 99 percent of the two cerebral hemispheres (Stephan, Bauchot, and Andy, 1970). This third brain is the seat of language, attention, memory, spatial understanding, and motor skills. In primates, and especially in human beings, an extremely large proportion of the cortex consists of *association areas*, regions that have neither motor nor sensory function and no direct connections outside the cortex (Rose, 1973). Association areas apparently act on information that has already gone through several stages of processing. Our logical thinking, then, comes from the neocortex; our emotions from older sections of the brain.

Dividing the brain in this way is probably too simplistic. Although human beings have retained the old structures, the functions have undergone changes (Rose, 1973). For example, although the limbic system is regarded as the source of emotions, parts of the cortex are heavily involved with emotional responses and with our recognition of emotions in others (Geschwind, 1979).

Psychologists who look at the evolution of intelligence as a gradual increase in learning capabilities ascribe increased human capabilities to the possession of large areas of uncommitted cortex (Rose, 1973). According to Harry Jerison (1973), intelligence is a natural development of the brain's work—the creation of a world to explain the mass of incoming and outgoing information processed by the brain. Part of this creation is the integration of information about the same object—information derived from vision, hearing, smell, and touch. This integration is possible because of the evolutionary transfer of much of the sensory function to the new, large cortex, which gave the sensory systems access to one another.

THE DEVELOPING BRAIN

The mature human brain is so large in proportion to the rest of the body that babies must be born with an exceedingly immature brain. If the brain were any larger at birth, a fetus could not pass uninjured through the birth canal (Magoun, Darling, and Prost, 1972); but because the brain is not capable of complex functioning at birth, human babies are helpless for a much longer period than the young of other primates. This immaturity is probably one reason human beings live so long compared to other animals. Although great apes and human beings alike spend about nine months in the uterus, apes finish growing in eleven years and live to be about thirty-five, whereas human beings grow for nearly two decades and live more than seventy— and sometimes as many as one hundred—years.

Brain Growth and Development

At birth, the baby's brain has all its *neurons,* or nerve cells, but is only about 25 percent of its adult weight and size. *Glial cells* continue to form after birth. These cells seem to play an essential role in the nourishment of neurons and in the development around each neuron of a sheath of *myelin*—a fatty substance that keeps nerve impulses channeled along the neural fibers and reduces the random spread of impulses from

one fiber to another. For the first two years the brain grows rapidly, reaching about 75 to 80 percent of its mature size. This rapid growth is due in part to increases in the sizes and shapes of existing glial cells (Bullock, Orkand, and Grinnell, 1977), in part to the formation of new ones, and in part to development within the neuron. The increased number and complexity of connections among neurons also add to brain growth, as does the continued formation of myelin around the neural fibers.

Although most of the myelination of fibers is complete after two years, some myelin sheaths continue to develop, and the nerve endings within and between cortical areas continue to grow in number and size at least until adolescence (Yakovlev and Lecours, 1967). When a child is about four, the fibers that connect the cerebellum to the cerebral cortex are mature. The cerebellum, as shown in Figure 7.1, is part

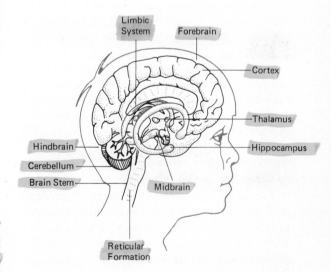

Figure 7.1 The human brain evolved from simple structures into an organ consisting of three interconnected units: the hindbrain (or reptilian brain), the midbrain (or paleomammalian brain), and the forebrain (or neocortex). Without the forebrain, logical thought would be impossible.

of the brain stem, and the connecting fibers permit the fine control of voluntary movement involved in such skills as writing. Myelination continues in the reticular formation—the core of tissue that runs through the brain stem and filters incoming stimuli—and in some parts of the cortex as late as the third decade of life.

The course of brain growth is genetically fixed and proceeds in an orderly and patterned way. The major pathways that connect parts of the nervous system and brain and are responsible for the sustenance of life are fully functional at birth. As other neural circuits develop, the cells show a great variety in shape and size, and their conducting fibers are relatively small and short. In keeping with nature's blueprint, each region of the brain eventually becomes characterized by specific types of cells arranged in specific patterns. As the connecting fibers spread, the distance between the cells of the infant's cortex increases, and the enlarged surface of the cortex continues to fold and become increasingly wrinkled (Rose, 1973).

The immature appearance of the cortex at birth indicates that much of a baby's behavior during the neonatal period may be primarily reflexive. Jesse LeRoy Conel's pioneer studies (1939–1963) of postnatal development of the cerebral cortex revealed the sequence of maturation during the first few years of life. Certain areas of the brain control particular sensory and motor functions, and these areas develop at different rates. As soon as the specific area in the cortex develops, the corresponding functions appear in the infant's behavior.

Thus postnatal development of the cortex can be followed in two ways. One is the sequence in which the functional areas of the brain develop; the second is the advancement of body functions corresponding to each of these areas (Minkowski, 1967). The early stages of development are characterized by an orderly sequence, in which the primary areas of the cortex begin to function efficiently. First, the primary motor area, in the precentral gyrus, develops; then the primary sensory area, in the postcentral gyrus

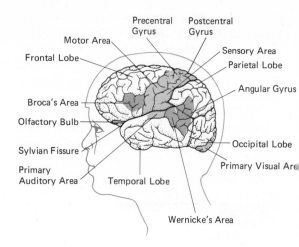

Figure 7.2 Language, attention, memory, spatial understanding, and motor skills are located in the cortex, which is immature at birth. This drawing shows the left hemisphere of the mature cortex, where—for most people—language is located in Broca's and Wernicke's areas.

(see Figure 7.2). Next, the primary visual area, at the back of the head in the occipital lobe, develops; and it is followed by the primary auditory area, at the side of the head in the temporal lobe. At first, these primary areas function at a simple level. For example, babies can control some of their basic body movements, and they can hear and see. However, the cortical association areas, which must develop before babies can integrate and interpret the stimuli they encounter, lag behind the corresponding primary areas.

The cortical control of behavior develops sequentially. Whereas most of the cerebral cortex thickens during the baby's first three months, the primary motor area develops more rapidly. Again, the cephalocaudal and proximodistal developmental patterns hold true; cortical control of the head, upper trunk, and arms appears before that of the legs; and cortical control of arm movements appears before babies can use their hands skillfully. The other primary cortical areas also develop in sequence, and babies are capable of controlled movement and simple visual and auditory functions. At this time, the cells of the motor and sensory areas rapidly develop a sheath of myelin, speeding the transmission of nerve impulses.

When babies reach the age of six months, the primary motor and sensory areas are still the most advanced, but other areas of the cortex are beginning to catch up. There is marked growth in the cortical motor areas that control the hands, upper trunk, head, and legs. Between six and fifteen months, growth of these motor areas slows down. Infants can then control their hands and arms, but control over the legs is not nearly so well developed. In fact, some children still do not walk at fifteen months. During the period from six to fifteen months, the visual association areas of the cortex continue to be more advanced than the auditory association areas. By the time children are two, however, the primary motor and sensory cortical areas are well advanced and the cortical association areas have developed further. This continued cortical development enables two-year-olds to integrate their own movements with the information they get from the environment, resulting in complex patterns of behavior, as when the toddler walks down a flight of stairs.

Neurochemistry

Neurons fire, transmitting an electrical impulse, or are kept from firing by the arrival of a *neurotransmitter*. About thirty of these chemicals act as messengers in the brain. When a nerve impulse travels along a neuron and arrives at a synapse, it triggers the release of a neurotransmitter, which travels to the adjacent neuron, where it changes the electrical activity of the nerve cell. Specific transmitters have specific effects, and depending on the nature of the transmitter, the change in electrical activity will either cause the neuron to fire or keep it from firing.

Since neurotransmitters are not randomly distributed throughout the brain but located in specific areas and along pathways, investigators have been able to implicate specific transmitters in various kinds of behavior (Iverson, 1979). Norepinephrine, for example, is found in the brain stem, the hypothalamus, the cerebellum, and the forebrain. It is believed to be involved in arousal, brain reward, dreaming, and mood. Serotonin, found in a portion of the brain stem, the hypothalamus, and other areas, may influence temperature control, sensory perception, and the onset of sleep. Dopamine, which is concentrated in the midbrain and forebrain, is believed to play a part in the regulation of emotional response and complex movement.

Dopamine also has been implicated in performance or memory — or both. Thomas Brozoski, Patricia Goldman, and their colleagues (Brozoski et al., 1979) taught monkeys to solve a problem involving a delayed spatial response. When dopamine was removed from the association area of the cortex, the monkeys no longer could solve the problem. It was as if that area of their brains had been sliced away with a scalpel. But when dopamine was restored, the monkeys were again able to solve the problem.

Little is known about the development of neurotransmitter function, and most research is limited — for obvious reasons — to rats, monkeys, and lower animal forms. We do know that the protein composition of the brain changes as children grow (Gaitonde, 1969) and that the synthesis of protein is intimately involved with both the production and the storage of neurotransmitters. In fact, some amino acids — the building blocks of protein — are known to be neurotransmitters themselves (Iverson, 1979).

At one time, researchers believed that by untangling neurochemistry they would find the "memory molecule" — a single substance that was presumed to be responsible for the consolidation of memory. But the memory molecule has remained elusive, and as Dan Entingh and his associates (1975) point out, the physical basis of memory is probably a complex chain of

metabolic reactions involving a number of substances. RNA (which carries the genetic information required for protein synthesis) and protein metabolism both seem to be involved in
the long-term memory storage. The appearance
of a new stimulus, such as a flickering light,
leads to changes in the metabolism of RNA, and
learning a task leads to protein metabolism.
When the synthesis of protein is inhibited, animals fail to form long-term memories. However,
other substances have also been implicated in
the process. Most research at present, say Entingh and his associates, focuses either on the
control of gene expression within neurons or on
biochemical reactions at the synapses between
neurons.

An example of the latter research is a series
of studies with lower animals by Eric Kandel
(1979) and his associates. Kandel's group studied
a motor response and the habituation of the
sensory neurons that control it. Habituation is
a form of short-term memory that soon disappears. Kandel's work indicates that when an
animal habituates to a stimulus, the neurons
involved release a smaller quantity of transmitter, thereby decreasing the signal to the next
neuron and leading to a temporary drop in the
efficiency of the synapse. In the equivalent of
long-term, or enduring, memory, synaptic connections were still inactive more than a week
after the animal had habituated. Kandel concludes that long-term memory can be explained
by an enduring change in synaptic effectiveness,
that it requires surprisingly little training, and
that short- and long-term memory both involve
the same mechanism—a depression in the transmission of the impulses that cause cells to fire.

Electrical Activity

As neural connections develop and myelination
progresses, changes also take place in the brain's
electrical activity. This aspect of brain functioning can be studied in babies and children, since
it is a relatively simple matter to attach electrodes to the scalp and record activity in various
parts of the brain. As we saw in Chapter 5, at
birth the brain shows characteristic electrical
wave patterns when a baby is awake or sleeping.
When babies are two or three months old, they
begin each sleep period with quiet sleep instead
of going immediately into REM sleep as they
do at birth. Other regular changes in electrical
activity, including a typical pattern that occurs
during the transition from wakefulness to sleep,
appear during the last half of the first year, but
it is not until a child is about nine or ten years
old that the patterns assume an adult form
(Gibbs and Gibbs, 1964).

Robert Emde and his colleagues (1976) have
been trying to establish a connection between
the development of infant wave forms and the
appearance of certain emotional expressions, but
so far their data show no close relationships.
Alpha waves, which appear in adults when the
eyes are closed and little information processing
is going on, are present at birth, but the rhythm
appears to follow a course of gradual change
throughout childhood, assuming an adult form
when a child is between ten and fifteen years old.

Another form of electrical activity, called
evoked potential, is a measure of the brain's response to a new sight or sound. When Robert
Hoffman (1978) recorded changes in brain activity evoked by showing either checkerboards
or blank patterns to babies between the ages of
six and ten weeks, he discovered that the control of such sights shifts from a subcortical location to the visual cortex at about two months.
The magnitude of the brain's response to visual
stimulation shows a marked increase when the
child is five to seven years old, and a further
change in magnitude when the child is about
fifteen (Dustman and Beck, 1966). Complex
computer analyses of evoked potentials are now
being used to assess learning disabilities; they
are discussed in Chapter 13.

Yet another wave form—one that occurs
when a person waits expectantly to do some-

thing—first appears shortly after a child is six or seven and increases its stability as the child grows older (McCallum, 1969). Just what changes in neural organization underlie the emergence and development of this and other wave forms is unknown, but their existence suggests a complex pattern of maturation.

HEMISPHERIC SPECIALIZATION

The two halves of the brain have specialized functions. Even the apparent physical symmetry of the two hemispheres turns out to be an illusion, as Norman Geschwind (1979) has demonstrated. Geschwind examined a hundred human brains and found that the length and direction of the sylvian fissure are different in the two hemispheres and that part of the language area on the left side of the brain is noticeably larger than that same area on the right. The difference is not a recent development: casts made from fossil skulls indicate that Neanderthal man had an asymmetrical brain; and the brains of great apes—but not monkeys—also show evidence of asymmetry in the sylvian fissures. The difference is also apparent in the human fetus, which indicates, says Geschwind, that the enlarged language area in the adult brain is not a response to the development of linguistic competence; rather, the left hemisphere's linguistic talents may have a solid anatomical base. As we shall see, the asymmetry of the brain has a bearing on handedness, on language, on differences in information processing, and on cognitive differences between the sexes.

Dividing the Work

Each hemisphere of the brain receives sensations from and controls the voluntary muscles on the opposite side of the body (see Figure 7.3). For example, the left hemisphere controls the right hand and foot. Although each ear is connected to both halves of the brain, the strongest link is to the opposite hemisphere, which means that sounds from the right ear are interpreted by the left side of the brain. The eyes are more complicated. The visual field of each eye is split, so that images in the right half of each eye's field go to the left brain, and vice versa. So far, the division is symmetrical—each side of the brain handles half the body and half the visual field. The asymmetry appears when we move away from sensation and motor activities and examine complex forms of information processing, such as those involved in language, music, and spatial perception.

LANGUAGE In right-handed people, language is located in the left hemisphere. The two major sites are Broca's area, on the left side of the frontal lobe near the part of the motor cortex that controls the muscles used in speaking (face, tongue, lips, jaw, throat), and Wernicke's area, on the left side of the temporal lobe, between the auditory cortex and the angular gyrus—an area that seems to be involved in the connection of sounds and sights (Geschwind, 1979). A bundle of nerve fibers connects Broca's and Wernicke's areas.

The special role of this part of the brain has been discovered through the study of victims of strokes, brain tumors, and head injuries. When Broca's area is damaged, people have trouble speaking but can make themselves understood; their words come out slowly, and their sentences are not grammatical, nor are they complex. These patients seem to understand language, but research has shown that their apparent understanding is based on context and redundancy of information. When they must decode a message by processing the structure of a sentence, they understand little (Gardner, 1978). When Wernicke's area is damaged, words flow freely and sentences are grammatical, but they often fail to make sense and generally in-

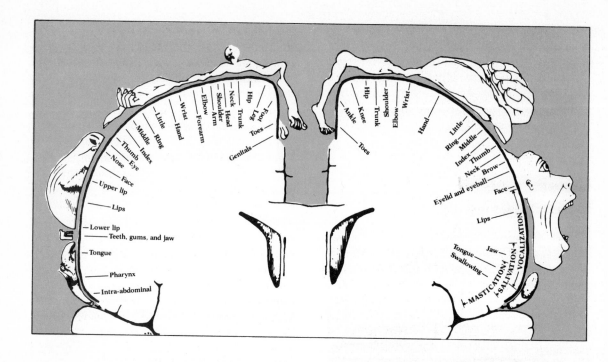

Figure 7.3 In this diagram, the right side of the brain is sliced through the motor and sensory areas of the cortex. The left side of the drawing locates areas that receive sensory information from various parts of the body; the right side locates the relative amount of brain space devoted to various motor functions.

clude nonsense syllables. These patients have no trouble understanding the structure of sentences; their lack of comprehension comes in the area of meaning (Gardner, 1978).

Such language disruptions are called *aphasias.* A patient with Broca's aphasia, asked what kind of work he had done, answered very slowly, "Me . . . build——ing chairs, no, no, cab—— in——ets," taking forty seconds to get the words out. A patient with Wernicke's aphasia, asked the same question, replied, "We, the kids, all of us, and I, we were working for a long time in the . . . you know . . . it's the kind of space, I mean place, rear to the spedwan" (Gardner, 1978).

A baby's ability to speak follows the maturation of cortical tissue in the language areas, just as the ability to control his or her body follows maturation in the motor cortex. Brenda Milner (1976) has traced the maturation of Broca's area and indicates that the emergence of speech accompanies cell maturation and the growth of neuronal connections there. The area appears to mature from the bottom up, with the two deepest of the six cortical layers beginning to mature when babies are about a month old. Uniquely human thought processes are believed to be dependent on the top three layers of cortical tissue, and about the time babies begin to learn their first words, myelination is spreading through the third of these layers. By the time children begin to put words together, this layer

The strides these young children make in acquiring language are accompanied by changes in Broca's area of the left hemisphere, where connections are spreading between neurons and myelination is progressing rapidly. (© Linda Ferrer 1981/Woodfin Camp & Assoc.)

of Broca's area is mostly myelinated, a process that is complete by the time children are about four. During this entire period, connections between neurons are spreading, with an especially rapid burst of growth about the time children learn to put two words together.

MUSIC AND SPATIAL PERCEPTION The right side of the brain also has its area of specialization. The perception of melodies and other nonspeech sounds—such as coughing,

laughing, and crying—seems to be processed in the right hemisphere (Kimura, 1975). The perception and analysis of visual patterns also seem to be the work of this hemisphere. People who have had their left temporal lobes removed have trouble remembering words, but their memories of melodies, faces, spatial locations, and abstract visual patterns is as good as ever (Geschwind, 1979). People with damage to the right hemisphere have trouble drawing, finding their way from one place to another, and building models from a plan or picture (Kimura, 1975). Their emotional responses may also be inappropriate, and they cannot detect emotion in the speech of others; they are unable to tell, for example, whether a statement is made in a joking or angry fashion (Geschwind, 1979). Because of this localization, right hemisphere damage often leads to inappropriate and disordered behavior, as if the patient's world had gone awry (Gardner, 1978).

Some researchers believe that each hemisphere processes information in a different fashion, with the left hemisphere handling sequential, logical processing, and the right handling simultaneous, intuitive processing (Ornstein, 1978). In this view, each hemisphere can process any kind of material, but each processes certain kinds more effectively. Joyce Schwartz and Paula Tallal (1980) believe that the left hemisphere's efficiency in language may come in part from its speed in processing rapidly changing events. When speech is slowed perceptibly, they have found, it can be processed in the right hemisphere. As research goes on, it becomes apparent that although certain areas are specialized in their function, many areas have overlapping functions, which interact to produce integrated behavior (Gazzaniga, 1975).

The Important Connection

The two halves of the brain are connected by the *corpus callosum*, a wide, arched band of myelinated fibers. If this connection is completely severed, as has been done surgically to stop seizures in some epileptics, the left brain literally does not know what the right brain is doing. (See Figure 7.4.) When a special apparatus flashes pictures or words to only the left visual field, for example, these split-brain patients will say they have seen nothing. The left hemisphere, which processes language, has not seen the material. If they handle an object, such as a spoon, with the left hand and are not allowed to look at it, they will deny that they have ever handled the spoon; but with the left hand, they will point out the spoon as the object they have handled (Gazzaniga, 1977).

At birth the corpus callosum is not completely formed, and it matures very slowly, being one of the last systems to myelinate. Since myelination is not complete in this area until after a child is ten years old, say David Galin and his associates (1979), it is reasonable to wonder how integrated the world seems to a young child. Galin's group tested three- and five-year-old right-handed girls in order to discover how early certain kinds of information are transferred between the hemispheres. They covered small, two-inch-square pillows with various fabrics whose textures varied—such as rayon, wool, linen, and denim. With the child placed so that she could not see the pillow, they rubbed a

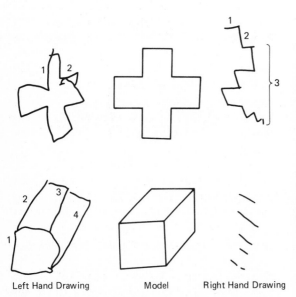

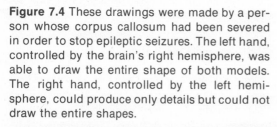

Left Hand Drawing   Model   Right Hand Drawing

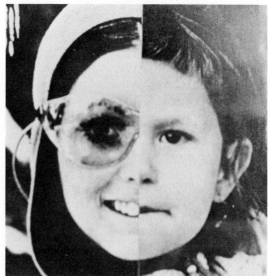

Figure 7.4 These drawings were made by a person whose corpus callosum had been severed in order to stop epileptic seizures. The left hand, controlled by the brain's right hemisphere, was able to draw the entire shape of both models. The right hand, controlled by the left hemisphere, could produce only details but could not draw the entire shapes.

(SOURCE: From "The Split Brain in Man" by Michael S. Gazzaniga, *Scientific American*, August 1967. Reprinted by permission.)

When patients with a severed corpus callosum are shown this composite photograph of a woman and a little boy, then asked to select the picture that they have seen from a group of six other photos, patients say "the child"—which is the picture the left half of their brain has perceived. But asked to *point* to the picture they have seen, they will invariably select the photo of a woman with spectacles—the picture the right half of their brain has perceived. (© Philip Daly 1967)

fabric over one of her hands. Using either the same or a different fabric, they next rubbed either that same hand or the other hand. The child's job was to say whether the two fabrics were the same or not. Although five-year-olds made the same number of correct guesses whether the fabrics were rubbed on only one hand (sending messages to only one side of the brain) or on both hands (sending messages to both sides of the brain), three-year-olds found the judgment extremely difficult when both hands were involved. They did as well as the five-year-olds, however, when only a single hand was involved.

This study shows that although the hemispheres may function autonomously in very young children, communication between them improves greatly by the time the child is five years old. Galin's group tested only the sense of touch, which is a very simple kind of transfer, and they point out that the corpus callosum of five-year-olds may not be mature enough for the transfer of more complicated information — such as that involving evaluations and decisions.

LATERALIZATION

It was once thought that *lateralization* (the establishment of functions in one hemisphere or the other) had not begun at birth and that the brain was not completely lateralized until a child reached adolescence (Lenneberg, 1967) — a judgment based on cases of childhood brain damage and its effect on language learning. Recent studies, however, have found evidence of asymmetry as early as researchers have chosen to look for it; and in some areas, lateralization appears to be complete at a young age. In addition to establishing specific functions in each hemisphere (see Figure 7.5), lateralization includes the establishment of *cerebral dominance.* In people with left-hemisphere dominance, the right hand and the right ear become more proficient than the left; whereas in people with

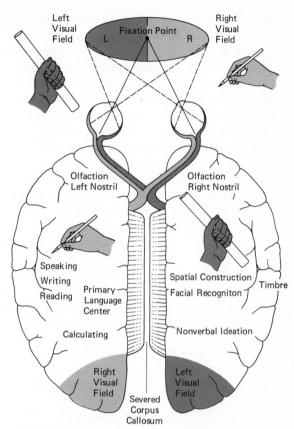

Figure 7.5 Each side of the brain controls half of the visual field; in addition, each hemisphere performs some tasks better than the other. When the corpus callosum is severed, as shown in the drawing, one half of the brain literally does not know what the other half is doing.

right-hemisphere dominance, the left hand and the left ear are generally more adept. But as we shall see, the division is not always as neat as theory would have it.

The Course of Lateralization

Differences in the way the brain processes linguistic and nonlinguistic auditory stimulation appear to develop very early in life (Molfese, Freeman, and Palermo, 1975). When infants hear consonant-vowel sounds or extended passages of speech, their brain-wave recordings show greater cortical activity over the left than over the right hemisphere. When they hear musical chords or passages of music, however, the right hemisphere shows increased cortical activity compared with the left hemisphere. More recent studies by Dennis Molfese and Victoria Molfese (1979) found that even among newborn infants, special mechanisms within the left hemisphere detect and analyze the sounds of human speech. The investigators played speech syllables while newborns slept and recorded the evoked potentials from each hemisphere. Upon analysis, it became clear that the two hemispheres were processing the sounds differently. Although both hemispheres had some capacity to process the sounds, the left was faster than the right and was the only hemisphere to process some types of sounds.

To establish which hemisphere handles the processing of spoken communication, researchers also use a *dichotic-listening technique,* in which two stimuli are presented at the same time, one to each ear. Although the test is also regarded as a measure of ear dominance, an individual is more likely to report hearing the stimulus that was transmitted to the hemisphere where language is processed (Studdert-Kennedy and Shankweiler, 1970). Studies using this technique indicate that right-ear superiority becomes established quite early in the majority of children. It has been found, for example, that when children hear such nouns as "ball," "cup," and "dog," they already show right-ear preference by three years, the youngest age tested (Ingram, 1975b). After seven, the advantage of the right ear does not increase relative to the left (Geffen, 1976); but as language abilities improve, children are more likely to be able to report the stimuli directed simultaneously to both ears. Paul Mirabile and his colleagues (1978) found that the ability to report both syllables increased steadily until children were eleven years old, but that between eleven and fifteen there was no further improvement.

Although some studies have indicated that spatial operations have been established in the right hemisphere by the time a child is five years old (Carter and Kinsbourne, 1979), others indicate that spatial ability is lateralized between eight and ten years. In an experiment conducted by Randall Flanery and John Balling (1979), right-handed children and adults were asked to slip their hands beneath a curtain and feel geometric forms cut from a sheet of linoleum. First the children felt a form with one hand, then they felt either the same or a different form with the other hand. The task was to report whether they had felt the same or different forms. First and third graders were no better with their left than with their right hands, but beginning with the fifth grade, the left hand was clearly superior at discriminating the three-dimensional forms. Fifth graders and adults were better at identifying forms with their left hands, even though they often said they could explore the shapes better with their right hands.

Handedness

A puzzle in the field of motor development is handedness. Only 5 to 10 percent of the world's adult population are left-handed, although a full 15 percent of preschoolers are "lefties." The frequency of left-handedness in both identical and fraternal twins is significantly higher than it is among single births (Hicks and Kinsbourne, 1976). But there is no known genetic or constitutional basis for handedness (Hardyck and Petrinovich, 1977). However, according to Geschwind (1979), Marian Annett, a British researcher, proposes that right-handedness is influenced by the presence of a single allele in a gene pair (a concept discussed in Chapter 4), and that there is no corresponding allele for left-handedness. If the right-handed allele is not present, the use of the right or left hand will be randomly determined. On the other hand, the facts suggest at least a partially experiential basis for handedness. Rhesus monkeys, who do not encounter human society, split half and half into left- and right-handers; and continued breeding of right-handed animals does not increase the percentage of right-handers among their offspring (Geschwind, 1979).

Handedness begins to become evident in the latter part of the first year. Almost as soon as infants can use their two hands independently, most of them prefer the right. Several findings suggest that this preference develops according to a timetable. Immediately after birth, a tendency to turn rightward is apparent in most babies (Kinsbourne and Swanson, 1979), and when young babies turn their heads, they will extend an arm in the direction in which the head is turned. This asymmetrical posture, called the tonic neck reflex, predicts which hand they will later prefer, because the arm they extend reflexively is likely to be that of the dominant side. By about three months, most infants tend to hold a toy longer when it is placed in the right hand than when it is placed in the left; and by about six to nine months, most babies prefer to use the right hand when reaching for an object that is directly in front of them. Douglas Ramsay (1979) has found that by fifteen months, when a xylophone baton is placed in the left hand, babies tend to transfer it to the right in order to tap the instrument before them. Those who keep the baton in the left hand tap the xylophone more slowly than those who transfer the baton to the right hand.

Because in nearly all adult right-handers and some left-handers the left side of the brain is responsible for the production and comprehension of language, several investigators (e.g., Bay, 1975) have suggested that both the onset of handedness and the beginning of speech may be due to the establishment of the left hemisphere's dominance in the control of motor functions. Handedness and speech certainly appear to be connected. From about twelve months, most infants begin to use their hands in coordination, adopting a consistent right- and left-hand strategy when faced with a task that requires both hands (Ramsay, Campos, and Fenson, 1979). The preference may develop as early as ten months or as late as seventeen

months. In exploring toys with movable parts, right-handed babies are likely to hold the base of the toy in the left hand and manipulate its movable parts with the right. This is just about the time most babies begin to talk. In a longitudinal study, Ramsay (1980) found that this consistent strategy appeared either at the same time or just before babies first put together dissimilar syllables to form words ("daddy," "baby," "pretty").

Children continue to make definite improvements in the adeptness and accuracy of their preferred hands. When Donna Piazza (1977) asked three-year-olds to tap out a given sequence with their fingers, most showed greater ability with the right than with the left hand. This superior right-handed performance reflects greater experience and practice with the preferred hand; but it also indicates an increase in the dominance of the brain's left hemisphere and specialization in the serial organization of motor skills.

Although right-handed children show agility with their preferred hands, they are likely to perform certain skills better with the left. Dianna Ingram (1975a) found, for example, that by the time children are three, they do better with the left hand than with the right when they try to imitate hand postures modeled by another person. Blind children scan braille better with the left hand than with the right (Hermelin and O'Connor, 1971); but this left-handed superiority is what we would expect, since the left hand is controlled by the brain's right hemisphere—the hemisphere that is superior at processing spatial information.

Research on left-handers has produced mixed findings, perhaps because only about 60 percent of the people who think they are left-handed are solely left-handed when tested. The brains of most left- and right-handed people appear to be organized differently; although about 60 percent of left-handers process language in the left hemisphere, nearly all right-handers do. The rest use either the right hemisphere or both sides of the brain to process language. This

The cause of handedness is unknown, but the dominant right hand is usually accompanied by a dominant left hemisphere and often by a dominant right ear and right eye as well. The connection in left-handers is less clear. (© Camilla Smith)

apparent difference in brain organization showed up in a study by J. Lomas and Doreen Kimura (1976), who found that when right-handers tap with the right hand it interferes with speech, but when they tap with the left hand, it does not. However, whichever hand left-handers tap with, tapping interferes with speech.

Developmental research on sighting dominance — that is, which eye's muscles control the point on which both eyes focus — suggests that sighting dominance may become established earlier than ear or hand dominance. In studies of sighting dominance, Stanley Coren (1974) carried out an experiment in which a light

shining from directly between and in front of the eyes was gradually brought toward the face. The eye that suddenly stopped converging or that diverged was the dominant eye. Coren found that a majority of year-old infants showed sighting dominance when tested in this manner, and that the incidence of right-eye dominance did not change among older children. But not all right-handed adults are right-eyed; among adults, as among children, approximately 65 percent of the right-handed show right-eye dominance (Dziadosz and Schaller, 1977).

A large minority of children and adults show no expected associations among handedness, ear or eye preference, and cerebral dominance. In one study of three- to five-year-old right-handed children, Merrill Hiscock and Marcel Kinsbourne (1977) found that only 60 percent showed a right-ear dominance when listening to numbers. In another study of three- to five-year-old right-handers, Ingram (1975b) found no relation between ear preference and the hand preferred for gesturing during speech. Because mixed patterns of dominance occur frequently among normal children and adults—and might even be associated with superior abilities in processing various types of information (Kershner, 1974)—it is clear that interaction between the two hemispheres and the rest of the brain is quite complicated.

Sex Differences

There are indications that brain development differs in boys and girls. Jesse LeRoy Conel (1963) found some evidence that at about age four, neural tissue grows and matures earlier in a girl's left hemisphere and in a boy's right hemisphere. Another study (Taylor, 1969) suggests that the female brain matures more rapidly and that hemispheric dominance emerges earlier than it does in the male brain.

Girls show an early advantage in verbal abilities. After surveying studies of sex differences, Eleanor Maccoby and Carol Jacklin (1974) concluded that boys appear to catch up with girls at about three years of age, but that by the time they are ten, girls are again superior on all tests of verbal ability. And their superiority continues to increase, at least through high school. Girls are better at comprehending complex written material, at understanding complex logical relations expressed in verbal terms, and at the verbal aspects of divergent thinking—a measure of creativity that involves the production of unusual responses. Boys, on the other hand, are better at higher mathematics (but not at arithmetic); the difference has fully emerged by adolescence, and it remains even when boys are compared with girls who have taken as many mathematics courses as the boys have. Male superiority on tests of spatial ability is also firmly established by early adolescence.

Corinne Hutt (1972) is among those who have tried to show that the earlier dominance of the left hemisphere in girls explains their superior verbal abilities. There is also speculation that boys demonstrate superior spatial abilities because the left hemisphere becomes dominant later, and less completely, in males than in females. This hypothesis is supported by more recent research, which suggests a greater right-hemisphere specialization in boys than in girls for visual-spatial and other nonverbal skills. Sandra Witelson (1976), for example, had children explore by touch alone two differently shaped objects presented at the same time, one to each hand. The children then tried to identify the objects they had felt with each hand by selecting ones like them from a group of six variously shaped objects. Witelson found that by the time they were six, boys found it easier to identify shapes with their left hands, whereas girls identified shapes equally well with either hand.

Somewhat different results appeared when Joseph Cioffi and Gillray Kandel (1979) had boys and girls from six to fourteen years old identify three-dimensional objects—shapes like those used by Witelson, two-letter words (TO, IT), or paired consonants (CM, HC). In this study, boys and girls were generally equal in their ability to identify most stimuli, and the older the children, the more accurate their identifications. When Cioffi and Kandel looked closely at their results, however, they found some differences in the way each sex processed the material. Both boys and girls identified nonsense shapes better if they felt them with their left hands and words better if they felt them with their right hands, and neither sex showed an advantage at these tasks. When it came to the paired consonants, however, boys did better using the left hand, whereas girls did much better using the right hand. The boys apparently processed the consonant pairs as if they were shapes, the girls as if they were linguistic stimuli—a difference that could affect reading skills. The researchers suggest that the difference is a matter of degree. The two hemispheres' specializations for language and for spatial processing appear to be a relative superiority, they say, and not an ability that is limited to one of

The brain appears to develop differently in boys and girls, and these girls may use both hemispheres in visual-spatial tasks whereas the boy may rely on his right hemisphere. (© Robert V. Eckert, Jr./EKM-Nepenthe)

the two hemispheres. There is, of course, always the possibility that information may have been passed back and forth through the corpus callosum.

In another study, Peter Wolff and Irving Hurwitz (1976) found that after children are about five years old, girls are more accurate with both hands than are boys when asked to reproduce a series of taps. Taken together, the results of the studies described seem to indicate either that boys use the right hemisphere more than girls do in performing visual-spatial tasks or that girls use both hemispheres in such tasks.

These differences between the sexes may depend on a connection between the rate of brain maturation and sexual maturation. Since thir-

teen-year-old girls were still using both hemispheres in identifying objects by touch in Witelson's experiment, she concluded that girls use both hemispheres to process spatial information at least until adolescence. Studies by Deborah Waber (1976, 1977) take a different approach to the subject. Waber studied adolescent boys and girls and found that, regardless of sex, those who reached sexual maturity early performed better on verbal than on spatial tasks, whereas those who reached sexual maturity late performed better on spatial than on verbal tasks. Boys and girls who reached puberty late were better at spatial tasks than those who matured early, but the reverse was not true; early puberty did not give the early maturers an advantage over late maturers on tests of verbal ability. Waber proposed that the differences she found are due to differences in the rate of sexual maturation. Girls generally mature earlier than boys, and Waber suggests that the effects of sex hormones on the brain at puberty, rather than biological differences at birth, may account for general male superiority on spatial tasks. If she is right, it would mean that whatever neural structures are responsible for hemisphere dominance must be especially sensitive to sex hormones.

If the reported differences in hemisphere dominance between the sexes are biologically based, can these differences be modified by experience? Studies have found that on visual-spatial tasks, which are performed more efficiently by the right hemisphere, training improves performance among girls but not among boys (Connor, Serbin, and Schackman, 1977). This suggests that any biological differences in cerebral organization are likely to be influenced in a complicated way by experience. It also suggests that although right-hemisphere tasks may not come as easily to girls as they do to boys, girls may be as capable as boys of acquiring them. Some investigators (e.g., Wittig and Peterson, 1979) have more recently suggested that sex-based differences in cognitive performance and brain function, although measurable, are neither large nor impressive.

PLASTICITY

The developing brain is not rigid. As a child grows, functions that have been impaired as a result of brain damage tend to be restored or to become established in other parts of the brain. This plasticity of the nervous system means that experience itself can modify the tissue of the developing brain.

Stimulation

The relationship between growth of particular cortical areas and the development of motor function is correlational. Since correlations do not tell us what is cause and what is effect, some authors have argued that the baby's use of his or her body and nervous system causes growth of appropriate brain areas, rather than brain growth leading to increased physical and mental control. Steven Rose (1973) is among those who suggest that the barrage of sensory information that assails the newborn when the infant emerges from the shelter of the uterus leads the cortex to grow and neural connections to develop.

Experiments with animals indicate that stimulation—or the lack of it—can affect brain development. Mark Rosenzweig and his colleagues (1972) carried out a lengthy series of experiments in which they raised rats under conditions either of sensory enrichment (new toys every day, space, a view of the laboratory, and company) or of sensory deprivation (no toys, small cage, nothing to see, and a solitary existence). When the brains of these rats were later examined, Rosenzweig's group found that the brains of the privileged rats had heavier and thicker cerebral cortexes than the brains of the underprivileged rats, and they found a difference in the amount and activity of two enzymes.

The cortexes of the privileged rats also were heavier in relation to the rest of the brain and had fewer and larger neurons, and more glial cells. The privileged rats also had many fewer synapses in a particular area, but each synapse was larger and thicker, indicating increased activity. When Rosenzweig's group reared other rats in a large enclosure that resembled a natural environment, their brains had developed even more than those of their litter-mates who had been kept in the enriched laboratory environment. In an opposite approach, David Hubel and Thorsten Wiesel (1963) found that prolonged rearing in the dark led not only to a failure of neural connections to develop in kittens' brains but also to an atrophy of connections that were present at birth.

R. A. Cummins and his colleagues (1979) have suggested that some neurons are "environment-dependent" and will not develop if an animal's cortex is not generally aroused by experience. They go on to suggest that there is a developmental ceiling for brain development and that once that ceiling is reached, additional stimulation will not increase brain growth. Because these studies have been conducted with animals, no one is absolutely certain what happens in the developing human brain. A certain degree of maturation may be necessary before stimulation has its effects, however, because studies of premature human babies show that they reach various motor milestones at what would be the same age as full-term babies if age were calculated from the moment of conception rather than from the time of birth. On the other hand, as a result of their early birth, the premature babies have received an extra month or two of external stimulation (Douglas, 1956).

Recovery From Brain Damage

The plasticity of the baby's nervous system may be the result of its extensive, rapid growth.

It has been found that when infants are born with a malformed major brain tract, their nervous system may correct for it, possibly by developing the same function in a different area. In addition, when a baby suffers brain damage, the child often recovers quickly and shows no apparent aftereffects (Searleman, 1977).

The most extensively studied aspect of recovery from brain damage is in the area of language function. Eric Lenneberg (1967) studied twenty-five case reports of children who had suffered brain damage from accident or illness at ages ranging from twenty months to eighteen years. In children who were less than three when their brains were damaged, language learning came to an abrupt halt, only to begin all over again from the beginning. Such a child once again babbled, produced single words, and then advanced to two-word phrases. The process of recovery was one of language acquisition. Children who were three or four went through a period when their language learning was interfered with; but they soon recovered and continued the course of language acquisition. Children between the ages of four and ten went through a period of aphasia similar to that suffered by adults; then the aphasia subsided and the child's grasp of language returned. Once children reached puberty, the picture changed. Those who were injured early in adolescence regained language but had to search for words and often uttered inappropriate words or sounds, whose emission they appeared unable to control. After fifteen or so, recovery was like that of adults. In some cases there was a temporary aphasia, which gradually cleared as physiological functions were restored. In other cases, there was permanent aphasia of varying degrees. Lenneberg suggests that with young children, damage to the left hemisphere simply leads to a switch of language function to the right side of the brain. With older children, there is a period of speech disturbance that is overcome within two years, as language function on the right side is gradually strengthened. With adolescents and adults, whose brains have lost most of their plasticity, some degree of damage may well be permanent.

More recent studies have indicated that Lenneberg was too pessimistic and that the adult brain retains some degree of plasticity. Aaron Smith (1978) studied eighty adult aphasics who had received language therapy and fifteen who had received no therapy. Language function improved significantly in aphasics who had received therapy, although on tests of nonlanguage function they did not improve. The control cases showed either negligible gains or slight losses. Smith believes that patients who improve have transferred some degree of language function to the right hemisphere.

Ian St. James-Roberts (1978), who has reviewed both animal and human studies—including the cases examined by Lenneberg—has concluded that the baby's brain is less plastic and the adult brain more plastic than most researchers have believed. He suggests that the brain, like any other organ, tends to heal itself and that disruptions of behavior immediately after an accident or disease tell us nothing about the nature of tissue damage. Instead, the immediate disturbances reflect a general disruption of the central nervous system. There may have been no cell destruction at all, and once the disruptive influences have cleared, the brain recovers. Where there is cell destruction, the brain may be able to repair itself by regenerating portions of nerve cells, so that old connections are reestablished or new connections are established on the other side of damaged tissue. St. James-Roberts also indicates that brain damage due to head injuries is much more likely to be temporary than injury due to disease, strokes, or any other internal damage.

LEARNING DISORDERS

It has been estimated that 3 percent of the population cannot learn to read at all (Gardner, 1975). A much larger proportion experience difficulties in school, difficulties that seem related to central nervous system functioning, not to mental retardation. Two of these conditions are developmental dyslexia and hyperactivity.

Developmental Dyslexia

Children with developmental dyslexia have no trouble talking, recognizing numbers, and understanding instruction in mathematics, science, or history; but they have enormous difficulty trying to read, write, or spell. Their basic problem seems to be an inability to connect written symbols to the sounds they make. As a result, they are reduced to learning words as units; they simply cannot sound out a word from its letters (Gardner, 1975). Dyslexic children often try to read words from right to left and tend to confuse letters that differ only in their spatial position, such as "d," "b," "q," and "p."

After testing dyslexics for lateralization, Sandra Witelson (1979) concluded that children with this affliction have developed spatial abilities in both hemispheres and that the processing of spatial information in the left hemisphere interferes with language ability. Among the battery of tests Witelson used with dyslexics was the identification of shapes by touch. She found that dyslexics are as good at identifying shapes with the right hand as with the left. Since lateralization appears to be present from birth, Witelson believes that instead of being the result of a lag in development, as some researchers have suggested, dyslexia is the result of a different kind of brain organization.

Paul Rozin (1976) has tried to solve the problems of dyslexic children by focusing on the lack of connection between sight and sound. Reading a phonetically based alphabet, he says, involves access to the phonological system, which is tightly wired into the specialized speech system. Some children find this process — connecting the auditory system to the visual system used in reading — extremely simple; others find it extremely difficult. This problem does not occur with a pictorially based language such as Chinese, Rozin indicates; he points to the prevalence of reading disability in the United States and the virtual lack of it in Japan, where the written language includes a proportion of Chinese-type characters.

With Lila Glietman, Rozin has devised a system in which dyslexic children first learn to interpret pictures, then move to "reading" regular drawings that depict each word (a tin can for the word "can," for example). See Figure 7.6. Once they have mastered this stage they begin to focus on sounds and soon go on to building words in which each syllable is a different drawing (picture for *sand* + picture for *witch* = sandwich). Finally, the children graduate to blending letters. Rozin has used this method successfully to teach reading to inner-city first-grade children who seemed unable to learn by conventional methods.

Hyperactivity

Hyperactivity is a childhood disorder that afflicts five to nine times as many boys as girls. Between 1 and 5 percent of the population have been diagnosed as hyperactive, and it has been estimated that 600,000 American schoolchildren take drugs to control the condition (Weiss and Hechtman, 1979).

Hyperactive children generally are extremely restless. As toddlers, they crawl, run, and climb incessantly; in middle childhood and adolescence, they find it difficult to sit still, and they fidget continually. Because they find it hard to sustain their attention, they fail to complete tasks they begin. And they perform poorly in unsupervised situations. Hyperactive children are impulsive: they talk out of turn, interrupt others, have trouble playing games that involve taking turns, seem unable to tolerate frustration, and fight with other children.

As James Swanson and Marcel Kinsbourne (1979) point out, almost any child shows every symptom linked with hyperactivity at some time. In order to be labeled hyperactive, such

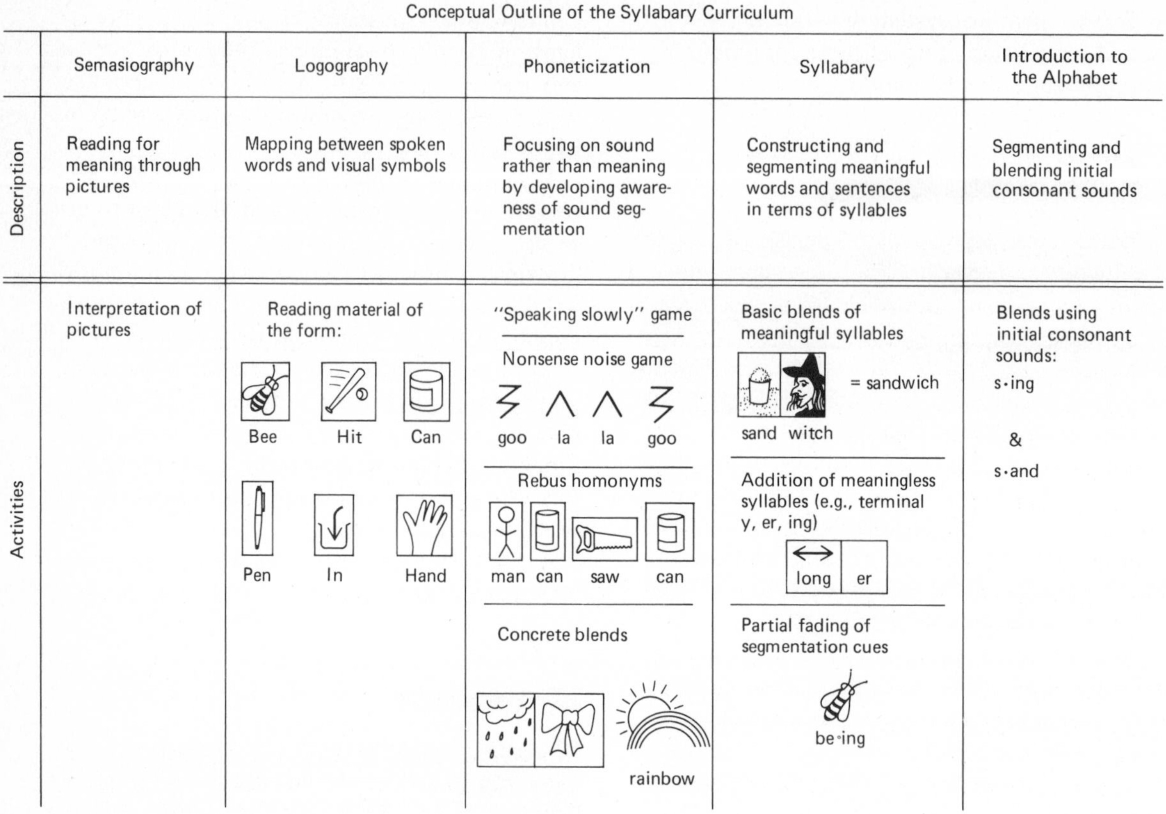

Conceptual Outline of the Syllabary Curriculum

	Semasiography	Logography	Phoneticization	Syllabary	Introduction to the Alphabet
Description	Reading for meaning through pictures	Mapping between spoken words and visual symbols	Focusing on sound rather than meaning by developing awareness of sound segmentation	Constructing and segmenting meaningful words and sentences in terms of syllables	Segmenting and blending initial consonant sounds
Activities	Interpretation of pictures	Reading material of the form: Bee Hit Can Pen In Hand	"Speaking slowly" game; Nonsense noise game: goo la la goo; Rebus homonyms: man can saw can; Concrete blends: rainbow	Basic blends of meaningful syllables: sand witch = sandwich; Addition of meaningless syllables (e.g., terminal y, er, ing): long er; Partial fading of segmentation cues: be·ing	Blends using initial consonant sounds: s·ing & s·and

Figure 7.6 Some dyslexic children, who cannot connect sight and sound, have learned to read through this method devised by Paul Rozin and Lila Glietman. Children first interpret pictures, then read drawings that stand for words, before they are introduced to the alphabet.

(SOURCE: From "Conceptual Outline of the Syllabary Curriculum," by Paul Rozin, in "The Evolution of Intelligence and Access to the Cognitive Unconscious," in J. M. Sprague and A. N. Epstein (eds.), *Progress in Psychobiology and Physiological Psychology*, Vol. 6. New York: Academic Press, 1976. Reprinted by permission.)

behavior must occur constantly and in inappropriate situations. Because of the wide overlap between "normal" and "hyperactive" behavior, a principal problem is diagnosis. It has been suggested that the school situation, in which children are required to sit still for long periods of time, may be responsible for what appears to be a higher than normal incidence of hyperactivity in this country (up to 5 or 6 percent of children in some city schools) (McGuinness, 1979).

No one is sure just what causes hyperactivity. At one time, researchers thought it was the result of structural damage to the central nervous system, so many referred to it as *minimal brain damage* (MBD). Later it was decided that the brain's structure was probably intact, but that the way it processed information was faulty, so MBD came to mean minimal brain *dysfunction*. Others said children with hyperactivity suffered from learning disabilities and attached that tag

What Happens When the Drug Wears Off?

Hyperactive children often are treated with stimulant drugs. The practice is controversial, some charging that drugs are prescribed indiscriminately, that they have become a substitute for parental control, or that they may mask some other neurological disorder (Schrag and Divoky, 1975). As noted in the text, the treatment often seems to be effective while children are taking the drugs; some parents and teachers say that as many as 90 percent of children receiving such treatment show marked improvement in their behavior at school and at home (Whalen *et al.*, 1979), but researchers who have tested children in laboratories have found that only between 60 and 70 percent showed improved performance with drugs (Swanson and Kinsbourne, 1979).

It is supposed that the "normal" state of hyperactive children is one of underarousal. The drugs work at subcortical levels, increasing the level of arousal and permitting children to sustain their attention and to inhibit impulsive responses. Hyperactive children who have taken one of the stimulants respond faster and make fewer unnecessary responses than those who have no drug in their systems (Douglas and Peters, 1979). Studies have shown, however, that the drug wears off rapidly and must be taken at least three times a day for its effect to be consistent (Swanson and Kinsbourne, 1979).

The rapid dissipation of stimulant drugs from the system carries with it another problem, that of state-dependent learning. Both animal and human studies have shown that what is learned under the influence of certain drugs, including alcohol and tranquilizers, tends to be forgotten when the drug wears off, although it may be recalled if another dose of the drug is taken (Overton, 1969).

James Swanson and Marcel Kinsbourne (1979) have discovered that drugs given for hyperactivity tend to have the same effect. They had hyperactive children learn to associate pictures of animals with their locations in a hypothetical zoo. The task required them to concentrate for fifteen to twenty-five minutes while sitting in the same place and following the instructions of an adult—a condition that approximates normal classroom situations. Half the children took Ritalin; the other half took a placebo (an inactive substance made to look like the drug they normally took). Hyperactive children who had taken Ritalin made fewer errors while learning the location of each animal than did hyperactive children who had taken a placebo. But when the conditions were changed the next day, the state-dependent effect turned up. Children who had been switched from Ritalin to a placebo seemed to have forgotten everything; they made as many errors in trying to recall the locations of the animals as they had the day before when they first learned them. Children who were still taking the drug, however, remembered the locations well, making few errors in their attempts to recall what they had learned. Since what children on Ritalin remember is linked to the presence of the drug in their bodies, it is no wonder the drug has no long-term effect, indicate Swanson and Kinsbourne. These researchers are now exploring the state-dependent effects of stimulant drugs on other kinds of information processing, such as spelling and reading comprehension.

Since all normal children show some symptoms linked with hyperactivity, diagnosing a child as hyperactive must be done with caution. (© Suzanne Szasz)

to them. Hyperactive children do often have learning problems, but many learning disabilities have nothing to do with hyperactivity. The confusion in terms has led to a confusion in the search for a cause and even for an exact description of the disorder (Douglas and Peters, 1979). Today, the American Psychiatric Association

(1980) calls the disorder an "attentional problem, with or without hyperactivity."

Hyperactivity has been attributed to genetic factors, to brain damage, to an imbalance of neurotransmitters (especially dopamine and norepinephrine), to food additives, to lead, and to allergies. It has been suggested, on the one hand, that hyperactive children are simply extreme examples of an inherited temperamental type (Swanson and Kinsbourne, 1979) and on the other, that lagging brain development — as shown in EEGs that do not become normal until adolescence — is the basis of the disorder (Weiss and Hechtman, 1979). It may be that hyperactivity is a term covering a flock of disorders that manifest themselves in similar ways. Virginia Douglas and Kenneth Peters (1979) describe hyperactive children as impulsive creatures who have an unusual need for stimulation and difficulty in concentrating — especially on dull, repetitive tasks.

Treatment of hyperactivity varies. Among the methods used are diet, stimulant drugs (especially Ritalin and amphetamines), behavior modification, and cognitive training — in which children are taught skills that lessen their tendencies to act impulsively. All treatments appear to work for a short time, but none has been shown to have any long-term benefit (Swanson and Kinsbourne, 1979).

Hyperactive children who have been followed into adolescence continue to deal with the world in an impulsive manner (Weiss and Hechtman, 1979). Although on the average they had an impulsive life style, a year's less schooling, and a much higher involvement in motorcycle and automobile accidents than adolescents in a control group, some of the problems of the hyperactive group seemed to ameliorate as they got away from school. Although their high-school teachers continued to rate them as inferior to controls, employers found no difference between hyperactive adolescents and controls on any measure — an indication that the setting may have had a good deal to do with the decision that hyperactive children are a problem.

SUMMARY

1. Human brains are larger in proportion to body mass than the brains of our early ancestors. As the brain evolved, the old structures shrank in relative size and new ones developed, which assumed some of the old functions and took on some new functions. The newest part of the brain, the cortex, is responsible for language, attention, memory, spatial understanding, motor skills, and logical thought.

2. As specific areas in the cortex develop, the corresponding functions appear in a baby's behavior. About thirty different chemicals act as messengers in the brain, conducting nerve impulses from one neuron to the next. Little is known about the developmental course of neurotransmitters, although we do know that brain protein changes as children grow and that protein plays a part in both the production and the storage of transmitters. As children grow, electrical activity in the brain changes, with various patterns reaching adult forms at ages varying from six to fifteen years.

3. Each side of the brain receives sensations from and controls the voluntary muscles on the opposite side of the body. Each hemisphere also appears to have specialized functions, with the left hemisphere more efficient than the right at language, and the right hemisphere more efficient at analyzing visual patterns, music, spatial locations, and emotions. The corpus callosum, which transfers information between the hemispheres and perhaps integrates a person's world, is not fully myelinated until a child is ten years old.

4. Some evidence of lateralization (the establishment of functions in one or the other of the hemispheres) is present at birth, and it apparently increases during early and middle childhood. Handedness, which may be due to either genetic or experiential influences, begins to develop in the latter part of the first year. About 40 percent of all left-handed people process language in the right hemisphere.

5. The brain develops somewhat differently in boys and girls, which may be one reason that girls are generally superior to boys in skills relating to language and boys are better at higher mathematics and spatial tasks.

6. It may be that some neurons will not develop if a baby's cortex is not aroused by experience. A baby's and a young child's brain appears to be more plastic than the brain of an adult, although the adult brain is capable of some repair. The brain repairs damage — perhaps by switching functions to different areas or perhaps by regenerating portions of nerve cells and making new connections around damaged tissue.

7. Children with developmental dyslexia cannot connect written symbols with the sounds they make, a condition that may be the result of a lag in development or of a different kind of brain organization. Hyperactive children, generally boys, are impulsive, seem to have an unusual need for stimulation, and often find it difficult to concentrate their attention. The cause of hyperactivity is unknown, misdiagnosis is common, and none of the treatments has a permanent effect.

PART 4

The Development of Language

Language enhances communication, but it is very much more than a means of conveying our emotions or immediate wants. Without language, nothing like human society could exist; for the ability to describe and explain—in speech, or in the marks on clay tablets or paper—allows human evolution to progress along cultural lines. Each generation does not have to re-invent the accomplishments of generations past. Language gives human beings the means to control one another, whether by request or command, by flattery or deceit, or by explanation. And as we shall see, language increases the power of memory and of thought. Without language, we should lack the lessons of past generations, the soaring heights of poetry, the opportunity to live other lives in story. Small wonder, then, that the acquisition of language is one of the most important aspects of human development.

Language: Self and Society

A toddler who had learned to get between-meal snacks by saying, "I want a cookie," one day discovered that her requests, although perfectly phrased, no longer worked. "You don't need a cookie," her mother would say, handing her a carrot stick. After several days of futile attempts to get a mid-morning cookie, the little girl tugged at her mother's skirt and said plaintively, "Mommy, Mommy, I *need* a cookie." This small girl's utterance was a social act, designed to have a specific effect upon the listener. As we shall see, language develops out of such social contexts, in which people use words to get things done.

By the time they are four years old, normal children all over the world have mastered the basic grammar of one or more of the world's thousands of different languages. Although each child hears a different set of sentences from the adults and children that he or she interacts with, all children exposed to a language learn to understand other speakers of that language. And the children end up with the same pronunciation, grammar, and vocabulary as the rest of their speech community. This means that each child in a speech community arrives at the same basic linguistic rules.

In order to understand just how the infant who can only babble soon becomes a master of a complicated language, it is necessary first to know something about the nature and function of language. In this chapter, we shall discuss the

Although animals do communicate with one another, none of their communication systems qualify as language because they lack semanticity, productivity, and displacement. (Miriam Amsterman/Animals, Animals)

nature of our uniquely human language and discover what qualities distinguish it from the communication of animals. After seeing how each of the various aspects of language lends itself to a different kind of study, we shall move on to a discussion of language function. There are, we shall find, private uses of language; and without language, our memory and thought processes would be impoverished. Next, we shall explore communication, the public use of language, discovering that long before babies utter their first words, language has begun to indoctrinate them into their culture. Finally, we shall look at social influences on language and note that socioeconomic and ethnic differences have their own effects on the way we speak.

HUMAN LANGUAGE

Language is a system of communication used within a particular social group, and no society —animal or human—can exist without commu-

nication (Burgess, 1975). How does the language of human beings differ from the communication of animals? After all, a worker bee dances on the floor of the hive to tell its fellow workers how far and in what direction to fly for nectar (Von Frisch, 1967). A father quail calls to warn his foraging family of approaching danger. Rats use chemical signals to communicate, aquatic insects use surface waves, land insects use vibrations, fish use electricity, and fireflies exchange light flashes. The members of different species also can learn to communicate. A dog whines, barks, and wriggles to ask its master for dinner, a game of ball, or a walk. A species of woodpecker learns to peck out a particular code to specify which of five kinds of food the bird wants from a researcher (Griffin, 1976). This communication between different species is particularly impressive when it comes from a chimpanzee that uses its hands, plastic chips, or a computer to answer a question or to ask for a drink. Yet, as the accompanying box indicates, even this last example falls short of language as most theorists view it.

The Properties of Human Language

Human language, suggests Roger Brown (1973), is set off from the communication systems of animals by three important properties: semanticity, productivity, and displacement. These properties are found in every human language, be it English, Russian, Chinese, or Urdu.

Semanticity refers to a language's meaningfulness—the fact that the symbols of the language represent an enormous variety of people, objects, events, and ideas. A mynah bird may mimic human speech perfectly, but it does not use these sounds in any meaningful way, so it cannot be said to possess language. And although the dance of the honey bee communicates meaning, the number of things that bees can "talk" about is quite small.

Productivity, the second property of language, is the ability to combine a finite number of words into an unlimited number of sentences. Except for common clichés, such as "How are you?" and "Have a nice day," almost every sentence we hear or speak is brand new (Chomsky, 1972). The productivity of language means that its speakers can communicate any kind of information about any topic in the world. Productivity appears to be limited to human beings, for none of the chimpanzees who have learned to use symbols can pass such a test of their ability to communicate.

Displacement, the last essential property of language, is the ability to communicate information about objects in another place or another time. Displacement is present in the child's language from the time he or she can ask for a cookie that is in the kitchen or for Father, who is at the office. Displacement is the property that allows us to transmit information from one generation to another so that we do not have to rediscover all knowledge every thirty years or so. The bee's dance uses displacement in denoting the location of nectar, but as with semanticity, displacement in the language of honeybees is limited to the subject of nectar.

Looking at Language

Human language is a system of social communication that uses sound to transmit meaning. As we have seen, it is also immensely productive, and can talk about near and distant places, past and future events, and abstractions. Developmental psychologists have generally approached language acquisition by looking at only one or another of these properties, and the one they choose to examine determines the sort of research they will do. These major avenues of language study are phonology, semantics, syntax, and pragmatics.

Phonology, or the study of speech sounds, concentrates on the sound patterns of language. Each language combines speech sounds, called *phonemes*, in some ways but not in others; and when a language fails to make a distinction between certain sounds, its native speakers do not notice the distinction themselves. The Japanese language, for example, makes no distinction between "r" and "l," so that when Japanese speak English they generally confuse the two sounds, saying "Herro" for "Hello," or "butterfries" for "butterflies." Similarly, English speakers make no distinction between the "t" in "tar" and the "t" in "star," so that when they learn certain Indian or African languages, they consistently substitute one of these sounds for the other (Fry, 1977). Because in these latter languages a change in the "t" sound changes meaning, English speakers often think they are saying one word when native speakers are hearing another.

Languages also use stress, tone, and intonation to affect meaning. In English, the intonation pattern is important; whether an utterance ends on a rising or falling note, for example, determines whether the utterance is a question or a statement. In Mixteco, the tone of a word determines its meaning; thus a certain sound spoken in a low tone means "mountain," and the same sound spoken in a medium tone means "brush" (Brown, 1958).

Research in developmental phonology concentrates on the child's progress in detecting and producing the sounds of speech. Investigators study what sounds or combinations of sounds children can detect; how their ability to detect various sounds changes with age and experience; and what sounds they produce, and when and in what order they produce them.

Semantics, or the study of meaning, reflects Brown's first essential property of language; it focuses on the content of language and on the meaning of various words and combinations. Researchers who study semantic development are interested in the way children form concepts — learning to map the word "cat," for example, onto the variety of four-footed animals they see running about, so that when they hear the word they immediately know that it refers to black cats and white, to cats with long or short hair, to big cats and little ones, but not to dogs, hamsters, skunks, or raccoons. Research in semantics also encompasses such topics as how children learn the meaning of prepositions ("under,"

Do Chimpanzees Talk?

For centuries, scientists and ordinary citizens agreed that it was language that set human beings apart from the rest of the animal kingdom. From time to time, unconvinced researchers have worked diligently with chimpanzees, hoping to prove that the gulf between species is much narrower than had been assumed.

Perhaps the most famous "talking" chimpanzee is Washoe, who began her language lessons with Beatrice and Allen Gardner (1969) at the University of Nevada. Washoe learned a limited amount of ASL (American Sign Language), the language of hand signs used by deaf Americans to communicate. Washoe learned 132 signs, which she combined in strings such as "Please sweet drink" and "Key open please blanket" (at the bedding cupboard). Her use of words showed the overextension common to the language of young children. For example, taught the sign "hurt" for scratches and bruises, Washoe extended it to red stains, a tattoo-like decal on the back of someone's hand, and her first sight of a human navel. But Washoe's words did not add up to language (Klima and Bellugi, 1973). The chimpanzee paid no attention to word order and apparently lacked the productivity that syntax gives to language.

Sarah, a chimpanzee trained by David Premack, communicated by "writing" with plastic symbols on a board. Sarah learned to understand compound sentences, obediently putting an apple in a pail and a banana in a dish after "reading" the symbols "Sarah insert apple pail banana dish" (A. Premack, 1976). Sarah's sentences followed a regular word order, and she even passed a test with an experimenter who did not know her language and therefore could give her no cues. Sarah answered questions correctly, although —like a small child—she seemed upset at working with a strange person who did not understand her language (D. Premack, 1976).

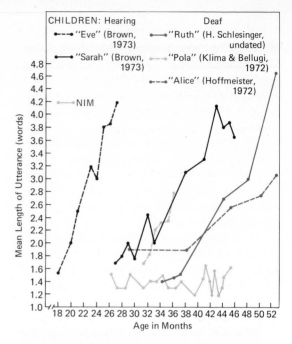

The difference between chimpanzee and human speech is shown clearly in this graph comparing the length of utterances of the chimpanzee Nim with those of two hearing and three deaf children.

SOURCE: From *NIM*, by H. S. Terrace. Copyright © 1979 by Herbert Terrace. Reprinted by permission of Alfred A. Knopf, Inc.

Her accuracy dropped somewhat, but so does that of a child placed in a threatening or strange situation. Sarah's language included displacement: given the written instruction "brown color of chocolate" to introduce the color brown, then told "take brown," she correctly chose the brown disc from a group of four.

Lana, a chimpanzee who was taught a computer-based language by Duane Rumbaugh (1977), "typed" her messages, which appeared on a lighted display as she struck the keys. The words she learned to "read" were lexigrams, made up of geometric signs. Lana had to adhere to a correct word order and signal the end of a communication with a period. The computer rejected ungrammatical constructions; so when she made a mistake, Lana often struck the period key to clear the machine and begin again. Lana learned stock sentences, into which she could insert the appropriate noun or verb, and she used them to converse about food, drink, and other desires. Once she even asked the computer to tell her the name of a strange object (a box of M&Ms candy) so she could ask for it, thus using language for an additional function (Rumbaugh and Gill, 1976).

Chimpanzees seemed to be getting closer and closer to real language—until Herbert Terrace (1979) worked with Nim and discovered that the chimpanzee knew less than his trainers thought. Nim learned 125 signs in ASL and put them together in two-word combinations. He even learned to substitute the signs "bite" and "angry" for physical aggression with trainers he had become attached to. But when Terrace analyzed videotapes of Nim with his trainers, the psychologist discovered that his chimpanzee could not qualify as a speaker of ASL. No matter how large Nim's vocabulary became, the average length of his utterances remained the same— between one and two words. A long string of words, upon analysis, seemed to be a simple pile up of all the words that might get the chimpanzee an orange ("give orange me give eat orange me eat orange give me eat orange give me you"). Nim rarely (less than 10 percent of the time) expanded upon what his trainers said. (Most three-year-old children expand on nearly half their parents' utterances.) Nim was primarily an imitator. What is more, Nim simply did not understand turn-taking, an essential nonverbal aspect of language that children learn long before they can talk.

The team that taught Lana recently threw additional cold water on the concept of chimpanzee language (Savage-Rumbaugh, Rumbaugh, and Boysen, 1980). They reviewed the major chimpanzee work and essentially agreed with Terrace, although their doubts run even deeper than his. Both Lana and Washoe, they say, have clearly reached the linguistic level of a nine-month-old child, in that they use their communication systems to control the behavior of their trainers. Nim, Washoe, and Lana, say this group, use symbols to make requests for contact, play, food, and change of location. In contrast, a child in the two-word stage does not simply demand things but uses language to comment on the situation as well. A human child would not limit herself to saying merely "More milk" or "Give milk Linda," but throw in such comments as "All gone," "Spill milk," "Pour juice," "Pretty cup," and "Linda do."

These researchers contend that, as yet, chimpanzees use words simply as replacements for their natural gestural system, which in the wild gets them reassurance, food, sex, grooming, and games. A chimpanzee that says "you me sweet drink give me" is a long way from a child who says, "Johnny's mother gave me some Kool-Aid." Lana's trainers have lost their early euphoria about chimpanzee language, doubting that chimpanzees have attained symbolization and suggesting that the chimpanzees may have accomplished no more than a pigeon that has learned to peck the proper key to get corn. In fact, using a similar but much simpler system than Lana's, Robert Epstein, Robert Lanza, and B. F. Skinner (1980) taught pigeons to carry on a spontaneous "conversation" about hidden colors.

But the researchers have not given up. They note that Lana did produce novel, grammatical sentences, not gibberish, indicating some comprehension of a symbol system. They suggest that researchers have concentrated too much on language production and not enough on making the chimpanzees demonstrate that they understand symbols. By 1980, no chimpanzee had yet met all the criteria (displacement, semanticity, and productivity) for real language.

"over," "on," "in," etc.), how they learn to distinguish between such words as "more" and "less," whether children understand more than they can say, and how adults' and children's meanings for words differ.

Syntax, or the structural principles that determine the form of sentences, reflects the second essential property of language — productivity. The syntax of a language is what makes the language productive, for it dictates the rules for combining words. Most combinations of words do not work. If the last sentence had been written as "Words most work of not combinations do," it would have been incomprehensible; but because the sentence as first written follows English rules of combination, its meaning is clear.

These rules vary from language to language. In English, for example, "Mommy kisses Baby" and "Baby kisses Mommy" have different meanings because the order of the words is different in the two utterances. But in Russian, the equivalent of "Mommy kisses Baby," with the three words in that order, could mean either that Mommy gets kissed or that Baby gets kissed, depending on whether "Mommy" or "Baby" has a particular sound on the end. So a Russian one-year-old must learn to pay special attention to the sounds that come at the end of words, whereas an American one-year-old must learn to pay special attention to word order.

Researchers who focus on syntax study the child's gradual grasp of grammar. They may be interested in the way a child forms the past tense or plurals, in the child's understanding of the passive sentence or the indirect object, or in the way a child comes to ask questions involving the use of auxiliary verbs ("Can cows fly?").

Pragmatics, or the study of language's social purposes, looks at the way language is used to get things done. When language is used for communication, each utterance is a social act, and the words are chosen because of assumptions and intentions on the part of the speaker. If the act is successful, the utterance will have the desired effect on the listener. The effect can be as

simple as getting the salt at the dinner table or as complicated as persuading someone to change his or her mind about an important issue.

Research in pragmatics centers on social interaction, examining the context of speech to see how the immediate situation affects both the expression and understanding of language. Much recent research in pragmatics has focused on infants, tracing the way that language emerges from earlier methods of communication, such as touching, pointing, and gazing.

THE PRIVATE FUNCTION OF LANGUAGE

Despite the emphasis of pragmatics, communication is not the only function of language. Human language serves an equally important private function by allowing us to translate our experiences into symbols, to remember experiences better, to think about abstractions, and to integrate our mental processes.

Representation

One of the ways human beings deal with the world is to represent experience in thought so that it may be used at a later date. We may think in images; but once we can translate our experiences into the symbols of language, our mental powers are greatly enhanced by the ease with which symbols can be processed and manipulated. Symbols give us the power of displacement; because they can be manipulated in the absence of whatever they represent, we can reason, remember, plan, and meditate, and we can solve complex problems quickly and efficiently.

According to Jerome Bruner (1964), the shared symbol system of language is conventionalized and transmitted by the culture, and the development of symbolic representation systems is a major component of cognitive growth. In one study by Bruner and his colleagues, five-to seven-year-old children were asked to rebuild a matrix of nine plastic glasses arranged by both height and diameter (as shown in Figure 8.1), after they had watched the experimenter remove all the glasses from the board. The five-year-olds rebuilt the matrix as easily as the seven-year-olds, although they took more time. When the matrix was transposed, however, so that the glass in the lower left corner was moved to the lower right, most seven-year-olds could rebuild it, but none of the five-year-olds could.

The key to whether a child would be able to rebuild the transposed matrix appeared in the child's language. When asked to tell how the glasses were originally arranged, children gave a dimensional (higher-shorter), a general perceptual (bigger-little), or a confused (higher-little) description. Regardless of age, those who confused terms from the two modes were twice as likely to fail at building the transposed matrix as those who used either the dimensional or the general description. The ability to manipulate symbols allowed the children to produce new structures based on the matrix's original organization.

Language also keeps children from being overpowered by the immediate perceptual attributes of their world. At first, children cannot separate words from the world they see around them. If a two-year-old who is seated on the carpet with a friend is asked to say "Jason is standing up," the little girl will say, "Jason is sitting down." The youngster reports the sight before her eyes instead of the words that contradict it, because meaning for a young child is fused with what he or she sees. But as language develops, it frees children from the immediate environment, allowing them to control and direct their own behavior (Vygotsky, 1962).

A study in which children were asked to say which of two glasses was fuller and which emptier demonstrated this effect. Two identical glasses were filled with the same amount of water and a tall, narrow glass was placed beside them. After Françoise Frank (1966) had screened the glasses from view, she poured the contents

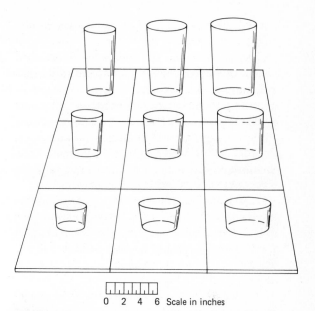

0 2 4 6 Scale in inches

Figure 8.1 The increased cognitive flexibility that accompanies language acquisition was illustrated in an experiment using these glasses. Five-year-olds had no trouble replacing them in their original arrangement, but when asked to transpose the arrangement, they always failed. Most seven-year-olds had little trouble with the new task, and their level of language facility predicted whether they would succeed.

(SOURCE: From J. S. Bruner, "The Course of Cognitive Growth," *American Psychologist*, 19 (1964), 1–15.)

of one glass into the tall, narrow glass and then asked children to compare the amount of liquid in the two glasses. Four-year-olds who had said both glasses held the same amount of water changed their minds when the screen was removed; five-year-olds did not. According to Bruner, the four-year-olds relied heavily on perceptual attributes (the levels of liquid), whereas five-year-olds had a verbal formula based on action, not perception ("You only poured it") to shield them from the overpowering appearance of the water levels before them.

A more radical notion about the power of language holds that language shapes and directs our thinking, rather than simply providing a means for representing our thoughts. This concept, called linguistic relativity, was proposed by Benjamin Lee Whorf (1956). According to Whorf, the vocabulary and grammar of a language in large part determine the way its speakers interpret their perceptions and experiences. In this view, then, language determines its speaker's ideas of time, matter, and space—even directing the form science takes in a culture.

The Whorfian hypothesis has not been generally accepted, but many researchers credit Whorf for calling attention to the complexity of social, cultural, linguistic, and cognitive interaction (G. Miller, 1978b). It is generally accepted that language influences our perception of the world, helping to determine what things in the world we notice and what we ignore. The more important a concept or category is for a culture, the more words a language has to describe it and the more precise and differentiated the perceptions of it by the speakers of the language. For example, Arabs have many words for camel; Eskimos, for snow; Americans, for car. The way a language carves up the world, then, may influence what we are likely to notice or do in a certain situation, but it does not limit the ways in which we *can* perceive it (Pollio, 1974).

Thought

Although we sometimes think in images, much of our thought is in the form of language—in that silent, condensed inner speech that consists of words turned into thought (Vygotsky, 1962). This inner speech helps us organize and integrate the processes of perception, memory, and problem solving, and allows us to understand and control our activities. Without it, our thought would be rudimentary and animallike. In fact, Lev Vygotsky believed that thought in infancy was like the thought of chimpanzees. He suggested that during the first part of life, speech and thought develop separately. Thought takes the form of images or of sensorimotor concepts

such as those proposed by Jean Piaget (see Chapter 2); the child may know words, which are used to label objects, but not language. Around the age of two, speech and thought join, and children's behavior changes. Language gives children independence from the immediate situation, allowing them to plan solutions and carry them out, to search for new means to solve problems instead of being limited to objects already present. Language gives children control over their own behavior, freeing them from the impulsive, spontaneous movements of apes (Vygotsky, 1978).

Not until thought and speech meet can children understand syntax; and until children grasp the syntax of a language, Vygotsky believed, they cannot use the structure of thought. As he put it, "grammar precedes logic" (Vygotsky, 1962). Children learn to handle abstract thought by first learning and using the language structures that express it. For example, children learn the structure of subordinate clauses (clauses that begin with such words as "because" and "although") long before they are able to grasp the structure of meaning indicated by those forms. But until children can express this scaffolding for thought, they cannot begin to understand and manipulate the kinds of relationships the clauses express.

Memory

Language can improve our ability to remember an object, an action, or an idea. Putting a concept into words seems to help us store the information in memory in a form that enables us to retrieve it. Most people have figured this out and repeat to themselves things they want to remember. Young children do not know this, but by telling them what to say, it is possible to make their memories more efficient, as Brian Coates and Willard Hartup (1969) have shown in their studies with four- and seven-year-olds. These investigators showed the children movies in which a man went through a series of twenty actions (such as building a tower of blocks, shooting a popgun at the tower, and whirling a hula hoop on his arm). Prior to running the film, Coates and Hartup told the children they would later have to imitate the model's actions. When asked to demonstrate the actions, four-year-olds who had watched the movie passively did worst. Those who had followed the experimenter's suggestion and described the man's actions in their own words as he performed them did better. But those who had repeated the words when the experimenter described the man's actions did best of all. Seven-year-olds did better than four-year-olds, no matter what technique was used. Apparently, they had already discovered that labeling is a good memory aid, and when they appeared to be watching the movie passively, they were mentally harnessing the power of language to help them remember what to do.

THOUGHT AND THE EMERGENCE OF LANGUAGE

A child's understanding of the world lays the basis for development of the ability to understand and to speak a language. It is obvious that a child who remained at the intellectual level of the neonatal period, when actions are primarily reflexive, would never learn to speak, and that a child who regarded the world as an extension of him- or herself would have little to talk about. Before children can use words meaningfully, they must have some notion that there is a world of enduring objects and people, and that people can act on objects. These notions develop during the first year of life.

A child's understanding of one aspect of causality, the use of tools, was related to the emergence of language among American and Italian babies studied toward the end of their first year by Elizabeth Bates (1979) and her associates. Babies who tugged at a supporting cloth in order to get an object they wanted, or who used sticks as tools to reach a desired toy, generally had larger vocabularies than babies who did not understand the use of tools to obtain a goal.

Imitation was also a good predictor of the baby's use of language. By the time they have celebrated their first birthdays, most babies are imitating events long after they have occurred, and Jean Piaget (1951) reported many instances of such imitations among his own children. For example, when his daughter Jacqueline was sixteen months old, she was impressed by an eighteen-month-old boy's tantrum. As Piaget described it:

> He screamed as he tried to get out of a play-pen and pushed it backwards, stamping his feet. J. stood watching him in amazement, never having witnessed such a scene before. The next day, she herself screamed in her play-pen and tried to move it, stamping her foot lightly several times in succession.

Piaget pointed out that because Jacqueline did not imitate the boy's behavior until the following day, she must have stored some representation of the event in her mind, acting it out in imitation much later. Just as one-year-olds can imitate events some time after they have experienced them, so they can use words some time after they have heard them. The abilities to imitate and to store internal images of sights and sounds are necessary prerequisites for the development of language.

A child's first words also emerge about the same time that he or she begins to use symbolic gestures and to engage in make-believe play. A baby girl who pushes a little stone along the table, pretending that it is a car, or rubs her hands together, pretending she is washing, has demonstrated symbolic play. Such play, as well as the sort of manipulative play in which babies build towers of blocks or stack wooden rings on a stick, is closely related to both the baby's use of words and his or her comprehension of others' speech (Bates, 1979).

Tool use, imitation, and both symbolic and manipulative play are implicated in the emergence of language. There is some evidence that when these capacities are absent, babies do not acquire language (Bates, 1979). Apparently, the same underlying intellectual capacities are nec-

These toddlers' imitation of adults they have seen cooking indicates that the youngsters have stored some representation of the act in their minds—an ability that is a necessary prerequisite for the development of language. (© James R. Holland/Stock, Boston)

essary for any of this complex behavior to develop.

THE PUBLIC FUNCTION OF LANGUAGE

In the absence of other people, we could survive without language. Our utterances are meant to communicate meanings to others, and we learn to use language socially in many ways for many purposes. We express emotions, describe ob-

jects or events, exchange ideas, ask questions, give commands, and tell stories. And sometimes we lie. Communication, then, is the public function of language.

If communication is to be smooth, we must understand the purpose of others' speech. But speakers are not always direct in the way they phrase their requests, commands, or assertions. For example, if a small boy's mother wants him to pick up his blocks, instead of saying "Pick up your blocks," she might use an indirect way of getting her son to clean up the living room floor. She might say "I wish you'd pick up those blocks" or "Why not pick up those blocks?" or "Haven't you forgotten something?" Children seem to understand indirect speech very early, and only rarely do they misinterpret it (Shatz, 1974; Garvey, 1975). It may be that very young children do not process the entire utterance but only its core, hearing and acting on "pick up the blocks"; or it may be that they have learned to interpret such forms as "Can you" or "I wish" or "Would you mind" or "Why not" as commands (deVilliers and deVilliers, 1978).

Children communicate as well as receive communications from others, and if they are to be effective, they must be able to fit their language to the immediate situation. As Jesse Delia and Barbara O'Keefe (1979) have indicated, children must know when to speak formally and when to speak colloquially. Once they can construct a sentence, they must know how to fit their utterances into the stream of conversation. They must learn how to interpret any violations of conversational rules. For example, if a person violates the turn-taking rule, is the interruption meant to communicate vital information or is the interrupter simply rude?

Finally, children must develop the ability to recognize the perspective and the needs of others, realizing how much information the other possesses and what he or she expects from the conversation. As their facility for language manipulation grows, children begin to adapt their language to a specific audience or situation. When they are requested to do something they understand and are capable of doing, children as young as four can modify their language appropriately, as Rochel Gelman and Marilyn Shatz (1977) found when they asked four-year-olds to explain the workings of a toy to two-year-olds. The older preschoolers described the toy much as an adult would. One four-year-old, explaining the way a dumping station with trucks and marbles worked, said:

> I gave you it. You want to have something funny? Put the marbles in here. Put the marbles in here. I'll give you the marbles. Now pour them in here. Go up here. And pour them in here. Now we have to dump it. Dump it. No, not in here. Pour it in here. Pour it in here. OK? That's funny. No, not like that. I'll do it. See, Sara?

The four-year-olds used repetition and simple, short sentences, modifying their messages to fit the limited capabilities of their pupils. They also adopted a "show-and-tell" approach, describing and demonstrating what the younger children were to notice and do. Yet when they explained the same toy to peers or adults, four-year-olds tended to use long sentences, to talk more about their own thoughts, and to ask the listener to provide information or clarification.

In another study, four-year-old boys went a step farther, adjusting their explanations of how a toy worked according to the individual responses of their two-year-old pupils (Masur, 1978). The more responsive the speech of the two-year-olds, the longer and more complex the sentences of the four-year-old teachers.

The ability to adapt language to a listener's needs develops gradually during childhood. When youngsters are unfamiliar with the demands of a situation, unable to understand the instructions, incapable of remembering what they are supposed to do, or preoccupied with figuring out an experimenter's wishes, they often cannot formulate an understandable message. They then make no allowances for a listener, appearing to assume that others see, hear, or feel exactly as they do.

THE SOCIAL FOUNDATIONS OF LANGUAGE

When language is a social act, that is, one in which the speaker is trying to accomplish something, its efficient use requires that both speaker and listener know more than the structure of the language and the meaning of its words; the social conventions that make communication possible also become important. Children learn these conventions as they acquire the language itself, in interactions with older human beings, usually their parents. In studying the development of this knowledge, researchers look at the emergence of intent in the baby's actions, at the context in which language is used, and at the social interaction in which the baby's understanding of the cultural context of language is forged. Long before children speak, they learn to manipulate the context of their actions according to rules they have acquired in activities with their caregivers.

Intention

Newborn infants communicate, but their messages are sent without intent. Their early cries are simply signals of distress, indicating that they are hungry, wet, uncomfortable, or in pain. Despite this lack of intent, the wails generally succeed in remedying the problem, and milk, a dry diaper, or cuddling customarily arrives in response to them.

After this successful, if unwitting, communication, babies develop clear intentions but do not try to communicate them to others. At about two or three months, for example, babies who see an attractive object dangled before them show their eagerness to grasp the object. They open and close their mouths, move their heads, and wiggle their bodies, behaving just as they would if they had the object. Within another month or so, if a toy is dangled before them, they will reach for it. In neither case, however, do babies make an attempt to get assistance from an adult. Similarly, when given a toy that requires adult assistance, babies will hit at the toy, push it, or throw it instead of indicating a need for help.

Somewhere around nine or ten months, babies who want a toy that is out of reach begin behaving in a very different way They look at a nearby adult, then at the toy, then at the adult again. If there is no response, they may fuss loudly to attract the adult's attention. Very soon thereafter, the grasp toward the elusive toy becomes an intentional signal, perhaps a repetitive opening and shutting of the hand, and the fussing sound becomes short, regular noises that change in volume and insistence depending upon whether the adult responds. This moment, says Elizabeth Bates (1979), is a great one in the dawn of language. It shows the child's intent to communicate as well as his or her realization that there are mutually agreed on signals, such as pointing, that can be used for mutually agreed on purposes. Earlier the baby may have wanted to communicate but lacked any shared notion of conventional ways to express that intention. Now that the baby has grasped this notion, the way is open for the first words.

Seeking help is one of the major intentions that govern most of a baby's communication. Indeed, most of a baby's communicative needs are encompassed in only four intentions, says Jerome Bruner (1980), and this limitation simplifies both the baby's job in learning to communicate and the caregiver's task in deciphering the baby's communications. In addition to seeking help, babies intend to persuade adults to look at something with them, achieving and regulating joint attention. Babies also intend to increase affiliation, enjoying the exchange of gestures, sounds, and facial expressions. Finally, babies intend to induce others to join them in their make-believe play. These intentions develop in a social context, with the caregiver playing an active role.

The Role of the Caregiver

Babies' knowledge of the cultural conventions that surround communication begins in the interaction of baby and caregiver. Almost from the beginning, parents respond to their babies' movements and sounds as if they were meaningful, attribute intent to their gurgles and coos, and encourage babies to take their turn in "conversation." Much early learning of language convention takes place in dialogues between caregiver and infant, and at first the caregiver supplies both sides of the conversation. As a result, even though babies may not be trying to communicate, they are learning something about the nature of human communication. For example:

Infant: (smiles)
Mother: Oh, what a nice little smile! Yes, isn't that nice? There. That's a nice little smile.

By pointing to a doggie in the picture, this baby shows a grasp of the notion that people communicate by means of agreed-upon signals, a cognitive advance that opens the way for the baby's first word. (© Ira Berger 1978/Black Star)

Parents' responses to the infant's sounds and gestures encourage any attempts to communicate. (Linda Rogers/Woodfin Camp & Assoc.)

Infant: (burps)
Mother: What a nice wind as well! Yes, that's better, isn't it? Yes. Yes.
Infant: (vocalizes)
Mother: Yes! There's a nice noise (Snow, 1977a).

During such exchanges, parents pay close attention to the baby's reactions, and as the infant's competence increases, the conversations change. More and more participation is demanded from the baby — first babbling, then words. The parent may repeat a question until the infant supplies an answer.

Carrying on a conversation requires children to master other conventions as well: they must learn to take turns, speaking at the proper time and not interrupting their partners; they must learn to make eye contact and to indicate that they are paying attention. Turn-taking and other nonverbal conversational skills grow out of early games, such as peek-a-boo, in which baby and adult share experiences and exchange roles in ritualized and predictable ways. At about six or seven months, babies seem to learn that certain signals in adult speech mean that something

the adult is attending to is worth looking at; from that moment joint attention becomes easier (Bruner, 1980). Shortly thereafter, the baby learns to follow the adult's gaze to find the object. In a study with Michael Scaife, Bruner (Scaife and Bruner, 1975) found that between eight and ten months, two-thirds of the babies would follow an adult's gaze and look intently at whatever was the focus of the adult's attention. By the time they were a year old, all babies did this. Such shared gazing paves the way to shared linguistic reference and the acquisition of words.

Parents also speak in special ways to their babies. In the early months, this altered manner of speaking consists of exaggerated pitch, loudness, and intensity, exaggerated facial expressions, extension of vowel length, and emphasis on certain words (Stern, 1977). At about ten months, just when the baby shows an intent to communicate, parents lapse into a kind of speech that has been called "baby talk" or "motherese" (Gleason and Weintraub, 1978). In baby talk, adults typically speak more slowly, use simple sentences, replace difficult consonants with easy ones, substitute nouns for pronouns, and repeat words, phrases, or whole sentences. As in the earliest speech to infants, pitch and tone change, as the adult seems to be both conveying affection and capturing the child's attention for the task at hand. Baby talk appears in cultures around the world; its presence has been documented in at least fifteen cultures, and it is used by parents, strange adults, and older children alike (Ferguson, 1977).

Adults also talk to children primarily about the here and now. They comment on what they are doing or what the infant is doing or is about to do. They limit their vocabularies, and they select words that are most useful for the child — words that relate to what children are interested in. As Roger Brown (1977) puts it, the adult is trying "to keep two minds focused on the same topic."

The result of baby talk is, however, anything but babyish. The content and the intonation of the communication is childish, but the dialogue pattern is strictly adult (Bruner, 1978). Without it, children might never become competent users of language.

The Uses of Conversation

During the preschool years, children's conversation with their caregivers continues to be a major influence on their skill at communicating. Once they begin putting several words together, the children's side of the conversation grows, and instead of replying with "Yeah" or "Dat" or "Baby shoe," they make suggestions and bring up new topics.

Sometimes conversation goes well and a two-year-old maintains his or her side of the talk over twenty or more turns, always responding appropriately. At other times, conversation breaks down and the child either lapses into silence, resorts to repeated "Huhs," or makes an irrelevant comment — as when one thirty-month-old boy replied to "Which is your ball?" with "Drink copee" (Brown, 1980). After studying the transcripts of conversations between twenty-one young children and a pair of developmental psychologists, Brown concluded that the content of adult-child conversations was their least important aspect. As he points out, when an adult says, "What's this?" and the child replies, "A

rabbit," the adult has learned nothing about the picture book they are sharing but a good deal about the little girl's assumptions and linguistic knowledge.

Children's relevant responses reassure the adult conversational partner that the pair share certain cultural beliefs, which form the background of the conversation. The child's contributions reveal his or her linguistic competence and knowledge, so that adults use these conversations as a running check on the child's progress. Research has shown that most parents are good at predicting their preschoolers' level of linguistic proficiency (Gleason and Weintraub, 1978).

When conversation does break down, adults are alerted to gaps in the child's understanding and adjust their own conversation to compensate (Brown, 1980). If the missing part is small (suppose the little girl had identified the rabbit as a mouse), they try to help by filling in whatever information the child needs. But if the breakdown is due to a more general problem of understanding, as in the small boy's irrelevant "Drink copee," the adult holds back but tries the same sort of situation again later. Instead of launching lengthy tutorial sessions, says Brown, adults use small efforts spread over long periods of time.

Although parents often correct gross errors in a child's choice of words or pronunciation, they are usually more interested in the truth of an utterance than in its syntax (Brown, Cazden, and Bellugi-Klima, 1968). For example, in a longitudinal study of several children, when one girl wanted to indicate that her mother was also female and said, "He a girl," her mother replied, "That's right." But when another young girl said, using passable grammar, "There's the animal farmhouse," her mother corrected her because the building was a lighthouse.

As a result of such experiences, children become more skillful at adjusting their speech to conventional usage. As Susan Ervin-Tripp (1976) points out, they learn to stay on the topic by using such words as "and" and "because." They learn to soften their requests, adding "please." They learn to time their speech so it

Children adapt their language to the audience or situation, speaking one way to an adult, another to a two-year-old, and yet another to their peers. (© Menschenfreund)

does not overlap or disrupt what their partner says, and to keep the conversation focused on the matter at hand by planning what to say next. Gradually, they learn the convention that when they change the topic, they are supposed to indicate the shift. By about eight or nine, they are likely to signal a change by saying something like "Oh yeah, that reminds me. . . ."

The Importance of Context

Every communication is affected by *context*, which includes the beliefs and assumptions of the speaker concerning the setting of his or her remarks; the prior, present, and future actions and remarks of both speaker and listener; and the knowledge and intentions of everyone involved (Ochs, 1979). Language itself can serve as context, as when the speaker's choice of a language style, whether formal, colloquial, distant, or affectionate, affects the way an utterance

is interpreted. Both adult and child respond to context and use it to interpret the intentions of the conversational partner.

HOW ADULTS UNDERSTAND INFANTS Communication succeeds during the early stages of language because adults are good at guessing a child's intentions. Although children give some clues to their intentions in intonation and gesture, the ongoing context provides vital information, and early one- and two-word utterances can be understood only if their context is known. For example, on hearing a recording of the word "door" spoken with an emphatic intonation, we would not be able to tell whether the infant speaker wanted the door opened or closed or merely wanted us to pay attention to the door. But if we were watching a toddler stand in front of a closed door and knew that on the other side of the door her father was repairing a light switch, we would know immediately that the emphatic utterance, "Door," meant that we had been asked to open it.

The process of deciphering a child's language is made easier by the fact that children — like the adults who talk to them — speak about the here and now, so that immediate context is a nearly infallible guide to meaning. Context plays such a dominant role in the infant's early speech that by relying on it, adults can frequently predict what children who are limited to one-word utterances will say next. These children often have more than one word in their vocabularies that could apply to a situation, but they will select their word by the criterion of informativeness, according to Patricia Greenfield (1979). Information that is regarded as certain is not mentioned; whatever cannot be taken for granted will be the topic of conversation. "Certain" information is information that is certain to the child, not the adult, for children at this level of development generally assume that adults share their perceptions.

Suppose that an eighteen-month-old boy is playing with a toy car, running it across the top of a table. He would not say "car" because the

When this little girl says "door," it is safe to assume that she wants the door opened, but without the context it would be impossible to decide whether she meant "Open the door," "Close the door," or "There's a door." (© Michael Weisbrot & Family)

car, being in his possession, is certain. Since the car can be taken for granted, he would direct his comment at its action, saying "hmmm" or "beep-beep" or whatever word he uses to imitate the sound of a car. Should the toddler's car fall off the table, he would say "car," because the car has suddenly become uncertain. However, having once mentioned the car, it becomes part of the context and therefore certain. Now he is free to comment on his elusive toy and might say "down" or "fall" or "gone."

When commenting on a person's actions, young children take the person for granted and talk about the action. Sitting on the kitchen floor and wishing to comment on the fact that his

mother is fixing lunch, the same little boy would say "Lunch," not "Mommy." But if his mother left the room, she would become uncertain in the child's scheme of things and the comment would be "Mommy," no matter how interested he was in his mother's action. Since, as Greenfield points out, adults and children appear to analyze a situation similarly, the boy's mother understands his comments during play and responds appropriately, making communication possible.

HOW CHILDREN UNDERSTAND ADULTS

If children are to understand what others are trying to accomplish with language, they must be alert to the social, or pragmatic, meaning of the utterances they hear, and they must often disregard the literal meaning. As we saw earlier, children while still quite young show a comprehension of indirect utterances, quickly picking up their blocks when Mother says, "Haven't you forgotten something?"

According to Marilyn Shatz (1978), instead of decoding the language they hear according to the syntactical arrangement of the words and their meaning, very young children do whatever seems appropriate, given the immediate social context. When the context is ambiguous, they assume that language demands action. In her study, Shatz tested the comprehension of two-year-olds with commands, questions, and simple declarative sentences spoken in a neutral fashion. She found, for example, that whether she said, "Fit the ball into the truck," "Can you fit the ball into the truck?" or "The ball fits into the truck," most children responded by putting the ball into the truck.

When she manipulated the context by setting up a situation that clearly demanded information from them, however, children responded appropriately. Using a toy telephone, she either steered the child toward action (saying such things as "Push the button" and "Ring the bell") or toward information (saying such things as "Who talks on the telephone in your house?" or "Can Daddy talk on the telephone?"). Asked the test question, "Can you talk on the telephone?" children in the action setting generally responded by talking on the play phone. Children in the information setting generally said "Yes" and left it at that, or else said "Yes" and then proceeded to demonstrate their ability. In other words, in the first situation, "Can you talk on the telephone?" was interpreted as a command; in the second situation, it was interpreted as a request for information. When words and actions work together to make simple action inappropriate and the giving of information appropriate, children will provide the information.

A child's interpretation of another's utterance may also depend upon his or her status in relation to the speaker. When the words come from a parent, a teacher, or another adult, five-year-olds are likely to treat simple declarative statements or ambiguous questions about their ability to carry out an act as indirect commands. By the time they are in the second grade, however, they pay more attention to the form of an utterance and respond to requests, commands, ambiguous questions, and statements in different ways (Olson, 1980).

Context continues to guide children in other ways. Five-year-olds are attentive to the implicit information in others' remarks and use it to frame their own utterances. Younger children, however, generally ignore such implicit information. This difference appeared in a study of three- to five-year-old Canadian children conducted by Verne Bacharach and Mary Luszcz (1979). Before showing the children a series of pictures, the investigators commented in a way that was meant to guide the children's responses to the command, "Tell me about the picture." Showing the picture of a horse pulling a wagon, for example, the investigator sometimes prefaced the command with "Did you know horses can do a lot of different things? Horses can run. Horses can eat hay." At other times the investigator said such things as "Did you know there are a lot of different kinds of animals? A cow is an animal. A rabbit is an animal."

Young children generally ignored the content of the remarks, responding in both situations with "Horse" or "It's a horse" or "Wagon." But the five-year-olds structured their remarks around the content of the comments, in the first instance saying such things as "It's pulling a wagon," and in the second, "That's a horse." This developmental change may lie in the five-year-old's increased linguistic skills or in the ability of the older child to hold information in immediate memory long enough to respond. Or it may be that three-year-olds are biased toward identifying objects no matter what the context. Whatever the reason, by the time children are five, they are skilled at taking others' remarks into account when communicating.

THE SOCIAL INFLUENCES ON LANGUAGE

Since children acquire language in the family, the influence of social class and ethnic group is bound to be seen in the child's style of speech. By their example, parents pass along not only their own language standards but also the standards of the society of which they are a part. In a heterogenous society such as the United States, these standards are not uniform. Thus the prevailing language varies from subculture to subculture, from region to region, and from one socioeconomic group to another. Although differences are not deficits, these social influences may lead to difficulties when children start school.

Social-Class Differences

The attitudes of parents toward language, the richness of their vocabularies, their responses to a child's attempts at speech, and the amount and kind of conversation that takes place in a home are likely to affect children's attitudes toward speech and to influence their success in formal education. Language style, vocabulary size, and ease of expression may all show evidence of socioeconomic class. Studies that compare the language use of children indicate that children from the more advantaged sections of society score higher on tests of pronunciation, vocabulary, and sentence structure than do children from lower socioeconomic groups (R. Hess, 1970). Tests that show such variation in language style do not, however, indicate that lower-class children have an inferior grasp of their language's basic structure.

Children from different social classes also show differences in their expressive language. Individuals in lower socioeconomic groups tend to express themselves with gestures in situations where those in higher socioeconomic groups use words (Miller and Swanson, 1966). Related language differences appeared in a series of studies by Basil Bernstein (1962, 1966). Bernstein analyzed the speech of sixteen-year-old boys from the English lower and middle classes, who were matched for intelligence. He discovered that the middle-class boys produced more elaborate descriptions, used a wider vocabulary with more nouns, and spoke fluently, making short pauses in their utterances. The boys from the lower socioeconomic class made fewer distinctions, used more common words, especially pronouns, and made longer pauses in their speech. As a result, the descriptions by the middle-class boys were less tied to context than those by the lower-class boys and made fewer assumptions about the listener's knowledge.

This sort of difference appears to vary with such factors as the topic boys are asked to talk about, the setting, and the purpose (Higgins, 1976). For example, when an inner-city black child of eight was interviewed in a test situation, the boy answered in monosyllables, his replies consisting largely of reluctant "Nopes" and "Hmm-ms." But when the boy was seen in a less formal setting, where the researcher sat on the floor, passed around potato chips, introduced taboo words to indicate it was safe to say anything, and asked another child to join the conversation, the boy's utterances lengthened, he used complex grammatical constructions, and he was an eager participant in the conversation (Labov, 1969b).

Dialects and Language Development

In a society such as ours, made up of many ethnic groups, language variation can be extreme. In some areas, English is not spoken in the home—as in the French-speaking Cajun area of Louisiana or in the large Spanish-speaking areas of the American Southwest and New York City. Children who speak Spanish at home often find themselves faced with a language problem when they enter the school system, but the Hispanic problem is straightforward. Teachers can recognize Spanish as a legitimate language and many see their role as introducing the Spanish-speaking child to a second language he or she will need to succeed in the larger society.

In contrast, children who grow up speaking a dialect of English, such as Black English, sometimes receive little sympathy when they reach the classroom. For many years, teachers and some researchers regarded Black English as a debased form of Standard English, calling it "not merely an underdeveloped version of English, but . . . a basically non-logical mode of expressive behavior" (Bereiter et al., 1966). Analyses of Black English have shown that such a characterization is simply wrong.

In linguistic terms, Black and Standard English are minor variants of the same English language; in developmental terms, acquisition of the two dialects follows similar patterns. For example, studies by Dan Slobin and Claudia Mitchell-Kernan (Slobin, 1975) of black children in the Oakland, California, ghetto show no serious differences between the basic pattern of language development in the ghetto children and in the children studied by Roger Brown at Harvard. The Oakland children spend most of their time learning language from the older siblings and playmates who watch over them during the day. This situation is common in cultures around the world, however, and seems to have no effect on the basic rate at which a child acquires syntax. The two dialects (Oakland and Harvard) are especially close at the preschool period and are roughly equivalent on functional

Table 8.1 DIALECT DIFFERENCES IN NEGATIVE UTTERANCES OF PRESCHOOL-AGE CHILDREN

Oakland Children	Harvard Children
That's not no bathroom.	It wasn't no chicken.
I'm not doing nothing.	I wasn't doing nothing.
I don't get no whipping.	I don't want no milk.
Nobody wasn't scared.	But nobody wasn't gonna know it.
Why bears can't talk?	Why I can't put them on?
But Renée or nobody wouldn't peel me no kinda orange.	Nobody won't recognize me.
Why she won't sit up?	Why we didn't?
	Why it's not working?
Nobody wouldn't help me.	No one didn't took it.
I don't have no suitcase.	It don't have no wings.
Never I don't get no whipping.	I never won't get it.

(*Source:* The Oakland examples are drawn from unpublished data of Claudia Mitchell-Kernan, and the Harvard examples from unpublished data of Roger Brown.)

and grammatical grounds—as is shown in the example in Table 8.1.

During later childhood, the dialects diverge; but even at the adult level, the difference is only superficial, as William Labov (1973) has pointed out. Schoolteachers often criticize Black English because it apparently lacks the verb "to be." Labov (1969a) has shown, however, that the verb occurs in many places in Black English and that its omission follows a strict rule. Speakers of Standard English often contract "to be" to a simple "-'s" in the present tense ("He's big" rather than "He is big"). Wherever Standard English can contract, Black English can—but does not always—omit the verb ("He big"). Such an omission does not indicate that Black English lacks an important part of English grammar. Wherever it is impossible to contract "to be" in Standard English, it is impossible to delete "to be" in Black English, as shown in Table 8.2. When speakers of Standard English want to emphasize a statement, they put heavy stress on the verb ("He IS big"). In this situation, "is"

also appears in Black English, and the Black form is the same as the Standard.

Given differences as subtle and superficial as these, it is difficult to believe that the use of Black English indicates anything more than a difference in sociocultural background. However, the vocabulary, pronunciation, and style of Black English label the child speaker in the eyes of the middle-class speaker of Standard English. Sometimes communication breaks down entirely. If a black child tells his teacher, "Dey ain't like dat," the teacher may assume the boy has said, "They aren't like that." Instead, the message the child intended was, "They didn't like that." When this happens, the teacher all too often decides that because the child's speech is unintelligible, he is unintelligent. A vicious circle is set up. Because the teacher expects the

Table 8.2 EXAMPLES OF *BE* IN TWO DIALECTS OF AMERICAN ENGLISH

Black English	Standard English
Deletion	*Contraction*
She the first one.	She's the first one.
But he wild.	But he's wild.
You out of the game.	You're out of the game.
We on tape.	We're on tape.
He always complainin'.	He's always complaining.
He gon' try to get up.	He's gonna try to get up.
Nondeletion	*Nondeletion*
I was small.	I was small.
You got to be good.	You've got to be good.
Be cool, brothers!	Be cool, brothers!
He *is* an expert.	He *is* an expert.
Is he dead?	Is he dead?
Are you down?	Are you down?
Is that a shock or is it not?	Is that a shock or is it not?
I don't care what you are.	I don't care what you are.
Do you see where that person is?	Do you see where that person is?

(*Source:* Adapted from William Labov, "Contraction, Deletion, and Inherent Variability of the English Copula," *Language,* 45 (1969), 715–762. The Black English examples are drawn from Labov (with some abbreviation), and the Standard English equivalents have been supplied for the purposes of this comparative table.)

boy to do poorly, the child fulfills the teacher's expectations and fails.

One way to break the circle is to instruct middle-class teachers in Black English so that they can better understand their students. (This suggestion, of course, applies equally to teachers of Hispanic students and to the teachers of any students who at home speak a different language or dialect from that taught in school.) Despite its richness as a language, Black English has major consequences for success in American society. Unless its young speakers are helped to come to terms with the Standard dialect, they will lack a basic tool for social and economic advancement.

Compensating for Different Backgrounds

Social environments differ in regard to how well they match the school environment. As we have seen, speakers of Black English are at a disadvantage when compared with middle-class children whose socioeconomic background has led them to acquire the motivations, habits, speech forms, and vocabulary and pronunciation skills demanded by the school system. The mismatch between home environment and school that has been observed among social groups in various countries is not based purely on linguistic factors but is related to other environmental features as well.

Studies of Norwegian children show that social settings can affect intellectual development in different ways. Marida Hollos and Philip Cowan (1973) compared isolated Norwegian farm children with the children of families of similar size and educational background in a small village and in a medium-sized town in Norway. The farm children spent most of their time watching others or playing alone. They had few toys. Their mothers neither prompted nor encouraged them to talk, and there was no storytelling or discussion. The children interacted with other adults only at mealtimes and in the evenings, which were largely devoted to television.

Hollos and Cowan found that the basic language development among these isolated farm children was similar to that of village and town children, in spite of the latter groups' many more opportunities for verbal interaction. The greater language experience of the village and town children put them ahead of the farm children in one area: they were more advanced in their ability to take a viewpoint other than their own. But the farm children were ahead of town and village children in their ability to think logically about physical properties and their relationships. Both abilities are important for schooling and necessary for development.

Thus it seems that the verbal environment affects only some aspects of cognitive development. Assumptions that "cultural deprivation" or poverty results in language deficits, and that deficient language delays or blocks full cognitive development apparently need to be reexamined. Such premises have been the basis for many compensatory education programs for lower-class minority children in the United States (Bereiter and Engelmann, 1966). Yet most studies indicate that all children learn the basic rules of language equally well, according to universal patterns of development. In this sense, there is no such thing as a language deficit in child development, only a language difference.

The problem of schooling, therefore, is neither one of teaching the child to think nor of teaching the child to speak. Instead, it is a matter of finding out which aspects of cognition need stimulation for a particular child or group of children and then devising the appropriate means (not necessarily verbal) to foster those facets of intellectual growth.

In the last few years, such specific programs for developing language skills have been developed. Some have used procedures based on behavior-learning theories, including instructions, adult modeling, social approval, and other rewards. The results indicate that such programs can improve specific language skills—

Although they have many fewer opportunities for verbal interaction, children who grow up on isolated farms develop language at the same time and in the same way as children who live in towns and cities. (© Jim Smith)

increasing the rate of children's spontaneous speech and its correctness, teaching them to time their conversation appropriately, and improving their storytelling skills and their skill in describing their own behavior.

SUMMARY

1. Human language is set off from animal communication systems by three important properties: semanticity, productivity, and displacement. In attempting to understand how children acquire language, researchers generally focus on one of language's four levels: syntax (or structure), phonology (or sound), semantics (or meaning), and pragmatics (or social use).

2. The private functions of language are representation, thought, and memory. Once children can represent events in the world with linguistic symbols, they can solve a greater range of problems and their information-processing powers expand. A command of language also enhances memory and helps us to understand and control our actions.

3. Language does not appear until a child reaches the appropriate level of cognitive development. Since tool use, imitation, and symbolic and manipulative play invariably emerge about the time a child begins to speak, all seem to draw on the same underlying mental capacities.

4. The public function of language is communication — to express emotion, to pass along information, to ask, demand, beg, plead, apologize, and so forth. In order to communicate efficiently, children must understand the rules of conversation, the needs and knowledge of others, and how to fit their language to the immediate situation.

5. Language acquisition begins in the social interactions of baby and caregiver. The intent to communicate emerges at nine or ten months, when babies begin to seek the help of adults in accomplishing their goals. Parents introduce children to language through baby talk, conversations, and games, and the conversational experiences of infants and young children teach them the cultural conventions of language. All communication is affected by context, and both children and adults rely on it when interpreting language.

6. Research on social class and dialects indicates that although there are no major differences among children in their acquisition of basic grammar, environmental variations affect pronunciation, vocabulary, fluency, and certain other skills. Such language differences are not an indication of language deficits.

Language: Sound, Sense, and Structure

How did you like the hospital?" one kindergarten boy asked his friend, who had just returned to school after a bout with pneumonia. The five-year-old thought for a minute, then said, "It was awful. I didn't eat anything. The food was hateable." From years of hearing language used, this kindergartner had mastered an English rule for the formation of adjectives from verbs. Since "squeeze" produces "squeezable," "hug" produces "huggable," and "love" produces "lovable," it was only reasonable that the boy should infer that "hate" produces "hateable."

Such an achievement demonstrates a child's grasp of syntactic rules, and in this chapter, we shall discuss some of the explanations that have been proposed to explain the achievements of children in deciphering their native language. We shall examine the way a baby responds to speech sounds and how the baby's own sounds change from babbling to words. We shall see that words may hold different meanings for children, and we shall look at the way in which children increase their vocabularies. We shall discover the significance of infants' progress from one- to two-word utterances and the way they master the basic grammatical machinery of their language. We shall find that young children tend to impose regularities on language beyond those that exist and that they devise their own strategies for figuring out statements. Finally, we shall approach language as play, discovering that children's appreciation of riddles shows a clear developmental progression.

THEORIES OF ACQUISITION

Before children can use language to communicate, to think, and to remember, they must acquire it. As we have seen, the acquisition of language begins in early infancy, in the interactions between the baby and his or her caregiver, and the process is guided by — and is the result of — cognitive development (Snow, 1977b). But precisely how that cognitive development — a result of maturation and experience — interacts with social experience to produce a competent speaker is a matter of debate. Several explanations have been advanced to explain how children acquire language, but none has satisfactorily accounted for all facets of language development. These explanations, which derive from various assumptions about child development, can be divided into biological, mechanistic, and functional theories of language acquisition.

Biological Theories

According to Noam Chomsky (1975, 1979), language development is primarily a matter of maturation because the structure of language is laid down in our genes. All human languages, despite their surface differences, share an underlying deep structure, which he calls a universal grammar. This grammar consists of principles, conditions, and rules of sound, meaning, and structure. Since biological constraints characterize the grammar children will construct, they take the bits and pieces of language they hear, analyze them, and fit them to the universal grammar. Only in this way, says Chomsky, can we explain how children in a given community, who each have entirely different — and mostly fragmentary — language experiences, come up

with the same rich, complex language system. In this view, language is partly predetermined, in the same way that genes determine the pattern of sexual maturation, and — given experience — children will invariably acquire language.

When maturation is considered the determining factor in language acquisition, the reference is to maturation of the brain. Eric Lenneberg (1967), convinced that maturation is the key to language acquisition, believed that there is a sensitive period in human development when language can be learned. The period begins when children are about two years old and lasts until they reach sexual maturity. At that time the ability to learn a language declines, and by the late teens it is difficult — or even impossible — to acquire a first language. The end of the sensitive period, said Lenneberg (1973), coincides with the maturation of the brain; once brain tissue is fully differentiated, it loses plasticity and can no longer make the adjustments that the acquisition of language requires.

There is some evidence to support this view. Until they are sexually mature, most children who suffer damage to the brain's left hemisphere recover the ability to talk; but adolescents and adults who receive similar injuries do not. Since, as noted in Chapter 7, language is located in the left hemisphere for most people, this phenomenon points to maturation as a critical factor in the development of language. In children, said Lenneberg, even though the left hemisphere handles most language function, the right is still involved in speech; and because the brain tissue is still plastic, it can assume all language function when the left hemisphere is damaged. Similarly, retarded children keep improving their grasp of language until they reach sexual maturity, which comes later among retarded than among normal children. Once retarded children mature, their language development ceases; they can still learn new words, but their grasp of syntax remains just where it was when they reached puberty and the sensitive period ended.

Recent studies have led some researchers to

question the concept of a sensitive period for language development. Some evidence indicates that brain lateralization is complete by the time children are five (Carter and Kinsbourne, 1979), and other research indicates that a child is born with the left hemisphere more proficient than the right at processing language (Molfese and Molfese, 1979).

If there is a sensitive period for language learning, it does not apply to the acquisition of a second language. Under a strict application of Lenneberg's theory, children under twelve should find it easy, and their parents and adolescent siblings should find it extremely difficult, to acquire a second language. Folklore keeps this idea current, but a recent study by Catherine Snow and Marian Hoefnagel-Höhle (1978) among English-speaking families that had moved to the Netherlands failed to support it. Adolescents learned Dutch the fastest, and three- to five-year-olds (who should have been the star pupils) were the slowest to learn, falling far behind their parents' fluency in Dutch. In fact, learning the new language caused the preschoolers' fluency in English to drop sharply.

But the concept of a sensitive period may be valid if applied only to the acquisition of a first language. The case of Genie, a California girl who grew up in almost total isolation, indicates that a first language can be acquired after sexual maturity but that the language will not be the rich, fluent system spoken by other members of the speech community (Curtiss, 1977). Genie was discovered when she was nearly fourteen, and her social experience had been limited to spoonfeeding from her almost blind mother. No one spoke to her, and whenever she made a noise, her father beat her. Although Genie was severely disturbed and had no language, she acquired English. The acquisition was difficult, however, and Genie's language has remained abnormal. She understands normal language, but she does not produce some of its basic structures. Her speech is rule-governed and productive, however, and she speaks of people and objects that are not present. Genie's case, therefore, supports a weak version of Lenneberg's theory (Curtiss, 1977), indicating that acquiring a first language after the brain is mature is difficult but not impossible.

Mechanistic Theories

According to B. F. Skinner (1957) and to Sidney Bijou and Donald Baer (1965), who are strict learning theorists, language is simply verbal behavior that is reinforced by the action of another person. The random babbling of babies, which springs from a genetic predisposition, gradually changes to words through the processes of shaping and conditioning. Because mothers generally talk to their babies while they care for them, using words to express affection, a mother's speech becomes reinforcing. Babies can also reinforce themselves by listening to their own vocalizations. As they mature and gain control over their speech apparatus, babies begin to direct the sounds they produce, and the more closely their babbling resembles their mothers' speech, the more reinforcing their vocalizations become. When babies babble, their mothers often reward them with attention, adding further reinforcement.

When babies begin to label objects in the world, their parents reinforce them with attention or approval. The reinforcement is for the sound itself, but the child soon responds to the sight of the object (dog, chair, shoe) with the label. Other words are learned because the child receives tangible rewards for producing them, as when the words "cookie" or "bottle" are followed by the objects they represent.

Social-learning theorists would add that imitation plays a major role in the acquisition of speech. Parents serve as models for their children, who imitate the speech they hear. As noted in Chapter 2, imitation does not have to be immediate. A child can learn by observing and imitate the forms of adult speech when a later occasion warrants it. Both comprehension and speech, says Albert Bandura (1977), are based on observational learning.

Although reinforcement and imitation undoubtedly contribute to the acquisition of individual words, mechanistic theories of language acquisition have been challenged on the ground that children learn more than words. They develop rules that allow them to produce and interpret an endless variety of novel sentences. Children produce sentences that are different from the sentences they hear. When a small girl says "All-gone sticky" after washing her hands, or "I seed two mouses," she is not imitating forms she has heard others use. Indeed, the latter sentence shows the child's attempt to force on language a rule-governed regularity it does not possess.

Social-learning theorists maintain, however, that children do imitate the structures they hear. Such sentences as "I seed two mouses," says Bandura (1977), simply indicate that children "model too well," slavishly applying the forms they have heard others use. Delayed selective imitation, argue Grover Whitehurst and Ross Vasta (1975), explains children's acquisition of language structure. In fact, by reinforcing four-year-olds each time the children indicated their understanding of sentences with both direct and indirect objects (e.g., "The boy gives the puppy the bone"), Whitehurst (1974) was able to get them to use similar constructions in their own speech.

Functional Theories

Researchers who support functional theories of language acquisition agree with biological theorists that maturation is an important factor and that children cannot acquire language until they reach a certain cognitive level. They also agree with mechanistic theorists that social interaction is the place to look for the beginnings of language. But they believe that innate mechanisms cannot, by themselves, explain the child's grasp of language, and that the basis for linguistic competence goes beyond conditioning and observational learning to include all nonlinguistic aspects of human interaction: turn-taking, mutual gaze, joint attention, context, assumptions, and cultural conventions. The forms of language are acquired, says Elizabeth Bates (1979), in order to carry out communicative functions.

Pragmatics is seen as the key to language development, with the nonlinguistic aspects of interaction providing the prespeech bases of language. As we saw in Chapter 8, these aspects send children a long way on the path to human communication before they say their first words. Instead of the unfolding of preprogrammed behavior, language becomes the product of the child's active interaction with an environment provided by other human beings (Gleason and Weintraub, 1978). These other human beings are tuned to the child's linguistic needs, and their speech meshes precisely with those needs.

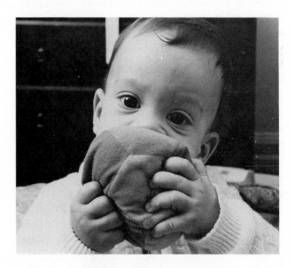

Whether language is primarily a matter of maturation, reinforcement, imitation, or general human interaction, this baby will progress in a predictable pattern from babbling to words to speech. (© Michael Weisbrot & Family)

As Jean Berko Gleason and Sandra Weintraub point out, the cognitive development of children can result from their interaction with the physical world, but they cannot acquire language through simple exposure to it as passive listeners.

In one case, where a child heard no simplified baby talk, language development was drastically slowed. J. S. Sachs and M. Johnson (1976) studied the hearing child of deaf parents who used only sign language with him. Although the child heard a good deal of adult speech on television, when he was four his language lagged far behind that of other children. He had only a small vocabulary, probably learned from playmates and from television jingles. It has also been found that children who watch television programs in a language other than their own do not seem to acquire the second language (Snow *et al.*, 1976). The speech they hear is probably too rapid, it is not aimed at the child's immediate situation, and of course no attention is paid to the child's reactions.

Perhaps, suggests Jerome Bruner (1980), interaction with adults who adapt their speech in special ways acts as a primer that cues a preadapted, innate process instead of triggering a preformed set of structures for language, as Chomsky proposes. Children may begin their language acquisition by using the context of a situation to figure out what speakers are trying to accomplish. In this view, language competence grows out of familiar situations, such as seeking help or establishing joint attention — situations that provide frameworks in which children learn to make their intentions plain and to interpret the intentions of others.

SOUND

In order to acquire language, babies must first separate the sounds of the human voice from other noises in the environment. Then they must distinguish between the sounds of speech and the coughs, whistles, throat clearings, and other noises produced by the adults around them. Finally, they face the task of breaking down the stream of speech into meaning.

Listening to Sounds

The job of acquisition is made easier by the fact that babies seem born prepared to attend to speech. Babies only a few days old prefer human voices to other sounds, as Earl Butterfield and Gary Siperstein (1974) discovered when they gave babies a chance to hear music. By sucking a pacifier, the babies could turn on tape-recorded music. The babies sucked to get musical reinforcement, and they sucked more to hear voices singing with music than to hear melodies without accompanying voices. These babies were actively selecting sound over silence and human sounds over nonhuman ones. Within the first month of life, human sounds take on added significance; for the sound of a person talking will stop a baby's cries, but the sound of a bell or rattle will not (Menyuk, 1971).

The first specific sounds an infant notices may be those words that receive the heaviest emphasis and that often occur at the ends of utterances. By six or seven weeks, an infant can detect the difference between syllables pronounced with rising and falling inflections. Very soon, these differences in adult stress and intonation can influence a baby's emotional states and behavior. Long before babies understand the words they hear, they can sense when an adult is playful or angry, attempting to initiate or terminate behavior, and so on, merely on the basis of such cues as the rate, volume, and melody of the adult's speech.

Just as significant for language development as the response to intonation is the ability to make fine distinctions between speech sounds. In a series of experiments, Peter Eimas and his colleagues (Eimas and Tartter, 1979) have shown that one-month-old babies can hear the difference between the sounds "ba" and "pa"; by two months, they can distinguish between "ma" and "na" and between "dae" and "gae." Other investigators have found that six-week-old infants can tell the difference between "bad" and "bag" (Jusczyk, 1977). These studies all used a similar method—a method based on the knowledge that babies will suck on a nipple at a constant rate as long as nothing new or startling strikes their senses, but that a sudden change in stimulation will cause them to suck at a more rapid rate. By giving babies a pacifier attached to electronic recording equipment, researchers are able to monitor a baby's rate and intensity of sucking. They repeatedly present a sound, such as "ba," to the baby until sucking reaches a stable rate; that is, until the baby has habituated to the stimulus. Then they switch to a slightly different sound, such as "pa," and babies immediately suck faster, indicating their ability to distinguish between the two closely related sounds. Such studies suggest that babies come into the world prepared not only to attend to speech but also to make precisely those discriminations among human sounds that are necessary if they are to acquire language.

Young babies cannot make all the necessary sound discriminations. Rebecca Eilers, Wesley Wilson, and J. M. Moore (1977) found, for example, that a three-month-old seems not to hear the difference between "s" and "z" at the ends of syllables, or between "sa" and "za." In addition, babies may lose their ability to detect differences that do not appear in the language about them (Eimas and Tartter, 1979). These two trends indicate that both experience and inborn ability play a role in the decoding of speech sounds.

Using sound differences to signal a difference in meaning develops later than the ability to detect differences between sounds heard in isolation, as Olga Garnica (1973) found in a study of eighteen-month-old infants. She gave the children colored blocks with features pasted on them, naming each block with a nonsense syllable, such as "bok" or "pok." When asked to put the "pok" under the blanket, few of the

infants seemed to hear the difference between the "b" and "p" sounds that newborns notice. After several training sessions, however, three times as many children made the distinction between "bok" and "pok." Apparently, children can learn to pay attention to distinctions they do not ordinarily notice, when there is a reason to do so.

Producing Sounds

Despite their sharp discrimination, it usually takes nearly a year before babies can produce sounds that can be identified as words. It is much more difficult for them to acquire motor control over the muscles and organs involved in producing speech than it is for them to perceive auditory distinctions (McCarthy, 1954). The progression from crying to babbling to speech follows the same sequence in most infants, but many pass through the linguistic developments earlier or later than the ages suggested in Figure 9.1.

A baby's first sounds are cries. After about three weeks, his or her vocalizations gradually increase in frequency and variety. Some sounds are only physical and digestive mouthings and gurglings; but by the second month babies invent new noises, from squeals to Bronx cheers, and repeat them again and again in a circular fashion (P. Wolff, 1969). Sounds of joy, called cooing, also may appear at this time, usually when babies seem happy: after eating, while watching a smiling face, when listening to singing, and while looking at or handling objects.

Infants in institutions with few adults around make fewer spontaneous noises and may not even cry as much as other babies, because crying is part of a child's social interaction. If no one comes to answer a cry, crying becomes a useless vocalization. When adults respond to the sounds a baby makes in play, the frequency of those sounds increases. In a series of experiments with institutionalized babies, Harriet Rheingold, Jacob Gewirtz, and Helen Ross (1959) used

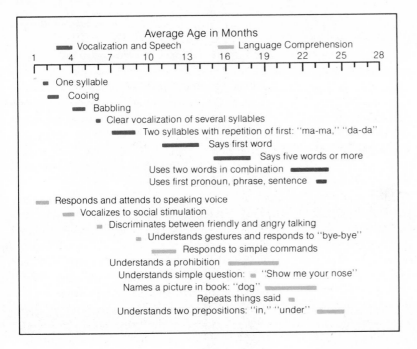

Figure 9.1 Highlights of language development during the first two years of life. Some infants may not show all the linguistic developments indicated. The average ages shown are approximations, and the length of the bars reflects the range in average ages that different researchers have reported for a particular linguistic development. (Adapted from Lenneberg, 1967; McCarthy, 1954; and Bayley, 1969)

simultaneous smiles, sounds, and light touches to the abdomen to condition babies' vocalizations. They did not reinforce coughs, whistles, squeals, snorts, fusses, or cries of protest. The reinforcement, which closely resembled a common variety of adult-infant play, quickly doubled the babies' responses.

Babbling begins around the age of five or six months, when babies produce sequences of alternating vowels and consonants, such as "bababba." These sound sequences give the impression that the baby is uttering a string of syllables. Such repetitions indicate that the

baby's control over speech musculature has greatly improved. This control, along with the coordination of sound production with sound perception, is probably the primary function of babbling. When babies feel certain patterns of motor activity involving throat, tongue, and lip muscles, they associate the movements with the sounds they hear themselves making. As babies gain motor control, babbling seems to follow the same rules and constraints that govern the development of words (de Villiers and de Villiers, 1978). As infants near the end of the first year, for example, they tend to babble consonants singly instead of in clusters, to put consonants at the beginning instead of at the end of a "syllable," and to drop final consonants. They also tend to switch the production of consonants from the back to the front of the mouth, shifting from babbles in which "g" and "k" sounds are frequent to those full of consonants formed with the tongue and lips—such as "b," "p," "d," and "t"—the consonants that are found in children's early words (Oller *et al.*, 1976).

Much early babbling appears to be sheer

motor play, as indicated by the fact that deaf babies babble in the same way as babies who can hear. But because the babbling of normal six-month-old babies shows a greater diversity of sound than the babbling of deaf infants, we can suppose that hearing speech sounds stimulates the baby. Soon after six months, deaf infants stop babbling, whereas hearing infants go on to greater diversity and experimentation in their speech play (Lenneberg, 1967).

Nevertheless, babbling may not be directly related to the acquisition of any particular native language (McNeill, 1970a). Babbling includes many sounds that adults do not make and that the baby may not be able to make a year later; nor can the early babbling of children from different language communities be distinguished from one another.

Near the end of the first year, however, intonational variations begin to appear in the child's vocalizations. Now the rising and falling pitch of his or her utterances becomes more and more like adult speech; the babblings of an English baby now sound like English, while the babblings of a Russian baby sound like Russian. At this time infants may produce long, complex sequences of meaningless sounds with the pitch contour of adult sentences. These sequences may appear when older infants are pretending to read or to talk to a doll.

Unlike babbling, first words do not sample a wide range of sounds. Indeed, when babies first begin to speak, they may be unable to imitate sounds they made earlier in playful babbling. First words tend to be short—one or two syllables—and each syllable generally consists of a consonant followed by a vowel. First syllables may be produced when infants simply release their lips while vocalizing. The first distinction among consonants that infants make is often between a sound such as "ma," which they produce by releasing air through the nose with the lips together and then opening the mouth, and "ba," which they produce by suddenly letting the air out between their lips. Once they have reached this point, they may be able to say "mama" and "ba" as distinct words; they are then ready to build a vocabulary.

The pronunciation of first words is not stable. If a baby's first word is something like "ba" for "ball," its pronunciation will vary from "bee" to "bow"; the consonant will also vary: it may be "pa," "va," "da," or "tha" (Ferguson and Farwell, 1975). Because a listener may expect to hear the sound "ball," he or she may believe the baby has a stable pronunciation of it. In fact, although babies can perceive the differences among sounds in adult speech, it takes a great deal of effort on their part to figure out how to produce the complex of sounds that correspond to adult words.

Because infants have few consonants at their command during the second year, their store of syllables is small and they often repeat them. For example, a year-old girl may say "pa-pa" or "bi-bi" or "car-car." Also, when she utters two different words with different meanings, they may sound the same because her small collection of syllables offers few possibilities for different word forms. She may say "ba" to imitate the words "ball," "bird," and "flower." The first time she says "ba," her mother or father will probably say "ball" when a ball is nearby or "bird" when a bird flies by. Such auditory reinforcement helps the infant to shape her "ba" until at last she does say both "ball" and "bird."

Struggling with Sounds

The work of decoding and reproducing the sounds of speech does not end with the child's first words; many preschool children and some young schoolchildren have trouble articulating certain sounds. A common problem in English, for example, is the confusion between the consonants "r" and "w,'" so that the child consistently says "west" instead of "rest" when it is naptime at nursery school.

Some children apparently do not notice any difference between the sounds they confuse, but they are in the minority. In an experiment John

Locke (1979) conducted with three- to six-year-olds who confused initial "r's" and "w's," one-third of the group, when shown a picture of a common garden implement, agreed that it was indeed a "wake" — pronounced thus by an adult. But the rest of the children had no trouble distinguishing between the sound "rake" and the sound "wake" when an adult pronounced them, and they denied that a rake was a "wake" — although adults perceived them as saying exactly that in their speech.

Quite a few children who make speech errors respond in this way, often becoming indignant if adults substitute the children's sounds in their own speech. Such indignation is embodied in a conversation with a three-year-old girl reported by Wick Miller (1964). Miller began the conversation by asking the child her name:

Child: Litha.
Miller: Litha?
Child: No, *Litha*.
Miller: Oh, Lisa.
Child: Yes, Litha.

In some cases the child's exasperation can be explained by the fact that children *are* making a distinction in their speech that adults do not detect. When Judith Kornfeld (1971) subjected children's speech to spectrographic analysis, she found that two-year-olds who seemed to be saying "gwass" for both "glass" and "grass" were not producing a real "w" sound and that the sounds they made for "l" and "r" were consistently different from each other when analyzed by machine instead of by human ear.

Despite this actual difference in the child's production, tests have shown that when children hear their own recorded speech, most of them perceive it as adults do. In another study, John Locke (Locke and Kutz, 1975) showed five-year-olds pictures of a wing, a ring, and a king and asked them to point to the correct picture and label it when they heard the experimenter say the names. Later, as children heard their own naming of the objects played back, they again

pointed to the pictures. All children could point to the correct picture when they heard the experimenter say the label, and children who customarily made the "l-r" distinction in their own speech also could identify the pictures from their own recorded labels. But children who had confused the sounds in their own speech pointed to the wing picture whether their taped voices were ostensibly saying "wing" or "ring." In other studies, Locke (1979) has found that children who say "wing" for "ring" when looking at a picture of a ring, if asked immediately, "Did you say 'wing'?" will reply "No."

Children who confuse these sounds in their own production but not in their comprehension of them may be failing to process their own speech sounds. However, Locke thinks it more probable that the children do process their speech sounds but pay little attention to the auditory and kinesthetic feedback from them, relying instead on their knowledge of their own intentions and on the context of the situation.

FOUNDATIONS OF MEANING

Although some babies begin to use a variety of single words toward the end of their first year, most will pass their first birthdays with a vocabulary of no more than three words. Before their second birthdays, their vocabularies begin to increase at an amazing speed, which will continue for years. The best guesses of researchers put the rate of increase among children of average intelligence at more than twenty words a day (G. Miller, 1978a).

First Words

Babies' first words carry on the patterns of behavior and intent they have developed during the prespeech period. As we saw in Chapter 8, babies seek help, persuade adults to look at things with them, engage in emotional exchanges, and induce others to join them in play. Before they accomplish these acts with the aid of labels attached to objects and actions in their world, babies pass through a phase when a single sound performs many functions at once. This effect shows clearly in Table 9.1, which gives a child's first seven words. When this little girl said "uh," for example, and pointed to a toy that had fallen, she was simultaneously referring to the toy, expressing her concern that it had fallen, and requesting that it be given back to her. In this case, a single, undifferentiated utterance referred, expressed, and demanded at the same time. As we shall see, once a child can combine several words in one utterance, these functions will become differentiated in speech.

An infant's first real words generally are names of objects and indicate the baby's recognition, first, that objects are worth talking about and, second, that they have names (Nelson and Nelson, 1978). Early vocabularies vary markedly according to the interests of young children and of those around them, but the first words usually express the same basic notions (K. Nelson, 1973). Most commonly, babies begin by naming *movers*—common objects that can move on their own and can manipulate other things. These include people, vehicles, and animals. Babies also refer

Table 9.1 THE FIRST SEVEN "WORDS" IN ONE CHILD'S LINGUISTIC DEVELOPMENT

Utterance	Age In Months	Meanings
uh?	8	An interjection. Also demonstrative, "addressed" to persons, distant objects, and "escaped toys."
dididi	9	Disapproval (loud). Comfort (soft).
mama	10	Refers vaguely to food. Also means "tastes good" and "hungry."
nenene	10	Scolding.
tt!	10	Used to call squirrels.
piti	10	Always used with a gesture, and always whispered. Seems to mean "interest(-ed), (-ing)."
deh	10	An interjection. Also demonstrative. Used with the same gesture as above.

Source: Adapted from David McNeill, *The Acquisition of Language: The Study of Developmental Psycholinguistics* (New York: Harper & Row, 1970), p. 22; based on material from Werner F. Leopold, *Grammar and General Problems in the First Two Years,* Speech Development of a Bilingual Child: A Linguist's Record, Vol. 3 (Evanston, Ill.: Northwestern University Press, 1949), p. 6.

The predominance of movers (objects that can move on their own) and movables (objects that can be moved) among first words reveals how infants perceive and arrange their world. (© Suzanne Szasz)

frequently to *movables*, objects that can be moved and manipulated but which cannot move independently. These include toys, food, articles of clothing, and household items. Such things as locations and objects used as tools (such as spoons) are less common early words. The form of these early words allows us to infer quite a bit about the way infants perceive and arrange their world (Clark and Clark, 1977); and as we shall see in Chapter 11, the baby's attention to movement and to the use of objects may play an important role in the development of concepts.

The Structure of Meaning

No one is certain just how children go about structuring word meanings; and when children first learn a word, its meaning may be very different from the conventional meaning attributed to it by adults. Sometimes a word means much more to children than adults believe, and sometimes it means less. Such differences in word meaning go unnoticed unless a child's error makes the discrepancy obvious.

OVEREXTENSION Young children sometimes extend the meaning of a word in their small vocabularies to cover objects or actions for which they have no word. This widespread application of a word, called *overextension*, is not illogical, for there is generally some perceived similarity of form or function among the objects or events to which the word is applied (E. Clark, 1973). Overextension is a fairly common practice, and analyses of parental diaries and observations of young children indicate that from 20 to 34 percent of a child's early words are extended in this fashion on some occasion (Nelson *et al.*, 1978). For example, one little girl used a single word to refer to a dress, a coat, a white hat, and the carriage she rode in, and to ask to take a walk or to report she had taken one. In this case, the mother's use of the word while dressing her small daughter to go out may have led the girl to include in its meaning all the re-

lated events and experiences for which she had no separate names.

Language and thought are so intertwined that when we examine children's meanings of words, we are examining the way they sort out their worlds. After analyzing many of the nineteenth- and twentieth-century diaries kept in various languages by linguist and psychologist parents, Eve Clark (1973) has discovered six major categories that young children use to bring order to the world: (1) *movement*, as when "sh" was extended from the sound of a train to all moving machines; (2) *shape*, as when "mooi" was extended from the moon to all round objects; (3) *size*, as when "fly" was extended from a specific insect to bits of dirt, specks of dust, all small insects, the infant's own toes, crumbs of bread, and a toad; (4) *sound*, as when "koko," a Yugoslav infant's word for a crowing cock, was extended to all music and even to a merry-go-round; (5) *taste*, as when "candy" was extended to mean cherries and then to refer to anything sweet; and (6) *texture*, as when "bow-wow" was

"Bow-wow" may enter this baby's vocabulary as the word for dog, but until the child has words for the rest of the animal kingdom "bow-wow" may be overextended to refer to horses, cows, goats, sheep, and cats as well. (© Michael Weisbrot & Family)

extended from a real dog to a toy dog, then to a fur piece with an animal head, and finally to all fur pieces.

As children acquire new words and have new experiences, they reorganize their early word meanings. Clark charts this development for a single word, showing its course in a young boy's experiences with the word "bow-wow." He first learns to apply "bow-wow" to dogs, but he soon uses it to refer to many animals—dogs, cows, horses, sheep, and cats—perhaps basing his meaning of the word on shape and movement. When he learns the word "moo," the little boy distinguishes cows from other animals, apparently dividing the animal kingdom into two categories: cows ("moo") and other animals ("bow-wow"). As the boy learns more animal names, he keeps subdividing the general class, "bow-wow," so that eventually he has separate names for dogs, cows, horses, sheep, and cats.

At each step, the available animal names take on a more precise meaning, based on those features the youngster uses to distinguish animals. For example, at one step, the concept "bow-wow" may include the feature of small size—because "bow-wow" refers only to fairly small animals such as dogs, cats, and sheep, whereas the concept "moo" and "gee-gee" (horse) may include large size among their features. In this process, the global meanings of infants' first words narrow as they learn new words and begin to attend to new features of objects and events. Each time they learn to notice and apply a new feature to the world, such as small, living, soft, and so forth, they may restructure the meaning of a number of words (McNeill, 1970a).

Children's overextensions may not always signify a true confusion of meaning. They may know that the word does not actually apply to the new object they have just named, but lacking the correct word, they reach for the nearest label in the same semantic neighborhood. Children who overextend words in speaking often understand the same words in a much more restricted fashion. Janice Gruendel (1977) has found that youngsters who refer to all animals as "bow-

wow," for example, when asked to point to the "bow-wow," will always pick a dog from a group of animals and never point to a cat or a sheep, even though they themselves use the term to refer to those animals. It is as if, she says, in comprehension a word denotes a single concept (such as dog), while in production it denotes the entire category of which the concept is a member (animals). In addition, overextensions may not always be examples of naming. Sometimes it appears as if the child is calling attention to similarities, as when a youngster calls a grapefruit a moon (roundness). If the child's grasp of language were firmer, he or she might say "It's like a moon" or "It's round" (Nelson et al., 1978).

UNDEREXTENSION   Another clue to the way children structure word meanings is a feature that is the opposite of the very young child's tendency to overextend meanings. Children also tend to underextend meanings of words, applying to a term only part of the meaning it has for adults. Children of all ages underextend words, but since the practice generally goes unnoticed, it has been studied primarily among older children. A child may know the word "food" perfectly well, for example, and asked what it means, say in the functional sort of definition that is prevalent among children, "Food is to eat." Yet asked if a cookie or a lollipop or ketchup is food, the child will say no. The child probably has never heard anyone refer to ketchup, cookies, and lollipops as food and may have established a central meaning for the term different from that held by adults. Food might mean, for example, "things to eat that are good for you," or "fruits, vegetables, meats, and cereal." The underextension arises when children come upon a poor example of a term—items that are a long way from the central meaning they have for the word (Anglin, 1978).

Children add verbs to their vocabularies more slowly than they add nouns, and for that reason, verbs are frequently underextended. Nouns are often concrete and their meaning is bounded by their physical nature. In contrast, verbs express relationships that depend upon abstract concepts; thus learning the meaning of a verb requires a child to learn the abstract relations involved (Gentner, 1978). In the sentence "The teacher gave Scott a gold star," for example, a child can see the teacher, the star, and Scott, but must abstract the relationship between the teacher's initial possession of the star, Scott's final possession of it, and the way the star passed from one to the other (freely? by coercion?), and so forth.

According to Dedre Gentner, children learn verbs in the order of their complexity and, until they know the meaning of a complex verb, will underextend it, representing just those aspects of it with which they are familiar. To test this proposal, she asked a group of children who were between three and eight years old to act out such sentences as "Make Ernie buy a car from Bert," using dolls, toy cars, and play money. The youngest children could act out the meanings of "give" and "take"; children who were a little older could act out "pay" and "trade"; but only the oldest children could act out "buy," "sell," or "spend money." Younger children most frequently acted out "buy" as "take" and "sell" as "give." As Gentner points out, such children have acquired enough of the meaning of "buy" and "sell" to know that objects change hands in a certain direction, but they are unaware of the monetary nature of the transaction.

This sort of development could be traced in another study, in which John Miscione and his associates (1978) tested three- to seven-year-olds on their knowledge of "know" and "guess." Most three-year-olds simply have no knowledge of the words' distinct meanings, say the investigators. They use "know" and "guess" indiscriminately and either randomly choose one or else use the one that has been more common or regarded as more desirable in their experience. Sometime after four, the words begin to separate in meaning, and children use "know" to mean both "know" and "guess successfully," while using "guess" to mean "guess unsuccessfully." Next, they go through a phase in which "guess successfully" is added to the meaning of "guess" but not applied consistently. Finally, around five or later, they use both words correctly on all occasions. This development shows how closely language and cognition are linked, say the investigators, because in order to use "guess" correctly, children must have advanced to a level of abstraction where external appearances and physical outcome (the success or failure of the guess) no longer dominate their thoughts or the meaning of their words.

THE USE OF ERRORS Children's errors of comprehension and production are frequently used as clues to semantic knowledge, for researchers assume that errors indicate a child's lack of knowledge or the inability to retrieve a word from memory (Bowerman, 1978). In some studies, however, the reason for children's misunderstandings is unclear. For example, Margaret Donaldson and G. Balfour (1968) found that young children confuse the words "less" and "more." The researchers constructed two apple trees from cardboard, on each tree putting six hooks from which red cardboard apples could be hung. After hanging a different number of apples on each tree, they asked three-year-olds which tree had more (or less) apples than the other. Preschoolers treated the two words as synonyms, answering every question as if both words meant "more." Donaldson and Balfour assumed that the children knew only that "more" and "less" had to do with amount, but not that they were opposites. Later research, however, indicated that children may not have gone by the meaning of the words but used context to decipher the researcher's questions. Susan Carey (1972) found that if she asked three-year-olds to "Make it so the glass has *tiv* in it," substituting a nonsense word for "more" or "less," the youngsters generally added water to the glass. Carey suggests that the context of the remark made during an obvious test led the chil-

It All Depends on Where You Stand

It is surprising enough that children master the underlying rules of language by the time they start school. It is nothing short of astounding that as toddlers they have already begun to learn the deictic function of words, a complicated aspect of semantics. *Deictic words* change their meaning because they locate things in reference to the speaker. "I" and "you," "my" and "your," "here" and "there," "this" and "that," "right" and "left," all reverse meaning depending upon who is talking. Understanding this change would seem to be a perplexing task, but children pick it up — and without anyone explaining it to them.

Very early in the second year, they learn to discriminate between "I/you" and "my/your." This ability to shift perspective appears to grow out of the turn-taking and role interactions with primary caregivers (Bruner, 1978), which were discussed in Chapter 8. From observation, Jill and Peter deVilliers (1978) decided that toddlers also had some inkling of the distinction between such expressions as "here" and "there." As they point out, when a small boy is told from across the room by his mother that his toy truck is "over here," he immediately trots to her vicinity to begin his search. But since in this case context might reveal meaning, the two researchers invented a game to test the discrimination.

In this hide-and-seek game, children sat across from an experimenter. Between them was a low Styrofoam wall; on each side of the wall was an overturned cup. While children closed their eyes, candy was hidden under one of the cups. Then the experimenter told the children where the candy was concealed, using a deictic expression ("The M&M is on *this* side of the wall"). Even three-year-olds were adept at translating from the speaker's perspective into their own and had no trouble with "here/there," "my/your," and "this/that."

But other studies have found that children are slow to extend comprehension of "this/that" to all situations. For example, in one study, half of the seven-year-olds were not always sure of the distinction between "this" and "that," even though they had been using the words for years (Webb and Abrahamson, 1976).

dren to understand that they were to do something with the amount of liquid in the glass and that adding water was a more typical response than pouring it out.

But errors, especially errors of production, are not always instances of misunderstanding, believes Melissa Bowerman (1978). Instead, they may simply be slips of the tongue by knowledgeable children. When she recorded the speech of her preschool daughters, she found that the girls began to use words incorrectly weeks or even months after they had been using them properly. When Christy was three and a half, for example, she said at bedtime, "I don't want to go to bed yet. Don't *let* me go to bed," confusing "let" and "make." And two-year-old Eva, finding her big sister's juice glass empty, said, "Then *put* her some more," confusing "put" and "give."

The girls were insensitive to the errors they made, never tried to correct them, and sometimes used the same word correctly only a few minutes after they had used it improperly. They rarely confused nouns; most of their errors were confined to verbs, prepositions, and adjectives that bore some relation in meaning, such as "behind" and "after" or "take" and "put." Bowerman suggests that children learn individual words without recognizing their similarity of meaning and that the errors do not appear until youngsters become aware of the similarity. As previously unrelated words move together in the organization of the child's vocabulary, they may put a strain on the child's ability to plan and monitor speech, so that when they search for a word, they select the wrong one from the same semantic neighborhood.

Meaning in First Sentences

Even when infants can speak only one word at a time, they appear to understand the longer utterances of their parents and older siblings. Their single-word utterances may also mean a good deal more than they can say at one time. Toward the end of the one-word period, infants often produce a series of separate one-word utterances that seem to relate to a larger meaning, although they speak each word with a falling intonation and pause between the words. For example, an eighteen-month-old girl described by Ronald Scollan (1979) held her foot above his tape recorder, looked up at him and said "tape" and then "step," as she threatened to step on the machine.

Within two months, this child was putting together two words with ease, saying such things as "drink soup" and "see Ron," with no pause between the words. The emergence of this two-word stage seems to be the result of an increase in neurological capacity, so that the child can process two words before forgetting the first. Now, although the child's level of understanding has not changed, he or she can put more information into a single statement.

The two-word stage is significant because it represents a striking advance in children's ability to code their understanding in linguistic terms and to project their ideas into the world of human interaction. Yet, with two-word sentences at their disposal, children still mean more than they can say in one utterance. For example, a small boy who wants his father to throw a ball cannot express the entire thought in a single statement. He can say "Daddy throw," "Throw ball," or "Daddy ball"; but he cannot say "Daddy throw ball." So youngsters again resort to stringing together short utterances to express a longer thought—as did the little girl in Scollan's study, who said such things as "Bathtub. Scrub it," and "Scary monster. Read dat."

Early language development has been studied in many different cultures, and everywhere the picture is the same. Sometime before their second birthday, children start to put two words together to express the same range of basic concepts that universally form the core of human language. Indeed, a large part of later language development is primarily a matter of elaborating and refining basic notions that are already present at this early age.

Expanding Vocabularies

Children's semantic development is a gradual process, and considering the speed with which

These nursery-school children are at the stage of rapid semantic development, when about twenty new words are mastered each day. (© Jean-Claude Lejeune/The Stockmarket)

Cataloging the Two-Year-Old Mind

These basic meanings expressed during the two-word stage come from data collected among children who speak English, German, Russian, Finnish, Turkish, Samoan, and Luo (spoken in Kenya). It would probably be possible to compile the entire list from two-year-old speakers of any language.

Identification "See doggy." An extension of the simple pointing responses that babies make during the prespeech period and the naming responses of the one-word stage.

Location "Book there." Words such as "here" and "there" signal the location of an object.
"Baby chair." "Dollie down." The juxtaposition of two words with no preposition indicates the relationship of being in, on, or under something else.

Recurrence "More write." "Another bang." "Book again." Used to indicate the presence, absence, and repetition of things and objects. Such utterances are among the first sentences a child speaks.

Nonexistence "All-gone ball." "Milk all-done." Indicate the disappearance of an object or the cessation of an action.

Negation "Not cat." "No water." Negative constructions used to contradict an adult utterance, to avoid a possible misunderstanding, or to reject the imposition of an adult desire.

Possession "Daddy coat." "Daddy chair." In a similar situation, infants at the one-word stage may say only, "Daddy."

Agent, action, and object "Daddy throw." (agent-action). "Throw ball" (action-object). "Daddy ball." (agent-object).

new words are added to their vocabularies, it seems safe to assume that at any time there are many words whose relevance they roughly grasp, but whose precise meaning they have not worked out (G. Miller, 1978a). By intervening in that development with the introduction of a single word, we can follow at least the beginnings of the process. At the Rockefeller University nursery school, where researchers were interested in the way children mastered the domain of color, that is exactly what researchers did. When considering color, points out George Miller (1977), the logical assumption is that children first learn the names for individual colors

and then learn that the general term for all color names is "color." But that is wrong. Children recognize words as terms representing color long before they know that the couch is brown and the blanket is pink. Asked the color of a ball or a plate, says Miller, most children will reply with a color term, even if they have not yet connected the right names with the various colors. The three-year-olds who attended the Rockefeller University nursery school had the most trouble learning white, gray, black, and brown; but they did not necessarily learn the primary colors before they learned pink, orange, or purple.

Although infants understand that agents act on objects, at the two-word stage they can express only two terms of this three-term relationship in a single sentence.

Action-location "Sit chair." "Mama sit." "Mama chair." Infants can talk about an action and at the same time specify where the action takes place only if they do not want to say anything else about the situation.

Action-recipient "Give papa." Infants can talk about who is to benefit from various actions.
"Cookie me." Even when the imperative verb remains unspoken, the demand is clear.

Action-instrument "Cut knife." Indicates that infants have some notion of the use of instruments to carry out actions.

Attribution "Red truck." "Big ball." Such utterances, in which nouns are modified with attributes, appear slightly later than other basic relationships.

Questions All the preceding sentence types become simple questions (in most languages) when infants say them with a rising intonation. In addition, infants generally possess several question words, especially "where," which they use simply with nouns ("Where ball?") or verbs ("Where go?").

SOURCE: Adapted from R. Brown, *A First Language: The Early Stages* (Cambridge, Mass.: Harvard University Press, 1973); D. I. Slobin, "Children and Language: They Learn the Same Way All Around the World," *Psychology Today,* 6 (July 1972), 71–74+; D. I. Slobin, "Cognitive Prerequisites for the Development of Grammar," in C. A. Ferguson and D. I. Slobin (eds.). *Studies of Child Language Development* (New York: Holt, Rinehart and Winston, 1973), pp. 175–208.

In an attempt to discover how children learned a new color term, Miller reports, Susan Carey and her associates painted a cup and tray an olive shade and introduced them into the school routine. In order to make sure that no child used learning from outside the school, they decided to call the color "chromium." Before the term was used, most children called the olive cup and tray "green." During the course of ordinary activities one day, an investigator used the term ("Please bring me the chromium cup") but made no attempt to teach it. The children had no trouble understanding the reference, because all that was needed to comply with the request was the knowledge "not the red one" or "not the blue one."

The word was not mentioned again. Six weeks after their single exposure to the word "chromium," the children were given a color test, in which they named color samples. One of the colors was olive. Eight of the fourteen children gave a response to the olive chip different from the one they had used before they heard the term chromium (two simply said they did not know the color's name; six used a new color term). After only one casual experience, more than half the children had learned that olive is not green and had begun to restructure their terminologies for the color domain. When we consider that these children are mastering twenty words a day and are working on many other chromium-type items, it is difficult not to be amazed at their linguistic feats.

THE CHILD'S GRASP OF SYNTAX

In order to become a competent speaker, a child must develop a command of syntax, especially of grammar. Grammar does not mean the schoolbook rules of how to speak "properly," but the rules that all of us know implicitly and use to organize our words into sentences. It is this knowledge of inflections, prepositions, word order, and so on that makes it possible for us to produce and understand sentences outside of any immediate physical context. The development of grammatical knowledge actively occupies the child from two to five, but some of the rudimentary grammatical tools are present before that time.

First Syntactic Devices

The first syntactic devices to appear in the child's speech are the basic tools of human language: intonation, word order, and inflection. By the time children come to the end of the two-word stage, they have a sure command of these devices and are ready to master the grammatical subtleties of their particular language.

INTONATION Infants at the one-word stage rely on intonation to communicate the intent behind a single word. When one-year-olds use intonation in this way, it is clear that they are not using their word simply to label an object, as Figure 9.2 indicates. Paula Menyuk and Nancy Bernholtz (1969) recorded the word "door" as spoken by an infant on three different occasions. When the tape was played, listeners had no trouble agreeing when the child made a declaration, made an emphatic statement, or asked a question. When the child used a falling pitch, listeners judged the utterance as referring to a door. When the word was uttered with a rising intonation, listeners interpreted it as a question. And when the intonation rose sharply and then fell, it was heard as an emphatic assertion or demand. Thus, the single word "door" could mean: "That's a door"; or it could mean "Is that a door?" or "Are you going to open the door?"; or it could mean "Open the door!" or "Close the door!"

Toward the end of the two-word stage, another intonational device develops — the use of stress to convey meaning. When saying "Baby chair," for example, a child may emphasize the first word, saying "BABY chair" to indicate possession ("That is baby's chair"); or the child may emphasize the second word, saying "Baby CHAIR," to indicate location ("Baby is in the chair") or destination ("Put baby in the chair").

WORD ORDER In English and in many other languages, the order in which words are spoken partly determines their meaning. English sentences typically follow a subject-verb-object sequence, and as soon as children understand this basic rule, they can distinguish between the meanings of "Tickle Daddy" and "Daddy tickle," because English speakers place the verb before the object. In Germany, however, very young children follow the rules of German word order and consistently place the object before the verb in two-word utterances (Roeper, 1973).

Instead of producing a random collection of words, using their two-word limit in any order, children use their knowledge of word order to establish the meaning of word combinations. For example, children who want Daddy to throw a ball will use some two-word combinations ("Daddy throw," "Daddy ball," "Throw ball") but not others ("Ball Daddy," "Ball throw," "Throw Daddy").

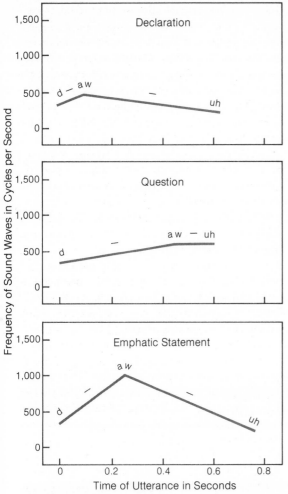

Figure 9.2 Three intonation patterns for the word "door" spoken by an infant at the one-word stage. (After Menyuk, 1971)

Children also use word order to understand the speech of others. Asked to act out simple sentences (such as "The cat kissed the dog"), in which word order is the only cue to meaning, children who can only speak sentences of two words will correctly portray the sentence (deVilliers and deVilliers, 1973). Similarly, linguists, parents, and other children use their own knowl-edge of word order to decipher the speech of children in the two-word stage.

When children first combine two words, individual differences appear in their grammatical constructions. Martin Braine (1976) argues that as children enter the two-word stage they discover different patterns of word order. One child may communicate the idea that an object is at a particular location by naming the object first and the place second ("Baby chair"); another may first discover a pattern in which the place comes first ("Here baby," "There book"). Some children prefer to combine two content words, as in "Play bed" and "Doggie bark." Others begin by combining content words with pronouns in most of their utterances, as in "I finish" (Bloom, Lightbown, and Hood, 1975).

INFLECTION Grammatical markers, such as the possessive "-'s" and the past tense "-ed," that are added to words to change their meaning are called *inflections*. Compared with other languages, English uses few inflections, and children begin to learn them early. Their mastery of the plural and the possessive, for example, soon makes it possible for them to indicate the differences between "Baby's chair" and "Baby chairs." To establish contrasts in meaning that English expresses by word order, some languages use differing inflections, and children who learn these highly inflected languages are quick to acquire the endings. For example, the direct-object inflection (in which the endings of nouns determines whether Mommy or baby does the kissing in "Mommy kisses baby") is one of the first endings that children pick up in learning such languages as Russian, Serbo-Croatian, Latvian, Hungarian, Finnish, and Turkish (Slobin, 1973).

The Development of Rules

To discover children's knowledge of grammar, some developmental psychologists observe and record children's natural speech, noting well-formed utterances, omissions and errors, and utterances children produce that they probably have never heard. Others set up situations in which children must either produce certain language forms, such as passive constructions, or else demonstrate that they can understand them.

DEMONSTRATING RULES When observing young children, researchers use indirect evidence to infer a child's knowledge of the rules. Each time children correct their own language, for example, they show that they believe certain combinations of words are incorrect — revealing they have a sense of grammatical norms (W. Miller and Ervin, 1970). A small girl, catching a glimpse of herself in a mirror, might say, "I see me in the mirror . . . I see myself in the mirror," or, on another occasion, "I seed . . . saw it." Such revealing instances are relatively rare, but they are the first signs of a child's ability to think about the form of language; they begin to appear about the time children are two years old (E. Clark, 1978).

In a major longitudinal study of language development, Roger Brown, Courtney Cazden, and Ursula Bellugi-Klima (1968) observed three children, whom they called Adam, Eve, and Sarah, over a period of several years. Brown and his colleagues selected these children because they were just beginning to combine words into two-word utterances and because their speech was clear and easy to understand. The researchers visited the children regularly, recording everything they said and everything that was said to them.

In the recorded dialogues, it was easy to trace the child's gradual grasp of English syntax. For example, in a single dialogue between two-year-old Eve and her mother, both participants made requests, formulated positive and negative statements, and asked questions. However, interesting differences appeared between the speech of the adult and that of the child. Certain elements that were systematically missing from Eve's speech were present in her mother's sentences. Eve's mother used auxiliary verbs (forms of ' to be," "to do," and so forth) wherever English syntax requires them. These grammatical elements were not present in Eve's speech. Eve, for example, said "It time," whereas her mother said, "It's time." Although the child's speech lacked the required auxiliary verb, it was understandable.

Within three months, Eve's language showed a dramatic change. She was using auxiliary verbs in negatives, questions, and statements. Her sentences were longer and more complex, and she was joining simple sentences together with such words as "when" and "and." She still made errors, of course, and some of these errors revealed that she was beginning to figure out the rules of English. For example, she said, "Then Fraser won't hear her too," where an adult would say, "Then Fraser won't hear her either." There is an odd rule in English that changes "too" to "either" in negative sentences (for example, it is correct to say, "Fraser will hear her too"). Eve had not figured out this rule for negative statements, but her use of "too" indicated that she understood the general function carried out by both "too" and "either."

FIGURING OUT RULES After studying research on language acquisition in many cultures, Dan Slobin (1973) concluded that children approach language with a set of seven beliefs that they apply to the words they hear. These beliefs, which Slobin calls *operating principles*, may determine which linguistic constructions are easiest for a child to learn.

The first principle is, *Pay attention to the ends of words.* In the languages Slobin studied, children learned suffixes (such as "-ed," "-ing," "-s," in English) more rapidly than they learned prefixes. This principle is essential in languages such as Russian, and it also plays a role in English. Its existence was demonstrated when

Stan Kuczaj (1979) tested preschool children with a nonsense syllable, which he alternately placed at the beginning and end of words. For example, some children heard "The boy drove the ip-car" while others heard "The boy drove the car-ip." With some children, the syllable "ip" was always given the meaning "big"; with other children it was always given the meaning "red." Whether "ip" meant "big" or "red," children who heard the syllable as a suffix found its meaning easier to learn than children who heard it as a prefix. Either children process word endings better than initial sounds or they pay attention to endings because such attention has paid off in the past.

Another operating principle involved in Kuczaj's study was one that states, *The phonological form of words can be systematically modified.* In the study, the same suffix ("ip") was systematically added to nouns, altering their sounds, and most children found it comprehensible.

The remaining operating principles are, *Pay attention to the order of words* (a principle we saw followed in the two-word stage), *Avoid interruption or rearrangement of linguistic units, Mark underlying semantic relations clearly, Avoid exceptions,* and *The use of grammatical markers should make semantic sense.* This last principle, Slobin believes, is demonstrated in the difficulty children have learning grammatical markers that denote gender but are purely arbitrary. This convention is not common in English, because English generally uses the neuter designation for inanimate objects and does not require the ending of adjectives to conform to the gender of the noun. But some languages do use this rule. In Spanish, for example, where pens are feminine and pencils are masculine, it is *una pluma blanca* (a white pen), but *un lapiz blanco* (a white pencil).

Not all of these operating principles have been tested in experimental situations, so there may be exceptions. But the principles provide a helpful framework for examining the development of grammar.

Overregularization

When children appear to be following the principle "Avoid exceptions," they are revealing the extent to which they have control of certain language rules, and many of their language errors can be viewed as attempts to make the language more systematic than it actually is. For example, Eve's use of "too" in both positive and negative utterances was a regularization of English, in which negative statements are an exception to the general rule. Overregularization in English shows most clearly in children's errors with the past tense of verbs and the plural form of nouns.

VERBS   The regular way to form the past tense for English verbs is to add "-ed": "walk, walked"; "ask, asked." However, many common verbs form their past tense in an irregular manner: "go, went,"; "come, came"; "drive, drove"; "break, broke." Investigators in the field of child language have found that children often learn a number of these irregular past forms as separate words at an early age and produce correct sentences: "It broke"; "Daddy went out"; "I fell." After using these correct past tense forms for many months, they discover the rule for forming regular past tenses; the irregular form may then disappear from their speech, to be replaced by overregularized forms. The child of three or four now may say, "It breaked"; "Daddy goed out"; "I falled."

As children get older, a curious pattern of redundant usage develops. Five- and six-year-olds begin to drop such forms as "eated," "goed," and "maked," and in their place may use a doubled past form, like "ated," "wented," and "maded" (Kuczaj, 1978). By the time children are seven, they have abandoned the redundant form; most have ceased to overregularize common verbs in any way.

What looks like regression in younger children is actually a sign of progress in the child's analysis of English. Clearly, children have not heard the overregularized forms from their parents; instead, they have constructed the forms to conform with the regularities they have noticed in the speech of others. And so a change from "went" to "goed" indicates that children have, on their own, discovered a regular pattern in English and are using it in their speech. They are avoiding exceptions and, by insisting on indicating the idea of the past in a regular way, are also marking semantic relations clearly — another operating principle (Kuczaj, 1978).

During these periods of overregularization, a child's speech seems remarkably impervious to gentle efforts at correction, as the following conversation reported by Jean Berko Gleason (1967) shows:

Child: My teacher holded the baby rabbits and we patted them.
Mother: Did you say your teacher held the baby rabbits?
Child: Yes.
Mother: What did you say she did?
Child: She holded the baby rabbits and we patted them.
Mother: Did you say she held them tightly?
Child: No, she holded them loosely.

Although his mother substituted the correct verb form twice in this short dialogue, the little boy persisted in repeating "holded" — tenaciously clinging to his own linguistic structure. Apparently, regularity is more powerful in its influence on children than are previous practice, reinforcement, and immediate imitation of adult forms. The child at this level of development seeks regularity and is deaf to exceptions (Bellugi, 1970).

As children gradually become aware of their overregularization errors, the correct form seems to filter in and out of consciousness. Dan Slobin (1978) reports a conversation with his young daughter, who was in the transitional phase. Slobin asked her if the baby-sitter had read a

book the previous night and Heida replied, using first the correct past tense, "read," then switching to "readed." During the exchange, Slobin said, "That's the book she readed, huh?" His own overregularization alerted Heida to the correct form and she replied in an annoyed tone, "Yeah . . . read!" following up with the comment, "Dum-dum!" As Slobin persisted in using "readed," Heida finally protested, "Will you stop that, Papa?" Although Heida was shifting back to "read," she may still have been saying "goed" and "maked," because children eliminate their overgeneralization errors slowly. They must learn, one by one, that only a single past form exists for each irregular verb (Kuczaj, 1978).

PLURALS The formation of plurals is another area in which children tend to overregularize. The English language has several ways to indicate whether a speaker is talking about one or more objects. English has three regular plural forms: s (as in "roots," "books"), z (as in "barns," "bees"), and ez (as in "horses," "matches"), and a child must learn that the rules for using these three endings depend on the final sound of each word. English also has some irregular plural forms, many of them common words: "feet," "mice," "men," "children." These irregular forms, like irregular verb past-tense forms, must be learned as separate vocabulary items.

A child's knowledge of the rules for forming plurals may be tested in a manner devised by Jean Berko (1958). In this test, an investigator shows a child some object for which there is no name, such as a large stuffed toy of unfamiliar shape. The investigator names these objects with possible nonexistent English words. She presents the child with one object and says, for example, "Here is a wug." Then she puts down another, similar object next to it and says, "Now there is another wug. There are two _____?" The child obligingly fills in the nonexistent word, "wugs," pronouncing it "wugz" if he or she knows the appropriate rule for forming plurals in English.

From observations of free speech, researchers have found that the child who has been correctly using some irregular plural forms ("feet," "men," "mice") may, for a time, overgeneralize the newly discovered rules of formation and say "foots," "mans," "mouses"—another example of the kind of overregularization that we saw earlier in the child's use of verbs. Here again, a child may learn the irregular form but apply the plural rule anyway, saying the redundant "feets," "mens," "mices."

Comprehending Complex Constructions

Children often develop their own simple rules for figuring out the meaning of sentences, although these strategies sometimes lead a child into misinterpreting certain kinds of sentences, such as those using passive constructions. Children hear many simple declarative sentences, each containing an actor, an action, and the object of that action: "Mommy is eating soup"; "Jane feeds her doll"; "Scott spilled the milk." In each of these sentences, the relationship between the actor ("Scott"), action ("spilled"), and object of the action ("milk") is expressed by word order. In passive constructions, however, the word order is reversed, and in the sentence "The milk was spilled by Scott," the object of the action ("milk") is the first noun in the sentence, and the actor ("Scott") the last.

Children's comprehension of sentences can be revealed by giving them objects to manipulate and asking them to act out the statements they hear. For example, the investigator may ask the child to act out "The truck follows the car." Using a toy truck and a toy car, most two- and three-year-olds can act out such declarative sentences; but asked to demonstrate a passive sentence, such as "The truck is followed by the car," even four-year-olds are seldom correct. In

fact, most four-year-olds carry out the opposite action each time, relying on word order.

Children apparently go through several strategies before they arrive at the complex rules of English grammar. Their changing understanding showed clearly in a study devised by Thomas Bever (1970). He gave children between the ages of two and four a toy horse and a toy cow and asked them to act out sentences such as the following:

1. The cow kisses the horse.
2. It's the cow that kisses the horse.
3. It's the horse that the cow kisses.
4. The horse is kissed by the cow.

Two-year-olds acted out the first three sentence types correctly, but their performance was random on the fourth (passive) sentence. They were as likely to have the horse kiss the cow as to have the cow kiss the horse. Bever suggests that when two-year-olds hear a noun followed by a verb, they assume that the noun is the actor. This noun-verb sequence is heard as a single perceptual unit meaning "actor-action." But if another word (or words) interrupts this simple sequence, as in sentence 4, the strategy fails and the children make a random choice of actor.

Four-year-olds, according to Bever, have developed a different strategy, in which they hear the first noun in a sentence as the actor and the noun following the verb as the object of the action. This strategy leads them astray in such sentences as "It's the horse the cow kisses," so in Bever's study they did worse than two-year-olds in this situation, generally picking the horse as the actor. In following their strategy, four-year-olds process a passive sentence as if it were an active sentence with some extra, uninterpretable parts. Thus, in this study, they consistently reversed the interpretation of passive sentences and acted out sentence 4 by having the horse kiss the cow.

Word order may not be the only cue children

use. Henrietta Lempert (1978) found that young children also use the animateness of the nouns involved to judge the meaning of passive sentences. In her study, when both subject and object were either animate or inanimate, the question did not arise. But when the sentence mixed animate and inanimate forms ("The ball is hit by Mickey Mouse"), three- and four-year-olds systematically chose the inanimate noun as the subject (acting out the sentence as "The ball hits Mickey Mouse," but correctly acting out "Mickey Mouse is hit by the ball"). The five-year-olds in her study had given up this strategy, generally giving correct demonstrations of passive sentences. Other studies indicate that not until the school years do children understand passive constructions in which the verb involved is not an action verb ("Donald Duck was liked by Goofy") (Maratsos *et al.*, 1979).

Passive sentences are not the only constructions that give children trouble. When active sentences are complicated, even nine-year-olds may resort to word order, interpreting the noun that most closely precedes the verb as the subject (C. Chomsky, 1969). For example, they interpret "Sally promised Mother to wash the dishes" as meaning that Mother washed the dishes.

Children do not progress directly toward adult grammar but instead construct and discard a variety of provisional grammars as they go along. As a result of these changing strategies, sentences that are correctly interpreted at one age (for example, the two-year-olds' correct understanding of "It's the horse that the cow kisses") may be misinterpreted at a later age.

Although children have mastered much of their language's grammar by the time they are four, they will continue to add to their knowledge of complex syntactical structures during the school years (Palermo and Molfese, 1972). This seems to be true regardless of the language they are learning and regardless of the setting in which they have been exposed to it (Slobin, 1975).

PLAYING WITH LANGUAGE

The basic rules of language are stabilized by kindergarten age, but as children move through the school years they become increasingly competent conversationalists, able to talk about remote and hypothetical events, quick to under-

The ability to lie effectively without getting caught marks the mastery of language, requiring a child to be aware of the listener's knowledge, the most convincing information, and an effective way to phrase it. (© Timothy Eagan 1981/Woodfin Camp & Assoc.)

stand complicated and indirect statements. According to Jill and Peter deVilliers (1978), this line of progress reaches it maximum development when the child learns how to lie effectively. As these researchers point out, in order to lie without getting caught, the liar cannot be bound by circumstance and must be aware of a listener's knowledge, of what information would best convince an audience, and of the most effective way to convey that information.

Children very early become aware of the power of the word, and quite small children indulge in language play. Preschoolers may explore the sound of words, chanting or singing a word or phrase while changing its stress or syllabic division. Catherine Garvey (1977b) describes a three-year-old boy who chanted "dune-buggy" over and over, becoming so absorbed in his word play that he forgot about the small model of a dune buggy that initiated his game. Children also play with word structure and with nonsense syllables, assigning funny names (Mrs. Fingernail, dingba, poopa, Uncle Poop) to themselves, to their playmates, or to imaginary people.

Riddles are a favorite form of word play, and children's earliest riddles fail to meet adult standards, for they are simply descriptive questions, such as "What's yellow? A banana." Five- and six-year-olds repeat such questions over and over, reveling in the capacity of language to refer to things in the world (Kirschenblatt-Gimblett, 1979). Children at this age cannot decipher incongruities, and some see riddles simply as questions with arbitrary answers. For that reason, their riddles often baffle adults: "Why did the donkey slam the door? Because the kangaroo was purple!"

Many riddles and jokes are based on the fact that words and phrases have more than one meaning. In order to appreciate the humor, children must be aware of the multiple meanings of a word or phrase and see how an unanticipated meaning resolves ambiguity. Thomas

Shultz (1974) regards a riddle as a misleading question followed by an incongruous answer. The listener must figure out how the incongruity makes sense; the pleasure comes when the child succeeds in resolving a problem by explaining the incongruous answer.

In his study of riddles, Shultz systematically studied children's appreciation of riddles at the ages of six, eight, ten, and twelve. The children heard a series of riddles, each having three possible answers. For example:

Why did the farmer name his hog Ink?

1. Because he kept running out of the pen.
2. Because he kept getting away.
3. Because he was black.

In answer 3, the incongruity is removed; the hog was named Ink because he was black. In answer 2, the incongruity remains but is not resolved; the answer is arbitrary and pure nonsense. In answer 1, however, the incongruity is resolved in a way that plays on words. A clearly discernible change in the child's appreciation of humor appeared between the ages of six and eight. Six-year-olds found the arbitrary, nonsensical answer humorous, whereas eight-year-olds appreciated the resolution of incongruity based on word play.

Daniel Yalisove (1978) extended Shultz's approach, testing riddle comprehension and liking among nearly 600 schoolchildren in grades one through ten. He discovered that first graders prefer reality riddles, that is, riddles that involve neither word play nor absurdity but that are based on a conceptual trick. For example, "How many balls of string would it take to reach the moon? One, but it would have to be a big one" tricks the listener, who at first assumes he or she is being asked to consider normal-sized balls of string. As in Shultz's study, riddles based on linguistic ambiguity were most popular in the fifth grade. But seventh, eighth, and ninth graders preferred absurd riddles, such as "How can you fit six elephants into a VW? Three in front and three in back."

Yalisove suggests three stages in the comprehension of riddles. In the first, strongest among first graders and lingering among a number of third graders, children interpret the riddle as a test of their ability to tell the difference between the sensible and the silly. In the second stage, which is strongest among third graders, children focus on the reasonableness of the answer and attempt to explain away the incongruity of the answer. They seem to be unable to tolerate the idea of the absurd, the illogical, or the implausible. In the third stage, which begins in the sixth grade and becomes increasingly prominent, children acknowledge the incongruity and then justify it on the basis of a special rule. Only the older children perceived the structural elements of each category of riddle.

Riddles demand linguistic sophistication, both in the telling and in the appreciation of their ambiguity. They show the link between language and cognition, and as we move on to the study of cognitive development, we shall see how important language is in the development of memory, thinking, and intelligence.

SUMMARY

1. The major explanations of language acquisition are biological, mechanistic, or functional. In biological theories, language is the result of maturation, and the basic structure of human language is genetically determined, requiring only exposure to language to develop. In mechanistic theories, language development is a result of conditioning and observational learning. In functional theories, language is a combination of maturation and social interaction, developing from the nonlinguistic communication between infant and adult.

2. From the first month of life, babies pay special attention to the speech they hear. Despite their ability to discriminate among sounds, it usually takes about a year for them to acquire sufficient motor control to be able to produce identifiable words. They acquire this muscular control first through crying and later through babbling. By the end of the first year, a baby's intonation patterns resemble his or her native language. The pronunciation of first words is erratic, but through reinforcement, word forms gradually stabilize.

3. The infant's first words generally name objects, and these early words are often overextended in meaning. Although they overextend words in speaking, infants' understanding is generally specific. Older children underextend words, applying only part of its accepted meaning to a term.

4. Infants often know and mean more than they can say. Although two-word sentences communicate more information than single-word utterances, they do not represent a new level of thinking. By the time they are two, infants can usually put several words together and can express and understand an impressive range of basic universal concepts.

5. A rudimentary grammar appears in the child's language toward the end of the two-word stage. It includes the basic tools of human language: intonation, word order, and inflection. With these first grammatical devices, the child is ready to master the further subtleties of his or her native language, and approaches the understanding of its structure with a series of operating principles that make some linguistic conventions easier to learn than others.

6. Young children attempt to simplify language by making it more systematic than it actually is. In English, for example, children tend to overregularize the past tense of verbs ("breaked") and the plural form of nouns ("foots").

7. The ways in which children comprehend speech also indicate an increased knowledge of grammatical rules. Over time, children appear to construct and discard a variety of provisional rules and may correctly interpret a certain kind of sentence, such as a passive one, at one age but not at another.

8. The child's development as competent linguist has fully flowered when he or she has learned to lie effectively, a demanding linguistic skill. Even small children play with words, and as their grasp of language becomes sophisticated, they begin to appreciate the incongruity at the heart of riddles, and the resolution of that incongruity.

PART 5

The Development of Cognition

We cannot see cognition, hear it, or touch it, but we can see, touch, and hear its products: speech, intelligent action, human artifacts, music, art, literature, and science. We know of its existence in ourselves but can only infer its existence in others from their actions. Perhaps the best way to describe cognition is to say that it encompasses all mental activity—from the perception of a pricking pin to the creation of the Mona Lisa or *Anna Karenina*. By the time we complete the tale of cognitive development, we shall have seen children as remarkably active organisms, curious about the world and themselves and eager to make sense of both, constructing from their varied experiences new hypotheses about how its parts fit. We shall see children as architects of time, space, and objects, and as designers and users of symbols. Cognition is the vehicle by which infants become intellectually accomplished adults.

Development of Sensation and Perception

An eight-year-old boy often runs errands for his mother. Grocery list clutched tightly in hand, he walks the six blocks between his house and the market, crossing streets and turning twice to reach his destination. Carrying his bag of groceries, he retraces his steps and hands over the sack to his mother, who rewards him with a quarter. Only a few years ago, this boy could not have navigated the route from his house to the store, nor would his mother have trusted him to do so. But gradually he has developed the ability to move around surely through the world, first orienting himself by landmarks—Mrs. Wilson's house, the fire station, the big apple tree on the corner where he must veer left—then slowly developing a concept of the route he knows so well that he follows its landmarks almost without thinking about them. The development of such mental maps is an advanced perceptual skill that builds on the elementary perceptual knowledge of infancy.

In this chapter, we shall first discuss the child's sensory development, noting anatomical changes in the eye and ear and the development of sensory capacities. We shall briefly examine the development of smell, taste, and touch before returning to the important area of visual perception. We shall watch the development of depth perception, and size and shape constancy in the infant and note how rapidly these skills become apparent. We shall see how the sophisticated skill of cognitive mapping develops from the way babies learn to orient themselves in space. Next we shall consider the perception of pictures, asking how children learn to see a three-dimensional scene in a flat display, and examining two major theories accounting for that ability. Finally, we shall discuss coordination among the senses and the development of sensorimotor coordination. By the end of the chapter, it will be clear that there is more to perceiving the world than simply recording its multiple sensations.

SENSORY DEVELOPMENT

Investigations of cognitive processes are meaningless unless researchers know how well babies' and children's senses function. It is through the senses that the raw material of stimulation is transformed into information. Children rely on their eyes, ears, mouths, hands, noses, and skin to extract information about the sounds and sights, the pains and pressures, the tastes and smells of their world. Young children can tell us whether two objects look the same, one note is higher than another, or a liquid is sweet or sour. But this is not true of infants. In a test of vision, for example, a baby cannot say, "I see a red and yellow square." Researchers, therefore, must resort to careful monitoring of infants' behavior during an experiment, watching to see if the baby's gaze strays from the stimulus. To detect visual responses, they also use instruments to measure such things as changes in the electrical potential of the retina, changes in brain waves, shifts in eye movements, or changes in reflections on the cornea.

Hearing

Sound is a major source of environmental information for the developing infant. Auditory perception is important in learning to understand and speak language and in determining the location of people or events. However, babies do not hear as acutely as adults. Some receptor cells in the inner ear, especially those responsible for the transmission of high-frequency sounds, are still immature at birth (Hecox, 1975). And although the auditory nerve is well myelinated at birth, the auditory cortex — that part of the brain where sound is interpreted — is quite immature. In addition, during the first few days of life fluid in the middle ear hinders the transmission of sounds. Despite the fact that the baby's ear is developed at birth, the external auditory canal, the eardrum, and the middle-ear cavity do not reach adult dimensions until the baby is at least a year old.

The frequency and intensity of sounds interact to determine babies' responsivity to them, and babies appear to be especially unresponsive to shrill tones, which have a very high frequency. Adults cannot hear sounds above 20,000 cycles per second or below 10 cycles per second unless the intensity of the sound is immense, and they are most responsive to sounds in the region between 1,000 and 3,000 cycles per second. So are babies, but their threshold is about fifteen decibels higher than that of adults. At 3,000 cycles per second, an adult can hear a sound as soft as a whisper; at that same frequency, babies require the sound to be about as intense as normal conversation, although at 1,000 cycles per second they respond to the level of a whisper (Olsho, 1979). At 10,000 cycles per second, even two-year-olds are relatively insensitive to (shrill) notes that adults hear easily (Schneider, Trehub, and Bull, 1980).

In some respects, however, babies show incredible sensitivity. William Kessen and his associates (1979) found that babies between three and five months old not only are responsive to pitch but can imitate it. Mothers coaxed their babies to vocalize, then followed the vocalizations with a musical note, which the babies soon began to imitate. Trained musicians who judged tape recordings of the musical "conversations" rated every baby as doing well, and some babies were within a quarter tone of the notes they copied. The experimenters suggest that pitch matching is a natural ability that is often eroded or lost as children acquire language.

At a very early age, babies are sensitive to the sounds of language. As we saw in the discussion of language development (Chapter 9), babies as young as a month can distinguish between the sounds "ba" and "pa." They appear to separate speech from nonspeech and to process the speech sounds in a way that supports the conjecture that the human organism is prepared to detect and decode spoken communication (Eimas, 1975).

Jerome Kagan (1971) and his colleagues tested the extent to which eight-month-old boys could recognize familiar sounds. They read four sentences to each baby in the study. Two of the sentences used words, such as "smile" and "daddy," that parents frequently use in interactions with their babies, and the words were arranged in a meaningful way. The other two sentences were nonsensical. Kagan and his colleagues found that the babies responded differently to these different combinations of sounds. The meaningful sentences with familiar words brought about a higher rate of babbling in the babies than did the nonsensical ones. This effect occurred even when the person who read the sentences was a male stranger, whose voice was unfamiliar.

Toward the end of the first year, infants have progressed considerably beyond their auditory capacities of the first few months, which even then were quite impressive. At that time they were sensitive to such things as the frequency, duration, and intensity of sounds. By the end of the first year, however, they are also sensitive to the differences between various combinations of sounds and they recognize certain words, becoming increasingly sensitive to the meanings of the sounds they hear.

Smell and Taste

Smell and taste have received much less attention than vision and hearing, in part because they are difficult to study and in part because we know little about these senses in adults. Yet

Since birth this child has been especially sensitive to the sounds of language and depends upon hearing as a major source of information about the world. (© R. Lynn Goldberg 1980)

smell and taste are important and probably play a larger role in the infant's knowledge of the world than in that of the adult, whose experienced vision and reliance on verbal communication have made the use of the other senses fade in significance. Early human beings relied on taste to help them decide what to eat and what to reject. Since ripe fruits are sweet, green fruits are sour, and many poisonous substances bitter, our inborn preference for sweets once had real survival value. Being without soaps, deodorants, and perfumes, our ancestors also undoubtedly got more information about the world through smell than people do today.

The neonate seems to respond to strong smells as an adult does, and a baby's ability to discriminate among odors develops rapidly. As noted in Chapter 5, within a week to ten days of birth, most babies can detect the difference between the odor of their mothers' milk and that of a strange woman. Such discrimination indicates a highly developed sense of smell.

Taste has received more attention than smell, but most of it has been devoted to sweet flavors, since heavy consumption of sugar-laden food has aroused concern for public health. The more sugar researchers add to water, the more water newborns will drink. The newborn's enjoyment of sweets never disappears but follows a typical pattern. Babies and children like extremely sweet tastes; older adolescents and adults prefer less sweet tastes. When people are asked to rate four different sugar solutions that vary enormously in sweetness (see Figure 10.1), 50 percent of children say they like the very sweetest solution, whereas only 25 percent of adults and adolescents older than fifteen do. What is more, 25 percent of adults will choose the least sweet solution, but only about 15 percent of children like it best (Desor, Maller, and Greene, 1977). This study also points out the presence of individual differences in response to taste. Some people cannot taste a sweet flavor at all; others need a stronger or weaker concentration to show the same discrimination (Kare, 1975).

Learning also plays a major part in the detection of flavor, as Joel Grinker (1977) discovered

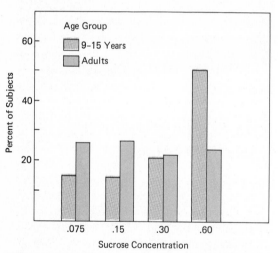

Figure 10.1 Although there is an inborn human preference for sweets, adults and older adolescents are less likely to enjoy extremely concentrated sweets, as shown in this study in which children and adults chose the solution they liked best.

SOURCE: From J. A. Desor, O. Maller, and L. S. Greene, "Preference for Sweet in Humans: Infants, Children, and Adults," in J. M. Weiffenbach (ed.), TASTE AND DEVELOPMENT. Bethesda, Md.: U. S. Department of HEW (DHEW Pub. # [NIH]77-1068), 1977.

when he added red food coloring to sweet solutions. Every child and adult in the study said that the sugar solution that looked like cherry Kool-Aid was sweeter than the same solution without the red coloring.

When it comes to salty tastes, newborns seem indifferent to weak solutions. Adding salty or bitter flavor to water does not affect a newborn's consumption, although adding a sour flavor will reduce the baby's intake (Desor, Maller, and Greene, 1977). Bitter or salty flavors must be intense before newborns reject them, and by the time babies are six months old, they even prefer slightly salty to plain water (Maller and Desor, 1974; Desor, 1975). By the time children are a year and a half old, however, they react as adults do and reject salty water (Beauchamp and Maller, 1977).

Touch, Temperature, and Pain

The responsiveness of babies and children to touch, temperature, and pain has received little attention. No one wants to hurt a baby, which is the only way to discover whether the infant responds to painful stimuli. But as Aidan Macfarlane (1977) points out, when the heels of newborns are pricked in order to obtain blood samples, babies pull their feet away, wail, tense their muscles, and turn bright red. In addition, their sleep patterns are often disturbed after such an experience. It seems clear that newborn babies feel pain.

As for temperature, newborns who are not hungry will sleep when they are warm and cry when they are cold (Macfarlane, 1977). In an experiment that totally controlled an infant's environment, B. F. Skinner (1972) reported that as a newborn, his young daughter seemed most comfortable without clothing at about 86°F.; when she was eleven months old, the most comfortable temperature for her naked skin was 78°. Skinner also found that his baby fussed when too warm and that lowering the temperature by a degree or two would end all signs of discomfort.

Babies are quite sensitive to touch; even a fetus responds to stroking around its mouth with a fine hair. Newborns react to air blown on the naked skin, but they find touch comforting as well. When a newborn baby is crying, a hand placed on the chest or stomach will often end the cries (Macfarlane, 1977). Before long, touch also becomes a way to learn. Babies less than a year old can learn to identify objects simply by touch. Sherri Soroka, Carl Corter, and Rona Abramovitch (1979) gave 10-month-old babies objects while they were in a dark room. One of the objects was a wooden ring, the other a wooden cross. After the babies had explored an object for two minutes without being able to see it, they were tested. Still in the dark and still unable to see the object, half received the same wooden shape and half received a shape they had never felt. Babies who got a strange shape manipulated it significantly longer than babies who were given the same shape they had held earlier, indicating that as they handled the first object, they acquired a good deal of factual information about it.

Vision

Newborn babies cannot see as well as adults. In fact, it is at least six months before the baby can see as clearly as an adult (Dayton *et al.*, 1964) and seven months to a year before the full range of the infant's visual capacities has developed (Cohen, DeLoache, and Strauss, 1979). But infants can see a good deal better than was once supposed. Within a few days, they have reasonably good visual acuity—at least at close distances.

ANATOMICAL CHANGES When babies are born, their eyeballs are smaller and less spherical than those of adults. The eyeball grows rapidly during the first two years, and its growth

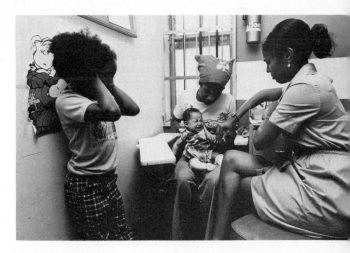

Young babies respond audibly to discomfort and pain, and their protests leave no doubt as to their sensitivity to touch and pain. (© Bohdan Hrynewych)

When B. F. Skinner's daughter spent her first months in this climate-controlled air crib, her fussing almost always stopped when the temperature was lowered slightly—indicating an early sensitivity to temperature. (Courtesy B. F. Skinner)

does not cease until the child reaches middle childhood, by which time it has doubled in size (Maurer, 1975). The baby's retina — where focused light stimulates cells that pass signals along the optic nerve to the brain — is fairly well formed at birth. That part of the retina which is responsible for color vision, however, is not fully developed. The neonate's color-sensitive cells are short and stumpy instead of long and slender, and few in number. It is four months before these cells have lengthened and become densely packed. The newborn's optic nerve is both thinner and shorter than the adult's, but the sheath of myelin, which speeds the transmission of signals, forms faster here than in other parts of the nervous system (Maurer, 1975). Myelinization of the optic nerve is complete by the time the baby is four months old. Although the visual cortex — that part of the brain where visual signals are interpreted — is underdeveloped at birth, all the neurons are present, if mostly unmyelinated (Cohen, DeLoache, and Strauss, 1979). The visual cortex functions at birth, but the neurons continue to change in size and shape and to become more differentiated. Myelinization in the visual cortex is not complete until children are at least ten years old. Control over the eye muscles comes slowly, and most babies are about seven weeks old before they have mastered the ability to converge their eyes on an object.

VISUAL CAPACITIES Vision may be babies' most important source of information about the environment during the early months of life.

There is still some uncertainty as to how soon babies can perceive color. As indicated in Chapter 5, the newborn infant may be color-blind. In experiments that separated brightness from hue, infants as young as two months apparently could see color in the yellow-blue range (Peeples and Teller, 1975). Such vision is similar to that of a partially color-blind person, who sees no difference between red and green. Subsequent experiments have indicated that by four months babies probably perceive colors as adults do,

seeing blue, green, yellow and red (Bornstein et al., 1976). These categories and infants' perceptions of them tend to correspond to the apparently universal and nonarbitrary psychological color categories used by older children and adults (e.g., Heider, 1972). Yet what the sight means to them is of course very different from the meaning the same sight will convey several years later (Haber and Hershenson, 1973).

Since the eyes of young infants are smaller than those of adults, their visual acuity may be poorer: the same stimuli fall on a smaller area of the retina, stimulating fewer cells (Maurer, 1975). As noted in Chapter 5, the newborn can best discriminate objects and patterns at a distance of nine inches. Acuity improves, until a six-month-old infant can probably see as clearly as an adult. At first, the visual field is quite narrow; babies can see objects directly in front of them, but when an object is more than thirty degrees to either side, they are unable to detect it. By the time they are seven weeks old, however, their peripheral vision expands, so that they can detect an object as far as forty-five degrees to the side (Macfarlane et al., 1976); this gives them a visual field of ninety degrees, about half that of an adult's. In another five or six weeks, they will be able to tell the difference between two objects placed to the side, but the objects can be no more than thirty degrees off center (Maurer and Lewis, 1979). Adults use peripheral vision to guide eye movements and to decide what they will look at directly. Although by the time they are four months old, babies can integrate peripheral and central vision to some extent, and both systems are mature by the time babies are six months old, no one is certain just how well the systems interact in a six-month-old (Cohen, DeLoache, and Strauss, 1979).

DEVELOPMENT OF VISUAL PERCEPTION

There is a good deal more to vision than detecting differences in pattern, color, or outline.

The human visual system is complex, and the explanations for many aspects of adult vision remain unresolved (Haber, 1978). Somehow a baby comes to perceive a three-dimensional world, to perceive objects as the same size and shape even when their images cast different shapes on the retina, and to understand their physical relationship to a place in space.

Depth Perception

We live in a world of three dimensions. Although the human retina is a two-dimensional surface, the solidity and depth of the world is apparent to us. Recent innovative research has begun to establish the time at which infants begin to perceive the three-dimensional quality of the world. It is possible to create the illusion of depth by presenting a different image to each eye. Thirty years ago, Hollywood went through a vogue of movies that simulated a third dimension. The audience viewed the picture through a pair of cardboard glasses with one lens of red cellophane and the other of green. Without the glasses, the image on the screen was blurred; with them, the picture appeared to have solidity and depth. This same technique has furthered research in visual perception. Bela Julesz (1971) combined it with computers that generate paired displays of red and green dots, called anaglyphs. Viewing the two slightly different displays through a pair of glasses like those used with 3-D films fuses the images, and a three-dimensional form appears. The advantage of using the computer-generated dots lies in the fact that there are no familiar forms to give the viewer cues — only perception of the third dimension allows a shape to emerge in the display.

Robert Fox, Richard Aslin, and their associates (1980) showed two-and-a-half- to six-month-old infants a series of anaglyphs in which the solid forms changed position and seemed to move across the screen. As the anaglyphs appeared, the investigators tracked the babies' eye movements. The youngest babies' eyes followed the changing shapes no better than chance; obviously they either saw nothing or were not interested in whatever they did see. But older babies did progressively better, and by six months, most babies were tracking the forms a good part of the time. When tested with anaglyphs that could not be fused to produce depth, babies' performance dropped to chance. Depth perception appears to emerge gradually, beginning at about three and a half months. Earlier research showed that by the time they are two or three months old, babies would rather watch a sphere than a flat disc (Fantz, 1966), indicating an awareness of difference in depth among these babies, if not an appreciation of it.

Other findings indicate that some time between three and six months is the closest one can come at present to fixing a date for the emergence of depth perception. In an experiment with three-and-a-half- and five-month-old-babies, Albert Yonas and his colleagues (1978) used a projected image of another kind — a solid object that appears to come directly at the viewer — to establish the existence of depth perception. All infants looked intently at the image, their eyes converging on the illusory missile that seemed ready to strike them. But only the five-month-old infants either reached out toward the object or blinked and withdrew their heads as the object appeared to draw near.

The intimation that they are about to be hit is not the only three-dimensional warning that babies respond to; they also use visual cues to save themselves from such dangers as falling off tables or chairs. In a novel experiment, Eleanor Gibson and Richard Walk (1960) studied infants' use of depth information by placing the infants on what appeared to be the edge of a cliff. Their experiments showed that an infant who is old enough to crawl will not crawl over the edge of a visual cliff, even to reach his or her mother. Because the infants in these experiments were between eight and twelve months old, it is difficult to say whether the behavior simply represented a maturation of vision or whether some learning was also involved. Subsequently, however, Sandra Scarr and Philip

The World of Blind and Deaf Children

The baby who is born blind depends on smell, sound, taste, and touch for information about the world. Since visual stimulation provides so much of the sighted baby's knowledge, it is not surprising to find differences in development among blind children. The blind baby cries, laughs, and smiles spontaneously, just as the sighted baby does. Daniel Freedman (1974) studied several blind babies and discovered that their first social smiles, which come in response to voices, touch, or the squeaking of a familiar toy, are extremely fleeting—much like the reflexive, early smile of both sighted and blind babies. By the time the babies are six months old, their smiles are normal. At about three months, like sighted babies, blind babies wiggle their hands before their eyes as if they were observing them, but this response soon drops away. Instead of reaching for objects at about six months, as sighted babies do, blind babies reach for noisy objects at about eleven months (Fraiberg and Bayley, 1974). They generally do not walk until they are more than fifteen months old.

Their lack of sight may give blind babies less reason to explore the world. Once they learn to move about on their own, they may develop the use of echolocation (navigation by using the echo from sound bounced off the surroundings). Many adult blind make their way surely through the world in this manner, sometimes clicking their tongues or snapping their fingers to create echoes (Gibson, 1969). Thomas Bower (1977) discovered that a sixteen-week-old blind baby he studied was already beginning to develop this sense. The little boy made sharp, clicking noises with his lips and tongue and turned his head to follow a ball that Bower dangled soundlessly in front of him.

Early imitative play among blind children is limited to mimicking sounds. As preschoolers, blind children show only a rudimentary imitation of actions; instead, they repeat conversations they have overheard or taken part in (Mogford, 1977). Blind children also begin to play house with dolls much later than sighted children and impute neither personality nor an imaginary life to their dolls (Fraiberg and Adelson, 1973).

If blind children suffer in the development of play and mobility, deaf children suffer in the area of language development. For the first six months, babies who are born deaf develop just as hearing babies do, babbling and cooing; consequently, parents generally are very slow to realize that their child cannot hear. However, to the trained observer the babbling of deaf babies sounds different, for deaf babies tend to persist in certain sounds whereas hearing babies run through a wide range (Lenneberg, 1967).

Because they never hear their own voices, when deaf children develop spoken language, the intonation patterns, pitch, and loudness will be wrong, although the same qualities in their laughter and babbling will sound perfectly normal (Lenneberg, 1964). Children who are deaf from birth tend to be

Salapatek (1970), using the visual-cliff apparatus designed by Gibson and Walk, found that infants begin to use depth cues to avoid edges shortly after they reach seven months of age, but only if they have begun crawling before that time. When two-month-old babies are placed on the deep side of the cliff, their hearts slow down, suggesting they make some sort of discrimination related to depth. When nine-month-olds are placed on the deep side, however, their hearts

poor readers, frequently reading at about a fourth-grade level when they graduate from a high school for the deaf (Locke, 1978). But if taught sign language, the deaf are skilled conversationalists. One deaf child of deaf parents had learned sixty words in American Sign Language by the time she was twenty-two months old (Newman, 1974), and three-year-olds may know as many as three hundred signs (Brill, 1974). In contrast, the six-year-old deaf child without sign language generally knows ten to fifty intelligible words (Lenneberg, 1967).

Where cognitive functioning is not dependent on language, deaf children equal the achievement of children who can hear. In one test of concept formation, seven- to twelve-year-old children had to learn "sameness," "symmetry," and "opposition" (Furth, 1961). The deaf and hearing children did equally well on "sameness," which both groups presumably had encountered and a concept for which deaf children have a sign. The deaf children did slightly better on "symmetry," a concept that neither group was likely to have encountered and one that hearing children rarely develop before they are twelve. When it came to "opposition," the hearing children did much better, perhaps because of the large number of oppositional words (short-long, little-big) in their vocabularies. The spontaneous play of deaf preschoolers is intelligent, imaginative, and appropriate for their age level (Lenneberg, 1967). They enjoy pictures, and their cognitive development as revealed in play seems comparable to that of hearing children.

When language is not required for understanding, deaf children do as well as hearing children no matter what the task. (© Alan Carey)

speed up, suggesting they are afraid (Campos, 1976). This discrepancy suggests that not the detection of depth but experience in crawling is necessary before an infant learns that the visual cues of depth may signify danger. More recent research indicates that the fear of depths emerges just after the baby develops the ability to move about (Campos *et al.*, 1978).

How does a baby develop an appreciation of the third dimension? Babies, like adults, may

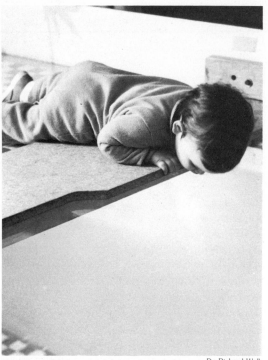

Dr. Richard Walk

When placed on this visual cliff, seven-month-old babies generally crawl across the glass covering the "shallow" side (*top left*) without hesitation; but faced with what appears to be a sudden drop (*top right*), they balk and will not crawl over the glass covering the "deep" side (*bottom*) even to reach their mothers. (Courtesy Dr. Richard Walk)

use various cues to perceive the existence of depth (Rock, 1975). Using only one eye, a viewer picks up information in three ways: from *perspective*, the effect that makes a two-dimensional drawing appear to have depth; from *accommodation*, as the lens of the eye changes with every change in the distance of the object being viewed in order to keep the image sharp; and from *motion parallax*, the changing separation between images of objects located at different distances. With both eyes working together, a viewer uses *convergence*, the changing angle of the eyes' gaze as an object is closer or farther

away; and *binocular disparity*, the separate images seen by the left and right eyes that fuse to form a single three-dimensional image. Eleanor Gibson (1963) believes that the perception of depth at an edge is inborn and matures as soon as locomotion is possible, given normal conditions of development. She used the visual-cliff technique with many species and found that rats, chickens, lambs, goats, pigs, turtles, puppies, kittens, and monkeys all avoid the deep side of the apparatus as soon as they are able to move about. That motion, rather than the fusion of two images, may be the critical factor in the development of depth perception is indicated by an experiment in which a baby born with only one functioning eye responded to the visual cliff just as infants with two eyes do (Walk and Dodge, 1962).

Perceptual Constancies

Objects stimulate the eye in very different ways, depending upon their angle in relation to or distance from the viewer. Yet all human beings interpret the objects and people in their world as unchanging, no matter where in the visual field they happen to be. When, for example, a two-year-old boy walks through the aisle in the department store with his mother, he knows that the teddy bear seated on the distant counter is just the right size to cuddle in his arms, despite the fact that the image it casts on his retina indicates the toy is about the size of a peanut. And when he drops the quarter his mother has given him to spend and it rolls on its side before coming to rest, he sees the coin as round, even though it casts an oval image on his retina. The invariant teddy bear is an example of size constancy; the rolling quarter, of shape constancy.

The newborn infant does not perceive the world in this way, but the year-old child certainly does. Developmental psychologists have devised ingenious experiments in their attempts to find out just how soon perceptual constancies develop.

SHAPE CONSTANCY The emergence of shape constancy comes sometime after two months but before nine months. Results appear to depend upon the experimental techniques used. Thomas Bower (1966a) conditioned two-month-old infants to turn their heads to the appearance of a wooden rectangular block by rewarding them with a bout of peekaboo each time they turned to the block. After they had been turning their heads regularly to the block, which had always been placed at an angle of forty-five degrees to the side, Bower showed them the block placed directly in front of them, a wooden trapezoid (which would cast the same retinal image as the block in its original position) directly in front of them and the trapezoid at an angle of forty-five degrees. The babies tended to respond to the block placed in the new position but not to the trapezoid, regardless of its position. Bower concluded that two-month-old babies possessed "some capacity for shape constancy." (See Figure 10.2.)

When tested by other techniques, however, shape constancy has not appeared in infants this young. Albert Caron and his associates (1977) showed one of several geometrical forms to three-month-old babies until they habituated. After they had ceased to respond to the original shape, which was either a square or a trapezoid placed at various angles, the experimenters showed all babies a vertical square. The researchers reasoned that if the babies had developed shape constancy, both the babies who had originally watched the vertical square and those who had seen the same square tilted back would be bored and pay little attention to the square. But all the babies, except the ones who had seen the same vertical square, responded as if they were seeing something new. None showed shape constancy.

Another experiment with three-month-old babies showed glimmerings of shape constancy. Michael Cook and his colleagues (1978) also used habituation, displaying either wooden forms painted white or photographs. They discovered that young babies could tell the difference be-

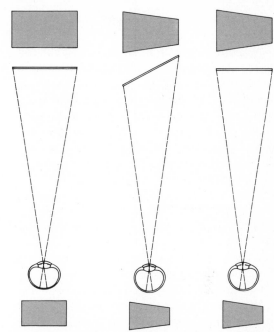

Figure 10.2 Seen in a parallel plane, the rectangle (*left*) projects a rectangular shape on the retina; placed at a slant (*center*), the rectangle projects the same trapezoidal shape as the trapezoid when seen in a parallel plane (*right*). Bower used this effect to test infants for shape constancy.

SOURCE: From T. G. R. Bower, "The Visual World of Infants." Copyright © 1966 by Scientific American, Inc. All rights reserved.

tween a cube and a photograph of a cube, and between a cube and an L-shaped block. But the babies appeared to see no difference between the cube and a trapezoid or between the cube and a wedge. In experiments with older babies, infants who were allowed to manipulate a wooden shape as well as look at it displayed shape constancy at nine months, but not at six months (Ruff, 1978).

Experiments in which babies habituated to photographs lowered the critical age to seven months. Leslie Cohen (1977), who used photographs of faces, found that seven-month-old babies showed shape constancy, but four- or five-month-olds did not. He showed the babies photographs taken at an angle, so that the face was a three-quarter profile, then tested the babies with a photograph of the same face looking directly at them. In order to show shape constancy, Cohen found, babies had to see a number of three-quarter views of the same face. Babies who saw only a single three-quarter view acted as if the full-faced photograph were a new and interesting person.

Presenting babies with two-dimensional photographs may be too difficult a task for younger infants. Eleanor Gibson and her associates (1978) tried habituation in an entirely new way and came up with a situation that is closer to that of the rolling coin. They discovered that five-month-old babies saw a foam-rubber disc as the same whether it rotated directly in front of them (either horizontally or vertically) or at an angle. But when the foam rubber was distorted so that it appeared to have a rippled surface, the babies reacted as if it were a new object, showing that they expected the object to be rigid in all conditions — constant not only in shape but also in texture.

Shape constancy may emerge sometime toward the middle of the baby's first year, although no one who has tested for it has used a technique that babies would find as appealing as Bower's peekaboo game. Perhaps giving babies a reason to display perceptual skills would enable researchers to detect those skills earlier.

SIZE CONSTANCY The size of the retinal image gives a viewer no clue as to the actual size of an object, yet by the time babies are a few months old, they appear to judge accurately the sizes of objects in their world. Somehow they realize that the farther away an object is, the smaller it will appear. The five-month-old babies who reacted to the illusory projectile as if it would strike them showed depth perception, but they showed size constancy as well.

In an experiment to test for size constancy, Bower (1966b) again conditioned two- and three-month-old babies to turn their heads by using a peekaboo reward, this time requiring the infants to look at a white, twelve-inch paper cube that was placed about three feet away. Next he showed the baby the same cube at nine feet, then a thirty-six-inch cube at both three and nine feet away. (The thirty-six-inch cube at nine feet stimulates the retina just as the twelve-inch cube does at three feet, and if the baby is relying on retinal image, responses should be the same as to the original stimulus.) Babies worked most for their peekaboo when the twelve-inch cube was in its original position and *least* when the larger cube was in the farther position (a change of both size and distance), indicating some grasp of size constancy. Furthermore, babies did just as well when they were allowed to use only one eye. Similar experiments, however, have indicated only that babies respond more to near objects than to distant ones, so that it cannot be firmly stated that such young babies have demonstrated size constancy (Cohen, DeLoache, and Strauss, 1979).

In experiments that test size constancy, five-year-olds err by about 4 percent in their estimates, six- to eight-year-olds are off by only 1 percent, and adults may make estimates that are wrong by as much as 17 percent, tending to estimate distant objects as larger than they actually are (Gibson, 1969). It may be that the sophisticated realization of the difference between perceived and actual size tends to throw off adults who consciously try to allow for its effects in experiments.

Work with babies and with the young of other species indicates that size constancy develops without the experience of moving around in the environment — at least as far as objects in motion are concerned (Rock, 1975). Peter Bryant (1974) believes that we establish size constancy for stationary objects by using the relation between the object and its background. Even though the retinal image of the teddy bear on the toy counter gets larger as the little boy approaches, its relation to the size of the counter, the clerk, and the other toys remains the same.

Space Perception

Human beings take for granted their ability to find their way through the world to distant places and back again. The mental maps that make such navigation possible are the product of a cognitive skill that has its roots in the infant's developing ability to orient him- or herself in space. As Piaget observed (1954), babies begin their orientation by locating objects in reference to themselves, and moving the infants around will mix them up. For example, Linda Acredolo (1978) placed six- to sixteen-month-old babies in the center of a curtained space with windows on both the right and left sides. When a buzzer sounded, an experimenter appeared at one of the windows, called the baby's name, and demonstrated an entertaining toy. Babies soon learned to look at the window (which was always the same one) as soon as the buzzer sounded. Then the baby's chair was moved so that the exciting window was on the infant's opposite side. But when the buzzer sounded, six-month-old infants turned their heads just as they had before and wound up looking at the empty window—directly away from the entertaining experimenter. Even when Acredolo placed a large star beside the experimenter's window, infants who had learned to look to the right persisted in looking right and infants who had learned to look left persisted in looking left, despite the fact that they now had a landmark that told them where they could expect to see the toy. By the time they were eleven months old, however, babies had begun to break out of this egocentric frame of reference. Half of them looked at the appropriate window—but only when they had a star to use as a landmark. By the time they were sixteen months old, about a

third of the babies could find the right window even without a landmark, and nearly all of them looked in the appropriate direction when they had a star to guide them.

Babies begin to crawl at about nine months and walk at about a year, so it is probable that their experiences in moving their own bodies around the world help infants learn to orient themselves in space. Babies apparently learn to orient themselves at home almost as soon as they can crawl, for Acredolo (1979) also found that whereas nine-month-old babies tested in a laboratory persistently used themselves as the only reference when looking for objects, tested at home they did as well as the sixteen-month-olds had done in the laboratory.

But babies find gravity even more of a help than their own bodies, as John Rieser (1979) discovered when he conducted an experiment similar to Acredolo's. This time the babies were in a round room with four windows directly in front of them so that the babies had to look up, down, or to one of the sides. Even newborns are sensitive to cues that indicate their heads are tilted in respect to gravity (Prechtl and Beintema, 1964). With the baby seat tilted at a forty-five-degree angle, causing the babies to lean to one side, they would, Rieser presumed, be sensitive to the body cues that signified gravity. It appears that he was right, for babies in the tilted position used gravity to orient themselves, looking, for example, at the door that was in its original position relative to gravity rather than relative to their own bodies. Babies who were not tilted tended to act as they had in Acredolo's study.

If, as seems probable from studies with infants, babies learn the spatial structure of their environment by using the information they glean from their own movements within it, how do children leap from looking in the appropriate place for a toy to navigating through the neighborhood and the wider world? The first step is learning to rely on landmarks to guide the way (Siegel, Kirasic, and Kail, 1978). Eleven-

If this toddler strays away from his father, he will not be able to find his way back, but before long he will be able to use landmarks to make his way surely through the neighborhood. (© Len Speier 1981)

month-olds in Acredolo's study were just beginning to use the large star in this manner, and in another of her studies (1977), half the three-year-olds and all the five-year-olds did just that, finding a hidden trinket by using normal landmarks instead of using their own bodies as a guide. When Acredolo added a blatant landmark to the trinket's hiding place, the number of three-year-olds who could ignore their bodily cues jumped to 75 percent.

Most studies of young children find that preschoolers are not very good at making their way around without significant landmarks (e.g., Acredolo, Pick, and Olsen, 1975), but in such studies the children are usually tested after only one exposure to a strange environment. When they are familiar with a place, kindergartners move about as surely as fifth graders. Given only a single walk through a model town, kindergartners could not reconstruct the layout nearly so well as fifth graders; but when each group took three walks through the town, the five-year-olds were as accurate at reconstructing the display as the ten-year-olds (Siegel, Kirasic, and Kail, 1978).

Once a child has learned to use landmarks, routes—series of landmarks—are the next step in the development of cognitive maps. Learning to follow a route through their neighborhood is much easier for kindergartners than reconstructing a layout. All children must do to make their way from home to school or to the store is to recognize the landmarks along the path. Alexander Siegel, Kathleen Kirasic, and Robert Kail describe routes as a kind of spatial glue that connects the landmarks and gives shape to the spatial representation. The child progresses from knowing that a landmark is familiar to knowing where the landmark has been seen. If one puts the development of cognitive maps into information-processing language, the ability to recognize landmarks and associate them with bearings is part of the child's system of cognitive hardware; the ability to organize them into routes through space and time is software—a map-making program.

The estimation of distance is another skill of cognitive map making. In a study conducted at a boys' camp, nine- and ten-year-olds were as accurate as adults in estimating the distances between various locations in the hilly terrain of the camp (Cohen, Baldwin, and Sherman, 1978). Both children and adults overestimated distances when there were hills or barriers of some kind between locations and underestimated the distances when the land was flat and no barriers were present. Estimations of distances along a route appear to be linked with the ease of travel along the way.

The ability to use landmarks appears to precede the ability to choose them efficiently. Gary Allen and his associates (1979) showed slides of a walk through a commercial neighborhood to children and adults (see Figure 10.3). Asked to select scenes that would most help them remember where they were along the walk,

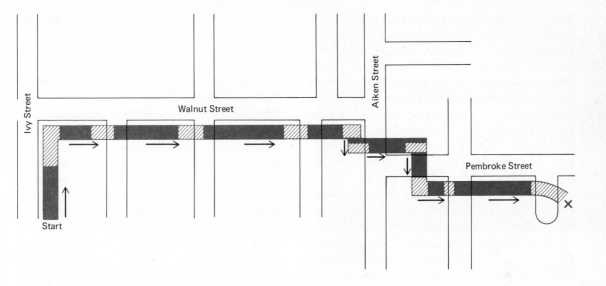

Figure 10.3 By looking at slides, children and adults took an imaginary walk through a commercial neighborhood. When asked which scenes would most help them remember where they were along the walk, adults but not children generally chose the critical landmarks (designated by diagonal shading).

SOURCE: From G. L. Allen *et al.,* "Developmental Issues in Cognitive Mapping: The Selection and Utilization of Environmental Landmarks," *Child Development,* 50 (1979), 1062-1070. © The Society for Research in Child Development, Inc.

second graders tended to choose colorful awnings or shop displays that closely resembled other locations; fifth graders did somewhat better, and adults picked critical landmarks, such as those indicating changes in bearing. When given a selection of slides chosen by their peers and asked to rank the pictures by their distances from a given point along the route, second graders did poorly; and they made as many mistakes when adults chose the slides. Fifth graders did little better than second graders with slides chosen by their peers, but given slides picked by adults, they ranked the scenes as accurately as adults did (see Figure 10.4).

The ultimate skill in cognitive map making is

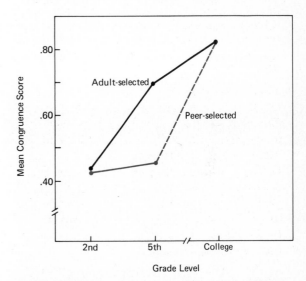

Figure 10.4 Regardless of whether they or adults selected critical landmarks, second graders could not decide where along a familiar walk the markers belonged. Fifth graders did poorly when peers selected the landmarks, but extremely well when they were selected by adults.

SOURCE: From G. L. Allen *et al.,* "Developmental Issues in Cognitive Mapping: The Selection and Utilization of Environmental Landmarks," *Child Development,* 50 (1979), 1062-1070. © The Society for Research in Child Development, Inc.

to integrate various routes into a survey map of a larger area, so that the routes from home to school, school to market, market to home, movie to fast-food restaurant, are integrated and children can make their way from any one point in the area to any other. The child's developing ability to accomplish this feat over a period of years resembles the performance of adults each time they are faced with a new situation: first, landmarks; then uncoordinated routes; then an integrated map that fits within an objective frame of reference. The capability to construct such cognitive maps probably depends upon the maturational state of the child's nervous system, the demands of the environment, and the child's motivation for having the map; the capability develops in synchrony with the child's other cognitive skills (Siegel, Kirasic, and Kail, 1978).

PICTURE PERCEPTION

Our world has three dimensions; it is deep, solid, and filled with motion. Pictures — whether paintings, drawings, or photographs — are two-dimensional: motionless lines and colors on a flat surface. The question of interest to psychologists is, What are the mechanisms by which we easily recognize a drawing as a representation of reality and perceive a three-dimensional scene in pictures? Developmental psychologists also want to know whether the skill is learned, and if so, how early children acquire it.

Gestalt Wholistic View

Gestalt psychologists (Koffka, 1931) claim that we interpret pictures by means of organizing principles that result from the brain's natural organizational processes. Although they agree that maturation and learning are involved in the development of perception, Gestalt theorists re-

ject the idea that we learn to see pictures by gradually building up associations. Instead, they claim that the perceptual process works by sudden reorganizations — mental rearrangements of the perceptual field along the lines of our innate organizing principles.

In this view, children interpret whatever is before them according to these natural relationships. They group elements that are close together, the principle of *proximity*; they also group elements that are generally alike in form, the principle of *similarity*. They tend to expect the next element in a group (such as dots forming a curve) to follow the line taken by the rest, the principle of *continuity*; they supply any broken or missing lines in a figure, the principle of *closure*; and they see objects that move or change together as a unit, the principle of *common fate*. As a result of these principles, children — like adults — perceive wholes, shapes, and forms and tend to disregard parts, points, and lines. They distinguish figures from the ground in which they are set, and presented with an ambiguous figure, they will impose a form on it.

Young children's perceptions are under control of these organizing principles, agreed Jean Piaget (1969), but that is because their attention is captured by dominant features in the picture, and these features are determined by the innate organizing principles. As children grow older, he said, they develop new cognitive processes, so that by the time they are six or seven years old, their attention no longer is caught by dominant features and they can act mentally upon the picture, exploring it visually, analyzing it, and integrating its features.

By using ambiguous pictures, David Elkind (1977) and his associates tested which interpretation of picture perception was correct. Children from four to eleven years old looked at pictures that could be seen in two ways, for example, as a tree or a duck. (See Figure 10.5.) First one element of the picture is seen as the figure and the other as the ground, then they reverse. If Gestalt psychologists were right, per-

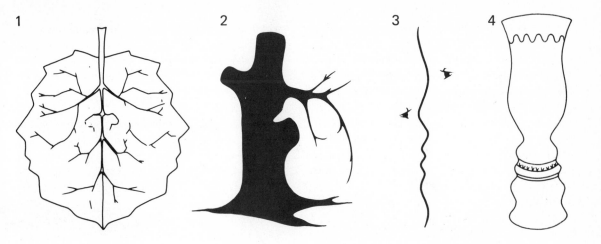

Figure 10.5 Ambiguous pictures such as these can be seen in two ways by reversing figure and ground. The older children are, the easier they find it to reverse figure and ground and to switch back and forth from tree to duck, as in Number 2.

SOURCE: From D. Elkind, "Perceptual Development in Children," in I. L. Janis (ed.), CURRENT TRENDS IN PSYCHOLOGY. Los Altos, Calif.: Kaufmann, 1977.

ceptual reorganizations should make the pictures reverse most rapidly and easily for young children. But if Piaget was right, the cognitive processes that emerge around the age of six or seven would make older children much more adept at seeing the reversal in such pictures. In this experiment, Piaget's prediction proved to be correct; Elkind and his associates found that the older the children, the more easily they reversed figure and ground.

Piaget (1969) found fault with Gestalt perceptual theory on other grounds. He agreed that the first impression a child has of a picture (the figurative whole) is the result of innate organizing principles; but he argued that the final impression the child derives after examining the picture carefully (the operative whole) was a reconstruction of pictorial elements based on the same cognitive processes that allow children to

switch figure and ground. Once again his position was supported in a study by Elkind and his associates (1977), in which children looked at pictures that consisted of large figures made up of smaller wholes (such as a man made from pieces of fruit or a scooter made from candy canes and lollipops). See Figure 10.6, p. 250.

When they looked at the pictures, young children generally saw only the fruit or only the candy. Some, however, saw only the larger figures. The young children lacked the cognitive development that would allow them to recognize that a picture could have more than one meaning. A four-year-old, therefore, tended to see apples, pears, grapes, and bananas; but a nine-year-old would describe the same picture as "a man made out of fruit." Some five- or six-year-olds could see both, but only one at a time. Such a child might say, "Some fruit. No, I mean a man." When asked to name the fruit they had mentioned, five-year-olds would deny there was any fruit in the picture. Nine-year-olds integrated the various aspects of the picture, constructing an operative whole that allowed them to see both fruit and man. From his studies, Elkind concluded that although the organizing principles described by Gestalt psychologists operate across the life span, cognitive development allows older children and adults to

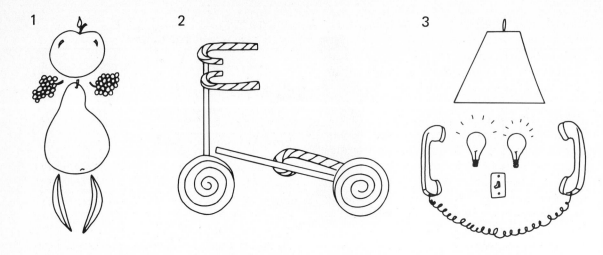

Figure 10.6 When young children look at pictures like these, they can see only the fruit, the candy, or the appliances. By the time children are nine, cognitive advances permit them to organize the shapes so that they can see, for example, both fruit and man.

SOURCE: From D. Elkind,"Perceptual Development in Children," in I. L. Janis (ed.), CURRENT TRENDS IN PSYCHOLOGY. Los Altos, Calif.: Kaufmann, 1977.

organize the visual field in other ways. These alternative methods of organization can become as automatic as the Gestalt principles.

Gibsonian Differentiation View

Another explanation of picture perception has been offered by Eleanor Gibson (1969), whose views have become extremely influential. Gibson says that perception is not organized along innate lines but is a matter of extracting information from sensory stimulation. Human beings do this, she proposes, by selecting from the environment its permanent, unchanging features and the relationships between them; by filtering information so that irrelevant or changing features are ignored; and by visually exploring the environment, then selectively attending to various aspects of it. As babies grow, they notice ever more specific details of things they see, making finer and finer distinctions. Pictures contain much of the same information as is present in objects, and babies use the same methods to discover the distinctive features of pictures as they use to perceive real objects. The perception of a realistic scene, therefore, requires no special learning, and babies learn to differentiate pictured objects at the same time that they learn the distinctive features of real objects.

Her view is supported by the study of an infant who had seen neither pictures nor photographs, nor heard them referred to (Hochberg and Brooks, 1962). The baby learned words from seeing natural, solid objects in the environment. When the little boy was nineteen months old, he was tested with line drawings of objects he had seen, such as shoes, skates, and airplanes. The experimenter showed him the drawings, and although the infant had never before seen a pictorial representation, he was able to identify the objects. Afterward he showed the same skill with photographs. Gibson argues that the little boy's accomplishments indicate that we do not need to learn to perceive pictures through associating them with real objects and that as soon as babies learn to scan the edges of objects, they apply that skill to a drawing.

Studies with even younger infants also support the Gibsonian proposal that no special learning is required to perceive pictures. Judy DeLoache and her associates (1979) showed five-month-old babies two identical dolls for one minute; then they showed the babies a colored photograph of one of the dolls they had been watching along with a colored photograph of a different doll. The babies preferred to look at the photograph of the new doll, indicating that they recognized the similarity between the other doll and its photograph. Next, the investigators tested the babies' ability to recognize a similarity between drawings and photographs. Again, after looking at colored photographs of a woman's face, the babies — given the choice of a line drawing of the woman in the photographs and a line drawing of another woman — chose to look at the strange woman. These babies apparently were extracting and storing the features common to the photograph and the line drawing.

Judging depth in pictures, according to Gibson (1969), does depend on learning; the child must learn to disregard information that betrays the flat nature of the picture and to attend to cues that indicate depth. First-grade children judge relative distances in pictures just as adults do, and their judgments are consistent (Flavell, 1963).

Children need more information than adults do to recognize an incomplete figure; as Gibson points out, young children seem to need continuity of line when following a contour with their eyes. Studies with fragmented outline drawings have shown that neither adults nor children can recognize a fragmented picture if the distinctive features are missing (Murray and Szymczyk, 1978). Adults are more efficient than children at recognizing incomplete pictures and require less detail, but this is probably because adults attend to finer details and use more efficient methods of visual search, scanning more

systematically and sampling the entire picture more widely than children do.

SENSORY AND SENSORIMOTOR COORDINATION

Vision does not work in isolation; the senses and motor abilities of the healthy infant work as a team (Gibson, 1969). Jean Piaget showed that by the latter part of the first year, infants construct notions of objects in terms of their combined touchable, tastable, smellable, hearable, seeable, graspable, and reachable characteristics. Indeed, everything nine-month-old babies can reach enters the mouth, there to be explored with tongue and lips. Babies are tireless reachers, graspers, and handlers of objects, which they study not only with their eyes but also with their fingers.

Because most events or objects provide multiple kinds of stimulation, infants discover that one kind of sensation signals that sensations of other kinds are probably near them in space or in time. If they hear a sound, they learn that it pays to look because they may see some interesting sight. According to Morton Mendelson and Marshall Haith (1976), babies come into the world prepared to learn about relations between sights and sounds. Mendelson and Haith studied babies less than one week old, measuring the babies' glances by the position of reflected infra-red lights on the pupils of their eyes. The researchers found that the sound of a male voice increased the amount of time the babies kept their eyes wide, increased their eye control, and caused them to look more at the center of their visual fields and to scan with smaller eye movements. The sound appeared to make the babies alert to possible visual stimulation. When the researchers played a repeating tape recording of a man reading an excerpt from a children's poem by A. A. Milne, they found that the babies looked in the direction of the voice when it began; but as the voice continued, their gaze gradually tended to wander away from the sound.

Among two-month-old babies, sights are such a strong attraction that they can overpower sounds. Jeffery Field and his associates (1979) studied young babies to see if they expected a definite correlation between what they saw and what they heard, using the spatial relationship between the sight of a researcher's face and the sound of a female voice reading poetry to detect the babies' expectations. Babies responded quickly to the sight of a researcher's face, whether it was accompanied by a voice or not. And when the face came from one side of the baby and the voice from the other, babies ignored the voice, betraying no signs of surprise or disturbance at the displaced sound. If there was no competing visual stimulus, babies consistently turned their heads toward the voices, but not as quickly. At two months, therefore, babies may use sounds to aid in visual search.

Babies may also expect a synchrony between voice and lips. When ten- to sixteen-week-old babies heard nursery rhymes recited, they looked intently at the investigator when her lip movements were synchronized with the words of the rhyme; but when the two were out of synchrony, the babies' attention flagged and their gaze wandered (Dodd, 1979).

Nancy Bayley (1969) found that many babies this young will search with their eyes for the source of a sound that is outside the field of vision. Fifty percent of the normal two-month-old infants she observed moved their eyes in apparent search when an unseen bell or rattle sounded. However, they did not necessarily look for the source in the correct direction. The more precise ear, eye, and head coordination required to turn the head and look in the correct direction for the sound source developed somewhat later in the babies that Bayley studied. Half of all four-month-old babies did this, and almost all had reached that level of inter-

sensory and sensorimotor cooperation by the time they were six months old.

The association between sight and sound appears firmly established by four months, for an infant of this age searches visually for a parent whose tape-recorded voice is played in the infant's hearing, even when the face and voice are separated in space and are not synchronized (Spelke and Owsley, 1979). In another study, Elizabeth Spelke (1979) gave four-month-old babies the choice of watching two films: a continuous game of peekaboo or a woman's hands playing toy percussion instruments. Although babies looked from one film to the other, whenever the accompanying soundtrack carried the music of the toy band, their gaze switched to the percussion instruments. In a similar study, babies of this age generally looked at film that was synchronized with the soundtrack and ignored the other (Bahrick, Walker, and Neisser, 1978).

Spelke (1979) also showed four-month-old babies movies of a yellow kangaroo and a gray donkey bouncing across the grass. The bounces of one were accompanied by thumps, the other by a clanging gong. The films and soundtracks were run in several combinations, both in and out of synchrony, and by their visual searches, it was apparent that the babies detected the connection between simultaneous sound bursts and visible impacts. Spelke concluded that at the first sight of a strange object, infants perceive a unity in motion and sound by detecting their temporal relationship.

This relationship between sight and sound has been studied among older children by Alice Vlietstra and John Wright (1971), who were curious about children's ability to transfer information from one sense to another. The researchers wondered if learning how to tell differences between intensities of sounds makes it easier for youngsters to tell differences between intensities of visual stimuli. If young children come to understand that the quality "stimulus intensity" can be perceived by any of

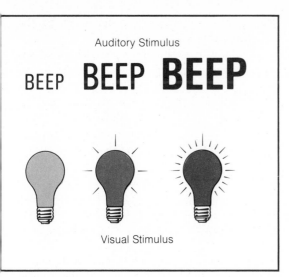

Auditory Stimulus

BEEP **BEEP** **BEEP**

Visual Stimulus

Figure 10.7 After learning to discriminate among different intensities of sound, young children found it easier to discriminate among comparable differences in intensities of light, indicating transfer of experience from one sense to another, as discussed in the text.

their sense organs, then their experience with intensity in one sense, such as hearing, should transfer to a different sense, such as vision. (See Figure 10.7.) However, if experience with intensity does not transfer from one sense to another, children would find their experience with sound of no help when they tried to discriminate between the intensity of two visual stimuli, such as two lights of varying brightness. When Vlietstra and Wright tested children who had learned to discriminate the intensity of sounds, they found that the skill did indeed transfer to another sense; the children found it easier to discriminate differences in visual intensity provided that the same general levels of intensity were considered correct in both tasks. Such transfer helps children coordinate the information they gather through their separate senses into increasingly complex perceptions of the world.

Another important coordination that develops in the first half-year is that between the eyes and the hands. We take it for granted that our hands will reach out the proper distance to touch or grasp objects that appear in our line of sight. But it is not until they are four and a half months old that half of all infants are able to touch a cube that is placed in front of them on a table, and not until they are six months old are virtually all infants that skilled.

The importance of this eye-hand coordination is reflected in the view of many students of infancy and early childhood that the origins of intelligence lie in the sensorimotor experiences and developments of infancy. For example, Piaget's books (1952b, 1954) on infancy are full of vivid descriptions and perceptive interpretations of age changes in infants' sensorimotor coordination and of their link to concepts of objects, space, time, and causality.

By the time they are eight months old, babies can transfer information from touch to sight. Peter Bryant and his colleagues (1972) devised a pair of semiround objects that were identical except for a small square notch in the end of one. When activated, either of the objects could make a "bleep." Both objects were shown to babies—who ranged in age from six to twelve months—while they sat in their mothers' laps, then were taken away. Without the baby being able to see the objects, one of them was placed in his or her hand. While the infant held it, it was made to bleep, then it was removed. When both objects were shown again, about two-thirds of the infants reached without hesitation for the particular object they had just handled, indicating their ability to translate information from a tactual to a visual mode.

Other studies in which babies must transfer information from touch to sight have led researchers to suggest that the ability is a good indication of cognitive development. Susan Rose and her colleagues (1978) have discovered that by the time they are a year old, full-term, middle-class babies can make the transfer. If they are kept from seeing an object but allowed to explore it with their mouths or hands, they will later recognize the object by sight. But premature infants (even though they are tested a full year after their expected birth date) cannot manage the transfer; they cannot recognize on sight objects they have only touched. They do, however, recognize objects they have been allowed to look at but not touch. It may be that the full-term infants studied had processed the events in their world more rapidly and efficiently than the preterm babies had.

Some of the intersensory and sensorimotor coordinations that emerge during the first year of life clearly reflect the infant's experiences. For example, by the time she is a year old, a baby girl has learned that she must fully extend her arm to reach a stuffed animal one foot away, because in the past she has not been able to grab a toy at that distance without reaching for it. On the other hand, maturation of the visual and motor functions in the central nervous system also may contribute to the development of the four-month-old's visually directed grab for an object. All these coordinations improve during the second year of life, because infants have greater opportunities to use them on the diversity of objects and events they encounter.

There is considerable evidence that a youngster's ability at tasks of intersensory recognition improves dramatically between the ages of three and six (Abravanel, 1968; Blank and Bridger, 1964; Zaporozhets, 1965). In one study V. P. Zinshensko and A. G. Ruzskaya (see Zaporozhets, 1965) presented children of three, four, five, and six with abstract forms that they were permitted to explore by touch but could not see. These researchers then tested the children to check their visual recognition of the objects that they had explored with their fingers. At about age five, there was a sharp improvement in performance. This improvement in intersensory coordination probably develops because the mental images of five- or six-year-olds become increasingly detailed and precise as a result of their exposure to objects and their sophisticated methods of exploration.

SUMMARY

1. Since babies cannot describe their sensations, investigators must monitor their reactions closely, often relying on instruments that measure physiological changes. Babies do not hear as well as an adult; a sound must be about fifteen decibels louder for them to detect it. They are also insensitive to very shrill tones but very sensitive to the sounds of language.

2. Babies and children like extremely sweet tastes, a preference that declines slightly by the time they reach adolescence. Although little. research has been done into infants' sensitivity to pain, it is clear that they feel pain and respond to touch and temperature change.

3. Although babies can see better than once was thought, their vision is not as clear as an adult's until they are about six months old. Depth perception emerges gradually, sometime between three and six months. Once babies begin to crawl, they use depth cues to keep from falling over edges. Shape constancy emerges toward the middle of the baby's first year, and size constancy probably develops about the same time.

4. Babies first locate objects in reference to their own bodies, but once they begin to crawl about, they start to use landmarks. Learning to move about surely through the wider world depends upon the use of cognitive maps, which develop from a reliance on landmarks, to the ability to follow a route, then to the integration of various routes into a mental map of a larger area.

5. In the Gestalt view of picture perception, children interpret what they see according to

innate principles of organization. Perception develops not through learning but through a series of insights. The older child's superior ability at reversing figure and ground indicates that cognitive development is also important. In the Gibsonian view, children notice unchanging features in the environment and pay increasing attention to specific details. Picture perception requires no special learning, for it involves the same process of extracting information from sensory stimulation as does the perception of the solid, three-dimensional world.

6. Young babies seem prepared to learn to connect sights and sounds, and by the time they are four months old can connect them appropriately. By eight months, they can make the transfer between touch and sight, recognizing visually objects they have handled but never seen.

Development of Attention, Representation, and Memory

An eight-year-old girl was being interviewed by a researcher studying what children know about memory. "What do you do when you want to remember a phone number?" he asked. The reply was immediate. "Say the number is 633-8854," said the girl. "Then what I'd do is—say that my number is 633, so I won't have to remember that, really. And then I would think, now I've got to remember 88. Now I'm eight years old, so I can remember, say, my age two times. Then I say how old my brother is, and how old he was last year. And that's how I could remember that phone number." The researcher took a deep breath. "Is that how you would most often remember a phone number?" he asked. "Well," said the eight-year-old, "usually I write it down." This child's advocacy of sophisticated strategies quickly gave way to the practical external aid of pencil and paper, but her knowledge of the way the memory system works is impressive. Mary Anne Kreutzer, Catherine Leonard, and John Flavell (1975) received the child's advice in the course of an interview study of children and memory.

Memory makes life as we know it possible. Without memory, there would be no learning, no problem solving, no continuity to life. We would greet each new experience without information from the past to guide our actions, and we would be unable to plan for the future. Lacking memory, a mother would not recognize her own baby; indeed, human relationships could not exist.

Although the basic ability to remember develops during the first two years of life, a young child's memory is inferior to that of an adolescent or an adult — primarily because young children have not yet developed efficient ways to put information into memory or to get it out again when they need it. Yet once a child has firmly committed something to memory, he or she will remember it as well as an adult.

In this chapter, we shall examine the development of memory, starting with attention and the way babies scan objects and choose what they will look at. We shall discuss the various ways children represent objects in memory; we shall see them move from physical, to visual, to symbolic representations and watch the way their concepts develop. We shall discover that memory is not a passive reflection of events but an active construction that can be reinterpreted and to which new information can be added. We shall examine the various types of memory and the development of strategies by children and adults to ensure that material is registered in the memory system and that it can be retrieved. Finally, we shall see how rapidly children themselves learn about memory and discover what makes remembering easy or difficult.

ATTENTION

People do not and cannot attend to all the stimuli in their environment. Selective attention begins almost at birth, and the kinds of stimuli and the way babies look at them change in predictable ways. Researchers assume that babies look at what interests them most; for that reason, studies have focused on their eye movements and the length of time they look at various objects.

Scanning

Babies are born ready to acquire information through their eyes. As noted in Chapter 5, neonates plan their looking patterns, searching for edges of objects with broad, jerky sweeps of the visual field. In the first few weeks, there is no inspection of entire shapes; a baby's attention is captured by a single feature or a few features (Salapatek, 1975). Even when there is something around they like to look at, babies seem unable to shift their eyes to it once their gaze encounters an edge. For example, Robert Fantz and Simon Miranda (1975) found that although the newborns in their experiment generally liked to look at bull's-eyes, they would not look at them if the target was enclosed in a large white square. Apparently their eyes stopped when they found the edge of the square. By the time they were two months old, however, babies crossed the square in order to gaze at the bull's-eye.

The same sort of scanning takes place when babies have the opportunity to look at a human face. Daphne Maurer and Philip Salapatek (1976) found that month-old babies tended to look at the edges of a face, staring at an ear, the chin, or the line of the hair; but two-month-olds inspected internal features, such as an eye, the nose, or the mouth. Other researchers have found that by about two months, infants pay increased attention to the internal features of the face, especially the eyes (Hainline, 1978). Whether the face is moving slightly from side to side or remaining still, talking or silent, two-month-old infants concentrate their scanning around the eyes (Haith, Bergman, and Moore, 1977). Not even the extra mouth movements that accompany speech draw attention from the eyes to the mouth.

It may be that babies begin to look past the square to the bull's-eye and shift their gaze from the edge of the face to the eyes when visual control shifts from subcortical regions of the brain to the visual cortex, as it does at about two months of age (Hoffman, 1978). This maturation allows them to habituate to, or become bored with, the features that first catch their gaze, and then become receptive to features at the edge of the visual field (Salapatek, 1975). The reason may also be social; for at about two months, babies' first social smiles appear and they may have come to see the face as a meaningful entity instead of as simply a collection of features. By this time, perhaps the eyes in a face have taken on social meaning and babies have learned that fixing their attention on the eyes keeps the sound of a human voice going. Throughout the first year, the infant's perception of the face appears to rest on a gradual discovery of its unchanging features and an integration of its parts into a meaningful configuration (Fagan, 1976; Haaf, 1977).

As children mature, their scanning patterns reflect their interests, their expectations about the visual world, and their strategies for acquiring visual information (Day, 1975). Young children tend to scan unsystematically unless the display they are viewing has a pattern of its own. For example, with J. Weiss, David Elkind (1977) pasted pictures onto cards. On one card the pictures (which included such familiar objects as an ice-cream cone, a parrot, a chair, and a hat) were glued down randomly; on the other, the pictures formed a triangle. Given the random card and asked to name the objects, five-year-olds omitted some pictures and named others twice; they read off the objects in no particular order. Eight-year-olds, however, made no errors—either of omission or commission—and read off the objects from left to right and top to bottom. With the triangular picture, five-year-olds were just as accurate as the eight-year-olds. They began at the figure's apex and read off the objects, following the pattern of the triangle.

Young children not only fail to scan systematically but also tend to stop scanning before they have obtained all the information they need. This showed clearly in a study with five- to nine-year-old children who were given outline drawings and asked to decide whether they were the same or different (Vurpillot, 1968). Some of the houses were identical, but others were not; the difference was always to be found in one of the windows: sometimes a window was curtained or had blinds or a bird cage hanging

in it. When five-year-olds compared houses, they did not start at the top and compare each pair of windows in turn, nor did they look at every window. But nearly every one of the oldest children in the study did just that, scanning both systematically and exhaustively.

Although older children scan more exhaustively, they are also more efficient and stop scanning once they have all the information they need for a task. As children grow older, they scan more rapidly—because they are processing visual information more rapidly, because they are integrating the information across glances, or because each fixation of their eyes picks up information from a wider field (Day, 1975).

All children scan downward, but until they are about five, their attention is caught by the focal point of a picture or pattern and they begin their downward scan from that point. Children who are more than five years old begin scanning from the top of a display, no matter where the main point of interest lies (Day, 1975). The context affects younger children's scanning patterns in other ways as well; when irrelevant information is added to a display, younger children find it difficult to identify figures or patterns.

All these changes in visual strategy, Mary Carol Day (1975) points out, are also found in the changing strategies children use to identify objects by touch—indicating that central cognitive processes direct children's acquisition of information through their senses.

Selectivity

Despite our wishes, some objects and events seize our attention: a building in flames, a pedestrian in a clown costume, the flashing light and siren of a patrol car, the roar of a subway train. Other sights and sounds we attend to by choice, filtering out stimuli that might distract us from our task. It is possible for attention to be focused so intently that even violent, disruptive stimuli are shut out. For example, a surgeon in a Chicago hospital concentrated so deeply on his cutting and stitching that he was unaware part of the ceiling had fallen. Only after the last suture was in place did he notice the plaster on the floor behind him (Csikszentmihalyi, 1976). Not everything we notice is remembered; but the stimuli we shut out—that is, the things we do not notice—cannot be processed and stored in memory. For that reason, psychologists are interested in the conditions that capture attention and how present situations interact with past experiences to make us likely to attend. With infants, the problem is determining whether they are paying attention at all.

In Chapter 5 we saw that given a choice, newborn infants will look at patterns rather than at plain stimuli; but they are also willing to stare at a blank panel for fifty seconds. On the other hand, one- and two-month-olds fuss, cry, or fall asleep when shown a solid black screen (Salapatek, 1975). During the first two months, babies prefer simple black-and-white patterns to color, movement, or a flickering light (Fantz, Fagan, and Miranda, 1975). This preference then declines rapidly.

During the third month of life, significant changes occur in the visual world of the infant (Kessen, Haith, and Salapatek, 1970), and studies of scanning indicate that as their ability to discriminate improves, babies begin to watch strange objects in preference to familiar ones. For example, Joseph Fagan (1971) showed infants of five, seven, and ten weeks of age visual stimuli, some already familiar to the babies and others new to them. He found that seven-week-olds preferred the familiar stimulus, whereas the ten-week-olds preferred the novel one.

These preference changes are largely the result of biological maturation, a development that became apparent when Fagan, Robert Fantz, and Simon Miranda (1971) tested the visual preferences of infants born four weeks before they were due and others born at full term. When eleven weeks old, the premature babies did not behave like eleven-week-old full-term

infants. In fact, the premature babies did not behave like eleven-week-old full-term infants until they were fifteen weeks old. Despite similar visual experiences, the premature babies could not respond to the familiar-novel dimension of visual information until their visual systems had reached a certain level of biological maturation, enabling them to remember that a stimulus had been seen before.

Novelty is sometimes not as attractive as discrepancy; some investigators have found that babies prefer objects or patterns that are somewhat similar to things they have seen before but are neither completely novel nor identical (Kagan, 1978). By the time babies are three or four months old, the informational properties (such as discrepancy or novelty) of an event become as important as its physical properties (such as content, movement, or complexity) in seizing and holding attention (Cohen, 1976; Cornell, 1975; Kagan, 1976).

Stimuli that attract the attention of infants come to bore them after a while, and babies shift their attention to another stimulus or fall asleep. This process of habituation and the response to novel stimuli are basic to the infant's ability to learn. Unless the infant can remember a stimulus, there can be no conditioning, no adaptation, no learning of any sort (McCall, 1971). Evidence of such learning appeared among three-month-olds studied by Allen Milewski (1979), for they recognized simple patterns even when those patterns changed in size or position. The infants who habituated to a pattern of three dots (either placed in a line or made to form a triangle) paid no attention to changes in the space between the dots (which changed the size of the pattern) or changes in the portion of the screen on which the pattern was displayed. Changes from one pattern to another, however, did attract renewed attention.

The effect of learning on selective attention was especially clear among four-month-olds studied by Judy DeLoache, Margaret Rissman, and Leslie Cohen (1978). Whenever a light in front of them blinked, these babies could see a

Television and Attention

Most children do not begin to watch television in the sense of systematically following a program until they are about two and a half years old (Anderson, 1979). Before that time, they appear to have their attention captured for a minute or two at a time but soon return to their play or to interacting with their mothers. Daniel Anderson believes that until they are thirty months old, children simply lack the cognitive ability to grasp the meaning of related images and sound. He regards children's television viewing as a blend of passive and active cognitive activities, but probably more active than passive.

Older children often play with their toys while they watch television, but they divide their attention, frequently glancing at the screen. Whether or not a child pays attention to the screen depends upon the sound, camera techniques, and content of the program and on the behavior of peers. Anderson has found that children's voices, peculiar voices, women's voices, sound effects, applause, laughter, and a change in the quality of the sound attract a preschooler's attention from toys to the screen. Such sounds tell children that the program is changing or that whatever is going on will interest them. They then watch until the program becomes incomprehensible or boring. Men's voices, on the other hand, seem to inhibit children's attention. They do not look up when a man's voice accompanies the picture, because the adult male voice indicates to them that the program is abstract or of interest only to adults.

Camera techniques can also affect children's attention. Elizabeth Susman (1978) found that four-year-olds stop watching when the camera zooms in for a close-up, and she suggests that the zoom removes the focused material from the visual flow of events and interferes with the young child's processing of part-whole relationships.

Not all the aspects that determine attention come from the set; the behavior of peers can draw young children's attention. Children remain sensitive to what their peers are doing and use their behavior as a cue as to whether a program is worth a look. When children watch together, visual attention to the program decreases with group size, and when one child looks at the set, looks away from it, or makes a remark, the other child or children do the same (Anderson, 1979).

This apparently selective viewing seems actively controlled by the child, who does not watch what he or she cannot understand. But watching a set for a longer time seems to have no effect on the young child's comprehension. Elizabeth Lorch, Anderson, and Stephen Levin (1979) had five-year-olds watch *Sesame Street* under two different conditions, either just with their parents or with their parents and a selection of attractive toys. The children with the toys watched the screen half as much as did the children who had nothing to play with, but subsequent tests indicated that both groups remembered about the same amount.

Not all a child's television viewing is active. Anderson and his associates have found what they call "attentional inertia," in which the longer children watch a television program, the more probable it is that they will continue to do so (Anderson *et al.*, 1980). In this process, attention is not bound to content, for it does not change when a program made up of segments, such as *Sesame Street*, switches from one segment to another. Anderson's group regard attentional inertia as the opposite of habituation, and they describe it as an involuntary response to a somewhat unpredictable, meaningful, dynamic stimulus. This sounds rather like the "plug-in drug" described by television's critics, but Anderson's group do not see children as the victims of hypnosis. Instead, they regard the phenomenon as a way for a child to keep processing material he or she does not understand, allowing the child to venture into unknown cognitive territory, perhaps to make an intellectual discovery.

slide by turning their heads. The babies turned their heads more rapidly to see an interesting, complicated slide than to see a simple one. In fact, when they were allowed to see interesting slides, they began to anticipate them. When the light blinked, they turned their heads faster than the projector could show the slide. By behaving in such a manner, say DeLoache and her associates, babies are actively attempting to control their visual experiences.

As thought processes become more sophisticated in early childhood, children show a sharp improvement in their ability to shift their attention, particularly in response to the verbal instructions of others.

Most, though not all, children between the ages of four and six tend to pay greater attention to the form of objects than to their color; children between two and three generally prefer color to form (Stevenson, 1972). These preferences affect a child's ability to discriminate among objects and events. If young children are required to sort objects of various colors according to their shapes, children who initially attend to shape find this task fairly easy, and those who first attend to color find the task more difficult.

Confronted with a problem that requires sustained attention to one or two properties and deliberate ignoring of other irrelevant information, the four- or six-year-old is usually less effective than the eight-year-old in solving the problem (Osler and Kofsky, 1965). Younger children tend to respond to irrelevant cues, which of course hinders their performance. Also, they are not as proficient as eight-year-olds in classifying information into categories that are relevant to the task, and as noted earlier, their search strategies are not as efficient.

The school experience surely plays some part in the development of selective attention, for when children enter school, they are constantly presented with tasks that require them to pay sustained and formal attention to relevant parts of material to be learned and to ignore irrelevant parts. For example, in learning to read, children

Between the ages of six and twelve, children become increasingly better at focusing their attention, and part of this development is probably a result of the sustained attention required by various school tasks. (© Suzanne Szasz)

must pay close attention to the shapes of letters and to their sequential order. The boldness of the print and the slant and size of the letters are usually irrelevant. A "P" is a "**p**" is a "*p*," but a "rose" is not a "sore" is not an "eros"; nor is an "o" identical to a "q" or a "c."

Children's performance on selective-attention tasks continues to improve with age. In one study of seven- to thirteen-year-olds, John Hagen and Gordon Hale (1973) assigned a simple learning task. The children were told that they would have to remember the *location* of some pictures that they would see. Then each child was shown a row of picture cards. On every card were two pictures, one of a common household object, such as a television set or a lamp, and one of an animal, such as a camel or a cat. The experimenter turned the cards face down and showed the child a "cue card" with one of the animals or one of the objects on it. Children were then asked to point to the one card in the set face down in front of them that pictured the same animal or object. The number of correct matches over a series of these trials was the measure of a child's *central learning*. After children were tested on picture location, which was the task given them, they were asked if they remembered which objects had been paired with which animals in the set of cards. The correct recall of the pairings measured a child's *incidental learning*.

Children who scored high on incidental learning must have paid attention to features that were irrelevant to the task described to them. Conversely, children who scored low on incidental learning must have paid little attention to the irrelevant aspects. It is reasonable to infer, therefore, that children who scored high on central learning and low on incidental learning are more selective in their attention. As instructed, they concentrated exclusively on location and hence learned little or nothing about the pairings.

As Figure 11.1 shows, there was a straightforward correlation between a child's age and his or her performance on the central-learning task. The older the child, the higher his or her memory-for-position (central-learning) score. On the other hand, while all children scored lower on incidental learning than on central learning, there were no significant differences in

Figure 11.1 In Hagen and Hale's study of children's attention and learning, there was an increase with age in the average number of pictures identified correctly on the basis of their location (central-learning task). The inset (*top left*) is a sample of the cards used in the study. The average number of pictured pairings of animals and objects remained relatively constant until age thirteen, when it dropped sharply (incidental learning). At about age twelve, a child's selective attention becomes so powerful that extraneous material is excluded. (Adapted from Hagen, 1967)

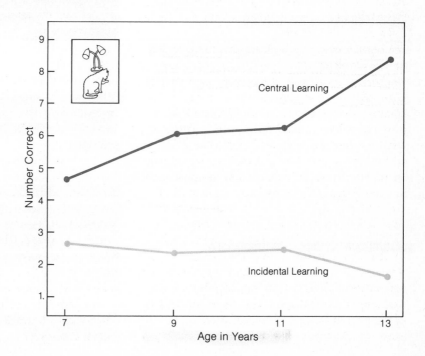

incidental-learning scores for children from ages seven through eleven, and among twelve- and thirteen-year-olds the incidental-learning scores actually dropped.

From these findings, it appears that even the youngest children are capable of directing their attention to the central aspect of a task and that this capacity continually improves with age. Because incidental learning does not increase with age, it seems that as children grow older, they become more competent at selective attention, focusing on only the relevant features of a clearly defined task. At about the age of twelve, selective attention seems to become so powerful that children exclude irrelevant material from consciousness, learning less about incidental features than they would have several years earlier. As children mature, then, their past experiences lead them to concentrate on what they expect will be the relevant aspects of a situation. In the process, as the rest of the chapter will show, attention, perception, and memory become increasingly intertwined.

REPRESENTATION

In order for children to remember people, objects, and events, they must have some way to store the information so that they can retrieve it at the proper time. A six-year-old boy recognizes Aunt Ellen, remembers Mother's promise to go to the circus, and decides whether he would rather go and play at a friend's house or stay home and watch television, by relying on his *representations*—the models he constructs to store information in memory.

Systems of Representation

According to Jerome Bruner (1973), when people construct a model for information storage, they retain aspects of the event they think will prove useful and discard aspects that appear to have no future use. There are three kinds of representational models: enactive, iconic, and symbolic. These systems develop consecutively as the child grows, each depending on the previous system for its emergence, and each demonstrating the child's increased ability to differentiate self from the environment. No system is ever discarded, and events that have been represented in one of them can be translated into either of the other two. All three systems are to some extent affected by cultural conditioning.

ENACTIVE REPRESENTATION Young babies cannot separate themselves from the world and the objects within it. To them, "The world is what I do with it" (McCall, 1979b). For this reason, the earliest way of representing an event is through *enactive representation*, or motor responses. As Bruner puts it, the child literally defines events by the actions they evoke.

Perceptions and actions are so intertwined that during the middle of the baby's first year, the infant finds it difficult to separate them. When a seven-month-old girl drops her rattle, she continues to shake her fist as if it still clutched the toy, expecting the action to bring back the rattle. The baby relies on enactive representation, as did the babies in the last chapter who could turn to the toy-show window only by using their bodies as a guide. But adults also rely on enactive representation for such skills as tying knots, typing, riding a bicycle, playing the piano, and the routine aspects of driving.

ICONIC REPRESENTATION Toward the end of the first year, babies begin to distinguish between themselves and the world. According to Bruner, they develop *iconic representation*, or imagery, mentally visualizing objects that are out of sight. Perception and action can be separated; the infant can imagine a lost toy without going through the motions connected with it. The ability to form images greatly expands the infant's world.

Iconic thought continues to dominate the thinking of young children, even after they have acquired language (Bruner, Olver, and Greenfield, 1966). Children store most information in images, not words. For this reason, their thought is inflexible. For example, although they can recognize and reproduce three-dimensional arrangements, they cannot mentally manipulate them. If an experimenter asks them to reproduce a complicated arrangement of graduated blocks, they can do so exactly; but if asked to rearrange the display so that the tiny block that was on the left is on the right, they cannot do it.

By the time children are seven, they have ceased to rely so heavily upon iconic representation, but they will never discard it completely. When Stephen Kosslyn (1978) asks adults, "What shape are a Doberman pinscher's ears?", they tell him that in order to answer the question, they mentally picture the dog and then inspect its ears.

SYMBOLIC REPRESENTATION The ultimate and most powerful means of representation is *symbolic:* words and symbols, whether language itself or the artificial languages of number and logic. Symbols are both arbitrary and remote; a word does not resemble the thing for which it stands, as does the visual image. Symbols can also be detached from the objects they represent and be manipulated, as they are in language.

Language is powerful because it is highly productive; its rules for the formation of sentences allow the child not only to represent experience but to transform it as well (Bruner, 1973). As we saw in the unit on language, the two-year-old knows words but not the productive rules of combination. Until children acquire a grasp of syntax, words serve primarily as pointers, even though the pointing might be toward an unseen cookie in the kitchen.

With symbolic representation, children develop an increasing capacity to attend to multiple aspects of the environment and to track several sequences at one time (Bruner, Olver, and Greenfield, 1966). Symbols compress meaning so that much more can be held in the immediate consciousness at one time. They also free children from the tyranny of immediate experience—as we saw in Chapter 8, where children who relied on internalized words were not overpowered by sights that contradicted what they knew to be true, as younger children were.

Bruner's belief in the power and primacy of language contrasts with Piagetian theory, for Bruner believes that language is at the root of the increase in problem-solving skills that appears in children around the age of six, whereas Piaget maintained that language is merely a symptom of the change and not its source (Anglin, 1973).

Building Concepts

A *concept* is a symbol with many examples. The symbol "dog," for example, is a concept that stands for all the dogs in a little boy's world; but the symbol "Prince" refers only to his own puppy. When children develop concepts, they are developing the ability to separate a symbol from its specific reference and to understand that the symbol itself possesses independent attributes (four legs, furry coat, tail, and a bark) that embrace many references. Concepts allow children to divide the world into categories, simplifying its overwhelming diversity and giving the child a way to deal with the unfamiliar. Once children have categorized scalloped potatoes as food or a dachshund as a dog, they can make inferences about them, in the expectation that the items share properties common to their class (Anglin, 1977). Food can be eaten and is likely to taste good; dogs wag their tails, chase balls, and bark.

But how do children (and adults, for that matter) discover what objects belong to what category, and how do they place new members into the correct class? Eleanor H. Rosch (1973) suggests that each concept is built around a "core meaning," which consists of the very best examples of the concept. The core examples are surrounded by other members of decreasing similarity to those in the center. (See Table 11.1.)

In exploring the nature of concepts, Rosch gave adults and children sentences concerning category membership ("A pear is a fruit") and noted both the accuracy of their answers and the time required to produce them. Statements about central members of a category ("An apple is a fruit") were answered faster than statements about peripheral members ("A prune is a fruit") by both adults and children, supporting the idea that a category is built around core examples

Table 11.1 CATEGORIES AND MEMBERS USED IN REACTION TIME EXPERIMENT

Category	Member	
	Central	Peripheral
Toy	Doll	Skates
	Ball	Swing
Bird	Robin	Chicken
	Sparrow	Duck
Fruit	Pear	Strawberry
	Banana	Prune
Sickness	Cancer	Rheumatism
	Measles	Rickets
Relative	Aunt	Wife
	Uncle	Daughter
Metal	Copper	Magnesium
	Aluminum	Platinum
Crime	Rape	Treason
	Robbery	Fraud
Sport	Baseball	Fishing
	Basketball	Diving
Vehicle	Car	Tank
	Bus	Carriage
Science	Chemistry	Medicine
	Physics	Engineering
Vegetable	Carrot	Onion
	Spinach	Mushroom
Part of the body	Arm	Lips
	Leg	Skin

Source: From Eleanor H. Rosch, "On the Internal Structure of Perceptual and Semantic Categories," in T. E. Moore (ed.), COGNITIVE DEVELOPMENT AND THE ACQUISITION OF LANGUAGE. New York: Academic Press, 1973. Reprinted by permission.

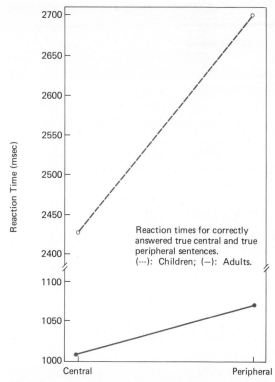

Figure 11.2 Both children and adults needed more time when judging whether peripheral members belonged to a category than when judging central members (see Table 11.1), indicating that concepts are built around core meanings.

SOURCE: From Eleanor H. Rosch, "On the Internal Structure of Perceptual and Semantic Categories," in T. E. Moore (ed.), COGNITIVE DEVELOPMENT AND THE ACQUISITION OF LANGUAGE. New York: Academic Press, 1973. Reprinted with permission.

(see Figure 11.2). And children made significantly more errors on peripheral than on central members of a category, supporting the idea that central examples are learned first. Rosch concludes that in most cases, categories are processed in terms of their similarity to central members of the group (see Table 11.2) and that adults (but not young children) use the abstract criteria (feathers, wings, beaks, two legs, lays eggs, flies) that determine group membership only to decide whether a doubtful example belongs to the group ("Is a penguin a bird?").

Table 11.2   JUDGMENTS OF "GOODNESS OF CATEGORY MEMBERSHIP"

Category	Member	"Exemplari-ness" rank	Category	Member	"Exemplari-ness" rank
Fruit	Apple	1.3	Vehicle	Car	1.0
	Plum	2.3		Boat	2.7
	Pineapple	2.3		Scooter	2.5
	Strawberry	2.3		Tricycle	3.5
	Fig	4.7		Horse	5.9
	Olive	6.2		Skis	5.7
Science	Chemistry	1.0	Crime	Murder	1.0
	Botany	1.7		Assault	1.4
	Geology	2.6		Stealing	1.3
	Sociology	4.6		Embezzling	1.8
	Anatomy	1.7		Blackmail	1.7
	History	5.9		Vagrancy	5.3
Sport	Football	1.2	Disease	Cancer	1.2
	Hockey	1.8		Measles	2.8
	Wrestling	3.0		Cold	4.7
	Archery	3.9		Malaria	1.4
	Gymnastics	2.6		Muscular	
	Weight			dystrophy	1.9
	lifting	4.7		Rheumatism	3.5
Bird	Robin	1.1	Vegetable	Carrot	1.1
	Eagle	1.2		Asparagus	1.3
	Wren	1.4		Celery	1.7
	Chicken	3.8		Onion	2.7
	Ostrich	3.3		Parsley	3.8
	Bat	5.8		Pickle	4.4

Students ranked members as to how good an example each was of its category. Rankings ranged from 1.0 (the best example) to 7.0 (extremely peripheral). There was general agreement, indicating that the structure of categories is quite similar among members of a culture. (Source: From Eleanor H. Rosch, "On the Internal Structure of Perceptual and Semantic Categories," in T. E. Moore (ed.), COGNITIVE DEVELOPMENT AND THE ACQUISITION OF LANGUAGE. New York: Academic Press, 1973. Reprinted with permission.)

As yet, psychologists are not sure how children decide on the core examples of concepts. It is generally agreed that both the perceptual qualities and the function of objects are important in concept formation, but debate continues over which aspect is dominant. Katherine Nelson (1979) believes that children base the core of their concepts upon function, grouping objects by their uses and actions. The process begins before a child has acquired language. Once the child has organized a concept in terms of its function (dogs run, bark, wag their tails, bite),

he or she progresses to the next step: identifying the perceptual features that define it (dogs have furry coats, four legs, a tail). Only after the concept is developed in this way does the child attach a name to it. In the process, says Nelson, children may rely on features that are not truly relevant, leading them to include objects that do not belong ("A wolf is a dog") or omitting objects that do ("A Mexican hairless is not a dog"). For this reason, children's and adults' concepts frequently differ.

Function continues to dominate among pre-

Asked to define an apple, this child would probably reply, "You eat it," since the function of objects appears to play an important role in young children's acquisition of concepts. (J. Berndt/Stock, Boston, Inc.)

schoolers (Nelson, 1978). Asked to respond to a word with "the first word you think of," four-year-olds will respond to "bread" with "eat." The dominance of function over perceptual information also shows when young children are asked to define an apple. Out of fourteen children, ten replied "eat" but only one said "fruit." Three others mentioned perceptual qualities (skin, seeds), but edibility—the apple's function from the child's standpoint—was obviously its most important characteristic. However, if children are asked, "Tell me what you know about apple," they begin to produce per-

ceptual information. As children grow, says Nelson, their concepts cease to be dominated by function. Older children respond to word association requests as adults do, with other class members, synonyms, opposites, or the name of the class. To the word "bread," they might reply "food" or "butter"; to "apple," the response might be "fruit" or "pear."

Other investigators, although they agree that function is often the essence of concept meaning, believe that perceptual features are more central than Nelson allows. Jeremy Anglin (1977) speculates that young children initially rely on perceptual features, developing some sort of visual image of a concept such as apple or dog or car, based on the first object in the class the child hears named. As they grow older, children supplement the iconic representation with a symbolic storage of the attributes that determine the concept. In the case of dog, the attributes might be furry coat, four legs, a tail, barks, wags its tail, bites. In this theory of concept formation, the child's original representation is never lost. It is simply supplemented with increasingly exact, abstract, and more highly differentiated descriptions.

Older children who know the attributes that determine a concept (food is edible, clothes are wearable) sometimes exclude peripheral items from it (such as lollipops and hats). Anglin believes that children often fail to coordinate their knowledge of class membership with the attributes that determine membership, and he points out that preschool children often have difficulty in specifying the critical attributes of a familiar concept.

Studies in another vein indicate that the way children categorize their world may be affected by their experience in formal schooling. Formal education teaches children to organize the world in increasingly abstract and logical ways, and perhaps speeds the switch from function to abstract criteria as a basis of classification (Cole and Scribner, 1974). In one study, Kpelle rice farmers grouped items by function but could not explain their grouping by citing a common attribute or by giving a category name to the group. Putting together a net, pot, pepper, okra, and peanut, these Africans would say, "The net is for fishing, the okra and peanut are cooked in the pot." But Kpelle who had attended school assigned category labels (utensils, clothes) easily. And when Michael Cole (1978) asked illiterate Yucatecan farmers to sort objects, they often placed a knife with bread or onion, reflecting the way they used knives in their daily life. But the farmers understood categories, even if they did not use them. Asked to pick out the utensils from a group of objects, they grouped the knife with the spoon.

Operative Representation

When children retrieve information, one would expect it either to match the stored representation or to have deteriorated. But Jean Piaget and Bärbel Inhelder (1973) believe that in some instances, a child's representation gets better, not worse, as time passes. This improvement appears to be the result of an interaction between memory and cognition, and the changed representation is known as *operative representation*, for it is the result of the child's mental operations on stored representations, generally iconic. For example, Piaget and Inhelder showed children a group of ten sticks of various lengths and asked them to draw the arrangement from memory. After six months, the same children, asked to redraw the sticks, often produced copies that were closer to the original display than were their first drawings. Apparently, memory is not passive, simply serving up a faithful representation of original perceptions. Instead, as children's comprehension develops, their memories change to conform to their new understanding. According to Piaget and Inhelder, memory actively and selectively constructs the past, using schemes (or mental operations) borrowed from intelligence.

Some studies have supported Piaget and Inhelder's explanation. Hans Furth, Bruce Ross, and James Youniss (1974) showed children ranging in age from five through nine years a

picture of a glass tilted from the horizontal base to a forty-five-degree angle, as in Choice A of Figure 11.3. The children were told: "This is a glass with cola in it. It is tilted and on a table. Now draw this picture on your paper, just the way you see it here."

Many children do not realize that the level of liquid remains horizontal with respect to the table even though the glass is tilted. They have not yet acquired this particular understanding of spatial transformations, even though they have seen numerous tilted glasses of milk, water, juice, and cola. Piaget would say that they have not yet developed the operative scheme of spatial coordinates, referring to the mental operations of middle childhood's concrete operational period, in which children apply logical thought to concrete objects.

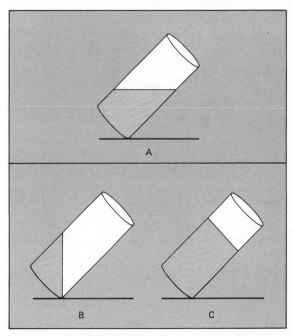

Figure 11.3 A tilted-glass experiment like that carried out by Furth, Ross, and Youniss. (*A*) Depiction of the actual angle of the level of liquid in a tilted glass. (*B* and *C*) Depiction of the angle reproduced by two children. (Adapted from Furth, Ross, and Youniss, 1974)

At varying intervals, the same children again drew the tilted glass. Furth and his associates found that the oldest children always did better than the rest at reproducing the drawing. In sessions held six months later, however, twenty out of the one hundred and sixteen children drew more accurate pictures than they had drawn shortly after they saw the picture of the glass. Only 17 percent of the children showed this improved memory; but the finding goes against our expectations that recollections will remain the same or else deteriorate over time. The investigators maintain that, during the six-month interval, these children had acquired a more sophisticated understanding of what happens to the level of contained liquids. As they developed the necessary operative schemes, they reconstructed their representations. When memory did improve, it was by stages; no child made a sudden leap from primitive reconstruction to perfect recall. Inhelder (1976) concludes that children represent in their memories not what they see but their own understanding of the model before them. The child's memory appears to be the product of an active process in which advances in cognitive maturity modify the information the child stored earlier.

The fact that memory is active does not mean that it always improves. In many cases, children in both experiments did worse, not better, after six months had passed. For example, in one experiment children who had seen four matches in a straight row and, below them, another four matches arranged in the rough shape of a "W" (see Figure 11.4), sometimes added extra matches to their drawings or lengthened the matches that made up the "W" in order to make the two rows equal in length (Inhelder, 1976). Because their operative schemes for number and spatial systems were developing at different rates, suggests Inhelder, the two schemes were in conflict. As a result, memory was dominated by a tendency to equalize the lines in the direction of the more advanced scheme.

Operative representation may not always affect memory in the way that Piaget and Inhelder

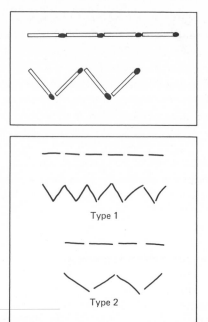

Figure 11.4 In a test of operative representation, children had to draw displays they had seen six months earlier (*top*). The performance of a number of children deteriorated, and they equalized the lines with no regard for the number or length of the matches (*bottom*).

SOURCE: From *Studies in Cognitive Development: Essays in Honor of Jean Piaget,* edited by David Elkind and John H. Flavell. Copyright © 1969 by Oxford University Press, Inc. Reprinted by permission.

suggest. Although most studies have shown a correlation between children's understandings of the various physical principles involved in the models and their later drawings, Lynn Liben (1977) has found that some children reproduce the models accurately even if they have done poorly on previous tests of their understanding. Further, changes in understanding do not always result in improved drawings, nor do improved drawings always reflect changes in understanding. The operative theory of representation and memory, therefore, looks promising but is not yet completely understood.

MEMORY

Memory, or the retention and recall of past experience, forms the basis of cognition. Systematic investigations of its development in children have covered how they acquire, store, and retrieve information, how well they retain it, and how well they understand the workings of their memory processes (Kail and Hagen, 1977; Ornstein, 1978). This research has generally been founded on assumptions based either on a Piagetian view or on an information-processing view.

From Piaget's point of view, memory cannot be separated from the rest of intelligence, and the way to understand memory is to understand the development of cognition in general. In the discussion of operative representation, we saw some implications that follow from his view of memory as an active construction of the mind that is tied to mental patterns of action.

From an information-processing point of view, memory is the transfer of information within the child's cognitive system. Researchers study the various processes involved in the transfer, expecting that an understanding of the mechanisms of memory will increase our understanding of cognition (Perlmutter, 1980).

Many information-processing theorists (e.g., Atkinson and Shiffrin, 1968) divide the hardware of the memory system into three types of memory storage: *sensory registers*, where information is literally recorded but decays within three to five seconds; *short-term store*, a temporary, working memory, where we are conscious of the active information; and *long-term store*, where information is held permanently. The strategies we use to help us remember information are part of the software that keeps information flowing through the system. Developmental differences in memory, according to this view, result from the techniques children use to make sure information does not get lost in the early stages of memory, and to ensure being able to get it back out of long-term memory. These techniques are fairly well developed by the time children are twelve or thirteen years old (Naus, Ornstein, and Hoving, 1978).

Some information-processing theorists (e.g., Cermak and Craik, 1979) prefer to ignore possible structures in memory and instead concentrate on various stages of processing, from initial pattern recognition of stimuli to the extraction of meaning and the elaboration of relevant information. In this *levels-of-processing* approach, incoming information is thought to be processed at deeper and deeper levels of analysis, from a shallow perceptual level to a deeper semantic level. Information that receives only a shallow analysis soon decays and is forgotten; information that is analyzed at a meaning level is retained. Researchers who adopt this approach attribute developmental differences in memory to increasingly skillful ways of storing material at deeper levels. As a child gets older, this ability improves (Naus, Ornstein, and Hoving, 1978).

Psychologists who apply a dialectical approach to memory are comfortable with a levels-of-processing explanation but believe that memory develops in a process of continuous interaction among the various aspects of a child's intelligence (such as memory, understanding, role-taking skills) and the child's memory strategies. Each time the child acquires a new goal or strategy, the context of development changes. For this reason, dialectical psychologists believe that memory must always be considered in multiple contexts: the situation, the goals of the child, the child's personal history, and the history of the society (Meacham, 1977).

Taken together, studies of children's memory seem to indicate that the hardware, or storage capacity, of a child's memory does not change greatly with age. Once something is lodged in memory, a preschooler will probably remember it as well as an adult. The major changes are in the child's software, or memory processes. As children age, they develop increasingly sophisticated programs for *encoding* (putting information into memory) and *retrieval* (getting it back out again).

RETENTION

Material that children (or adults) retain is stored in enactive, iconic, or symbolic representations. Whatever approach psychologists use to study memory, they agree that children demonstrate their retention of material by recognition, by reconstruction, or by recall.

Recognition

Recognition requires only that we perceive an object as something that has been perceived in the past. It is the simplest form of memory retrieval, for it takes place in the presence of the original object. Because of this simplicity, Piaget regarded recognition as a primitive process that is found in many lower animals, including frogs, fish, lizards, and birds (Piaget and Inhelder, 1973). A familiar example of recognition in action is a multiple-choice test. Given three possible answers, the task is to recognize the correct response, as opposed to recalling the answer on a completion test. According to Piaget, recognition is based on perception and on patterns of simple motor actions; therefore it is within the capacity of very young infants. Recognition is also the simplest form of memory from the standpoint of information processing. In order to recognize a person or a toy, a baby must only match a present perception with a representation in memory, a relatively simple operation (Perlmutter and Lange, 1978).

As noted in Chapter 5, the newborn infant is capable of remembering a stimulus for five to ten seconds and of detecting a difference between that memory and a subsequent stimulus. Research on visual recognition among infants relies on attention, assuming that babies will pay more attention to unfamiliar objects or patterns than to those they have seen before. When babies look at patterns for a specified length of time, gradual improvements appear with age in their ability to retain a memory. But when they are allowed to look at the patterns until they lose interest, two-month-old babies do as well as older babies at recognizing them. This suggests that although it may take young babies more time to acquire information about stimuli, once they have acquired it, they are as good as older babies at retaining it.

Habituation studies indicate that babies first sort out the people in their world by using age and sex to separate them. Given two thirty-second periods to study the photograph of a baby, five-month-olds recognize the photo when they see it along with the photo of a round-faced, bald man (Fagan and Singer, 1979). Since they base their memories on features that define sex and age, they can recognize the difference between photographs of men and women, or babies and adults; but shown photographs of two men, they cannot recognize the one they have seen. By seven months, however, they can make this distinction.

John Werner and Marion Perlmutter (1979) have concluded that although once information is processed, retention appears to be fixed, individual differences in processing visual information are present from birth. When babies look at a pattern until they are bored, suggesting that they have encoded the information, those individual differences no longer affect recognition. Babies begin forgetting almost immediately, probably within fifteen seconds; but traces of a memory may last for hours or even weeks (Werner and Perlmutter, 1979). Studies have found that babies as young as two months old recognize stimuli they have seen the day before (Martin, 1975).

Repeated exposure to stimuli may serve to keep information in an infant's memory. A recent study may help explain the phenomenon. Three-month-old babies were allowed to see (but not operate) a mobile they had learned to power several weeks earlier by kicking their feet. The next day, given the opportunity, they immediately began working the mobile. Babies who had not seen the mobile the day before the test showed little recognition and had to relearn its operation (Rovee-Collier *et al.*, 1980). The

Very young infants show evidence of recognition, the simplest form of memory, and daily reencounters with familiar objects explain why infant memory may be sustained over long periods of time. (Peter Vandermark/Stock, Boston, Inc.)

fact that such reencounters are a regular part of daily life but an element absent in most experiments may mean that laboratory studies have tended to underestimate the persistence of memory in young babies.

As babies grow, it takes less and less time for sights to register in memory. At any age, however, the more complex the stimulus, the longer it takes to become familiar with it (Werner and Perlmutter, 1979). In one study, toddlers between the ages of twenty-nine and forty-four months looked at pictures from a single conceptual group, such as animals, until they tired of watching them. Then they were shown the same six pictures, six additional pictures of animals, and six pictures from an entirely differ-

ent group, such as fruits. The toddlers looked least at the familiar animal pictures, most at the fruits. Because the new animals seemed less interesting than the fruits, the researchers assumed that the toddlers not only remembered the pictures they had seen but also generalized their familiarity to other members of the same group (Faulkender, Wright, and Waldron, 1974). But as Perlmutter (1980) has pointed out, in infant recognition studies and in studies like this one, there is no way to tell whether children realized they had seen the familiar pictures before. It is possible that the differences in attention are automatic and do not reflect a conscious awareness of memory.

Toddlers can tell a researcher if they have previously seen an object, so Nancy Myers and Perlmutter (1978) studied the way recognition develops in preschoolers by showing youngsters eighteen small, attractive objects. Later the children looked at thirty-six objects: the eighteen they had seen before and eighteen new ones. Two-year-olds were correct in their judgments on 81 percent of the objects; four-year-olds on 92 percent. Both groups were extremely accurate at realizing they had never before seen an object; two-year-olds did about as well as four-year-olds. But four-year-olds were more accurate at recognizing familiar objects, an indication that during early childhood there is some improvement in children's ability to represent or to retain the memory of objects.

By the time children are ready for school, their recognition memory is very good, at least for simple stimuli. With more complex stimuli, requiring skilled scanning and registration of information, they may not do so well (Perlmutter, 1980). Children's lack of experience may also hinder their recognition skills. Adults recognize unfamiliar pictures better than five-year-olds do, but five-year-olds are as proficient as adults in recognizing pictures of familiar objects (Nelson and Kosslyn, 1976). As for retention itself, once information is processed, age may not have any effect on the length of time a memory is retained.

Reconstruction

Their studies of children led Jean Piaget and Bärbel Inhelder (1973) to suggest that there is an intermediate form of producing retained material, which they call *reconstruction*, or the reproduction of the organization of an object previously seen. Reconstructive memory requires children to take material (sticks, matches, checkers) and arrange it to resemble a model seen an hour, a week, or six months previously. Children's reconstructive memory is superior to their recall, said Piaget, because when children manipulate concrete objects, they intentionally repeat the natural order of events, calling their action schemes, or patterns of motor skills, into play. In the studies described in the earlier section on operative representation, for example, children who reconstructed the models they had seen, using sticks or matches, were more accurate than children who drew the models.

Even children younger than those Piaget tested show strong reconstructive memory. When toddlers were asked to reconstruct a display of eight small toys, replacing each toy in the correct compartment of a plain wooden box, both two- and three-year-olds did well. Each group got 75 percent of the toys in the right slot. But when researchers substituted an eight-room dollhouse for the plain wooden box, two-year-olds did worse and three-year-olds did better. The younger children may have been distracted by the interesting dollhouse, so that their attention was not on the original task of remembering where the toys were placed. The older children may have used the various locations in the dollhouse as an aid to memory (the ball goes in the kitchen) (Cohen, Perlmutter, and Myers, 1977).

Recall

Recall, the most complex of the ways people demonstrate memory, takes place in the absence of the material remembered. It is a goal-directed, cognitive skill that appears to be stimulated by environmental demands (Perlmutter and Lange, 1978). When a society requires well-organized recall, its members develop the skill, using supports provided by the culture—an example is the memorizing of epic poems that preserve the history of a nonliterate culture. Unlike recognition, which appears to be similar in all groups, recall varies according to the requirements of a culture (Cole and Scribner, 1977).

Piaget and Inhelder (1973) believed that recall is impossible in children who are less than a year old, because it depends upon symbolic functions. (Unlike Bruner, Piaget includes mental imagery in the category of symbols.) Internalized images reinstitute the memory on a symbolic level rather than as action, as in reconstruction. For this reason, the emergence of recall is a significant step in cognitive development. Described in information-processing terms, recall requires children to generate material internally. Recall, if it is to be efficient, involves special skills to establish the material in memory so that it may be retrieved (Perlmutter and Lange, 1978).

Babies less than a year old have shown some degree of representational skills in their daily lives. Daniel Ashmead and Marion Perlmutter (1980) collected examples of infant recall by having parents keep diaries of incidents in which their seven- to eleven-month-old infants showed any evidence of it. For example, at her father's suggestion, an eleven-month-old left the room, got her doll, brought it back to the living room, and played with it. The babies remembered the location of household items and conducted searches for missing people or objects; they remembered bathing and feeding routines; and they remembered social games, such as peekaboo. While her nine-month-old son was sitting in his highchair, one mother said, "Peekaboo." The baby immediately held his bib in front of his face. On another occasion, an eleven-month-old, on hearing the telephone ring, headed as fast as she could toward the phone and tugged on the cord.

Babies apparently have some power to recall objects or events, but since recall is most easily

When this infant smiles delightedly at the sight of grandfather, recognition has been demonstrated; but should the infant initiate a game of peekaboo or patty-cake, the demonstration is one of recall. (James R. Holland/Stock, Boston, Inc.)

assessed by verbal descriptions of unseen material, infant recall is difficult to test. For that reason, no children less than two and a half years old have been tested for verbal recall. Although both recognition and recall improve during the preschool years, recognition is good from the beginning, whereas recall is extremely poor among two-year-olds.

Preschoolers are beginning to organize their memories around concepts, as Perlmutter and Myers (1979) found in a series of studies with three- and four-year-olds. The children saw nine small, attractive objects. Sometimes each object was from a different conceptual category (bell, clock, drum, flag, horse, leaf, pen, star, truck); the rest of the time there were three objects from each of three different categories (animals, utensils, transportation). The experimenter played the "remembering game" by showing each object to the child, labeling it, and replacing it in a box. When asked what they

remembered seeing, neither three- nor four-year-olds could recall many of the objects, even though they knew that the ones they did remember they would be given to take home. Three-year-olds tended to remember about two items; four-year-olds remembered three or four items. Both groups did better on the list of related objects, indicating the conceptual organization of their memory. What is more, when the experimenter provided conceptual cues ("Do you remember any more animals?"), their recall improved even more. Most children showed an "echo-box" effect; that is, they remembered the very last object they had seen, as if that were the only item stored in their immediate memory.

Their incompetence at recall may be due to a number of factors that affect memory. Preschoolers appear to be ignorant of strategies (such as rehearsal or clustering) that help register information in memory. They may be limited by their inappropriate search tendencies (such as their propensity to recall the last object shown). They may have difficulty in internally generating material. Finally, their limited verbal ability may limit their production of available information (Perlmutter, 1980).

Preschoolers are rarely required to engage in deliberate memorization of the sort demanded by laboratory studies. They all sing advertising jingles and nursery rhymes, however, and their recall of parental promises seems almost perfect. When three- and four-year-olds were studied in their homes, they showed an amazing amount of recall about their experiences (Todd and Perlmutter, 1980). The recollections were both spontaneous and in response to a researcher's question. Most episodes were social, involving the preschoolers themselves or other people. Only 12 percent of the incidents they recalled involved objects, the favorite focus of laboratory research, and 11 percent involved the antics of cartoon characters. Almost half the events the children recalled had taken place within the preceding month, although a third of them had happened more than three months before. Older children produced more spontaneous recollections than did the younger children, and those

Motive and Memory

If memory is not a frozen photograph but an active construction, perhaps people's motives affect what they remember. Michael Moore, Jerome Kagan, and Marshall Haith (1978) tested that conjecture with a group of eight-year-olds and came up with some surprising results. The children's teachers rated their pupils on four motives: hostility to peers, dominance, academic mastery, and affiliation. Children who were rated extremely high or extremely low on the motives took part in the study. On one day they listened to a group of sentences and on the next day chose from sentence pairs the ones they had previously heard. What the children did not know was that none of the sentences on the test was among those they had heard the day before. Instead, each sentence was constructed to reflect one of the four motives.

On the first day, the children heard twenty neutral sentences, for example, "The child's favorite drink was Coca-Cola." On the following day, they were asked whether they could recall any of the sentences. None could. Then the experimenter and the child together read two sentences that reflected motives, one displaying a motive judged to be particularly strong in the child and the other judged to be particularly weak. The four motive sentences for the sample neutral sentence were, "The child was mad at his friend for not sharing his Coca-Cola" (indicating hostility to peers), "The child could drink Coca-Cola faster than anyone" (indicating dominance), "The child was allowed to have Coca-Cola because he improved in school" (indicating academic mastery), and "The child liked to share Coca-Cola with his friends" (indicating affiliation). On 70 percent of the sentences, children selected the one that reflected their own strong motive as the sentence they had heard, indicating that motives do affect the way a child remembers.

This finding is not an isolated event. Studies investigating the nature of eyewitness testimony have found that asking loaded questions about a previously witnessed event can change a person's memory of it. Elizabeth Loftus and J. C. Palmer (1974), for example, showed the film of a traffic accident to a group of adults. Later they asked some of the viewers, "About how fast were the cars going when they hit each other?" The rest were asked, "About how fast were the cars going when they smashed into each other?" People who heard "smashed" estimated the speed of the cars as faster than people who heard "hit." A follow-up interview a week later was even more enlightening. Buried in a series of questions about the filmed accident was, "Did you see any broken glass?" There was no broken glass in the film, but people who had heard "smashed" were twice as likely to say they had seen glass as people who had heard "hit." Studies like this have persuaded researchers that when we recall an event, we use inference and construction to fill in the gaps—and perhaps we use our motives as well.

recollections were more likely to involve unusual events, as opposed to the everyday occurrences that dominated the younger children's free recall.

When children enter school, their recall continues to improve. The improvement is not the result of an improved ability to retain information but of the use of various strategies to help them remember (Hagen and Stanovich, 1977). As we shall see in the next section, children often develop the ability to use these aids before they actually employ them.

STRATEGIES

When people know they must remember something—a telephone number, a name, the amendments to the Constitution—they use various strategies (such as rehearsal or mnemonic rhymes), either at the time they encode the material or at the time they retrieve it or both. The importance of strategies cannot be overemphasized, because they are a major factor in the improvement of memory over the years. Young children do not use strategies, and in cases where strategies are not required for efficient performance on a memory task, preschoolers do almost as well as adults (Brown, 1975).

Strategies are not used in isolation. As we saw in the section on attention, selectivity and scanning techniques can be very important in focusing attention. As children grow older and become more skilled at selecting important information and excluding what is unimportant, and as they learn to scan exhaustively and efficiently, they use memory strategies to better advantage.

This girl is using the encoding strategy of rehearsal in order to memorize her numbers in English as well as in Spanish. (Elizabeth Crews/Stock, Boston, Inc.)

Encoding

Memory tasks are problem-solving situations in which strategy is the means to the goal of recalling specific information (Flavell, 1970). Memory strategies help move material from short- to long-term storage, or—from a levels-of-processing view—either maintain the information at a given level or else lead to its being reprocessed at a deeper level (Ornstein and Naus, 1978). The encoding strategies most studied by developmentalists are rehearsal, imagery, and organization.

REHEARSAL *Rehearsal* is the repetition of material that is to be memorized; it can be done silently or aloud, and its use clearly increases with age. In their study of preschoolers' recall,

Christine Todd and Perlmutter (1980) found that three- and four-year-olds engaged in a certain amount of rehearsal, which took the form of discussing events with their parents. But the strategy was not used intentionally.

Rehearsal increases rapidly during the school years. Told to remember words, objects, or pictures, five-year-olds do not rehearse the material, but ten-year-olds almost always do. The development of this strategy appeared in a study by John Flavell, David Beach, and Jack Chinsky (1966), in which they had five-, seven-, and ten-year-old children memorize pictures of common objects. The children looked at the pictures, then closed the visor on a "space helmet" for fifteen seconds. Afterward, the visor was lifted and the child selected from a group of pictures the ones he or she had been asked to recall. The visor did not obscure the children's lips, and during the fifteen-second interval, investigators watched and recorded any lip movements. A few five-year-olds and nearly all the ten-year-olds silently named the pictures during the interval. Children who moved their lips remembered more pictures than children who did not.

The fact that a child does not use verbal rehearsal does not mean the child *cannot* use it. In a similar study, T. J. Keeney, S. R. Cannizzo, and Flavell (1967) found that when children who did not spontaneously move their lips were instructed to whisper the names of objects they were to remember, their performance improved. It appeared, said the investigators, that the memories of the non–lip movers were as good as those of the lip movers, but the non–lip movers suffered from a *production deficiency*. That is, they possessed the capability to rehearse material and to profit from the rehearsal, but they did not use it. Nor were they about to adopt the strategy. Given another test and allowed to memorize material in any way they liked, most of the young children who had rehearsed only when instructed to do so stopped using the strategy.

Shown a series of pictures and asked immediately or after a very short delay to recall as many as they can—in any order—children of almost any age generally recall the last picture they have seen. Since the test comes close on the heels of the pictures, the last picture is still lodged in the short-term storage, so it is not surprising that children remember it. Older children are likely also to recall the first picture they saw, a tendency that indicates they have been rehearsing the list.

As children grow older, their rehearsal techniques change (Ornstein and Naus, 1978). Third graders, for example, repeat a single word over and over, in rote fashion. Older children repeat a series of words, as shown in Table 11.3. But when third graders are instructed to repeat three different words at each rehearsal, they remember almost as many words as older children do. The difference that remains between the two groups is apparently due to the content of the rehearsal, as shown in Table 11.4. Third graders cling to the same two words (generally the first two in the list) and change the third word in each repetition. Sixth graders mix up the words so that they rehearse the entire list.

Older children also use rehearsal time differently (Hagen and Stanovich, 1977). Given as long as they like, older children use more time than younger children do. They also often test themselves, deliberately looking away from the material they are to memorize and attempting to repeat the list. Even in adulthood, some people use rehearsal more effectively and in a more sophisticated manner than others do. By itself, rehearsal is not always the most efficient way to encode material, but as we shall see, it can be combined with other strategies.

Table 11.3 TYPICAL UNINSTRUCTED REHEARSAL

Word Presented		Eighth Grader	Third Grader
1.	yard	yard, yard, yard	yard, yard, yard, yard, yard
2.	cat	cat, yard, yard, cat	cat, cat, cat, cat, yard
3.	man	man, cat, yard, man, yard, cat	man, man, man, man, man
4.	desk	desk, man, yard, cat, man, desk, cat, yard	desk, desk, desk, desk

Source: From P. A. Ornstein, M. J. Naus, and C. Liberty, "Rehearsal and Organizational Processes in Children's Memory," *Child Development*, 26 (1975), 818–830. © The Society for Research in Child Development, Inc. Reprinted by permission.

Table 11.4 TYPICAL INSTRUCTED REHEARSAL

Word Presented		Sixth Grader	Third Grader
1.	apple	apple, apple, apple	apple, apple, apple, apple
2.	hat	hat, apple, hat, apple, hat, apple	hat, apple, hat, hat, apple
3.	story	story, hat, apple, story, story, hat, apple	story, hat, apple, story, hat, apple
4.	dog	dog, story, hat, dog, dog, story, story, hat	dog, hat, apple, dog, hat, apple
5.	flag	flag, dog, story, flag, dog, story, flag, dog, story	flag, hat, apple, flag, flag, hat
6.	dish	dish, flag, hat, dish, flag, hat, dish	dish, hat, apple, dish, dish, dish

Source: From M. J. Naus, P. A. Ornstein, and S. Aivano, "Developmental Changes in Memory: The Effects of Processing Time and Rehearsal Instructions," *Journal of Experimental Child Psychology*, 23 (1977), 237–251. Reprinted by permission of Academic Press.

IMAGERY *Imagery* is the visual association of two or more things that must be remembered. Suppose a child must memorize a list of paired words: cat/ice cream, ball/moon, baby/statue, tree/fork. Later the experimenter will give the child the first word in the pair and the child's job is to respond with the second. If the child connects the two words in a visual image, for example, imagines the cat licking an ice-cream cone, the ball bouncing high over the moon, the baby perched on the top of a statue, and a fork hanging from a tree, it will be much easier to recall the second word of the pair. Children discover this strategy much later than they do other strategies (Flavell, 1977), and some may never arrive at it by themselves.

Like other strategies, however, imagery can be used with instruction by young children who would never use it spontaneously. Even kindergarten children can make use of such imagery, although it does not improve their recall as much as that of older children (Reese, 1977). It may be that young children cannot "read" such images. Shown drawings that connect the two words for them, young children of the 1970s were better able to use them as memory aids than were nursery-school children a decade before. H. W. Reese (1977) believes that television programs, specifically *Sesame Street*, may have accelerated children's cognitive growth and consequently their ability to use imagery. Other studies have found that when the experimenter labels the pictures, preschoolers recall more of the paired words but schoolchildren—even first graders—do not (Means and Rohwer, 1974). The older children apparently label the pictures for themselves, so the experimenter's aid is unnecessary.

Imagery may be an effective memory aid because it strengthens the association between two things to be remembered. Or perhaps people who use it code the compound images two ways (in images and in words), thereby increasing the likelihood that material will be recalled. Or, from a levels-of-processing view, it may be that the elaboration required to form the compound images leads to processing at deeper levels of the memory system.

ORGANIZATION One of the most effective memory strategies is *organization*, the grouping of items around some common element. Adults can hold approximately seven elements ("bits" of information) in their short-term stores at a time, but by grouping information, they can increase their access from seven bits to seven groups (Miller, 1956). When memorizing a list, adults generally organize the words into semantic categories. Asked to recall them, instead of retrieving each word separately they recall them in groups—all of the furniture items, then the vehicles, then the musical instruments, and so on.

Despite the fact that even preschool children's memory is aided by semantically organized material, children this young do not spontaneously organize material as well as older children. Researchers test for organization by giving children a series of objects, pictures, or words, then asking them to recall items from the list in any order. Recalling words in groups that have a common feature indicates that the child has clustered the items. Sometimes researchers encourage children to sort items before they attempt to recall them. In these circumstances, the way young children divide the pictures or objects shows that their groupings often differ from those of older children or adults. Young children use a great many categories and place few items in any one category. They may take a long time to sort the items; they may group items according to a story line instead of by semantic category; and they sometimes find it difficult to explain why they assign items to certain groups (Moely, 1977).

With organization, as with rehearsal, there is a production deficiency. When items are presented in small blocks, a category at a time, preschoolers tend to remember by categories. But if the items are presented one at a time, with just a few items in each category, not even six-year-olds do much organizing (Furth and Milgram, 1973). Five-year-olds can sort items into categories when asked to do so, but they do not use the information to help them remember (Moely, 1977). When children are required to recall list items category by category, they remember more, but they will not use the same organizational technique to memorize a new list (Scribner and Cole, 1972).

Since young children who do categorize often use categories different from those an experimenter would choose, researchers have also studied how children organize unrelated material on their own. Faced with an array of objects, pictures, or words that have no semantic relation, children must impose their own organization on the material. Garrett Lange (1978) points out that under these circumstances, children five to twelve years old show little inclination to organize their recall. Lange believes that children generally fail to organize items when they are trying to learn them; and when they do organize the material, they do not use the organization extensively when trying to recall. As we shall see in the next section, children often know more than they recall.

Retrieval

Often a name or date that we know perfectly well is tucked away in memory becomes stuck in long-term storage. Try as we might, it will not transfer into working memory. Later, unbidden, it surfaces when we no longer need it. Such a commonplace event indicates that the ability to encode information does little good if we are unable to retrieve it. When children begin to use strategies, their ability to transfer material through the memory system improves. Strategies for retrieval can be simple (the resolution to keep searching for an item that does not immediately turn up in working memory) or complex (the planned use of intricate encoding strategies to simplify later retrieval).

An obvious strategy is the use of an external cue, such as the string tied around a child's finger as a reminder to ask a parent for lunch money or a senator's list of words to aid the recall of arguments to be made in a campaign speech. In a study that explored young children's ability to use external cues, 25 percent of the three-year-olds spontaneously used photographs to remind them of toys that had earlier been matched with the pictures, although they had to turn over the photographs that were lying face

In order to recall their lines from long-term memory, these children rely on cues, in this case the words or actions of the other actor. (J. Berndt/Stock, Boston, Inc.)

down on the floor; 75 percent of the five-year-olds did the same. But even after the experimenter showed the other children how to use the pictures, 30 percent of the three-year-olds could not manage to do it (Ritter *et al.*, 1973).

A similar study with schoolchildren indicated that six-year-olds may still find the deliberate use of external cues difficult. Akira Kobasigawa (1974) showed children twenty-four pictures drawn from eight categories. Along with the pictured items in each category, the children saw a related card that could be regarded as a cue for the category. Three animal pictures, for example, were accompanied by the picture of a zoo. When the children were allowed to use the cue cards during the recall period, only a third of the six-year-olds elected to use them, and they did so inefficiently. They recalled one item from a cue card, then stopped searching their memory and moved on to the next card. Older children, on the other hand, tried to remember as many items as they could before moving on to the next card. But the younger children had stored more information than they could re-

trieve unaided. When the experimenter showed them each cue card and asked them specifically to recall all three items, the differences vanished. Six-year-olds recalled as many items from the list as did eleven-year-olds. In another study, when Kobasigawa (Tumolo, Mason, and Kobasigawa, 1974) placed three squares on the cue cards to remind children that there were three items in each category, six-year-olds improved dramatically, but eight-year-olds showed no difference. Apparently the older children were already applying the cue of number to their memories.

Eight-year-olds who spontaneously used number to help them remember the items in a category were generating their own internal retrieval cues. Other internal cues are category names. Lists that have been organized by category for encoding can be remembered as a group if the category name is generated. This technique was used by H. Salatas and Flavell (1976) in an attempt to come nearer to the way memory functions outside the laboratory. Except for shopping lists and school exams, rote memorization is not a feature of daily life. Most of the information we recall is used in contexts different from those in which it was acquired. Therefore, Salatas and Flavell arranged a study in which children had to reorganize material they had learned but could do so by using category names as internal cues. First the children learned a list of words by category and were tested again and again until they could recall every item in each category. Then Salatas and Flavell asked them such questions as, "Which ones are small enough to fit in this box?" To answer the question, children had to retrieve each category, go through the items, decide which objects would fit, and list them aloud. Out of thirty-six six-year-olds, only one managed this complicated task; but nine out of thirty-two nine-year-olds could do it, and most of a group of college students automatically produced the requested items. When Salatas and Flavell told the children exactly how to go about the mental search, more than half the nine-year-olds could answer the question but few of the six-year-olds could.

Apparently most six-year-olds and many nine-year-olds cannot conduct systematic searches of memory, then report selectively concerning items that fit specific requirements (Kobasigawa, 1977).

METAMEMORY

Children are unlikely to make deliberate use of memory strategies unless they have some understanding of the way memory works. This understanding is called *metamemory*, and even three-year-olds show a glimmer of it. Told to remember where a toy is hidden, they look at or touch the hiding place and in some way make that place distinctive from the rest of the room. Three-year-olds who are not given instructions to remember do not (Wellman, Ritter, and Flavell, 1975). Three-year-olds also know that noise makes remembering more difficult and that remembering a few items is easier than remembering many (Wellman, 1977).

But remembering where a toy is hidden and memorizing a list of words are very different tasks. In the former, the goal is retrieving an attractive toy; in the latter, the goal is recall. As Flavell and Wellman (1977) point out, the three- or four-year-old may not realize that being asked to memorize words or objects requires the child to do something special with those items and that the child's job is to do something now that will be of questionable use later.

By the time children are in kindergarten or first grade, they know what it means to learn, remember, and forget. Kreutzer, Leonard, and Flavell (1975) interviewed kindergarten and first-, third-, and fifth-grade children in order to discover their understanding of how memory works. Most of the youngest children were aware that events that happened a long time ago were hard to recall, that meaningless strings of items such as telephone numbers are quickly forgotten, and that once something is learned, it is easier to relearn the same material than to learn something new. These young learners realized that they could plan their study time to help their memory and even proposed deliberate schemes, such as careful inspection of the items to be learned. They also proposed and understood the use of external memory aids such as other people, tape recordings, written notes, or even a string on the finger to help them remember.

Third and fifth graders were firmer than younger children about what they knew and had acquired additional information about memory. They not only recognized that time affects memory, but they also understood that more study time helps recall and having to learn more items will hinder it. They realized that these two factors interact, so that a short study of a short list leads to better recall than long study of a long list.

A major difference between young and older children is the ability to plan. Older children are better at forming and maintaining a memory goal and using strategies to help them reach it (Flavell, 1977). But memory is more than knowing about strategies. As children learn more about the workings of the memory system, such stored knowledge can influence the way they handle material, leading them to integrate it with previous knowledge and process it at a deeper level, thereby increasing its availability (Cavanaugh and Perlmutter, 1980).

Metamemory is one of the newer approaches to the understanding of memory, having been recognized as a major area of memory studies only about a decade ago. Although we have learned much from it and from other memory studies, our understanding of children's memory is far from complete. Most research has involved the memorization of lists, which, although assumed to illuminate the important components of memory, may leave important parts of the picture in deep shadow. Taking memory out of its normal context may lead us to underestimate youngsters' capabilities. Soviet psychologists (e.g., Yendovitskaya, 1971) believe the young child's memory is involuntary and depends upon an understanding that is stimulated by cues in the real world. Preschoolers approach a researcher's memory task in a different manner from schoolchildren, whose educational experience has accustomed them to structured memory tasks. A child who has been memorizing spelling lists and multiplication tables may regard recall as a plausible end in itself and not only as a means to a goal. A child or adult who has never been to school may take a dim view of recall as a goal, and so perform far below his or her capabilities. As was pointed out earlier, the child's own history and the history of the culture have powerful effects on the development of memory.

SUMMARY

1. Selective attention begins almost at birth, and the kinds of stimuli and the way babies look at them change in predictable ways. By about two months, babies switch from scanning the edges of a face to scanning its features, especially the eyes. Five-year-olds still scan unsystematically, tend to stop scanning before they have all the information they need, and have their attention grabbed by a picture's focus of interest. Eight-year-olds, on the other hand, are efficient, rapid scanners, who scan patterns from the top down, regardless of the picture's center of interest.

2. As babies' ability to discriminate among sights improves, they begin to watch strange objects in preference to familiar ones. Young children find it hard to ignore irrelevant information; but as children get older, they focus so intently upon central information that they remember less incidental information than do younger children.

3. Children store events in memory by constructing a model, called a representation. Representations are either enactive (a motor response), iconic (a visual image), or symbolic (a word or symbol). These systems of representation develop consecutively, each depends on the previous system for its emergence, and events that have been represented in one system can be transferred to another.

4. Children divide the world by grouping together items with similar qualities, perhaps building each group (animals, colors, utensils, etc.) around a core meaning, which consists of the best example of the category. Young children base their categories on function, grouping objects by their uses and actions, although perceptual features also play an important role. Older children and adults reorganize their concepts, using semantic bases of classification. Formal education may play an important role in speeding the classification switch from function to semantics.

5. Recognition is the simplest way of remembering, and from a very early age babies can recognize objects they have looked at for a long time. Once information is processed by the memory system, age appears to have no effect on the length of time a memory is retained.

6. Children can also reconstruct models or patterns from memory, a skill that is more difficult than recognition but easier than recall, the most complex demonstration of memory. At about eleven months, some babies seem to show recall. Although preschoolers do poorly at laboratory tests of recall, their recollections of their own experiences are good.

7. One reason older children and adults seem to have a more efficient memory is their use of memory strategies, either at the time they encode material or at the time they retrieve it from storage. Strategies keep information flowing through the memory system and may take the form of rehearsal, imagery, organization, or internal or external cues.

8. Three-year-olds show traces of metamemory, a knowledge of how memory works. By the time children are in kindergarten, they know quite a bit about the process. As children learn more about the memory system, they begin forming memory goals and consciously using strategies. As a result, they integrate new material with old, process it at a deeper level, and remember more.

Development of Thought

One four-year-old girl's favorite birthday present was an electric train, which came with a small, circular track. Later, her grandparents arrived for a visit bearing a big box filled with track — straight track, curved track, crossovers, and switches. There was also a large piece of plywood, on which her father screwed down the new layout securely so that the little girl could play with her train whenever she liked. As the last screw went into place, the child's mother said, "Later we'll get some little trees and houses and telephone poles and glue them down on the board. Then it'll look like a real little town." The little girl's eyes glowed. "Now?" she asked. "No, later," repeated her mother. The four-year-old accepted the postponement gracefully, but in less than fifteen minutes she came into the kitchen where her mother was preparing lunch. "Is it later enough yet?" she asked. The child's concept of time bore little resemblance to that of her mother, and as we shall see, it would be a number of years before she would be able to understand the relation between time and actions.

The development of children's concept of time is one example of the changing ways in which children think about the physical and social world — a subject that has been most extensively described by Jean Piaget, whose theory was discussed in Chapter 2. He saw the individual as progressing from the reflexive neonate who could not distinguish between self and world to the adolescent who could apply logical thought to abstract situations, solving problems in a rational, scientific manner. That progression, he believed, was the result of the child's spontaneous activity; and as we explore the development of children's thought processes, it will become clear that much research in cognitive development is either a continuation of Piagetian theory or an attempt to challenge it.

In the last two chapters we traced the development of perception, attention, and memory; in this chapter we shall explore changes in the way that children apply these aspects of cognition when they think about the physical world. Young children, we shall find, learn concepts in a manner very different from that used by older children and adults, and the process of learning universal rules is a lengthy one that builds upon the associations children learn in the first few years of life. As we examine the development of thought, we shall follow the progression of children through the stages that Piaget set forth, noting some of the major developmental tasks of each stage. Finally, we shall look at the way children develop an understanding of three concepts: time, number, and causality (the relationship between cause and effect).

LEARNING TO THINK

In the course of cognitive development, a boy grows from an infant whose memories last for a few fleeting seconds to an adolescent who tests hypotheses in a rigorous, scientific manner. As his nervous system matures and his experiences deepen, the boy's concepts gradually develop. Learning theorists believe that he observes the effects of his own actions and those of others, and that he extracts regularities from the multiple, seemingly chaotic events in his world (Bandura, 1977). As the boy's information-processing skills develop, he can reason about what he observes, using knowledge he has built up from watching television, attending school, and interacting with others, and by deducing new information from the store of knowledge he already possesses. In order to understand how this happens, it is helpful to see how children learn concepts and extract rules.

Learning Concepts

The way children develop new concepts, believes Tracy Kendler (1979), undergoes a radical shift shortly after they start school. This is about the time that children enter Piaget's concrete operational period and begin to apply logical thought to concrete objects and situations. Until then, children and rats appear to learn in the same manner; they form relatively direct associations between the stimuli in the world and their responses to them. Each time their actions are reinforced, their tendencies to repeat that action increase. Each time their actions are not reinforced—or are punished— their tendencies to repeat that action diminish. As children acquire language, however, they begin to represent events symbolically and to transform their perceptions mentally. Instead of transforming their perceptions directly, they process them as examples of a category (Kendler and Kendler, 1975). This means that children first respond mentally to stimuli, then mentally generate another stimulus based on their store of concepts. The new cognitive stimulus thus affects their response to the perceived stimuli. In short, they are thinking about what they have seen. Because of this developmental difference in learning, one can use the results from animal experiments to predict the way a three-year-old will learn, but when applied to college students, predictions based on conditioning are generally wrong.

These conclusions have come from studies of *discrimination learning*, in which a person sees two stimuli and must choose between them. A correct choice brings a reward—a marble for a bright child, the reinforcement of knowing you are right for the college student. Incorrect choices bring nothing except the knowledge that one has failed at the task.

In a typical experiment (see Figure 12.1),

Development of Discrimination Learning

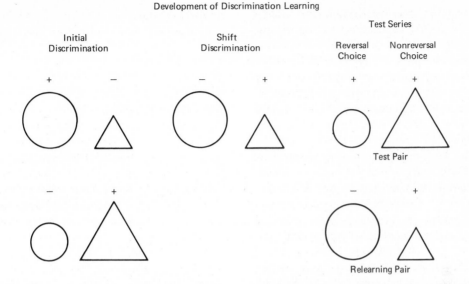

Figure 12.1 In the study of discrimination learning discussed in the text, children learn in the initial phase that "big" is correct and "small" is incorrect. In the shift phase, both "small" and "triangle" are correct. Whether a child's criterion shifts from "big" to "small" or from "big" to "triangle" is revealed in the test phase, and the choice helps indicate whether simple operant conditioning or thought was involved in the process.
SOURCE: From T. S. Kendler, "The Development of Discrimination Learning: A Levels-of-Functioning Explanation," in H. W. Reese and L. P. Lipsitt (eds.), ADVANCES IN CHILD DEVELOPMENT AND BEHAVIOR, Vol. 13. N.Y.: Academic Press, 1979. Reprinted by permission of the author and publisher.

children see two shapes (a large circle and a small triangle) and choose one of them. In this case, the large circle is the correct choice. The next pair of shapes is a small circle and a large triangle; the large triangle is correct. The child's task is to learn that the "big" shape, whether a circle or a triangle, is always correct. After the child has correctly chosen "big" ten times in a row, the experimenter abruptly shifts the rules; now the small triangle is correct, so that using either "small" or "triangle" as a basis of judg-

ment is correct. After the child learns to choose the small triangle in the pair — which is shown again and again — the important part of the experiment begins. The investigator sets about discovering whether the youngster has reversed the concept (now choosing the small stimulus instead of the large one) or whether the child has switched and is now judging by shape instead of size (now choosing a triangle instead of a circle). Rats and small children apparently learn by a gradual strengthening of their tendency to choose the particular instances that have been reinforced. Thus they find it extremely difficult to reverse the concept (change from big to small). The reversal is difficult because they have never been rewarded for choosing small objects, but half of their rewards have come for choosing triangles. Therefore they will nearly always switch to the concept of shape. Older children, on the other hand, learn in a manner that allows them to think about the problem and the dimensions that have been reinforced. Thus the older they are the easier it is for them to reverse their concepts. Like adults, they are more likely to switch from big to little than from big to triangle. Presumably, they are already attending to shape.

Kendler (1979) believes that the schoolchild's more sophisticated approach to discrimination learning is the result of applying the logical skill of hypothesis testing to the problem. As children attempt to solve the puzzle posed by the experimenter, they test one dimension after another, using their errors for guidance, until they have the answer (Trabasso and Bower, 1968). The basic rule for hypothesis testing is a simple decision rule: stay with your choice if you win, switch if you lose. Three- and four-year-olds do not use this rule; but most of them gradually learn to do so. Children who use hypothesis testing, on the other hand, jump from being generally wrong to being always right. The proportion of children who do this rises steadily through the school years until, by the time they are eighteen, nearly all use the win-stay, lose-switch rule.

There is some indication that a few five-year-olds and most six-year-olds use or can be taught to use hypothesis testing. In a discrimination experiment, Joan Cantor and Charles Spiker (1979) found that 26 percent of the kindergartners and 32 percent of the first graders they tested spontaneously used hypothesis testing. But among children who were given direct instruction, 38 percent of the kindergartners and 75 percent of the first graders used it.

From an information-processing point of view, the difference in the way children learn concepts indicates that they move from the young child's shallow processing to the adult's practice of processing important material at deeper levels. From a broader perspective, children move from the kind of learning that is explained by strict learning theory to the kind of mental operations that fit comfortably into an organismic view of the world (although social-learning theory also sees thought as transforming the child's responses to stimuli).

Learning Rules

Learning is generally considered an obvious, specific change that takes place before our eyes.

Many four-year-olds can print the letters of their names and count, one by one, the pennies and dollar bills they have saved to buy a new game. (They still cannot manage to count pennies and nickels and dimes and quarters together.) Changes in general capabilities, however, are considered development. Although a four-year-old girl watched her mother carefully divide the bottle of cola, she happily accepted the tall, narrow glass in the belief that it contained more cola than the squat glass her older brother took. According to Piaget's theory, the child did not understand the concept of *conservation;* she did not realize that irrelevant changes in the physical appearance of objects do not affect their quantity. In another year or two, as a result of cognitive development, she will progress to a different stage of thinking and will no longer be fooled by the different shapes of glasses.

Some learning theorists believe that this change in a child's understanding is not the result of a movement from one stage of cognitive development to another, but the cumulative effect of learning. The distinction between learning and development is primarily one of time, believes Robert Gagné (1968), and slow, cumulative learning can explain a child's eventual grasp of logical rules such as those that govern irrelevant changes in the appearance of substances—whether glasses of cola, balls of clay, or rows of coins. Although Gagné is not proposing that logical rules are simply the result of conditioning, he does suggest that conditioning lies at the bottom of a great hierarchy of learning, and that changes in general capabilities take place when children learn new, complex rules.

The path to these rules begins with conditioning—associations between stimuli and their responses. These associations build up into chains—both motor and verbal—and the child learns to make discriminations. Objects have characteristic dimensions, textures, tastes, and smells, for example. They can be thrown, dropped, and manipulated in certain ways. Discriminations lead in turn to concepts—the concepts of "surface," "container," "liquid," and so on. From the concepts come simple rules, such as that one can pour liquid into a container, and that liquids assume the shapes of their containers. Simple rules lead to complex ones and eventually, by a lengthy process of recognition, recall, and the transfer of what the child learns from one situation to another, a developmental change occurs.

Each new association, concept, and rule, points out Gagné, is learned under different conditions, because as learning accumulates, the child has more and more information stored and available in memory. By the time a child is ten years old, most associations already have been established and much of the child's learning now consists of rules and concepts. The eventual learning of rules and concepts, of course, depends upon the ability to recall all those discriminations, chains, and associations it took the child so many years to learn.

In Gagné's view, the understanding that irrelevant transformations in appearance can be reversed, which is basic to conservation and which Piaget regards as evidence of qualitative changes in the child's thinking, is evidence of accumulated concrete knowledge. In the case of liquids, it is knowledge the child has gradually piled up through years of experience with liquids and with containers of various widths and heights.

THINKING LOGICALLY

Because Piaget has given the most comprehensive picture of cognitive development, a convenient approach to logical thought is an examination in terms of his system. As indicated in Chapter 2, Piaget believed that a child is not capable of logical thought until the age of seven or eight. However, the logical thought of the school years does not suddenly spring into being. It is based on concepts laid down during the first two stages of life. It is hard to imagine, for example, that a child could understand conservation without developing the understanding that objects continue to exist when out of sight—a key task of the sensorimotor stage of infancy—

or without developing the understanding that people who change their clothes or hair color are the same individuals—a major developmental task of the preoperational stage of early childhood.

Although the schoolchild develops logic, he or she uses it only in regard to tangible objects. For this reason, Piaget described the schoolchild's thought as concrete operational. The thought of adolescents, who can apply formal logic and manipulate abstract relationships, he called formal operational.

Sensorimotor Thought

During the sensorimotor period, which covers approximately the first two years of life, a major task is that of separating self from the world. Babies cannot distinguish between their own bodies and the objects and people in the world around them until they are about a year old and have reached the fifth of Piaget's six substages of this period (the six substages are discussed in Chapter 2). Not until babies reach this fifth substage did Piaget consider their behavior "intelligent"—an intelligence based on perceptions and motor skills, hence sensorimotor intelligence.

Out of their sensory, perceptual, and motor interactions with the environment, babies gradually develop the *object concept*—the understanding that objects remain the same although they may move from one place to another and that they continue to exist when out of sight. These interrelated ideas of object identity and object permanence are not fully developed, Piaget believed, until the latter part of the second year, when the baby reaches the sixth and last substage of the sensorimotor period.

Piaget noted that if an object being watched by a baby of less than four months disappears from view, the baby tends to act as if the object had never been there. It is as though an object exists only when it is being immediately perceived. During the next four months or so, however, a baby in Stage 3 often initiates a visual search for an object he or she has seen

Play and Problem Solving

Allowing children to play freely can help them learn to solve problems. The advantages that play gives children in a problem-solving situation was evident in a study that required preschoolers to discover a way of retrieving a piece of chalk from a box without getting up from their seats at a low table. The transparent plastic box, whose lid fastened with a J-shaped hook, rested across the table from the child, too far to be reached by stretching or with one of the sticks that lay on the table. In order to reach the chalk, children had to clamp together three pieces of wood with two C clamps that lay on the table, nudge the hook open, and insert the end of the stick in the box.

Children who were allowed to play freely with ten sticks and seven clamps before they were given the problem were just as likely to sólve it as children who watched an adult demonstrate how to clamp the sticks together to extend their length. The playing children were not simply exploring the materials, because they did such things as use the sticks to form letters and to construct a house with the aid of the clamps. It was not the act of playing itself that led to the children's solutions, propose Kathy Sylva, Jerome Bruner, and Paul Genova (1976), but the self-initiation that is a part of free play—and an essential part of problem solving. Playing with the materials also gave the children a chance to practice flexibility and reduced the amount of stress they might otherwise have felt when presented with the problem.

In a similar study, Peter Smith and Susan Dutton (1979) asked four-year-olds to get a marble out of a box under conditions much like those in the previous experiment. This time, instead of using clamps to join the sticks, children had to insert the sticks into holes bored in the face of wooden blocks. Reaching the box required the joining of only two sticks. As in the previous experiment, children who had played freely with the materials and those who had been given training in joining sticks both solved the problem faster than children in a control group. But Smith and Dutton then pushed the children further; they moved the box so far away that the children had to join several sticks in order to reach it. In this new situation, those who had simply "played" with the materials solved the problem significantly faster than children who had been given training, and far fewer of them required hints. Most of the children in the control group showed little interest in solving the new problem, and they needed many hints in order to find a solution. As Bruner (1972) has proposed, free play appears to make children much more adept at combining familiar ways of action to solve new problems.

disappearing from view. At this point in the development of the object concept, the object seems to continue existing for the baby only if the infant sees the object starting to move away. When a cover is dropped over an object held by a baby who is in Stage 3, the baby either withdraws the hand or behaves as if he or she does not know the object is still grasped in the hand.

Other researchers have confirmed that at four months, babies respond to the disappearance of objects in a new way. For example, Alastair Mundy-Castle and Jeremy Anglin (1969) conducted an experiment in which an object appeared on an infant's right and rose vertically out of sight. Then an identical object dropped down on the infant's left and fell out of sight, while the one on the right again rose into view.

After watching a number of such cycles, infants of less than four months simply looked from side to side in order to see the objects. But older babies assumed that a single object was traveling on a circular trajectory. Their eyes followed a path that corresponded to the possible path of the object. For these babies, the moving object continued to exist, even though it was out of sight. What is more, unlike younger babies, the four-month-olds looked back to the right (where last seen) if the object did not appear, as predicted, on the left.

In observations of his own children, Piaget (1952b, 1954) found that during the last four months of their first year, his children searched for objects that they saw him place behind a screen, but they searched in a limited fashion. For example, Piaget moved a toy behind a screen while his child was observing. The child retrieved it. Piaget made his move in the game again, and the child again responded appropriately. This was repeated several more times. Then Piaget, with his child attending to his actions, hid the toy behind a screen located in a different place. Yet the child insisted on searching for the toy in the original location. Piaget concluded that the child failed to search in the new location because babies in Stage 4 cannot dissociate the objects of the world from their own actions on them and that babies remember a place solely in terms of the movement they made when first retrieving the toy.

Because this reaction by the baby is basic to understanding the development of the infant mind, researchers have tested Piaget's explanation in an attempt to discover the nature of the baby's error. Other researchers have found that babies continue to reach toward Point A even when the toy is not hidden but remains plainly visible at Point B (Butterworth, 1977) and also when a toy different from the one hidden at A is hidden at B (Evans and Gratch, 1972).

Explanations vary widely. Babies may simply learn that Point A is the "toy place" (Gratch, 1975). Or the error may depend in part on memory, because babies rarely make it if they are already reaching for the toy as it is being hidden or if they are allowed to reach for it immediately after it has been hidden at B (Gratch et al., 1974). Or babies may not be searching for the toy at all but seeking to reinstate action patterns (a reach toward a certain point) that earlier brought them pleasure (Flavell, 1977). J. G. Bremner and Peter Bryant (1977) found that nine-month-old infants tended to remember the response that won them the toy but not the place where the toy was hidden, an explanation that supports Piaget. As the discussion in Chapter 10 indicated, until babies move about and explore the world on their own, they tend to locate objects in reference to themselves, so they repeat their earlier successful grasp, reaching where the toy

At six months, babies have not developed the object concept, so that when the toy elephant that has captured this baby's attention (left) is hidden from view, the infant seems unaware that the fascinating toy is still on the tray before her (right). (George Zimbel/Monkmeyer Press)

previously lay in respect to their own bodies.

Bremner and Bryant have also offered a simpler explanation. Babies may know that the toy is now at Point B, but lack the control that allows them to inhibit an established learned response.

According to Piaget, not until the last sub-stage of the sensorimotor period will babies look in all possible places for a hidden object. Until that time, he maintained, they have not completely developed the object concept.

Charles Brainerd (1978), who has reviewed the relevant research, concludes that despite extensive experimentation, the issue of whether babies fail to keep searching for hidden objects because they lack the object concept or because they lack the skills required to continue the search has not been settled, and that Piaget's belief that development of the concept is not complete until the second year of life has not been disproved. No matter how the issue is resolved, once the concept has been established, babies regard people, places, and objects as existing separately from themselves and as not depending on their behavior.

Preoperational Thought

Despite the obvious superiority of the preschooler's thought to that of the infant, the preoperational child lacks logic. Piaget saw thought at this period as intuitive, inflexible, focused on individual events, and contradictory. These qualities indicate that the cognitive processes are not *operations* (which are by definition flexible, rigorous, and logical thought), hence the period is called the *preoperational stage.*

The concept of *identity*, which develops during the preoperational period, is vital to the appearance of logical thought. It consists of understanding that objects and people remain the same, even if irrelevant properties are changed. A six-year-old girl understands that her friend can put on a gorilla mask and still be her friend, that her mother can change her hair color and

still be Mother, and that a girl can have her hair cut and wear boys' clothes and still be a girl—a concept that is also important in the development of sex roles, which are discussed in Chapter 17. But when this same girl was only three, and firmly entrenched in preoperational thought, she would have believed that her friend in a gorilla mask was no longer her friend but some strange and terrible creature.

In order to test children's understanding that

A three-year-old who watches familiar children don their Halloween masks will be frightened at the terrifying monsters, because a child in the preoperational stage lacks the concept of identity and thinks that the masked children are no longer his or her friends. (© Harvey Stein)

an animal cannot change its species, Rheta DeVries (1969) put masks made of fur and rubber on a cat's head. One mask was that of a dog, the other that of a rabbit. DeVries showed the cat to children whose ages ranged from three to six. Three-year-olds identified the cat as whatever species its head resembled. Whenever masks were put on or removed, these children believed that the animal's species had changed from cat to dog to rabbit and back. Children a little older would say that the cat would remain a cat, but once the mask was in place they would change their minds. The sight of a dog's head on a cat's body — even though the animal's body never left their field of vision — overwhelmed their earlier assertions that its species would remain unchanged. Only the five- and six-year-olds maintained that the cat was a cat no matter what kind of mask it wore.

Apparently, the concept of identity develops very slowly during the preoperational period. Its beginnings can be seen fairly early. Preschool children do accept the identity of their own bodies; they realize that despite their increase in size, pictures of their younger selves are "still me" and that when they are big enough to go to school, the schoolchild will be "me." But in the case of a plant, they say, "It grew, but it isn't the same any more; here it's a little plant and there it's a big plant. It's not the same plant" (Piaget, 1968). By the time they are seven, however, they admit to the identity of the seedling and the mature plant.

Concrete Operational Thought

The child who crosses the threshold of the concrete operational period has come to what Piaget (Piaget and Inhelder, 1969) called the "decisive turning-point." For the first time, thought is logical, although only when applied to concrete objects and situations. Since children's cognitive processes are also flexible and rigorous, they qualify as operations. Among the operations that develop during this period are the principles of conservation, transitivity, and class inclusion.

CONSERVATION Once children understand that objects continue to exist and that superficial changes in the appearance of objects do not change their basic identity, they are ready to grasp the principle of conservation. Children who are "conservers" understand that irrelevant changes in the external appearance of objects have no effect on the object's quantity — its weight, length, mass, or volume.

In the best-known test of conservation, children watch an experimenter fill two glasses of the same size and shape to an equal level with colored water. The children are asked whether the two glasses contain the same amount of water. When the children assert that the amounts are the same, the researcher pours the water from one glass into a shorter, broader glass, so the levels of colored water in the glasses differ. A four-year-old boy, asked whether each glass now contains the same amount of water, says "No! This one has more water in it because the water is higher." But a seven-year-old girl is not fooled. She points out that the squat glass is shorter, but that it is also broader; she understands the concept of conservation of quantity. She knows that if she pours the water back into the tall glass, the level will be just where it was before.

The seven-year-old has acquired what Piaget called the concrete operation of *reversibility:* the understanding that irrelevant changes in appearance can be reversed and that such changes tend to compensate one another. For example, as the water level falls in the short, broad glass its quantity also spreads out.

At one time, many developmental psychologists believed that children who gave erroneous replies in the experiment with the glasses of colored water had clearly demonstrated that they did not understand the conservation of quantity. But researchers have begun to question this conclusion. For one thing, when chil-

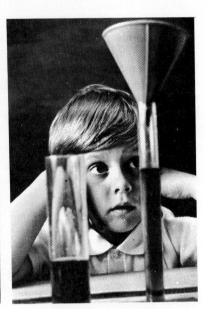

In a standard test of conservation, a boy watches carefully as water from one of two wide beakers is poured into a narrow container (*right*); then he is asked whether the squat and the narrow containers hold the same amount of water (*left*); unless he understands that irrelevant changes in appearance can be reversed, the boy will say that there is more water in the narrow container. (Courtesy *The New York Times*)

dren are allowed to pour the colored water themselves, more of them solve the problem correctly. For another, Margaret Donaldson (1979) has pointed out that the conditions of the experiment push the children toward the wrong answer. When the experimenter pours the water, he or she generally says, "Now watch what I do," indicating to the child that the change is important and will affect whatever follows.

The influence of the experimenter appeared when Susan Rose and Marion Blank (1974) conducted a version of the conservation experiment in which they did not ask the child about the quantity of the two items *before* they manipulated their appearance. They suspected that asking the same question both before and after

the manipulation might suggest to children that they should change their answer. When they tested six-year-olds with only the final question, they found that the children not only made fewer errors on the task at hand but also scored much higher a week later when tested in the manner devised by Piaget.

It appears that changing the way a test is presented may allow additional children to demonstrate their grasp of conservation. In Piaget's view, however, not even the most skillful teacher can teach four-year-olds that pouring water into a short, squat glass does not change the amount of water, or that twisting a necklace into a curve does not affect its length. Although he agreed that learning takes place during cognitive development, Piaget maintained that all a child can learn is to apply cognitive structures (such as reversibility) he or she already has acquired to new contents (Brainerd, 1978), and since four-year-olds lack operations, they cannot learn to conserve. Yet a number of investigators (e.g., Brainerd, 1977; T. Rosenthal and Zimmerman, 1978) have been able to teach three- and four-year-old children to pass conservation tests.

There may be an explanation that reconciles

the two views. Preschoolers who appear to understand conservation may not be mentally reversing the change in appearance, but simply maintaining their belief in the object's identity (Acredolo and Acredolo, 1979). Such an explanation squares with the results of a study by Gilbert Botvin and Frank Murray (1975), which showed how children who fail to conserve weight, mass, and number on standard tests learn the concept from other children. Botvin and Murray put children in groups of five, each made up of three nonconservers and two conservers. A researcher first asked each child to answer the same series of questions about weight and mass conservation, so they heard one another's answers. The group then talked over their explanations and agreed on an answer to each conservation problem. After they had reached an agreement, the researcher questioned each child.

Most of the nonconservers, including an additional group of children who merely watched and listened to the group, learned to conserve mass, weight, and number. During the earlier group discussions, original conservers tended to explain conservation by talking about the reversibility of the change, whereas the new conservers tended to give "identity" explanations, noting that nothing had been added to or subtracted from the original amount, or that the change had been irrelevant. Botvin and Murray interpret the change as the result of modeling, suggesting that when the models gave correct answers, they produced mental conflicts in the other children, which prodded them into reorganizing their thinking. In this case, the first grasp of conservation relied on an understanding of identity, not of reversibility, which may be the way most children develop their comprehension.

Piaget's experiments (Piaget and Inhelder, 1969) on children's notions of conservation reveal an interesting phenomenon. Although seven-year-olds realize that the mass of an object, such as a piece of clay, does not change when the clay is stretched or compressed, they may fail to realize that its weight and volume also remain unchanged. Piaget found that children always acquire the various kinds of conservation in the same order. First a child understands conservation of quantity; then, at about the age of nine or ten, he or she grasps the notion of conservation of weight; and finally, at about ten or eleven, the child realizes that there is also conservation of volume, in the sense that the amount of water displaced by an object is not affected if its shape is changed (Piaget and Inhelder, 1941). Other researchers have confirmed Piaget's basic findings about the sequence of these acquisitions (Sigel and Mermelstein, 1966; Uzgiris, 1964).

Children as old as nine may not transfer their realization that changing the shape of an object does not affect its weight to other kinds of transformations. For example, many children who pass the weight conservation test when an object's shape is altered still think that butter loses weight as it melts and that water becomes heavier as it freezes (Lovell and Ogilvie, 1961).

Developmental psychologists are still far from understanding exactly how children acquire conservation concepts or why they seem to acquire them in a particular order. Conservation is an extremely complex cognitive skill, which Susan Carey (1974) sees as developing from two sources. First, as the nervous system matures, children's ability to process information increases (that is, they can handle more bits of information at once, they can process it more rapidly, etc.). So all children get better at conservation simply by getting older. Second, children acquire the pieces of knowledge that allow them to understand and solve problems of conservation. Once information-processing abilities have matured somewhat, children can be taught by practice or observation, as were the children in Botvin and Murray's study.

Even without formal schooling, children constantly experience the heaviness or lightness of objects they lift, push, or pull. They "know" from their handling of objects, although they may not realize that they know, that things do not get heavier or lighter if their shape or color changes. Many children conserve weight in the sense of maintaining constant muscular pressure when they lift a ball of clay that has just been elongated, even though, if asked, they would state that its weight had changed. Thus they may demonstrate a working knowledge of conservation, just as they daily demonstrate their fluency as speakers of language. But they cannot explain their knowledge, just as they cannot explain the rules of syntax they use each time they speak.

TRANSITIVITY Another skill Piaget placed in the concrete operational period is *transitivity*, or the making of logical inferences based on separate observations. Told that Scott is older than Jennifer and that Jennifer is older than Mark, concrete operational children infer that Scott must be older than Mark. This deduction requires a child to join two instances of the relational concept "older than." Like conservation, transitivity does not suddenly appear full-blown. In order to handle the inferences the task requires, children must first understand *seriation*, or the ordering of objects by size or weight. In a seriation test, a child arranges a row of sticks in ascending or descending order of length, or a row of coins in order of size—from dime to half-dollar—or threads different size beads on a string to make a necklace of graduated sizes.

Once children can arrange objects in order of size, they are ready to develop the more sophisticated skill of transitivity, in which they arrange and compare objects in their heads. According to Piaget, this concept requires operational thought and is rarely found in children younger than seven. He tested children's grasp of the concept in the following manner:

> We present two sticks to a child, stick A being smaller than stick B. Then we hide stick A and show him stick B together with a larger stick C. Then we ask him how A and C compare. Preoperational children will say that they do not know because they have not seen them together—they

have not been able to compare them. On the other hand, operational children . . . will say right away that C is bigger than A, since C is bigger than B and B is bigger than A [Piaget, 1970a].

The reason young children fail the test may be because it also measures such factors as language ability and memory, which are unrelated to transitivity (Brainerd, 1978). Piaget required that a child not only give the correct answer but also explain each inference logically, a skill that may be beyond the scope of some children who otherwise would pass the test. The factor of memory may be even more critical. Young children may fail to infer the proper relationship between sticks A and C because by the time they reach the third (inferential) step of the experiment, they have forgotten the information given during the first two steps. (See Figure 12.2.)

Peter Bryant and Tom Trabasso (1971) decided to find out if memory played an important role in four-year-olds' failures to make correct inferences. Instead of asking the child about the relationship between three sticks, they used five. Bryant and Trabasso constructed four one-step comparisons (A and B, B and C, C and D, D and E) in which three of the sticks occur as both the larger and smaller members of pairs. This precaution ensured that a child could not pass the test simply by recalling that the word "bigger" was the only adjective connected with the larger stick in most of the comparisons.

In the initial training stage, children learned and remembered the four direct comparisons. When asked to compare B and D in their heads, 78 percent of the four-year-olds, 88 percent of the five-year-olds, and 92 percent of the six-year-olds made the correct inferences, indicating that memory is crucial to the task. This result seems inconsistent with Piaget's belief that children cannot grasp the concept of transitivity until they have reached the concrete operational stage.

In subsequent research, Trabasso (1977) studied children to find out how they process the

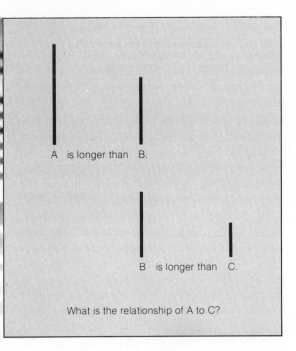

Figure 12.2 Example of a transitivity problem, which requires the joining together of two instances of the relational concept "longer than."

knowledge needed to solve the problem. He discovered that children (like adults) do not store the information the way they learn it—as four separate pairs. Instead, they recode the information, constructing an internal representation of the entire group of sticks, perhaps as a list, perhaps as a visual image. When asked to compare lengths, they "read" the answer off their representation. If children stored the information by pairs, they should be fastest at retrieving comparisons they had learned directly (B is longer than C), but they are not. The more widely separated the sticks, the faster children can answer questions about them. They can, for example, report the relation between B and D (an inference) more quickly than they can report the relation between B and C, which they memorized.

Although it takes a four-year-old much longer than it does a seven-year-old to learn the four comparisons, once the child understands and remembers them, the four-year-old is as accurate as an adult in making mental comparisons. Because their successes, their errors, and their comparative reaction times are similar, Trabasso (1975) concludes that the cognitive processes of adults and children are quite similar, and that memory and the young child's heavy dependence upon linguistic context are responsible for the failures of young children on the traditional tests.

However, John Flavell (1977), who agrees that children solve problems of transitivity earlier than has been commonly believed and by using a different cognitive process than has been supposed, points out that the results of research such as Trabasso's indicate that the stick problem apparently does not require concrete operations for its solution. If children (and adults) are simply reading off the answers from a mental image, they are solving the problem without using inference. Piaget, therefore, may be wrong about the young child's ability to solve the stick problem but correct in maintaining that young children cannot reach such conclusions when inference rather than internal visualization is required.

CLASS INCLUSION The child's knowledge that a superordinate class (animals) is always larger than any of its subordinate classes (cows, dogs) is also considered a concrete operation by Piaget. If this operation, *class inclusion*, has been mastered by a youngster who has eight lemon drops and five licorice drops, the child will agree that lemon drops are candy and that licorice drops are also candy. The child's mastery of class inclusion is demonstrated when the youngster claims to have more candy than lemon drops.

Although preschool children know perfectly well that lemon drops and licorice drops are both candy, they will stoutly maintain that they have more lemon drops than candy. (See Figure

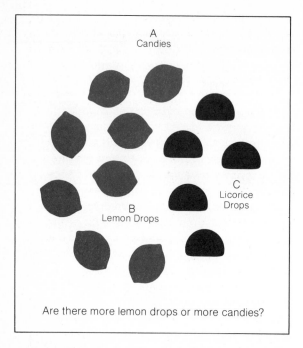

A
Candies

C
Licorice
Drops

B
Lemon Drops

Are there more lemon drops or more candies?

Figure 12.3 Young children are likely to have difficulty reasoning about the relation of a part or parts to a whole, and, if shown a collection of lemon drops and licorice drops, they are likely to say that they have more lemon drops than candy.

12.3.) Piaget (1952a) explained this by saying that young children cannot think of both an entire class and a subclass at the same time; therefore, they cannot compare them. Presented this way, the problem is even more difficult than Piaget supposed. Some investigators (e.g., Winer, 1980) have discovered that many children are at least ten years old—not seven—before they can solve traditional class-inclusion problems.

A variation on the lemon and licorice drops experiment indicates that part of the children's problem may lie in language, not in concept. James McGarrigle (see Donaldson, 1979) tested forty-eight children, who were about six years old, with four toy cows. Three of the cows were black and one was white. McGarrigle placed all

the cows on their sides and told the children they were sleeping. When he asked the standard Piagetian question, "Are there more black cows or more cows?" only 25 percent of the children correctly answered "More cows." But when asked, "Are there more black cows or more sleeping cows?" 48 percent of the children correctly said, "More sleeping cows." The inclusion of an adjective that encompassed the entire class enabled many more children to compare class with subclass. In another study, when all the classes involved were stated ("Are there more pets or more dogs or more cats?"), the number of children who answered correctly jumped from 5 percent to 55 percent (Ahr and Youniss, 1970). Finally, when the terms "more" and "less" are cast aside and the problem is rephrased in practical terms, even preschoolers do well at class inclusions. Shown three M&Ms and two jelly beans and asked, "Do you want to eat the M&Ms or the candy?" many three-year-olds showed they understood by promptly eating all the candy (Siegel *et al.*, 1978).

The way children encode information about the objects goes a long way in determining whether they can answer the questions. Tom Trabasso and his colleagues (1978), who have approached class inclusion from an information-processing standpoint, explain that children can encode a display of five plastic cows and three horses as only the superordinate class (animals) or as two subordinate classes (cows and horses) or hierarchically (both as animals and as the subordinates, cows and horses). Unless children use this last type of coding, they cannot solve the problem.

There are various ways to encourage hierarchical coding, and Trabasso's group mentions some of them. Labeling the superordinate and subordinate classes increases the number of first and second graders who pass the tests from 60 to 70 percent. Adding another superordinate class (fruit) with two subordinate classes (apples and oranges) to a display of animals (dogs and cats) also increases the number of children who know there are more animals than dogs and

What's in a Name?

When it comes to solving conservation and class-inclusion questions, it appears that there is a lot in a name, and that using collective nouns instead of class nouns radically changes the performance of children on such problems. Young children often have great trouble with problems that require them to compare subordinate with superordinate groups. Given three plastic cows and one plastic horse and asked whether there are more cows or more animals, they nearly always say, "More cows."

Ellen Markman has shown, however, that children think differently about groups and about numbers when researchers refer to them using collective nouns. For example, Markman (1973b) showed a picture of dogs to six- and eight-year-olds. She described the picture as a family of dogs, calling the two large dogs the mother and father, and the four small dogs the babies. Then she again referred to the dogs as a family and asked children who would have more pets, a person who owned the baby dogs or one who owned the family. Sixty percent of the children who heard the dogs described as a family said that someone who owned the family would have more pets. Among children who did not hear the use of the collective noun, almost all said that someone who had the little dogs would have more pets. In a later study, Markman and J. Seibert (1976) found that using collective nouns (forest, band, crowd, pile) instead of class nouns (trees, musicians, people, bricks) increased from 45 to 70 percent the number of children who could answer class-inclusion questions about the groups.

More recently, Markman (1979) has discovered that the same effect changes performance on number conservation problems. She arranged toy soldiers in two equal rows, then rearranged one of the rows so that the one-to-one correspondence was destroyed. Twice as many four-year-olds who were asked "Does your army have as many as my army?" answered correctly as those who were asked "Do you have as many soldiers as I do?" It is clear that thinking of rows of objects as collections instead of classes greatly increases the number of young children who pass number conservation tests.

As Markman and Seibert see it, the internal structure and the psychological integrity of collections improves the children's ability to answer questions that compare the part to the whole. A collection is semantically different from a class, because members of a collection are related in some way. A family requires relations between its members that a group of people does not; an army requires relations that soldiers do not; a pile of blocks requires a relation that "blocks" do not. Gelman and Gallistel (1978) point out that the logic of classes allows the child to focus on individual members, whereas the logic of collections requires them to pay attention to the collection itself. They simply cannot apply the collective noun to the subordinate class.

more fruit than apples. The sight of the fruit with the animals prompts the child to compare the two classes and to identify the superordinate sets, leading the youngster to encode all items hierarchically.

Trabasso's group believes that class-inclusion questions are not simply tests of logical ability or even of semantic knowledge, but that they mix hierarchical class concepts with language comprehension, counting ability, and decision making. If the child codes the information properly, the comparisons can be made by a three-year-old; if the child does not use a hierarchical coding, even a ten-year-old will find the going rough. However, the finding that encoding plays a major role does not conflict with Piaget's analysis, since only with hierarchical coding can a child think of the objects as being both class and subclass members, and only older children appear to use hierarchical coding spontaneously.

Formal Operational Thought

Children generally enter the stage of formal operations around the age of eleven or so, but Piaget (Inhelder and Piaget, 1958) believed that the abstract, scientific thought that characterizes the period and that he regarded as the culmination of cognitive development is not firmly established until children are about fifteen years old. The central feature of formal operational thought is the conception of possibilities that lie outside the immediate environment.

Although Piaget often wrote as if all adolescents develop formal thought, he agreed that in some cultures adult thinking might never develop beyond the level of concrete operations (Piaget, 1976b). Indeed, studies suggest that formal thought is neither as inevitable nor as universal a step in development as is the concrete thought of childhood (Neimark, 1975). Research in other countries indicates that abstract categorization and reasoning may not be an inevitable outcome of growing up but the direct result of formal education. In some societies few people develop the ability to reason from hypotheses. In Turkey, for example, formal thought appears in city dwellers but not in residents of primitive villages (Kohlberg and Gilligan, 1971). On the basis of numerous studies in Africa and Latin America, Michael Cole (1978) has concluded that formal education changes the mind in several ways: people group things into general categories according to formal rules (cow, dog, horse) instead of according to their function (cow, pasture, milk); they use these classes to solve problems and to

Studies using simple weight problems have indicated that children can reason systematically long before they enter the stage of formal operations. (Courtesy *The New York Times*)

organize their recall; and they treat problems in logic as hypothetical puzzles instead of as questions of fact or interpretation. Although literacy does not guarantee the development of formal thought, some children show these changes after as few as three years of schooling. Nine years of formal education, Cole discovered, will bring about the changes in most children.

Patricia Greenfield and Jerome Bruner (1966) attribute the greater evidence of formal thought in societies with schools to the fact that schooling promotes training in written language, a view that is similar to Cole's. Writing forces a child to separate thought from objects and thus may encourage children to let their symbolic processes run ahead of concrete fact, developing the capacity to think in terms of possibility instead of actuality. In modern societies with widespread school systems, more middle- and upper-middle-class adolescents show formal thought than do adolescents from working- and lower-class backgrounds, and adolescents in upper socioeconomic classes develop this thought earlier (Dulit, 1972; Peel, 1971).

Although formal thought is not a universal characteristic of adolescence, its development constitutes a change of primary importance for the individual. Because it allows adolescents to speculate about what might be instead of accepting things as they are, its appearance can signal profound changes in their identities and in their social relations.

TESTING FOR FORMAL THOUGHT An experiment that was conducted by Inhelder and Piaget (1958) illustrates differences among problem-solving approaches based on preoperational, concrete operational, and formal operational thought. (See Figure 12.4.) The investigators gave elementary- and high-school students strings of different lengths and objects of different weights, which the children could attach to a rod so that they swung like pendulums. Inhelder and Piaget pointed out to the children that each of the various possible pendulums would swing through its arc at a different speed. The problem was to explain the differences in speed. The four intuitively plausible causes are (1) the weight of the object, (2) the length of the string, (3) the height from which the object is released, and (4) the force of the initial push.

Inhelder and Piaget were primarily interested in the thought processes of the children as they tried to solve the pendulum problem. Of the four possible factors, only the length of the string affects the speed of the pendulum. A child can discover this solution either by methodically trying all possible combinations of the four factors (varying a single factor with each trial) or by imagining trials of all possible combinations of factors.

The youngest children, six and seven, almost

Figure 12.4 Illustration of a pendulum problem. The child is given a set of weights (*pictured at bottom*) and a string that can be shortened or lengthened (*as pictured at left*). The task is to determine which factor or factors account for the speed with which a pendulum traverses its arc. (After Inhelder and Piaget, 1958)

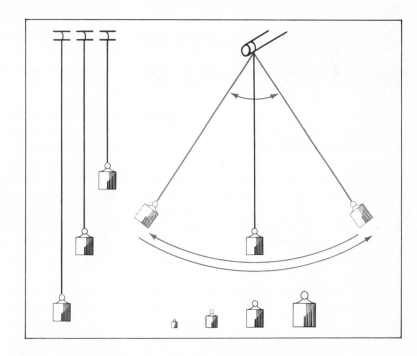

always concluded that the force of their own initial push determined the pendulum's speed. They did not approach the problem methodically; they failed to set up an experiment in which they varied each of the factors separately. It was hard for these children, who were judged to be in the preoperational stage, to imagine that the motion of the pendulum could be independent of their own thrusting.

Children between eight and thirteen, who were in the concrete operational period, were somewhat more systematic, but not systematic enough to solve the problem. At first they varied some but not all of the factors, having particular difficulty with weight. They also accurately judged the differences in the pendulum's movements—but not until the experimenter showed the way could they isolate the effect of one factor from the effect of others. They did not generate on their own a set of procedures that specified all possible combinations of the four factors. As a result of these limitations, they concluded that the length of the string is one determining factor but not that it is the only relevant one. They found it particularly difficult to exclude factors.

Only the fourteen- or fifteen-year-olds anticipated all possible combinations, tested them experimentally, and deduced not only what affects a pendulum's speed but also what factors are irrelevant. On the basis of experiments such as this, Inhelder and Piaget concluded that adolescent thought is characterized by the ability to hypothesize and to deduce.

Although Inhelder and Piaget found that eleven- and twelve-year-olds usually fail to solve the pendulum problem, Robert Siegler, Diane Liebert, and Robert Liebert (1973) have developed a training procedure that successfully taught even ten-year-olds the skills that enabled them to solve it. They conclude that Piaget is correct in stating that ten- and eleven-year-olds do not usually solve such problems on their own but that this does not mean that such problems

are beyond children's intellectual grasp. Just as four-year-olds can be taught to understand conservation, a ten-year-old can learn to perform some of the mental activities that often do not develop until adolescence.

ROOTS OF SCIENTIFIC THOUGHT

When Siegler found that children in the concrete operational stage could learn to use the methods of formal thought, he searched for its origins in early childhood. Inhelder and Piaget (1958) acknowledged that the foundations of formal thought were laid in early childhood but took the position that young children could not reason in a scientific manner because they lacked the necessary logical structures and because their understanding of physical relationships was unsystematic.

In a series of studies that explored scientific reasoning, Siegler discovered that children could reason systematically much earlier than had been supposed. Presented with a simple problem in physics, the three-year-olds guessed randomly, but about half of the four-year-olds and nearly all of the five-year-olds consistently applied a single, simple rule (Siegler, 1978). For example, asked to predict which arm of a balance scale would go down if the lever was released (see Figure 12.5), the rule these children applied was that if both sides of the scale have the same number of weights, the scale will be in balance; otherwise the side with the greater number of weights will go down. (They did not realize that this rule will work only if the weights are the same distance from the fulcrum.) Siegler discovered that although eight-year-olds generally operate by the same simple rule, many of them develop more sophisticated rules when given problems that require them—but five-year-olds do not. The older children would, for example, learn to allow for the distance of the weights from the fulcrum except when the combination of weights and distance was so complicated it required arithmetical computation.

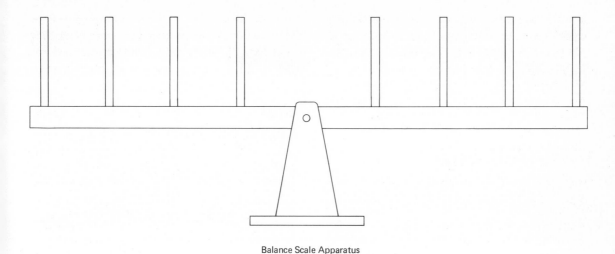

Balance Scale Apparatus

Figure 12.5 By using various weights on this balance scale and asking children which arm would go down if the lever was released, Robert Siegler discovered that children could reason systematically much earlier than had been supposed.

SOURCE: Reprinted with permission of the editor and publishers from R. S. Siegler (ed.), CHILDREN'S THINKING: WHAT DEVELOPS? Hillsdale, N.J.: Lawrence Erlbaum Associates, 1978.

In another experiment with three- and four-year-olds who were random guessers, Siegler (1978) released the lever after each of their guesses. When the child's prediction was right, he said, "Very good. You were right." When it was wrong, he said, "No, that's not right. Look carefully at the balance scale to see if you can figure out what would have told you the right answer." Ten seconds later, he proceeded to the next problem. After a series of such problems, more than half the four-year-olds, but none of the three-year-olds, began to use the simple rule of weights to guide their predictions.

Siegler discovered that a major reason for the three-year-olds' failure to profit from their experience with the scale was the way they encoded the problem. In a test of their memories for the placement of the weights, he found that most of the four-year-olds, but none of the three-year-olds, could remember the number of weights placed on each arm of the scale. When he taught the three-year-olds to encode the weights, they too learned from their experience with the scale and began to use the simple rule so prevalent among five-year-olds. In the same way, Siegler taught five-year-olds to encode the distance of the weights from the fulcrum and found that they then performed as well on the scale problem as most eight-year-olds. But not until adolescence can children learn to use the most sophisticated rule, which requires computing the relation between weight and distance, and even then, Siegler found, they require both instruction and external memory aids. College students need only the instruction or the aid in order to adopt the rule.

As Siegler points out, something very important happens to children between the ages of three and five: when faced with new problem-solving situations, they begin to generate and apply systematic, rule-governed strategies. He divides scientific reasoning into two major phases: from birth to age five, and from age five to adulthood. As noted earlier, this is exactly the way Kendler divides human approaches to the learning of concepts.

UNDERSTANDING

The adolescent in the stage of formal operations understands the concepts of time, number, and causality. Adolescents deal with past and future, manipulate negative numbers, and can predict the consequences of physical actions. They have no trouble thinking about the civilization of ancient Egypt; they are trying to decide which college to attend a few years hence; they solve problems involving distance, time, and speed; and they know just where to hit the cue ball to send a billiard ball spinning in any direction. All these concepts developed slowly, and it is possible to trace their beginnings back to babyhood.

Time

The young infant with a memory of only a few seconds has no awareness of time, but within six months, the baby's repetitive shaking of a rattle or banging of a cup indicates that he or she is beginning to develop a primitive concept of duration. Toward the end of the sensorimotor

By the time adolescents enter the formal operational period, they will be able to predict the path of a ball, taking into account the angle of the cue and the place where it strikes the cue ball. (© Len Speier 1979)

period, as the baby's memory develops, the concept of time broadens.

It will be a good many years, however, before the baby's concept of time matches that of an adult. When Piaget (1971b) queried one- to four-year-olds about age, for example, they believed that age could be determined by size and that when trees or people or dogs stop growing, they stop getting older. The children looked at a series of annual pictures of an apple tree and a pear tree. The pear tree was planted a year later but grew faster than the apple tree. By the fifth year, it was larger and bore more fruit. As long as the apple tree was larger, the children agreed that it was older; but as soon as the pear tree surpassed it, even the five-year-olds insisted the pear tree was older. A five-year-old might agree that the apple tree was five years old and the pear tree was four years old and that a five-year-old child is older than a four-year-old but still insist that the pear tree was older "because it had more pears."

The concept of time is intertwined with the concepts of speed and distance, and according to Piaget (1970a), although there is a primitive intuition of speed, time is an intellectual construction: the relation between an action and the speed with which it is accomplished. Some children, said Piaget, think that "faster" means "longer." Because preoperational children cannot discern the proper relationship between speed and action, they believe that faster means getting more done, and getting more done means they have to spend more time. For them, whether they walk briskly to school, run, or dawdle, it always takes the same time. In one of Piaget's (1970a) experiments, the investigator took a little doll in each hand and—when the child said "Go!"—hopped them along the table, side by side. The dolls started at the same time and stopped at the same time. When they covered exactly the same distance, the preschoolers agreed that the dolls had stopped and started at the same time. But if one doll covered a greater distance than the other, the child denied

that the dolls had stopped at the same time, saying that the doll that did not go as far had stopped first. The investigator could get the child to agree that one doll was not still going when the other stopped, but the child still argued that the dolls had not stopped at the same time because one of them had not gone as far as the other. Children only a little older said that both dolls had started at the same time and stopped at the same time, but insisted that one had walked a longer time because it had gone farther.

After a lengthy series of experiments involving speed, time, and distance, Piaget concluded that children could not develop a mature concept of time until they had mastered three operations that are parallel to those involved in logical thought: seriation (discussed in the transitivity section), in which the child learns to order events in time; class inclusion, in which the child learns that lunch follows breakfast and dinner follows lunch, and that the time from breakfast to dinner is longer than the time from breakfast to lunch; and measurement of time, which derives from a synthesis of the first two operations.

Robert Siegler and Dean Richards (1979) carried out an experiment with five- to eleven-year-olds similar to some done by Piaget, using two parallel train tracks and toy locomotives. Five-year-olds judged time (and speed and distance) by the stopping points of the train, just as they had in Piaget's train experiments and just as they did in the experiment with the hopping dolls. No matter where the locomotives started or stopped, no matter how fast or how slowly they traveled, the five-year-olds insisted that the one which stopped farther along the track had traveled longer (had gone a greater distance at a faster speed). Although Piaget had found that eight-year-olds have developed mature concepts of speed and time, taking speed, time, and distance into account in the motion of toy trains, Siegler and Richards' experiment provided different evidence. They found that while many eight-year-olds and most eleven-year-olds have developed speed and distance concepts, few understand the concept of time. These researchers suggest that, contrary to Piaget's findings, the concept of time develops much later than the concept of speed—sometime after the eleventh year.

Number

Young children do not understand the concept of number as Piaget defined it, although they may be efficient counters. Piaget (1965) was not interested in whether children could count, add, or multiply; his definition of the number concept required that children be able to reason about number *without* counting. This kind of understanding does not develop until children reach the concrete operational stage, Piaget believed, because it goes hand in hand with the development of logic.

A good deal of Piaget's research about understanding number focused on conservation experiments similar to those discussed in the section on conservation. Again, a change in the external appearance of identical objects seems to convince the young child that the total quantity of one has been altered. For example, place in front of a four- or five-year-old two rows of seven checkers each. Then ask the child if one row has more, less, or the same amount of checkers as the other. The child may correctly answer that the two rows have the same amount of checkers. Next bunch the checkers in Row 1 together. Ask the child if Row 2 has more, less, or the same amount of checkers as Row 1. To the surprise and chagrin of many parents who have tried to prove Piaget wrong by administering this test to their own clever children, most four- or five-year-olds respond quite emphatically that there are more checkers in Row 2 than in Row 1. They may retain this view despite their realization that if the checkers in Row 1 are returned to their original position, the two rows will once again have the same number of

checkers (Piaget, 1952a). These young children apparently believe that the number of checkers varies with the dominating perceptual feature of the row, in this case length or spread. However, by the time children are seven, they respond to the posttransformation question with an emphatic "Of course they are the same, you didn't add any or take any away, you just put them closer together." Some reply in a tone of surprise mixed with disdain at an experimenter who could ask such a silly question.

Piaget (1970a) believed that children originally establish the equality of the two rows by one-to-one correspondence between the checkers in each row, and that this correspondence is the basis for the notion of number. He did not expect to find the seven-year-olds' response among younger children, and indeed, few show it.

However, Rochel Gelman (1977) notes that children two and a half to five years old who may not seem to understand conservation on traditional Piagetian tasks do not totally lack the concept. If they are shown three checkers, for example, and then a fourth is surreptitiously added or one of the three is surreptitiously removed, the children show surprise and point out that a checker has been added or subtracted. If the checkers are surreptitiously spread out without changing the number, the children again notice the change but indicate that it is irrelevant, demonstrating their understanding of conservation.

Gelman does *not* claim that such results mean that the young child has the same abilities as the older child who demonstrates a grasp of the principle on a Piagetian task. Younger children show conservation of number only when the task uses five items or less. In judging whether two sets are equivalent, they first try to count the items in each set. In contrast, older children do not concern themselves with the exact number of items but simply consider the effect of a transformation apart from the specific number of items involved. Gelman and C. R. Gallistel (1978) have pointed out that judging the equality of two sets based on one-to-one correspondence is algebraic reasoning, that is, reasoning without using any actual numbers. Preschool children cannot reason in this way, they say, but young children do have a concept of number and they do apply principles of reasoning to numbers.

Gelman and Gallistel have traced the development of number and have found its beginnings among two-year-olds — although many two-year-olds can count only as far as two. These investigators believe that counting, like language, is a natural human function. Even young children who do not know the number words of their language count. Some use letters, some use their own words, others make up number sequences such as "one, two, three, eight, eleven" but always use them in the same way, that is, eight always functions as four, and eleven as five. When two-and-a-half-year-olds begin to count, they point at the objects they are counting or touch them and say their number words aloud. As they get older, they count to themselves and simply announce the result. Five-year-olds return to audible counting, however, if they must count a large array of objects.

Preschoolers, say Gelman and Gallistel, are flexible about what they will count. As long as they can assign some superordinate term or can simply classify the objects to be counted as "thing," they can count mixed groups (trees and flowers and chairs, or toys and books and candies) as easily, if more slowly, than they can count objects from the same group.

By the time they are four or five, children appear to develop insight into the principles that govern counting. They learn that it makes no difference where they start counting a set, and they are willing to count the objects one way and then another, beginning with a different object in the set each time. They can handle equivalences, identity, addition, and subtraction — but only with very small numbers of objects and always by counting. Not until they can focus on numerical relations, as opposed to number, will they pass tests of conservation.

As children move from numerical to algebraic reasoning, say Gelman and Gallistel, they go through three stages. First, they are not fooled by the rearrangement of objects but count the checkers in each group to get their answer. In the second stage, they say the rearrangement had nothing to do with number ("You just moved them"). They can reason that the rearrangement did not change the altered set but cannot compare the two. In the stage of full algebraic reasoning, they deal with the relation between the two sets and have attained the number concept as Piaget defined it.

Gelman and Gallistel's views are in some ways compatible with those of Piaget. They argue that preschool children have an operational concept of number, but they define the concept differently from Piaget. What he regarded as an operational concept of number, they see as an algebraic concept of number; but they believe, as he did, that the young child's failure to conserve reveals an inability to reason about numerical relations.

Causality

The earliest ideas of causality arise out of the circular reactions of the sensorimotor period, as infants develop a sense first of themselves, then of other people, as causal agents. By the time babies are into their second year, they begin to connect events. Piaget (1954) described the way his thirteen-month-old son, Laurent, searched for the cause of his moving baby carriage. Peering over the edge, the infant saw Piaget's foot slowly pushing it and smiled with satisfaction. In another few months, Laurent would expand his notion of causality from actions that affected himself to actions between people and objects that had no direct effect upon him. During the sensorimotor period, said Piaget (1930), infants move from a belief in magical causes — in the sense that objects obey their desires — to an awareness that their own behavior can be affected by others.

Preschoolers have developed precausal think-

Understanding Death

Children who are younger than two or three appear to have no understanding of death. When Maria Nagy (1948) studied 378 children in Budapest, Hungary, she found that their concept of death fell into three phases. In the first phase, which characterized children between three and five, children saw death as a sleep or a journey—only a temporary separation. In the second phase, between the ages of five and nine, death was personified. For some children, it was an angel; for others, an evil, frightening monster or a "death man." Although children at this age saw death as final, they believed that their own deaths could be avoided—all they had to do was to outrun the death man. In the final phase, beginning around the age of nine or ten, children realized the final and inevitable nature of death, seeing it as a permanent, biological process that happens to everyone.

The older children in Nagy's study had lived in war-torn Europe, when soldiers died in battle and civilians died in air raids. Their experiences might have influenced the rate at which they grasped death's irrevocable, universal nature. Children who grow up in a protected environment might develop the concept more slowly. Edward White, Bill Elson, and Richard Prawat (1978) examined the way five- to ten-year-old children in suburban American schools regard death. White and his associates read one of two versions of an old woman's death to the children. In the first version, Mrs. Wilson was a kind woman, nice to pets and children, who enjoyed reading newspaper comic strips. In the second, Mrs. Wilson was not kind; she was mean to her pets, never laughed, and yelled at children. After the children had heard the story, they were asked questions that explored their understanding of death's finality and universality.

Children's understanding of the universal nature of death was strongly linked to their cognitive development. More than 60 percent of the children who understood conservation

---

ing and simply do not believe in accidents. They search for a cause to explain every minor occurrence, and they ascribe thoughts, feelings, and life itself to inanimate objects (a type of belief known as *animism*). This aspect of children's thinking is reflected in many of their notions about the causes of such things as night and day, sun, moon, clouds, mountains, and rivers. Thread unwinds from a dropped spool because "it wants to." Slowly, over a period of several years, children develop more naturalistic explanations of causality. For example, Piaget (1930) described the way the explanation for cloud movements develops in children. Four- or five-year-olds, he said, believe they make the clouds move by walking. Six-year-olds believe clouds move because either God or adults make them move. Seven-year-olds believe the clouds move by themselves but at the command of the sun or moon. By this time, Piaget believed, there is at the back of the child's mind a motor scheme that prepares the way for the next development, when, at about the age of eight, children attribute the clouds' movements to the wind but explain that the wind rises out of the clouds ("They make air and the air chases the clouds"). Nine-year-olds do not know where the wind comes from, but they know that it pushes the clouds and that without it clouds cannot move.

Children gradually develop naturalistic explanations, suggested Piaget, through their interactions with machines. As they try to make toys function, produce physical effects, or overcome physical resistance in objects, they may learn about the nature of physical causality. If Piaget

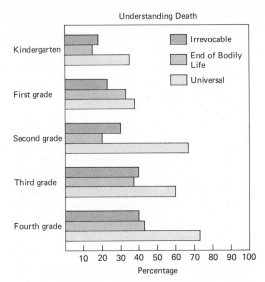

Understanding Death

Irrevocable

End of Bodily Life

Universal

Kindergarten

First grade

Second grade

Third grade

Fourth grade

10 20 30 40 50 60 70 80 90 100
Percentage

The sharp jump in the grasp of death's universality shows a connection with cognitive development; the slow growth in the grasp of death's finality indicates that the understanding is probably based on experience.

SOURCE: Adapted from Edward White, Bill Elson, and Richard Prawat, "Children's Conceptions of Death," *Child Development*, 49 (1978), 307–310.

believed that death came to everyone. But the idea that death was irrevocable and that it meant the end of bodily life showed no such connection. As the figure indicates, the big jump in understanding death's universality comes between the first and second grades, just where Piaget placed the transition from preoperational to concrete operational thought. Nagy's children seemed to have a surer grasp of death's finality than these American children did. Since this aspect of the concept does not appear to be strongly linked to cognitive development, the difference may lie in the gulf between the experience of the two groups of children.

Although the nature of the story read to the children did not affect their views of death's nature, it did appear to affect their belief as to why the old woman died. Among the children who heard of a mean woman's death, 22 percent said that she died because of her unkind acts; among those who heard about the death of a nice woman, less than 1 percent attributed her death to her behavior.

was right, it is no wonder that children resort to animistic answers when asked about complex natural phenomena. Asking preschoolers about what causes wind and rain, why rivers flow, how bicycles and other machines work is asking them to talk about things they have had little experience with (Gelman, 1978). Since they lack the knowledge, they make up animistic but plausible answers. When Michael Berzonsky (1971) questioned children about remote events, asking, for example, "Why does the moon change shape?" they generally gave precausal answers. When asked about familiar events, such as tires going flat, or flying kites, however, they usually gave physical, mechanical answers.

When given a series of three pictures (for example, a boy pulling a dog's tail, a dog biting a boy, and a boy crying), even three-year-olds can

correctly choose which picture represents the cause of the dog's actions (Kun, 1978). In another study (Gelman, 1978), Gelman and Merry Bullock gave four- and five-year-olds an opportunity to explain a physical event. They showed children a box with two handles on its side: one handle started a ball rolling down an incline; the other switched on a series of flashing lights that made it appear as if a single light were moving down the incline. The children watched the ball and the light move down the incline together and disappear into a second box. Three seconds later, a jumping jack popped out of this box. When children were given a chance to "make the jack jump," they chose to start the ball instead of the light. Their choice indicates that when trying to account for actions, children tend to choose a reasonable cause (a rolling ball

About the time children are in the second grade, they understand the universality of death, but the understanding that death is irrevocable and that it means the end of bodily life comes more slowly. (© Ken Heyman)

causes physical impact) over an unreasonable one.

Using easy problems that children solve early in life even though they cannot explain the forces involved, Piaget (1976a) explored the development of the child's growing awareness of causality.

In one study, he placed two small balls (A and B) in line with an English ninepin (a much smaller version of an American bowling pin) and had children first knock the pin over using both balls, then hit ball B with ball A so that both balls missed the pin, and finally knock over the pin when it was about forty-five degrees out of line with the two balls. Four-year-olds could do the first two tasks but could give no general rule. Seven- and eight-year-olds knew that they must make ball A hit the side of B if they wanted B to change direction, but they still failed at the third task. Nine- and ten-year-olds succeeded on all tasks and could generalize from the idea of hitting B at an angle to the rule that striking the ball at different points generates different directions, saying, "If you hit it more toward the edge of the ball, it goes more like that [correct direction]." Eleven-year-old children formulated a general relation between impact and direction, saying, "When you want it to go straight, you hit it in the middle; but if you can aim at the balls from another angle, they go off at another angle [the same angle]." The pendulum experiment described in the section on formal operational thought also shows the way the child's understanding of causality gradually develops, indicating that by the time children can reason abstractly, they can figure out the causes of actions by a process of systematic testing and deduction.

SUMMARY

1. Until children enter school, they appear to learn in the same way as rats do — by associating stimuli and responses. By the time they are five or six, however, children use symbols to transform their perceptions and begin to respond to mental events. Now they are thinking, and using simple hypotheses to test what they perceive. Development, or the switch from one cognitive level to another, may simply be the cumulative effect of learning that leads to the child's eventual grasp of logical rules.

2. During the sensorimotor period, children develop the object concept; and during the preoperational period, the concept of identity. Using these two major concepts as a base, children develop logical thought. Children in the concrete operational period apply logical thought to concrete events; they understand the concepts of conservation, transitivity, and class inclusion. Research indicates that these concepts can be taught much earlier than Piaget supposed, and that the way children encode what they see determines their ability to solve problems involving such concepts.

3. In the formal operational period, children apply logical thought to abstractions, considering possibilities outside the immediate environment. Such scientific thought is not universal but appears to depend on formal education. When children are about five, they begin to generate and apply systematic, rule-governed strategies and can be taught to encode problems in a way that enables them to solve problems they normally could not handle.

4. The concept of time develops much more slowly than the concept of number. Although Piaget believed that children do not understand number until they reach the concrete operational stage, research indicates that even preschoolers have mastered the concept. It is an algebraic, not an operational, concept of number that requires a higher level of understanding.

5. From a period in which they believe in magical causes, very young children move into precausal thinking, in which nothing ever happens by accident and inanimate objects have thoughts and feelings. Not until they are much older, said Piaget, do they develop the notion of physical causality. But preschool children do give naturalistic explanations for events in their daily lives; only when asked about remote phenomena do they resort to the animistic thinking found by Piaget.

Intelligence and Tests

Figan loved bananas, which were kept in a concrete box that fastened with a simple pin. Learning to pull the pin was an easy task for this chimpanzee, so Hassan, a member of the staff at the Gombe Stream Chimpanzee Reserve, cut threads in the pin and the handle so that the box would open only if the pin was unscrewed. Within a few months, Figan was deftly unscrewing the pin to get to the bananas. Next, Hassan put nuts on the ends of the screw. Now the nuts had to be removed before the pin could be unscrewed. In a short time, Figan had learned to remove the nuts in order to get to the pin. But problems remained. Once the lid was up, chimpanzees who ranked above Figan in the dominance hierarchy swarmed in for bananas, leaving him to go hungry. Figan soon learned not to open the box when other chimpanzees were in the vicinity. After removing the nuts and unscrewing the pin, he would sit, one foot holding the lid closed, and groom himself until all the high-ranking chimpanzees had gone. Jane Van Lawick-Goodall (1971) once timed a wait of more than half an hour, as Figan sat looking everywhere except at the banana box beneath his foot.

Such an anecdote provides a clear example of

adaptive behavior, evidence—if any was needed—that human beings have no monopoly on intelligence. If we keep in mind the fact that intelligence is more important as a species characteristic than as an individual characteristic, the topic can take on a very different nature, and the political and social controversy over tests that purport to measure intelligence—and over the concept itself—can be seen in perspective.

For this reason, we shall temporarily set aside development and spend most of this chapter examining the concept of intelligence itself. After reviewing the ways psychologists have described human intelligence, we shall look at several ways of studying the subject: the biological approach, with its emphasis upon evolution and adaptiveness; the cognitive approach, which emphasizes problem solving and logic; the psychometric approach, which focuses on individual differences; and the information-processing approach, which uses artificial intelligence as a way of understanding human intelligence. After considering the many influences that can affect a child's score on an intelligence test, we shall look at the lack of correspondence between the results of infant and child intelligence tests, and the greater—but not universal—stability of test scores later in life. Keeping in mind the fact that IQ scores often change, we shall investigate the use of the tests to predict success in school, discovering that they are efficient and effective at this task. Next, we shall look at the relation between academic intelligence and success in life, and between intelligence and creativity. When we turn to the modifiability of intelligence, we shall examine the concept of heritability, the influences of malnutrition or fetal exposure to alcohol, and the environmental influences that can depress the growth of a child's intelligence. We shall examine early intervention programs and discover that although they are successful, their effects generally fade when children leave the program. Finally, we shall consider specific environmental influences that can raise children's test scores.

THE PROBLEM OF INTELLIGENCE

A major problem in the study of intelligence is the lack of agreement on just what "intelligence" is. For as long as anyone can remember, psychologists have been arguing over its definition. Sixty years ago, an entire issue of the *Journal of Educational Psychology* was given over to a symposium devoted to that question. The definitions of intelligence suggested then by psychologists ranged from the ability to "carry on abstract thinking" through "an acquiring capacity," "a group of complex mental processes," "the power of good responses from the point of view of truth or fact," and the "ability to learn to adjust oneself to the environment" to "general modifiability of the nervous system" (Resnick, 1976). The discussion continues today, and some psychologists have suggested that intelligence is "whatever intelligence tests measure." Until a better definition comes along, most psychologists would accept the proposal that intelligence is based on the ability to benefit from experience and the ease with which a person can learn a new idea or new behavior. As we shall see, one reason we lack a formal definition of intelligence is that psychologists have approached its study from such divergent premises.

The Nature of Intelligence

Many developmental psychologists have paid little attention to the study of intelligence, because theorists of human development are primarily interested in the ways in which people are alike, and—to many—the concept of intelligence implies individual differences (Guilford, 1973). When Piaget spoke of intelligence, for example, he referred to cognitive functions that are shared by the entire species, paying little attention to whether their speed, efficiency, or capacity differs among individuals. Some psychologists who have focused on the study of intelligence, however, are primarily concerned with individual differences in cognitive functioning and with the measurement of those differences.

SPECIES INTELLIGENCE When looked at from the standpoint of the species, intelligence is the disposition to behave adaptively when faced with the demands of the environment. The intelligence level of any species is the result of its evolutionary history, in which animals that could not adapt simply did not survive long enough to have any descendants. Among the various species, intelligence appears to fall along a continuum from simple pattern recognition through expectancy, understanding, intention, awareness, thought, and consciousness. Donald Griffin (1976), who has studied birds, fish and bats, believes that animals probably have significant mental experiences, and that the distance between human and animal intelligence is more one of quantity than of quality.

As species become more intelligent, the proportion of fixed behavior decreases and the influence of learning and insight becomes more and more important (Lorenz, 1965). Knowing that an organism is an octopus, a dog, a chimpanzee, or a person, for example, tells us a good deal about its relative intelligence and provides a rough indication of what can be expected from it. As Donald O. Hebb (1949) points out, a dog shows superior intelligence by outstripping a rat or a hen in passing obstacles and reaching a goal by the shortest route. But a dog seems incredibly stupid when compared with a chimpanzee, who can use tools and will, for example, stack boxes in order to get food that is hung out of reach. And even the dullest human being who is able to earn a living is far more intelligent than the cleverest chimpanzee. At the species level, however, differences in intelligence among members of the same species are slight.

INDIVIDUAL INTELLIGENCE When we look at human intelligence, the concept becomes

Chimpanzees show an impressive level of intelligence because they appear to solve problems by insight; that is, instead of relying on trial and error, they grasp the relationship involved. (UPI)

exceedingly complex, says David Wechsler (1975), although any normal twelve-year-old understands the ordinary meaning of the term. Wechsler, who devised a widely used intelligence test, refuses to pin a technical definition on intelligence, believing that it refers to behavior that is intentional, goal-directed, rational, and worthwhile. This last quality, he admits, means that judgments of intelligence are necessarily subjective and will change as the values of society change.

The more closely psychologists look at individual differences, the more fragmented the picture becomes. Alfred Binet, a French psychologist who practiced at the beginning of the twentieth century, supposed that intelligence is a general ability to understand the world and to reason about it. However, he believed that the best way to discover individual differences was to use three concepts: (1) there is a goal or direction to the mental processes involved; (2) intelligence involves an ability to show adaptable solutions; (3) intelligence involves a selectivity of judgment and a self-criticism of choices (Chaplin and Krawiec, 1974).

Charles Spearman (1927) agreed with Binet that there is a factor of general intelligence, which he called "g," and that it involves seeing and manipulating the relation between bits of information. He believed, however, that intelligence also includes specific abilities—"s"

factors—and he used a system called factor analysis to detect them. In *factor analysis*, the scores people make on a variety of tests are correlated, in the belief that when the scores show strong correlations, they are measuring a common mental ability. It is often further assumed that the mental abilities discovered through factor analysis are characteristic of human intelligence. Over the years, the number of abilities thought to comprise intelligence has varied from 2 to 120. Louis Thurstone (1947), for example, used factor analysis to show that intelligence consists of seven primary abilities: verbal comprehension, word fluency, number, space, memory, perceptual speed, and reasoning.

According to J. P. Guilford (1973), intelligence is much more complicated than Thurstone's seven factors indicate. Guilford's structure-of-intellect model includes five kinds of intellectual processes (*operations*), which people use on four different classes of information (*contents*) to produce six different forms of information (*products*). (See Figure 13.1.) This means that there are 120 factors (5 × 4 × 6) involved in intelligence. Operations include cognition, memory, divergent production, convergent produc-

Figure 13.1 Guilford's structure-of-intellect model, in which intelligence is divided into 120 potential abilities; the three-dimensional arrangement shows the relationship of the abilities to one another.

SOURCE: From J. P. Guilford, "Theories of Intelligence," in *Handbook of General Psychology,* B. B. Wolman (ed.), © 1973, p. 636. Reprinted by permission of Prentice-Hall, Englewood Cliffs, N.J.

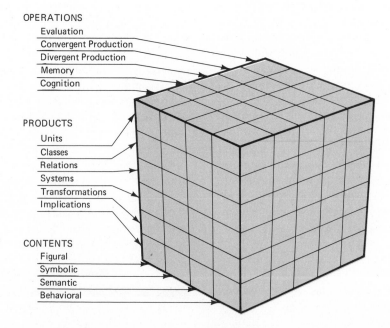

OPERATIONS
Evaluation
Convergent Production
Divergent Production
Memory
Cognition

PRODUCTS
Units
Classes
Relations
Systems
Transformations
Implications

CONTENTS
Figural
Symbolic
Semantic
Behavioral

tion, and evaluation; contents may be figural, symbolic, semantic, or behavioral; the products may be units, classes, relations, systems, transformations, or implications. Guilford's theory of intelligence goes beyond traditional academic skills. For example, divergent thinking—one of Guilford's operations, which he describes as "the generation of logical alternatives"—can lead to low scores on most intelligence tests, which measure convergent thinking, or "the generation of logical necessities." Divergent thinking involves remote associations and is often regarded as a measure of creativity. Convergent thinking produces conventionally accepted responses.

Another view of intelligence was proposed by Raymond Cattell (1968), who suggested that there were two major kinds of intelligence: fluid and crystallized. Fluid intelligence is relatively unaffected by cultural differences; it is a broad relation-perceiving capacity. Crystallized intelligence is a related group of abilities (verbal, numerical, reasoning) that are acquired through cultural experiences, especially through formal schooling. Cattell has tested deckhands and farmers who have for one reason or another missed schooling and finds that they sometimes score much higher than college professors on tests of fluid intelligence but do poorly on tests of crystallized intelligence, where professors excel.

Cattell used factor analysis in developing his approach and concluded that the two kinds of intelligence are made up of twenty-three different factors. John Horn (1970), who worked with Cattell in developing the distinction between the two kinds of intelligence, indicates that some of the twenty-three factors involved, such as figural relations and associative memory, primarily affect fluid intelligence. Others, such as verbal comprehension and mechanical knowledge, primarily affect crystallized intelligence; yet others, such as number facility and formal reasoning, are related to both kinds of intelligence.

Traditional intelligence tests do not distinguish between the two major kinds of intelligence. Therefore, children who have not been adequately exposed to the majority culture will not do as well on them as they do on a test of fluid intelligence, which is supposed to be "culture-fair." Even much of the material on a test of fluid intelligence is learned, says Horn, but the learning is incidental and not directed by the culture, as in the child's spontaneous exploration of the environment. Over the years, the two kinds of intelligence develop differently. Some of the abilities that make up fluid intelligence decline in old age, while some factors involved in crystallized intelligence may increase.

Biological Perspective

It is impossible to study intelligence without raising biological questions, believed Piaget (1971a). Although his own research adhered to the cognitive approach, he was aware of the biological underpinnings of thought and said that in the end knowledge must be interpreted in terms of biology, whether it was the development of knowledge in the individual or the evolutionary development of knowledge in the human species.

Biologically based approaches to the study of intelligence examine intelligence in terms of the species and its evolutionary history. For example, Sandra Scarr-Salapatek (1976) suggests that the sensorimotor intelligence of infancy evolved very early and that it has changed little since that time. To support her proposal, she notes the similarity between the abilities of ape and human babies. There are few intellectual accomplishments in the first eighteen months of a human infant's life that are not paralleled in the life of an infant chimpanzee.

As a result of the species' evolutionary history, human babies are genetically prepared to learn the typical sensorimotor schemes of infancy and to combine them in innovative and flexible ways. During the first eighteen to twenty-four months of life, cognitive growth appears to be highly canalized (a concept discussed in Chapter 6 in relation to physical growth), so that neither individual heredity nor minor environmental influences have much effect on its development (Scarr-Salapatek, 1976; McCall 1979a). Intellectual development during the period appears to follow a path common to the entire species. Unless infants live in a severely deprived environment, one not typical of human life, they will develop similarly. And since early intellectual development is highly canalized, infants who suffer early deprivation will tend to catch up when placed in a normal environment as has been found among babies who spent the first year or so in institutions or in a highly restricted environment in rural Guatemala (Kagan, 1978).

An ethological view of intelligence is taken past infancy and applied to children by William Charlesworth (1976), who regards intelligence as the species' latest attempt to adapt to the everyday challenges of its evolutionary niche. Intelligence according to Charlesworth, is a disposition — the result of evolved cognitive processes acting on a store of learned knowledge. He believes that although we can never measure intelligence directly, we can measure intelligent behavior, the behavior that is called forth when a child or an adult encounters a problem in daily life. Coping with life on an inner-city street requires intelligent, adaptive behavior, and behavior that has developed in response to life in a protected suburb might not be adaptive in a city surrounding. In order to understand intelligence, we should — in Charlesworth's view — be applying to human beings the methods ethologists use with animals, especially field studies, which were described in Chapter 3.

Charlesworth has begun the spadework, observing toddlers at home and at school, in the hope of identifying the major cognitive processes used to deal with problems and discovering how contextual and emotional factors either hinder or aid the solutions. In one of his observations, for example, a toddler rides his tricycle along the sidewalk until he comes to an incline. The little boy tries to pedal up the slope, but begins to roll backward. He climbs off his tricycle, pushes it up the incline, climbs back on and pedals off. The entire process, from encounter to solution, took fifteen seconds. From such observations of behavior, suggests Charlesworth, it will be possible to discover how many problems children encounter as they go about their daily lives, the nature of the problems, how they deal with them, their rates of success or failure, and the extent to which other people help or hinder them in their solutions.

Charlesworth believes that data derived from ethological observations not only show the nature of a child's intelligence but also broaden the general study of intelligence, in which adaptive interactions with the environment have been generally ignored.

Cognitive Perspective

Despite the biological strain in his own theory, Piaget was the major exponent of the cognitive approach to intelligence, which examines intelligence at the species level, focusing on the mental processes involved in problem solving and logic. Piaget would have considered Chapter 12 of this book as devoted to the development of intelligence, for he used the terms "intelligence" and "thought" interchangeably.

In Piagetian theory, babies are born without intelligence, for intelligence is the consequence of interaction with the environment. Intelligence first appears in the third stage of the sensorimotor period, when the baby repeats actions in order to make interesting sights last. At first, a baby's intelligence is "empirical," because things in the environment, not deduction, control it. Toward the end of the sensorimotor period, when a baby's consciousness of the relation between his or her actions and the behavior of objects leads to the first deductions, intelligence becomes "systematic." Once this happens, a baby uses mental combinations to invent ways of handling new situations. Without this sensorimotor experience, intelligence cannot develop.

Just how much sensorimotor experience is required for the development of intelligence is uncertain. At first glance, it would appear that a case cited by Margaret Boden (1979), in which a middle-aged woman who was born without any functional use of her limbs attained full intellectual development, would challenge Piaget's theory. But Piaget (quoted in Kopp and Shaperman, 1973) saw such individuals as posing no problem for his theory of intelligence, because such people can control their mouths, move their eyes, and turn the head and trunk. According to Piaget, although such children lack the ability to move their hands or run about, their use of assimilation and accommodation in eating, drinking, and perceptual activity is enough to maintain intellectual development.

In the cognitive approach to intelligence, the researcher's interest lies in the qualitative analysis of the structures that underlie intelligence, in order to "discover the actual operational mechanisms that govern such behavior and not simply to measure it" (Piaget, 1953). Piaget was interested in intellectual competence, not intellectual performance — what is optimally possible for a person to do, not what that individual does in a specific situation (Boden, 1979).

Psychometric Perspective

In contrast to cognitive approaches, which focus on intelligence at the species level, researchers who take a psychometric view focus on individual differences. The field of *psychometrics*, or mental testing, began when Alfred Binet tried to develop a test that would pick out children whose cognitive function made it impossible for them to learn in regular classrooms. It was hoped that his test would also indicate the sort of special instruction that would enable these children to profit from schooling. This marked the beginning of a strong movement centered on individual differences in intelligence.

The psychometrics movement has no theory of human development; instead, intelligence tests are practical tools, constructed so that most children of a specific age can answer questions specified for that age level and so that scores on the test correlate highly with success at school.

At one time, psychologists in the field of psychometrics assumed that intelligence was a general capacity and that their tests measured a general aptitude. Today many psychologists believe that intelligence is made up of a host of abilities and that tests measure only a few of them. Ulric Neisser (1976) has suggested that the tests tap only academic skills and that we should be careful to distinguish academic intelligence from intelligence in general. Many academically talented people, he points out, behave stupidly in everyday life, and there is no evidence to indicate that they are better at conducting their lives than the academically dull.

As the psychometric movement developed, factor analysis became one of its basic tools, and many measures of intelligence are constructed around it. Latterly, however, its value in analyzing intelligence has been questioned by Robert Sternberg (1977), who claims that factor analysis falls short on four counts. Two of his basic criticisms are statistical; they amount to charges that with this method, it is difficult to compare theories of intelligence. Depending upon how factor analysis is used, different factors emerge as components of intelligence. In his two nonstatistical criticisms he maintains, first, that factor analysis deals only with responses to questions and cannot throw light on the cognitive processes used to arrive at those answers; second, he points out that although intelligence (and its component abilities) exists within the individual, factor analysis analyzes patterns of individual differences among groups of people. Although he regards it as an aid to the study of human abilities, Sternberg believes that factor analysis can never be used to discover the underlying components of mental ability — the aim of its proponents.

Information-Processing Perspective

Most psychologists who apply information-processing approaches to the study of intelligence are interested in intelligence at the species level — writing computer programs, for example, that simulate the way children solve conservation problems. Recently, however, some psychologists have been exploring the possibility of applying information-processing theory to the investigation of individual differences — simulating the kind of thought that is tapped by intelligence tests and identifying the differences in basic processes that account for variety in human performance.

For example, Earl Hunt (1976) proposes that individual differences may exist in the speed with which people can manipulate information in working memory, or transmit it from place to place within the total system, or how efficient they are in shifting the burden of information processing from one component of the memory system to another, or how rapidly a stimulus arouses codes stored in long-term memory. In his own work, Hunt has investigated the speed with which people can retrieve items from long-term memory. He has discovered that college students (all of whom have attained a certain level of verbal ability) can be divided into high-verbal and low-verbal groups. Although there is no difference in the amount of time it takes these students to detect similarity or difference between two stimuli, high-verbal students are significantly faster in retrieving a conceptual code from memory. In another study reported by Hunt, both groups were asked to recall lists of "meaningless" syllables. When the syllables did not make up a word ("ark" "ler"), high- and low-verbal students performed similarly; but when the syllables could form a word ("prob" "lem"), the high-verbal group was much more efficient, indicating that the conceptual nature of the code is important. And when the syllables were presented rapidly, the gap between high- and low-verbal students increased.

It has been suggested by John Carroll (1976) that information-processing theory be applied to the results of factor analysis, in an attempt to discover what specific processes underlie each of the various factors that make up intelligence. Individual differences, he suggests, can appear in the rules used by the information-processing system, in the speed with which information is handled, in the processing capacity, or in the contents of long-term memory. When Carroll analyzed twenty-four factors, he discovered that eight of them involved operations and strategies in either short-term memory or some kind of sensory buffer; one factor involved storage and retrieval from intermediate-term memory, and fifteen involved long-term memory — search, retrieval, or its contents.

Sternberg (1977; 1979) agrees with Hunt and Carroll that looking at intelligence within an information-processing framework gives the most promise for understanding it. He suggests a *componential analysis* of human abilities, in which both the components (the steps that one goes through to solve a problem) and the metacomponents (the higher-order processes that one uses to decide *how* to solve the problem) are analyzed. Sternberg believes that the ability to solve analogies is a good measure of intelligence and that when such solutions are analyzed at the level of components, individual differences among components in the solution process may be found.

Using a sample analogy, WASHINGTON is to ONE as LINCOLN is to: (a. FIVE, b. TEN, c. FIFTEEN, d. FIFTY), Sternberg lists six steps in the problem-solving process. First, the solver must *encode* the terms of the analogy, identifying each and retrieving relevant attributes from long-term memory. If he or she does not encode the names as those of Presidents whose pictures appear on currency, the solution progresses no farther. Next, the solver must *infer* a relation between the attributes of WASHINGTON and ONE. Inferring that Washington is the first President instead of the portrait on the dollar bill ends the solution at this step. Third, the solver must *map* the relation that links the Washington half of the analogy with the Lincoln half (Presidents of the United States whose pictures are on currency). The fourth step is to *apply* the relation between WASHINGTON and ONE to LINCOLN and each of the suggested answers, a step that requires recall of the information that Lincoln is portrayed on a five-dollar bill. If this analogy is given to a person from a different culture or to a young child, of course, that information is unlikely to be stored in long-term memory. The fifth step is to *justify* one of the four options as preferable to the other three. A person who did not encode the problem as one involving currency might look for SIXTEEN—Lincoln's position in the chronological list of Presidents—and not finding that, settle for FIFTEEN on the grounds that his or her memory was slightly defective. Finally, the solver *responds* with the justified answer.

Individual differences can appear in the speed with which a person performs each of these steps, in the strategies the person uses, or in the contents of long-term memory. For example, Sternberg has found that people's strategies differ in the proportion of possible attributes that they encode and then compare during the later steps of the solution.

Although a test based on analogies offers a promising way to explore intelligence among older children and adults, it could not be used with young children. Sternberg notes that until children are nine, they seem unable to carry out the mapping component of the solution, and they are not skillful at it until they are about eleven or twelve—about the time they should be attaining formal operational thought. In addition, children's strategies change with age. Younger children encode as few attributes as possible during the first step. As children grow older, they encode an increasingly greater proportion of attributes. Third- and sixth-grade children appear to solve analogies by association, choosing the answer that has the closest relationship to the key term. Ninth-grade and college students rely on reasoning processes, solving analogies by inference (Sternberg and Nigro, 1980).

Analogies examine intelligence at the component level. Once we begin analyzing intelligence at the level of metacomponents, says Sternberg (1979), our views of intelligence may have to change. It is possible that intelligence tests succeed when they measure not only the speed and accuracy of the processes used to solve problems (components) but also the speed and accuracy with which the method of solution (metacomponents) is chosen. When intelligence tests fail, it may be because they are measuring only componential speed and accuracy and not the speed and accuracy of the metacomponents.

THE MEASUREMENT OF INTELLIGENCE

If they are successful, says the author of the Wechsler series of intelligence tests, intelligence tests measure "the capacity of an individual to understand the world about him and his resourcefulness to cope with its challenges" (Wechsler, 1975). As we shall see, that is exactly what some psychologists believe that present ways of measuring intelligence fail to do.

Most of the innumerable tests a person takes over the course of a lifetime are not intelligence tests. Many are tests of achievement, and they measure what the person already has learned. Tests of intelligence are supposed to be aptitude tests—tests that measure the broad range of a child's ability to learn new scholastic skills. But most intelligence tests are heavily based on general cultural knowledge, so that the aptitude of some children is not fairly tested by them.

The results of an intelligence test are generally given in terms of an intelligence quotient, or IQ, a number that represents a child's performance relative to the performance of numerous other children who have previously been tested under the same conditions. Given the way that intelligence tests are constructed and standardized, the IQ score is simply a descriptive statistic relating a child's present performance to that of other children of his or her chronological age.

Many factors determine a child's intellectual

This youngster is part of a longitudinal study that follows children from nursery school through elementary school; the study includes periodic assessments of intellectual development. (Cary Wolinsky/Stock, Boston, Inc.)

In this test, the boy is asked to arrange the pictures in sequence so that they tell a story, demonstrating his ability in a way that does not require verbal skills, but does presuppose a familiarity with bicycles. (© Anne Chwatsky)

performance, among them biological change, general education, life experience, motivation, and personality. In addition, external influences at the time of the examination, including the manner of the examiner and the attitude of the child, can affect the child's performance. It is risky, therefore, to make important decisions about a child's future based on only one assessment—or even several assessments—of his or her intellectual abilities (McCall, Appelbaum and Hogarty, 1973).

When properly used, however, the IQ score is an efficient and accurate summary of the degree to which a child has learned the concepts and rules of middle-class Western society. The IQ score is useful because it predicts fairly well how easily a boy of eleven will master the elements of calculus or history when he enters college. Tests are revised periodically to ensure that the questions contribute to the accuracy of this prediction. If questions predict school success, they are kept; if they do not, they are thrown out. Also, if questions distinguish between the sexes, generally being answered correctly only by boys or only by girls, they are discarded. Because of the test's purpose, the eleven-year-old is asked to define "shilling" rather than "peso." He is asked to state the similarity between a fly and a tree, rather than the similarity between "fuzz" and "Uncle Tom." He is asked to copy a design, rather than to defend himself against the neighborhood bully.

Present IQ tests are biased toward measuring skills that upper- and middle-class white Americans value and teach, but that is no reason to discard them. Instead, the parent and teacher should appreciate the arbitrary content of the test. If the primary objective is to predict a child's success in school subjects, then the IQ test is the best instrument psychologists have yet devised. But if the goal is to measure an individual's total cognitive functioning, it would be best to look elsewhere.

For many years psychologists thought that an IQ score measured practically everything of importance in cognitive development. Performance on an IQ test was taken as an index of creative abilities, productive thinking, and problem-solving abilities. Along with this faith in the IQ test went a belief that it was not possible to train mental capacities. Evidence and experience have modified these ideas about IQ, and attempts to develop new kinds of tests are under way. In California and in Canada and Great Britain, psychologists are working on intelligence tests based on Piaget's experiments with children, in the hope that tests grounded in a comprehensive theory of mental development will make it possible to assess children's cognitive levels without comparing them specifically to other children (Tyler, 1976).

Despite the fact that present intelligence tests measure only certain aspects of cognitive functioning, they are as yet the only objective measures we have. For that reason, as we explore other areas of intelligence — its stability, its relationship to various aspects of life, and it susceptibility to modification — we shall use the results of such tests as our reference.

STABILITY AND CHANGE IN INTELLIGENCE

Since tests are reasonably good predictors of success in school and at work, we would expect IQ scores to remain stable throughout life. This is not always so.

IQ Tests in Infancy

Scores on intelligence tests given in infancy bear little resemblance to the results of tests given during the childhood or adult years. In the Berkeley Growth Study — a longitudinal study of sixty-one children — IQ testing began when the babies were a month old. As the year wore on, babies who scored low on early tests tended to catch up with the high-scoring babies (Bayley, 1955). There was no relation between test scores at the end of that year and those the babies made in the first few months, although, as Nancy

Bayley suggests, the abilities measured — alertness, reaction to stimuli, sensorimotor coordination, vocalization, the recognition of differences — may reflect motor abilities more than mental capacities. Thus the results may not accurately predict later cognitive behavior.

Scarr-Salapatek (1976) has proposed that sensorimotor intelligence is indeed different in quality from later intelligence, and that it is independent of the cognitive skills that evolved later in human history. If this is so, the lack of any correspondence between scores on infant intelligence tests and later test scores becomes understandable. Another major difference between infant and child intelligence tests lies in the relative unimportance of language on the former and the overwhelming stress on verbal ability in the latter.

Despite low correlations between scores on infant intelligence scales and later IQ, infant tests can be valuable tools. They effectively detect severe mental retardation. Thus the correlation between infant and childhood IQ scores is somewhat better for retarded than for average or superior babies (McCall, 1979a). Infant IQ tests also identify babies who may need extra attention because of various factors connected with the fetal environment or with birth complications. Drawing an analogy between such uses and the practice of weighing a baby, Robert McCall points out that knowing a baby's weight at six months does not help us predict the infant's weight as an adult, but it does help a physician decide whether the baby needs medical assistance.

IQ Tests in Childhood

Once children have reached the toddler stage and begin to use symbols, they might be expected to show more stability in their IQ scores. And they do. As soon as children begin to talk, the stability of IQ scores does increase. Tests of older children rely heavily on verbal items and abstract-symbolic reasoning, and correlations between IQ scores at ages six and eighteen

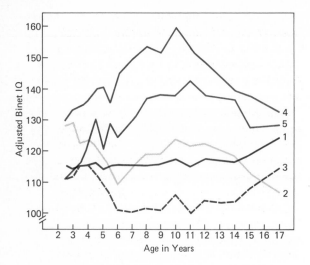

Figure 13.2 In the Fels Longitudinal Study of development, IQ scores over the years fell into five different groups, each with a characteristic pattern of change. The most nearly stable group (Group 1) contained the most individuals, but the average child showed a change of 28 IQ points between ages two and seventeen.

SOURCE: From R. B. McCall, M. I. Appelbaum, and P. S. Hogarty, "Developmental Changes in Mental Performance," in *Monographs of the Society for Research in Child Development,* Serial no. 150, Vol. 38, No. 3. University of Chicago Press, 1973. © The Society for Research in Child Development, Inc.

A New Wave of Intelligence Tests?

If a new approach to the assessment of cognitive processing fulfills its developers' hopes, traditional intelligence tests will one day be obsolete. Their place will be taken by a computer that analyzes children's brain waves. Researchers at New York Medical College's Brain Research Laboratories (Karmel, Kaye, and John, 1978) use a forest of electrodes to gather information from throughout a child's brain as the child listens to and watches various types of computer-produced stimulation. As the child undergoes a battery of more than ninety tests, processing sensory, perceptual, and cognitive information, the computer evaluates the child's evoked potentials, comparing them with average reactions to the same measures. When a child's brain waves are significantly different from those of the average child of the same age, the computer print-out alerts the technician.

Behind the test is an attempt to unite information about perception and information processing developed by psychologists with knowledge of brain function discovered by neuroscientists. E. Roy John and his colleagues call their approach *neurometrics,* as opposed to the psychometrics of the intelligence-test approach.

Cells in many parts of the brain, not simply cells in a specific region, are involved in all kinds of learning, says John (1976). Because

are at least .80. (1.00 would indicate that children who get high scores at age six always get high scores at age eighteen.)

Nevertheless, many children show large changes in score. When the intellectual development of 140 typical mid-American children was followed at Fels Research Institute, investigators found that the IQ of the average child shifted over a range of almost 30 points between the ages of two and a half and seventeen years (McCall, Appelbaum, and Hogarty, 1973). See Figure 13.2. One child out of seven showed a shift greater than 40 points.

In this group of children, investigators found different patterns in IQ shifts over the years. The largest group (45 percent of the children) showed relative stability in their scores, which tended to increase slightly as they grew. The remaining children showed either general declines or general increases during the preschool years. Parents of children in the group that

the neurometric test averages information from all parts of the brain, it is much more sensitive than the ordinary EEG. For example, computer analysis of evoked potentials successfully identified twenty of a group of twenty-five epileptics (ten of whom showed no signs of epilepsy on an ordinary EEG), twenty-two of a group of twenty-five stroke patients (fifteen of whom had normal EEGs), and twenty-four out of twenty-five people with brain tumors (ten of whom had normal EEGs) (Goleman, 1976).

When used to diagnose school-related problems, the neurometric test may be faster and more accurate than traditional intelligence tests. John and his colleagues (Karmel, Kaye, and John, 1978) administered a two-minute portion of their fifty-three-minute Neurometric Battery to 172 boys between seven and eleven years old. Among the boys were sixty-two who had earlier been classified as "learning disabled." The computer analysis of only two minutes of data did as good a job of separating the learning-disabled boys from the normal boys as did the battery of intelligence tests that had taken several hours to administer. Both methods can distinguish between the two groups, but the psychometric method produces false diagnoses more often than does the neurometric method.

The Neurometric Battery does more than simply note whether a child's brain activity is normal; it can pinpoint specific disorders.

The test can also indicate whether a child's problem is sensory (he or she may simply need glasses) or involves information processing. Some of the items on the test battery, such as the spontaneous brain waves, provide a general measure of the brain's state. For example, Bernard Karmel, Herbert Kaye, and John believe that an abundance of delta waves (slow brain waves that—except among young children—appear only during sleep) indicate a maturational lag that manifests itself in general learning difficulties. Excessive theta waves (another slow brain wave) indicate a lag in the child's control over attention, which is manifested as a short attention span and perhaps an extra susceptibility to environmental stimulation—typical hallmarks of the hyperactive child. Other items measure specific functions, such as pattern perception, perception of complex relationships, short-term memory, spatial relations, attention, concept organization, representation of geometric forms, and word recall.

Some schools in New York State are now using the Neurometric Battery on an experimental basis. Should it prove as accurate as preliminary experiments have indicated, assessing the cognitive function of the next generation of schoolchildren may be simple. Each child would sit with the computer for an hour, listening to music and watching television programs that are accompanied by a series of flashes, clicks, and taps (Goleman, 1976).

showed no substantial IQ changes demonstrated no extreme behavior on any of the visits investigators made to the children's homes; but there was a strong correlation between parental behavior and larger shifts in IQ. Children whose parents used severe punishment (which may have caused fear and resentment) and children whose parents punished very lightly (so that punishments were inconsequential) both showed IQ declines. Children whose parents pushed them to achieve, were clear in their policies, and provided firm but not severe discipline showed general increases in IQ.

Sudden major shifts in IQ tended to come when children were about six and ten years old. As noted in the last chapter, there appears to be a change in the way children learn at about age five or six, which may be a factor in the first shift. McCall and his associates point out that many of the ten-year-old shifts were dips in scores among very bright children. They speculate that the children they studied might have been turned off by a restrictive school curriculum aimed at the average child.

Apparently the IQ score of the average child varies almost as much during childhood as do scores among a group of unrelated people (McCall, Appelbaum, and Hogarty, 1973). But despite frequent changes in IQ scores over childhood, different tests given at fairly close intervals do produce similar scores; for example, tests given at age fifteen correlate .96 with tests given at age eighteen (Bayley, 1949). Although many IQ scores remain stable, others may go up or down, and changes may continue in later life. For example, in several longitudinal studies, a number of people continued to show gains in their IQ scores at age fifty (Bayley, 1955).

WHAT IQ SCORES TELL US

Given that IQ scores can change dramatically over time, can intelligence tests really predict performance? When scores from these tests are compared with what children and adults actually do in school, in life, and with their creative talents, the results are mixed.

Success in School

Tests that purport to measure intelligence are at their best when predicting success or failure in school. This should not be surprising, since such predictions are exactly what the tests were developed to make. IQ scores correlate about .70 with school grades (McClelland, 1973), making them the best single predictor of success in school for children of all socioeconomic levels (McCall, Appelbaum, and Hogarty, 1973). Tests predict success better in some academic areas than in others. For example, among high-school students, the Stanford-Binet scale correlates over .70 with reading comprehension but drops to just below .50 with geometry (Bond, 1940). The IQ test generally does the job of predicting, quickly and efficiently, how well a child can profit from regular classroom instruction. The tests are better at predicting elementary- and high-school performance than college or graduate-school success, because the farther a person moves up the educational ladder, the less varied the group that is competing for grades, and the more important such factors as personality, perseverance, and distraction may become. The correlation of less than 1.00 between school success and IQ scores warns us, however, that there will always be some errors in prediction; in the case of some children, the tests will not demonstrate their true potential.

There are some good things to be said about the use of IQ tests in school: they have saved many children from being placed in classes for the retarded; they have indicated whether a child's problems in school have behavioral or intellectual roots; they have selected gifted children who would otherwise have lost out on extra educational opportunities; and they have provided a way for children from disadvantaged families to move out of poverty (Hyman, 1979). In fact, Leona Tyler (1976) suggests that widespread use of IQ tests may have accelerated the breakdown of the class structure in society by identifying exceptionally able individuals in the lower socioeconomic classes.

There are also some bad things to say about the use of intelligence tests in the schools: they have been used to excuse bad education for minority groups; they have saddled children with a "retarded" label when all the children lacked was exposure to the dominant culture (Mercer, 1972); and they have set in motion self-fulfilling prophecies, by persuading teachers that children could not profit from instruction (Rosenthal, 1973).

IQ tests are fairly accurate at predicting a child's success or failure in school, because the tests were developed to make such predictions. (Robert Eckert/EKM-Nepenthe)

Success in Life

IQ scores are reasonably good predictors of occupational success (McCall, Appelbaum, and Hogarty, 1973). If IQ scores among various occupational groups are compared, the average IQ of accountants and lawyers, for example, is more than 20 points higher than the average IQ of miners and farmhands (Harrell and Harrell, 1945). The connection, however, is not as clean as it appears. Robert McCall (1977) compared childhood IQ scores of almost 200 men and women from the Fels Study (see Figure 13.3) with their education and occupation at age twenty-six. He found that correlations got increasingly better until the children were about seven years old. At that time, they reached about .50, remaining fairly stable afterward. Although a correlation of .50 indicates some correspon-

dence between whatever the tests measure and occupational success, it is not high enough to be used to predict an individual child's performance. According to McCall, 64 to 84 percent of the difference in these children's adult status was *not* accounted for by childhood IQ scores.

The correlation between years of schooling and IQ scores is generally about .55, indicating that the role of IQ in predicting occupational success may lie in its facility at opening the door to college enrollment. But in the Fels Study, children's IQ scores did not predict eventual educational level as well as did the factor of father's education, which correlated .62 with eventual educational levels. McCall suggests that bright but disadvantaged children often have no opportunity to continue their education, whereas upper-income children who are not as bright often go on to college.

IQ score, then, is no sure predictor of education or income; some farmers have IQ scores higher than those of most lawyers. What is more, correlation between IQ scores and proficiency on the job is as low as between .20

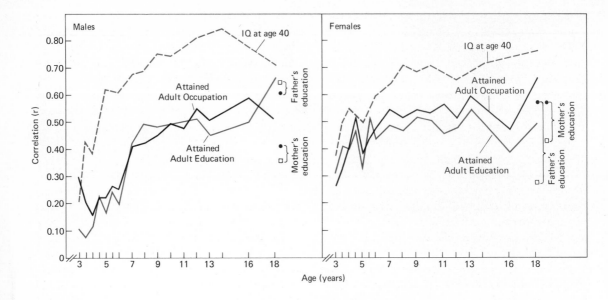

Figure 13.3 As children age, IQ scores become better predictors, although IQ predicts adult IQ much better than it predicts occupational or educational status. Open squares show parental correlations with occupation; filled circles show parental correlations with education. Father's education is a better predictor of boys' occupations than IQ is.

SOURCE: From R. B. McCall, "Childhood IQ's as Predictors of Adult Educational and Occupational Status," *Science*, 197, July 29, 1977. Copyright © 1977 by the American Association for the Advancement of Science. Reprinted by permission of author and publisher.

and .25 (Jensen, 1970). Although a minimum IQ is required for certain occupations, once that is attained, there is no indication that higher scores bring greater success. In a survey of mathematicians, for example, the IQs of those who were doing exceptionally fine research were no higher than the scores of other mathematicians (Helson and Crutchfield, 1970).

A look at the exceptionally gifted throws more light on the relative importance of IQ in a person's life. In the 1920s, Lewis Terman (1959) began studying more than 1,500 California schoolchildren with IQ scores of 135 or more (their average IQ was 150). As adults, this group of children ranked higher than average on almost any positive measure one could imagine: education, professional standing, social status, income, health, and happiness. Of the more than 800 males, 125 had earned either Ph.D.'s or M.D.'s; 100 were engineers; 85 were lawyers. They were also creative. By 1959, the men and women together held 230 patents; they had written more than 90 books and 350 short stories and plays. They ranked lower than the national average in two categories: mental illness and suicide.

In 1968, investigators separated the extremely successful and the unsuccessful from the rest of this gifted group and found that those at the top had IQs that averaged 6 points higher than those at the bottom — not an impressive difference (Oden, 1968). The greatest difference between the top and bottom groups fell in the areas of personality and motivation — not intellect. General personality adjustment and a need to achieve were both much stronger in the top group. Despite high IQs, some of those in the bottom group failed college.

The group was checked again in 1972, when their average age was sixty-two (Sears, 1977). This time, investigators wanted to know what had given these intellectually gifted people the most satisfaction in their lives. Although the men indeed found a great deal of satisfaction in their careers, they rated the satisfaction derived from their family lives as most important to them. Investigators checked early records to discover what factors predicted occupational and family satisfaction and discovered that neither advanced degrees, occupational success, nor financial rewards were the important criteria. Instead, men who showed a general optimism about life, a zest for occupational combat (measured by ambition and liking for work), and a feeling of self-worth were the men who derived greatest satisfaction from their careers.

In the area that gave these men their greatest satisfaction — their families — the factors that accompanied high satisfaction were mental health, social adjustment in elementary school, high-school activities, feminine tastes and interests, admiration for their parents, and high scores on a marital aptitude test. Robert Sears, who supervised the 1972 study, suggests that the men probably derived great satisfaction from their careers because their IQs permitted them both a high degree of autonomy in choosing which profession they would enter and in the way they behaved once they were members of that profession. He also notes that even the gifted find their greatest satisfaction not in work or in intellectual pursuits but in their relations with other people.

Creativity

From the abundance of inventions, stories, books, and plays produced by the Terman group of gifted men and women, we might suppose that a high IQ is necessary for creativity.

That is true only in part. Once a certain minimum IQ is reached (and that IQ varies depending upon the area of creativity), intelligence as measured by tests does not distinguish between highly creative and representative writers, architects and scientists (Barron, 1968). Researchers at the Institute for Personality Assessment and Research studied such groups, comparing highly creative professionals in each occupation with professionals who were not especially distinguished. Although the men and women they studied were in the upper 5 to 10 percent of the general population in IQ, once they reached that level, there was absolutely no relationship (a zero correlation) between IQ and creativity. The average IQ of the novelists, poets, essayists, mathematicians, architects, research scientists, and engineers studied hovered between 135 and 140, but it varied by field. Generally, the

Although creative people are generally intelligent, intelligence does not guarantee creativity, and no IQ test can identify a future Alicia de Larrocha, Itzhak Perlman, or Jean-Pierre Rampal. (Jean-Claude Le Jeune/Stock, Boston, Inc.)

more highly verbal a field, the higher the IQs of its practitioners.

Amy Lowell once subjected herself to a word-association test, and the psychologist who administered it reported that the poet "gave a higher proportion of unique responses than those of any one outside a mental institution" (Bingham, 1953). This correlation has shown up in other situations. Among the architects studied by the Institute for Personality Assessment and Research, one of the best predictors of creativity was scores on a word-association test; unusual associations correlated .50 with creativity (MacKinnon, 1962).

Personality and childhood circumstances also separated the highly creative architects from ordinary architects. Although less imaginative architects had IQs just as high as their creative peers, the outstanding architects tended to be more open to their own feelings and emotions, self-aware, and open to experience, and to have feminine interests. As children, the highly creative tended to identify either with both parents or with neither, and their mothers tended to lead active lives, sometimes having their own careers. The families moved frequently, and during childhood and adolescence, the creative architects often felt alone, shy, isolated, and solitary; they dated little as adolescents. Discipline was consistent, and the family had clear standards of right and wrong, but the children were expected to develop their own ethical codes. These aspects of childhood correlated .36 with high creativity. Such studies indicate that although creative people generally score high on intelligence tests, intelligent people are not necessarily creative.

MODIFIABILITY OF INTELLIGENCE

Intelligence expresses itself in the ability to benefit from experience. It is generally assumed that each person has a ceiling, a point above which he or she will be unable to profit from experience in a particular activity, and that this ceiling is governed by environmental and hereditary factors.

Heredity

The hereditary influence on intellectual abilities was discussed in Chapter 3. There we noted that the more closely two people are related, the higher their IQ scores correlate. As Table 13.1 shows, the correlation between the IQ scores of two children who are unrelated and reared apart is −.01, essentially zero. Correlations between siblings, fraternal twins, and parents and

Table 13.1   CORRELATIONS OF INTELLIGENCE TEST SCORES

Correlations Between	Median Value
Unrelated Persons	
Children reared apart	−.01
Children reared together	+.20
Collaterals*	
Second cousins	+.16
First cousins	+.28
Uncle (or aunt) and nephew (or niece)	+.34
Siblings, reared apart	+.46
Siblings, reared together	+.52
Fraternal twins, different sex	+.49
Fraternal twins, same sex	+.56
Identical twins, reared apart	+.75
Identical twins, reared together	+.87
Direct Line	
Grandparent and grandchild	+.30
Parent (as adult) and child	+.50
Parent (as child) and child	+.56

* Descended from the same stock, but different lines.
Source: Based on estimates reported in John C. Loehlin, Gardner Lindzey, and J. N. Spuhler, *Race Differences in Intelligence,* San Francisco: W. H. Freeman, 1975; and in Arthur Jensen, "How Much Can We Boost IQ and Scholastic Achievement?" *Harvard Educational Review,* 39 (1969), 49.

children are all similarly strong, about .50. In each of these cases, the two individuals involved share half their genes.

Although environment plays a potent role in these correlations, studies of adopted children have shown that environment alone does not account for them. Correlations between the IQ scores of adopted children and their biological parents are greater (approximately .35) than between those same children and the parents who reared them (.00 in some studies; from .09 to .16 in others) (Honzik, 1957; Scarr-Salapatek, 1975; Skodak and Skeels, 1949). In fact, there is little difference between the correlations for adopted children and their biological parents and the correlations for children reared by their own parents (see Figure 13.4).

When we look at the average IQ scores of these same children, the effect of environment on intellectual skills becomes apparent. Their average IQ scores are closer to the average scores of their upper-middle-class adoptive mothers than to the average IQ scores of their impoverished biological mothers. In one study, the average IQ score of the biological mothers was 86, but the average IQ score for the children was 106, a score near the estimated IQ of the parents who reared them. Clearly, IQ scores are likely to improve if people are in a rich environment, for such surroundings allow intellectual abilities to develop near the upper limits of their reaction range, a concept discussed in Chapter 3.

Each person has a reaction range for IQ of at least 30 points. Since a negative environment during childhood and the prenatal period can so hinder the development of a child's IQ, it is probably safe to assume that genetic influences on IQ are much smaller among lower-class children than they are among middle-class children (Scarr-Salapatek, 1971).

Despite these findings, psychologists and ordinary citizens alike continue to argue about the genetic contribution to tested IQ performance. A few years ago, Arthur Jensen (1969) heated up the nature-nurture controversy by claiming that 80 percent of the differences among the IQ

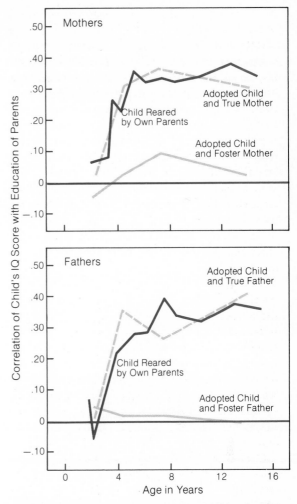

Figure 13.4 Correlations between children's IQ scores and estimated IQ scores of parents. Reddish lines are based on Skodak and Skeels's research, and the other lines are based on research by Honzik. Note that in this research parents' educational level was used as a rough estimate of their IQ score because it was not possible to administer a test to each parent. The two top lines in each graph show that as children get older, their scores correlate more closely with their true parents' scores. The bottom line in each graph shows that there is little or no change with age in the low correlation between adopted children's scores and those of their adoptive parents. (Adapted from Skodak and Skeels, 1949; after Honzik, 1957)

scores of individuals can be traced to differences in their genetic backgrounds. Others countered that a close examination of the data reveals so many problems in untangling genetic and environmental influences that there is little evidence for any genetic component to IQ (Kamin, 1973; M. Schwartz and Schwartz, 1974).

When we look at Jensen's claim that the heritability for IQ is .80, we find a number of problems. First, the statement implies that in a group of individuals, only about 80 percent of the *difference* in their scores—not 80 percent of their entire scores—is associated with differences in their genetic make-up. No one has claimed that 80 percent of an individual's entire IQ score is "determined" by genetic make-up and 20 per-

cent by environment, as if 80 of the 100 points in an average child's IQ score was contributed by genes. Most behavioral geneticists agree that it is impossible to put a number on the proportion of behavior that is inherited (Scarr and Weinberg, 1978). A complex and interdependent set of genetic and environmental circumstances that scientists are only beginning to understand causes the child's test performance.

Second, as noted in Chapter 3, a heritability estimate of .80 depends on the nature of the samples used to calculate it. Heritability may not be the same among blacks as among whites, among upper-middle-class individuals as among the poor, among individuals tested in the 1930s as among those tested in the 1970s or 1980s.

Third, because of the way genetic research must be done with human beings, often involving variation in both hereditary and environmental influences, the accuracy of that estimate of .80 heritability, even in the specific samples tested, is questionable.

Fourth, even if human heritability for IQ were .80, this finding does not suggest that attempts to stimulate or improve intellectual functioning would be fruitless. It may be difficult to change intellectual ability or it may not, depending on whether we can discover which experiences are most important for its development. In a study of more than 100 disadvantaged black infants who were adopted by white middle-class families, researchers found that as schoolchildren, their IQ scores were higher than the national average for both black and white children (Scarr and Weinberg, 1978).

Health and Nutrition

In earlier chapters, we saw that physical factors can retard intellectual development. One of the most damaging factors is fetal alcohol syndrome. When the syndrome was first detected in France, investigators reported that afflicted children did not outgrow the associated problems. By the time they were in school, they had short atten-

Genes and environment work together in the development of intelligence; children in the Kennedy family, for example, grow up in an environment that allows intelligence to express itself at the high end of the reaction range and that also strongly emphasizes achievement. (J. Berndt/Stock, Boston, Inc.)

Occasional meals of fast food will not affect the developing intelligence of children, but children who are consistently malnourished are likely to show lower IQ scores than children whose diets are nutritionally sound. (© Alan Mercer)

tion spans and were unable to continue an activity for very long (Lemoine *et al.*, 1968). Their reported IQ scores indicated borderline mental retardation—about 30 points below average. Eight out of twelve children of alcoholic mothers studied at the University of Washington were retarded and three more had scores that indicated borderline retardation; only one had a normal IQ score (Streissguth, 1976). In a California study, 75 percent of the children of alcoholic mothers showed signs of mental retardation compared with 22 percent of a control group (Jones *et al.*, 1974).

The initial physical problems of babies with fetal alcohol syndrome are generally complicated by a poor environment that includes poverty and general disorganization in the home. Many factors interact to intensify or lessen the effects of fetal exposure to alcohol (Rosett and Sander, 1979). For example, middle-class children of alcoholic mothers seem less likely to show severe retardation, another indication of the powerful effect of a good environment, even on physical factors.

Severe malnutrition also can affect intellectual development. When such malnutrition occurs early in life, its effects are often long lasting. Babies suffering from kwashiorkor (discussed in Chapter 6) were tested on infant intelligence scales during and after their hospital treatment (Cravioto and Robles, 1965). Of the twenty babies tested, fourteen made higher scores after treatment; the six who failed to improve were the youngest babies in the group. If kwashiorkor is allowed to go untreated for more than four months among young infants, they may be severely retarded and later treatment is unlikely to correct the condition (Cravioto and Delicardie, 1970). Some children are unable to absorb basic nutritional requirements from their food. This condition, called "failure to thrive," also affects IQ; seventeen out of nineteen infants who had the condition showed severe mental retardation in childhood (Pollitt and Granoff, 1967).

Some babies who are born "small-for-gestational-age" suffer from malnutrition, but the effect on intellectual development apparently can be lessened by a good environment. In a survey of 17,000 births in Great Britain, babies whose birth weights were below the fifth percentile for their gestational age—regardless of the cause—had lower scores on tests when they were seven years old (Butler, 1974). First-born children of professional parents, however, showed only slight impairments, whereas later-born children of parents in low socioeconomic classes showed large impairments. Other studies have shown that children of diabetic mothers (who tend to have a higher rate of small-for-gestational-age births) showed significantly lower IQs, on infant tests when they were eight months old and on standard IQ tests when they were four years old (Churchill and Berendes, 1969). Finally, when all the children born on the island of Kauai in

Hawaii during 1954 and 1955 were followed, those who had suffered birth complications were twice as likely to have low IQ scores on tests given at twenty months and at ten years as babies whose births were uncomplicated (Werner, Berman, and French, 1971). One reason may be that a baby who is born malnourished often is treated differently. As we saw in Chapter 5, the premature baby is less attractive in appearance, in cry, and in social interactions than the normal baby.

Environment

Children from low socioeconomic classes consistently score 10 to 15 points below middle-class children on IQ tests. Psychologists have been investigating, first, what causes these lower scores among disadvantaged children, and second, what can be done to change the children's environment so they can develop their intellectual potential.

CLASS DIFFERENCES IN IQ   There are no class differences in intelligence scores among babies. For the first eighteen months of life, white and black, lower- and middle-class babies all score about the same on infant intelligence tests (Golden and Birns, 1976). This is true whether the tests are the standard infant scales or newer tests based on Piagetian tasks. As noted earlier, tests given in infancy do not predict the IQ scores of children or adults, perhaps because sensorimotor intelligence is radically different from later intelligence.

Class differences in IQ scores begin to appear at about eighteen months, and may come from the child's physical surroundings, from the quality of parent-child interaction, from the level of nutrition and sanitation, or—as is most likely—from the interaction of all of these factors. The effects of malnutrition already have been mentioned.

A child's physical surroundings may affect IQ in several ways. The homes of disadvantaged preschoolers are often disorganized and unpre-

Differences in nutrition, sanitation, physical surroundings, and the quality of parent-child interaction probably combine to account for the social-class difference in IQ scores, a difference that is not present during the first eighteen months of life. (© Rick Smolan)

dictable (Bradley and Caldwell, 1976). Lower-class infants are also more restricted; their mothers are more likely than middle-class mothers to confine them to a playpen instead of allowing them to explore their world (Tulkin and Kagan, 1972). This is understandable, in view of the fact that the homes of lower-class infants are more likely to be crowded, with more people and their possessions crammed into fewer rooms. The middle-class infant, on the other hand, often has his or her own room and is likely to live in a home where there is also space to place forbidden or dangerous objects safely out of an infant's grasp. The profusion of toys pressed on middle-class infants may also encourage cognitive development.

Theodore Wachs (1976) has found that freedom of exploration is very important in cognitive development but that three other home factors also play a role: the availability of toys, papers, magazines, books, mobiles, and other items that provide visual and tactual-visual stim-

(UPI)

ing more to their mothers' words; whereas lower-class infants make no such distinction (Lewis and Freedle, 1973), perhaps indicating more advanced communication skills among the middle-class babies.

Asked to read books to their young children just "as you would at home," mothers in one study displayed another social-class difference related to language (Rossman *et al.*, 1973). Middle-class mothers seemed to enjoy the project, read the whole story through before discussing it, and related the pictures to the story. Lower-class mothers often failed to finish the story and did not relate pictures and story. Compared with lower-class mothers, middle-class mothers used more complex, explicit language, explained more, asked their children more questions, and responded more often to their children's questions. Taken together, these studies indicate that the major component of IQ tests — language — is also the area of greatest class difference in maternal-infant interaction. Thus it is not coincidental that class differences in IQ appear just at the time that language starts to play its overwhelming role in development.

Other class differences add to these physical and social distinctions. If children are highly motivated to improve the quality of their intellectual skills and have high standards for intellectual mastery, they are likely to score higher on tests than if they are not highly motivated or have low standards. Because middle-class children are more consistently encouraged than lower-class children to learn to read, spell, add, and write, a child's IQ, social class, and school grades all should be positively related. This is generally the case. In addition, the personality attributes of children who do well in school (persistence, lack of aggression, and responsible behavior) are similar to the characteristics of children from middle-class homes. In Chapter 15, we shall see other basic class differences in child rearing that may contribute to IQ differences.

ulation; the presence of a variety of objects a child can explore; and the presence of toys that produce interesting sounds and sights. Finally, Wachs found that a high level of background noise — a common aspect of small, crowded lower-class living quarters — correlates negatively with IQ. That is, children who live in homes filled with inescapable noise tend to have lower IQs, an example of the negative effects of too much, rather than too little stimulation (Parke, 1978).

The quality of interaction within the home is another possible source of social-class difference in IQ. The only clear-cut class difference in mother-infant interactions falls in the area of language. During the first year of a baby's life, middle-class mothers respond more to their babies' vocalizations with vocalizations of their own (Golden and Birns, 1976). Mark Golden and his associates (1974) found that lower-class infants tend to respond to their mother's speaking with their own simultaneous babbling, whereas middle-class infants quiet and listen to what their mothers are saying. Other studies have found that middle-class infants differentiate between their mothers and other people, respond-

EARLY INTERVENTION PROGRAMS
Programs designed to help disadvantaged chil-

Intervening with Television

When in 1967 planning began for *Sesame Street,* it was hoped that the series would help prepare disadvantaged children to do well in public schools (Lesser, 1974). Subsequent studies showed that the program may have had a pronounced effect on young children's developing cognitive skills and their symbolic representations. Preschoolers who regularly watched *Sesame Street* made large and important gains in these areas, as shown by tests that measured the children's knowledge in such areas as letters, numbers, geometric forms, body parts, and their matching, sorting, and classification skills (Ball and Bogatz, 1972). The children studied were three, four, and five years old, and they were middle as well as lower class. Children were tested in their homes before *Sesame Street* went on the air. At the time of the first test, scores generally ranked by age. After the second test, a year later, scores tended to rank by exposure to the program, with three- and four-year-olds who watched more than five times a week doing better than five-year-olds who saw it three times a week or less. These results, say Samuel Ball and Gerry Ann Bogatz, suggest that three- and four-year-olds are capable of learning most of the skills taught in the kindergarten classroom.

Among a group of 100 children from poverty areas who were matched for age, IQ, home background, and scores on the first

test, those who watched the program regularly consistently outstripped the nonviewers, making scores on the second test that were about 40 points higher than those made by children who never saw the program. Finally, when children from poverty areas were compared with middle-class children, all heavy viewers made large gains and watching *Sesame Street* modified the effect of social class. The regular watchers among the lower-class children did about as well as middle-class children who watched the program two or three times a week, and much better than middle-class children who never watched the program. In fact, children from poverty areas who watched Big Bird and his friends at home did just as well on the tests as children who were enrolled in Head Start programs and watched *Sesame Street* in the classroom.

dren overcome the effects of their early environment vary greatly. Their aim is not to increase children's IQs, but to keep the initial levels from dropping. A number of programs have succeeded in holding up scores for at least three years (Belsky and Steinberg, 1978). Many of them began as part of Project Head Start and were funded by the government. Some used day-care centers, some were carried on in infants' homes, some focused on the children themselves, others worked primarily with parents.

A home-based program directed by Ira Gor-

don (Gordon and Guinagh, 1974; Guinagh and Gordon, 1976) worked primarily with parents. On weekly home visits, mothers of young babies were taught to carry out Piagetian-type activities, beginning with manipulative and exploratory sensorimotor games, later moving into preoperational games involving such concepts as object permanence. When the infants were two years old, they attended playgroups that met in one of the homes for another year, when the program ended. The children who completed Gordon's three-year program scored significantly higher on IQ tests at age six and on achievement

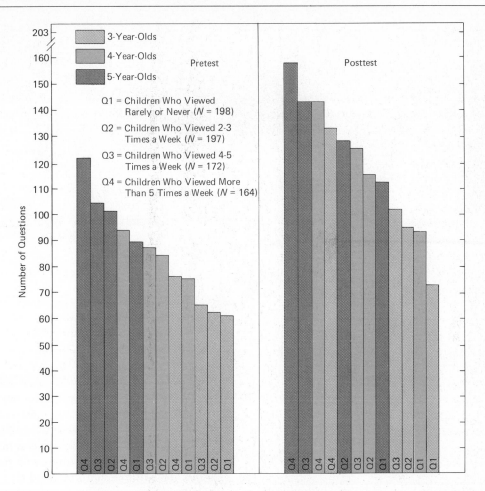

Before disadvantaged preschoolers watched *Sesame Street,* their scores on cognitive tests ranked by age; after watching the program (posttest), they ranked by exposure to *Sesame Street.*

SOURCE: From S. Ball and G. A. Bogatz, "Summative Research of *Sesame Street:* Implications for the Study of Preschool Children," in A. D. Pick (ed.), *Minnesota Symposia on Child Psychology*. Vol. 6. University of Minnesota Press, Minneapolis. Copyright © 1972 by the University of Minnesota.

tests at age eight than did children in control groups.

A center-based program directed by Bettye Caldwell (1970) focused on children, taking infants as young as six months and keeping them at the center all day, five days a week, until they began school. The program concentrated on language development, and teachers carefully labeled objects and actions for the children, spoke to them often, and read to them before they were a year old. Children who entered this program showed IQ gains of 14 to 18 points over children in control groups, and those entering after they were three years old tended to do slightly better than those who came in at six months old. But, as with most intervention programs, the comparative gains in IQ scores tended to fade as children reached school age.

Again and again, hopes have been dashed as whatever good the intervention programs had done faded away soon after children graduated from them (Horowitz and Paden, 1973). However, a study by Richard Darlington and his associates (1980) followed nearly 1,600 Head Start graduates of eight separate preschool programs. The children ranged in age from nine to nine-

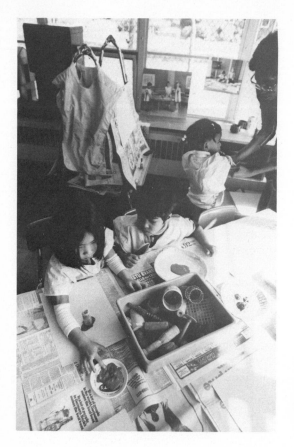

Follow-up studies have found that although IQ gains from Head Start programs fade in about four years, children who attend such programs are less likely to fail in school than disadvantaged children who do not attend. (© Robert V. Eckert, Jr./EMK-Nepenthe)

teen. The investigators compared children who had attended the programs with other children from the same area who had not. Head Start graduates, they found, were less likely than controls to be relegated to special education classes or held back in school (24 percent as compared with 45 percent). The rates varied, and the differences between children who attended Head Start and children who did not was even greater in some areas. In Gordon's program, for example, held in an area where 62 percent of the

disadvantaged children are either held back or placed in special education classes, 39 percent of the Head Start children had such failure at school. But when it came to IQ scores, the programs failed to change the picture. Gains still faded gradually, until most had disappeared four years after a project's close. It would be amazing, however, if intervening for a few months in a child's life consistently overcame the influence of the 24-hour-a-day environment. Certainly, children in the intervention programs have experienced less academic failure than other disadvantaged children.

ENVIRONMENT AND THE INDIVIDUAL Not all changes in a child's IQ over the course of a lifetime are the result of a steady influence. Although socioeconomic factors provide a powerful pull in the same direction throughout childhood, we have seen that the same child may show a variation of 30 points between the ages of two and a half and seventeen. It may be that specific events interact with a child's skills and motivations to cause major changes in the abilities tapped by the tests (McCall, Appelbaum, and Hogarty, 1973).

Sometimes the process can have positive results. For example, a male teacher who has a deep interest in the space program has an eleven-year-old boy for a pupil whose divorced father lives in another city. The boy identifies with the teacher, adopts the teacher's interests as his own, applies himself to mathematics and science, reads widely about the space program, and shows a large jump on an IQ test the following year. A ten-year-old girl, whose brother is captain of the football team, finds that she can get her own share of family attention by studying hard and making the honor roll; her IQ score soars. In the same quest for attention, she could have chosen to play the flute in the school orchestra or to rebel against family standards; but this year — perhaps because of a television program she saw, a book she read, or her observations of her parents' reactions to a scholarship winner—she chose to apply herself to academic subjects. A year or two earlier or later, the young boy and girl may have reacted differently. Different children may not respond to similar situations in the same way. McCall and his colleagues believe that such influences may be especially potent on children who are already making above average scores on IQ tests.

As we have seen in this chapter, intelligence is not a fixed quantity that can be measured at age six or eight or eighteen and then remains stable for the rest of life. Instead it is flexible, develops out of the individual's interaction with the environment, and is responsive to physical, social, and emotional stimulation, and to motives, fears, and expectations. Intellectual ability reflects evolutionary history, genetic endowment, culture, and family circumstances, whereas IQ scores reflect intellectual performance at a specific time under the influence of the immediate situation. It is no wonder that psychologists continue to argue over the concept of intelligence and how it relates to IQ tests.

SUMMARY

1. When looked at from the standpoint of the species, intelligence is the disposition to behave adaptively when faced with the demands of the environment. Differences in intelligence among individuals become negligible when compared with differences in intelligence among species. Human intelligence has been regarded both as a single, general capacity and—when measured by factor analysis—as made up of as many as 120 factors.

2. Human intelligence has been analyzed from at least four perspectives. Biological analysis looks at the purpose of intelligence in species survival. Cognitive analysis focuses on problem solving and logic, examining what human beings can do under the best of circumstances. Psychometric analysis tries to measure individual differences in intelligence. And information-processing analysis applies computer models to human cognition, regarding individual differences as variations in the speed, content, or efficiency of specific parts of the information-processing system.

3. Intelligence tests, which produce a score in terms of IQ, measure a child's performance in relation to the performance of other children who have been tested under the same conditions. IQ tests measure how well a child has learned the concepts and rules of middle-class Western society, and any questions that do not predict school success are eliminated from the tests.

4. Scores on infant intelligence scales bear little resemblance to later IQ scores, perhaps because sensorimotor intelligence may be very different from later intelligence. Although IQ scores become more stable as children grow older, scores may shift by as many as 30 or 40 points during childhood.

5. IQ tests do an efficient job of predicting school success. They also correlate highly with vocational success, although the correlation may be due to the fact that the higher a person's IQ, the more likely he or she is to receive advanced education. Although certain professions require a minimum IQ, once that level is reached, higher scores do not bring greater success.

6. Heredity plays a role in intelligence, but its full expression requires an optimal environment. It is likely that genetic influences on IQ are much smaller among lower-class than among middle-class children. Severe malnutrition, the fetal alcohol syndrome, low birth weight, and a disadvantaged environment can all depress IQ scores. Early intervention programs, such as Head Start, appear to lessen the rate of school failure among disadvantaged children. Specific environmental events may interact with children's skills and motivation to cause changes in individual IQ scores.

PART 6

Social and Personality Development

Babies are social creatures from birth. In the tight world of the family circle, where they interact primarily with parents and siblings, they become attached to their caregivers, learning from them some of the constraints society will later impose. In these close first relationships, children develop a sense of social competence that enables them to explore confidently the toddler's world of peers, teachers, and nursery school and later move into the wider world of schoolchild and adolescent. But influence runs both ways. From their earliest interactions with their caregivers, babies are influencing others, contributing to the development of their parents, siblings, grandparents, and every other person with whom they have contact. The process of personality and social development goes on as long as life itself.

The Emerging Self

W hen Karen was a year old, her mother once took her to the university experimental room, where she played happily with toys. From time to time she looked up at her mother, who sat on a nearby chair, showed her a toy and, on one occasion, babbled at her. The door opened and a strange woman entered and sat beside Karen's mother. Karen smiled briefly at the stranger and continued to play, although she occasionally looked at the stranger. When her mother left the room, Karen got up, toddled toward the door, stopped, looked at her mother's empty chair and the handbag beside it, then sat down again. After some hesitation, she accepted a toy from the stranger and played with it, glancing from time to time at the closed door. When her mother returned, Karen greeted her with delight.

Karen behaved as many babies do in this situation. She was curious about the stranger but somewhat wary. Later, after the stranger departed, her mother again left the room and Karen found herself alone. The stranger reentered and this time her presence tipped Karen's reaction from wariness to fear, bringing on tears. On her mother's next return, Karen clung closely to her. Karen's reactions demonstrated her attachment to her mother, attachment being a special bond between adult and infant that appears to be universal among human beings. The bond takes different forms, but its absence or unreliability signifies a major problem in social development.

In this chapter, we shall look at the baby's first social bond with primary caregivers and discover that there are wide differences in the form this attachment takes. We shall find that attachment plays an important role in the baby's developing trust in the world, in feelings of competence, and in a growing sense of self. We shall see that early experiences lay the groundwork for the developing personality, but that these first experiences are not irreversible. By the end of the chapter, we shall understand the function of attachment in the development of the growing child's individuality.

ATTACHMENT

A human baby arrives on the social scene prepared by millions of years of primate evolution to respond to the sights and sounds of people and to behave in ways that elicit responses from them. Ethologists (Bowlby, 1969; Ainsworth *et al.*, 1978) have argued that by causing adults to stay nearby or to rush to the baby's side and provide necessary care, the baby's inborn tendencies play an active role in ensuring survival. Adults, in turn, have been prepared by evolution to respond to the baby's signals, providing care and giving the child early opportunities for social interaction.

These built-in biases are the building blocks for complex systems of social behavior that begin in the family. In most cultures, the closest relationship of all is between mother and infant. They are involved for a time in a close symbiotic relationship in which the child is almost an extension of the mother's being. It is no surprise, then, that investigators have taken a keen interest in the development of the special bond between infant and caregiver called *attachment*.

The Stages of Attachment

The development of attachment takes months to appear, requires a complex intermeshing of infant and caregiving behavior, and is subject to much variation. Attachment in human babies refers to the early love relationship between baby and caregiver (usually one or both parents), and developmental psychologists study it by examining the kinds of behavior associated with such a relationship. The signs of attachment include smiling and joyous greeting when the caregiver appears, and crying when he or she leaves. One of the most important aspects of behavior that signifies attachment is that it is directed toward some people and not toward others. According to ethologist John Bowlby (1969), in developing an attachment, the child passes through three stages. These stages begin with indiscriminate social responses that gradually become specific. In the first stage, which lasts until babies are about two months old, they respond to anyone; in the second, found in babies from two to about seven months old, babies prefer familiar people but do not protest when either parent leaves and can be comforted by others. In the third stage, which begins at about seven months and lasts until a baby is two or two and a half years old, attachment is strong and separation from a caregiver leads to the baby's distress.

INDISCRIMINATE SOCIAL RESPONSIVENESS At first, newborn babies can summon aid only by crying. A baby's wails bring milk, dry clothes, an end to physical discomfort, and the pleasure of close human contact. Infants in this first stage of attachment will accept aid and comfort from anyone. The indiscriminate stage of responsiveness lasts for about two months (see Figure 14.1). Toward the end of this stage, babies develop a social smile and at the same time often begin to babble.

This additional means of communication allows the baby to initiate, prolong, or end social interaction. A smile and a coo will often keep an

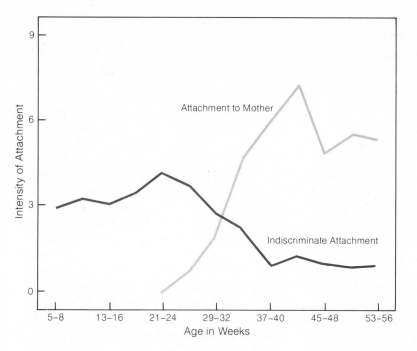

Figure 14.1 During the early weeks of life, most infants prefer not to be separated from the person they are with regardless of who that person is. Such "indiscriminate attachments" begin to decline about the same time that infants start to show preferences for specific persons, such as their mothers. (Adapted from Schaffer and Emerson, 1964)

adult near; by falling silent and turning away, a baby can shut off communication. If an infant can so influence the behavior of others, then babies have some control over their early social experiences. Karen, for example, came into the world with the predispositions common to all infants. But she also possessed her own bundle of individual characteristics, such as her levels of activity and general irritability. Her temperament interacted with her experiences to develop her own unique self.

DISCRIMINATE SOCIAL RESPONSIVENESS During the next few months of life,

babies develop the ability to discriminate among the adults who come into contact with them. They continue to smile at familiar faces as often or even more frequently than they did earlier, but the smiling at strange faces that was so prevalent at about two months drops off or even disappears. Harriett Rheingold (1969) has suggested that the talking, smiling human face, with its changing expression and movements, interests and attracts a young baby. Gradually, through a variety of experiences, the faces of principal caregivers come both to elicit positive emotional and social responses in the baby and to reinforce them.

For many years, both learning theorists and psychoanalysts assumed that babies develop close bonds with their caregivers because the caregivers feed them, satisfying the babies' physical needs. J. P. Scott (1962) has noted that this assumption can lead us to an unromantic conclusion: infants love us only because we feed them. Research with monkeys has demonstrated, however, that there is more to attachment than being fed. In one series of studies by

Attachment and Down's Syndrome

When a baby is born with Down's syndrome (a chromosomal abnormality discussed in Chapter 4), parents face a difficult adjustment. Having anticipated the birth of a normal infant, they discover they are the parents of a child who will always be different in appearance, will have moderate to severe mental retardation, and may also have associated physical problems such as poor vision, cardiovascular defects, or problems with respiration. At one time, such children were shunted away to institutions and some mothers never saw their babies again. Today, most infants with Down's syndrome are reared at home, and about half of them reach adulthood (Stein, 1975), although few can ever be independent.

Robert Emde and Craig Brown (1978) have studied families who were adapting to the birth of a baby with Down's syndrome and have found that the adjustment goes through regular, predictable phases and that the process of attachment is complex. Instead of building their feelings of love and caring on prenatal anticipations, parents go through an initial period of mourning, grieving over the loss of the normal baby who was not born. At the same time, they face adjustment to life with a baby who will always be different and who will require enormous amounts of medical, physical, and emotional care. Only after the first grief is over can parents attach themselves to their real child. During the baby's first few months, parents may deny their child's disability. The baby may turn over in the crib early, and this apparent physical precocity often gives parents hope that the diagnosis was mistaken.

In the normal course of attachment, a baby's social smiles and alert eye contact generally lead to an upsurge of positive emotions toward the child, strengthening the bonds of attachment. But the first social smiles of the Down's infant are delayed, and when they come, they may diminish the parents' love and delight and set off a second wave of grieving. The baby's smiles are dampened. The cheeks and eyes fail to crinkle, the eyes never brighten, the arms and legs fail to move in the bicycling motion that conveys alertness and anticipation to parents. In addition, the baby generally shows poor eye contact. The alert, communicative gaze that leads parents to speculate about their child's feelings and thoughts is absent.

Since there are marked individual differences among mothers, including varied

Harry and Margaret Harlow (1966, 1969), infant monkeys were raised in cages with two surrogate mothers. One mother substitute was covered with soft terry cloth; the other was of hard wire mesh and was equipped with a feeding mechanism. If feeding were the most important factor in attachment, the infant monkeys would have spent more time expressing their attachment to the wire "mother," which fed them. But the monkeys spent much more time clinging to the cloth mother, which gave them no nourishment at all.

The monkeys seemed genuinely attached to the cloth mother. Given a choice of things to observe in a machine that allowed them to see various objects, they looked at the cloth mother much more often than they looked at the wire mother. Monkeys raised under normal condi-

strengths of a mother's sense of self and her experiences with her own mother as a child, development of a mother's attachment to her baby can be relatively easy or extremely difficult. And since Down's infants vary in responsiveness and degree of disability, the infant's contribution toward the bond will vary. Some mothers, point out Emde and Brown, are primed to be loving and tender. They require little responsiveness from their baby.

Emde and Brown describe one mother who spent hours with her baby during his first seven weeks in intensive care, slipping her arm under the small body that was connected to wires, drains, and catheters, and patting him gently on the bottom. Despite Leo's many physical problems, his visual development was above average for such babies; by three months he could track a face and had developed a dull social smile. His mother had no difficulty developing an attachment. She learned to coax smiles and responses from Leo, took pride in her baby, and saw his slow development as ensuring a longer dependent babyhood.

Another mother started out poorly. She refused to see her baby for several days and held Linda only once during her two weeks in the hospital. The mother was filled with anger and anxiety, and expressed thinly veiled death wishes toward her small daughter. Neither parent at first called Linda by her name and the outlook was not hopeful. But when small Linda began social smiling, the tenuous parental bond strengthened. Her ability to track objects and to make eye contact were good, and her eyes brightened when someone drew near. Her responsiveness was enough to get the attachment process safely underway.

The outcome is not always happy. Emde and Brown describe one case in which a young mother was never able to develop a strong attachment to her baby. The mother spent the first six months of her baby's life in a chronic depression, intermittently expressing hostile wishes toward tiny Martha. If Martha had physical problems, it was because she was angry at her mother. Martha was an extremely unresponsive baby, who at five months was smiling only infrequently to touch and voice. At six months, when Martha began to make some eye contact with her mother, a positive attachment began to develop, only to be ruptured by the baby's pneumonia, which required a three-week stay in the hospital. After much frustration and despair, Martha was put in a foster home. By the time the little girl was nearly two years old, her mother agreed to give her up for adoption.

tions rarely chose to look at either artificial mother. When monkeys raised with artificial mothers were put in strange places or when frightening objects were placed near them, they ran to the security of the cloth, but not the wire, mother. At first the baby monkeys seemed terrified, but when allowed to cling to their cloth mother, they soon calmed down. Eventually, the monkeys used the cloth mother as a base for exploration, leaving to manipulate strange objects but returning frequently to cling to their soft, snuggly mother, as monkeys raised with real mothers do. The wire mothers were never used in this way.

Monkey babies may have became attached to the terry-cloth mothers because contact is important to the formation of attachment in monkeys. At birth young monkeys cling to their

mothers; it seems as natural to them as scanning and vocalizing are to human infants. A soft terry-cloth mother encourages clinging, but a cold, hard mesh mother does not, and the differences lead to lasting effects. After a year's separation, a monkey will run to embrace its soft terry-cloth mother, clinging passionately to its soft form. But after a similar separation from a wire mother, monkeys show no affection at all when they are reunited. Although attachment in human beings and in monkeys follows a similar pattern, the response of a human baby to his or her mother develops more slowly than the infant monkey's attachment to its mother.

Feeding undoubtedly can increase the development of attachment, but only if the feeding experience is pleasurable. Unless caregivers are sensitive to babies' signals and respond to them appropriately, feeding may give babies the physical nourishment their bodies require but withhold their social nourishment. Such a caregiver would function like a monkey's wire mother.

Although babies at this second stage of attachment are beginning to differentiate the world into the familiar and the strange, they have not yet developed a true attachment to any person. Babies as young as three months old can tell their mothers from strangers. Nevertheless, if the baby is left with a sitter, the infant is unlikely to protest. Not until infants understand that other people continue to exist after they disappear from view (the concept of object permanence discussed in Chapter 12) will they develop the intense bond that signifies true attachment.

SPECIFIC ATTACHMENT Attachment to specific people may develop as early as six

When frightened by a toy bear (*top*), monkey babies in the Harlow experiment ran to the cloth-covered mother for comfort (*middle*), rejecting the wire mother that fed them (*bottom*). (Harry Harlow, University of Wisconsin Primate Center)

348

months, and most babies have formed their primary attachments by the time they are eight months old. By now they realize that the same people react to their needs in the same predictable ways. This realization is probably related to the baby's development of object permanence. Silvia Bell (1970) found that most babies are aware of their mothers as objects who continue to exist when out of sight slightly before they demonstrate such an awareness with physical objects. Although there is some question as to whether person permanence appears before object permanence in all situations (Jackson, Campos, and Fischer, 1978), it may be that because the comings and goings of the human caregiver are related to the satisfaction of the baby's needs, the baby pays special attention to the location of this very important "object." Bell also found that babies who had developed secure and stable attachments to their mothers were aware of their mothers as permanent objects earlier than were babies with less stable attachments. Furthermore, babies who acquired the concept of person permanence early also developed the concept of physical object permanence early, suggesting that understanding in the social realm has positive effects on understanding in the physical realm.

An infant boy who knows that his mother exists even when she is out of the room can also creep across the floor, following her from living room to kitchen. He no longer must lie in his crib or sit in his playpen, waiting for his mother to respond to his cries. Because he can now seek out his mother and father, the infant can take on some of the responsibility for maintaining the close proximity to adults that helps ensure his survival.

The Function of Attachment

The basic function of attachment is, as noted earlier, to keep the infant alive. Important as its protective function is, attachment works in other ways to help the child develop essential social and cognitive skills. This secondary function becomes clear when one examines the four complementary systems that coordinate the behavior of child and environment (Lamb, 1978). The first is the *attachment behavioral system*, which has just been discussed. The second, the *fear-wariness system*, which helps the baby avoid people, objects, or situations that might endanger life, is often called wariness of strangers; it is discussed later in this section. The third, the *affiliative behavioral system*, encourages a baby, once the initial wariness of strangers has been overcome, to interact with people outside the immediate family. This system promotes the baby's social development, a necessity in a social species like humanity. The fourth and last, the *exploratory behavioral system*, allows the baby to explore the surrounding world. Exploration of the environment is necessary if the growing child is to develop competence. The presence of a secure and reliable attachment figure provides the baby with emotional security, allowing the affiliative and exploratory systems to operate. If the attachment figure is missing or unreliable, the fear-wariness system takes over, and the dis-

Infants with secure attachments learn that their parents are predictable and reliable; the basic trust that develops in such relationships generalizes to other people. (David Austen/Stock, Boston, Inc.)

Theories of Attachment

Psychoanalytic Theory
Sigmund Freud based his psychoanalytic theory of attachment on the infant's instinctual drives and saw the child as choosing the caregiver as a primary love object. In Freud's view, this relationship develops out of the infant's initial self-preoccupation, or *narcissism,* as the caregiver satisfies the baby's needs and gratifies the desire to suck that is the principal pleasure of infancy. Gradually, babies become attached to those who feed, care for, and protect them.

Adaptation Theory
John Bowlby is a British child psychiatrist who proposes a theory of attachment based on ethological thought, although he also draws on post-Freudian psychoanalytic views. He sees evolved predispositions on the part of both the infant and the adult caregiver as interacting to ensure the infant's survival. Bowlby suggests that certain stimulation (a human face, a human voice, a strange object) evokes specific behavior in the infant (smiling, alertness and scanning, crying). The infant's behavior, in turn, releases complementary behavior in the adult. Thus an infant's smile may trigger a smile in the adult and perhaps a strong attraction to the infant as well. Bowlby sees attachment as one of four behavioral systems that operate in infancy. The other three are the fear-wariness system, which helps the baby avoid life-threatening people or situations; the affiliative system, which encourages the baby to interact with people outside the immediate family; and the exploratory system, which allows the baby to explore the surrounding world.

Mary Ainsworth's view of attachment is heavily influenced by John Bowlby's theory. However, Ainsworth focuses not simply on behavioral systems and the nature of the bond that underlies those systems but on individual differences in the quality of the attachment

tressed baby will refuse to investigate new people and new places, making it difficult for the child to develop a sense of competence or mastery.

Secure attachments between babies and caregivers appear to have influences that go far beyond the family circle. As babies learn that their parents are predictable and reliable, they develop basic trust. Trust is usually assumed to be something a person possesses, an inner attitude. Yet trust reflects a system of interaction with the social world. Trust generalizes to other people and helps determine the quality of a baby's future interactions with others. As noted in Chapter 2, the establishment of trust is seen by Erik Erikson as the baby's major developmental task, allowing the child to tolerate frustration and to delay gratification. The emotional warmth that accompanies a secure attachment makes parents more effective models and their approval a more potent reinforcer, increasing the likelihood that experience within the family circle will have the effects parents desire (Lamb, 1978).

Separation Distress

After attachment has developed, a baby tends to cry and stop playing when left in an unfamiliar place. The child may reach out for the attachment figure when he or she leaves and

relationship that develops between infant and caregiver. Ainsworth has also pointed out that attachment is not a unitary phenomenon and has distinguished the existence of three different types of attachment: secure, ambivalent, and avoidant.

Behavior-Learning Theory

Sidney Bijou and Donald Baer are behavior-learning theorists who see attachment as complex behavior that is established and maintained through reinforcement. In this view, attachment develops because the adult caregiver and the infant each reinforce the other's behavior, thereby exerting some control over each other. The caregiver feeds and cares for the baby and provides interesting and satisfying stimulation, so that the caregiver's presence becomes reinforcing. In turn, the baby's responses—coos, gurgles, and smiles, and the cessation of cries—reinforce the caregiver's attention, communication, and other behavior connected with attachment.

---

later may crawl or walk in pursuit of the figure. This distinctly negative reaction to being parted from an attachment figure is called *separation distress*.

Although the age when separation distress first appears varies from culture to culture, it seems to be a universal phenomenon. Ugandan babies begin to protest as early as six months if they are separated from their mothers (Ainsworth, 1967). Separation distress among Guatemalan babies, on the other hand, emerges a bit later and shows a developmental pattern similar to that of North American babies (Lester *et al.*, 1974). Distress begins to appear at about eight or nine months, reaches a peak at around twelve months, then declines.

Placed in a strange situation, most nine- to twelve-month-old babies are likely to show concern that their primary caregiver be present and nearby. For example, Mary Ainsworth and Barbara Wittig (1969) found that babies in a strange situation first establish contact with their caregivers. Somewhat later they venture out on short forays into the strange environment, exploring bits of it but always returning to their caregivers between expeditions.

For example, when a mother brings her eighteen-month-old infant on a first visit to a friend's home, the infant clings to (indeed, hides behind) the parent. Only after the infant has become accustomed to the new setting is he or she likely to let go of the mother's leg. This reaction is similar to the way both cloth-surrogate-reared and normally reared young monkeys behaved in a strange environment.

On the other hand, caregivers are more than security bases. When Rheingold and Carol Eckerman (1970) placed infants in a new situation, the babies showed not distress but joy and excitement, leaving their mothers to explore their new surroundings and returning to share their fun. Thus it is undoubtedly true that babies use attachment figures both to reduce their fear and to share in the pleasures of life, and it seems that the same general pattern of behavior serves both purposes.

Wariness of Strangers

Wariness of strangers, a manifestation of the fear-wariness system, usually develops a month or two after specific attachments begin. Babies appear to go through four phases in their reaction to strangers. At first they do not discriminate between strange and familiar persons. Later they respond positively to strangers, although less positively than to familiar people. Then they go through a period of reacting to strangers with fear if an attachment figure is present, looking back and forth between the

If this child were only two or three months old, she might be content on Santa's lap, but this little girl is showing an extreme wariness of strangers—a reaction that develops in the latter part of the first year and lasts for a good many months, becoming especially sharp in strange surroundings. (David A. Krathwoh/Stock, Boston, Inc.)

stranger and the caregiver as though comparing the strange person with the familiar one. At this time, babies merely become sober and stare at the stranger. It is not until they are around eight months old that some babies respond to strangers with fear and withdrawal, looking away, frowning, whimpering, or even crying. This reaction is particularly intense when a baby's attachment figure is absent (Ainsworth, 1967).

George Morgan and Henry Ricciuti (1969) investigated both the developmental timing of fear in the presence of strangers and the calming effect of a caregiver's presence. They found that at eight, ten, and especially at twelve months, a baby responds more positively to the approach of a stranger if seated on his or her mother's lap than if four feet away from her. At four or six months, however, a separation of four feet makes little or no difference; the baby

responds positively to the stranger in either case.

Another influence on babies' reactions to strangers has to do with the manner of approach. As Mary Anne Trause (1977) found, if strangers pause before walking up to a year-old baby, the baby is more likely to smile and less likely to show distress than if the stranger walks rapidly over to the infant. Apparently, the slower approach gives babies time to judge whether the stranger presents a probable source of danger. As Alan Sroufe (1977) has pointed out, most babies become fearful if a stranger touches them, reaches for them, or picks them up. When babies are given time to evaluate the stranger, their curiosity and affiliative tendencies can come into play.

But the fear-wariness system does not operate in isolation. By the time babies are nine months old, their memories have begun to develop and the effect of past experiences may change their response to strangers from simple wariness to fear (Bronson, 1978). Indeed, in Trause's study, babies were less friendly toward a stranger on a second visit, suggesting that babies connected the appearance of the stranger with a separation from their mothers that was part of the first experiment.

The characteristics of the stranger may also have an effect. As Alison Clarke-Stewart (1978) has suggested, once the stranger acts—or fails to act—toward the child, the situation becomes social interaction, and the stranger's sex, appearance, and manner of behavior will influence the behavior of the child. She points out that in experiments in which strangers act out a rigid script, babies display more wariness or fear than in experiments that allow strangers to interact naturally.

Fear of strangers, like separation distress, appears sharpest when the baby is in an unfamiliar setting. Babies are much less likely to show wariness in their own homes than when they are observed in a laboratory. Russel Tracy and his colleagues (1976) studied babies from the time they were three weeks old until they were more than a year old. The babies were observed in their own home for four hours every three weeks. Tracy and his associates found that once babies began to crawl, they tended to follow their mothers from place to place and to play comfortably in the presence of strangers. Although no baby at any age ever followed a stranger, few cried or showed other distress at a stranger's approach. Babies also engage in more exploration and vocalize more freely at home than they do in the strange and perhaps frightening surroundings of the psychologist's laboratory.

DIFFERENCES IN ATTACHMENT

Babies' reactions to strangers indicate that not all infants develop the same kind of bond with their caregivers. Mary Ainsworth and her colleagues (1978) have discerned three major kinds of attachment bonds: secure, avoidant, and ambivalent. After a separation from their mothers and a meeting with a stranger, babies with *secure* attachments actively seek out their mothers when they return, and contact with their mothers quickly ends the distress. Less securely attached infants fall into two major groups: *avoidant* infants, who shun contact with their mothers upon being reunited, and *ambivalent* infants, who alternate between seeking contact with their mothers and angrily squirming to get away from them.

The extensive study carried out by Ainsworth's group found a consistent connection between a year-old baby's attachment and a mother's style of caring for her baby. Securely attached babies had mothers who were highly responsive to their infants' cries, smiles, and other signals. They held their babies tenderly and carefully, and were flexible in their interactions. They were accepting, affectionate mothers, who cooperated with their babies' efforts instead of interfering with them.

Avoidant babies had mothers who were in-

sensitive to their babies' signals. They avoided close bodily contact with their babies, were rigid in their interactions, and rarely expressed affection. Instead, they often allowed their anger and irritation to show.

Ambivalent babies had mothers who were relatively insensitive to their babies' signals, but who were not as rejecting as the mothers of avoidant babies. They held their babies closely, but were awkward instead of tender. They rarely showed affection. These mothers appeared to handle babies primarily to attend to the infants' needs.

As a result of their experiences with their caregivers, babies apparently develop expectations about the caregiver's predictability and reliability (Lamb, 1981). These expectations are reflected in the quality of the baby's attachment and the baby's socialization. Securely attached babies respond cooperatively to their mothers, cry little, are affectionate, and are neither spoiled nor overdependent. They show a balance between independence and harmonious interaction with others (Ainsworth, Bell, and Stayton, 1974).

Ainsworth's group found that babies appeared to be more influenced by their mothers' responsiveness than mothers were influenced by the characteristics of their babies. But the effect of an infant's characteristics on a caregiver have often been overlooked. As we saw in Chapter 5, research has established the presence among infants of various activity or temperament types that affect the emotional quality of the mother-infant interaction. A study by H. Rudolph Schaffer and Peggy Emerson (1964b) indicates that babies who actively resist cuddling tend to develop attachments later than cuddlers do. "For some infants," say Schaffer and Emerson, "it appears contact is not comforting." Cuddlers have a more intense attachment to their caregivers throughout the first year of life than noncuddlers do, but this difference seems to disappear during the second year, apparently as a result of the infant and mother adapting to each other's style. In Schaffer and Emerson's study, babies who actively resisted contact did not always prevent social interaction between themselves and their parents. Instead, each baby and his or her parents gradually evolved a system of social interaction that did not depend on physical contact. The intensity of these attachments bore no relation to feeding, weaning, or toilet-training practices. Once again, maternal responsiveness and the amount of mother-child interaction were related to attachment. Babies were more strongly attached to mothers who responded rapidly to their needs and who spent more time interacting with them.

Because the distress and comfort of infants and their parents are likely to be reciprocal, a fussy baby can be especially difficult for parents. Studies show that parents of babies who fuss frequently are likely to wait longer before responding to their baby's cries than do parents of babies who fuss infrequently (Dunn, 1977). This may be analogous to the tale of the boy who cried wolf; parents of fussy babies may interpret their signals of distress as being simply bids for attention, or if the babies do not quiet easily, the parents may decide that since responding has little effect, they may as well ignore the babies' cries until they become too loud to disregard. Babies who quiet easily, on the other hand, are likely to reinforce their parents' attention and make them feel more secure as caregivers. In this connection, Susan Goldberg (1977) notes that because parents need to feel they can respond to their baby's signals and satisfy his or her needs, the baby whose signs are easy to read enhances the parents' feelings of competence. Thus the baby whose signals say clearly, "I'm hungry," "I'm bored," or "I'm wet," who sucks vigorously and smiles freely is also the one who is most likely to make parents feel successful and important.

IT'S NOT ALWAYS MOTHER

Even in the same culture, no two sets of parents have precisely the same attitude toward their children, nor do they rear them in exactly the same way. As we have seen, the responsiveness of the parent to an infant's signals is crucial to the kind of bond the infant forms. An ambivalent or avoidant bond, however, is still a form of attachment. Schaffer and Emerson (1964a) found that, whether the mother-infant interaction consists primarily of caregiving activity or of social play, the attachment that develops seems equally strong.

Although most research on attachment has focused on the bond between infant and mother, there is evidence that babies become attached to more than one person. Babies in the original Israeli kibbutzim, for example, became attached to both mother and *metapelet*, the primary caregiver in the kibbutz nursery (Fox, 1977). Only recently has the bond between babies and fathers become the subject of research.

Fathers as Attachment Figures

Studies show that the attachment between babies and fathers is also strong and that it might serve needs that are not met in the infant-mother relationship. In traditional nuclear families, fathers spend little time with young babies. Hence they have been regarded as relatively unimportant in their children's early social development. It appears, however, that infants become attached to both parents at about the same time and that a father's function goes beyond the role of occasional mother substitute (Lamb, 1978c).

Fathers become as deeply attached to their infants as mothers do. As caregivers, they have been found to be nurturant and competent, and their involvement with their babies tends to complement that of the mothers. During the first few days in the hospital, for example, middle-class fathers and mothers tend to spend an equal amount of time with their newborn babies. Both fathers and mothers look and smile at their babies, talk to and kiss them, explore their bodies, and give them their bottles. Given

Fathers are deeply attached, competent caregivers, who engage in a great deal of rough-and-tumble play with babies, whether they are boys or girls. (Jean Boughton/The Picture Cube)/(© R. Lynn Goldberg 1980)

the opportunity, lower-class fathers also appear to be nurturant and competent with their newborn babies (Parke and Sawin, 1976). When, for example, their baby shows distress during a feeding, both father and mother show their sensitivity in the same way; they stop the feeding, look at the baby, and pat the infant solicitously.

Fathers are not only likely to be attached to their infants and involved in their development during the first two years but also to interact with the babies in a different manner from the pattern shown by mothers (Lamb, 1977). Most of the time, mothers pick up their babies to care for them; when fathers pick them up, it is generally to play. Mothers play such traditional games as peekaboo and pat-a-cake; fathers engage in rough-and-tumble play, regardless of the infant's sex (Lamb, 1976b).

Perhaps in response to the differences in the ways fathers and mothers behave with babies, when infants from twelve to eighteen months are with both parents in a stressful situation, they will go to the mother (Lamb, 1976a). But in other situations, babies either show no preference or prefer their fathers. When alone with either parent in a stress-free situation, a baby is likely to smile at him or her and vocalize more frequently than the baby does when both parents are in the room. In addition, in terms of overall interaction, when observed in their homes, infant boys generally show a preference for their fathers, whereas infant girls may prefer either parent (Lamb, 1976c).

Multiple Caregiving

In today's world, multiple caregiving is a frequent form of infant care even among babies who are not in institutions. Does the lack of a central caregiver mean that a baby will suffer from discontinuous or inadequate interaction? Research by Michael Rutter (1971) indicates that when the main attachment figure shares caregiving with other people, as when mothers work or when the baby is part of an extended

When Fathers Are "Mothers"

It is generally taken for granted that mothers are the primary caregivers, the major influence on the baby's developing personality. Even researchers who study the effect of fathers on babies' cognitive and social development typically conduct their investigations in traditional two-parent families, where they have found consistent differences in the ways that mothers and fathers interact with their infants. However, a study by Tiffany Field (1978) looked at fathers who were primary caregivers.

Field compared twelve fathers who were primary caregivers with twelve traditional mothers and twelve fathers who played the traditional role of secondary caregiver. All the parents were white, middle-class, and college-educated. The parents brought their four-month-old babies to a laboratory where the baby sat in an infant seat opposite the parent. Field asked the parents to pretend the pair were at home, playing together at the kitchen table. Then the parent was left to entertain the baby while videocameras operated, taping three different three-minute interactions.

Whether the parent was a father or mother, there was no difference in the amount of talking that went on. Babies had their noses wiped, their burps mopped up, and their needs attended to whether a father or a mother was present.

But Field found significant differences among the three groups. Primary caregivers—whether father or mother—laughed less and smiled more than did the fathers who were secondary caregivers. They also imitated their babies' grimaces more often and mimicked their vocalizations in the high-pitched style that is a characteristic of baby talk.

Fathers, whether primary or secondary caregivers, played more games and poked at their babies more than mothers did. The fathers also held the babies' arms and legs less than did mothers. Fathers of sons played more games and did more high-pitched mimicking than did fathers of daughters.

The similarities that distinguished parents who had the primary responsibility for a baby's care from fathers who did not led Field to speculate that many observed father-mother differences may be the result of the different amounts of experience mothers and fathers traditionally have with their infants. Parents who spend a good deal of time with their babies, she suggests, imitate their offspring more because they have learned that babies enjoy being imitated. They imitate grimaces instead of laughing because grim-

family, children will thrive as long as the other caregivers provide stable relationships.

Research (e.g., Gewirtz, 1965) indicates that many of the children reared in Israeli kibbutzim show normal social and emotional development. In the past, infants in kibbutzim were often reared communally in residential nurseries by several caregivers and saw their parents for only a few hours a day or on weekends. In such arrangements, the kibbutz caregiver saw to the daily needs and training of the child, and the parents primarily provided emotional gratification (Beit-Hallahmi and Rabin, 1977). Again the conclusion emerges that parents may be absent for significant amounts of time without radically influencing attachment patterns, as long as someone who cares is present.

There is little evidence that infants reared by multiple caregivers will develop differently from those reared by a single caregiver. Although Zambian infants are reared by multiple caregivers, their development of attachment and

aces are characteristic of a four-month-old infant.

But some male-female differences emerged from a study in Sweden, where legislation has made it financially possible for parents to share caregiving responsibilities. Michael Lamb and associates (1982) studied fifty-two middle-class families, half of whom were traditional and half of whom either shared or reversed the responsibilities for child care. Interviewed shortly before the birth of their babies, the traditional and nontraditional couples fell neatly into two groups. The traditional fathers found work more fulfilling and parenthood less fulfilling than their wives did. These fathers planned little involvement in the care of their babies. In the nontraditional families, the fathers found work less fulfilling and parenthood more fulfilling than their wives did. These nontraditional fathers planned extensive involvement in the care of their babies.

Despite the difference in attitudes, the fathers' behavior in both types of families was more alike than different. When the babies were three and eight months old, the investigators observed each parent alone with his or her baby for an hour. Behavior divided by gender. Mothers in both kinds of families touched, tickled, kissed, and tended their babies more than the fathers did. They also smiled and talked to the infants more. Whether these gender differences are the result of biology or socialization remains open to speculation, as does the question of the possible effects of such differences on the infant's personality.

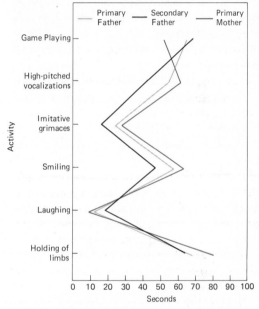

SOURCE: Adapted from T. Field, "Interaction Behaviors of Primary versus Secondary Caretaker Fathers," *Developmental Psychology,* 14 (1978), 183–184.

stranger wariness follows a course similar to that of infants reared by a single caregiver. Studies of infants in day care have failed to find any evidence that such care interferes with the development of attachment to mothers or other primary caregivers. In one such study, Richard Kearsley and his associates (1975) followed twenty-four day-care and twenty-eight home-reared infants from the time they were three and a half months until they were twenty-nine months old. The babies were from white and Chinese-American families who were both working- and middle-class. The investigators found no differences in the amount of separation distress shown by the day-care and home-reared infants, and in both sets of babies, separation distress peaked around nine months and again around thirteen months.

As we shall see in the next chapter, most studies of day care have been undertaken in excellent centers, often those connected with universities. These day-care centers offer en-

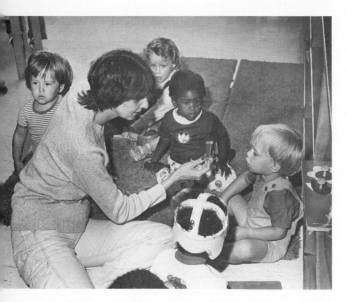

Early studies found that life in institutions had harmful effects on both intellectual and social development, but later studies have shown that when given intellectual stimulation and consistent care, as they are in this foundling hospital, children develop normally. (The New York Foundling Hospital/Center for Parent and Child Development)

riched programs and are not simply custodial institutions. In high-quality programs, infants develop normally, both emotionally and intellectually; the bond between mother and infant remains intact; and children have broad opportunities to interact with peers (Belsky and Steinberg, 1978). However, in the only study to assess the quality of day-care centers, 11 percent of the 280 nonprofit centers and 50 percent of the 103 proprietary centers were rated as "poor" (Keyserling, 1972).

A more serious challenge to an infant's well-being is a loss or lack of mothering. Early studies of children reared in institutions found devastating effects on their social and intellectual development, but it is now clear that these unfortunate children suffered from a general lack of the stimulation necessary to social and cognitive growth as well as from the absence of a single stable caregiver. The babies in Lebanese institutions discussed in Chapter 6 showed gains in cognitive growth as well as in physical development when interesting objects were introduced into their lives for only a few minutes each day.

Research with monkeys also suggests that development can follow a relatively normal course in the absence of a parental relationship. Monkeys raised without mothers or mother surrogates but with other baby monkeys for company were more normal in their adult social and sexual behavior than were monkeys raised with a surrogate mother but without peer contact. These findings support Lawrence Kohlberg's (1969) suggestion that it is the opportunity for pleasurable social interaction that is important to the infant's social-emotional development, not a specific tie to a caregiver.

Not all infants who suffer maternal deprivation are able to cope with their loss. An infant whose attachment to a primary caregiver has been ruptured may develop depression, or an extreme sadness. The British child psychiatrist John Bowlby (1953) has observed what he regards as depression in fifteen- to thirty-month-old healthy infants after they had been separated from their families and placed in a hospital or other residential institution. After an initial phase of active protest and crying, such an infant falls into a phase of despair. The baby becomes withdrawn and inactive, makes no demands of the environment, cries intermittently though without specific cause, and seems to feel increasing hopelessness and sadness. Later, the depressed infant gradually moves out of this phase into one of increased emotional distance. Now he or she interacts in a pleasant but shallow manner with institutional caregivers, and when parents visit, the baby responds in an aloof and detached way. If the separation is only temporary, such children when they return home may continue for a time either to treat their parents as strangers or to cling to them excessively and refuse to be left alone (Schaffer, 1977).

Temporary ruptures of the attachment relationship rarely appear to have long-lasting effects, however. Bowlby (1956) found that boys and girls in middle childhood who had been hospitalized for long periods during their first two years showed no obvious signs of impaired relationships with their parents.

CLASS, CULTURE, AND PERSONALITY

Although children, no matter what their social class or culture, become attached to their caregivers, parent-child relationships vary widely across classes and cultures. And differences in this basic relationship can have lasting effects on children's development.

Jerome Kagan and Steven Tulkin (1971) have studied the influence of social class on maternal attitudes and behavior. Their observations of ten-month-old babies showed some similarities across classes: both middle- and lower-class mothers held, tickled, kissed, and bounced their babies. But other maternal behavior often differed. A middle-class mother was more likely than a lower-class mother to vocalize within two feet of her baby, imitate the baby's sounds, engage in prolonged "positive interaction," give verbal rewards, and encourage her baby to walk. About two-thirds of the lower-class mothers in the study used food to soothe their irritable babies, whereas less than one-third of the middle-class mothers solved problems with food.

When Kagan and Tulkin tested these babies in the laboratory, they found no class differences in the babies' levels of reactivity to meaningful and meaningless speech. However, middle-class babies quieted more dramatically to highly meaningful speech with a high degree of inflection than to other stimuli. In addition, they were more likely than lower-class children to look at a stranger after hearing such speech.

Middle-class infants also quieted more to their mothers' voices than to strangers' voices, and they vocalized more than lower-class infants did after listening to recordings of their mothers' voices.

Parent-infant relationships also vary across societies. Urie Bronfenbrenner (1970) has described some of the differences between the Soviet Union and the United States in the parent-infant relationship and the socialization of children. Russian babies receive significantly more physical handling than their American counterparts do. Breast feeding is virtually universal in Russia, and babies are held most of the time, even when not being fed. Russian babies get much more hugging, kissing, and cuddling than American babies do, but at the same time they are held much more tightly and are allowed little freedom of movement. Russian mothers are generally much more solicitous and protective, and their efforts to protect the baby from discomfort, illness, or injury curtail the baby's mobility and initiative. Such differences in child rearing across cultures can have subtle but deep effects on personality development.

THE DEVELOPMENT OF SOCIABILITY

Although attachment to parents is of primary significance in the life of the infant, the spectrum of significant relationships soon broadens. By the time a little girl reaches a year and a half she must contend with her older brother as a potential threat or aid to her well-being, just as she must contend with his playmates, her own playpen peers, and possibly her younger siblings. It is within the first two years of life that we find the beginnings of sociability. During the development of this aspect of personality, babies regard other human beings with varying degrees of warmth, positive expectations and trust, depending upon their early experiences. The development of social skills begins with the emergence of a self-concept, efforts to achieve competence, and the demand for autonomy.

Self-Concept

From their early experience, infants appear to develop a first crude sense of "me" and "not me." These experiences begin in the first hours of life, for detailed studies of interactions of babies and their mothers reveal that a baby is a social creature from birth (Sander, 1977; Schaffer, 1977). Although they may not be aware of their changing responses, most mothers quickly learn to read their babies' cues and adjust their own behavior so that the baby takes the lead in their interactions. During these turn-taking experiences, babies control the rate, level, and nature of their experiences (Stern, 1977).

The infant's sense of self forms an increasingly noticeable and integral part of his or her sociability from the latter part of the first year. As a result of cognitive development, infants become conscious of themselves as separate and distinct persons. This blossoming self-awareness in turn influences their interest in others and how they relate to them.

The baby's developing sense of self has been explored in a series of studies by Michael Lewis and Jeanne Brooks (Brooks and Lewis, 1976; Lewis and Brooks, 1974, 1975). They found that by twenty to twenty-four months, babies have developed a self-concept, readily recognizing themselves and other people, reacting in terms of the gender, age, familiarity, height, and facial features of others. In one experiment, infants as young as seven months stared with apparent surprise at a midget. Their eyes widened, their eyebrows arched, and their mouths rounded, as if they expected a small body to have a child's face.

In order to test infants' recognition of themselves, Lewis and Brooks placed babies before a mirror after first surreptitiously dabbing rouge on their noses. No babies under a year seemed to recognize that the smudged nose in the mirror

belonged to them, but among babies from fifteen to eighteen months, 25 percent immediately touched their noses, and by twenty-four months, 75 percent grabbed for their noses as soon as they looked in the mirror. When a similar study was carried out among children with Down's syndrome, most were nearly three years old before they reached for their noses (Mans, Cicchetti, and Sroufe, 1978). This delay in self-recognition among retarded children indicates that self-awareness is closely related to a child's level of cognitive development.

The development of self-concept also shows in the reactions of infants as they look at pictures or videotapes of themselves and others. Lewis and Brooks found that babies looked longer and smiled more at their own pictures than at any others and that they reacted most to videotapes of themselves. They vocalized and imitated themselves twice as much as they imitated strange babies, blinking, waving, and sticking out their tongues. It appears that infants as young as nine months can recognize and react with pleasure to themselves and that they are especially responsive to those who are most "like me."

Striving for Competence

As infants' skills and sense of self develop, they find increasing satisfaction in acting on, exploring, and getting to know the social world. Rheingold and Eckerman (1970) point out that although infants show distress at being left by their parents, they show no distress when they leave attachment figures to explore. When Eckerman and Rheingold (1974) placed ten-month-old babies in an unfamiliar environment and gave each the opportunity to approach and touch an unfamiliar toy or person, babies promptly approached the toys and played with them. They rarely made physical contact with the strangers; instead they looked at the strangers and smiled. These results suggest that looking and smiling at people serve an exploratory function similar to touching and manipulating toys.

Apparently, early exploratory behavior does not depend upon gender; it is a function of age. Rheingold and Eckerman (1970) recorded children's forays from their mothers, placing forty-eight children between one and five years old in an L-shaped yard behind a house, which allowed children to leave their mothers' field of vision. Although there were wide individual differences among children who were two or older, researchers could predict from the age of the child how far a boy or girl would travel from his or her mother. The investigators suggest that during the second year of life there is a decline in the infant's need for physical contact, a decline that is motivated by the desire to be competent, to know the social and object world: to touch, take apart, put together, figure out toys and other objects, and to evoke responses (smiling or attention) from new people. Novelty, complexity, and change—interesting new stimulation—draw infants away from the comfortable familiarity of attachment figures. But this new independence does not signal the end of attachment. The desire to be close to familiar and loved people and the desire to try out new experiences and expand one's competence appear to coexist throughout the life of the individual. An infant who is secure in his or her attachments feels safe to explore and to develop a sense of self as an independent agent or a causer of effects in the world. From their explorations, infants bring back new knowledge and abilities that they may incorporate into increasingly differentiated and interesting interactions with familiar and cherished others.

Autonomy

The first concentrated push toward autonomy, or independence, appears toward the end of the second year, when infants enter a period of social development that drives parents to despair. The baby becomes reluctant to agree with anything parents suggest and the consistent response to all questions or commands is "No!"

This "negativistic crisis" grows out of the infant's awareness of a mental distinction between self and others, a distinction between his or her own will and the will of others. Until now, infants have had to depend on caregivers for the satisfaction of most needs, in what David Ausubel (1958) has called *executive dependence:* the parent acts as an executive arm, instrumental to the infant's needs. As infants become aware of their own competence and effect on the world, they strive for *executive independence,* or autonomy. They want to do things for themselves. The negativistic infant is attempting to discover the limits of his or her center of activity and initiative: the self. Parents frequently note that

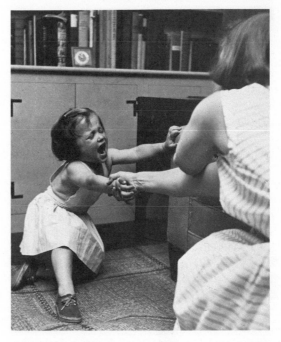

Toward the end of the second year, when infants begin to become autonomous, they go through a period of negativism when they clash continually with parents in an attempt to discover the limits of their own competence. (© Suzanne Szasz)

the clash of wills seems to be conflict for conflict's sake; the infant is concerned not with an issue but with a principle.

This developing sense of control, competence, and autonomy will be important throughout children's lives. It appears to underlie what will later become their *locus of control*, the degree to which they believe that they or others control their fate. People with an internal locus of control generally believe that they are responsible for what they do and that they can affect what happens to them. People with an external locus of control generally believe that what they do makes little difference and that other forces — such as luck, fate, or powerful other people — determine what happens to them.

ATTACHMENT AND LATER PERSONALITY

As babies move into the second year of life, society begins to apply its pressures. In the next chapter we shall see that parents are the major socializing agents and that as toddlers show greater competence and increased independence, their parents will expect an accompanying growth of responsibility. Toward the end of the second year, for example, infants may find themselves subjected to toilet training.

If a secure attachment to parents allows infants a greater scope to explore the world and to interact comfortably with other people, then we would expect this bond to influence later social development. Some investigators have found such a connection, indicating that babies with secure attachments become competent, independent toddlers.

Leah Matas, Richard Arend, and Alan Sroufe (1978) presented two-year-olds with increasingly difficult problems, the last of which — weighting a lever to lift a piece of candy from a plastic box — was beyond the capacity of a two-year-old to solve. They found that children who had been rated as securely attached when they were twelve and eighteen months old attacked the

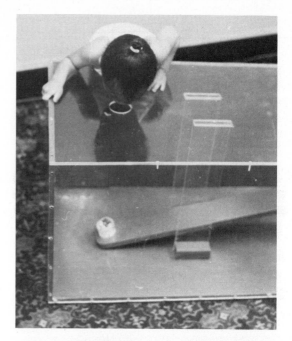

Weighting a lever to get the piece of candy from this plastic box is beyond a two-year-old's problem-solving ability (1), but a securely attached youngster like this little girl accepts her mother's advice (2), tests the lever (3), weights it with a block (4), retrieves the candy (5), and enjoys it. (© L. Alan Sroufe)

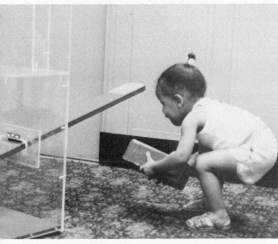

problems with an enthusiasm and persistence not generally present among children who had earlier been rated as either ambivalent or avoidant in their attachments. When they reached the insoluble problem, securely attached children were less likely to throw tantrums and more likely to accept help from their mothers than were the children with insecure attachments.

Differences in maternal behavior were just as pronounced. When their two-year-olds faced the difficult problem, mothers of securely attached children generally offered small hints that allowed the children to feel they had solved the problem themselves. Mothers of insecurely attached children, on the other hand, tended to allow their toddlers to become frustrated before they offered help, and then the mothers often solved the problem themselves.

In another study, children who had been rated on the quality of their attachments at fifteen months were observed in a nursery-school situation at three and a half years (Waters, Wippman, and Sroufe, 1979). The preschoolers who had been rated as having secure attachments were less hesitant and withdrawn than the insecurely attached children. They were also more likely to be leaders, to suggest play activities, to have their company sought by other children, and to be sympathetic to the distress of others. Striking differences in personal competence and other aspects of personality related to self-concept also appeared among the toddlers. Those who had been securely attached were more self-directed, displayed greater curiosity about new things, showed greater enjoyment in learning new skills, pursued their goals more forcefully, and were less likely to behave in a turned-off, "spaced-out" manner than were the insecurely attached children.

It is important to note that the children in both studies lived in stable environments, where both parents were present in the home. Studies of children whose parents are divorced or who live in families that have moved frequently or faced sporadic unemployment would probably

Studies have found that babies who develop secure attachments to their parents become competent, independent preschoolers, who are curious about new things and enjoy learning new skills. (David Powers/Stock, Boston, Inc.)

uncover quite different patterns of personality, showing different degrees of continuity. Nevertheless, as we shall see, early experiences are not irreversible.

EARLY EXPERIENCE

The notion that early experience is of primary importance for later life was popularized by Sigmund Freud (1917). His idea that certain experiences during infancy are crucial for personality development has been adopted by developmental psychologists whose theoretical outlooks are otherwise quite different.

Types of Effects

Much of the evidence demonstrating the effects of early experience comes from studies of animals. Severe restriction or deprivation of experience in early infancy has striking effects on behavior in animals, and much of this behavior

seems to persist into adulthood. These deprived animals are often quite different from normal animals in both social and emotional development. For example, puppies who spent their first few months in isolation from other puppies and from human beings showed "bizarre postures and a tendency to be unresponsive to playthings, people, and other puppies" (J. Scott, 1967). A less extremely deprived puppy will behave more normally but may have an intense fear of strange people and strange situations. Chimpanzees reared in a restricted environment also are more timid, especially in novel situations (Menzel, Davenport, and Rogers, 1963).

If impoverishment of the early environment can have such strong effects, we might expect that an enriched early environment would also have a major impact on animals. A variety of evidence suggests that this is so. Whereas restriction often produces fearful animals, extra stimulation at an early age often produces animals that are bolder than normal (Denenberg, 1966), even when the extra stimulation consists of mild electric shocks. In addition to being bold, animals raised in enriched early environments also tend to be curious in new situations (Forgus, 1954). Such evidence indicates that in some species, early experiences have important and enduring effects on the way animals respond to the world.

Limits on Effects

Although early learning can have pervasive effects on later development, some research suggests that the connection is more complicated than it appears. A brief look at imprinting in animals and at the development of fear and laughter in babies indicates that there are strong constraints on the effects of early experience.

SENSITIVE PERIODS Many animals form strong, long-lasting social attachments, but research has led some investigators to conclude that such attachments can form only during a sharply restricted period of life, called a *sensitive period*. In some species of birds, this attachment, called *imprinting*, forms when a baby bird, fresh from the shell, sees and follows a moving object. In the normal course of events, the first thing a baby bird sees is its mother, so that

The first moving object these baby geese saw was ethologist Konrad Lorenz. As a result, they became imprinted on him, following Lorenz around as if he were their mother. (Thomas McAroy/Time-Life Pictures Agency, © Time, Inc.)

the bird becomes imprinted to her; but birds also have become imprinted to human beings, rubber balls, and other objects. A bird overcomes substantial obstacles in order to follow this object (or others like it) and shows great distress when the object is out of sight (E. Hess, 1964). A young bird will try to feed the object to which it is imprinted and may even use it as a model for a suitable mate (an effect that has introduced complications into the lives of certain ethologists). But imprinting occurs only during a sensitive period shortly after the animal's birth, and the attachment can be changed. Ducklings that were imprinted to human beings have changed their attachment to mature ducks (E. Hess, 1972), and William Mason and M. D. Kenney (1974) managed to switch a young monkey's attachment from another monkey to a dog.

Some theorists have suggested that the bond between human babies and their mothers develops in the same way that baby birds or goats or sheep become imprinted to their mothers. If this were true, it would have significant implications for child rearing. But as we have seen, human attachment is far more complicated and diverse than animal bonding. The importance of the imprinting phenomenon lies in two implications: first, that sensitive periods might exist in human beings during which certain kinds of learning, such as language acquisition, must occur if they are to take place at all; and second, that experiences during infancy can have enduring effects on a child's later development, as Freud maintained. As we trace the social development of children, it will become clear that early experiences are important but do not irrevocably determine the way a child develops.

OTHER CONSTRAINTS Although strong emotions may affect human learning, an emotion requires some learning if it is to develop. Consider, for example, some of the complex relationships that are involved in the development of fear. A startled and wailing neonate is not truly afraid. Although sudden loud noises, un-expected events, and physical pain may produce crying, distress, and avoidance reactions in new-borns and very young babies, their responses are not fear in the sense that we use the term.

True fear requires a rather sophisticated level of cognitive development, and several studies have demonstrated the cognitive underpinnings of the emotion. To be afraid, babies must be able to hold the feared object in memory, and the sight of the object must call up the per-ceptual and emotional experiences that were connected with it in the past. Later, the mere mention of the object will be enough to evoke fear.

Changes in the nature of children's fears re-ported in early studies by Arthur Jersild and Frances Holmes (1935) clearly indicate the in-creasing importance of cognitive development (see Figure 14.2). For example, no children less than two years old were afraid of physical harm, and few were afraid of the dark, being alone in the dark, or imaginary creatures; but a signifi-cant percentage of four- to six-year-olds feared these things. Such fears, in contrast to "fear" of sudden loud noises, require imaginative re-constructions based on the generalization of past experience.

Similar developmental trends appeared in a study by Sandra Scarr and Philip Salapatek (1970). They reported that between the ages of five and eighteen months, there was an increase in infants' fear of strangers, of a grotesque mask, and of heights (as measured by the visual-cliff technique described in Chapter 10). These fears could develop only after the infants learned about the familiar and safe aspects of their en-vironments. During the same period, there was no increase in infants' fear of loud noises or of a jack-in-the-box that suddenly popped up at them.

Suppose that when a baby girl was six months old her older brother suddenly thrust his head over the side of her crib and made a grotesque face. Would she scream with fear? She might laugh at her brother's face but scream at the

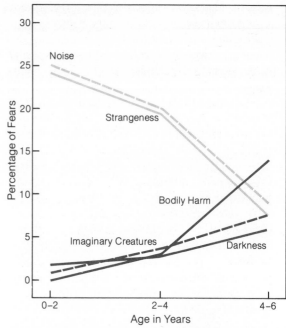

Figure 14.2 Developmental changes in the na-ture of children's fears as indicated by their responses to different objects and situations. (Adapted from Jersild and Holmes, 1935)

same behavior in a stranger. Laughter and fear both seem to occur in response to a stimulus that is unfamiliar or incongruous in comparison with a familiar standard of reference.

Such responses appeared when Alan Sroufe and Jane Wunsch (1972) studied the develop-ment of laughter during the first year of life; they found that babies laughed when confronted with a mask instead of becoming fearful, as the infants in the Scarr and Salapatek study had done. The discrepancy was the result of two important differences between the studies: the mask that elicited laughter in the Sroufe and Wunsch study was human-looking and was worn by the baby's mother; the mask that elic-ited fear in the Scarr and Salapatek study was nonhuman and was worn by the experimenter. Sroufe and Wunsch speculated that an incongru-ous event arouses tension that, depending on the circumstances, will either lead to crying and avoidance or be released in laughter.

Findings such as these on fear and laughter suggest additional limitations to the notion that early learning experiences automatically establish enduring personality dispositions. They indicate, just as the imprinting data do, that an infant or a child is not always open to the same learning experiences. They also suggest that the same learning experience may produce different effects, depending on the infant's genetic inheritance, maturational state, cognitive growth, past experiences, and present surroundings.

A secure attachment, then, does not protect a child against all future environmental insult, nor does an insecure attachment doom a child to become withdrawn and inept at solving life's problems. Nevertheless, it seems clear that a secure attachment gives a child an advantage at the starting line.

SUMMARY

1. In studying personality development, psychologists have paid special attention to attachment, the primary bond between infant and caregiver. This early love relationship takes months to develop, and ethologists have suggested that it passes through three stages, so that a baby who is initially comforted by anyone can finally be comforted only by specific attachment figures.

2. The basic function of attachment is to keep the baby alive; but attachment is thought to be only one of four complementary behavioral systems, which are expressed in attachment, fear or wariness, affiliation, and exploration. As the infant develops a primary attachment, separation distress and wariness of strangers may appear. These reactions seem to depend on the quality of the infant's attachment to the caregiver, the situation, and the characteristics of strangers.

3. The attachment bond differs in quality, and there appears to be a connection between the characteristics of a bond and the style of care given the baby. Securely attached babies actively seek out their mothers after a separation and are quickly comforted by them. Insecurely attached babies may shun contact with their mothers or else may be ambivalent, alternating between seeking contact and angrily squirming away.

4. Mothers are not the only attachment figures. Babies also become attached to their fathers, and this relationship may serve needs not met in the infant-mother relationship. Some babies have many caregivers, but as long as the relationships are stable, babies thrive and attachment develops along the same course seen among babies with a single caregiver.

5. Social class and culture affect the attitudes and behavior of the primary caregiver. There are, for example, consistent class differences in language usage between American mothers and infants, and there are consistent cultural differences in the amount of physical affection and freedom given babies in the United States and the U.S.S.R.

6. Babies are social creatures from birth. As their sense of self develops and as they become motivated by a desire for competence, infants generally need less physical contact with their parents. The two-year-old's negativistic behavior represents a concentrated push for autonomy.

7. Although early experience can have pervasive and enduring effects on later development, investigations of early learning and behavior suggest that there are strong constraints on the effects of early experience. These constraints may involve sensitive periods in development as well as maturational state, cognitive growth, and previous experience. Just as important is experience that follows early deprivation or crisis.

The Child Within the Family

Three-year-old Jennifer pushed a chair to the kitchen cabinet, quietly climbed to the formica counter, and stood on her tiptoes, stretching her hand up, up, toward the clock that hung on the wall. There was no crystal over the dial and her small fingers could just reach the hands. She was industriously pushing the minute hand around the dial when her mother entered the room. "Jennifer," said her mother, "just what are you doing?" Jennifer looked over her shoulder, slowly lowered her hand, and said, "You should watch me." In three years, Jennifer had clearly built up a set of expectations—not only as to what was permitted but also as to the proper role for parent and child. She had also learned that a response that made her mother laugh was likely to eliminate—or at least ameliorate—any possible punishment.

In this chapter, we shall trace the development of the child within the family, examining the role of the family in socialization, the ways in which various styles of discipline affect children, and the influence of brothers and sisters on the growing child. We shall compare the social development of children placed in good day care with that of children reared at home. We shall discuss the effects of a father's absence from the home and compare it with the influence of marital discord. We shall look at the powerful effect social class has on child-rearing practices and at the stresses and strengths of black families. We shall examine child-rearing practices in nontraditional families, and finally, we shall look at failed rearing in the form of child abuse, discussing the part that parents, children, and society play in the problem.

THE PROCESS OF SOCIALIZATION

The process of absorbing the attitudes, values, and customs of a society is called *socialization*. Slowly, the growing child is pressured to behave in approved ways and to conform to cultural standards. During the first few years of life, the family is the major agent of socialization. By encouraging appropriate behavior and discouraging behavior that is unacceptable, parents transmit the culture to their offspring. The family's power is considerable. Children depend upon their parents for material wants: food, clothing, shelter, and other physical necessities. They also depend upon them for attention, affection, physical contact, and play. Because the manner in which parents fulfill children's physical and psychological needs affects children's behavior, parental control exerts a strong influence on the kind of person a child becomes.

But parents are not the only agents of socialization. From the very beginning, television brings the wider world into the home, reinforcing or negating parental influence. Brothers and sisters also play an important role in early socialization, and as we shall see in the next chapter, once children start school the effect of parents and siblings is modified by peers, teachers, and other adults. In addition, children's appearance, health, and temperament will affect not only how they respond to others but also how others approach them. Socialization, like other aspects of development, grows out of the interaction of many influences.

The socialization process differs across cultures, but many psychologists believe that four basic mechanisms operate in all children in all cultures. These mechanisms are (1) the desire to obtain acceptance, affection, regard, and recognition; (2) the wish to avoid the unpleasant feelings that follow rejection or punishment; (3) the tendency to imitate the actions of others; and (4) the desire to be like specific people whom the child has grown to respect, admire, or love (identification).

PARENTS

As babies approach the end of infancy, the role of parents changes. Instead of playing with them and attending to their needs, parents begin to demand that their children do certain things and refrain from doing others. By now, children's increasing mobility and sureness, their burgeoning mental powers, and their growing grasp of language make it possible for them to understand parental instructions and to follow parental suggestions. These new abilities also make it possible for children to refuse parental demands. The way the conflict between children's wishes and those of their parents is resolved has a profound effect on the behavior and personality of the growing child.

Style of Discipline

Few parents set out deliberately to "socialize" their toddlers; instead their first demands and restrictions are aimed at making family life possible. They attempt to instill a sense of responsibility in their children in order to guard them from danger, to protect the parents' belongings from destruction, and to teach the children to fit into family routines (Sears, Maccoby, and Levin, 1957). The way parents teach their children to stay out of the street, to refrain from scribbling on the walls, and to eat with a fork instead of their fingers will in part depend upon their attitude toward children. If they believe that children are full of dark urges that must be stamped out, they will use harsh, authoritarian measures of control. If, on the other hand, they believe that children are naturally good — perfect little buds that will unfold to form beautiful blossoms — they will abdicate attempts at discipline, allowing their child freedom for self-actualization. In truth, few parents are as extreme as either of these two examples would indicate, but styles of discipline do fall along that continuum.

No matter what approach parents take, they establish and maintain discipline by a system of rewards and punishment. In addition, parents serve as models of acceptable behavior. But despite years of study, psychologists' search for the most successful combination of disciplinary techniques has not resulted in the discovery of a foolproof method of socialization.

The most extensive research has been conducted by Diana Baumrind (e.g., 1968, 1972b) and her associates, who have spent twenty years studying disciplinary styles among parents of preschool children in an attempt to discover the connection between the way children are reared and their personalities. The investigators gathered information on parents from lengthy interviews, standardized tests, and observations in the home. They also watched the children in nursery school and talked to teachers and parents. The styles of most parents, Baumrind found, fit one of four patterns: authoritarian, permissive, nonconformist, or authoritative (Lamb and Baumrind, 1978).

To the *authoritarian* parent, obedience is a virtue. When a child's actions or beliefs conflict with the parent's view of right conduct, the child is punished forcefully. Respect for authority, work, and the preservation of order are important. The child must accept without question the parent's word on matters of right and wrong. As preschoolers, children of such parents tend to be overprotected and dependent. Daughters tend to set low goals for themselves and to withdraw in the face of frustration, whereas sons tend to be hostile.

The *permissive* parent avoids control, relying on reason alone and consulting children about policy decisions. The permissive parent is nonpunitive, accepting, and affirmative, and makes few demands for household responsibility and orderly behavior. Children are allowed to regulate their own activities and are not encouraged to obey externally defined standards. Despite the difference in disciplinary style, children of permissive parents resemble children reared by authoritarian parents, and tend to be dependent. Again, daughters set low goals, withdrawing in the face of frustration, and sons tend to be hostile.

Baumrind (Lamb and Baumrind, 1978) speculates that the children of permissive and authoritarian parents turn out similarly because both types of parents tend to shield their children from stress, thereby inhibiting the development of assertiveness and the ability to tolerate frustration. Passive permissiveness on the one hand and overprotectiveness on the other both produce dependent children.

The *nonconformist* parent, like the permissive parent, is against authority and authoritarianism but exerts more control and may demand high performance in some areas. As preschoolers, daughters of nonconformist parents are like the daughters of permissive and authoritarian parents: dependent children who set low goals for themselves and cope with frustration by withdrawing. The sons, however, are much more independent than sons of permissive and authoritarian parents; and they tend to set high goals for themselves.

The *authoritative* parent agrees that control is necessary but uses reason as well as power to achieve it. When directing the child's activities, the authoritative parent uses a rational, issue-oriented method and encourages verbal give-and-take, which the authoritarian parent does not tolerate. As a result, children experience firm control, in which necessary rules are enforced, their own demands are resisted, and they receive guidance. But in addition, their individuality is encouraged and they have ample opportunity to try out new skills. The aim is responsible conformity with group standards without the loss of independence (Baumrind, 1972b). Daughters of authoritative parents tend to be independent and socially responsible; the sons are also socially responsible but no more independent than average. According to Baumrind, the children's social responsibility develops because the parents impose clearly communicated, realistic demands on their children.

Most parents, believes Baumrind (Lamb and Baumrind, 1978), want to produce *instrumentally competent* children—children who are "self-assertive, friendly with peers, and not intrusive with adults," a combination of social responsibility and independence. In their attempts to produce such children, parents use different disciplinary styles, but all of them implement their styles with the use of punishment, rewards, and modeling.

Regardless of disciplinary style, parents who produce instrumentally competent children punish them often. Authoritative parents (who are most effective at producing instrumental competence) include corporal punishment among their disciplinary techniques. But neither they nor other parents rely exclusively on physical punishment. Parents also punish by scolding, social isolation, withholding expected rewards, and the withdrawal of affection. No matter what kind of punishment is used, to be effective, it should come immediately after the misbehavior and the child should know exactly why he or she is being punished. If, for example, a three-year-old girl is spanked when her mother catches her smearing fingerprints on the wall, she should be told clearly that the spanking is for disfiguring the wall, not for using her brother's fingerpaints without permission. Discipline should also be consistent; to punish for painting the wall one day and to ignore it the following week only confuses a child.

Again, regardless of disciplinary style, punishment from a warm parent may be more effective

When a child must be disciplined, punishment from a warm parent appears to be more effective than punishment from a parent who is cold. (Robert Eckert/EKM-Nepenthe)

than punishment from a parent who is cold. Baumrind found that warmth, when associated with the firm control of authoritative parents, appears to produce socially responsible children. In a large study of five-year-olds, Robert Sears and his associates (Sears, Maccoby, and Levin, 1957) found that although most warm mothers did not use frequent physical punishment, those who did claimed that it worked. Relatively cold mothers who relied on physical punishment were much less likely to say that it was effective. Both studies, then, point to the importance of parental warmth.

Punishment is applied when children misbehave. But children are often good, and parents can support good behavior with reinforcement. Rewards for good behavior need not be tangible. Dimes, cookies, and special treats may be effective, but so are smiles, nods, pats, praise, hugs, or even tone of voice. In the study by Sears and his associates, warm mothers were especially likely to use lots of praise and tangible rewards with their children.

In addition to rewards and punishment, an extremely powerful influence on children's behavior is what they see their parents do. In Chapter 2, we noted that children imitate models; parents are permanent models for their growing children. They are powerful dispensers of rewards and punishment, and when they are warm and nurturant as well, they are precisely the kind of model that researchers have found to be most effective. Children who have been allowed time to develop a rewarding relationship with an adult model engage in far more imitation than children who have not (Bandura and Huston, 1961). When parents encourage their children's identification with them and approve of their attempts to imitate them, the modeling becomes even more effective. As we shall see in Chapter 17, identification with the parent of the same sex is a factor in children's learning of sex roles; in Chapter 18, we shall examine the role of identification in the development of morality and aggression.

In their investigations of child rearing, both Baumrind and Sears studied young children, with Baumrind concentrating on preschoolers and Sears on five-year-olds. To see if different methods of rearing had lasting effects, both researchers followed up the children they had studied. Baumrind found that by the time her preschoolers were nine years old, the differences in social competence among the groups had narrowed, so that although the distinctions remained, they were not nearly so striking (Baumrind, 1975). When Sears checked up on the children he had studied after a lapse of seven years, he found that twelve-year-old high achievers with high self-concepts generally had warm parents who had used reason and discussion with their young children instead of authoritarian control (Sears, 1970). The parents were also likely to discipline their children by using social isolation or withholding expected rewards, rather than by spanking or the withdrawal of their love. However, the high-achieving girls — but not the boys — tended to have permissive mothers, a finding that contradicts the results among Baumrind's preschoolers.

Predicting the Outcome

Placing the long-term results of these two studies side by side shows how difficult it is to single out the precise parental traits that lead to competent children and then write a prescription for successful child rearing. Perhaps as children grow, they require different sorts of responses from their parents, so that the kind of parental behavior that encourages competence at eight months would not encourage its development at three years. If we look again at infants who are developing attachments, we find that neither warmth nor firmness nor permissiveness but *sensitivity* is the single most important factor in producing a secure bond. To be sensitive to a baby's needs, a parent must interpret the baby's signals and respond effectively.

It may be that sensitive parents behave differently with their children over the course of childhood. If preschoolers are to become socially competent, for example, the last thing they need is to have every desire met. In the studies of toddlers, we saw that sensitive mothers who responded quickly to their babies' needs encouraged their two-year-olds to solve problems by themselves (Matas, Arend, and Sroufe, 1978). It was the mothers of insecurely attached babies who stepped in and solved their toddlers' problems. This indicates that parental sensitivity probably consists not in instant responsiveness but in empathic understanding of a child's needs. If that is the case, then parental behavior would change as the child developed; empathic parents would understand when their children needed guidance and when they should be allowed to strike out on their own (Lamb, 1981).

No matter how empathic, consistent, and reasonable parents are, however, there is no guarantee that their methods will produce a socially competent child. A child's personality results from an interaction between his or her own temperament, parental style and personality, and influences from the rest of the culture —which become progressively stronger after the child starts school. The methods a parent uses may be a response to the child's temperament, not a cause of it. One study that followed children from birth found that it was not children with difficult temperaments or children whose parents had maladaptive styles who needed psychiatric help, but children whose temperaments did not match their parents' styles. Disturbances arose when parental demands ran head on into children's temperamental characteristics, placing the children under heavy stress (Thomas, Chess, and Birch, 1968). The best that psychologists can do is to point out what patterns of parental behavior are connected with what sorts of children. They cannot, however, establish any sort of cause-effect relationship.

SIBLINGS

Until children start school, their brothers and sisters are their primary, if not their sole, playmates. Few studies have examined the interaction of siblings from the standpoint of socialization, but it would be amazing if the steady companionship did not play a major role in a child's socialization. Numerous studies have shown, however, that birth order appears to affect later personality.

Most of the available research indicates that first-borns tend to be conservative, anxious, highly verbal, high achievers, who are nurturant but domineering toward their younger siblings (Sutton-Smith and Rosenberg, 1970). Later-born children tend to be autonomous, flexible, tolerant, empathic, and popular with peers. In many studies of sibling influences, investigators give children or adults tests of various kinds and then look to see how highly their scores correlate with birth order. Other studies look at adult outcomes, for example, checking sibling patterns among Rhodes scholars or among people listed in *Who's Who*. In one such study, Frank Sulloway (1972) found that in major scientific controversies of the past, such as the battle over Darwin's theory of evolution, first-born sons tended to uphold the status quo whereas later-born sons tended to take the side of the challenging new theory.

Whether a child is male or female, surrounded by siblings of the same or opposite sex, or has one or many siblings also has a profound effect on personality development. Researchers have begun to look carefully at the way young sisters and brothers behave toward each other. A pair of studies by Michael Lamb (1978a, 1978b) indicate that preschoolers may facilitate their younger siblings' mastery of the physical world. Lamb observed infants with their preschool siblings, first when the infants were twelve months old, then again six months later. He found that on both occasions the babies carefully watched their older siblings, then often took over toys the older children had abandoned and imitated them. The older children talked to their baby brothers and sisters and offered them toys. Although boys touched their young siblings more than girls did, the girls were more sociable and nurturant and paid more attention to the infants.

One thing babies with older siblings learn quickly is that force is not an effective method of getting their way. The preschoolers in Lamb's studies were more likely than infant brothers or sisters to hit or snatch a toy away, and the babies did little hitting or grabbing. Younger siblings' reluctance to use force was reaffirmed in another study, in which eighteen-month-old babies who had older siblings were less likely than babies without siblings to grab toys from peers and squabble with them (Easterbrooks and Lamb, 1979).

Although Lamb's studies took place in a lab-

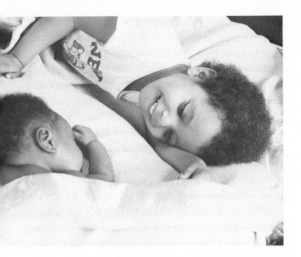

Siblings play important roles in one another's lives; the presence of a preschool brother or sister advances a younger sibling's mastery of the physical world. (© Suzanne Szasz)

Older sisters are generally more sociable and nurturant with baby brothers and sisters than are older brothers. (EKM-Nepenthe)

oratory setting, a study done in the home by Rona Abramovitch and her associates (Abramovitch, Corter, and Lando, 1979) also found that siblings play an important role in one another's social lives. Older boys hit, kicked, bit, and pinched their infant siblings more than older girls did; but the girls were every bit as likely to tussle over a toy, tease, threaten, or tell their mothers about their younger brothers' and sisters' misbehavior. And the older girls again played the nurturant little mother. Abramovitch found, as Lamb had, that the infants did most of the imitating; but she points out that the older children did 20 percent of it, banging play dough on the table, blowing cake crumbs, or dancing around in imitation of the infants.

Despite the thread of aggression that ran through the studies, none of the investigators felt that sibling rivalry was a dominant feature of the relationships. This observation agrees with lifelong studies of sibling relationships, which indicate that siblings tend to be egalitarian, close, and frank with one another, and to understand one another's problems (Cicirelli,

1979). Sibling influences tend to be very strong through the early school years and then diminish, only to reassert themselves in late adolescence and early adulthood.

VARIATIONS ON A THEME

Most research on personality development has focused on children in intact, white, middle-class families in which the father is the primary breadwinner. Such families, although they may conform to the American ideal, are not a majority in this society. Children live in a variety of ethnic groups, social classes, and family arrangements. Some children live with one parent, some have stepparents, some spend most of their waking hours in day care, some live amid continual marital conflict, and some are raised in nontraditional families. All these variations on the familiar theme provide experiences for the growing child that can affect the socialization process.

Day Care

A child in day care is both separated from primary caregivers for most of the day and subjected to the influence of many peers and substitute caregivers. It seems logical to assume that these circumstances influence the socialization process in some way.

The number of children in day care is growing, and the proportion of children under two that are enrolled is increasing at a rapid rate. In 1977, a survey of 2,536 day-care centers turned up an enrollment of 897,700 children; of these, 4.5 percent were under two years old (Connell, Layzer, and Goodson, 1979). While total enrollment in day-care centers had increased by 23 percent in eight years, enrollment of children under two had increased by 32 percent. These nearly 900,000 children represent only a small portion of the children in day care. Nursery schools and day-care centers together account for only 11 percent of the children in substitute care. The best estimates of the Office of Child Development indicate that 26 percent of children who need substitute care have a baby-sitter other than a relative come into their homes and another 16 percent are taken to someone else's home (*National Childcare Consumer Study*, 1975). We know almost nothing about either the quality or the effects of this kind of care, although a large study recently conducted in England indicates that children who are taken to a sitter's home fare less well than children in day-care centers, and that one-third of the children who spend their day in a sitter's home become withdrawn and passive (Bruner, 1980b).

Nor is much known about the effects of other forms of day care. When Jay Belsky and Laurence Steinberg (1978) reviewed the research that had been done, they concluded that it is impossible to judge the effects of day care on the basis of the scant evidence that is available. Research to date has been largely confined to high-quality care in centers connected with universities, where the daily program is designed to foster cognitive, emotional, and social development. Except for a single study (Moore, 1975),

no one has looked at any effects of day care that might linger or appear after the preschool years. In addition, comparisons of children in day care and those who are reared at home are generally invalid because parents who put their children in day care and parents who do not usually differ in their attitudes—toward day care, toward the maternal role, perhaps even toward children themselves. And finally, most research has consisted of testing children—usually in laboratories. Few researchers have explored the possible effects of day care on the family.

Bearing these limitations in mind, Belsky and Steinberg in their review of the research assessed the effects of high-quality day care. In the area of cognitive development, there appear to be no lasting effects—good or bad—upon most children. Even the intellectual gains stimulated by the highly enriched curricula appear to vanish soon after a child leaves the program. Disadvantaged children, however, do appear to profit from these programs, as the discussion in Chapter 13 indicated. Such children do not show the decline in IQ that generally appears among poor children.

Children's emotional development does not seem to suffer as a result of day-care experience. The attachment to their mothers of children in day care remains strong, and there appear to be no long-range effects on the mother-child relationship.

In the area of socialization, several studies have shown that children in day care get along better with their peers than home-reared children do; and the single study that followed children into adolescence found that this effect lasted: boys who were enrolled in day care before they were five years old were high in sociability and liked by their peers (Moore, 1975). This rosy picture has been tempered by other studies, which found that children in day care are more aggressive and impulsive than other children and less cooperative with adults (Schwartz, Strickland, and Krolick, 1974), indicating that early day care may retard one part of socialization—the acquisition of adult cultural values.

When Mother Works

An ever-increasing proportion of children grow up in families where the mother works outside the home. Traditionalists have warned that the trend threatens the foundations of the family; others have been equally loud in claims that a mother's employment has no effect on the growing child. Research indicates there is no clear answer.

A recent study examined the cumulative effects of maternal employment among a group of ten-year-olds. Included in the study were more than 200 children, who came from both working- and middle-class families. The mothers of half the children had worked steadily since the children entered elementary school; the mothers of the other half had never worked. Dolores Gold and David Andres (1978), who conducted the study, found mixed effects related to maternal employment, some of them heartening.

Most children of working mothers, for example, are less bound by sex-role stereotypes than children of mothers who do not work. Ten-year-olds whose mothers worked saw much greater similarity between men and women in personality traits, behavior, jobs, and authority. The effect was strongest among girls. Working-class boys, however, tended to see the world through stereotypical glasses even when their mothers worked. Although they were less stereotypical in some of their attitudes than working-class sons whose mothers had never been employed, they were much less egalitarian than other children of employed mothers. This may have had some connection with the way the mothers themselves felt. The more content a mother was with her employment, the more egalitarian her child was, and working-class mothers of sons were not at all content to be employed.

When it came to school, sons of middle-class employed mothers did the worst of any group on achievement tests, having special trouble with verbal achievement. Middle-class daughters of employed mothers did the best of any group, but only slightly better than middle-class daughters whose mothers did not work. Working-class boys of employed mothers disliked school much more than any other group, but their dislike was not reflected in their scores, which were the highest of any of the boys.

The father's involvement with his children turned out to be another key to school success. When fathers were involved with their children, the grades and educational aspirations of the children whose mothers worked both climbed. But—except for middle-class sons—this positive correlation was not found among children of mothers who did not work.

In general, children's adjustment was not affected by their mothers' employment. As groups, the children of employed and unemployed mothers did not differ. Any problems that did appear were limited to boys. More working- than middle-class fathers whose wives worked reported problems with their sons' behavior in school; these fathers rarely described their sons as cooperative or ambitious. On the other hand, middle-class fathers whose wives worked tended to describe their sons as confident. There was one troubling trend: the longer a middle-class mother had been employed, the poorer the adjustment of her son. It may be, as others have speculated, that maternal employment makes it difficult for boys to identify with the male sex role.

The clearest finding of this study is that there is no single effect of maternal employment. Whether a mother's job has benign or harmful influences on her child's socialization depends upon the interaction of other factors: social class, whether the mother works steadily or sporadically, how she feels about her job, and the involvement of the father with his children.

When children who have been in day care later enroll in school, they may be less involved in educational activities than other children. Belsky and Steinberg believe that the marks of day care on the social development of children reflect the values of individual day-care centers and hence are probably program-specific.

Good day care may have less impact on socialization than does social class or ethnic group. A study by Jerome Kagan and his associates (1978) that followed Chinese and Caucasian, middle- and working-class children for two and a half years concluded that attendance at a high-quality day-care center had almost no effect on the infants. Ethnic and class differences were much larger than differences between children who attended the center and those who were reared at home. Kagan's group recommends that babies who are to attend a day-care center should be enrolled either between the ages of one and seven months or after they are fifteen to eighteen months old. This rule ensures that babies will not have to cope with additional stress during those months when they are subject to especially severe separation distress.

The second recommendation to come out of the Kagan study is that each caregiver should be responsible for no more than three infants or toddlers. In the survey cited earlier (Connell, Layzer, and Goodson, 1979), the average number of children per staff member in day-care centers was 3.9 for infants under seventeen months and 5.9 for toddlers from eighteen to twenty-four months. In fact, some licensed day-care centers had as many as 10 infants or 14 toddlers assigned to each caregiver. No research has examined the effects of day care under such conditions.

Most studies have focused on the children themselves, but the change in family life that follows when an infant or preschooler is removed from the home for a good part of the child's waking hours undoubtedly has some effects on the family. Those effects appear to be mixed, but the research is scanty. Some investigators have found that extended enrollment in full-time day care may cause mothers to lose interest in their children (Fowler and Kahn, 1974, 1975). Others have found positive changes in marital relationships (Meyers, 1973) and in the family's economic circumstances (Elliott, 1973).

Father Absence

Although the lengthening life span means that fewer parents are lost by death, the increased divorce rate has led to more and more children being reared in single-parent homes. As a result, their entire early socialization escapes the influence of one gender. In this century, custody has almost always been given to the mother, so that research has focused on the consequences of life without father. Differences regularly turn up between groups of children who have fathers and those who do not, but how much of the discrepancy is due to the father's absence and how much to other factors is unknown.

The area of most intensive study has been sex-role development. Experimenters have been concerned that a growing boy's masculinity or a girl's femininity might be impaired by an absent father. An investigation into the effects of temporary, early father absence indicated that boys whose first two years were spent without the presence of a father were less aggressive and less independent with their four- to eight-year-old peers than boys who had never been separated from their fathers (Stolz et al., 1954). These boys, whose fathers were away during World War II, tended to be submissive or to be hostile in immature ways. At the time of the study, however, the boys' fathers were back in the home, so the boys' behavior may have been related to some factor other than their fathers' absence.

A study that looked only at first-born, lower-class boys—both black and white—indicated that the permanent loss of a father after a boy was six years old had little effect on his independence, his dependency on adults, his aggression, or his sex-role preference (Hetherington,

1966). But boys who lost their fathers before they were four were not aggressive and tended to make feminine scores on a sex-role test. They also liked nonphysical, noncompetitive activities (reading, working puzzles, watching television, collecting things) and preferred checkers, cards, or Monopoly to physical sports. A subsequent review of the effects of father absence agreed that early father absence appears to weaken or retard (but not prevent) the acquisition of the male sex role (Biller, 1976). There is, however, no firm evidence to indicate that boys who grow up in fatherless homes will become men with an inadequate masculine identity (Herzog and Sudia, 1973).

Evidence on the effects of father absence on a girl's sex-role development is scant. Henry Biller's review turned up conflicting conclusions. Some studies found that girls are less affected than boys by the absence; others found that girls from broken homes tend to reject the role of wife and mother or have difficulties in achieving satisfactory sexual relationships. It may be that the father's early departure affects girls as it does boys but that the influence does not show until girls reach adolescence. Mavis Hetherington (1972) found that working-class adolescent girls who had lost their fathers before they were five seemed uncertain about their actions around males. When taking part in an interview, they were either painfully shy (if their fathers had died) or excessively seductive (if their parents had been divorced). But middle-class college women who had lost their fathers before they were five did not show the same inappropriate responses to males (Hainline and Feig, 1978). Either middle-class girls have wider opportunities than working-class girls to learn how to behave with the opposite sex or else practice in socialization during high school helps most girls overcome the problem. We will return to the topic of sex-role development in Chapter 17.

Boys who grow up without fathers do not seem to do as well in junior-high school as other boys, even when investigators control for the difference in IQ (Shelton, 1969). Among girls,

on the other hand, performance does not seem to be as affected. Some studies that report detrimental effects on school performance are done shortly after the divorce and may simply be reflecting the immediate impact of a father's departure, not the lasting influence. As with sex-role development, early absence appears to have the deepest effects. In a study of Harvard students, father absence appeared to affect scores in mathematic but not in verbal aptitude (Carlsmith, 1964). When fathers were present throughout boyhood, math scores were generally higher than verbal scores—a typically masculine pattern. When fathers were absent early—and for a long time—verbal scores tended to be higher than math scores, a typically feminine pattern. The earlier a father stepped out of a boy's life and the longer he was gone, the lower the student's math aptitude score in relation to his verbal score. A late, brief absence, however, sent math scores zooming.

Some studies find that boys without fathers also run the risk of becoming juvenile delinquents; other studies find no connection. The available figures are simply too confused for us to be able to say with any certainty that children in fatherless homes are more likely than other children to become delinquent. According to Elizabeth Herzog and Cecelia Sudia (1973), who reviewed the studies, father absence is less of a factor in juvenile delinquency than are the climate and tone of the home and the kind of supervision the child receives. They agree that there is probably a greater frequency of delinquent behavior among boys without fathers but contend that the increase is so small as to have little social significance.

Growing up without a father obviously leaves some mark on a child, but no one can say how long the effects last. A myriad of other factors can heighten or ameliorate the impact of the absence. The age of the child at the time of the father's departure, the length of the absence, the presence or absence of siblings, whether siblings are younger or older, and of the same or different sex, the presence or absence of a stepfather, the socioeconomic level of the home, the mother's reactions to the father's departure, the ability of the mother to exercise supervision, and community standards — all these factors are inextricably woven together in such a way that makes it impossible to tease out the single strand of socializing influence marked "father absence."

Marital Discord

Growing up amid marital strife also affects the socializing process and may be more damaging to children than growing up in a one-parent home. According to Michael Rutter (1979), family discord and disharmony have been strongly linked with delinquency and severe behavior problems in children. Divorce, which often follows a stormy marriage, is also a common factor in the background of delinquent children, but the death of a parent is not. The implication is that not the loss of the parent but the discordant, stressful relationships are critical. Ending a bad marriage ultimately seems to benefit the children. Following a divorce, children's problems tend to get worse; but two years after the divorce children have fewer problems than children who continue to live in an atmosphere of marital strife (Hetherington, Cox, and Cox, 1978). Among juvenile delinquents, those from intact but strife-ridden homes are much more likely to relapse into delinquency than children from broken homes or children from intact homes without serious problems. The influence extends into later life, for people from unhappy homes have a higher than average rate of poor marital adjustment and divorce.

In addition, boys appear to be more vulnerable than girls to the effects of marital discord. Boys with delinquency and behavior problems are more likely than girls to come from families characterized by marital conflict.

By itself, marital discord is not likely to damage a child, however. Rutter points out that studies of general populations show that children in families suffering only from marital discord show no higher rates of psychiatric disorders than children who live in harmonious families. But if another stress is added to the discord, the risk of a child developing some psychiatric disorder is four times as great.

Class and Cultural Differences

Differences in social class and ethnic group within a single society, as well as differences among cultures, further complicate attempts to make concise statements about the way the family socializes the growing child. The values and life styles of families in various subcultures differ, as do their resources and financial security. As a result, families live in such different worlds that, as Melvin Kohn (1979) has said, they develop "different conceptions of social reality, different aspirations and hopes and fears, different conceptions of the desirable." And what parents believe is desirable will strongly influence their child-rearing practices.

Parents at all social-class levels, says Kohn, want their children to be honest, happy, considerate, obedient, and dependable. But there is a definite class split when it comes to autonomy. Parents in higher social classes also want their children to be responsible, self-controlled, and interested in how and why things happen. Parents in lower social classes also want their children to be neat, clean, and good students. The effect is to encourage autonomy in one social class and conformity to authority in the other.

Children from different classes do not start life differently, but they are treated differently by their parents. Working-class mothers talk less to their toddlers than do middle-class mothers, intrude more into their activities, and tend not to explain punishments and prohibitions. In a study of ninety first-born Caucasian children, Jerome Kagan (1978) and his associates watched the children at home with their mothers on several occasions. They found that lower-class mothers issued a prohibition every five minutes, whereas "No" or "Don't touch that" came only every ten minutes from the middle-class mothers. Although this difference may sound trivial, it indicates that lower-class children hear twice as many prohibitions as do middle-class children, and the cumulative effect could be substantial. Kagan suggests that this sort of difference in training is one element that helps middle-class children become more autonomous.

By the time youngsters enter nursery school, the lessons in autonomy and conformity have taken hold. Middle-class children are likely to believe that they have some control over what happens to them; lower-class children tend to believe that their efforts will have little effect (Stephens and Delys, 1973). The middle-class child is developing an internal locus of control, whereas the lower-class child is developing an external locus of control.

All parents punish their children, but the conditions of punishment differ from one social class to another. Working-class parents tend to punish their children on the basis of the consequences of the child's misbehavior, whereas middle-class parents generally punish on the basis of the child's intent (Kohn, 1979). Working-class parents, for example, who punish for fighting may not punish brothers and sisters for arguing. Middle-class parents, however, are likely to treat fighting with a neighborhood child and arguing with a sibling similarly. Such differences appear about the time the child is six years old. Distributing punishment in this manner is in line with parental values. A parent who values autonomy will judge misbehavior in terms of the reasons a child misbehaves. Parents who value conformity to authority, on the other hand, will judge misdeeds in terms of whether the act violates the rules that have been laid down.

By the time they are adolescents, middle-class children are likely to believe that they can achieve occupational status and other external symbols of success through their personal ef-

forts. But the middle class splits in an important respect. The experiences of adolescents from upper-middle-class families (professional and managerial occupations) are likely to have prepared them for careers, and they grow up believing in the importance of delaying gratification in the interest of future success (Mischel, 1976). They are also likely to value their cognitive competencies, because the social roles they are being socialized for involve using the head more than the hands (R. Hess, 1970).

For the most part, adolescents from lower-middle-class families (semiprofessional, semi-managerial, white-collar, and skilled-craft occupations) look forward to jobs, not careers. They value individualism and take an activistic stance toward the world and their future in it. However, lower-middle-class adolescents and their parents are likely to see that future in terms of the security, stability, and respectability that jobs bring rather than in terms of opportunities for development, intrinsic satisfaction, or self-actualization.

Both upper- and lower-middle-class adolescents tend to share the attitudes and beliefs that correspond to those demanded by schools and colleges (Douvan, 1956). Thus the idea of prolonged schooling is likely to make sense to both groups.

The proposal is less likely to find favor with adolescents from working-class families (semi-skilled and unskilled blue-collar workers) or from lower-class families that depend on irregular employment in marginal work roles or on welfare funds. Going to college, thereby delaying immediate gratification in the interest of future success, is not likely to make much sense to these adolescents. Adolescents from lower-class families tend to adjust their occupational plans to what they think they can hope to achieve; when they look around them, they are unlikely to expect much from life.

Among many working-class families, employment is valued as a means of providing goods and services to the extended family, and family loyalty may stand in the way of any action, such as going away to school, that may weaken family bonds. Fathers of working-class families take pride in their regular employment, but they rarely move up; the tasks they perform are simple, specialized, circumscribed, and repetitive. If they work in a factory, the pace and rhythm of work are imposed from above by supervisors and technicians. The worker on the assembly line is rewarded for following orders and coordinating his work with the rest of the line, not for showing self-direction, individuality, or innovative techniques (Blau, 1972). It is not difficult to see how conforming to authority came to be an important aspect of working-class life.

Child-rearing practices also vary from culture to culture, and the influence of a society's general economy on its values shows most clearly in agricultural, fishing, and hunting societies. In a study of 104 societies, most of them non-literate, Herbert Barry, Irvin Child, and Margaret Bacon (1959) found that knowing whether a culture tends to accumulate and store food surpluses or to consume the food as it is obtained allowed them to predict what qualities would be inculcated in children. Societies based on animal husbandry, for example, train children to be responsible and obedient; they do not stress achievement, self-reliance, and independence. Carelessness in animal management or innovation in herding techniques can threaten a family's food supply for months ahead. Hunting and fishing societies, where few means exist to store the day's catch, stress achievement, self-reliance, and independence; they place little stress on responsibility and obedience. In these societies, innovation carries no penalties and initiative pays off immediately.

In the Soviet Union, obedience and discipline are highly valued. Parents use a combination of reason and praise, backed up by the withdrawal of love, to instill these qualities in their children. According to Urie Bronfenbrenner (1970), the difference between American and Russian discipline lies in the "emotional loading" of the parent-child relationship in the USSR. Russians are more demonstrative than Americans and quick to withdraw affection when a child misbehaves. As a result, the child feels that he or she is ungrateful and has betrayed an affectional bond.

Black Families

Many children in black families face stresses that are not considered in studies of white, middle-class family life — stresses that may result in different patterns of socialization. Black children are more likely to live in the central city (80 percent live in urban areas, 60 percent in the inner city); more likely to be poor (black adult unemployment is twice that of whites); more likely to have both parents working at low-paying, precarious jobs; less likely to be living with both parents (52 percent have both mother and father in the home); less likely to have a father at home (35 percent of black families are headed by women); and more likely to be illegitimate (illegitimacy rates are six times as high among blacks as among whites) (McQueen, 1979). Stresses apparently interact, each additional stress greatly increasing the strain on growing children. And added to all these burdens on black children is the burden of racism.

Despite these hazards, many black families are healthy, cope effectively with their problems, and rear competent children. Robert Hill (1971) has found a number of strengths that enable black families to overcome negative social and economic conditions. First, kinship bonds, by tradition, are especially strong. In times of trouble, the extended family steps in with money, advice, and services; and both child and adult relatives are accepted into the extended family. Second, both husbands and wives have a strong work orientation and both participate in decision making; when the husband is present, the black family is not a matriarchy. Third,

Children in black families face stresses that children in white, middle-class families never encounter, but black families also have additional strengths, including especially strong kinship bonds. (© Ken Heyman)

all members of the black family are characterized by a strong desire to achieve: to get a better education, better job, more income. This urge is not, however, generally matched by the conviction that improvement is possible. Finally, many black families rely on the church, which helps maintain the values of respectability, perseverence, and achievement.

Albert McQueen (1979) studied black families in Washington, D.C., to see how these strengths affected them and to determine just what strategies distinguished those who coped successfully from those who did not. All the families were poor or near poor, but some, whom he called the *troubled-poor*, had difficulty feeding and clothing their children and paying the rent. The others, the *future-oriented poor*, seemed able to handle their economic problems. The future-oriented families were more likely than the troubled-poor to be headed by males: 85 percent compared with 65 percent. Both types of families aimed at improving their economic lot, wanted to rear their children well, and wanted

good family relations, but the future-oriented devoted more of their resources to family goals. Although all the families wanted to improve the quality of their lives, none of the mothers was striving to get into a higher socioeconomic bracket. Mothers in future-oriented families had high aspirations for their sons: 40 percent wanted their sons to finish college and 33 percent believed their sons would do so; 63 percent wanted their sons to have upper level white-collar jobs. Mothers in troubled-poor families were much less ambitious: 26 percent wanted their sons to finish college, but only 11 percent believed they would do so; 40 percent wanted their sons to move into upper level white-collar jobs. McQueen speculates that mothers in the future-oriented families were attentive, encouraging, and supportive of their sons.

The parents in the future-oriented families had much stronger links with the church than those in the troubled-poor families. Despite their near poverty, 35 percent of the future-oriented families were buying their own homes and 25 percent had savings. None of the troubled-poor had savings, and only one family was buying a home. The future-oriented families showed a major difference in their dealings with extended kin. They were self-reliant and neither borrowed nor lent money. When they ran out of money, they simply "made do," whereas most of the troubled-poor turned to kin. This factor, McQueen believes, enabled the future-oriented families to manage their financial resources to achieve their goals. The borrowing and lending patterns of the troubled-poor made them perpetually insolvent, deeply affecting their and their children's social world and expectations.

The stresses peculiar to black families may account for a disparity in Baumrind's (1972a) studies of child rearing. She found that black girls respond differently from white girls to disciplinary techniques, so that in black families, authoritarian — not authoritative — parents produce instrumentally competent girls.

Nontraditional Families

In the late 1960s, Americans began experimenting with variations on the traditional nuclear family theme. Some young people chose to live together without marriage, some joined communes that serve as extended families, and some—both men and women—decided to rear their children as single parents. Such a variety of environments should lead to widely differing socialization practices; but a recent study of 200 families by Bernice Eiduson (1979) and her associates, which compared most of these groups, found that any can provide a nurturant atmosphere for a child.

SOCIAL-CONTRACT FAMILIES In comparison with the traditional family, unmarried couples tend to be unstable; but they are more stable than communes. During the three years Eiduson studied what she calls *social-contract families*, fifteen of the fifty unmarried couples broke up; another eight decided to marry. Life in an unmarried household tends to be loose and unscheduled, and income derives from a combination of seasonal jobs supplemented by welfare. Literacy appears to be high; stereos, records, books, and pictures are found in all the homes. Child care is intense, and babies go everywhere with their parents. Mothers breast-feed, generally for a long time, and fathers participate in child care. Sex roles are egalitarian, and parents value interpersonal relations as well as achievement for its own sake, above materialistic goals.

COMMUNES Communes vary widely; they can be large or small, rural or urban, religious or secular. Some encourage—or at least tolerate—bonds between parents and children, others try to stamp them out. Because of these differences, which affect family functioning, Eiduson separated the communes she studied into five types: Christian religious communes, Eastern religious communes, families with charismatic leaders, agricultural communes, and urban communes.

In Christian religious communes, children are regarded as future evangelists and their development is supervised with that goal in mind. By the time they are two or three years old, they are given responsibilities. Discipline consists of spanking followed by hugging, and the spanking is done with religious sanction and without guilt. Babies are often left with caretakers while the parents are sent on religious missions.

Life in a commune is very different from life in a nuclear family, but a study of babies in communes indicates that the infant's biological and social needs appear to take precedence over communal regulations so that the babies develop normally. (© Rick Smolan)

Although caretakers change frequently, babies are expected to take the changes in stride. Christian communes are not egalitarian; parents and children are expected to adhere to sexual stereotypes.

In communes that center around Eastern religions, parents are expected to rear their own children. The commune provides an outline for life; the parents translate it into child-rearing practices. The father's role does not differ from that of the traditional nuclear family; fathers appear at mealtimes and in the evenings but spend their days working for the religious order. Child care is left to the mother, although commune members may baby-sit. Commune practices steer children into stereotypical sex roles.

In "families" that center about a charismatic leader, children may be reared in radical ways. The family's child-rearing philosophy is likely to be experimental and erratic, and few caregivers are trained. The nursery in which children live may concentrate on intellectual stimulation, on hedonism, or on destroying special bonds between parent and child on the ground that they make the child too dependent. Eiduson suggests that in this sort of family, close ties between parent and child are seen as weakening the child's tie to the group.

In agricultural families that are part of the back-to-nature trend, children have the freedom typically found on farms. Their lives are regulated by the demands of farm life, and the children participate in many of their parents' activities. Adults in these communes have strong inner discipline; they are efficient, conscientious, and determined, and they work hard. These same qualities are carried over into their child-rearing practices.

Families that have sprung up in the cities are informal and relaxed. Child rearing is casual, spontaneous, and impulsive, and there are few demands on the child to conform. Children may sleep in their parents' room or in a nursery. They may be in day care or in a nursery group, or they may have a baby-sitter; the idea is to free the mother for other activities.

All the communes tended to be unstable, but the agricultural and urban families lost more members during the three years of Eiduson's study than did the other types of living arrangement.

SINGLE-MOTHER HOUSEHOLDS The single mothers Eiduson studied were unmarried, not divorced. Some were professional women who had decided to have a child. These mothers were economically and psychologically self-sufficient and maintained social relations within the community. Children generally were cared for in private homes while the mother worked, and mother and child spent most of their free time together. An extremely close emotional attachment and dependency developed between these women and their children.

The unwed mother whose child was not planned generally had economic problems. She combined welfare with temporary work and often shared quarters with another woman, or with a man — who may or may not have been sexually involved with her. The child was often regarded with ambivalence and pushed aside in favor of the mother's adult relationships. But she valued the child as tangible proof of permanency in the center of a haphazard existence. The child generally attended a day-care center.

Some unmarried mothers elected to return to the home of their own parents. Such mothers were psychologically and economically dependent upon their parents; mother and baby simply became two additional family members in the parents' home. The grandparents generally were ambivalent about the child, whom they saw as a reminder of their daughter's rebellion. Sometimes these children were left temporarily with the grandparents and were reared as the only children of older "parents," with the indulgences that accompany such a position.

COMPARING NONTRADITIONAL FAMILIES In all these nontraditional families,

Eiduson found, children develop normally through the first year of life. They were average in both motor and mental skills, and there was no difference between any of the groups and a control group of traditional nuclear families. Even when the family's official policy was that of shared caregiving, the child-mother unit remained basic. Eiduson speculates that the biological and psychological needs of the baby take precedence over the social rules of a family.

There were no strong influences on the children's early intellectual or socioemotional development that distinguished the family types; but when babies were a year old, some characteristics within the families were linked with scores on mental and physical tests. Babies with several caregivers tended to make higher mental scores than babies with only a single caregiver. When the father or other women helped in child care, scores on the physical tests also tended to be high. Breast-feeding was also related to high motor scores; significantly more bottle- than breast-fed babies scored in the lowest 25 percent on the physical test.

At three years, children of single mothers scored lowest on a picture-vocabulary test. Children whose parents were traditionally married but had elected to live in one of the groups scored highest on this test. Eiduson speculates that this difference may arise because single parents possibly talk less to their children or because these children are less likely to hear adults talking to each other.

SINGLE-FATHER HOUSEHOLDS More and more fathers are gaining custody of their children, providing examples of socialization in the absence of a mother. The single-father family, however, has received almost no attention from psychologists. If boys are more likely to have problems when the father is absent, suggest Michael Lamb and Susan Bronson (1980), girls are more likely to have problems when the mother is gone. Unless there is an older sister with whom she can identify, a girl will lack a female role model. (It is possible, however, that

because the mother is absent, the daughter will be expected to assume some maternal responsibilities in the family, giving her an opportunity to learn the feminine role.) She will, as will a son, also miss the chance to see successful interaction between men and women, a deficit that also characterizes the single-mother household.

Puberty is likely to be a difficult time when a single father rears a daughter. Almost all fathers expect their wives to discuss matters of sexuality and menstruation with daughters, and they are extremely uncomfortable at the prospect of having to assume that responsibility. Girls, therefore, are likely to be without any individual adult counsel and guidance in the area of sexuality, and some evidence indicates that these girls are more likely than others to have an illegitimate pregnancy (Fox, 1978).

On the positive side, fathers encourage their daughters toward competence and success in careers. In addition, because the father is highly involved with the children, performing the duties that traditionally fall to the mother, both sons and daughters are likely to develop flexible views of masculinity and femininity (Lamb and Bronson, 1980).

This survey of nontraditional families makes it clear that children can be successfully socialized in a wide variety of living arrangements. Although the nuclear family approximates the ideal of this culture, the traditional mothering role can be assumed by fathers or even by several people. The human infant is active, flexible, and highly adaptive; and no matter what the family arrangement, peers, school, and television will ensure the growing child's encounter with cultural standards.

CHILD ABUSE

Sometimes the rearing process goes dreadfully wrong, and instead of successfully socializing their children by nurturing competent offspring, parents beat, maim, or kill them. According to the accepted definition, an abused child is one who has been physically injured because of intentional acts or failures to act on the part of his or her caregiver; and the acts or omissions violate the community's standards concerning the treatment of children (Parke and Collmer, 1975). Some years ago, few cases of child abuse were reported to authorities; but once the problem received public recognition, many states passed laws requiring the reporting of child abuse. As a result, the magnitude of the problem has become clear. From 1968 to 1972, for example, the number of cases reported in California jumped from 4,000 to 40,000; in Florida, from 10 to 30,000; and in Michigan, from 721 to 30,000 (Kempe and Kempe, 1978). As reporting rose, the severity of the cases reported dropped. In one survey of parents with children under three, aimed at discovering just how widespread abuse is, 3.5 percent of parents admitted having acted in such a violent manner that they could have injured their children (Gelles, 1978). According to the records of the National Center for Child Abuse and Neglect, during 1978 there were 614,291 cases of child abuse or neglect reported to the authorities in the fifty states.

Like any other outcome of child rearing, child abuse has no single cause. It appears to result from the interaction of many factors: the personality characteristics of the parents and whether they were abused as children, the socioeconomic strains on the family, the patterns of family interaction, the personality characteristics of the children, the isolation of the family, and the cultural acceptance of violence (Starr, 1979).

The Abusing Parent

It was once thought that child abuse had a simple explanation: psychotic parents beat or murdered their children. As more and more cases were investigated, however, it became clear that psychosis was rarely a factor in child abuse (Spinetta and Rigler, 1972). Studies that have focused on parental personality characteristics have come up with a number of traits that have been found in abusing parents; the only problem is that different studies have found different clusters of traits (Parke and Collmer, 1975). Child abusers have been found to possess one or more of nineteen traits, including a tendency to be rigid, domineering, impulsive, immature, self-centered, hypersensitive, low in self-esteem, or lacking in impulse control. That they cannot always control their aggressive impulses is obvious; the existence of child abuse is ample testimony to that defect. But most people possess at least one of the remaining eighteen traits, so that the list adds little to our understanding of the problem (Steele and Pollock, 1968).

Investigators generally agree that child abusers had wretched childhoods. They are likely to have been abused and neglected, and to have been deprived of basic mothering. As children, they learned from their own parents to be aggressive; and they learned, too, that parents criticize and disregard their young children while making demands on them (Parke and Collmer, 1975).

But knowing all this is not enough. Most people who show the various personality traits discovered in abusing parents do not batter their children. And not all people who were

The prevalence of child abuse has led to the formation of groups of former child-abusers who counsel one another, just as alcoholics come to one another's aid through Alcoholics Anonymous. (© Menschenfreund)

abused as children become child abusers; nor were all child abusers abused by their own parents.

A study by Ruth and Henry Kempe (1978) of 350 Colorado babies showed that the way parents of full-term babies behaved in the labor and delivery rooms could separate those who would not abuse their babies from those who *might*. (But the elimination of premature babies from the study may mean — as noted in Chapter 5 — that some of the likely candidates for battering were not considered.) Although extensive prenatal interviews and postnatal home observation were also part of the study, the parents' behavior just before and after the child's birth provided the best indicators of potential abusers. Signals that indicated parents who might abuse their babies were mothers who neither touched, held, nor examined their newborn infants; mothers who failed to use affectionate language or tones when talking about their babies; and mothers or fathers who made unfriendly or disparaging remarks about the baby's appearance, failed to look the new baby in the eye, seemed disappointed in the baby's sex, or were not loving toward each other.

Seventy-five of these babies (fifty judged as being at risk for battering and twenty-five judged as being unlikely to be battered) were followed for seventeen months. The study found that five children in the high-risk group were hopitalized for abuse or neglect; none in the low-risk group was hospitalized. Twenty-two children in the high-risk group had had at least one accident requiring medical attention; four in the low-risk group had had such an accident. Eight high-risk babies (including two in the hospitalized group) had been reported to Denver's Central Child Abuse Registry; none in the low-risk group had. The researchers' measures, then, had correctly selected a large group of babies who would not be harmed by their parents; but their predictions of babies who were at risk had included more "false-positives" — babies who would not be abused by their parents — than babies who would be abused. Un-

less other factors are present, the marked lack of affection apparently does not get translated into abuse.

The Abused Child

The child may play a part in bringing about or maintaining abuse from parents. A child's appearance or temperament may somehow increase the chances that a parent will be abusive. The child may learn, from parents or siblings, to act in ways that evoke abuse, or the experience of being battered may alter his or her behavior in such a way as to make future episodes of battering more likely.

As noted in Chapter 5, the premature baby runs a special risk. Babies with low birth weights have particularly aversive cries, they are less attractive than full-term babies, they require more parental care at home, they develop slowly, and the bonding process is often disrupted because the babies' precarious condition requires them to be separated from their parents and placed in special-care nurseries.

Not surprisingly, the experience of abuse affects a child's behavior. Carol George and Mary Main (1979) watched ten abused toddlers and ten toddlers from families under stress the first time they attended a day-care center. The two groups of children differed only in the fact that one group had been abused and the other had not. The battered toddlers were more aggressive than the other children; only the abused toddlers assaulted or threatened to assault the caregivers. Seven of the abused children but only two of the children who had not been abused harassed the caregivers, behaving in malicious ways that were intended to distress the caregiver. There is, of course, no way to tell whether the abused toddlers' aggression and harassment were the cause or the result of their parents' abuse.

Although the abused children approached their peers, they were much less likely to approach the caregiver. They frequently avoided

The Human Ecology of Child Abuse

The contribution of the family's social setting to child abuse is highlighted in a study by James Garbarino and Deborah Sherman (1980). These investigators compared two neighborhoods with similar socioeconomic and racial composition but with radically differing rates of child abuse. Given its socioeconomic make-up, each area should have had between 65 and 70 cases of child abuse during the year. Yet one neighborhood reported 130 cases while the other reported only 16. Garbarino and Sherman first interviewed "expert informants" (public health nurses, school principals, mailmen, clergy, etc.) about conditions in the neighborhoods, then conducted two-hour interviews with residents of each area. Differences between the two neighborhoods became clear.

There were no "latchkey children" in the low-risk neighborhood. A parent was likely to be present when a child came home from school. Families in the low-risk neighborhood assumed full responsibility for their children, but they also exchanged assistance and child supervision with neighbors. Neighborhood children were likely to be playmates. Discussing child abuse, an agency worker said, "There used to be a number of cases there, but now it will be real hard to find one."

Families in the high-risk neighborhood were socially impoverished. They tended to be isolated, and the mothers believed that fewer people were interested in their children's welfare. A school principal in the area said, "There are probably a significant number of 5 to 8 year olds at school who got themselves up this morning. They may or may not have been at their own homes, but they got themselves to school and took care of their needs."

In the low-risk neighborhood, families were likely to be involved with preventive agencies (such as Boy Scouts); in the high-risk neighborhood, involvement was likely to be with treatment agencies (such as Family Service Association). Despite similar economic resources, people in the low-risk neighborhood kept up their homes and their families, but houses and families were both run-down in the high-risk neighborhood.

When new families moved into the high-risk neighborhood, they tended to be families that already were functioning poorly. The already stressed families tried to get all they could from others while giving as little as possible in return. A visiting nurse said of the high-risk neighborhood, "There's stealing from each other." The negative neighborhood situation worsened existing family problems. As a result, families were threatened from without and within. Garbarino and Sherman point to a combination of family histories, economic pressures, and political forces that lead high-risk families to congregate in high-risk neighborhoods. The mix apparently sends the rate of child abuse zooming.

the friendly advances both of other children and of the caregiver, and often showed approach-avoidance. That is, in response to a friendly overture, they would crawl toward the caregiver, then suddenly veer away. Or they would creep toward the caregiver, carefully keeping their heads averted. Ann Frodi and Michael Lamb's study (1980) showing that abusive parents react aversively to smiling, friendly babies might provide a clue here. The apparent apprehensiveness of the abused babies may have developed from their having learned that *any* adult attention is sometimes followed by blows. Their negative responses to friendliness, however, might well help to maintain their parents' abuse.

Socioeconomic Stress

The family's social setting is a third factor that affects the incidence of child abuse. Careful studies in New York and Nebraska (Garbarino, 1976; Garbarino and Crouter, 1978) show that where socioeconomic support for mothers is poor, child abuse increases. Children are more likely to be abused or neglected when incomes and educational levels are low, when mothers head the household, when the neighborhood is unstable, and when day care is not available. When parents are under economic and social stress, when they have no relief from child care, when they have no support from friends, and when—from lack of education—they do not know where to turn for help, the impulse to strike out in response to a crying, whining, or aggressive child may be overpowering. But wiping out poverty would not eliminate child abuse. Although the rate of child abuse is higher among the poor, prosperous parents also abuse their children. Marital discord, employment worries, and other stresses of the affluent can also result in a battered child.

The Persistence of Abuse

Many child abusers learned as children that violence works. They were beaten by their own parents. The childhood home lesson that violence is an appropriate way to enforce rules or to reach one's goals was then reinforced by three-quarters of the programs seen on television (Gerbner, 1972). Having learned the lesson, abusive parents apply it inconsistently. One study found that abusive families lack guidelines for children's behavior and any consistency in discipline (Young, 1964). As a result, children never know when they will be punished or why.

Since erratic punishment is not effective, abusive parents are likely to intensify their use of force. According to Parke and Collmer (1975), abusive parents often justify their violence as necessary discipline, forget the harmful effects of abuse, blame the child for provoking them, label the child as incorrigible, "crazy," or "dumb," react to the child's pain with intensified aggression, and are encouraged in their attacks by approval or indifference on the part of their spouses.

In a study of abused children and their parents, both the abused children and children who had not been abused behaved similarly with their families when building with tinker toys, tossing bean bags, or discussing how they would spend lottery winnings (Burgess and Conger, 1978). Mothers of abused children, however, showed 77 percent more negative behavior than mothers in the control group. They also spoke less often to their children and had less positive contact with them. Fathers of abused children were much less likely to comply with the requests of either the mother or the children than fathers of children in the control group.

But Ruth and Henry Kempe (1978), who work with the National Center for the Prevention and Treatment of Child Abuse and Neglect, have found that most abused children are excessively compliant, passive, and obedient. They seem stoical and accept whatever happens. Others are negative, aggressive, and sometimes hyperactive. A third small group swerves between sweet, compliant behavior and unprovoked disruption and impulsiveness. These researchers believe that the abused children they have seen have failed to develop the basic sense of trust that Erik Erikson believes is the major developmental task for young children. Such children find it hard to trust adults, make only superficial friendships, and discard their new friends at the slightest hint of rejection. In school they are underachievers, generally poor at communication, lonely, and friendless. They are, in short, candidates to become child abusers.

SUMMARY

1. Socialization is the process by which the growing child slowly absorbs the attitudes, values, and customs of society. Parents and siblings both play an important role in this process.

2. Connections have been found between the disciplinary styles of parents and the personalities of their children, although it is impossible to say that any particular type of child rearing has a specific effect upon children. The authoritarian and the permissive parent both produce dependent children, perhaps because both kinds of parents tend to shield their children from stress. Nonconformist parents produce dependent girls and independent, high-achieving boys. Authoritative parents, who are firm but not repressive, produce independent, socially responsible girls and socially responsible sons with average levels of independence.

3. First-born children tend to be conservative, anxious, highly verbal, high achievers who are nurturant but domineering toward their younger siblings. Later-born children tend to be autonomous, flexible, tolerant, empathic, and popular with their peers. Studies indicate that the later-born children are helped in the mastery of the physical world by their older brothers and sisters. Sibling influence tends to be very strong during the early school years, then diminishes until late adolescence.

4. High-quality day care appears to have little effect on the emotional development of children, and children in day care get along better with their peers than children who stay at home. Children who begin day care early, however, may be a little slower in acquiring adult cultural values.

5. Growing up without a father has some effect upon children's personalities and socialization, but the depth of the impact depends upon a host of factors: the age of the child at the time of the loss, the presence of siblings, the sex of the child, the socioeconomic level of the home, the mother's reaction to the loss, and community standards. Marital discord may be worse in its impact on the child than the loss of either parent by death or divorce.

6. Parents in different social classes tend to treat their children differently, and the major effect is to encourage conformity to authority among working-class children and autonomy among middle-class children. The economy of a culture plays a major part in determining which values are stressed during socialization.

7. Black families face extra stresses, but they also have strengths that are not found in most white, middle-class homes. Some black families cope successfully with the stresses, handling economic problems that others find insurmountable and striving for upward mobility.

8. Children who grow up in a nontraditional family arrangement—whether a social-contract family, a commune, or a household headed by an unmarried mother—can produce children indistinguishable from children in traditional nuclear families, perhaps because the needs of babies seem to overwhelm unusual social rules. Households in which the only parent is a father may lead to competitive, career-oriented girls and to both sons and daughters who have flexible views of masculinity and femininty.

9. Child abuse has no single cause; it seems to result when personality characteristics of parent and child interact with socioeconomic stress, patterns of family interactions, and social isolation. The pattern of abuse tends to be handed down, and the lonely, friendless, isolated abused child often grows up to become a child abuser.

Social Competence in the Wider World: Peers and Achievement

One afternoon after school, Jan and Debby stopped at a local variety store. "Watch me," whispered Jan, as her hand snaked out, grabbed a handful of pencils from the counter, and dropped them into her schoolbag. Eleven-year-old Debby's eyes widened, but she said nothing. "Try it," Jan said. "It's easy." Debby hesitated. "Go ahead," Jan whispered, "are you a scairdy-cat?" Debby looked nervously over her shoulder, grabbed a pencil, thrust it under her sweater, and walked quickly out the door. Debby did not need the pencil; she did not even want it, but the demands of her peer were stronger than her wishes or her own sense of right or wrong.

The influences of a child's peers can be extremely important in shaping development. Some years ago, peers had little impact until a child skipped off to elementary school. Until then, brothers, sisters, and perhaps cousins, the boy next door and the girl across the street provided a youngster's only sustained contacts with other children. Today, about a third of all three- and four-year-olds meet their peers in regular, organized contact at nursery school. The power of the peer group has also increased at the other end of childhood. Fifty years ago, only about half of American adolescents attended high school; today nearly 95 percent are enrolled.

In this chapter, we shall trace the development of children as they move into the wider world, concentrating on the growth of social competence. First, we shall examine the role that peers play in the development of competence. We shall see that peers are also important in the development of other species and that research with monkeys can help clarify human development. We shall investigate the qualities that cause a child to be welcomed into the peer group, then trace the changing course and increasing importance of peers in a child's life. We shall discover that conformity to the group, which can seem so powerful in later childhood, declines during adolescence. We shall discuss the reasons some children become isolated from the peer group—and what can be done to end the isolation. Finally, we shall turn from competence in the peer group to the development of competence within the child, examining the way a child's assessment of his or her own competence influences academic achievement.

FROM PARENTS TO PEERS

Until children enroll in school, parents are the most important socializing force in their lives. When children develop a secure attachment to their parents (a concept discussed in Chapter 14) they become competent, independent toddlers. Some of the skills they develop within the family transfer to their contacts with others. As a result, they enjoy learning new things, play well with other children, and plunge into the day at nursery school with enthusiasm.

Three-year-olds who had developed secure attachments, Alicia Lieberman (1977) found, played more harmoniously with their peers than did insecurely attached toddlers. They were less likely to throw toys, fight, leave the room, or cry, and more likely to share toys, point out objects of interest, and laugh together than were insecurely attached children. Lieberman speculates that mothers who foster secure attachments

Preschoolers with secure attachments to their parents get along well with their peers, perhaps because their experiences have left them with positive expectations about play. (© Lawrence Frank 1969)

also encourage their children to play with others, and that these securely attached children enter into play with positive expectations.

As noted in Chapter 14, other studies have found a strong connection between the quality of a child's early attachment and his or her later social competence with peers. Ann Easterbrooks and Michael Lamb (1979) also found differences in social competence among securely attached eighteen-month-olds. Those who used their mothers as a base from which to explore the environment, maintaining contact with smiles, looks, and vocalizations, were more likely to play with a strange baby than were babies who seemed to need to stay near their mothers.

When children enter nursery school, their world changes from one populated almost entirely by giants to one in which a far greater number of people are near their own size and share their interests. The child for the first time has a real peer group, and the importance of that group steadily increases.

Much of what young children learn about their world they learn from other children, and most of what they learn, from whatever source, they practice and rehearse within the peer group. Thus, the peer group is the place where children perfect the roles that they will play in later years. During early childhood, a child's dependence on adults often decreases while dependence on peers (such as in seeking approval or asking for help) increases. In fact, well-adjusted youngsters tend to have a comfortable reliance on their peers (Emmerich, 1966).

PRIMATES AND PEERS

The role of peers as agents of socialization is not uniquely human. Students of primate behavior are generally convinced, both from laboratory studies and from studies conducted in the wild, that early contact with peers is necessary for the normal development of most primates. In fact, it is almost impossible to conceive of socialization among rhesus monkeys or chimpanzees in the absence of peer interaction. Because of this similarity across species, primate social interaction can provide insights that help clarify the role of peers in the socialization of the human child.

In many primate species, young animals spend much of their time in a play group consisting of other infants and juveniles. Within this group, young primates practice the behavior they will later be expected to perform as adults. It is here that primates perfect the intricate patterns of facial gestures and social threat. And it is here, by approach and mounting during play, that young primates learn adult sexual behavior. Rough-and-tumble play within the peer group also develops the aggressiveness that primates use both to maintain status and to defend the group against predators.

The animal research of Harry and Margaret Harlow (1969) and their associates helps us understand the role of peers in socialization. Infant monkeys raised in total isolation never learned to play the usual monkey games, and they never had the opportunity to acquire the social roles that they would need in later life. After six to twelve months of such isolation, these monkeys found it almost impossible to fit within a group when, as adolescents, they were introduced to others of their kind. They tended to remain isolated from the rest of the group; they rarely engaged in social play, and when they did, it was with other isolates. Even individual play was infrequent among monkeys that had been isolated for twelve months.

Such isolated monkeys encountered great difficulties when they became sexually mature. Males did not know how to approach young females (or even that it was females that they should approach), and the females did not know how to entice and yield to the males. Both males and females were abnormally aggressive. They attacked and bit young monkeys, which normally reared animals almost never do. They also launched attacks against the largest and most dominant adult males, an extraordinarily maladaptive action for an adolescent.

Clearly, these monkeys had severe social problems (Suomi and Harlow, 1975). To try to pinpoint the cause of the problems, researchers raised more monkeys, but each group was raised in a different manner. Some monkeys spent the first few months of their lives with their mothers but had no contact with any other monkeys. Another group spent the first few months of life only with other infant monkeys. The infants raised with only their mothers behaved in a far less abnormal manner than did the monkeys raised earlier in isolation. They were, however, less affectionate with peers and more aggressive than monkeys raised in a normal manner, and they tended to avoid social play,

Monkeys raised without their mothers and with only their peers for company at first developed strange patterns of behavior, such as clinging together in a line, but the monkeys soon went on to normal play. (Harry Harlow, University of Wisconsin Primate Laboratory)

Furthermore, the longer the baby monkeys were isolated with their mothers, the more abnormal their behavior.

Researchers had suspected that the peer-raised animals would show severe social problems, and for the first several days it appeared that their suspicions were correct. The infants simply clung together in a "choo-choo" pattern, as shown in the photograph above. This pattern soon broke up, however, and the monkeys established normal play. The later development of peer-raised monkeys was relatively normal. They showed affection and played normally, and they demonstrated only normal aggression toward monkeys in their rearing group. They were, however, aggressive toward other monkeys.

In view of the important role of parents in the rearing of both infant monkeys and human infants, these results are surprising. They seem to indicate that at least among rhesus monkeys, peers teach certain social skills that are not learned from parents.

PEERS AND COMPETENCE

Peer interaction allows even young children to test their skills and enhances a growing sense of self. As children grow, peers serve a number of important functions in their lives. They provide emotional security, set norms for behavior, instruct one another in cognitive, motor, and social skills, stimulate and encourage play, and help children adjust to life (Asher, 1978). Peers carry out these functions in two major ways: by reinforcement and by modeling. Even babies are affected by this social interaction.

Early Social Skills

In the past, many investigators simply did not look for social interaction between infants, perhaps because of the general belief that young babies are too egocentric for such sociability. Ask any park bench mother, however, and she will report that infants as young as nine months who meet regularly and explore the world together while their mothers talk will indulge in give-and-take with a toy, play peekaboo, or simply crawl after each other in follow-the-leader fashion. When Jacqueline Becker (1977) observed pairs of nine-month-old babies in their homes with their mothers present, she found that babies who were with each other for a period of ten sessions paid more attention to each other than to toys or to their mothers. As the sessions went on, the babies became increasingly involved with each other and played with each other more; their play also became more complex. The babies reached toward each other, followed each other, passed toys, and looked at each other far more frequently than did infants who played together for only two sessions. But the increased play and its greater complexity seemed unaffected by peer reinforcement. Behavior that was not rewarded increased as much as behavior that was. It may be that one baby served as a model for the other or, as has also been suggested, sustained social contact with another child may stimulate behavior that is natural to the species (K. Bloom, 1974).

The babies' increased social competence was not simply due to maturation, because it transferred to a new situation. When Becker placed the babies, one at a time, in a play situation with an unfamiliar infant, babies who had previously played with a peer for ten sessions played more with the unfamiliar baby than did babies who had previously played with a peer for only two sessions.

Toward the end of the first year, a baby begins to see peers as an even greater source of enjoyment. The one-year-old often passes a toy to a peer and displays obvious pleasure when the other child receives it. (That same object can quickly become the target of a tug-of-war, however, and the loser in the battle will scream in distress.) One-year-olds also stimulate each other to begin play sequences. For example, one infant starts banging on a table or taking toys out of the toy box and the others join in. As each new treasure is pulled from the box, mutual smiles break out. Real enjoyment seems to come from this mutual play.

Once infants have resolved their conflicts over play materials, they attend positively to peers. For the eighteen- to twenty-four-month-old, toys and playmates are more successfully integrated and social interactions begin to predominate. Infants modify their behavior to adjust to playmates' activities. For example, Judith Rubenstein and Carollee Howes (1976) found that seventeen- to twenty-month-old playmates who met regularly with each other in their own homes not only played freely and made few demands on the adults present but also seldom squabbled over toys. Play between a pair of playmates was also more intricate and constructive than solitary play by either member of the pair or play by a single baby and his or her mother.

Peer Reinforcement

One important way in which children influence one another is through actions that support or encourage behavior. When children praise another child's behavior, join in the activity, imitate the first child, comply with his or her requests, or simply watch attentively, the likelihood that the first child will repeat the behavior is increased. The kinds of responses that reinforce an activity such as aggression, however, differ from those that reinforce an activity such as sharing. And because of differences in past experience, one child may respond to a sort of encouragement that has no effect on another. Nevertheless, such responses as praise and affection reinforce most children in most situations.

The way a child initiates social interaction helps determine whether the overture will be reinforced (Leiter, 1977). When a child approaches others in a friendly manner, smiling or pleasantly suggesting an activity, most other children will agree. But if the child uses demands or coercion, the amount of compliance drops sharply; many children will threaten, hit, or shove the child instead of agreeing to his or her requests. Others simply ignore the child. Sometimes, however, coercive children do get reinforced, as when other children agree to their demands or plead with them, crying or begging them to stop. Children who whine, beg, or cry when making requests generally get ignored.

The way children distribute social reinforcers seems to be strongly related to their popularity within the peer group. Popular youngsters approach others in a friendly manner and are generous with praise and approval. Rosalind Charlesworth and Willard Hartup (1967) found, for example, that popular young children who frequently were supportive of other children tended to distribute their approval among nearly

Play and Socialization

Even nine-month-olds engage in social interaction and squabbles over toys. It was once assumed that infants begin with solitary play, then move on to parallel play—in which two children play side by side, each intent on his or her own toy and each perhaps keeping up a running commentary that amounts to thinking aloud—and finally, group play develops. This sequence of development was put forth when investigators concentrated on egocentrism in young children to the exclusion of children's rudimentary ability to understand others. When preschoolers have an opportunity to play with familiar peers, however, three-year-olds sustain conversations, pay attention to each other's play, and are responsive to their friends' requests (Garvey, 1977a).

When Anna-Beth Doyle, Jennifer Connolly, and Louis-Paul Rivest (1980) studied preschoolers at play, they found that social play among familiar peers was more frequent and carried on at a higher cognitive level than play among children who did not know each other. In addition, there was much less passive watching or solitary play when the preschoolers knew each other. Peter Smith (1978) studied preschoolers, observing them at play for a period of nine months. He found that parallel play is not always an inevitable step in the development of social play. Many children went directly from playing alone to playing with a group. This pattern of behavior was especially typical of three- and four-year-olds. Two-year-olds, however, often did go through a period of parallel play before they ventured into group play. Although parallel play decreases with age, says Smith, where it exists it continues throughout the preschool period.

Children who are playing house, doctor, bus driver, or any adult role are indoctrinating themselves into the culture, testing what they have learned about social roles without any of the physical, emotional, or economic consequences that accompany mistakes made when engaging in the real thing (Bruner, 1972). This function of social play was made clear several decades ago when Meyer Fortes (1938) noted that Tale boys practiced shooting barbless arrows at cornstalks, wood, and small birds—a safe preparation for the hunting with barbed and poisonous arrows that would be part of their adult responsibilities in that African society.

The play of young children builds on all the elements found in toddlers' play (Garvey, 1977a). As children practice a variety of roles and deal with the inevitable conflicts that arise, their egocentrism decreases and their skill in understanding others increases. Children begin to comprehend the effects of their actions on others and to see their playmates more as individuals and less as objects of play. As they differentiate among people, children's specific attachments increase and they form friendships that may be remarkably durable. Smith (1977) believes that one of the basic functions of rough-and-tumble play is that it serves to form and maintain friendships.

Adults watching rough-and-tumble play might believe that a fight was in progress, but the laughter, the expression on the faces of the children involved, the wrestling, and the jumping tell ethologists that the struggle is not aggressive and that there is no hostility involved. According to Nicholas Blurton-Jones (1976), such play—more common among boys than among girls—is similar to play among rhesus monkeys, where it is important in the development of the monkeys' social and sexual behavior. Like Smith, Blurton-Jones indicates that such violent play appears to gain friends more often than it loses them.

all their peers. This study also found a strong positive correlation between the amount of reinforcement children gave and the amount they received.

On the other hand, in another study Hartup (1964a) found that young children performed better at simple tasks when they disliked the child who praised their performance than when they liked the youngster. This connection between dislike and approval showed when Hartup had children carry out a task that required them to drop marbles through holes. Periodically, either the child's best friend or a child the marble dropper disliked expressed approval. Children dropped marbles faster when the disliked child applauded their skill than when the praise came from a friend.

The effectiveness of approval from a disliked child may have something to do with expectations. Joanne Floyd (1965) found that children who received unexpectedly large or small rewards in a sharing task changed their patterns of sharing more radically than children who got rewards they had more or less expected. Because children may expect their friends to approve their actions, the support merely meets the expectation. A child may expect disliked children to disapprove of his or her actions, however, so that approval from such children exceeds expectations and has a powerful influence on performance.

Children's playmates can also affect a child's aggressiveness. Gerald Patterson, Richard Littman, and William Bricker (1967) describe just how this process works in a nursery school. When attacked, 97 percent of the beleaguered children responded in one of two general ways: they either reinforced their attacker — by becoming passive, crying, or assuming a defensive posture; or else they punished the offending child — by telling the teacher, retrieving their property, or retaliating with an aggressive act of their own. When a physical attack met with passiveness, crying, or defensiveness, before long the young attacker generally tried new acts of aggression against the original victim. Counteraggression, on the other hand, often altered the attacker's behavior. The young offender was likely to act in a changed manner toward the former victim, to pick a different victim, or both.

Other studies of the ways in which children encourage one another's behavior have shown how closely children's actions are linked to reinforcement. For example, Robert Wahler (1976) selected five nursery-school children whose behavior was related in some way to encouragement from their peers. He then enlisted the aid of the children's friends. Wahler asked them to ignore their friend whenever he or she acted in a certain way. Within a few days, the selected behavior — whether talking, shouting, fighting, or cooperating — dropped. When Wahler told the children's friends to resume their usual treatment, the five children went back to behaving just as they had before the experiment began. Studies such as this one indicate that by remaining alert to established patterns of peer reinforcement, parents and teachers may be able to use peers to help solve problems within the group. As we shall see in Chapter 17, peers systematically use reinforcement and punishment to steer boys and girls into what they consider appropriate behavior for each sex.

Peer Modeling

Reinforcement and punishment are not the only ways in which children influence one another's behavior; modeling is also powerful. Seeing another child behave in a certain way can affect the behavior of a child for at least three different reasons (Bandura, 1977). First, the watching child may learn how to do something new that he or she previously either could not do (such as working a puzzle) or would not have thought of doing (such as riding a bicycle with "no hands"). Second, the child may learn what happens when one acts in a certain way — for example, that fighting gets children into trouble

A child's actions often influence the behavior of peers; when a child models such behavior as helping put chairs in a circle, other children are likely to imitate the action—either at that moment or on another occasion. (Bobbe Carey/The Picture Cube)

or that disobeying does not always bring punishment. As a result of this knowledge, the child's own behavior may change. Third, a model may suggest possible ways of behaving in a strange situation. For example, a child may stand around nervously at a birthday party until another child begins throwing cake. Immediately, the ill-at-ease child and others join the game. As we saw in Chapter 15, even babies imitate the behavior of their older siblings.

Preschoolers are most likely to imitate the behavior of a model immediately after they have observed it; but such immediate imitation declines sharply as children reach the school years, becoming rare among nine- to eleven-year-olds. In a study by Rona Abramovitch and Joan Grusec (1978), no matter what the age group, the more a child was looked at, the more the child was imitated. Children high in the dominance hierarchy were imitated most, and these children also imitated others. It may be, say the investigators, that imitating others is a good way of establishing and maintaining influence.

Since children often learn a new response and save it for an appropriate occasion, imitation of models is likely to be much higher than Abramovitch and Grusec found. The decline in immediate imitation among older children could have two causes: first, they may have other ways of gaining influence; second, they may be more likely than younger children to store a response until later. Being called a copycat is no compliment among children in elementary school.

Models can establish a situation that encourages compliance or disobedience, as Thomas Wolf (1972) found when he told young boys not to play with an attractive toy and then had another boy comment on the prohibition. Some children heard the boy say that he expected most boys would not play with the toy, others heard him say that he expected most children would play with the forbidden toy. The model's statements about probable disobedience apparently made playing with the toy an appropriate thing to do, for children who heard the model say that he expected disobedience disobeyed more often than the others.

Additional research has shown that the consequences received by a model affect watching children as if they had received those rewards or punishments themselves (Walters, Leat, and Mezei, 1963). If the model is reinforced, as when an aggressive child gets to keep a toy he or she has grabbed, children are likely to imitate the model themselves, grabbing another child's toy at the first opportunity. But if the model is punished, as when the grabber is scolded and made to return the toy, the watching children are unlikely to grab a toy themselves.

Peer models can induce positive behavior as well as aggression and disobedience. In one study by Hartup and Brian Coates (1967), while four- and five-year-old children watched, one of their classmates solved a series of maze-drawing problems and then shared the prizes he received with a mythical child from another class. The model was actually the experimenter's confederate and had been coached to give away most of his trinkets to the "other child." After the altruistic model had left the room, the experimenter asked the watching children to complete the same maze-drawing task, rewarding their solutions with trinkets and giving them an opportunity to divide their prizes with the "other child." As Figure 16.1 shows, children who watched the altruistic model gave away many more trinkets than did children in the control group who had not seen the model, providing straightforward evidence that peer models can influence a socially approved activity.

The effectiveness of a peer model varies, and in the Hartup and Coates study, two factors seemed responsible: the nature of a child's previous experience with the model and the nature of the child's interactions with the peer group.

Popular children (who are accustomed to receiving reinforcement) were more likely to imitate a child who had previously reinforced them than a child who had never given them attention or approval. But unpopular children (who are rarely reinforced) were readier to imitate a child who had never paid them any attention than a child who had reinforced them in the past.

Figure 16.1 The results of Hartup and Coates' study of children's altruistic behavior. Children had six trinkets that they could give away in each trial. In all four of the experimental conditions, children saw an altruistic model, and in each case they shared more trinkets in comparison with the children in the control group, who saw no model. In addition, popular children gave away more trinkets when the model they saw was a child who usually reinforced them, whereas unpopular children tended to give away more trinkets when the model they saw was a child who had never before shown them attention or approval. (After Hartup and Coates, 1967)

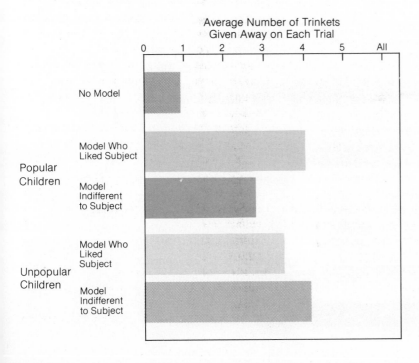

The kind of behavior modeled also affects the likelihood that children will imitate it. David Hicks (1971) had young girls watch a model and judge the model's behavior as either "awful" or "nice." Two months later the girls imitated behavior they had rated "nice" much more frequently than behavior they had rated "awful." Although modeling often establishes the appropriateness of actions children are unsure about, this study indicates that when children regard behavior as clearly inappropriate, they are unlikely to imitate it despite seeing a peer model it. Imitation seems most likely to occur when the modeled actions are so clearly "good" in the eyes of watching children that they are unlikely to be confused in their judgment of the action.

Since adults and peers can both serve as models, we might wonder which model a child is likely to follow when the examples conflict. Hartup (1964b) has noted that children who imitate models tend to do so whether the model is an adult or another child. But when it comes to learning new ways to express aggression, young children are more likely to imitate other children than adults (Hicks, 1965).

GETTING ALONG WITH PEERS

Whether children are comfortable with their peers will depend upon what they bring to the social system and the way others treat them. As we saw, children who emerge from secure and rewarding home relationships tend to be trusting and confident. They are also interested in and capable of initiating rewarding interactions and of receiving overtures from others. These characteristics correlate with a child's popularity as measured by *sociometric analysis*, a method that charts how often a child is chosen by peers as a preferred friend or companion (Campbell and Yarrow, 1961).

Children's behavior, the responses of others to them, and the expectations of all the persons

Good News on Integration

When elementary schools were first integrated, many people hoped that daily classroom contact would lead to increasing acceptance by children of other races. But sociometric analysis, in which children were asked to name their best friends, indicated that blacks almost invariably chose blacks and whites chose whites—even in schools that had been integrated for some time (Bartel, Bartel, and Grill, 1973). However, a study by Louise Singleton and Steven Asher (1979) shows that prospects for integration are better than gloomy predictions had led us to believe.

Singleton and Asher, assuming that acceptance rather than selection as best friend was the appropriate measure of integration, tested third-grade children in a midwestern city. Instead of asking them to name their *best* friends, they asked them to rate each of their classmates (on a scale of 1 to 5) as to how much they liked to play with them and how much they liked to work with them. Three years later, when the children were in the sixth grade, the test was repeated. At the same time, another group of third graders took the same test. All the children had been in integrated classrooms since kindergarten.

The news was mostly good. Each race in-

involved form an interlacing web, so that it is difficult to say which comes first or to establish a cause-effect relationship between a child's behavior and the responses of others to him or her. A number of additional factors over which children have no control—such as their appearance, their names, and their social skills—help determine their experiences within the group and their acceptance or rejection by their peers.

dicated a sturdy acceptance of the other, producing similar ratings for play and for work. Although children rated their own race higher, the difference was slight. Blacks indicated they liked to play and work with whites, and whites did the same for blacks. Gender played a larger role than race in the ratings. Boys rated boys of another race high, and girls low; girls showed the same pattern, with white children showing stronger cross-gender rejection of the other race than black children. As children moved from the third to the sixth grade, cross-gender rejection dropped among all boys but increased among white girls.

White children showed no greater preference for their own race in the sixth grade than they had in the third, but blacks were not as comfortable playing and working with whites by the time they became sixth graders. Singleton and Asher suggest that by the time they are eleven or twelve, blacks have become much more aware of their minority status and so make ingroup-outgroup distinctions, redrawing friendship lines with a greater emphasis on race.

Racial relations did not improve in the three years between the tests, indicating that natural contact has done all it can by the third grade. (The new third graders gave their classmates the same positive ratings as the sixth graders had done three years earlier.)

Singleton and Asher suggest, therefore, that curricula encouraging cooperation—which have improved race relations among fifth-grade children (Blaney et al., 1977)—might be instituted as early as the third grade.

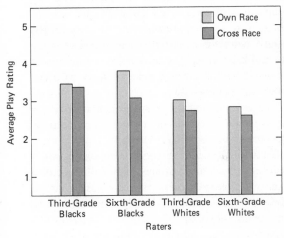

Black and white children attending integrated schools said they liked to play with children of the opposite race, although both showed a slight preference for their own race.

From L. C. Singleton and S. R. Asher, "Racial Integration and Children's Peer Preferences: An Investigation of Developmental and Cohort Differences," *Child Development*, 50 (1979), 936-941. © The Society for Research in Child Development, Inc. Reprinted by permission.

Names and Appearance

Even among preschool children, physical attractiveness is an asset and unattractiveness is a liability. Karen Dion (1973), for example, found that young boys and girls prefer attractive peers as potential friends and expect them to be friendly and nice, but they reject unattractive peers and expect them to be unfriendly and mean. In this respect, Judith Langlois and

Cookie Stephan (1977) found that kindergarten children and fourth graders generally hold the same views. They found, for example, that black, Anglo, and Mexican-American children see attractive peers, regardless of their race, as being more likeable, smarter, more friendly, and more willing to share than unattractive peers. Attractive Anglo children are particularly likely to benefit from shared social stereotypes, since they are likely to be perceived by all children, regardless of their race, as being the smartest, kindest, and happiest, and as doing the best in school. Attractiveness was, however, more important than ethnic background in determining the children's responses.

Research has shown that physique is also likely to influence a child's popularity. J. Robert Staffieri (1967) investigated the relationship between the popularity and the physique of boys from six to ten years old and found that muscular boys are more popular than boys who are skinny or plump. Most of the boys he studied wished for a muscular build in accord with the masculine stereotype.

Similarly, an attractive first name is likely to be an asset whereas an unattractive first name is likely to be a liability (McDavid and Harari, 1966). Children with attractive first names, such as John or Karen, are more likely to be popular with their peers than children with unattractive names such as Horace or Adelle. Herbert Harari and John McDavid (1973) found that children's names can bias teachers' judgments. In this study, they randomly assigned attractive names (e.g., David or Lisa) or unattractive names (e.g., Herbert or Bertha) to a group of fifth-grade essays of similar quality. When teachers then graded the essays, those with attractive names attached received marks that were a full letter grade higher than those that carried unattractive names.

In view of the expectations that names carry, it is understandable that children's self-concepts may reflect similar effects. Among sixth-grade boys, for example, those with desirable names had a more positive view of themselves, their abilities, and their interpersonal relations than boys with undesirable names (Garwood, 1976). Boys with desirable names also believed they could do better work and get along better with others in more situations, and they made significantly higher scores on a standardized achievement test.

An attractive name and appearance may enhance popularity, but they are not enough to secure the role of leader. Although popular children often become leaders in their peer group, children tend to be discriminating in their assignment of leadership roles. When children are organizing a baseball game, they generally listen to an athletically skilled child; when they are staging a play, they turn to an imaginative child. Thus in a study of leadership among a large number of six- to eleven-year-old children, C. Wade Harrison, James Rawls, and Donna Rawls (1971) found that the leaders generally tended to be more intelligent, active, aggressive, achieving, and socially adept than children who rarely led; in addition, leaders tended to be more competent in a specific area of development.

Social Skills

Name, appearance, ethnic background, and gender are not the only determinants of popularity. A child's skill in relating to his or her peers also plays a major role in determining popularity. As Steven Asher (1978) has pointed out, a child must be able to initiate new relationships and then maintain them. When elementary-school children pretended for researchers that they were meeting a strange child, popular children greeted the newcomer, gave or requested information, or invited the child to join in activities. Unpopular children were much less likely to do so (Gottman, Gonso, and Rasmussen, 1975). If the first meeting with a strange child goes badly, children who believe the rebuff is due to a misunderstanding will try again when they meet new children; children who believe they were rebuffed because they simply do not know how to make friends may avoid a new encounter (Dweck and Goetz, 1977).

Asher has compiled a list of maintenance skills that children use to keep a friendship going. They include the ability to sustain informative communications with another child, to analyze the effectiveness of their own communications and adjust their messages accordingly, to tell another child when his or her message is ambiguous, to interact in a positive manner, and

Although uncontrollable factors, such as name, appearance, ethnic background, and gender, can affect popularity, popular children are friendly and generous with praise and approval. (Jean-Claude Le Jeune/Stock, Boston, Inc.)

to manage interpersonal conflict. As already noted, popular children are friendly, and generous with praise and approval. Among nursery school children, they also tend to go along with the wishes of another child and often spontaneously offer their playmates toys or food (Hartup, Glazer, and Charlesworth, 1967). Popular children also help their peers — but they do it in accepted ways. Gary Ladd and Sherri Oden (1979) found that third and fifth graders who suggested highly unusual ways of helping other children tended to be disliked.

Children may be aggressive and still have friends; but if their blows or verbal abuse are seen as inappropriate by their peers, they will be disliked (Moore, 1967). Among nursery school children, as was reported in Chapter 2, the child on the top of the dominance ladder is rarely the most aggressive child in the group. A study of adolescent boys (Olweus, 1977) indicates that the popularity of bullies is average; they are

neither leaders nor are they rejected. At nursery school, the scapegoats are children who do not remain on their rung of the dominance ladder; but among adolescents, the scapegoats are social isolates who do nothing to provoke the attacks of bullies. In Olweus' study of Swedish adolescents, the bullies were physically strong, the scapegoats physically weak.

The personal and social consequences of popularity show up in other ways. Herbert Harari and John McDavid (1969), for example, recruited both a popular and an unpopular child as collaborators and had them carry out prohibited acts in the classroom, such as stealing money from the teacher. The other children in the class, who had watched what took place, were later called into the principal's office and asked what had happened. Half the children came in by themselves; the rest were accompanied by another child.

The principal questioned all the children, insisting that they tell on the culprit. When children were interrogated alone, all identified the guilty child. When the children were questioned in pairs, however, they refused to tell on the popular child but without hesitation told on the unpopular culprit. Children apparently realize that their actions in the presence of another child are likely to get back to their peers. Informing on a popular child could lead to their own rejection, whereas informing on an unpopular child is unlikely to have adverse personal consequences.

Children who are popular with their peers are likely to be popular adolescents as well; popularity rankings from year to year throughout childhood and adolescence generally remain stable (Roff, Sells, and Golden, 1972). One factor that continues to have an important impact upon popularity is physical attractiveness. But extreme attractiveness is no help when it comes to popularity with one's own gender, as Dennis Krebs and Allen Adinolfi (1975) discovered when they investigated friendship and dating choices of sixty male and sixty female residents of a student dormitory. Each resident chose the persons they liked and disliked most. The most liked persons were students who were attractive but not stunning. The most attractive students were most frequently rejected by members of their own sex; the least attractive students were chosen neither as the most nor as the least liked — they were simply ignored.

Popularity is also highly related to conformity to peer-group norms, customs, and fads. During adolescence, as in childhood, the characteristics having most to do with peer acceptance are those that define appropriate sex-typed behavior in our society (Hartup, 1970). Athletic participation and skill, standing up for one's rights, sexual prowess, and sometimes drinking prowess, are valued in the adolescent boy. The popular girl is one who is fun to be with and has interpersonal skills. Because these characteristics bring with them the positive consequences of peer acceptance, they are in turn strengthened. Thus, participation in peer activities reinforces sex-role learning. This continuity in socialization may be largely responsible for the general stability of popularity rankings.

CHANGING RELATIONSHIPS

As children develop, the nature of their interaction with peers changes. The infant plays beside and with another baby, making simple social overtures. When children enter nursery school or kindergarten, peers increase in importance. Children find a large number of schoolmates of their own age and, in elementary school, many others of slightly different ages. The new peer group includes children from different neighborhoods, children who would have remained strangers without the school setting.

Friendship

A wider group of acquaintances, however, does not necessarily lead to an increase in the number of close friends. During early childhood, chil-

The course of friendship changes during development. The relationship of these girls is based on shared activities; with adolescence, they will build friendships based on psychological sharing and intimacy. (Elizabeth Crews/Stock, Boston, Inc.)

dren tend to draw close to an increasing number of their peers; but during later childhood, their friendships increase in intensity rather than in number. They spend more time with their friends than they used to, playing after school at friends' houses or spending the night with friends. As they move into adolescence, the relation with their peers changes, and so do their friendships, moving from the congenial sharing of activities to psychological sharing and intimacy. Asked what they like best about a friend, young children mention play; they expect their friends to be entertaining. Adolescents and adults, however, expect their friends to be useful (Reisman and Shorr, 1978).

Investigators have found that similar personal characteristics are a major determinant of whether two people will form a friendship (Byrne, 1971). These studies suggest that obvious similarities are more important in the early stages of friendship but that a friendship is not likely to last unless the persons involved go on to discover that they see intentions, motives, causes, and characteristics in the same way. In the beginning of the relationship, friends tend to apply such categories as physical characteristics or people's roles or activities to assess others. If the friendship lasts, they tend to use psychological categories such as "sly" or "tries hard"; that is, they share a way of perceiving and thinking about the unobvious attributes of self and others (Duck, 1973, 1977).

Intimate friendships are not likely to develop in the relative absence of compatible psychological constructs. For example, Stephen Duck (1973) found that whereas only 5 percent of the twelve-year-olds he studied used psychological constructs to describe others, the number rose to 25 percent among fourteen- and fifteen-year-olds. Among college students, 63 percent described others in terms of psychological characteristics.

The developmental course of friendship does not contradict such a view. Friendships among girls appear to progress from the activity-centered pairs of late childhood and preadolescence to the interdependent, emotional, and conflict-resolving relationships of middle adolescence, finally becoming relationships that are less emotional, less an instrument for reducing conflict, and more a sharing of personalities, talents, and interests (Douvan and Adelson, 1966). It is the emotional friendships that Harry Stack Sullivan (1953) had in mind when he described *chumship* and indicated that such a same-sex relationship was necessary to the later development of heterosexual intimacy and mature sexuality.

Although male friends in college use similar psychological constructs, junior-high and high-school boys appear to be less concerned with the personal relationship involved in friendship. Their friendships are more like those found among preadolescent girls and involve a congenial companion with whom one shares the same reality-oriented activities (Douvan and Adelson, 1966). This gender difference is part of a larger pattern of gender-role differences that make interpersonal relationships in this society a major factor in the formation of female identity. Males are also more likely than females to spend their adolescent social lives in cliques and gangs instead of in pairs.

Peer Groups

Children come to have definite reactions to and expectations of other children (and of themselves, depending on how other children respond to them). Organization creeps into children's relationships, and two patterns are characteristic of later childhood, when the peer group takes on increased importance. The first is the elaboration of an ingroup-outgroup sense of belonging that is supported by special group activities and rituals and the exclusion of outsiders. Children learn to define their own special qualities and ways of behaving in relation to how the group acts and, frequently, in contrast to the way outsiders act. Fortunately, group organization is not rigid during these years, and many such cliques break up and reform, so that temporarily and arbitrarily excluded children may later slip into the fold. A second pattern of group interaction that soon emerges is the development of hierarchies. The dominance hierarchy present among nursery school children, which was discussed in Chapter 2, is joined by other ratings. Any child in a fifth-grade classroom can rattle off an ordered list of the smartest, most athletic, and most popular, and children show surprising agreement. The roles and positions that children take in peer-group play provide their training for the later assumption of adult social roles, and the ranking of children in their dominance hierarchies seems to predict general social competence (Hartup, 1979).

The structure of the peer group changes during adolescence to accommodate the development of sexual maturation and heterosexual behavior. At first the peer group is similar to the preadolescent gang; it is a clique of adolescents of the same sex. Then, about midadolescence, it becomes heterosexual, and each member generally establishes a significant relationship with a member of the opposite sex (Dunphy, 1963). Dunphy and other observers have also found that group members often deny the existence of a hierarchy within the group. This is not always the case, however, as is shown by a study of the way dominance hierarchies were formed at a summer camp (Savin-Williams, 1979).

In Ritch Savin-Williams' study of twelve- to fourteen-year-olds at a summer camp, dominance hierarchies in the boys' cabins were frankly recognized, but in only two of the four girls' cabins did the girls agree on the ranking of leaders and followers. Leaders among both sexes were self-confident, "cool," mature, athletic, intelligent, and popular. Boy leaders asserted themselves physically, argued with others, and tended to threaten and displace their cabinmates. Girls controlled by recognizing the status of their cabinmates, giving unsolicited advice and information to some and shunning or ignoring others. Leaders took the biggest pieces of cake at dinner, the preferred seats at discussions, and the best sleeping sites near the campfire at campouts. The rankings, says Savin-Williams, appeared to add stability and predictability to social relationships and to reduce group friction and overt aggression. Leaders took on group obligations; dominant girls, for example, often intervened in squabbles and patched interpersonal relationships.

Because leaders are useful to the group—their status depending upon some combination of personal attributes and material resources—the dominant position is not necessarily permanent. Changes in group goals are likely to lead to fluctuations in the hierarchy; as activities change,

Children's peer groups develop dominance hierarchies, which fluctuate as group goals change; the star pitcher and the home-run hitter who are near the top of this group may find themselves lower in the dominance hierarchy when baseball season ends. (Read R. Brugger/ The Picture Cube)

the resources of different members may become important (Sherif and Sherif, 1964). Thus status rankings over the months and years are less stable than popularity ratings.

CONFORMITY

No matter what status children hold in a group, group solidarity exercises a great deal of influence on their behavior. Competition within a group may decrease solidarity (Stendler, Damrin, and Haines, 1951), but Muzafer and Carolyn Sherif (1953, 1964) have found that evenly balanced competition between groups results in greater cohesiveness within each group. Although occasional rancor may appear just after a competitive defeat, group members generally become much closer to one another in competitive situations. Because competition between groups produces a cooperative atmosphere within an individual group, it is not surprising that it should promote group solidarity. However, in a field study of unbalanced competition among boys in a summer camp, when one group consistently lost, the losing group threatened to collapse in disharmony (Sherif and Sherif, 1953). Apparently, when the unpleasantness generated by defeat becomes constant, it simply overcomes any tendency within the group for members to cooperate.

Whether competition was balanced or unbalanced, it produced a considerable amount of friction between groups. The boys looked down on members of the other group, and the situation eventually exploded into open hostility. This intergroup hostility further strengthened group cohesiveness and increased the influence of the group over the behavior of its members. Further, boys who were not normally hostile participated in intensively aggressive acts for the sake of the

group. In such a case, it seems that the structured group has the ability to overpower any tendency children have developed toward self-judgment and to lead them to engage in behavior they would normally avoid.

The strong influence that peers can have on a child's behavior was clearly demonstrated in a study by Philip Costanzo and Marvin Shaw (1966), who asked children to compare the lengths of a pair of lines and identify the longer one. One line was obviously longer than the other, but all except one of the children were confederates of the investigators, and they chose the incorrect line. If the child denied the evidence of his or her senses and agreed with the obviously incorrect judgment of the group, the child had altered a personal judgment to conform to that of peers. As Figure 16.2 shows, a

Figure 16.2 Children's conformity to the judgments of a peer group. Both females and males show increased susceptibility to peer influence with age, until early adolescence; then it gradually declines. (After Costanzo and Shaw, 1966)

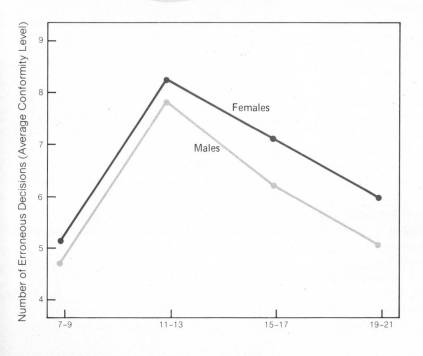

child's susceptibility to this form of peer influence increased with age, reached its peak during the preadolescent years, and then gradually declined.

A recent study by Thomas Berndt (1979) supports Costanzo and Shaw's finding that conformity to peers declines during adolescence. (See Figure 16.3.) Berndt found that children's tendencies to conform to their parents' wishes decrease from the third through the ninth grade, and that conformity to antisocial pressure from peers increases sharply from the third to the ninth grade, then declines during the high-school years. Among third graders, parents' wishes outweigh those of peers; where there is conflict, third graders generally conform to their parents' desires. Although peer influence increases among sixth graders, there seems to be no conflict between family standards and those of the peer group. Children apparently live in two worlds, each with its own standards. Conflict between those worlds is sharp among ninth graders, perhaps because the push toward antisocial behavior is strongest among these children. But among eleventh and twelfth graders, the conflict has eased; adolescents no longer feel compelled to conform to their peers' wishes. In addition, they are beginning to accept conventional adult standards for their behavior.

These findings conflict with some accounts of adolescent development, which assume that as a child reaches adolescence, conformity to parents' wishes decreases and conformity to peer wishes increases—in other words, that conflict between peer and parental standards inevitably accompanies adolescence. However, no available evidence demonstrates that the onset of adolescence necessarily means any decrease of conformity to parental demands. Adolescents conform to peers in matters pertaining to choice of friends, language fads, and clothes, but they conform to parental values in matters pertaining to achievement, such as academic performance and job or career aspirations (Brittain, 1963).

Studies by Denise Kandel and Gerald Lesser (1972) in the United States and Denmark indi-

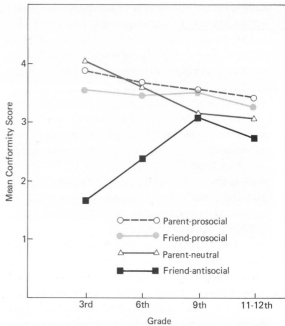

Figure 16.3 The course of antisocial peer pressure on children follows a characteristic course, rising sharply from third to sixth grade, then declining during the high-school years as adolescents begin to accept conventional standards.

SOURCE: From T. J. Berndt, "Developmental Changes in Conformity to Peers and Parents," *Developmental Psychology,* 15 (1979), 606-616. Copyright 1979 by The American Psychological Association. Reprinted by permission.

cate that in both countries parental influence on an adolescent's life goals is much stronger than peer influence. Although they confirmed earlier findings that adolescents rarely reward intellectual achievement in their peers, they also found that peers have less influence than parents on adolescents' future educational goals.

The rise and subsequent decline of peer influence has been studied by Hartup (1970), who suggests that peer influence may initially rise, as the growing child's ability to see things from the perspective of another increases. The later decline he explains by the children's ability to reinforce themselves. That is, as children interact with their peers, they begin to internalize the statements other children make about their behavior as well as the effects of peers' responses to them. And as they internalize the judgments of others, children develop the ability to evaluate their own actions and pay less attention to the judgments of their peers.

The continuing link between adult and adolescent standards is illustrated by studies of adolescent alcohol use. Every study of alcohol use has found that the drinking patterns of teen-agers directly reflect those of their parents and the community in which they live. About two-thirds of all adults in the United States drink on occasion, and drinking is more prevalent among persons of higher social status than among those of lower social status. Margaret Bacon and Mary Brush Jones (1968) found that most adolescents who drink tend to drink moderately, to begin drinking at home with their parents, and to follow the rules of alcohol consumption that their parents set. They also found that drinking among adolescents varies from 86 percent in Nassau County, New York, to 44 percent in rural Kansas. Other studies show that teen-age drinking patterns imitate adult drinking patterns: boys drink more than girls, city adolescents drink more than country adolescents; middle- and upper-middle-class adolescents drink more than working- or lower-class adolescents.

Because adolescents have learned from their parents and other adults to perceive drinking as an explicitly social activity, peer-group norms for acceptable drinking behavior tend to keep such behavior in line. Thus when adolescents drink in the secrecy of the peer group, social control is still present.

Smoking is one area where parental admonitions appear to have little effect, and most psychologists believe that peer pressure is a primary cause of adolescent smoking. Adolescents know about the risks connected with cigarettes, but since the effects do not appear for decades, they are not gravely concerned about the personal consequences (Evans, 1976). If peer pressure is indeed an important factor in adolescent smoking, then self-confident individuals should be the most resistant and therefore the least likely to smoke. A study sponsored by the American Cancer Society showed that this was true among boys but not among girls. Boys who smoked were less self-confident than boys who did not smoke, but girls who smoked were more self-confident than girls who did not. The girl smokers were also heavier smokers and more socially outgoing than the boy smokers, but the girls did not regard smoking as a social asset. Like many women, girls believe that by keeping them from eating, smoking helps them control their weight.

Adolescent use of other drugs alarms parents, but as with alcohol, adult behavior serves as a model. Adolescents have had more than a decade of exposure to adults whose behavior—whether legal or illegal—has been a model for their own experimentation and for the control

Peers often dictate an adolescent's choice of friends, language, and clothes, but their influence is much weaker than that of parents when it comes to the adolescent's attitude toward education or the choice of a career. (Carol Palmer/The Picture Cube)

of group behavior. But adults who smoke, drink alcohol, or take tranquilizers or barbiturates tend to ignore these connections and consider drugs as a purely adolescent problem.

The experience of other cultures shows that conflicts between parent and peer standards are not necessary; the peer group can function as a representative of adult society. Urie Bronfenbrenner's (1970) observations and studies in the Soviet Union indicate that Soviet children are brought up in a series of "nested social units" that carry the responsibility for a child's behavior, each concerned with a progressively larger number of children. For example, in the school, the units include the row of double-seated desks, the classroom, and the entire school; youth organizations are composed of similar units. Because the group is held responsible for the individual's behavior and administers formal rewards and punishments, children soon learn to adhere to society's standards and to subordinate their own interests to those of the group. The Soviet peer group functions under the guidance of the adult society. Bronfenbrenner points out that an earlier American experiment along the lines of the one carried out by Costanzo and Shaw (1966) shows how the process works. Morton Deutsch and Harold Gerard (1955) discovered that when a person's behavior affects only him- or herself, conformity in the line experiment runs about 33 percent. But when the entire group is rewarded for making the fewest errors, thereby intensifying group feeling, twice as many people conform to the obviously incorrect judgment.

SOCIAL ISOLATION

Not all children are accepted by their peers. Several studies conducted over a thirty-year period (Bonney, 1943; Gronlund, 1959; Hymel and Asher, 1977) have shown that when children are asked to designate their friends, about 10 percent of the children in a group are not named at all. But not all friendless children are shy, withdrawn isolates; some are aggressive children who interact as much as the rest. Indeed, studies have shown that there is little relationship between a child's acceptance by the group and his or her interaction with peers (Gottman, 1977). As we have seen, children's acceptance depends upon a number of factors.

Rejection by their peers may have greater consequences for children than simply the unhappiness that often accompanies social isolation. Isolates tend to drop out of school (Ullman, 1957); they are also more likely than the accepted child to have later emotional problems or to become juvenile delinquents. When researchers checked back eleven years after they had studied a group of third graders, they found that children who had been disliked by their peers were more likely to have developed emotional problems than the rest of the group (Cowen et al., 1973). Another study (Roff, Sells, and Golden, 1972) found that rejected middle-class and upper-middle-class children tended to become juvenile delinquents. Social isolation did not predict delinquency among lower-class children, and it has been suggested that because gang membership accompanied by delinquency is common at low socioeconomic levels, it washes out the connection between isolation and delinquency (Asher, 1978). That is, in a group where delinquent acts are considered part of normal social activities, peer acceptance may demand them.

Until recently, educators and psychologists did little to bring rejected children back into the group. After all, the withdrawn child does not disrupt the classroom, and teachers—who most often witness peer interaction—tend to be concerned about the child who interferes with classroom or playground activities, not about the social isolate. Realization of the possible social consequences of isolation has changed the picture, and various programs are now under way that attempt to bring rejected children into the group by using behavior modification, modeling, or coaching to teach isolates the social skills they need to get along with other children.

Approaches based on behavior modification

Children who are rejected by their peers are more likely than other children to drop out of school, develop emotional problems, or become juvenile delinquents. (John R. Maher/EKM-Nepenthe)

teach social skills by reinforcing children's attempts at social interaction. Sometimes a child already possesses these skills but does not use them. Ann, a bright, creative four-year-old enrolled in a Washington nursery school, was such a child. When Ann entered school, her advanced physical skills (climbing, jumping, riding) and her art activities, nature collections, original songs, advanced speech, and helpfulness brought praise and approval from teachers but not from the other children. Within a few weeks, Ann retreated from group play and spent most of her time seeking attention from adults, watching the other children from a distance, plucking at her lower lip or tugging her hair, and going off to "sleep" in a make-believe bed in the play yard.

When Eileen Allen, Montrose Wolf, and their associates (Allen *et al.*, 1964) were called in, they discovered that the techniques Ann used successfully to get adult attention necessarily isolated her further from her peers. Using simple behavior modification, the team had the teachers reinforce Ann only when she interacted with other children and ignore her when she was alone or seeking adult attention. Ann's behavior changed immediately. Instead of spending 10 to 20 percent of her time interacting with other children, she spent 60 percent of her time with the group. The children responded, and Ann seemed to enjoy her play. After several weeks, the teachers slowly phased out their reinforcement for peer activities, thereby putting Ann on an intermittent schedule of reinforcement. Ann continued to interact confidently with other children and seemed to have become a happy member of the peer group.

Allen and her colleagues point out that Ann's case is unusual because she already had learned appropriate social skills. Many social isolates have never learned how to interact successfully with others. But reinforcing social interaction and ignoring (thereby extinguishing) actions that interfere with it also helps such children learn social skills. These investigators say that children who lack social skills generally take several weeks to reach the level of social interaction that Ann achieved on the first morning of the behavior modification program. When rewards for social interaction are ended abruptly, however, children tend to retreat to their original isolation. It is important to transfer to intermittent reinforcement and then gradually fade the therapeutic rewards, allowing the natural reinforcement of group play to build up, as was done in Ann's case.

When modeling techniques are used, children watch filmed models who approach children at play and join in their activities. After withdrawn children have seen the filmed model, they may engage in role-playing, rehearsing the actions they have seen on the film. Modeling techniques have led to increased social interaction by withdrawn children; when observed a month later, children are still interacting at a high level (Evers and Schwartz, 1973).

In a program that combined social reinforcement with modeling techniques, however, the reinforcement seemed more powerful and longer lasting than the modeling section of the program (Weinrott, Corson, and Wilchesky, 1979). This study used peer reinforcement and group rewards in addition to rewards for the isolated children. By the end of the program, these first- to third-grade isolates were involved in as much social interaction as other children, and their peer activities extended to lunchroom and playground contacts. The formerly isolated children began to visit friends and to invite them to their own homes. Teachers said the children seemed happier, more alert, and eager to assume responsible tasks, although they did not show as much altruistic or cooperative behavior as other children, nor did they pay as much attention to others.

Coaching, the third approach to social isolation, directly instructs children in social skills. Sherri Oden and Steven Asher (1977) taught third- and fourth-grade children how to start playing a game; how to pay attention; how to take turns; how to share materials; how to reward other people by looking at them, smiling, offering help or encouragement. The children practiced the skills they had learned in play sessions with their peers. Afterward, the coaches met again with the children and went over the skills they had been taught. After a six-week program, the isolated children appeared to be accepted by their peers; a follow-up one year later showed that the acceptance had increased. The program's only visible failure was that it did not increase the number of "best friends" the isolates had.

No matter what kind of approach is used, the earlier the intervention, the better for the isolated child. It may be harder to change established patterns of withdrawal in older children; in addition, isolated children's peers may be slower to change their opinion of a withdrawn child (Asher, 1978).

COMPETENCE AND ACHIEVEMENT

The competence a child develops among peers can influence other areas of life. How peers respond to a young boy, whether they accept him, look up to him, or regard him as a scapegoat, will have profound effects on his own sense of control, competence, and autonomy. The boy's feelings about himself will affect the decisions he makes, the way he meets challenges and opportunities, and the impact of rewards and punishments along the way. Often it is not what happens to a child that bolsters or diminishes the sense of competence but the way the child explains the event to him- or herself. A child who feels incompetent will not be motivated to succeed. Although experiences with others deeply affect a child's feelings of competency and attitudes toward achievement, these experiences interact with early home influences. As with many aspects of personality, psychologists have traced the birth of a child's need to achieve, or *achievement motivation*, to the family circle.

Family Influence

Both mother and father influence a child's urge to succeed, but each plays a different role. When Marian Winterbottom (1958) studied mothers, looking for a link between achievement motivation and child rearing, she found certain clear differences between the mothers of boys with strong achievement motivation and mothers of boys whose achievement motivation was weak. The first group of mothers make more demands on their sons before they are eight years old and place more restrictions on them before they are seven — but the demands made are greater than the restrictions imposed. They expect their sons to do such things as hang up their clothes, make their beds, do well in competition with other children, attempt difficult undertakings without asking for help, cut their own meat, make their own friends, and select their own clothes earlier than do mothers of boys with weak achievement motivation. Mothers of boys with high achievement motivation also evaluate their sons' accomplishments higher and reward them more profusely than do mothers of boys with low achievement motivation. The mothers' expectations for their sons indicate that they train their children for both independence and achievement, and certainly there is likely to be some connection between doing things well and doing things by oneself.

But simply training a boy to be independent will not motivate him to succeed, report Bernard Rosen and Roy D'Andrade (1959), who watched parents interact with their sons. Mothers of boys with high achievement motivation stressed

achievement at the expense of independence and became emotionally involved as their sons worked at difficult tasks. They showed significantly more warmth — but also more rejection following a poor performance — and were more dominant than mothers of boys with low achievement motivation. They pushed their sons to succeed.

Fathers of boys with high achievement motivation stressed independence rather than achievement in their sons. They sat back and gave the boys hints instead of becoming involved as the mothers did. They were less rejecting, less pushing, and less dominant than fathers of boys with weak achievement motivation, who tended to be relatively rejecting, dominating parents.

Both the parents of boys with high achievement motivation had high aspirations for their sons, expected them to do well, believed they were competent problem solvers, and were interested in and concerned with their sons' performance. They also tended to be competitive and involved and to enjoy the problem-solving part of the study themselves. They showed more affection for their sons than did the parents of boys with weak achievement motivation, and they rewarded successful performance with warmth and approval.

In Brazil, where parents wait until their children are older to begin independence training and where the push to achieve comes later, boys' levels of achievement motivation are lower than they are in the United States (Rosen, 1962). Brazilian parents expect their children to show obedience and deference, and they surround them with indulgence and affection. As a result, suggests Rosen, Brazilian boys may begin with unrealistic expectations of success and then lose interest in achievement and competition after a few failures.

Although Robert Sears (1970) did not look specifically at achievement motivation, he found that among twelve-year-old boys whose early years were marked by warm parents and non-dominant fathers, self-concept and school achievement in reading and arithmetic tended to be high. For girls, there was no relation between father dominance and self-concept, but school achievement was linked to parental warmth.

Parental warmth may not be the best recipe for producing a girl whose achievement extends outside the classroom. Aletha Stein and Margaret Bailey (1973) reviewed studies of achievement in girls and concluded that girls are most likely to become independent high achievers when their parents are only moderately warm and moderately to highly permissive, and when they both reinforce and encourage the girls' attempts. Excessive maternal warmth, say Stein and Bailey, may produce a dependent girl, and some studies (e.g., Baumrind, 1968; 1972) have shown that early protectiveness on the part of parents produces girls who are passive and withdraw from situations that demand achievement motivation. Achievement is also encouraged when girls have high-achieving mothers as role models.

Expecting achievement from boys and girls, then rewarding their successes and punishing their failures appears to be intimately bound up with the development of achievement. Middle-class parents generally have higher expectations for their children than do lower-class parents. Asked how their four-year-olds would perform on four tasks, middle-class parents consistently predicted higher scores for their children than lower-class parents predicted for their children (Marcus and Corsini, 1978). Middle-class parents expected their children to make average scores, but lower-class parents believed their children would perform less well than the average child. In fact, middle-class and lower-class children made similar, average scores on the tasks. The low expectations held for their children by lower-class parents may be one reason that lower-class children tend to be low achievers in school.

Most research on achievement motivation has been done on boys, but research on another aspect of achievement has focused on what was originally considered a female phenomenon: the fear of success.

Fear of Success

Concerned because research into achievement motivation seemed unable to explain its development adequately in girls and women, Matina Horner (1969) suggested that women learn to fear success. They learn early that achievement in the world is aggressive and therefore masculine; if they compete, they may become less feminine (Tavris and Offir, 1977). And if they defeat males in competition, they may be punished. When women discover that aversive social consequences follow when they expend effort, persist in the face of obstacles, or compete and actually succeed, they may learn to withdraw from achievement situations—or avoid them. At the very least, they may learn to play down their accomplishments. They withdraw, then, not because they are afraid of failure but because they are afraid of success.

Subsequent research has shown that the situation is not quite that simple. Men and boys frequently show as much evidence of "fear of success" as girls and women do, and male college students who feel threatened by female competence score high on tests that measure fear of success, but their girlfriends do not (Tresemer, 1974). The standard test requires one to complete a story that begins with a male or female in a moment of high success. If that success is followed in the story by images of failure, the person shows "fear of success." Males tend to show greater fear of success when writing about a female in a nontraditional situation ("Ann finds herself at the top of her medical-school class") than when writing about a male in the same situation.

Believing that fear of success might reflect a

girl's or woman's attempt to avoid expected punishment for outperforming a male, John Condry and Sharon Dyer (1977) studied the impulse among fifth- to ninth-grade children. First children took a standard fear-of-success test. Their stories showed that fear of success declined with age in both sexes, but especially among girls. Fifth-grade girls showed much greater fear of success than did fifth-grade boys; by the ninth grade, they showed less.

Next, Condry and Dyer wanted to see whether fear of success showed itself in an actual competitive situation. Boys and girls, working by themselves but seated in pairs opposite each other, unscrambled anagrams as part of an "intelligence test." Afterward, they were taken to another room, one at a time, ostensibly for another test but actually to be told that they had "won" over their partner of the opposite sex. Then they returned to the testing room, where they were seated opposite the same partner and asked to unscramble more anagrams. If they feared success, they would not do as well on their second try with anagrams.

Fifth-grade girls and boys both improved on the second anagram test, and by about the same amount. The scores of seventh-grade girls plummeted, however, while the scores of seventh-grade boys improved. (See Figure 16.4.) Among ninth graders, boys' scores went up substantially and girls' average scores improved, but only by a slight amount. Placed in direct competition, neither girls nor boys in the fifth grade nor boys in the seventh and ninth grades showed any fear of success. But told they were outperforming a male, older girls retreated. Their achievement was severely affected, despite the fact that they understood they were taking an intelligence test that might be expected to affect their academic futures. Seventh graders simply withdrew from competition. When girls' scores were analyzed, however, ninth graders showed a curious pattern: half the girls improved and half showed disastrous declines.

Condry and Dyer believe their study of ac-

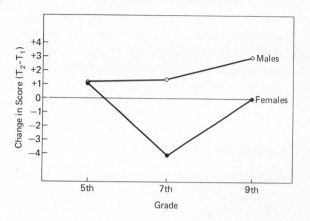

Figure 16.4 When children discover they have defeated a member of the opposite sex in an anagram game, adolescent boys and girls react differently to the news, and on a similar game seventh-grade girls show a pronounced fear of success.

SOURCE: From J. C. Condry and S. L. Dyer, "Behavioral Fantasy Measures of Fear of Success in Children," *Child Development*, 48 (1977), 14 17-1425. © The Society for Research in Child Development, Inc. Reprinted by permission.

tual behavior is in line with sex-role development. As we shall see in the next chapter, adolescents show increased adherence to stereotypical views of appropriate male and female behavior. Most seventh-grade girls have entered puberty. Ninth-grade girls, many of whom have reached the stage of formal operational thought, are able to break the restriction of stereotypes—although only half of them do so. The discrepancy between actual behavior (the anagram game) and performance on traditional fear-of-success tests indicates that results from tests purporting to measure fear of success may, as Condry and Dyer (1976) have suggested, be contaminated by common knowledge about the consequences that befall a girl or woman who steps too far outside the boundaries of accepted female behavior. That is, adolescents and women may attribute such fear to other females although they do not feel it themselves. The study does indicate that some adolescent girls and women may indeed be so upset by the thought of beating men at their own game that they retreat.

Explaining Achievement

Children's reactions to the world vary, depending on what they perceive as the cause of their behavior. If they believe that they get along with their friends or play games well because of their own ability and effort (an attitude linked to an internal locus of control), they learn to take pride in those accomplishments. If they believe their successes are due to outside factors over which they have little control (an attitude linked to an external locus of control), they are likely to take small satisfaction in whatever they do. And if they believe they have little success at games because of an inherent lack of ability, they are likely to avoid similar encounters in the future or to enter them expecting to fail.

By the time they are in kindergarten, most children have developed consistent explanations for the results of their efforts and social interactions. These explanations are likely to depend in part on their intelligence and socioeconomic level. Toni Falbo (1975) found, for example, that five-year-old middle-class children were more likely than working-class children to stress the causal relationship between a person's effort and success or failure at a task. Bright children generally explained success as being due to personal ability and failure as due to the difficulty of the task. Less bright children tended to explain success as being due to the ease of the task but used lack of personal ability to explain failure. Falbo points out that the bright children's explanations encourage them to perceive themselves as responsible for success ("I'm smart") and not responsible for failure ("It was too hard"). In contrast, less bright children's explanations encourage them to perceive themselves as responsible for failure ("I'm dumb") and as deserving no credit for their success ("It was just easy").

Studies by Diane Ruble and her associates (1976), however, indicate that failing at an easy task or succeeding at a hard one may not always have the predicted effect on younger children. Although ten- and eleven-year-olds felt bad about their failures, six-year-olds were not depressed when they failed. They continued to feel good, but not so good as when they succeeded. Four-year-olds were not fazed. Ruble's group suggests that children at this age may be so accustomed to failure because of their limited abilities and lack of coordination that another failure or two at solving puzzles just does not bother them. Not until children were eight years old did information about the difficulty of the task influence their reactions to it.

Children who do well in school generally attribute their success to ability ("I succeed because I'm smart") and their failures to effort ("I didn't work hard enough"). Because effort is a matter of personal control and can be changed, they perceive themselves as being able to overcome failure. Children who do poorly in school are likely to develop a different pattern of perceiving causation, attributing their successes to external events such as difficulty ("It was an easy test") or chance ("I was just lucky"). They are also likely to attribute their failures to ability ("I failed 'cause I'm dumb"). Since ability is a stable, internal characteristic, they are likely to see no reason to try harder on future occasions. Children who generally attribute their failures to a lack of ability may, after a new failure, suddenly become unable to solve a problem they had already mastered with ease (Dweck, 1978).

It is not success or failure that determines attitudes, then, but the causes to which one attributes the success or failure. The causes can be inside the person (effort, ability, mood) or outside (difficulty, conditions under which a task is performed, other people, luck). The causes can

How Teachers Teach Girls to Fail

Girls get higher grades in elementary school than boys do: they do just as well on tests of math achievement, and they outscore boys on tests of reading and verbal achievement. Yet girls are much more likely than boys to interpret the news that they have made a mistake as indicating their own lack of ability, when the information comes from an adult. They may respond to such news by failing at tasks they had performed easily in the past.

Carol Dweck and her colleagues (1978) had observed that teachers criticize boys indiscriminately but criticize girls primarily for inaccurate schoolwork and wondered if such differences in kind of feedback for each sex might be responsible for the tendency of girls to show learned helplessness.

They divided fifth-grade children into groups that received "boy" or "girl" criticism for mistakes in solving anagrams. Children who got "boy" criticism heard negative remarks that were devoted half the time to the inaccuracy of the child's solution and the rest of the time to their lack of neatness. The other children were given "girl" criticism, that is, all critical comments were devoted to the inaccuracies of the child's answers. Then each was given another task, which was halted three times and the child criticized for not working fast enough. After the third criticism, the children were asked to fill out a slip on which they checked the reason for their failure (I did not try hard enough; The man was too fussy; I am not very good at it). So that they would not end the experiment on a note of failure, all the children worked additional problems, for which they received considerable praise.

The results exactly followed Dweck's conjectures. Few of the boys and girls in the "boy" criticism group thought their own ability had anything to do with their mistakes: 80 percent of the girls and 50 percent of the boys said they had not tried hard enough, 20 percent of the boys said the man was too fussy. Both boys and girls in the "girl" criticism group reacted similarly: most attributed their failure to lack of ability, only a few thought they had failed because they did not try hard enough, none of the children blamed the experimenter.

Boys hear so much criticism directed at their sloppiness or laziness that given a new task, they discount past failures and expect that if they persevere, they will succeed. Girls, who have heard far less criticism but have taken it as an indication of a general lack of ability, embark on a new task with fewer expectations of success. Dweck suggests that such experiences may help explain why, after years of outscoring boys on math tests, girls begin to fall behind when they reach junior high school.

If children generalize from past patterns of criticism to areas outside the school, these experiences might help explain why, when they become adults, men attribute their successes to ability but women attribute theirs to good luck. If women believe they lack ability, they will tend to seek other explanations for success. Kay Deaux (1976) has found that at state and county fairs, men seek out games of skill (e.g., tossing coins into dishes) but women seek out games of chance (e.g., bingo). What is more, men and women have similar expectations of success when they begin a game of luck; but when they start to play a game of skill, men's expectations go up and women's come down.

also be stable (ability, task, difficulty) or unstable (mood, chance, unfamiliarity with task). One person's stable factor, however, may be another's unstable factor (Dweck, 1978). Larry, for example, may believe that he is inherently lazy and thus see his effort as impossible to change. But Robb may believe that his inability to win first chair in band can be overcome by practicing and never consider that lack of talent plays a part in his failure.

These different attribution patterns, of course, are likely to be linked with other differences in children's self-concepts (Coopersmith, 1967). Children who are successful and perceive themselves that way are likely to have a positive self-concept; they feel confident about themselves and their abilities. Children who are unsuccessful and perceive themselves that way are likely to have a negative self-concept; they lack confidence in themselves and their abilities, and feel unworthy.

Once children start school, they may find it necessary to revise their expectations of themselves, depending upon their academic performance and how it is evaluated (Entwisle and Hayduk, 1978). Some children may experience repeated disappointments and frustrations that lower their expectations; others may encounter success that raises their expectations. The biggest change for some children may be that, for the first time, they are evaluated in terms of how well they do in comparison with other children, instead of with their own previous performance.

Children who experience repeated frustration, failure, and punishment, and perceive these experiences as due to stable factors, are likely to believe that they can do little or nothing to change things. Because of this belief, they will fail to try even when situations are such that they can succeed. This inability to see any hope of success can easily lead to what has been called *learned helplessness* (Seligman, 1975). When this occurs, children no longer try to deal with problems because they have learned from repeated experience that what happens to them is independent of what they do.

The school experiences of girls are especially likely to promote learned helplessness, whereas school failure has little effect on boys. Carol Dweck (1978) explored the interplay between teachers and students and found that criticism followed stereotypical patterns. Teachers criticize boys more often than they criticize girls. Boys are told to pay attention, criticized for not following instructions, scolded for being messy, and told they just do not try hard enough. And when their task is criticized, almost half the time the hard words have nothing to do with its accuracy. Such indiscriminate criticism is often interpreted by boys as a signal that the teacher does not like them.

Neat, obedient little girls, on the other hand, are scolded much less often — but when the criticism comes, it is related to the accuracy of their schoolwork. Consistently placed in this situation, girls learn that they lack ability and boys learn that they will do well if they just try harder. Although boys may experience frequent failure and still perceive themselves as capable, girls may develop a sense of helplessness. As we move on to the discussion of sex roles, we shall see that gender affects every aspect of peer relationships and achievement.

SUMMARY

1. Boys and girls transfer to their contacts with other children the social skills they develop within the family. As children grow older, the importance of the peer group steadily increases, and it is here that children practice and perfect the roles they will play in later years.

2. Studies with primates show that contact with peers is necessary for normal development. Peers appear to teach one another certain social skills that are not learned from parents.

3. Play and interaction with peers begin before babies are a year old, and the interaction be-

comes an increasing source of enjoyment. Children influence one another by acting as models and by reinforcing and punishing one another's behavior. As a result, peers can either encourage or discourage such actions as aggression, disobedience, sharing, or cooperation.

4. A child's popularity is influenced by many factors over which he or she has no control, such as name or physical appearance. Social skills, something a child can learn, are also important determinants of popularity and they enable children to enter new relationships and then to maintain them.

5. The course of friendship changes during childhood, progressing from simply playing together to psychological intimacy. As the peer group takes on added importance, a special sense of belonging flourishes and hierarchies develop within the group.

6. Children generally conform to peer standards in matters of friendship, language, and clothing, but they retain parental values concerning their future goals. The tendency to conform to their peers rises throughout elementary school years, peaking in the ninth grade, then declines during high school. Peer and parental standards do not always conflict; in the Soviet Union the peer group acts under the guidance of adult society.

7. Not all children are accepted by their peers. Since isolates may drop out of school, have emotional problems, or become delinquents, ways have been sought to bring isolated children back into the group. Behavior modification, modeling, and coaching isolates in social skills have all been used with varying degrees of success.

8. Parents who expect achievement from their children, rewarding their successes and punishing their failures, are likely to have children with a strong urge to succeed. Girls may learn to withdraw from competition because success makes them appear less feminine. Children's attitudes toward their successes or failures depend upon the causes to which they attribute the outcome. If children fail repeatedly and believe their failures are due to enduring factors they cannot control, they may simply give up — a condition called learned helplessness.

Development of Sex Roles

Four-year-old Tommy walked into the nursery-school playroom for the first time. While waiting for the morning's activities to begin, he strolled over to the doll corner and picked up a doll similar to one that belonged to his sister. Tommy had three older sisters; he had often played house with them, and the familiar doll made him feel less uncomfortable in the strange surroundings. Just then a pair of boys burst through the door, stopped, and stared. Still carrying his doll, Tommy walked over to them. "Hi!" he said, smiling. There was no answering grin. "Look at the sissy," one of the boys said to the other, then the pair turned their backs and started toward the block corner.

Tommy will soon learn that boys play only with boy toys—especially at nursery school. Although he plays with dolls at home, he knows that he is a boy. He loves rough-and-tumble play and wears with pride his jeans and western shirt that are "just like Daddy's." Tommy is becoming a male psychologically by a complex process that is still incomplete. He is acquiring aspects of the male sex role and will rapidly learn that his peers have rigid ideas about permissible masculine behavior, ideas that he will soon adopt himself.

The shaping of a baby girl or boy into a firmly female or male adult is a lengthy and complex process involving hormones, learning, identification, imitation, and cognition. It is carried out by parents, friends, teachers, books, television, and most of the institutions of society. And it is helped along by the growing child, who seeks out and acquires behavior that seems appropriate to his or her gender. But the development of sex roles is not simply a cumulative process; the importance of being masculine or feminine ebbs and flows. Despite all the furor over sexist attitudes and behavior in our society, there are times in life when sex roles are not very important.

In this chapter, we shall consider the importance of sex roles and examine the biological and social forces that shape them. We shall discover that sex roles pervade every society and every aspect of life, explore the difference between sex role and gender identity, and examine the consequences of an insecure gender identity. We shall look at the relationship of sex roles to a person's life situation and, finally, consider the topic of androgyny.

THE PERVASIVENESS OF SEX ROLES

Every culture has established acceptable and unacceptable patterns of behavior and psychological standards for the sexes, and these sex-role standards are imposed at an early age. Sex roles pervade every aspect of life and most of our activities reinforce the distinction between the sexes. In all societies, men and women have different duties, different responsibilities, and often different pleasures. Together, they make up a culture's *sex roles*, which include aspects that are inseparable from gender (the potential to bear a child or impregnate another person) and aspects that have nothing to do with it (in some cultures only men plant crops; in others, only

women). Sex roles ignore many inherent sex differences. If they did not, most brain surgeons would be women, since females generally are superior to males when it comes to the delicate motor control required in neurosurgery.

Sex roles are inevitably interwoven with the status that society attaches to each role. Thus male dominance was one of the earliest bases of discrimination among human beings, presumably because survival among hunting and gathering tribes depended on the ability to move about unencumbered by childbearing and nursing. The burden of advanced pregnancy or of carrying a small child would make it impossible for a woman to throw a spear accurately or to run after game (Friedl, 1978). Male children have always been valued, and many cultures have regularly killed excess female babies at birth.

The superiority of the male sex role has been perpetuated by incorporating it into the customs, laws, and socialization practices of successive generations. A cross-cultural survey of tribal societies by Herbert Barry, Margaret Bacon, and Irvin Child (1957) disclosed that the more its economy requires physical strength, the more strongly society emphasizes sex differences in socialization. In most societies, whether ancient, primitive, or modern, the prestige of the task determines whether it is assigned to males or to females, with women often treated as if they were members of a minority group.

Somehow sex roles get translated into *sex-role stereotypes*—simplified, fixed concepts about the behavior and traits typical of each sex. Slight differences between the sexes, which are magnified by sex roles, become full-blown gender traits in the public mind. Stereotypical women talk and cry a lot; they are sociable, submissive, dependent, and timid. Men, on the other hand, are silent and stoic; they are aggressive, competitive, and independent, with an itch to achieve. Men and women who fit these stereotypes are rare, but as we shall find, young children readily acquire the concepts however militantly nonsexist their parents may be.

ROLES AND IDENTITY

A sex role is like an outer garment. It is the visible and socially prescribed manifestation — in speech, dress, behavior — of one's gender. A woman, for example, is not likely to settle an angry dispute with a right to her opponent's jaw, nor is a man likely to burst into tears when distressed. Sex roles vary from culture to culture and from time to time in the same culture. Thirty years ago, closely cropped hair was a symbol of masculinity; today, hair length has no necessary connection with sex role. Seventy-five years ago, femininity and skirts were inseparable; today, women wear jeans as often as dresses. But before children can wrap themselves in society's sex roles, they must first establish a sense of gender identity — a quite different concept.

Gender identity is invisible. It is the inner experience of gender, the unchanging sense of oneself as male or female (Money and Ehrhardt, 1972). Most developmental psychologists believe that gender identity is secure when a child not only understands the fact of his or her gender but also feels comfortable in the role. In this view, a person's degree of masculinity or femininity would be signified by the amount of satisfaction derived from being male or female (Lamb and Urberg, 1978).

In the view held by cognitive theorists, on the other hand, satisfaction has nothing to do with gender identity; it is largely intellectual, limited to the understanding of one's gender (Kohlberg, 1966). If gender identity is defined in this way, a male who had accepted the fact of gender but did not feel masculine would still have achieved gender identity. An eleven-year-old boy, for example, might know he is now and always will be male, but he might feel distinctly unmasculine because he does not care for football and finds the rough-and-tumble horseplay of his schoolmates distasteful.

Gender identity and sex role are the same in most cases; but sometimes there is little correspondence between the two. A woman who lacks a secure gender identity might, for that reason, adopt a highly stereotypical sex role. She may, for example, know she is female but take little comfort in the fact and not "feel" feminine. In compensation, she might go in for ruffles and timidity, play the cuddly, clinging vine, and never under any circumstances behave in an "unfeminine" way. On the other hand, those who flout prescribed sex roles, as in the case of the working wife and the house-husband, may nevertheless have secure gender identities.

THE DEVELOPMENT OF GENDER IDENTITY

Before babies learn to think of themselves as girls or boys, they must discover what a "girl" or a "boy" is. The voyage of discovery begins before they are aware they have embarked on it, for they are wrapped in pink or blue blankets in the hospital nursery and surrounded with sex-typed clothes and toys at home.

Learning One's Gender

Around the time they are eighteen months old and begin to acquire language, children learn gender labels and begin to apply them, generally relying on hair and clothes as clues. Two-year-olds can identify females as "girl" or "mommy" even when the pictured models have short hair or wear long pants. But as Spencer Thompson (1975) found, most two-year-olds are not convinced of their own gender. The children he studied did not always sort their own pictures appropriately by gender (as they did pictures of stereotypical males and females), nor did they always answer correctly when asked, "Are you a boy?" or "Are you a girl?" As we saw in Chapter 9, children are still learning the meaning of concepts long after they have a word for them. To a two-year-old, the label "girl" may be as idiosyncratic as "Susan" or "Lauren"; it is a name that applies to a lot of people, just as the child's caregiver and the caregiver of the little boy next door are both called "Mommy."

By the time they are thirty months old, Thompson found, most youngsters know their own gender, although 25 percent of them are still likely to have trouble sorting their pictures and answering gender questions about themselves. Three-year-olds have no trouble with questions about the gender of themselves or others. They seem to realize that they—and all other people—are either male or female.

According to Lawrence Kohlberg (1966), this rudimentary sense of gender identity is only the first step. He believes the process is not complete until the child realizes that gender is constant: boys always become men and girls always become women, and maleness or femaleness cannot be changed. When Kohlberg asked children if a girl could become a boy if she wanted to, most four-year-olds said that she could. All she had to do was to cut her hair and wear boys' clothes. Kohlberg reports that one young boy, just two months short of four years old, told his mother, "When you grow up to be a Daddy, you can have a bicycle, too [like his father]."

The sense of *gender constancy* develops between the ages of five and seven, when the child is also developing an understanding of physical conservation—a concept that was discussed in Chapter 12. As children come to understand that the amount of clay remains constant whether it is squeezed into a lump or rolled into a long string, so they understand that gender does not change—by dress or by magic. Because these concepts develop about the same time, says Kohlberg, a stable gender identity is primarily an intellectual accomplishment. A number of recent studies have explored this assertion.

In one such study, Dale Marcus and Willis Overton (1978) tested five- to eight-year-olds with the standard Piagetian conservation tasks involving clay of various shapes and the transfer of soybeans from a squat to a narrow container. Then, on another test, each child's sense of gender constancy was rated. For example, children looked at pictures of girls and boys and were asked whether the pictured children's gender remained constant as their clothes and hair styles were transformed. Marcus and Overton found that for most children, conservation preceded gender constancy. They also found that although the older a child, the firmer his or her assertion of gender constancy, brighter children developed the concept before less bright children did—an indication that a certain level of cognitive development, not simply a specific number of years of experience, is required for its understanding.

This child has developed a sense of gender identity; he knows that he is a boy and he seeks out male models and imitates them. (Karen Collidge/Taurus Photos)

Nor does experience with unclothed people appear to speed the development of gender constancy. Kohlberg (1966) reports that four- to seven-year-olds who had no trouble explaining "how you could tell [naked] boys from girls" were no more advanced in their understanding of gender constancy than were children who lacked an awareness of anatomical differences.

But cognitive development cannot by itself explain children's understanding of the concept. In another study of preschool children, Ronald Slaby and Karin Frey (1975) found children as young as three who understood that boys always become men and girls always become women, and children as young as three and a half who understood that gender could never be changed. In fact, in a group of children ranging from twenty-six to sixty-seven months, 25 percent understood the first concept and another 40 percent understood the second—an indication that children may develop a sense of gender constancy earlier than suggested by Kohlberg.

Once a child develops a sense of gender constancy, Kohlberg believes, the child seeks out sex-typed models, identifying with the opposite-sex parent and choosing same-sex friends and sex-typed clothes, games, and behavior (see Figure 17.1). Slaby and Frey did find that as children developed gender constancy, they paid increased attention to models of their own sex. In Marcus and Overton's study, however, children who understood gender constancy did not show Kohlberg's predicted increase in preference for sex-typed games and same-sex friends

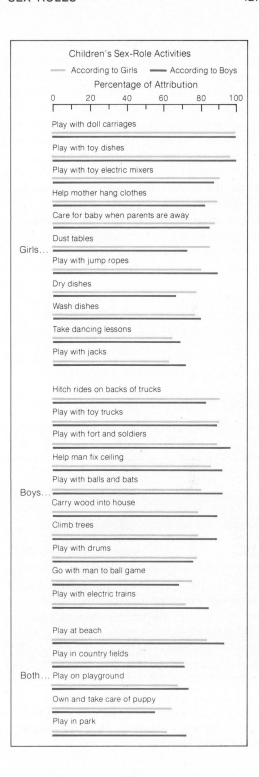

Figure 17.1 The effects of sex-role stereotypes on the way boys and girls classify childhood activities. As the chart shows, there is a high degree of agreement between boys and girls about the activities that are seen as the province of one sex or the other. For example, all boys and girls felt that playing with doll carriages is a girl's activity, and almost all saw playing with trucks as a boy's activity. (After Hartley and Hardesty, 1964)

and television characters; the preferences were already firmly established by the time they entered kindergarten. D. Z. Ulian (1976) found that six-year-olds who lacked gender constancy believed that unless one adhered rigidly to sex-typed activities, one's gender might change. Eight-year-olds, on the other hand, were more relaxed. They had an unshakable sense of gender constancy and believed it was all right for males and females to engage in activities typed for the opposite sex.

Gender constancy may not be necessary for the child to acquire a sturdy sense of gender identity. The rudimentary realization that one is a girl or a boy, a knowledge that children develop around age two, may be the crucial foundation. But the meaning that knowledge has for the child will indeed change over the years, and perhaps what Kohlberg has been studying are these shifts in meaning.

When Things Go Wrong

Not all children develop an appropriate sense of gender identity. A child whose gender identity does not coincide with his or her anatomical sex faces a miserable childhood, and things do not improve with maturity. People who grow up believing they have been trapped in the body of the opposite sex are known as *transsexuals*. Often they request surgery so as to change their exterior anatomy to conform to their inner feelings. And for every tennis-playing physician who has had such surgery and is written up in the press, there are thousands of other transsexuals living in a world gone wrong.

A transsexual is not a homosexual; homosexuals do not have disturbed gender identities. As yet, no one is sure just how the transsexual's inappropriate gender identity develops. It is not simply a matter of biology, wrong chromosomes, or inappropriate hormones. Socialization has a powerful influence on gender identity. John Money and Anke Ehrhardt (1972) report case after case in which children born with ambiguous genitalia have been assigned to one sex or the other and reared with secure gender identities. Also, after appropriate surgery or hormonal treatment, genetic boys have been reared successfully as girls, and girls as boys.

Nor is a confused gender identity simply a matter of the child's lacking a parent of the same sex with whom he or she can identify. Although the lack of a male role model may impede a young boy's development of masculine behavior, single parents generally rear boys and girls with appropriate gender identities. Nor does having a homosexual parent as a model seem to interfere with the development of gender identity. A study comparing the sons and daughters of lesbian mothers with children of heterosexual single mothers showed no difference between the two groups (Kirkpatrick, Smith, and Roy, 1979).

Learning one's gender begins early—so early that Money and Ehrhardt believe it a risky business to reassign a child to the opposite sex after the baby is eighteen months old. They believe that the critical period for establishing gender identity is from eighteen months, when the child begins to develop language, until three or four years. To switch a baby's sex during this period, they say, means that the child will understand his or her gender but will never be really comfortable with it. To switch a child's gender after age four is to risk serious disturbance.

Richard Green (1974), who has worked with many transsexual boys, has proposed a hypothetical pattern for the development of a male transsexual. Such a boy, he believes, is perceived by his mother as an unusually attractive baby. She showers attention on him, and when he begins to play with her shoes, cosmetics, or jewelry, she—and the rest of the family—finds the cross-sex play charming, giving the little boy even more attention. The father either is not present or does not object. About the time he is four, certainly by the time he is six, the boy habitually dresses in high heels, jewelry, cosmetics, and improvised dresses. Perhaps because of low hormonal levels, the boy shows little interest in rough-and-tumble play. This alienates his father, who labels him "mama's boy." The child prefers to play with girls instead of rough boys. His behavior becomes increasingly feminine, and he is teased by his peers. When he is about seven—generally at the instigation of a neighbor or a teacher—his mother brings him to a professional for help.

The early development of feminine behavior in boys with disturbed gender identity has been confirmed by other investigators (Bates, Bentler, and Thompson, 1973). Such boys stand out from their siblings. For example, Kenneth Zucker and his associates (1979) found that gender-disturbed children consistently played more with toys and clothes belonging to the opposite sex than did their brothers and sisters with normal gender identities.

It appears that a transsexual gender identity develops when biological, constitutional, and social forces combine to push a child into the role of the opposite sex. Not only is the young child reinforced for cross-sex behavior, but he or she feels more comfortable with it, perhaps because of hormonal or temperamental predispositions.

THE DEVELOPMENT OF SEX ROLES

Gender identity is closely connected with a child's sex role. As indicated, although the two may be at odds, generally they are the same. The influences that shape sex roles come from biology, parents, peers, teachers, the media—and the development of gender identity itself.

The Influence of Biology

In the absence of contrary instructions, the fertilized egg develops into a female. The information that turns the egg into a male is carried by the Y chromosome, which causes the neutral gonads of the fetus to develop into testes. The testes, in turn, produce the hormones that develop male sexual organs and keep female organs from developing. Male hormones also affect the developing fetal brain. Without their presence, the hypothalamus (a part of the midbrain close to the pituitary) will develop as female—that is, set to produce hormones cyclically, so as to maintain the female reproductive cycle, instead of continually, as in the male brain.

Some of the differences in male and female intellectual functioning were discussed in Chapter 7; here, the question is whether male hormones also leave permanent traces on the developing personality. It seems clear that they do, although the traces are neither as many nor as deep as once was thought.

Ovarian hormones are not required for stereotypical female behavior to develop. Babies with Turner's syndrome—in which there is a single X (female) chromosome but neither a second X (as in normal girls) nor a Y (as in boys)—look like girls when they are born. But they have no ovaries and therefore no ovarian hormones. They are, of course, reared as girls. Such children seem, if anything, more feminine than normal girls; they show less interest in athletics, fight less as children, and are more interested in such personal adornments as jewelry, perfume, and hair styling. The interest in other sex-typed activities and the anticipations of marriage and motherhood of such children are similar to those of normal girls (Money and Ehrhardt, 1972).

But even a girl with a full complement of female hormones tends to show traces of masculine behavior when she has been inadvertently exposed to the male hormone androgen before birth. Anke Ehrhardt and Susan Baker (1975) studied seventeen girls who had received prenatal doses of androgen. The girls were genetically female, with normal female internal organs, but at birth their external genitalia appeared

If It's Wide Awake, Scowls, and Waves, It's a Boy!

For years, psychologists have been trying to establish the existence of male-female differences early, before the culture has had any chance to begin training baby boys to be masculine and baby girls to be feminine. Some studies have shown that boys cry more and sleep less, and that boys tend to be fussy. But because most baby boys in this country are circumcised while they are in the hospital nursery, many people have been reluctant to accept such findings, attributing them to postsurgical discomfort.

A study of newborn infants by Sheridan Phillips, Suzanne King, and Louise DuBois (1978) may help settle the controversy. These researchers observed twenty-nine infants at Long Island Jewish Hospital—fifteen girls and fourteen uncircumcised boys. The sexes were matched for type of delivery, Apgar scores, size, and maturity. Each baby was observed for two days, and data were collected at four different thirty-minute periods between feedings, both morning and afternoon. Each baby was watched a total of eight hours.

To make sure the observers did not know the babies' sex, the babies were given random labels (A or B) by the nurses, their hair was combed in a neutral fashion, and crib blankets of a neutral color were placed on the cribs. Nurses then moved the babies (two at a time) up to the glass nursery wall where the observers waited.

There were no significant sex differences in crying; boys and girls wailed about the same amount. But Phillips and her associates did find other significant sex differences. Boys were awake significantly more than girls. Boys grimaced more; that is, they raised their eyebrows, winced, wrinkled their brows, or contorted their faces without making any sound. And boys showed more low-intensity activity; that is, they turned their heads, waved their hands slowly, twitched, or jerked.

It is possible, say the researchers, that males are indeed slightly more irritable and prone to distress than females. A study by Howard Moss (1974) found that three-month-old boys fuss more than girls; the wakefulness and grimaces may be a forerunner of later fussiness.

In a more recent study, Raymond Yang and Moss (1978) found there was more continuity between the behavior of boys from birth to three months than in the behavior of girls. The correlation was between the newborn boys' gestational maturity, size, and autonomic stability at birth and their activity, alertness, and vocalizations at three months. Yang and Moss found no such connection for girls. These researchers suggest that the lack of stability among girls may be due to the fact that females are more receptive to early environmental influences—in other words, they learn faster.

masculine and had to be surgically corrected. Although the girls were no more aggressive than their normal sisters, most were tomboys—they showed a much higher level of rough, outdoor play and a disinterest in dolls, babies, and marriage. Ehrhardt and Baker speculate that fetal exposure to androgens results in a temperamental inclination to the rough-and-tumble, high-energy play regarded as "natural" for boys. But they believe that for that inclination to become

Although biology may produce such behavioral predispositions as an inclination to rough-and-tumble play among boys, environment has a profound effect on the development of sex-typed behavior. (© Ann Chwatsky)/(© Michael Weisbrot)

manifest, the environment must be one that permits — or encourages — such play, because it did not develop in all the androgenized girls. In addition, all the girls developed secure female gender identities.

There are certainly behavioral differences between the roles society prescribes for boys and girls, and much larger differences between the roles prescribed for men and women. But it is difficult to gauge the strength of the biological component. Eleanor Maccoby and Carol Jacklin (1974), who reviewed more than 1,400 studies of sex differences, concluded that when it came to personality, the only clear-cut difference between the sexes was in aggression. Males were definitely more aggressive than females in every culture studied; they were more aggressive from the beginnings of social play as toddlers, and they expressed it by both word and deed. Because of its universality and because aggression is affected by hormone levels, Maccoby and Jacklin argue that this one aspect of behavior indeed has a biological component. Other traditional behavioral differences between the sexes — activity, competitiveness, and dominance for boys; timidity, compliance, and nurturance for girls — were not resolved by their review. Some studies found the expected sex differences, others did not. It is, of course, possible that activity, competitiveness, and dominance are linked to aggression, and timidity and compliance — and even nurturance — to its absence.

It is probable that prenatal hormones predispose children toward certain kinds of behavior. In addition, the babies' anatomy and their temperamental predispositions lead others to treat them in ways that reinforce the behavior society expects from people of their gender.

The Influence of Parents

For the first few years, parents are the primary influence on a child's development. Whether the child is cared for full-time at home or left in day care, the bonds of attachment described in Chapter 14 are forged. If parents treat boys and girls differently, then a powerful force within the family pushes children into the appropriate sex role.

If we assume that parents treat their own children as they do the children of other people, the push begins early. When Caroline Smith and Barbara Lloyd (1978) videotaped mothers of first-born babies playing with a six-month-old, they discovered that adult behavior changed with the baby's gender label. Told the baby was a boy, mothers encouraged "him" with words to crawl, walk, and behave vigorously; if "he" did, they were likely to reinforce the behavior with their own activities. If they were told the baby was a girl, there was no verbal encouragement for motor activity, and the toy of choice was never a hammer.

Additional differences in adult behavior turned up in a study conducted by Hannah Frisch (1977). When fourteen-month-old infants were identified as boys, most adults encouraged them to large motor activity by putting them on a tricycle and choosing blocks for further play. When the babies were called girls, adults talked more to them and chose a doll or a baby bottle for play. Adults whose scores on an "Attitudes Toward Women Scale" indicated their sympathy with feminism were likely to get out the tricycle for "girls" or to play blocks with them; but they did not encourage "boys" to play with the doll or the baby bottle. The infants, for their part, showed no sex differences in behavior.

It is possible, of course, that when adults play with strange babies, they respond to the only information they have: gender and age. Mothers and fathers may be more likely to respond to their own infants on an individual basis, encouraging motor activity in girls who have

shown they like it and talking quietly to boys who prefer that. Such is the conclusion of Maccoby and Jacklin (1974), who found little evidence of sex-typed treatment of children — except in the area of toy choice. But as Jeanne Block (1976) has pointed out, many of the studies they reviewed were inadequate because they were done with extremely young children; others did not properly sample the expected differences in behavior; and yet others were of measures inappropriate to the age groups studied.

A number of studies have shown that by the time they are two, children show sex-typed differences in behavior. Toys by themselves can hardly produce gender differences. Susan Goldberg and Michael Lewis (1969) watched thirteen-month-old infants with their mothers and noted that the boys and girls played differently. The boys played more roughly with the toys than the girls did; they manipulated light switches and doorknobs instead of sticking with the toys provided; and when separated from their mothers by a picket fence, they tried to get around it. Baby girls played quietly with toys, stayed near their mothers, and when separated from them by the fence, cried. But the researchers also noted that the mothers encouraged different behavior in the children. Mothers of sons discouraged their children from touching them and suggested that the little boys play with toys that lay across the room. Mothers of girls, on the other hand, allowed their daughters to play near them and to touch them.

When Peter Smith and Linda Daglish (1977) watched English babies at home, first at twelve months and again at twenty-four months, they found that girls tended to play more with dolls and soft toys, and boys with transportation toys. The boys were more active in their play and more likely than the girls to do forbidden things, such as playing with wall plugs and climbing on the furniture. The sex-typed differences in play were already apparent at twelve months and did not increase appreciably over the next year. Smith and Daglish found one

Children generally identify with the parent of their own gender, and this identification helps a child build an appropriate sex role. (Frank Siteman/The Stockmarket)

major difference in parents' behavior—a tendency to discourage or punish boys more than girls.

But by the time children are two years old, Beverly Fagot (1978a) found, parents react in predictable ways to specific behavior. She watched twenty-four single-child families whose child was between the ages of twenty and twenty-four months. Each family was watched on five different occasions for a period of an hour, while Fagot closely observed the ways parents responded to the actions of boys and girls. Girls and boys were often reinforced or punished differently for the same behavior. Girls, she found, were never encouraged when they played with blocks; and only girls tended to be discouraged when they manipulated objects. As a result, while boys explored the physical world freely, girls might get criticized for it. Girls were encouraged to be helpers and to ask for assistance when they tried to do things. The differences in parents' responses were subtle, and these mothers and fathers were unaware

that they were training their girls to be dependent and their boys to be independent.

The same push toward early independence for boys showed in another study, in which Fagot (1974) found that mothers discouraged their toddler sons from following them around the house. Their daughters, on the other hand, were encouraged to stay near them. Other studies show that boys are allowed to investigate wider areas of the community without parental permission (Saegert and Hart, 1976) and that they are expected to run errands at an earlier age. When mothers of four-year-olds were asked at what age they thought children should be permitted to be independent, mothers of boys listed younger ages, compared with mothers of girls, for such behavior as crossing the street alone, using sharp tools, and going off to play without telling a parent the destination (Callard, 1964).

Some years ago, Robert Sears, Eleanor Maccoby, and Harry Levin (1957) studied 369 five-year-old children, questioning their mothers in depth about all aspects of child rearing. They found the largest difference between the socialization of boys and girls fell in the area of aggression. Boys were often encouraged to use their fists in neighborhood disputes—but to keep their fighting outside the home. More boys than girls were allowed to express aggression toward their parents. Indeed, the expression of aggression by girls was often squelched entirely. On the other hand, girls were more often disciplined with love—and its withdrawal—and boys with spanking. When this research is considered together with Fagot's studies, we see the independent, aggressive male and the dependent, helpful female already emerging.

Many developmental psychologists believe that identification with a parent of the opposite sex helps a child build an appropriate sex role. Freud believed that a boy switched his identification to his father in an effort to calm the emotional tempests of the stormy phallic period. Some learning theorists, on the other hand,

Theories of Sex-Role Development

Psychodynamic View

Sigmund Freud emphasized the notion that early childhood is critical in the socialization of the individual. During these years, the child's sensual pleasure is focused on the genitals, and the child's fantasies about gratifying these desires result in sexual conflict with the parent of the opposite sex. Whether this parent responds with warmth and affection to the child, thereby indirectly satisfying the child's desires, affects personality development. According to Freud, the oedipal conflict is resolved when the child comes to identify with the parent of the same sex, and this identification forms the basis for appropriate sex-role development, with the parent also becoming the model for the values that will be part of the child's adult personality.

Erik Erikson concurs with the view that peer and parental responses are important factors in socialization during early childhood. Appropriate sex-role behavior develops when a child identifies with the same-sex parent and assimilates the parent's behavior into his or her own personal identity. In Erikson's theory, parental support and encouragement when the child first attempts to acquire appropriate male or female behavior can help the child achieve a positive self-image and a strong personal identity. But parents are not the only people who fill this role; members of the child's peer group are also important.

Cognitive-Developmental View

Lawrence Kohlberg emphasizes cognitive development as the most important factor in socialization. He takes the position that identification with the same-sex parent develops only after a child acquires a sense of gender identity. Thus once girls or boys begin to think of themselves as girls or boys, they want to talk, think, and act as others of their sex do. In the process, they come to identify with their parents. In this view, although parents, peers, and other adults are important in socialization because they provide models and approval, children basically socialize themselves as they discover how to behave in competent, acceptable ways.

Social Learning View

Walter Mischel, a social-learning theorist who has concentrated on the development of personality, sees the process of socialization as continuous from infancy through childhood. By interacting with their environment, children learn to behave in increasingly complex ways and discover the consequences of their

think that boys switch their identification to their fathers when they realize that he controls the family power. But they are at a loss to explain why girls do *not* imitate the powerful parent. Other psychologists believe that by providing continuing contact with the opposite sex, mothers give boys and fathers give girls a chance to learn their own sex roles. As we saw in Chapter 15, most studies have shown that it is the father's presence that is critical, with many adolescent girls who grew up without fathers acting uncertainly around males, and many boys who lost their fathers quite early tending to be less traditionally masculine in their behavior.

Although not much concern is shown over girls who choose boyish activities, parents— especially fathers—become quite upset when

actions. In Mischel's view, sex-role development involves learning appropriate behavior, which in turn is modified by the consequences that follow when the child performs it. Parents act as models; they—as well as the child's peers and other adults—shape the child's behavior by the way they respond to his or her actions.

Adaptation View

John Money, a professor of medical psychology and pediatrics, regards sex role as the public experience of gender identity, and gender identity as the private experience of sex role. In his view, the development of gender identity is analogous to language acquisition, another biologically based human capacity whose expression is heavily influenced by society. Although gender identity must be learned, it is acquired very early, so that the period between eighteen months and three or four years of age may be regarded as the sensitive period for its establishment. The influence of prenatal hormones on the fetal brain produces behavioral traits that lead others to treat newborn infants in gender-appropriate ways, with the parents completing the social transmission of gender. However, gender identity is not sealed at birth, and if a switch to the opposite gender must be made for medical reasons, it is difficult to carry out after an infant is eighteen months old.

their young boys engage in girlish games. The pressure on boys to be "real boys" may translate into rigid sex roles during the early years. When more than a hundred preschool children were tested for their absorption of sex-role stereotypes and their knowledge of sex-appropriate behavior, boys tended to choose stereotypical toys and behavior for children but to be somewhat more relaxed about what adults

did (Edelbrook and Sugawara, 1978). Girls, on the other hand, chose a wide range of toys and behavior for children but were more restrictive when they described acceptable adult behavior. The investigators suggest two reasons for these discrepancies. Because boys are ridiculed for "sissy" behavior but girls are permitted to be tomboys, young boys may be more reluctant to engage in or to condone cross-sex activities. Regarding adult behavior, since most primary caretakers are mothers, girls have much more experience with adult women than boys have with adult males. Because fathers and other males are not around much, young boys may be less certain about the appropriate behavior of adult males.

The Implications of Gender Identity

The sure knowledge that one's gender is unchangeable has, believes Kohlberg (1966), a tremendous influence on the development of sex roles. He believes that the two- or three-year-old likes objects and toys associated with his or her own sex because of previous toys, playmates, and reinforcements provided by parents, which build on whatever innate tendencies exist. Thus a girl likes dresses and dolls because she associates them with herself; a boy likes toy trucks and masculine clothes for the same reason. At this early age, says Kohlberg, boys are still mother-oriented; they have not yet identified with their fathers.

Once children know their gender will never change, they decide they are happy with it—whatever the gender is. They believe the positive things they hear about their own sex and the negative things they hear about the opposite sex. They identify with the parent of their own sex and seek out—from all available sources—the behavior and attitudes that go along with that gender.

Parents are not the only models, however, as

a study by David Perry and Kay Bussey (1979) made clear. Eight- and nine-year-old children watched a group of men and women choose one item from pairs that had no connection with gender—between a plastic cow and a plastic horse, for example. Afterward the children were given a chance to choose for themselves. The more often models of their own sex had selected an item, the more likely children were to choose it. In a second study, children watched adult models make choices that were either sex-appropriate or sex-inappropriate; afterward, the models chose items that had no connection with gender. When later choosing from the latter set of items, children imitated according to the sex appropriateness of the models' first set of choices. That is, boys and girls imitated adults of their own sex who had earlier made sex-appropriate choices; they also imitated models of the opposite sex who had earlier made sex-inappropriate choices. Children apparently imitate adults whom they believe provide good examples of their own sex roles. In the study by Slaby and Frey (1975), six-year-olds who had developed gender constancy spent more time watching a movie character of their own sex than one of the opposite sex when, on one side of the movie screen a woman built a fire, popped corn, played a musical instrument, and drank juice, and on the other side of the screen a man did the same thing. But boys watched the man more than girls watched the woman.

Girls' tendency to watch the male as well as the female may be explained by their realization of where power lies. As children develop their sense of gender constancy, they are also becoming aware of the power and competence associated with the male sex role. Now girls no longer like their own sex better, but they continue to believe that girls are "nicer" and "prettier" than "bad" boys. So they decide, says Kohlberg, to go after the only kind of power they think society offers girls—the power one can wield through being attractive and good.

Children also make a moral judgment: compliance with sex-role stereotypes is good; flouting of stereotypes is bad. Whether they are middle-class or lower-class, white or black, have traditional or liberated parents, children adhere to this judgment. So despite enormous differences in adult behavior—and despite the wide overlap in male and female behavior—children gravitate to the narrow stereotypical examples.

Kohlberg's description is persuasive. However, as noted earlier, it places the development of a stable gender identity at a far later age than do other theories. A number of studies have shown that at four—sometimes as early as three—many children have already developed gender constancy and the attitudes that go along with it; long before this time, they have begun to behave in a stereotypical fashion.

The Influence of Peers

As we saw in Chapter 16, peers play an important role in the social development of young children; and now that an increasing number of youngsters are enrolled in some kind of day care, the influence of peers is more important than it traditionally has been. By the time they are three, children know "what boys do" and "what girls do" and they pressure one another to conform.

When three- and four-year-old boys played with dolls or played dress-up at a nursery school studied by Fagot (1977), they were criticized by their peers. And boys who persisted in such play were criticized five or six times as often as other children, no matter what the boys did. Occasionally girls would allow such a boy to join them in the play kitchen, but they too were mostly negative in their reactions. Boys who persisted in cross-gender play played alone almost three times as often as other children. Girls who played with boys' toys fared better. They were generally ignored by the other children and allowed to continue their play; when they returned to girls' activities, they were welcomed back into the group.

Although several researchers have noticed that young children criticize their peers for cross-gender play, until recently no one has measured the effectiveness of the criticism. In a pair of studies, Michael Lamb and his associates (Lamb and Roopnarine, 1979; Lamb, Easterbrooks, and Holden, 1980) found that three- to seven-year-old children punished one another in a number of ways. They criticized offending children, asked them to stop their actions, diverted them with another toy, stopped playing with them, complained loudly, or physically intervened to stop the play. Regardless of the kind of punishment inflicted, the offending child stopped cross-gender play almost immediately; but children punished while engaged in sex-appropriate play tended to keep playing longer.

The same sort of difference appeared in response to rewards. Regardless of the kind of reward their peers dispensed — praise, encouragement, imitation, or obedience — children kept on with their activity significantly longer if it was typed for their own gender than if it was inappropriate. These differences in children's reactions, suggest Michael Lamb and Jaipaul Roopnarine, also indicate that three-year-olds are well aware of sex typing, and that the punishment serves to remind, not to instruct, the child that he or she has crossed the sex-role boundary.

As children become older, they tend to change the way they punish other children who engage in cross-gender play (Lamb, Easterbrooks, and Holden, 1980). Three-year-olds are likely to stop playing with a boy who plays with a doll or a girl who begins hammering — perhaps simply indicating a lack of interest. Five- to seven-year-olds, however, let their disapproval be known; they often make direct attempts to change the offending child's behavior. But for most children, the physical presence of peers is unnecessary; simply believing that an activity is typed for the opposite gender is often enough to make

a child avoid it (Liebert, McCall, and Hanratty, 1971; Thompson, 1975; White, 1978).

The Influence of Teachers

In their role as instructor in sex differences, children's schoolmates are joined by another ally — the teacher. Even in nursery school, teachers unobtrusively push children into traditional sex roles — and most of them do not know they are doing it. Lisa Serbin and her associates (1973), for example, observed teachers in fifteen nursery-school classrooms and recorded how they behaved toward boys and toward girls. They found that teachers were helping to shape traditional sex roles, often unwittingly, by prompting and reinforcing independent, assertive behavior in boys and dependent, passive behavior in girls. In one classroom, for example, the children were making party baskets, a task that required them to staple a paper handle in place. The teachers provided instruction as the boys manipulated the staple gun and attached the handle. The teacher, however, was likely to take the basket from a girl, staple the handle to it, and hand it back. Serbin's group points out that most teachers do not realize that they demonstrate things and explain them more to boys than to girls and that they give boys more directions that require them to accomplish things on their own. From such findings, the investigators conclude that most girls learn to be submissive, to remain near an adult, and to be rewarded with affectionate hugs, whereas most boys learn to be assertive and to receive praise for being independent problem solvers.

Teachers in nursery schools also react to physical aggression in selective ways that are consistent with traditional sex-role development. They indicate by their reactions that they expect boys to fight, and they pay strong attention to them when they do — thereby inadvertently reinforcing aggression in young boys. When nursery school children engage in play that is regarded as the province of the opposite sex, teachers sometimes join peers in making the children feel uncomfortable (Fagot, 1977). Boys who dress up or girls who play outside in the sandbox are criticized. But when girls dress up, or boys hammer or play with blocks, the teacher joins in, suggests additional activities along the same line, or makes favorable comments. On the other hand, teachers are kindly disposed toward art activities and shower boys with approval when they cut, paste, or draw — although such activities are overwhelmingly favored by girls. This may be, says Fagot, who observed more than 200 nursery school children, because teachers see art activities as appropriate academic tasks.

When children's free play is observed, girls prefer playing with art materials, looking at books, inspecting objects, and watching people, whereas boys gravitate to wagons, tricycles, trucks, sandboxes, and rough-and-tumble play. As a result, when teachers steer children to the "cultural enrichment" of the nursery-school curriculum, they are pushing boys to do things that they would not choose on their own. Observations of nursery school teachers indicate that the more experienced the teacher, the stronger such pressure on boys (Fagot, 1978b). Experienced teachers reinforce both boys and girls more than 80 percent of the time for doing what girls prefer to do. Teachers without experience reinforce girls at a similar rate, but they reinforce boys equally for the active play the boys prefer and the literary and artistic play teachers wish they liked. The mismatch between early school curriculum and boys' inclinations may help explain why girls make better students early in their academic careers — and why more little boys than little girls dislike school.

But as school progresses, teachers take a hand in redressing the balance — again without knowing it. As pointed out in the last chapter, when boys fail, teachers generally criticize them for not trying. In contrast, when girls fail, teachers almost always criticize them for having the wrong answer. Because the criticism that girls receive focuses on the content of their work, they are likely to attribute their failure to lack of ability and may come to believe that their successes are simply lucky. Boys fail, hear that they should try harder, and may do so. As a result, teachers may be teaching girls to fail and boys to persevere in academic tasks, perhaps preparing both sexes to expect that males will solve problems for helpless females.

The Influence of the Media

In nonliterate cultures, children hear the exploits of heroes and heroines in song and story. The folksinger and the storyteller, with their tales of brave deeds and weaknesses, of loyalty and love, describe ideal models. In a media-saturated culture, models continually assault the child from every side. Television, books, movies, magazines, radio, and newspapers portray — in words or pictures — the approved sex roles for the society.

When two-year-olds turn the glossy pages of their mothers' magazines, pointing to the kitty in the catfood ad or the baby advertising paper diapers, they see in the pitches for soaps, floor waxes, canned soups, cigarettes, and cosmetics what boys and girls, mommies and daddies are supposed to do. Mommies are young and beautiful and spend most of their time at home or in the supermarket; daddies play tennis and ride horses through Marlboro country. What children see in magazines may help develop the sex-role stereotypes that are found in preschoolers; but those ads are a minor influence compared to the impact of the omnipresent television set.

TELEVISION Children at play often enact social roles they have taken from television, and they have plenty of time to absorb them. In 1976, half of American twelve-year-olds were watching six or more hours of television each day (Gerbner and Gross, 1976b). Children spend more time watching television than they do going to school. Television often serves as an unpaid baby-sitter, keeping preschoolers occupied while their mothers are busy.

For the most part, television is a purveyor of stereotypes. As Carol Tavris and Carole Offir (1977) have pointed out, when Wonder Woman is not saving the world, she works as a secretary; and the Bionic Woman teaches school. In addition, most television heroines, from Charlie's Angels to Police Woman, unmask villains by luck or accident. In children's programs, men are aggressive, constructive, and helpful; their activities bring them tangible rewards (Sternglanz and Serbin, 1974). Women, on the other hand, tend to be deferential, passive, and ignored; if they are too active, they are punished.

In television programs, women themselves sometimes get to be heroines. But few commercials shatter sex-role stereotypes. Except for the occasional woman bank manager and traveling sales representative, women in commercials either do housework or are sex objects. They defer to men's needs, wishes, and preferences. Men are the authorities, confronting women shoppers with twelve-hour cold capsules, correcting their choices of detergent, and delivering the smooth, authoritative voice-over pitches in commercials.

Since the average child watches more than 20,000 television commercials each year, the results of a study by Terry Frueh and Paul McGhee (1975) come as no surprise. When these researchers compared children's beliefs about sex roles and the amount of time they spent watching television, the investigators found that heavy viewers (children who watched more than twenty-five hours each week) had significantly more stereotypical notions than did children who watched ten hours or less each week. And the older the child, the more ingrained the stereotype.

BOOKS The other heavy media influence on children is the printed word — primarily readers and other textbooks, but also books a child reads for pleasure or for book reports. Children no longer grow up in the white, middle-class world of Dick and Jane, who once dominated American readers; but the stories still tend to be boy-centered, and the main character, when an adult, is generally a male. Even animal characters, from Peter Rabbit and the Three Little Pigs to Stuart Little and Ferdinand the bull, are usually male.

When Women on Words and Images (1972) examined 134 anthologies compiled as children's readers, they found five boy-centered stories for every two that featured a girl, and 147 occupations described as possible for boys but only 26 for girls. One reason boys predominate in such collections may be that, given the penalties from parents, peers, and teachers for cross-sex behavior, boys object vigorously to reading books that feature female heroines. As librarians know, boys will not read them and find it nearly impossible to identify with a heroine. But girls have no difficulty reading about Robin Hood or Johnny Tremaine.

Female characters are scarce in prize-winning picture books for young children. Over a five-year period, eleven times as many males as females were depicted in Caldecott medal winners and honor books, 95 male animals were portrayed for every female animal, and there were eight obviously male characters in the title for every three females (Gagnon, 1977). Things do change as children progress to books for older children. In the same five-year period, female heroines outnumbered males in Newbery medal winners and honor books. And from Jo March to Caddie Woodlawn to Karana, there are many resourceful girls to be found. In books that feature boys as protagonists, however, girls tend to be easily frightened, incompetent followers, whose problems are solved by resourceful, intelligent brave boys. Heroines in fairy tales have the same problem; they rarely succeed on their own — a handsome prince, a fairy godmother, or a passing woodcutter generally rescues them from sorrow or disaster.

SEXUALITY

With the onset of puberty, biology again becomes a strong force in development. Hormones, a sudden growth spurt, the development of secondary sexual characteristics, a new interest in sexuality and the opposite sex, and changed expectations from family, peers, and society come together to produce uncertainty and self-consciousness. Adolescents' bodies are changing rapidly—and in a way that dramatically announces their sexual maturation to the world. No longer "sexless" children moving through the placid latency period, they find themselves suddenly thrust into the genital period and beset by new role demands. In response, most children retreat to the safety of sex-role stereotypes.

Reactions to Physical Change

Understandably, physical changes of the magnitude experienced by adolescents have a significant effect on how they feel about themselves. Peer and social attitudes influence both boys' and girls' reactions to these changes. One important influence is that of the mythical *body ideal*, the body type defined by the culture as "attractive" and sex-appropriate. Peer and family expectations and portrayals in the mass media teach these ideal characteristics. William Schonfeld (1963) has pointed out that movies, television, advertising, and the worship of sports heroes perpetuate the reverence for the ideal body and encourage the disparagement of those whose bodies do not conform to the ideal.

Adolescents of both sexes are especially sensitive to any body characteristic that might be interpreted as sex-inappropriate. From childhood, boys and girls learn which physical attributes are feminine and which are masculine, and they show deep concern over any deviations from those stereotypes (Schonfeld, 1964). Adolescent boys are particularly concerned about such characteristics as a circle of fat

Hormones, sexuality, and changed expectations from others combine to send the uncertain adolescent back to the safety of sex-role stereotypes. (Christopher Brown/Stock, Boston, Inc.)

around the hips and thighs, underdeveloped external genitalia, or the development of subcutaneous tissue in the breast region. Although such developments as fatty hips and breast growth are normal and usually soon disappear, they are often a source of great embarrassment to a boy.

Herbert and Lois Stolz (1951) have identified certain physical characteristics that adolescent girls consider unfeminine. These include large hands and feet, a figure that is much too full or too thin, pigmented facial hair, and a large body.

Thus many of the normal temporary changes of adolescence may seem "unfeminine" to a girl. She grows body hair, her voice becomes lower, her hands and feet grow, and so forth. Eventually, however, a girl may be comforted by the fact that her friends are experiencing the same changes.

The developing adolescent whose body conforms to the cultural ideal has a social advantage. But extremely tall, skinny adolescents and extremely short, fat ones are likely to evoke negative reactions from their peers. For example, J. Robert Staffieri (1967) found that classmates more often chose well-muscled and thin adolescents as friends than fat ones. Evaluations by others generally have a strong influence on an adolescent's social relations and behavior.

Developmental psychologists Mary Cover Jones and Nancy Bayley (1950) and their colleagues have followed groups of early- and late-maturing boys from early adolescence through the fourth decade of life. The boys differed markedly in social and physical characteristics during the years from thirteen to fifteen. At the same chronological age, the early maturers were taller, stronger, more attractive, and better coordinated than the later maturers, and they tended to have well-muscled bodies. The late maturers tended to be thin and were more talkative, active, busy, and uninhibited, yet they also tended to be tenser and bossier than the early maturers. These findings suggest that late maturers possess less social maturity and that they use negative behavior to get attention, thereby compensating for their physical disadvantages. Additional studies support this interpretation. Late maturers also show a greater need for social acceptance, greater anticipation of rejection, heightened dependence, and negative self-concepts (Mussen and Jones, 1957).

Schonfeld (1964) points out that many of the physical characteristics of late-maturing boys, which the boys themselves may regard as evidence of inadequate masculinity, fall within the normal range of development. When such is

the case, a late-maturing boy need only wait until he catches up with his peers. But in the meantime, the values placed on athletic prowess and manly appearance (by boys and girls alike) may make him feel inferior to those who mature early.

The early maturer is more active in athletics and student government and has greater visibility in the school social system. The social advantages of early maturity also appear to continue into adulthood, when differences in physique no longer exist. In their thirties, early maturers tended to have higher occupational status, were more likely to work in supervisory or managerial positions, and reported more active social lives in clubs, organizations, and business (M. Jones, 1957). The differences that became apparent when the groups were in their late thirties suggest that early maturers achieve in a conforming way, whereas later maturers' achievements are more likely to be idiosyncratic. Early maturers are likely to be conventional in both thought and attitude; they continue to have social poise and to show responsibility. Late maturers appear to be more flexible and adaptive; they tolerate ambiguity better than early maturers (M. Jones, 1965). Thus, as Harvey Peskin (1967) suggests, it appears that the greater social advantage of early maturers may lead them to fix on their identity early in life, thereby producing conventionality.

Studies of early- and late-maturing girls suggest that the early-maturing girl has less prestige than other girls in early adolescence but that as the growth process continues, she comes to enjoy the social advantages of the early-maturing boy (Faust, 1960). At first, the early-maturing girl is somewhat conspicuous and is likely to be far out of step developmentally with boys of her own age. However, early maturity may be a source of satisfaction if a girl's favorite companions are also early maturers. At seventeen, girls who have matured early may have a more favorable view of themselves and may rate higher in popularity than they rated earlier in their teens. However, studies that follow early- and late-maturing girls into adulthood have not been especially revealing, presumably because in the past a woman's social life, status, and opportunities for achievement have depended on the status of her husband (Eichorn, 1963).

Retreat to Stereotypes

The adolescent retreat to sex-role stereotypes shows up at about the age of fourteen. How much of this change in behavior is directly attributable to hormones and how much to adolescent uncertainty in the face of new social pressure is unknown, but both presumably have some part in the process.

Despite their changed behavior, individual adolescents see themselves as less stereotypical than the rest of the world. In Katheryn Urberg's (1979) study of sex-role development, when twelfth graders described themselves, there was only one significant difference in their portrayals. Girls saw themselves as more dependent than boys did. But when adolescents described the ideal person, stereotypes abounded for both sexes. And their descriptions of the opposite gender were always more stereotypical than were their descriptions of their own gender. The pattern of sex-role stereotype development showed clearly in Urberg's study. Seventh graders and adults—whether twenty or sixty-five—had a similar and much less stereotyped view of males and females than did twelfth graders.

One place where the retreat to stereotypes shows clearly is in adolescents' responses to babies. Shirley Feldman, Sharon Nash, and Carolyn Cutrona (1977) watched eight- and nine-year-old children and fourteen- and fifteen-year-old adolescents react to a baby who was playing on the floor near them. The younger girls and boys showed a similar degree of interest, both in the playing baby and later in pictures of babies. But among adolescents, girls paid more attention to the live baby, and they

looked longer at pictures of babies and liked them more than did boys. Similar studies of adults have shown that this sex difference soon disappears.

When Ann Frodi and Michael Lamb (1978) measured children's physiological reactions to crying and smiling babies, they found no difference between the sexes, whether at eight or fourteen years. Children and adolescents showed the same increased heart rate and skin conductance when the baby cried; they felt distressed, irritated, and unhappy, and they were sorry for the infant. When the baby smiled, their heart rates slowed and they felt good about it. But when these same young people were sitting near a baby while they waited to take the tests, adolescent boys interacted less with the baby than did the younger boys, and adolescent girls interacted more than did the younger girls. The fact that there were no sex differences on biological measures while there were sex differences on measures of behavior indicates that sex differences in behavior may be not biologically based but learned.

Sex Roles and Sex Differences

Traditional childhood and early adolescent socialization generally provides girls with a greater degree of competence than boys in interpersonal relationships. For most girls, sexual behavior involves incorporating sexuality into a social role and an identity that already included capacities for tenderness and sensitivity. For most boys, on the other hand, the pathway to mature heterosexual behavior involves sexuality first; only secondarily does the capacity for concerned, tender, and loving sexual relationships develop. Thus cultural stereotypes and parental and peer socialization emphasize, to use Ira Reiss' (1973) terms, "body-centered" sexuality for the male and "person-centered" sexuality for the female.

There is a connection between this formulation and the pattern of sex differences that should not go unnoticed. Boys reach the peak of their sexual powers earlier than girls, even though girls reach menarche earlier than boys reach a corresponding level of development. Boys desire orgasm more often than girls; they resort more than girls to sexual fantasies; they are more responsive to sexual symbols; they reach a sexual climax in dreams more often; they require less constant physical stimulation to remain aroused; they more often have had sexual relations with more than one partner; they do not tend to insist, as many girls do, that there should be a feeling of affection between sexual partners; and they prefer to go steady less often than girls do (Kinsey et al., 1948, 1953).

Alfred Kinsey and his colleagues tended to explain differences in male and female sexual behavior in biological terms—by assuming, for example, a more urgent male sex drive. A more balanced view suggests that these differences are the result of a complex interaction among neurological, hormonal, psychological, and cultural factors. It seems clear that male and female sexual behavior is influenced by sex-role stereotypes and expectations just as much other behavior is. According to traditional American standards, the girl plays a passive role in sexual relations. The boy takes the initiative in petting. The girl accedes, and if the approach threatens to go beyond the limits she allows, she is expected to serve as a calming influence for both. In courtship, it is the man who is supposed to propose. Although our culture's sex-role stereotypes are gradually changing, few adolescents have escaped the social pressures that dictate appropriate sexual behavior for each gender.

As a result, a girl's first intense sexual experience usually occurs in a heterosexual context; a boy's first experience is likely to occur when he is alone. Among their peers, groups of girls are likely to support and encourage one another for interpersonal competence and romantic interests, whereas groups of boys are likely to support and encourage one another for erotic interests, responsiveness to erotic stimuli, and proclaimed erotic activity. Adolescent peer groups also are likely to reward popularity with the opposite sex with status (G. Schwartz and D. Merten, 1967). Thus during adolescence, both boys and girls learn to incorporate sexual behavior into their gender roles, but the experiences each brings to his or her relationships are likely to be quite different. Further, as William Simon and John Gagnon (1969) suggest, adolescent dating and courtship can be seen as a training process in which boys train girls and girls train boys in the meaning and context of each sex's commitment to the heterosexual relationship.

The evolutionary changes in American sexual behavior and attitudes can be seen as part of a more general movement toward equalitarianism and, therefore, may affect traditional gender roles. For example, after surveying these changes, Reiss (1973) concludes that the human sexual relationship is changing from an occasion for male satisfaction of body-centered sexuality to an equalitarian relationship that involves more than physical attraction. He notes that although people will continue to pursue sexuality for pleasure, the pleasure is more likely to be mutual and equalitarian.

SEX ROLES AND THE LIFE SPAN

We might expect that a child begins life completely ignorant of the components of a sex role, then—as the rewards and punishments of society pile up—the constraints of gender become tighter and tighter, so that people over sixty-five adhere to the most rigid stereotypes of all. But that is not the case. In fact once developed, the degree of conformity to sex roles does not even remain stable. Already we have seen that the stereotypes so dear to the heart of the four-year-old loosen during the latency period of middle childhood, only to tighten again during adolescence.

What appears to happen is that during certain periods of life it becomes useful for most people to live within the traditional sex roles. And during those times when a traditional sex role is useful for a person, there is also an accompanying societal pressure for him or her to conform. During adolescence, when boys and girls are uncertain about their sex roles, conformity helps ease the uncertainty. The same ebb and flow of adherence to sex roles appears to be a characteristic of the entire life span.

In a series of studies, Shirley Feldman and Sharon Nash and their associates (Feldman and Nash, 1978; Abrahams, Feldman, and Nash, 1978; Feldman and Nash, 1979) have shown that as their life situations change, adult men and women modify their attitudes toward sex roles and even their own self-concepts in regard to them. If this is the case, one would expect childless adults to be less interested in babies than parents are. When adults in their twenties and thirties were placed in a situation similar to that Feldman, Nash, and Cutrona used with adolescents, the responses to a live baby and the interest in baby pictures were almost identical in all groups: single men and women who were cohabiting, childless couples, and couples who were expecting their first child. But mothers of babies showed a high interest in the baby who was playing in the waiting room and spent a lot of time looking at baby pictures, although fathers did not. In addition, when tested on a sex-role inventory (which measures a person's degree of masculinity or femininity), mothers scored higher in femininity than did childless women, and fathers scored higher in masculinity than did childless men.

Parenthood usually makes sweeping changes in a couple's life, and during their child's infancy, parents tend to conform to stereotypical roles. As we saw in Chapter 14, mothers and fathers respond similarly to their newborn infants, but since mothers are expected to take primary responsibility for their babies, they spend more time with them than fathers do — and less time with their husbands than they did

before the baby's arrival. Fathers, on the other hand, often become more preoccupied with the economic necessities of life, because although the mother may plan to return to work eventually, for the present the father bears the responsibility of supporting three lives.

Similar connections between people's situations and their interest in babies continue throughout life. Parents of adolescents and parents whose grown children have left home display similar (minimal) interest in babies, although mothers always show slightly more interest than fathers. The level of interest rises sharply among grandparents, and grandmothers show the most interest of all. Again, when sex differences serve no purpose, they diminish.

Function cannot explain the increased interest taken in babies by grandparents, although the interest corresponds to stereotype. On the sex-role inventory, grandmothers are as high in femininity as other women but are higher in masculinity. Similarly, grandfathers are as high in masculinity as other men, but show increases in their femininity scores. This change in self-concept to include qualities of the opposite sex conforms to the proposal of David Guttman (1975). On the basis of studies in several cultures, he believes that the responsibilities of parenthood play an overwhelming role during much of adulthood, requiring men to become assertive and dominant and women to become nurturant and passive. But once their family responsibilities have been completed, older adults may indulge those qualities that have been suppressed in the interest of their children, with both sexes moving toward the middle ground of androgyny.

ANDROGYNY

In recent years there has been a trend away from stereotypical notions of masculinity and femininity for adults. In their place has come the concept of *androgyny*, a term that describes people who embrace the characteristics of both

Androgynous people see little psychological difference between the sexes, so that a man can feel comfortable under a beautician's hairdryer and a woman can build muscles without feeling she is less female. (Frank Siteman/Taurus Photos)/(© Lawrence Frank, 1980)

sexes. Their self-concepts allow them to be masculine or feminine, assertive or yielding, depending upon the appropriateness of a reaction to a specific situation (Bem, 1974).

If androgynous people are defined as those who are high in *both* masculinity and femininity — both competently assertive and securely sensitive to other people — we might expect an-

drogyny to lead to fuller human functioning. Janet Spence (1979) has found that androgynous people have the highest self-esteem of any group. She speculates that they are individuals with multiple talents. Because they are flexible, they can take on any role they choose or that their life situation demands. This may well be so, for some studies (Hammer, 1964; Helson, 1966) have shown that highly creative men and women tend to incorporate attributes of the opposite sex.

Androgynous people, believes Sandra Bem (1979), differ from traditionally masculine and feminine people in their beliefs about basic differences between the sexes. These beliefs influence both how they behave and how they interpret the sex-role behavior of others. According to Bem, since androgynous people see little basic psychological difference between the sexes, they process gender-related information differently and are less likely to interpret variations in people's behavior as attributable to gender.

For this reason, androgyny may not be possible for the very young. Regardless of what their parents do to counteract stereotypical sex roles, children tend to be traditional. As they work to establish a sense of gender identity, they search out sex-role differences. The possibility of androgyny may not open until children reach adolescence. Despite inner and outer pushes to conform, adolescents can accept the concept of androgyny provided they have developed formal operational thought, which was described in Chapter 12. Once the capability to think about abstract situations and to deduce conclusions from hypotheses is established, it becomes possible to consider the merits and drawbacks of traditional sex roles and to go beyond them.

Although many formal obstacles to the advancement of women in the economic and legal areas have been overcome, it is unlikely that society will either abolish or reverse gender roles. Most women will continue to be responsible for primary child care—although they may feel free to work and to share the chores with their husbands and (primarily female) day-care workers. And given that situation, most men will continue to bear primary financial responsibility while the children are very young. But the edges of stereotypes are likely to blur, with both sexes feeling less hemmed in by rigid restrictions than in former times.

SUMMARY

1. Sex roles pervade every aspect of life, and in every culture men and women have different duties, different responsibilities, and different pleasures. Slight differences between the sexes become magnified into sex-role stereotypes, simplified concepts about sex differences that resemble few people in the culture.

2 Sex roles vary from culture to culture and refer to the socially prescribed manifestations of gender; gender identity is one's inner experience of the self as male or female. Although the two usually correspond, sometimes they do not, as in the case of the househusband with a secure male gender identity.

3. The sense of gender constancy—the knowledge that one's gender will never change—appears to develop between the ages of five and seven, although some studies have found it among much younger children. Children whose gender identity is different from their anatomical sex are called transsexuals, a disorder that may result from a combination of biological, constitutional, and social forces.

4. Prenatal hormones may dispose male and female infants toward different kinds of behavior, but the way they are treated by others has an extremely powerful influence on gender identity and on sex-role development.

5. Parents appear to encourage independence in boys and nurturance and dependence in girls, and the work they begin is furthered by teachers. Peers also play an important role by reinforcing appropriate sex-role behavior and punishing behavior they see as inappropriate. The influence of the media may also be considerable, as books and television generally provide a steady diet of traditional sex-role portrayals.

6. With the onset of puberty, adolescents retreat to the shelter of sex-role stereotypes, perhaps influenced by both hormones and social pressures. Sexual behavior itself is influenced by stereotypes, so that adolescent boys and girls

bring quite different backgrounds and expectations to sexual experiences.

7. Conformity to sex roles is not stable. During certain periods of life—the preschool years, when children are developing their sex roles; the adolescent years, when they are learning to cope with the role demands of sexual maturation; and the years of early parenthood—traditional sex roles are useful and most people conform to them. When one's life no longer is built around the implications of gender, the strictures of sex roles drop away. Older adults appear to move toward androgyny, with men expressing feminine and women expressing male qualities that have been repressed.

8. Androgynous people embrace the characteristics of both sexes, being assertive or yielding as the situation demands. People who score high in androgyny see little psychological difference between the sexes and may process gender-related information differently. Although society is unlikely to abolish gender roles, both sexes face fewer restrictions today than they once did.

PART 7

Reweaving the Strands

The time has come to reweave the strands of cognition and personality that were unraveled in Parts 5 and 6. Although the results of a child's cognitive processing are heavily dependent on motivations, emotions, attitudes, and past experiences, and although the effect of experiences depends upon the level of a child's cognitive development, much of the discussion has proceeded as if the two strands of development progress in isolation. One place where the close weaving of the strands is most apparent is in the general area of social cognition, which includes moral development. The way children meet moral and ethical problems, their level of aggressiveness, their tendency to help others, can be understood only by looking both at socialization practices and at cognitive development. And the child's understanding of self, others, and society requires the application of cognitive processes to the subject matter generally covered in the chapters on socialization. By concluding the book with consideration of an area in which the strands are so tightly knit, we emphasize for a final time the interactive nature of human development.

Morality: From Rules to Conduct

Paul and Michael, both fifteen months old, were struggling desperately over a toy. First Michael, then Paul, tugged on the attractive plaything, each trying to capture it for himself. Suddenly Paul began to cry. At the sound of his friend's distress, Michael let go of the toy. But possession did not end the tears; Paul kept on sobbing. Michael studied his friend for a moment, then gave his teddy bear to Paul. Paul cried on. After another pause, Michael ran from the room and came back with Paul's security blanket. He offered it to his friend, who took it, then stopped crying. Somehow this infant realized that just as his prized teddy bear could comfort his own distress, Paul's security blanket would end his friend's unhappiness. This anecdote, reported by Martin Hoffman (1976), indicates that even an infant can be empathic and correctly assess and minister to another's needs. Empathy, which provides the link between moral development and altruism, is examined later in this chapter as an example of prosocial behavior.

In this chapter, we shall discuss moral development, distinguishing between moral behavior and moral reasoning, and looking at the effect of the immediate situation on moral behavior. We shall describe the psychodynamic and social-learning theories of moral development, as well as the social-evolutionary approach. After comparing Piaget's cognitive theory of moral judgment with the system developed by Lawrence Kohlberg, we shall consider the application of both to moral behavior. Next we shall look at the positive side of behavior, studying the development of empathy and its role in altruism. Finally, we shall look at aggression, examining its origins, the situations that evoke it, and the influence of television on antisocial behavior.

MORAL DEVELOPMENT

Children who learn to abide by the rules of their culture are generally considered "good." But how do they come to carry out rules that uphold their culture's values and to avoid breaking its prohibitions? And what is good? If being good simply means conforming to social standards, then a good Nazi was a moral human being in the Germany of the 1930s and 1940s. The valuation we place on human life and on justice will not allow us to accept such a totally relative position, one that requires us to regard slavery or genocide as moral if it is practiced and condoned by a culture. But whether right or wrong is whatever a culture says it is or whether there are universal moral principles or whether certain human moral predispositions take different forms in different cultures, children learn the rules of their own culture in basically the same way. Many psychologists agree that (1) babies come into the world as amoral beings, (2) they are active learners, (3) they acquire their first personal moral values and standards from their parents, (4) early moral edicts are tied to specific situations, (5) a child's early moral concepts and understandings differ from those of adults, and (6) a person's moral concepts and

understandings change with increasing cognitive sophistication and social experience.

Defining Moral Development

When researchers talk about moral development, they are often talking about two different things. By moral development, psychoanalysts and social-learning theorists mean just what parents, policemen, and the average citizen mean — behavior. These researchers focus on what children do and how that behavior changes as children grow. Much of their research involves lying, cheating, stealing, resisting temptation, and being willing to share possessions or to assist people in need. In contrast, cognitive theorists pay little attention to what children do. They are interested in how children think about moral problems and the kinds of judgments they make. Most of their research involves presenting stories that center on some kind of transgression or moral dilemma and asking children to judge the actors and explain why the children in the story are good or bad and whether they should be punished.

The basic problem is that the connection between what children or adults say is right in tests of moral reasoning and what they actually do is slight. Whenever researchers have found a relationship between moral reasoning and moral behavior, it has been modest. Walter and Harriet Mischel (1976) surveyed the existing research and concluded that it is difficult to justify claims of strong links between moral reasoning and individual action. They suggest that knowing people's moral reasoning allows one to predict only 10 percent of the variation in their behavior in different situations. For example, it is often possible to predict moral behavior just as accurately from a child's need for achievement or need for affiliation as from the child's level of moral reasoning. And the problem of prediction is complicated by the fact that a child will cheat in one situation and will not cheat in another.

Inconsistency in Moral Conduct

Although people continue to talk about moral conduct as a class of reactions that go together and are governed by some central controlling process such as conscience, it is plain that most of us behave inconsistently in situations involving moral problems. After surveying the research, Douglas Graham (1972) concluded that people are likely to show highly consistent moral conduct only when the range of situations that confronts them is restricted or when a high level of abstract thinking allows them to apply general principles over many varied situations.

More than fifty years ago, Hugh Hartshorne and Mark May (1928) conducted a landmark study of children's consistency in moral conduct and disappointed all those who would like to divide the world into moral and immoral people. In the course of their research, Hartshorne and May tested 11,000 schoolchildren for many types of moral behavior (such as cheating, lying, and stealing) in different contexts (such as tests, games, and contests) in widely varied settings (such as home, church, and playground). They found that children's moral judgments remained consistent provided that the questionnaires that measured them were administered in the same setting. When the setting was moved—for example, from a church to a clubhouse—the correlations between the two scores dropped drastically, making it appear that the children's basic moral codes changed when a given situation changed.

The children's moral behavior was even less consistent than their moral judgments. Hartshorne and May found that almost all children cheat some of the time and that knowing a child has cheated in one situation does not make it possible to predict whether the child will cheat in another. Expediency appeared to determine the decision. When it seemed safe and easy to cheat or when it appeared that other children cheated or approved of cheating, a child was more likely to cheat. For example, in some classrooms, many children cheated; in others, almost no one cheated. It also appeared that the child who cheats in the classroom is not necessarily the same child who tells lies there; nor is the child who lies to the teacher the same child who lies to peers. Finally, the relationship between children's moral judgments and their actual behavior was virtually nonexistent. Their results convinced Hartshorne and May that it was foolish to try to categorize children or adults as moral or immoral. The crucial question was not whether an individual would behave morally or immorally but rather when he or she would do so.

The children studied by Hartshorne and May did not, however, cheat at random. According to Roger Burton (1976), who reanalyzed these classic studies, they did establish individual predispositions to be honest or dishonest. Burton believes that children's learning experiences lead some of them to be relatively consistent in their honesty or dishonesty and others to be relatively inconsistent. Even when a child develops a general tendency to resist or to succumb to temptation, the conditions surrounding each moral choice will have a strong effect on the child's final decision.

Other research has not challenged these basic conclusions. For example, Robert Sears, Lucy Rau, and Richard Alpert (1965) compared six different tests of children's resistance to temptation in play settings. Almost all the resulting correlations were positive, but none indicated a very great degree of consistency, even though all were administered in the context of a play situation. A similar study of moral consistency led Wesley Allinsmith (1960) to conclude that a person with a truly generalized conscience is a statistical rarity.

Inconsistency in moral conduct should not be

Circumstances often determine behavior in situations involving morality. This child will steal if he thinks he won't get caught; another child might steal only if the payoff is enormous; and a third, only if the theft is easy. (© Sepp Seitz/ Woodfin Camp & Assoc.)

surprising. Moral situations involve strong and conflicting pressures, and only a slight change in these pressures may shift the proposed situation from moral to immoral in a person's judgment. Circumstances also influence people in different ways. For one person, the chances of getting caught may determine his or her behavior. For another, the magnitude of the payoff may be the determining factor. A third person's behavior may depend on the amount of effort involved. Although moral reasoning may become increasingly unified and consistent as a person develops, his or her behavior often depends on situational constraints. Moreover, moral conduct in one situation (resistance to temptation) is a behavior pattern different from moral conduct in another (the donation of money to a charity). Both are examples of moral behavior, but they are not necessarily governed by the same processes nor do they necessarily manifest themselves in a consistent fashion across individuals.

DEVELOPING MORAL BEHAVIOR

However inconsistently people behave, at times "conscience" keeps them from breaking moral codes. When they speak of conscience, however, people are referring to their feelings when they remember or anticipate some transgression. These feelings develop gradually during childhood, and babies who come into the world without any sense of right or wrong become eight-year-olds who "feel bad" when they disobey parents or teachers. In fact, the language of morality is full of terms that relate to feelings — terms such as "guilt," "shame," "anxiety" — and how people come to feel about their actions is a critical factor in the development of moral conduct.

Psychoanalytic theory describes *what* children learn in the process of developing a conscience; social-learning theory describes *how* they learn moral actions and under what conditions they are likely to put that learning into action. The two approaches to moral development, then, are complementary — one concentrates on content, the other on process (Hogan and Emler, 1978).

Establishing Guilt — The Psychoanalytic Approach

According to Freudian theory (see Chapter 2), the child's conscience, or superego, develops out of the oedipal struggle. Fearing the loss of parental love, children identify with the parent of the same sex. They strive to be like that parent in every way, copying behavior and incorporating moral standards and values. Once this is accomplished (at about six, or the beginning of the latency period), whenever children are tempted to violate a parental prohibition, they experience guilt—a form of self-punishment. The rules that once had to be enforced by the parent are now enforced by the child because they have become the child's own values.

If the psychoanalytic view is correct, then disciplinary techniques that keep the child uncertain about a parent's love (withdrawal of love, denial of rewards, and threats of ostracism) are likely to produce children who feel guilty when they violate parental standards. In a study of seventy-five cultures, John Whiting and Irvin Child (1953) found that societies in which parents used love-oriented techniques of discipline were indeed more likely to produce guilty children than were societies in which parents used physical punishment or ridicule. The relation, however, was weak.

Further support for identification as the basis of conscience turned up in the study by Robert Sears, Eleanor Maccoby, and Harry Levin (1957). They found that five-year-olds who were disciplined with love-oriented techniques developed strong consciences—but only if they had warm mothers. Children of cold mothers who relied on the withdrawal of love were unlikely to develop strong consciences.

Because the guilt that accompanies a strong conscience is unpleasant, children generally learn how to avoid or reduce it, and this learning is likely to take many forms. As children's ability to understand and to think increases and as they gain additional social experience, they learn new ways to manage guilt. And, although individual differences in this aspect of moral development are large, most children appear to develop somewhat similar ways of managing guilt (McMichael and Grinder, 1966).

One of the most obvious ways to avoid guilt is through self-control. For example, children can resist temptation and refuse to do something that is forbidden. If, however, they believe that they will succumb to temptation, they may learn to avoid guilt by not even thinking about forbidden things, because the thoughts themselves provoke guilt feelings.

As their cognitive sophistication increases, however, most children learn elegant ways of avoiding the guilt produced by their thoughts or actions. For example, if a boy hurts another person, he may define his actions in benevolent terms, saying, "I just did it for his own good." Or he may learn to avoid guilt and self-condemnation by telling himself that the other person is a "tattletale" or a "cheater." Other learned ways of reducing the unpleasantness of guilt appear equally effective. A boy may learn to confess his transgressions or to apologize for what he has said or done. Or he may learn to reduce his guilt by saying that his misbehavior was only half as bad as it could have been or as what others have done.

Some of these ways in which children and adults learn to handle their feelings of guilt and responsibility appear strikingly similar to what has been called the "just world hypothesis" (Fein, 1976). In general, people want to see the world as working in a consistent and just fashion, so that evil is punished and good is rewarded. Adopting this perspective allows people to see themselves as caring, helpful, and concerned human beings, no matter what happens to others. They have, therefore, a way to escape feelings of guilt or responsibility when someone else is the victim of an obvious wrong; if the world is just, the person must have deserved it.

Learning Moral Conduct— The Social-Learning Approach

Social-learning theorists believe that children learn moral behavior as they learn any other behavior—through a combination of rewards, punishment, and observation of models, mechanisms that were discussed in Chapter 2. Children discover that when they do or say things their parents approve of, they generally receive affection, and through conditioning, this affection becomes coupled with their feelings of self-approval. They also discover, however, that when they do or say things their parents dis-approve of, withdrawal of affection or punishment of some kind is likely to follow, and through conditioning, this punishment becomes coupled with their feelings of guilt and self-reproof. As a result of this kind of learning, children eventually may behave morally even though their parents or other people are not present. Gradually, their own thoughts and feelings replace rewards and punishments administered by others, and they come to regulate their own moral conduct. They are also likely to keep learning various ways of reacting to their guilt over actual or contemplated transgressions.

DISCIPLINE Studies have shown that the nature of the parental relationship, the explanation of the reasons for discipline, and the timing of punishment are all important factors in the establishment of guilt and self-regulation in moral conduct. According to Justin Aronfreed (1976), punishment (which includes rejection and disapproval) is an inevitable part of child rearing and without it socialization probably cannot take place—as we saw in Chapter 15. Mild physical punishment, coupled with a mild withdrawal of love, appears to establish guilt and self-regulation much more efficiently than does severe physical punishment (M. Hoffman, 1977a). A child can always avoid the brief unpleasantness of physical punishment merely by avoiding the punisher, but if a normally loving parent also withdraws his or her love, the punishment lasts until the love is restored. Children disciplined by severe and unexplained punishment are unlikely to develop an effective sense of guilt or self-regulation and instead only learn to behave so that they will not get caught.

Studies by Martin Hoffman and Herbert Saltzstein (1967), Aronfreed (1969), and others suggest that reasoning with children and pointing out the effects of their wrongdoing are at least as important as withdrawing love—possibly more so. Such verbal explanation and reasoning do two things: they encourage a child

Reason or Power— Not Always the Parent's Choice

The sort of discipline parents use with their children apparently affects children's behavior—including their moral development, as the discussions in Chapter 15 and in this chapter have indicated. For example, the use of reasoning with children has been linked with the development of altruism (Hoffman, 1975). But what if the influence runs both ways? An experiment by Barbara Keller and Richard Bell (1979) indicates that a child's behavior may go a long way toward determining the techniques parents use to instill codes of morality.

Keller and Bell trained three nine-year-old girls to behave in two entirely different ways. The first style was "person-oriented": the girls looked at adults' faces, smiled, and answered questions promptly. In the second, "object-oriented" style, the girls kept their attention on the materials before them (beads, small toys, etc.) and counted silently to five before answering adults' comments. Each girl learned both styles of behavior.

Twenty-four undergraduate college women, who were the subjects, were each instructed to interact with a child in an attempt to get

to take the role of others, and they help a child to internalize moral standards by providing thoughts to associate with his or her feelings and with the reward or punishment. As a girl (or boy) comes to understand how her behavior affects others and how their behavior affects her, and as she comes to adopt the moral thoughts and attitudes of her parents, she soon responds with self-approval to what are now her own correct thoughts and actions. She learns to use self-instruction and self-praise. And when

her to show some consideration for others. In order to give the student power over the child, the experimenter handed her a stack of poker chips, which could be exchanged for toys or books after the session. The student could award the child chips or take away chips the child already had.

Before the twenty-minute interaction period began, the student watched one of the girls through a one-way mirror as she ran through a memorized script with the experimenter. During this enactment, the girl behaved in either a person- or an object-oriented style. During the following session with the college student, the girl (while continuing to behave in the person- or object-oriented style) impeded whatever altruistic task the student was urging her to do. For example, she spent more time working on a pillow for herself than on one for a handicapped child.

When the videotaped sessions were scored, it was plain that the girls' manner of behaving had a profound effect on the college students. When speaking to a girl who behaved in a person-oriented manner, the students relied on reason, often referring to the consequences of the child's behavior. When speaking to a girl who behaved in an object-oriented manner, the students fell back on the only kind of power they had—references

to the poker chips that they could give or take away. The girls' behavior also affected the students' impressions of them. On a questionnaire they answered after the session, students rated the girls as significantly more attentive, responsive, attractive, cheerful, intelligent, and physically active when they had behaved in a person-oriented manner than when they had used the object-oriented style.

The results of this experiment indicate that children play an important part in determining the ways in which they are socialized. Children who smile are generally considered cheerful and attractive; children who respond promptly to questions are generally regarded as intelligent and active. These perceptions affect the people around them.

The process of parent-child interaction is surely a circular one. As noted in Chapter 5, the infant's initial responsiveness may set the tone for parent-child interaction, and the discussion in Chapter 14 pointed out the importance of a mother's responsiveness to her child. What combination of inborn tendencies, rewards and punishment, and level of cognitive understanding—in both child and parent—develops a highly person-oriented child is unknown. It appears, however, that the choice of disciplinary techniques is not arbitrary but dictated in part by the child's behavior.

faced with a temptation, such as a dazzling display of dials and push buttons on a color television set, the child may regulate her conduct by telling herself, "No. Don't touch. That's a good girl. I'm a good girl for not touching."

The timing of discipline appears to be especially important in the development of guilt and self-regulation. In studies by Richard Walters, Ross Parke, and Valerie Cane (1965), for example, children were punished either just as they were about to play with a forbidden object

or after they had begun to play with it. Afterward, the children were placed, one at a time, in a situation in which the same forbidden object tempted them. Generally, children who were punished early showed greater resistance than children who were punished late.

Similar results appeared in a study by Aronfreed (1976), who found that a majority of children who were punished as they reached for a toy did not touch the forbidden toy when they were left alone with it. Those who did pick it up succumbed only after a lengthy period. But children who were not punished until after they had picked up the toy began playing with the forbidden toy as soon as the experimenter left the room. Aronfreed suggests that when a child is punished early in the course of a transgression, enormous anxiety becomes associated with the *anticipation* of doing wrong, allowing the child's inner monitors to exercise control over behavior.

In a second study, Aronfreed found that children who were given a verbal reason (that the toy was "only for older boys") along with the delayed punishment resisted temptation much longer than children who simply experienced delayed punishment without a reason for it. And when the late punishment was accompanied by an explanation that focused on the child's intentions (the child "had wanted" to play with the toy) along with the reason it was not to be played with, resistance to temptation was as strong as when children were punished as they reached for the toy.

It is, of course, often impossible to punish children just before they begin to do something that is forbidden, but as Aronfreed's studies show, delayed punishment can be effective. Along with providing punishment, the parent must use words to recreate the transgression as fully as possible, sensitizing the child to his or her intention as well as to the consequences of the act. In this way, when the child is later tempted, anxiety will be generated *before* any transgression takes place, greatly increasing the chances that the child will resist temptation. By using this sort of approach, Donald Meichenbaum and Joseph Goodman (1971) have taught impulsive children with a history of getting into trouble to talk to themselves when they are tempted to do something forbidden. Using this kind of self-regulation, children end up modifying their own behavior.

MODELS As earlier discussions of modeling indicated, if models are warm, powerful, and competent (and in early childhood that is just the way parents are likely to seem), a child may well copy their behavior. But as we also saw in earlier discussions, what happens to the models a child sees also affects the probability that a child will imitate them. If the model is rewarded, the child is likely to copy the model and to expect a reward for behaving in the same way. If the model is punished, the child is unlikely to copy the behavior because he or she would expect to receive similar punishment. And if a model resists moderate temptation—especially if the model explains why he or she resisted—a child will forgo temptation, even when it means having to continue to work on a boring task (Grusec *et al.*, 1979).

One of the most important findings to come out of research on the observational learning of moral conduct is that an unpunished transgression appears to have the same effect on the watching child as a transgression followed by rewards. Children who see peers playing with forbidden toys are more likely to play with the toys than children who see no such transgression (Grosser, Polansky, and Lippitt, 1951). Apparently, when a child sees other children breaking a prohibition and getting away with it, the consequences the child anticipates for violating that prohibition change.

An experiment by Richard Walters and Ross Parke (1964) supports the idea that the absence of expected punishment may act as a reward. They showed films of a model playing with forbidden toys to several groups of children. Some of the children saw the model rewarded; some saw the model punished; others saw nothing—either good or bad—happen to the model. When these children were later placed in a situation similar to that depicted in the film, both those who had seen the transgression rewarded and those who had seen it go unpunished were more likely to play with the forbidden toys than children who had seen the model's actions punished or those in a control group who had seen no film.

All the children who saw the films learned the model's behavior, for when the experimenter indicated that no one would be punished for playing with the forbidden toys, children who had seen any of the films were more likely to play with the toys than children who had not seen the films. Thus it is apparent that those who did not copy the model's transgression were trying to avoid expected punishment.

Subsequently, Walters, Parke, and Cane (1965) also found that in certain conditions, only the prospect of punishment can keep a child from transgression. Once again, they showed children films of a model playing with forbidden toys, but this time the toys were so enticing that punishing the model was the only consequence that affected children's transgressions; the rest—

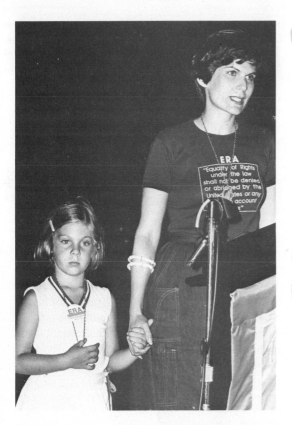

Parents provide powerful models for moral conduct, and if their actions reflect their words, their children are likely to copy them. (Jean-Marie Simon/Taurus Photos)

children who had seen the model rewarded, those who had seen nothing happen to the model, and those who had seen no film—could not resist the tempting toys.

When children watch a model go unpunished, two things happen. First, the punishment-free transgression suggests to them that the usual negative sanction does not apply in this situation, and they modify their own thinking accordingly. Second, the children then copy the model's violations because transgression is safe and because playing with the forbidden toys is rewarding. Consequences to a model can also affect other aspects of moral conduct. When children see a model go unrewarded for moral behavior, such as altruism, they will also fail to copy the model (Staub, 1975). Thus in a paradoxical sort of way, seeing moral behavior go unrewarded may decrease the rate at which it occurs, just as if the behavior were immoral and therefore punished.

Children who develop high standards of moral conduct, says Albert Bandura (1977), are likely to be children whose parental models keep high standards themselves, have reaped rewards because of their standards, demand that their children adhere to the same standards, and protect their children from different standards that might be held by their peers.

Solving Moral Problems— The Social-Evolutionary Approach

If we regard the traditional psychoanalytic approach as relying on inborn human tendencies and the social-learning approach as relying on environmental explanations, then the social-evolutionary approach is a combination of the two: through the interaction of inborn and environmental influences, the child develops by solving a series of problems that differ as his or her competencies develop. The major exponent of the social-evolutionary approach to moral development, Robert Hogan (1973, 1975; Hogan and Emler, 1978), regards this view as harmonious with Erik Erikson's theory of human development, which was discussed in Chapter 2.

According to social-evolutionary theory, the child passes through three stages in moral development. Each stage presents a new set of problems that must be solved, and the manner of the solution determines the child's attitudes toward morality. In the first stage, which lasts until the child is from three to five years old, the problem is to learn to live with authority. When the attachment between baby and parents is secure, says Hogan, infants will naturally comply with parental direction (Stayton, Hogan, and Ainsworth, 1971). Given warm but restrictive parents, such as the authoritative parent described in Chapter 15, children will have little difficulty in learning to live by the rules; they will comply with moral rules because of their respect for authority.

In the second stage, which lasts until late adolescence, the problem is to learn to live with others. Children must accommodate themselves to the largely unstated rules of the peer group, which requires the development of social sensitivity. Along with learning social interaction, children acquire a sense of justice. According to the Piagetian theory of moral judgment (Piaget, 1932), this sense of justice arises out of the cooperation of peers. Hogan, on the other hand, believes that it develops out of the injustices children encounter in the peer group. Only when older children adhere to the rules can younger children take part in games. By experiencing injustice at the hands of their elders, children come to understand why the rules they learned at home are important. Children comply with moral rules out of a sense of justice and from respect for peers.

When children are about sixteen years old, they enter the third stage, where the problem is learning to live with oneself. To solve the problem effectively, the adolescent must develop autonomy. The lessons of childhood are set within the framework of a philosophical or religious world view, and a person complies with them

regardless of pressure from peers or authority figures to transgress. The morally mature person, suggests Hogan, is one whose moral code represents a synthesis between moral intuition (confidence in higher laws that supersede human legislation) and moral rationalism (confidence in society's laws and rules). Adults comply with rules because they believe them to be sacred, valid, or historically sanctioned.

DEVELOPING MORAL REASONING—THE COGNITIVE APPROACH

Cognitive theorists pay little attention to whether people's conduct is moral or immoral or to how people feel about their actions; instead, cognitive theorists focus on how people reason about moral issues and how they justify their moral judgments. Just as social-learning theorists regard the development of moral behavior as a case of learning applied to a single realm, so cognitive theorists regard moral reasoning as a kind of thought that is subject to the same developmental constraints as the rest of cognition. In this view, until a child reaches an appropriate level of cognitive development, certain types of moral reasoning are impossible. The child in the sensorimotor stage, for example, lacks even a rudimentary appreciation of morality. Once the child moves into the preoperational stage and begins to use symbols, the beginnings of moral reasoning appear. Not until a child acquires formal operational thought are the highest levels of moral reasoning possible—and even then, there is no guarantee they will develop. The dominant theorists in the area of moral thought have been Jean Piaget and Lawrence Kohlberg.

Moral Judgment

Jean Piaget (1932) believed that, since morality is embodied in a system of rules, the best place to watch moral development is in children's

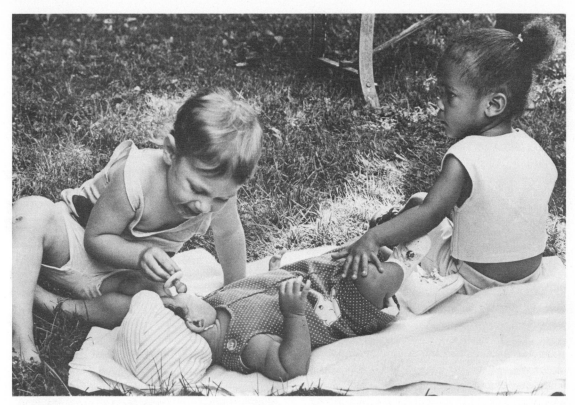

According to cognitive theorists, moral reasoning is impossible for children less than two years old; once they reach the preoperational stage, children can begin to appreciate the existence of right and wrong. (© Joel Gordon 1976)

games. Consequently, he spent a good deal of time watching children play marbles and talking to them at length about the rules of the game. He discovered that until children are two, there are no rules because there is no game; children simply handle marbles as they wish. From two until they are five or so, children imitate rules but do not try to win. Rules are regarded as interesting but not obligatory. From about six until they are ten, there is an attempt to agree on rules, but each child seems to play by a different set. Despite their contradictory accounts of the rules and their general laxity in following them, children of this age regard the rules as imposed from the outside by authorities. Rules are sacred, eternal, and untouchable; even to consider changing them is naughty. From ten to twelve, everybody knows the same rules and there is a regulation for every detail of the game. Although children respect the rules, they know that they may change them. Any change, however, must be the result of a consensus and also be consistent with the spirit of the game.

Piaget proposed that as children move from confidence in the eternal nature of rules to a belief in their mutability, they also tend to move from one major stage of morality to another. In the first stage, called the *morality of constraint*, duty consists of obedience to authority. Transgressors are punished by immanent justice, that is, wicked deeds inevitably bring punishment, even if it takes time or appears in the form of accidental injury. If a boy steals a quarter from his mother's purse and later cuts himself on a broken cola bottle, the cut is seen as punishment for the theft. Children operating under the morality of constraint judge an act by its consequences, not by the intentions of the actor.

The second stage, the *morality of cooperation*, develops from children's interactions with their peers. In judging transgressions, children believe the intentions of the actor are more important than the consequences of the act. Punishment is not inevitable, and when it comes, it should not be arbitrary. The wrongdoer should receive a similar injury (a punch in the nose for a child who hit another), suffer the natural consequences of the action, or make restitution for the wrong.

Piaget realized that both these moralities can exist side by side—that a child may apply the morality of constraint to one action and the morality of cooperation to another—but he believed that as children grow older, they tend increasingly to judge in terms of the morality of cooperation.

When Piaget studied moral judgment, one of his techniques was to have children listen to a pair of stories and judge the actors. In one story, for example, a child accidentally broke fifteen cups while opening a door; in the other, a child accidentally broke a single cup while getting into a cookie jar. Young children generally consider the child who did the most damage naughtier and deserving of more punishment. On the basis of such results, Piaget concluded that although children as young as three or four may be able to distinguish between accidental and intended acts, they are unlikely to use such information in making a moral judgment; instead they are likely to use the consequences of an act as the basis of their decision. According to Piaget, young children believe that transgressions deserve punishment, and because their parents punish most severely transgressions that do the greatest wrong, young children follow the same standards.

Recent research indicates that Piaget's results and interpretations are correct in some respects but not in others (Lickona, 1976). Cognitive immaturity does appear to be the source of the

young child's idea that rules are inflexible; as children grow older, they do increasingly judge by the intentions of the actor. The belief in immanent justice declines sharply between the ages of five and ten, and fifth graders simply do not believe in it (e.g., Suls and Kalle, 1979). But Piaget's belief that the morality of cooperation develops out of cooperative peer relationships has not been substantiated (Hogan and Emler, 1978), and children appear to be less consistent in judging acts by one of his two stages of morality than Piaget had expected (Lickona, 1976). In addition, the traditional pairs of stories used by Piaget are unlikely to provide a fair test of young children's understanding of a culprit's intent or their use of it in making a judgment. The stories require a child to remember and then compare two intents and two outcomes; the intentions of the actors are not stated clearly or explicitly in Piaget's stories, and the outcome is always stated last. When the stories are simplified so that only one intent and one outcome have to be considered at a time (e.g., Berg-Cross, 1975), and both intent and outcome are explicitly stated and systematically varied (e.g., Gottlieb, Taylor, and Ruderman, 1977), young children may show much more advanced moral reasoning than Piaget found. In such cases, young children not only can distinguish between accidental and intended actions, and between good and bad intentions, but they also can weigh both intention and consequence in making moral judgments (Surber, 1977). Even five- and six-year-olds can weigh the circumstances surrounding a misdeed and adjust the punishment accordingly (Darley, Klosson, and Zanna, 1978). They are also likely to distinguish between harm to human beings and other types of damage, and to judge the former more harshly (Elkind and Dabek, 1977).

As Piaget found, however, when young children are fully aware of the intentions behind an action, they still may base their moral judgments primarily on the result of an act. Rachel Karniol (1978) suggests that young children appear to learn, first, that acts based on bad intentions are naughty regardless of their outcome and therefore deserve punishment. But when a well-intentioned act does greater harm than an act with bad intentions, children may give the consequences greater weight than intentions in assessing punishment. This interpretation, according to Karniol, is consistent with the common socialization experiences of young children. That is, parents are more likely to punish consequences than to reward good intentions, so children are likely to learn early what others consider wrong; they learn to distinguish good behavior later and more slowly.

Stages in Moral Reasoning

Lawrence Kohlberg (1963, 1969) has proposed a provocative and appealing approach to moral thinking that is in part an elaboration and refinement of Piaget's ideas about the nature and development of moral reasoning. In Kohlberg's approach, a child or adult responds to a number of moral dilemmas, of which the following is an example:

In Europe a woman was near death from cancer. One drug might save her, a form of radium that a druggist in the same town had recently discovered. The druggist was charging $2,000, ten times what the drug cost him to make. The sick woman's husband, Heinz, went to everyone he knew to borrow the money, but he could only get together about half of what it cost. He told the druggist that his wife was dying and asked him to sell it cheaper or let him pay later. But the druggist said, "No." The husband got desperate and broke into the man's store to steal the drug for his wife. Should the husband have done that? Why? [1969, p. 379]

Using the responses to such dilemmas, as well as interviews that probe the reasoning behind them, investigators attempt to ascertain the nature of a person's moral reasoning.

Drawing on studies that have used this method, Kohlberg proposed a series of six developmental stages of moral reasoning, as illus-

trated in Figure 18.1 (p. 464). Notice that the stages differ in the reasons a person gives for making a decision and in the type of concerns that are indicated for self, authority, and/or society. As can be seen, it is not the decision concerning the theft of the drug but the form of its justification that identifies a person's stage of reasoning. A person at any stage may decide either way in a given situation.

Each succeeding stage consists of a more complex and balanced way of looking at the moral-social world. Children presumably advance through the stages in sequence; they must understand the reasoning typical of one stage before they can begin to understand the greater complexities of the next. As children move to a new stage of understanding, they must reorganize their thoughts and feelings, not just add new ones. Thus as a child advances through the stages, old moral-social relationships between the child and other people, and among people in general, acquire a new look.

As Figure 18.1 shows, the proposed six stages form three basic developmental levels of moral reasoning, distinguished by what defines right or moral action. The first two stages form what is called the *premoral level*, because value is placed not in persons or social standards but in physical acts and needs. The next two stages form the *conventional level*, with value placed in maintaining the social order and the expectations of others. The final two stages form the *principled level*, where values reside in self-chosen principles and standards that have a universal logical validity and therefore can be shared. Because the distinctness of each stage remains uncertain (Kurtines and Greif, 1974), we will focus on the levels of moral reasoning.

There is suggestive evidence that the levels are related to age. For example, Figure 18.2 shows that, among children from seven to sixteen, older children tend to be at more advanced levels. Moral statements that reflect the premoral level decrease with age. Those at the conventional level appear to increase until about age thirteen and then stabilize; statements that re-

		What Is Right	Reasons for Doing Right	Social Perspective
Premoral Level	Stage 1	To avoid breaking rules backed by punishment. Obedience for its own sake. Avoiding physical damage to persons and property.	To avoid punishment. The superior power of authorities.	Does not consider interests of others or recognize that they differ from actor's. Considers actions in terms of physical rather than psychological interests of others. Confuses authority's perspective with actor's.
	Stage 2	Following rules only when they are to someone's immediate interest. Acting to meet one's own interests and needs and letting others do the same. Right is what is fair, what is an equal exchange.	To serve one's own needs or interests in a world where other people also have their interests.	Aware that everybody has own interests to pursue and these conflict, so that right is relative (in a concrete, individualistic sense).
Conventional Level	Stage 3	Living up to what is expected by those close to you or to what people generally expect of those in your social role. "Being good" is important and means having good motives, showing concern about others. Keeping mutual relationships, such as trust, loyalty, respect, and gratitude.	The need to be a good person in your own eyes and those of others. Caring for others. Belief in Golden Rule. Desire to maintain rules and authority that support stereotypical good behavior.	Aware of shared feelings, agreements, and expectations, which take primacy over individual interests. Relates point of view through the concrete Golden Rule, putting yourself in other person's shoes. Does not yet consider generalized system perspective.
	Stage 4	Fulfilling the actual duties to which you have agreed. Upholding laws except in extreme cases where they conflict with other fixed social duties. Contributing to society, the group or institution.	To keep the institution going as a whole, to avoid the breakdown in the system. To meet one's defined obligations according to the imperative of conscience.	Takes point of view of system that defines roles and rules. Considers individual relations in terms of place in the system.
Principled Level	Stage 5	Being aware that people hold a variety of values and opinions, that most values and rules are relative to your group. Generally upholding these relative rules in the interest of impartiality and because they are the social contract. Upholding some nonrelative values and rights, such as *life* and *liberty*, regardless of majority opinion.	To keep one's obligation to law because of the social contract to make and abide by laws for the welfare of all and for the protection of all people's rights. To follow one's contractual commitment to family, friendship, trust, and work obligations. Concern that laws and duties be based on rational calculation of overall utility, "the greatest good for the greatest number."	Aware of values and rights prior to social attachments and contracts. Integrates perspectives by formal mechanisms of agreement, contract, objective impartiality, and due process. Considers moral and legal points of view; recognizes that they sometimes conflict and finds it difficult to integrate them.
	Stage 6	Following self-chosen ethical principles, which are those of justice: the equality of human rights and respect for the dignity of human beings as individual persons. When laws violate these principles, acting in accordance with the principles.	To adhere to universal moral principles and to keep one's personal commitment to them.	Recognizes the nature of morality or the fact that persons are ends in themselves and must be treated as such.

Figure 18.1

SOURCE: Adapted from Lawrence Kohlberg, "Moral Stages and Moralization: The Cognitive-Developmental Approach," in T. Lickona (ed.), *Moral Development and Behavior: Theory, Research, and Social Issues.* Holt, Rinehart and Winston, 1976. Reprinted by permission of author.

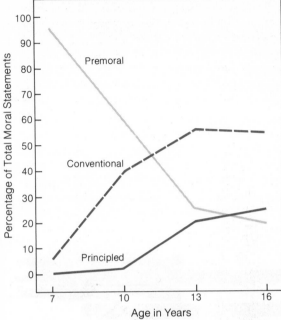

Figure 18.2 Changes with age in moral reasoning in a sample of American boys. (After Kohlberg, 1963)

flect the principled level appear to increase slowly after age thirteen, although they still constitute only a limited proportion of the judgments among sixteen-year-olds. Some college students, however, appear to regress to premoral levels, although Kohlberg (1970) reports that all the middle-class college students in his longitudinal study who had regressed later developed principled, postconventional morality.

In general, the speed with which children move from one level to the next appears to vary with their intellectual ability. Higher-level moral concepts and attitudes are acquired only in late childhood or in adolescence; apparently they require an extensive foundation of cognitive growth and social experience. Children and adolescents also appear to rate moral reasoning that is below their own level as inferior and that above their own level as better. However, they recall moral reasoning that is below their own

level more accurately than they recall reasoning that is above it (Rest, 1973; Rest, Turiel, and Kohlberg, 1969). It also appears that the ties between moral judgment and formal education are close. In most adults, moral judgment stops developing when they leave school, with no more than a third of high-school graduates at the principled level; a majority of those who continue with advanced study in philosophy, political science, and theology reason on the principled level (Rest, Davison, and Robbins, 1978).

Although a certain level of intellectual ability seems necessary for a given level of moral reasoning, intellectual ability in itself does not guarantee the development of higher levels of moral reasoning. In fact, a child's relative brightness and level of moral reasoning can combine to produce unexpected effects. In a study by Richard Krebs (1968), for example, it was found that among children who were at an opportunistic, premoral level of reasoning, those who were bright and attentive enough to see that they could cheat jumped at the chance. Among those children who were at a rule-oriented, conventional level of moral reasoning, however, the ones who cheated seemed to be those who were not bright or attentive enough to succeed by understanding and following the rules.

Kohlberg's theory has been criticized (e.g., Kurtines and Greif, 1974; Hoffman, 1979) on several counts: responses are difficult to score; the stages within a level are difficult to distinguish; all people do not appear to pass through the six stages in their given order, and some regress to earlier stages; there is no firm evidence that exposure to the reasoning of a higher stage will lead to a reorganization of a child's reasoning and an advance to that stage; the separate stages are not associated with distinctive patterns of behavior; the theory neglects the motivation of people faced with a moral dilemma; and the theory is biased toward a male, Western, individualistic culture.

Some of the inherent difficulties can be seen in the fact that Kohlberg (1976, 1978) has changed the rating of the Archie Bunker law-and-order mentality, originally considered an example of Stage 4 morality, to Stage 3, because, Kohlberg says, Bunker is more concerned with the small group ("people like us") than with society (Muson, 1979). This shift may eliminate part of the sex-related bias that appears to be built into the proposed sequence of stages. According to Kohlberg, moving the Archie Bunkers of the world from Stage 4 to Stage 3 has ended the results that typically placed more men than women in Stage 4.

Such a shift may eliminate part of the sex-related bias in the system, but other evidence suggests that the male bias remains built into Kohlberg's sequence of stages. Females do not show the expected pattern of movement through the stages (Gilligan, 1977; Holstein, 1976)—a difference that may be the result of socialization. The values of compassion, responsibility, and obligation are more likely to be stressed in the socialization of females than in that of males, but because Kohlberg has assigned these values to the conventional level of moral reasoning, females who base their reasoning on these values are automatically classified at a lower level of moral development.

In response to criticisms of his theory, Kohlberg (1976, 1978) and his associates (Colby, 1978) have recently revised the scoring method to make it more objective and easier to use; and other researchers have used his dilemmas to develop a more objective and simpler test (e.g., Rest, 1976). In his revisions, Kohlberg has proposed the existence of two types of reasoning (A and B) at each stage of development. Each type is presumed to reflect a different orientation to moral issues: Type A reasoning stresses literal interpretations; Type B emphasizes the intent of a rule, norm, or standard. Of the two, Type B is rated as the more advanced, as it is considered to be more balanced and developed. Stage 6 is no longer considered a separate stage by Kohlberg, because studies have failed to confirm its existence; it is now viewed as an extension of Type B reasoning at the fifth stage.

Findings based on the use of moral dilemmas continue to be questioned. Elizabeth Simpson (1974) and Sarah Harkness (1980) have pointed out that Kohlberg's theory is culturally biased and not universal, because it is based on a social organization and values that fit only Western culture. Simpson argues that because Kohlberg's approach focuses on issues of equality, rights, and justice, moral reasoning at a principled level fits only a constitutional democracy. In addition, the abstract thinking involved at this level is probably beyond most of the people in the world. It may be that like formal, abstract reasoning, principled moral reasoning requires formal education for its development.

This proposition is supported by Figure 18.3, which shows that although moral reasoning may develop in a similar way in various cultures (Kohlberg, 1968), principled reasoning appears primarily in the American sample. And in a study of Bahamian children and adolescents, not a single one reached the principled level of reasoning (White, Bushnell, and Regnemer, 1978).

CONSISTENCY IN MORAL DEVELOPMENT

Looking at the evidence, the pessimist is tempted to say that high levels of moral reasoning simply allow sophisticated excuses for dubious conduct. It is certainly true that principled reasoning does not guarantee honesty or loyalty, nor does it rule out deceit. The consistency of a child's conduct, and the link between conduct and reasoning, will depend upon the way that intellectual, social, and emotional factors combine during the course of moral development. At present, there is no way to predict the consistency of any individual's moral thought, feelings, and actions.

But as people move into the higher levels, there does appear to be a trend toward consistency. Research indicates that adolescents who have developed both formal thought and a principled level of moral reasoning are most

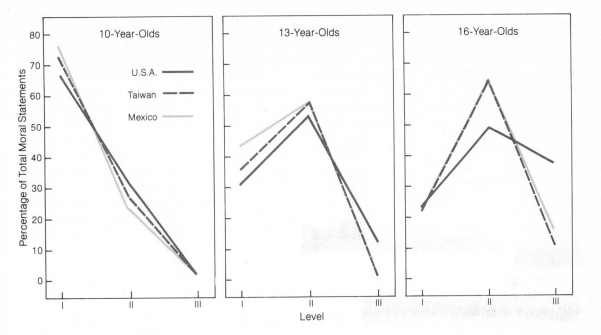

Figure 18.3 Changes with age in moral reasoning in three cultures: the United States, Taiwan, and Mexico. The sample from each culture consists of middle-class urban boys. Levels I, II, and III indicate, respectively, premoral, conventional, and principled levels. (After Kohlberg, 1968)

likely to show a high degree of both morality and consistency in what they think and do. For example, significantly fewer college students at a principled level of moral reasoning cheated in situations that required them to resist temptation than did those at a conventional or premoral level (Kohlberg, 1969). The adolescents at a principled level seemed to define the tempting situations as ones that involved an implicit contract based on trust, whereas those at lower levels seemed to respond to the looseness and permissiveness of unsupervised situations.

College students at a principled level of moral reasoning also appear to have shown a higher, more consistent level of moral conduct than other students in an experiment conducted by Stanley Milgram (1963). In this study, undergraduates were ordered to administer what they thought were increasingly severe electric shocks to a "victim," who was supposed to be a subject in a learning experiment but was actually a stooge. Only thinking characteristic of a principled level of reasoning clearly defines the situation as one in which the experimenter has no moral right to insist that pain be inflicted on another person. Accordingly, 75 percent of the students who had been judged to be at a principled level refused to shock the victim, but only 13 percent of those judged to be at lower levels refused to administer the shock (Kohlberg, 1970).

Finally, a study by Norma Haan, M. Brewster Smith, and Jeanne Block (1968) examined the possible relationship between moral reasoning and civil disobedience. They studied University of California students at the time of a sit-in that was part of the college protest movement in the 1960s. Of the students studied, 80 percent of those who were at a principled level participated, as compared with only 10 percent of those who were at a conventional level. But those of us who like neat categories of right and wrong will be disappointed; 60 percent of the students who were still at a premoral level also sat in. The premoral students reported different reasons for their actions from those given by the principled students. Consistent with their level of moral reasoning, the principled students reported concern with the basic issues of civil liberties and rights and of the relationship of students as citizens within the university community. The premoral students were also consistent, but they focused on the issue of their individual rights in a conflict with power. As the actions of both premoral and principled students show, similar conduct can result from widely varied moral reasoning.

PROSOCIAL BEHAVIOR

The discussion thus far has focused on keeping the rules, making moral decisions, discipline, and guilt. But there is another side to morality — acts that go beyond simply adhering to the rules and into the realm of prosocial behavior. Prosocial behavior, as defined by Paul Mussen and Nancy Eisenberg-Berg (1977), is action intended to benefit another person — but action that is taken without the anticipation of external reward. The action often involves some sort of risk, cost, or self-sacrifice on the part of the actor. Prosocial behavior includes cooperation as well as altruism. In this section, however, we will focus on *altruism*, which is defined as an unselfish concern for the welfare of others and springs from a combination of emotional distress at another's plight and an understanding of his or her needs.

Empathy

Without empathy, which is the vicarious identification with another's emotions, altruism would probably be impossible. A good many theorists believe that empathy develops through conditioning as the child comes to associate the pain or distress of another with his or her own

Teaching Empathy to Emotionally Disturbed Children

Many emotionally disturbed children find it impossible to put themselves in the place of another. Without this ability, neither empathy nor altruism can develop. A number of studies have shown that children who lack this ability (as measured by their role-taking skills or their skill in communicating effectively about matters another person cannot see) also lack social maturity (Cowan, 1966) and that socially deviant children (who already have run afoul of society's standards) lag behind other children of their age in developing these skills (e.g., Chandler, 1973).

Michael Chandler, Stephen Greenspan, and Carl Barenboim (1974) carried out a program among emotionally disturbed children in two institutions in an attempt to see if such children, who were described as antisocial and had been unable to adjust to school and home situations, could learn the skills upon which empathy develops. They worked with 48 children, chosen from a larger group of 125 institutionalized boys and girls who were between nine and fourteen years old and were neither psychotic nor retarded. The children were the most socially egocentric and noncommunicative children among the boys and girls in the two institutions.

After dividing the children into three groups, Chandler and his colleagues coached

painful past experiences. But Martin Hoffman (1976) believes that although simple conditioning plays a part in the development of empathy, the cognitive components are also vital. Hoffman (1979) believes that a child progresses through four stages in developing a full-blown ability to empathize with others.

In the first stage, which lasts most of the first

the first group in role-taking skills. For two hours every week during the ten-week program, these children developed, portrayed, and taped television skits that dealt with events in the lives of children. The second group of children learned communication skills. Their weekly sessions were spent playing games designed to increase their ability to communicate. Among their games were special versions of blindman's buff, treasure hunts that used walkie-talkies to pass information, and baseball games in which the ability of the pitcher and catcher to communicate determined a team's success. The third group received no training or treatment of any kind.

At the end of the ten-week program, all the children were tested again. Compared with children in the control group, boys and girls in the role-taking program made striking improvements in their ability to put themselves in another's place. The children in the communication-training program improved just as much in role-taking skills as did the children who were specifically trained to assume the role of another; in addition, their scores on tests of communicative ability were significantly better. Twelve months after training, the children still showed slight behavioral improvements compared with children who had had no training. (The ratings were made by members of the institutional staffs.) Although the long-term effects of training on behavior were slight, allowance must be made for the fact that the program was short and the children always remained under the in-

fluence of institutional and family forces that were operating before the training began.

Not all emotionally disturbed children lack empathic ability, and not all the children who participated in the program showed improvement; but the results of this experiment indicate that regular coaching in empathic skills might lead to meaningful improvements in social competence among a substantial number of emotionally disturbed children.

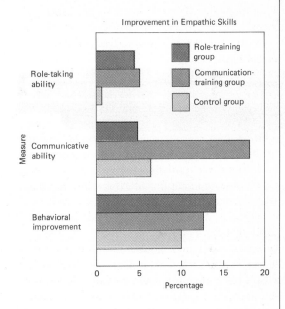

Improvement in Empathic Skills

SOURCE: From M. J. Chandler, S. Greenspan, and C. Barenboim, "Assessment and Training of Role-Taking and Referential Communication Skills in Institutionalized Emotionally Disturbed Children," *Developmental Psychology*, 10 (1974), p. 551.

year, an infant does not distinguish between the self and the person in distress. Hoffman describes an eleven-month-old girl who saw a child fall and begin to cry. The baby girl, looking as if she were about to cry herself, put her thumb in her mouth and buried her face in her mother's lap—her customary reaction to her own distress or injury. In the second stage, infants develop

person permanence and are aware that the observed distress is not their own. However, infants assume that the person in distress feels exactly as they do. In the anecdote about Paul and Michael that began the chapter, Michael's first response to Paul's tears was to assume that his own teddy bear would have as much meaning and comfort for Paul as it did for him. In the third stage of empathy, which children reach some time after their second birthday, an awareness develops that other people may have responses to a situation that differ from their own. Now children have a rudimentary ability to put themselves in another's place. The final stage of empathy, which develops in late childhood, includes an appreciation of others' feelings that goes beyond the immediate situation. The child becomes aware that giving a single meal to a starving person, for example, does not end that person's want.

Studies have demonstrated the link between empathy and altruism. As James Bryan (1975) explains it, children can be conditioned to experience the emotions of people they observe. Once this empathy is established, the act that makes the model joyful creates joy in the child and will either reinforce a child's altruistic acts or motivate the child to perform them. Bryan, together with Elizabeth Midlarsky (Midlarsky and Bryan, 1967), for example, conditioned primary-school-age girls by having a female experimenter assume a joyful expression and hug the girls each time a prize was sacrificed, on the supposition that the girls would feel happy themselves and come to empathize with the experimenter's obvious pleasure. Girls who were hugged by a joyful experimenter were more likely than girls who were not hugged or girls who heard no words of joy to sacrifice their prizes—even after the experimenter stopped hugging them and expressing joy. What is more, these girls made larger anonymous donations than other girls to poor children. Bryan points out that girls who were hugged—but by an experimenter who did not express joy—were no more likely to sacrifice prizes or give donations than girls who were never hugged. The same process increases the likelihood that a child will go to the rescue of another. Together with an experimenter, children were subjected to a painfully loud noise through earphones. The experimenter showed distress at the sound, hoping that the show of discomfort would lead the children to empathize with his distress. Later only the child heard the noise, and the experi-

menter gave up a chance to win a prize in order to end the offensive sound in the child's earphones, thereby modeling self-sacrifice. These children, when later placed in the experimenter's position, were more likely than other children to come to the aid of a third party who heard the sound—even if they had to sacrifice prizes (Aronfreed and Pascal, 1966).

In order to condition empathy, similar emotions must be aroused in both the child and another person—and almost at the same time. In addition, the child's actions must be able either to give the other person pleasure or to end his or her distress.

Role-taking is the purely cognitive accompaniment of empathy. Until children reach Hoffman's third stage of empathy, they will have difficulty in assuming the role of another, because most preschool children tend to be egocentric. But just as fifteen-month-old Michael managed to take Paul's role to the extent that he realized his friend's security blanket would comfort him, young children may be more capable

As children come to understand the feelings of others, they can also become altruistic, for empathy is a necessary step in the development of altruism. (Lyn Gardiner/Stock, Boston, Inc.)

than laboratory tests would indicate. Most research tasks that young children fail put a premium on verbal and cognitive skills, which they may lack, thereby masking their actual role-taking capabilities (Hoffman, 1976).

The importance of empathy cannot be overstressed. Although a child may develop empathic responses without becoming altruistic, a child will not be altruistic unless he or she has developed empathy (Mussen and Eisenberg-Berg, 1977).

Generosity

For the most part, children become more generous as they get older (Bryan, 1975). Older children are usually more willing than youngsters to share with others, whether they are sharing candy, toys, or money. This increased generosity appears to develop for several reasons. First, older children often find it easier to part with possessions simply because they do not seem quite so valuable. At the age of three, a child regards a dime as a huge sum that will bring the pleasures of bubble gum, candy or some trinket. Consequently, he or she will be reluctant to part with it. In contrast, the ten-year-old sees a dime as such an inconsequential sum that it can easily be given to others.

Second, older children have had more opportunities to learn that people are supposed to help others. They may have seen their parents donate to charities or do volunteer work in hospitals. They may have rung doorbells on Halloween to collect money for UNICEF. They may have heard people say that "A friend in need is a friend indeed" and that "It is better to give than to receive." Such experiences generally make it clear to children that their society places a premium on helping other people.

Third, as the last section indicated, older children are likely to be less egocentric than young children. Many have learned to take the perspective of others and to empathize with people who need help. Kenneth Rubin and Frank Schneider (1973) measured the egocentrism of their seven-

year-old subjects and then gave them an opportunity to donate candy to poor children and to help a younger child complete a task. The children who were better able to see things from another's viewpoint were more likely both to donate candy and to assist the younger child.

But the generosity that appears in the laboratory may diminish on the playground. Research reviewed by Bryan (1975) indicates that in competitive situations, ten-year-olds become less willing to sacrifice. Thus, parents who stress competition and individual achievement in their children may be retarding the development of altruism.

Most studies find that girls are more generous and empathic than boys, and the explanation may lie in sex differences in socialization (M. Hoffman, 1977b). Although generosity and empathy may not be correlated in a given situation (Elmer and Rushton, 1974), the two may be associated more consistently in the case of girls than of boys. Girls are more likely than boys to be taught to express their emotions, to be sensitive to the feelings and needs of others, and to be assigned responsibility for caring for other children. Girls are also more likely than boys to experience nurturance and help from others.

Various sorts of experiences, of course, may lead children to become generous. Obviously, anything that causes children to become less egocentric will be likely to increase generosity, but seeing another person act in a generous manner will have the same effect. For example, Joan Grusec and Sandra Skubiski (1970) found that children who watched an adult donate to charity were more generous in their own donations. However, when the adult simply said that the children should share their money with the charity, donations were markedly smaller than when the adult actually gave money. Verbal exhortations had strong effects on children's giving only among girls who had previously had a warm relationship with the adult who urged generosity.

Similarly, J. P. Rushton (1975) and other investigators have noted that exhortations increase only children's statements that people should be altruistic. They do not affect children's behavior. The lesson from these studies seems clear. If we want children to talk altruistically, we should talk altruistically ourselves. However, if we want them to behave altruistically, we should act in an altruistic manner. Children can learn hypocrisy just as they can learn altruism.

When combined with a warm relationship, exhortations to donate can induce generosity, as previously mentioned. Apparently, adult nurturance increases the effectiveness of other methods as well. In one study of young children, Marian Yarrow, Phyllis Scott, and Carolyn Waxler (1973) found that although any adult model could affect children's immediate behavior, children who saw a warm, nurturant model were still generous two weeks after they watched the generous adult. It seems that models who have strong, lasting effects on children are likely to be those who have close, rewarding relationships with the children—such as parents. Without such a relationship, examples are likely to have only a fleeting effect.

Giving Aid

Although giving aid is a second kind of altruism, it is quite a different form of positive behavior from generosity. While generosity is usually clearly defined, the circumstances in which aid may be appropriate are usually confusing and unclear. It may not be obvious to a child that an emergency exists, that responsibility for help rests on him or her, or even that the child is competent to help. As one might expect, this kind of altruistic behavior follows a different developmental course from that taken by generosity.

Ervin Staub (1970) has studied children's tendency to help in an emergency. He left children alone in a room for a few minutes; during this time, each child heard a crash and the sound of another child crying in an adjacent room. Staub noted whether the child either entered the room, presumably to give assistance, or offered unsolicited information to the experimenter about the sounds of distress that were heard. In contrast to the finding that older children are more likely to share, Staub found that children's tendency to assist a crying child first increased with age and then decreased. Staub suggests that the reason that few young children assist a child in distress is because they are less able to empathize with others in this sort of situation. As children get older, they are more capable of putting themselves in another's position, and so they are more likely to help in an emergency. In later childhood, however, children also become more sensitive to criticism and disapproval. Older children may be reluctant to help for fear of incurring an adult's disapproval, so that helping which seems to require breaking a rule (leaving the room) demands courage. This interpretation was supported by a slight change in the experimental situation. Simply telling a child that it was all right to sharpen a pencil in the other room increased the likelihood that a child would offer assistance.

In a subsequent investigation, Staub (1971) strengthened the case for believing that fear of disapproval affects a child's tendency to give aid. In a situation similar to the one in his earlier study, he found that children who had a warm relationship with the adult investigator were more likely to help than those who lacked this relationship. He suggests that because children believe that a warm, nurturant adult is unlikely to criticize them, the principal barrier that keeps older children from giving aid is removed. In this study, Staub also found that an adult example increases helping, and he speculates that this effect occurs because it demonstrates that the child will not be criticized if he or she leaves the room to help.

As with moral conduct, altruistic behavior depends upon the interaction of the immediate situation, the child's level of cognitive maturity, and his or her predisposition to help—which itself depends, in great part, on previous experience. Children with strong, solidly established, prosocial dispositions, point out Mussen and Eisenberg-Berg (1977), may donate to charity or come to the aid of a child in distress regard-

How Children
Postpone Pleasure

An important aspect of moral behavior is the ability to postpone immediate gratification. For example, an adolescent who cannot postpone pleasure may steal an appealing record, sweater, television set, or car because he or she is not able to pay for it immediately and cannot endure to wait until the required money has been saved. Although most young children want what they want immediately, research indicates that even three- or four-year-olds are capable of postponing their pleasure. However, research shows that their ability to do so varies with such factors as their mood and what they do while waiting.

Most studies of young children's self-control involve their desires for snacks or small toys, and their moods apparently affect their ability to wait for them. Bert Moore, Andrea Clyburn, and Bill Underwood (1976) asked some three- to five-year-olds to talk and think about things that made them sad; they asked others to talk and think about things that made them happy. Afterward, each child was given a choice between a less-valued treat (a round pretzel), which he or she could eat immediately, or a more-valued treat (a small lollipop) to be eaten several hours later. Children who talked and thought about sad things more often chose the pretzel, but those who talked and thought about happy things more often chose the lollipop. This suggests that negative moods may increase children's tendency to be impulsive, whereas positive moods may increase their willingness to be patient.

Other research shows that what children do while they wait affects how long they can delay gratification. Children are more likely to be willing to wait and to wait longer if they distract themselves by doing or thinking about something else. It has been found that children who sing, whistle, talk to themselves, play games with their hands or feet, and so on, are able to wait longer for something they want than children who do not distract themselves. Walter Mischel and Nancy Baker (1975) have found that the way children think about objects they want but must wait for can also play a part in how long they will wait. Mischel and Baker gave children a choice of eating one pretzel or marshmallow immediately or getting two pretzels or marshmallows if they waited. Children who thought about the pretzel sticks in front of them as being "little brown logs" or "crayons," or who thought about marshmallows as being "cotton balls" or "clouds," managed to wait for a relatively long time—an average of fourteen minutes. But those who thought about the "crunchy, salty, toasty taste" of pretzels or the "chewy, sweet, soft taste" of marshmallows gave up and took their single pretzel or marshmallow after an average wait of less than five minutes.

Around the age of seven, there appears to be a clear shift in children's own strategies for postponing pleasure (Yates and Mischel, 1979). Kindergarten children, given a choice, prefer to look at the actual rewards (pretzels, marshmallows) while they wait, a decision that makes the waiting difficult and one that reveals their cognitive immaturity. Second graders, on the other hand, prefer to look at pictures or objects that have no connection with the promised rewards, indicating that they have come to understand how frustrating the sight of the delayed reward can be. This change denotes a cognitive advance that allows children to work for distant goals by focusing on their abstract (a pleasant reward) rather than their concrete (specific taste) aspects.

less of the immediate situation. Children with weaker tendencies toward prosocial action may donate or help only when the immediate situation makes altruistic behavior easy.

The Influence of Television

When children watch television designed for them, they generally understand the prosocial messages embodied in the programs. For example, children who watched four episodes of *Big Blue Marble* showed changes in attitude toward the rest of the world. They perceived children in other countries as more like themselves and were less likely to endorse ethnocentric statements extolling the superiority of the United States over every other country (Roberts et al., 1974). In another study, 90 percent of the children who watched an episode of *Fat Albert* recalled at least one prosocial message from the program (Columbia Broadcasting System, 1974).

Aletha Stein and Lynette Friedrich (1975) have found, however, that recalling the message does not necessarily mean that it influences behavior. They showed four episodes of *Mr. Rogers' Neighborhood* to kindergarten children. The programs attempted to teach children to understand others, to express sympathy, and to help others and share with them. After viewing each episode, some children spent time with an adult, hearing a story that covered the material in the program and explicitly labeled it, and then answering questions. Other children replayed the story they had seen with hand puppets. A third group carried out both activities, and a fourth had activities with no connection to the program's themes. A control group saw neutral films.

All children who had seen the Mr. Rogers program learned from their experiences; they knew more about the prosocial themes than children who saw neutral films. But when placed with a child who needed assistance, most children were no more helpful than children who had seen neutral programs. Only those children who had had used the puppets and thus had

experience in taking another's role were likely to translate their learning into action.

Longer exposure to prosocial television appears to increase the likelihood that children will act on its messages. Children who watched Mr. Rogers saw only four shows. Preschoolers in another study who saw twenty shows (one episode from a commercial television program every weekday for four weeks) displayed the influences of the prosocial programs in their daily behavior (Rubenstein et al., 1974). The episodes were chosen from *Lassie, I Love Lucy, Gilligan's Island, The Brady Bunch*, and similar shows. Half the children saw episodes that were high in prosocial themes and low in aggression; the other half saw neutral episodes. Children who watched the prosocial episodes helped each other significantly more than the children who saw the neutral films. Boys were more willing to put aside attractive toys to help another child, and both boys and girls cooperated more with other children.

Longer exposure and role-playing both appear to increase the likelihood of prosocial television's affecting the behavior of young children. Other factors also play a part in increasing or dampening a program's effects, including a child's social class, previous typical behavior, incidents that call forth a particular response, and the consequences that follow when a child imitates the considerate, patient, or helpful behavior that has been modeled on the screen.

ANTISOCIAL BEHAVIOR

Antisocial behavior is a concern of parents everywhere. The amount of aggression that societies tolerate differs and their rules regarding its expression vary; but an important aim of socialization in every society is to teach youngsters how to manage feelings of hostility and anger.

The Causes of Aggression

There is a continuing debate over whether human beings have an inherent drive toward aggression. Konrad Lorenz (1966) believes that aggression is instinctual and that aggressive energy builds up in a person until a releasing stimulus allows its expression. In this view, aggressive behavior is therefore inevitable. But as Karl Moyer (1971) points out, what we know about human physiology tells us that, even if people have an inborn aggressive drive, the expression of aggression is not inevitable. The same mechanisms that strengthen impulses toward aggression also lessen them. For example, hormone levels first rise, then fall; and once hormone levels drop, the impulse to aggression passes. Such an explanation indicates that if socialization can teach people to control aggressive impulses during the peak period, aggression will not have to be expressed.

Whether aggression must be expressed or not, in Lorenz's view human violence is a distortion of a useful innate behavior that evolved to space human beings out over the vast available territory on this planet. With the human invention of lethal weapons, the instinct became maladaptive, leading to mutilation, murder, and war in the "defense" of mates, property, and territory. Some psychologists have adopted a version of this theory to study dominance hierarchies in children (Strayer and Strayer, 1976), adolescents, and adults.

Other researchers, especially John Dollard and his colleagues (1939), reject the idea of an innate aggressive force but believe in the existence of an aggressive drive. According to this *frustration-aggression hypothesis*, the aggressive drive is the result of a child's or an adult's frustration when someone or some thing interferes with their activity toward a goal. In its original form, this theory assumes that all aggression is the result of frustration, although frustration may be displaced on another person or object. When a child is punished by a parent, he or she may yank the cat's tail; or an adolescent who has been refused use of the family car may chop wood with a vengeance.

Seymour Feshbach (1964) modified the frustration-aggression hypothesis to distinguish between *hostile aggression* and *instrumental aggression*, a distinction that has been widely accepted. Hostile aggression aims at hurting another person, whereas instrumental aggression aims at retrieving or acquiring an object, territory, or privilege. Only hostile aggression is thought to involve frustration, and it is often not the injury itself that is the goal but the victim's pain. The sight of the suffering victim restores the aggressor's self-esteem. Children learn specific aggressive responses, but whether they will be expressed or inhibited depends upon the environment, as we saw in studies of modeling. Feshbach (Feshbach and Singer, 1971) also believes that aggressive fantasies can reduce hostile aggression, although they are not as effective as aggressive action.

Psychologists who accept behavior-learning theory reject the idea of an aggressive drive. They believe that aggression is conditioned behavior, which, like any other behavior, is controlled by the environment. The assumption is that, for example, a boy's habitual fighting is a response to the actions of others just before the act of hitting; and the immediate consequences of the blows will have a strong effect on whether the child will hit again in the same situation (Patterson and Cobb, 1973). If the victim cries, leaves the scene, or hands over the object of dispute, the aggressor is likely to hit again the next time he wants his own way. The boy's fighting is also reinforced by other responses: the victim's obvious pain, the attention the aggressive boy may get from his nursery school teacher, or the sudden cessation of his sister's teasing. In this view, much aggression is under the control of aversive stimuli, such as being ignored by a teacher or parent, being teased or laughed at, or being refused a toy or companionship. But if the environment changes so that the child no longer experiences the aversive stimuli, or if the aggression is no longer reinforced, aggressive responses will cease.

Most contemporary research into the causes of aggression is based on social-learning theory, which agrees that the environment is powerful but also takes into consideration the influence of models and cognitive control. In this view,

Behavior-learning theorists believe that children's fighting is controlled by the environment; the consequences of the blow that sent the child sprawling on the ground will help determine whether the young aggressor will hit out in his next playground argument. (Robert Eckert/EKM/Nepenthe)

The Development of Aggression

Children are expected to learn to control aggressive responses early. The earliest expressions of anger are the result of physical discomfort or are demands for attention (Goodenough, 1931). As soon as young children begin to throw tantrums, to hit, or to hurl toys about, parents generally impose restraints, and the socialization of aggression begins. In a study of 200 nursery-school quarrels, a shift in the way children handled aggression appeared with age (Dawe, 1934). The youngest children relied primarily on instrumental aggression, and the proportion of hostile acts increased with age. Specifically, H. C. Dawe found that whereas 78 percent of the interpersonal conflicts among eighteen-month-old infants centered on possession of toys or other objects, children of five or six years old quarreled over possessions only about 38 percent of the time. On the other hand, infants began only 8 percent of their quarrels with blows, bites, or hairpulling, whereas the five-year-olds started 27 percent of their quarrels with physical violence.

The way that children express aggression changes with their cognitive development. As indicated in earlier discussions, children under six generally find it difficult to imagine another viewpoint or to make inferences about people (Flavell et al., 1968). If hostile aggression depends on attributing negative intentions to people who frustrate them, then younger children would be less likely to show this kind of aggression. And younger children would also be less likely to regard frustration as a threat to their self-esteem.

Using this rationale, Willard Hartup (1974) tested and attempted to extend the earlier findings of Dawe. He observed children at play over a ten-week period and found that older children (from six to eight years) showed less total aggression than younger children (four to six years). This difference in total aggression was due primarily to the preponderance of instrumental aggression among younger children. As

aversive stimuli lead to emotional arousal. Whether a child responds with aggression will depend on how the child has learned to cope with stress and how effective these methods have been (Bandura, 1973). One child might seek help, another might try harder, a third might give up, a fourth might hit. Frustration or anger might increase the chances that a child will respond aggressively, but neither is necessary for aggression to occur. According to Albert Bandura, a culture that keeps frustration low, values aggressive accomplishments, provides aggressive models who are successful, and rewards aggressive actions will produce aggressive children who become highly aggressive adults.

he had expected, older children showed a higher proportion of hostile aggression. Hartup also found, as had Goodenough, that children shifted from physical to verbal aggression as they got older, confirming a change in both the form and the amount of aggression as children develop. As they get older and their acts of physical aggression are punished, children find more subtle ways of expressing aggression.

The socializing influences that lead children to be generous or helpful also teach them to behave aggressively. Watching someone behave in a violent or aggressive manner tends to make children behave aggressively, but it does not always do so. The situation itself helps decide whether a child will imitate such a model, as Marian Martin, Donna Gelfand, and Donald Hartman (1971) found in a study of one hundred children. The children watched a model go through a series of aggressive acts. During a later play period, children were most aggressive when a peer of the same sex was present. When an adult was present, a child at first showed little aggression; but if the adult failed to disapprove of the child's aggressive acts, the child became more and more aggressive. Apparently, the presence of an adult tends to inhibit aggression, but the inhibitions disappear if children become aware that their aggressive acts are acceptable, or at least neutral, in adult eyes.

Adult demands for obedience can overcome a child's inhibitions about aggression. When Jordanian children were told that they were teachers in a learning experience and that the learner (actually a confederate of the experimenter) must get a shock of increasing intensity each time he made a mistake, 73 percent of the children obeyed, delivering what they thought were shocks — even though the children believed the shocks were harmful (Shanab and Yahya, 1977). Although neither the age nor the sex of the children, who ranged from six to sixteen, made a difference in their behavior, girls were more likely than boys to say that they gave the shocks in order to obey the experimenter. Before condemning the children for obediently following the unethical demands of the experimenter, consider that Stanley Milgram (1974) surprised the psychological community in 1964 when he demonstrated that as many as 65 percent of the adults he studied would administer what they thought were severe, even lethal, shocks to an innocent person simply because an authority ordered them to do so in the course of an experiment. Clearly, under special conditions, people will behave in ways they ordinarily would reject.

Such conditions are rare. Under ordinary conditions, children consider the consequences before they respond to the demands of others. Their past experiences and their developing self-concepts affect their decisions.

Sex Differences in Aggression

Data gathered by developmental psychologists consistently show that boys are more aggressive than girls and that aggressive behavior is regarded as appropriate only for boys (Maccoby and Jacklin, 1974; 1980). In a study that followed eighty-nine children from early childhood to young adulthood, Jerome Kagan and Howard Moss (1962) found that the amount of aggressiveness tended to be stable in males over the years but that aggressive behavior declined in females. Because our society tolerates aggressive behavior in boys, there is not likely to be a systematic effort to change the aggressive characteristics they show in early childhood. On the other hand, as noted in Chapter 17, any display of aggression in girls is often stamped out by parents.

Other investigators have found that boys as young as two are more physically aggressive and more negativistic than girls. Studies with nursery school children show that by this age boys are quite selective in the targets of their physical assaults (Maccoby, 1976). Their victims are usually other boys, in particular those who give in; rarely is a girl the target of assault.

The consistency of findings that males are, on the average, more physically aggressive than females suggests possible biological contributions to such behavior, or other constitutional factors linked with gender that might predispose boys toward physical aggressiveness. Seymour Feshbach (1970) has suggested that the greater physical strength and more vigorous motor impulses of males may lead to different social experiences. Boys, for example, have greater success than girls in getting what they want by hitting. Also, parents more often frustrate a boy's impulsive acts, thereby stimulating his aggressive reactions.

The social environment can overwhelmingly influence the direction aggressiveness takes. Although physical aggressiveness is the hallmark of masculinity in many cultures (as exemplified by the warrior), patterns of aggression among both sexes vary widely from one culture to another (B. Whiting, 1963).

However, the fact that boys in our society are more noticeably aggressive does not mean that girls are nonaggressive. As Feshbach (1970) and others have indicated, forms of aggression differ according to sex. A variety of studies have demonstrated that from nursery school on, boys are likely to express aggression in physical ways, whereas girls are likely to scold or argue or use indirect forms of aggression, such as gossip, a concerted resistance to demands, and subtle forms of rejection. Girls who are overtly aggressive tend to be rejected by their peers and disliked by their teachers (Levitin and Chananie, 1972). Boys are just as likely as girls to meet disapproval for overt aggression, but because they are stronger and more active, their aggressive attempts are more likely to be successful.

Although girls and boys may differ in the extent to which they find aggression a useful and accepted way to solve problems, girls are just as capable of aggression. When Ann Frodi, Jacqueline Macaulay, and Pauline Thome (1977) reviewed numerous studies on sex differences in aggression, they found that in some circumstances women may be just as aggressive as men. In face-to-face encounters with another adult, women are less likely than men to engage in verbal or physical aggression. But in situations where aggression is justified, or when they can remain anonymous, women tend to be as aggressive as men.

The Power of Television

Over the past thirty years, American society has undergone a major shift in the way it introduces its young to the world. Before about 1950, young children's exposure to adult society was filtered by their parents. The young child knew about the culture from experience with the family, the neighbors, the occasional shopping trip, and perhaps from Sunday school or picture books. Now, most children witness televised murder, arson, muggings, and warfare almost from birth. Even when parents regulate their children's viewing habits, the network news and the Saturday morning cartoons deliver a dependable diet of murder and mayhem, presenting models who not only transmit new behavior but also may reduce inhibitions on antisocial behavior the child already has learned.

Numerous experiments have been conducted to assess the effects of television on children. Early studies by Albert Bandura (1973) and his associates showed that children can learn new ways to express aggression from television and similar media. D. Keith Osborn and Richard Endsley (1971) went further and investigated children's emotional reactions to various sorts of television programs. Children in this study saw four films depicting either human violence, cartoon violence, human nonviolence, or cartoon nonviolence and then talked about what they liked best and what was the scariest. The two violent films produced the most emotional reactions; the children remembered details of the violent films the best, and they found the human violence the scariest. But the film they liked best was the nonviolent cartoon. This study shows that watching television violence evokes emotional responses in children and influences them to remember the details of depicted violence.

Moving closer to the central question of whether television violence affects the way that children behave, the Office of the Surgeon General (1972) commissioned an exhaustive study of the effects of television violence but failed to reach any definitive conclusions. However, other investigations give some clues as to how television may affect behavior. For example, Robert Liebert and Robert Baron (1972) investigated whether watching television aggression would make children more willing to hurt another child. Liebert and Baron showed brief excerpts taken directly from regular television shows to boys and girls from five to nine years old. The excerpts were either violent and aggressive (a fist fight or a shooting) or exciting but non-aggressive (a tennis match). After they saw one of these programs, the children were given a series of opportunities either to hurt or to help another child by pushing a button. Each child was told that pushing one button would help another child (who was not actually present) to win a prize but that pushing the other button would hurt the child. They were also told that the longer they pressed either button, the more the other child would be helped or hurt.

Despite their brief exposure to these television shows, children who had observed the violent television sequence chose to hurt the other child for a significantly longer period of time than those who had watched the nonaggressive scenes. Obviously, this study uses a specialized definition of aggression, but it demonstrates that watching one kind of aggression may lead to aggression of a very different sort. It suggests that television programs depicting aggression may remove or reduce some children's inhibitions against committing violence—at least immediately after a child sees the program. Additional studies support this position (Leifer and Roberts, 1972).

The long-term effects of television violence may have been detected by Leonard Eron and his colleagues (1972), who found a significant relationship between the amount of television violence that third-grade boys watched and their aggression as rated by their peers. Even more impressive is their finding of a relationship between the amount of television violence that boys watched in the third grade and their later

aggression, at age nineteen. The investigators concluded that it was not merely that children who commit aggressive acts watch more television violence but that a preference for watching televised violence contributes to the development of aggressive behavior. What is more, nineteen-year-olds who continued to watch a good deal of violent television tended to believe that the crime stories and Westerns they saw were realistic portrayals of life. Therefore, the experimenters point out, these adolescents interpreted the violence they saw on television as an appropriate way to solve problems in daily life.

However, not all the research into the effects of television viewing supports the contention that there is a direct correlation between viewing violence and aggressive behavior. Feshbach and Robert Singer (1971) controlled the television diet for six weeks in three residential private schools and four institutions for boys with social, personal, or family problems. During this time, the boys watched television in groups for a minimum of six hours each week. Half the boys watched violent programs, the other half watched nonviolent fare, such as situation comedies and game shows. The results were unexpected. Whether or not the programs they had watched were violent, the upper-middle-class boys in the private schools showed no change in their aggressive behavior. But boys in the institutions who had been exposed to a steady diet of violence were *less* aggressive at the end of the study than boys who had watched nonviolent programs. The decrease in violence was greatest among overtly hostile boys who, on tests given before the study, were found to have few aggressive fantasies. This finding led Feshbach and Singer to suggest that watching aggression on television allows such boys to express some of their aggressive impulses vicariously, thereby reducing the chances that they will act aggressively. On the other hand, the aggressiveness of boys who watched no violence may be due to the fact that they were angered when their usual violent television fare was not made available to them.

Children's fascination with the Muppets provides a minor example of television's influence on growing children; there are indications that a steady diet of televised violence in childhood may result in the development of aggressive adolescents. (© David S. Strickler/The Picture Cube)

The Feshbach-Singer study examined only the short-term effects of television—and examined them only among thirteen-year-old boys whose years of television viewing had presumably already had some effect, whereas the study of Eron's group studied the cumulative effect of televised violence over ten years. Another study indicates that the long-term effects of heavy television viewing may sometimes be less violence, because heavy television viewing may teach people to become passive in the face of aggression. George Gerbner and Larry Gross (1976), who believe that television may teach

people to play the role of victim, found that, regardless of age, people who watched four or more hours of television each day tended to be significantly more suspicious of others and afraid of being involved in violence themselves than people who watched television two hours or less each day. (They also discovered that nearly half of the twelve-year-olds in their study watched at least six hours of television each day.)

At present, our knowledge of television's power to increase violence is confused. Part of the confusion that comes from conflicting findings in the fields of moral development can probably be traced to a point that has been made again and again: the developing child's behavior is a product of continuous interaction between constitutional forces and the child's own social environment. The older the child, the greater the accumulation of different experiences. For this reason, no two children will react to the same experience in precisely the same way.

SUMMARY

1. Although moral conduct is often viewed as a group of related actions governed by some central process such as conscience, research indicates that most people are inconsistent in what they say, feel, and do. Individual predispositions toward honesty or dishonesty appear to exist, but the aspects of each situation have powerful effects both on people's judgment of an action's morality and upon their behavior.

2. Psychoanalysts believe that moral behavior results from children's attempts to avoid the guilt that arises when they violate prohibitions imposed by parents with whom they identify. Social-learning theorists believe that children learn moral behavior through a combination of rewards, punishment, and the observation of models. The social-evolutionary approach sees moral behavior as the result of the child's solution of a series of moral problems: learning to

live with authority, learning to live with others, and learning to live with oneself.

3. Cognitive theorists believe that moral judgments depend upon cognitive development. Piaget saw childhood morality as passing through two major stages: the morality of constraint, which predominates among younger children, and the morality of cooperation, which is found among older children.

4. Developmental changes in moral reasoning have also been studied by assessing people's reactions to posed moral dilemmas. This approach has led Lawrence Kohlberg to propose that moral reasoning goes through a progressive series of stages: premoral, conventional, and principled.

5. Although principled reasoning does not guarantee honesty or rule out deceit, a trend toward consistency in moral judgment appears to develop among people who rely on higher levels of moral reasoning.

6. Empathy, which is essential for the development of altruism, appears to develop through four stages, from the infant's confusion between the person in distress and him- or herself to the older child's appreciation of others' feelings that goes beyond the immediate situation. The cognitive accompaniment of empathy is role-taking, which allows a child mentally to take the place of another.

7. Generosity develops as children find it easier to part with possessions and as they have opportunities to learn that one person is supposed to help another. Children are often slow to come to another's assistance because they are uncertain that an emergency exists, because they are unaware that any responsibility rests on them, or because they do not believe that they are able to help. The presence of warm, nurturant models is likely to increase both generosity and the giving of assistance among children.

8. Some psychologists believe that an aggressive drive is responsible for aggression — but only for hostile aggression, which aims at hurting another person. Other psychologists believe that aggression is conditioned behavior and that children who are reinforced for aggressive acts will continue to commit them. How a child responds to situations likely to evoke aggression will depend upon how the child has learned to cope with stress and how effective these methods have been.

9. Studies consistently show that boys are more aggressive than girls. Biological predispositions may well exist among males, but the social environment has a powerful influence on whether or how aggression is expressed. Findings regarding the influence of television on aggression are mixed, but violent programs may remove or reduce a child's inhibitions against committing acts of violence.

Social Cognition

Come on, I want a television for my room. Come on. Please. Daddy, come on. Buy me a television. I want one for my room. Come on. Come on, Daddy, I want you to. There!"

"Say, Dad, a lot of kids at school I know are getting televisions for Christmas. Can I have one? Gee, I know a lot of kids that want one, gee. I could really use it, you—for some of the educational programs, you know, that are on TV, and they're real good, and for homework at night some of our teachers want to watch 'em,

and—you know, Johnnie always wants to watch cowboys and . . . and everything, and I—I'll never get a chance to watch it down there, so why can't I have it in my room? C'mon, Dad, please."

The first plea came from a third grader, the second from a child in the seventh grade. Both had been asked by John Flavell and his associates (1968) to show how they would persuade their fathers to buy them their own television sets. The third grader's simple pleading becomes the seventh grader's triple pitch of education, family harmony, and what Flavell called the bandwagon approach (everybody's doing it).

The growth in understanding that makes this development possible forms the major part of this chapter on social cognition, which explores the way children come to know the social world. The process has many parallels with the general development of children's cognition, but here the understanding is of people and society instead of the physical world. The baby who sees the world as an extension of the self becomes the adolescent who understands the workings of social institutions and realizes that each person is unique, with his or her own and probably different feelings and opinions. That development is a lengthy one, but it begins with the understanding of the self. Consequently, we shall begin this chapter by looking at the development of self-concept during childhood and adolescence. We shall then see how children learn to understand others, examining their dawning realization that others neither see nor feel exactly as they do, and seeing how this development leads to fuller communication and a growing ability to put themselves in another's place. Finally, we shall watch the growth of the child's understanding of society, of law, and of convention, noting that this understanding, too, develops in a regular sequence, building on the child's understanding of others.

UNDERSTANDING ONE'S SELF

The discussion of such concepts as identity and self-knowledge in a chapter on social cognition might seem surprising. But the domains of self and other cannot be totally separated. Our interpretation of others' behavior comes from our knowledge of how they have acted in the past, from cues in the immediate environment, and from what we know about ourselves. For ultimately, we can only know about others' feelings and intentions by making inferences based upon our own perceptions, emotions, and knowledge.

SELF-CONCEPT

Babies distinguish themselves from the world very early, for by the time they are about two or three months old, they seem to recognize and behave differently toward different people (Lamb, 1981). Once that task is accomplished, the development of self-concept remains. The appearance of the baby's sense of self was dis-

cussed in Chapter 14, beginning with self-recognition. Babies' ability to recognize themselves in a mirror develops gradually, just as does the concept of object permanence. Bennett Bertenthal and Kurt Fischer (1978) found a high correlation (.84) between the two concepts, although sometimes they were equally advanced and sometimes object permanence ran ahead of self-recognition. There is good reason for the parallel development of the concepts. Without an awareness that objects and other people continue to exist when out of their sight, babies could not develop a sense of their own continuing identities. By about twenty to twenty-four months, you will recall, babies consistently touch a spot of rouge on their noses when they see their reflections in a mirror (Lewis and Brooks, 1975), indicating their awareness of self.

This rudimentary self-concept continues to develop as the child comes to understand that one is a boy or a girl, big or small, capable or not. Throughout early childhood, children increasingly come to perceive themselves in terms of concrete attributes—such as sex, age, activities, personal appearance, and possessions (Livesley and Bromley, 1973). Asked to describe themselves, they reply in terms of such attributes: "I'm Lauren" (name), "I'm four" (age), "I have a brother" (kinship), "I'm pretty" (physical appearance), "I play dolls" (activities), "I like ice cream" (likes), "I'm little" (size), and "I have a kitty" (possessions). Most frequent, however, are activities, in terms of habitual actions ("I sit and watch TV"), acts of competence ("I wash my hair myself"), and helpful acts ("I help Mommy") (Keller, Ford, and Meacham, 1978). Although these aspects of a child's self may seem superficial to an adult, they have great meaning for the child and form a basic part of his or her sense of being. They are closely tied to experiences with other people and the child's environment. And because young children take such a strong present-oriented view of themselves, their self-concepts necessarily reflect this here-and-now quality.

Children in middle childhood, however, can

In early childhood, self-concept is based on concrete attributes, such as sex, age, activities, appearance, and possessions, which are closely tied to the child's experiences with others. (© Leonard Speier 1981)

also see themselves in terms of what they have done and were like in the past, and what they might do and be like later. It is now that personal qualities begin to enter their self-descriptions, and a child might say "I'm shy" or "I'm a hard worker." In a study of first, third, and sixth graders, Don Mohr (1978) asked children to distinguish between themselves and others ("What would you have to change about yourself for you to become your best friend?"). He also got them to think about the stability of their self-concepts by inquiring about their future selves ("What will [will not] change about yourself when you grow up?") and their past selves ("What has [has not] changed about yourself since you were a baby?"). First graders relied primarily on external attributes in their answers to all questions; third graders divided their responses between external attributes and behavior. But by the sixth grade, children had almost given up referring to external attributes, responding mostly in terms of their behavior. Only sixth graders gave many answers that referred to internal states (feelings, thoughts, knowledge), and those replies came mostly in

response to questions about the stability of their identities.

In the early years, a child's relative lack of ability in any area may not affect his or her self-concept, for it is not until children are seven or eight years old that they begin to evaluate themselves by comparing their own and others' behavior. Diane Ruble and her associates (1980) had first and second graders arrange a series of cartoons to tell a story. After the children had finished their task, they were told how well they had done and how well their peers had done on the same task. Then the children expressed their feelings about their own performance by moving the mouth on a cardboard face so that it smiled, frowned, or remained neutral. (In order to have all children leave happy, those who were told they had done badly were later given another task on which they were told they did very well.) In judging themselves, first graders paid no attention to information about the performance of others. Second graders did allow the information to affect their judgments, but not on a predictable basis. In a second study, kindergartners and second and fourth graders could compare their success in a ball-tossing game with the scores of eight other children. This time, only fourth graders allowed information from social comparisons to affect their self-evaluations in any consistent or systematic way. Ruble and her associates suggest that five- to seven-year-olds are not especially interested in self-evaluation. They are aware of their limited abilities and lack of coordination, and comparisons and competition seem not to hold any importance for them. Their concern is in making sure they make some correct answers and get their fair share of rewards. Yet as we saw in Chapter 16, children's concepts of their own abilities come to have a profound effect on their achievement.

Adolescents take a far less simplistic view of themselves than children do (Livesley and Bromley, 1973; Montemayor and Eisen, 1977). There appears to be a qualitative change in self-descriptions around the age of thirteen or fourteen, and it may be the result of the adolescent's ability to consider possibilities. W. J. Livesley and D. B. Bromley found that adolescents use descriptive terms more flexibly and precisely than younger children do, often adding subtle qualifying and connecting terms. Most impressive in the self-descriptions written by adolescents is the change in organization. Adolescents select and organize their ideas in a coherent and complex fashion, whereas younger children's impressions are like beads on a string. In describing themselves, adolescents tend to refer to ambitions, aspirations, wants, needs, expectations, fears, wishes, self-reproaches, beliefs, attitudes, values, and comparisons with others. This change reflects the privileged information people have about themselves; but it also indicates the relation between cognition and self-concept, for it reflects the adolescent's grasp of formal thought.

As the concept of self develops, so does self-consciousness, a concern with what others think of one. This heightened self-consciousness, suggests David Elkind (1980), is the result of the young adolescent's belief that other people share the adolescent's own preoccupations with him- or herself and hence are always noticing the adolescent's appearance, behavior, and actions. Elkind and Robert Bowen (1979) studied fourth, sixth, eighth, and twelfth graders and found that self-consciousness shows a developmental trend. They asked children to consider themselves in a number of situations in which they would have to reveal either their "transient selves" (momentary appearance or behavior—such as soiled clothing or inadvertent acts—which people do not regard as reflecting their true selves) or their "abiding selves" (mental ability or personality traits that people regard as permanent aspects of the self). These two concepts of self, believe Elkind and Bowen, do not separate until children reach the concrete operational stage; for this reason, they did not test younger children. The imaginary situations involved either the transient self (a red, scraped, swollen face on the day class pictures are taken) or the abiding self (being watched while at work). Their answers revealed that in all situations eighth graders are much more self-conscious than either younger children or older adolescents—except for fourth-grade boys, who were just as reluctant to reveal their transient selves as were the eighth-grade boys. An eighth grader who went to a dress-up party in soiled clothing, for example, would either "stand in a dark place," "hold a hand over the stain," or arrange "to spill something" on the soiled clothing. Younger or older children were likely to say the stain would not bother them. Girls were more self-conscious than boys in every age group. An eighth-grade girl, placed in the stained clothing situation, might say that she would simply refuse to go to the party. However, with the exception of the fourth-grade boys, all the children were more reticent about exposing their "real" than their transient selves, perhaps because only aspects of the abiding self were linked with self-esteem on another test. In a similar study of eleven- to eighteen-year-olds in a rural school, self-consciousness continued to increase with age, so that twelfth graders were more, not less, self-conscious than eighth graders (Adams and Jones, 1981).

Identity

The eighth graders who were so hesitant about revealing themselves had just entered adolescence, when developmental changes often bring about a disruption of the concept of self. For this reason, Erik Erikson (1968) believes that establishing a concept of identity is the major developmental task of the period. Erikson's concept of identity has two facets. It refers to feelings about the self, or self-esteem, and to the relationship between one's self-concept and descriptions of one's self by significant others.

The childhood self reflects the immediate world of persons crucial to the child and is based on relatively simple identification with these people. Adolescents must often reexamine and reintegrate this self-concept so that it is consistent with their increased capacity for rationality, their moral values, and their capabilities.

There are wide individual differences in the

methods that adolescents may use to attain new self-concepts, which require them to incorporate their new physical and sexual attributes and the opportunities they present. One youthful solution involves a determined attempt to change society so as to bring it into line with the adolescent's principles and needs. Another solution is a systematic attempt to change oneself so as to fit into the existing system with less anxiety or discomfort. A third approach is the effort to carve out some special niche within society where the qualities of the self can be preserved, enhanced, or acted on.

Some developmental changes, however, can threaten the adolescent's integration of his or her childhood self-concept and lead to what Erikson (1968) called *totalism*, an organization of self-concept that has rigid, absolute, and arbitrary boundaries. Totalism makes adolescents particularly susceptible to totalitarian movements and to ideologies of the left or the right. According to Erikson, if adolescents feel their emerging identities severely threatened by historical or technological development, they become ready to support doctrines that allow them to immerse themselves in a synthetic identity, such as extreme nationalism, racism, or class consciousness, and to condemn the stereotyped enemy of their new identities. This tendency toward total immersion in a synthetic identity can take other forms, and it characterized the participation of many American adolescents in the civil rights movement two decades ago and, more recently, in opposition to nuclear power and resistance to registration for the draft.

UNDERSTANDING OTHERS

Once babies learn that objects and people have an existence of their own, they can begin to develop an understanding of others. The discussion of empathy in the last chapter indicated that children only gradually come to understand that the needs, wants, and beliefs of other people are

According to Erik Erikson, the participation of some (but not all) adolescents in the movement to ban nuclear power can be explained by totalism, which develops when adolescents feel their identities are severely threatened. (© Jean-Marie Simon/Taurus Photos)

different from their own. Until they achieve this understanding, they find it difficult to comprehend the behavior and emotions of another individual. Such understanding requires children to infer another's response by taking the other's role, that is, mentally putting themselves in the place of the other.

Piaget (1926) believed that the young child is trapped by *egocentrism*. Even after the young boy (or girl) can distinguish himself from the rest of the world, for example, he still believes that others see the world exactly as he does and that they experience his thoughts and feelings. Slowly, during both the preoperational and the concrete operational stages, the boy's (or girl's) social interactions with adults and with other children make him aware that his perceptions and reactions are not theirs. It is not until children are about nine or ten, said Piaget, that they escape from egocentric thought. As we examine children's gradual understanding of others, we shall find that the apparent egocentrism of preschoolers may be based not on the children's unawareness of others' reactions but on their lack of information, inadequate memory, or still developing language skills, which keep them from communicating their understanding. Such understanding is made up of several elements. If children are to understand others, they must comprehend what others are like, what others see and know, and how others feel.

Understanding What Others Are Like

If, as Piaget suggested, young children believe that others see, think, and feel exactly as they do, then their concepts of others would be much like their own self-concepts. Indeed, when children are asked to describe others, their descriptions do follow the same general course as their self-perceptions. Concrete attributes give way in middle childhood to personal qualities.

Between the ages of eight and twelve, there is a steady decrease in children's egocentric de-

scriptions of others (Honess, 1980). An eight-year-old's description of a friend is full of comments that either do not distinguish between the child and the friend ("We play together") or describe activities or attributes they have in common ("Matt collects stamps; so do I." "She sits with me"). By the time children are eleven, such egocentric descriptions have declined significantly, and comparison statements ("Susan is taller than I am"; "David doesn't lose his temper like I do") have increased sharply, as have non-egocentric and abstract descriptions. Carolyn Shantz (1975) suggests that the developmental trend from describing people's surface appearance toward describing them in terms of inner qualities is much like the development of conservation. Clothing, hair styles, and possessions may change, as the level of cola changes when poured into the squat glass, but a person's values, beliefs, and inner qualities are likely to remain steady despite surface alterations.

Contrary to expectations, the occurrence of egocentric descriptions rises again among thirteen-year-olds. Terry Honess (1980) suggests that although adolescents' statements take the same egocentric form as the eight-year-old's "We play together" or "She sits with me," they have a different conceptual base. The adolescent often qualifies a description ("We *try* to wear the same clothes") or indicates an interpersonal involvement ("We share our troubles"). Such statements may reflect not egocentrism but the development of intimate friendship discussed in Chapter 16.

In other studies (Livesley and Bromley, 1973), adolescents show a greater ability to analyze and interpret the behavior of others and an increased concern with making their descriptions convincing. That is, in describing another person, only adolescents would report an impression and hastily add a qualifier to keep a listener from drawing the wrong conclusion. For example, a fifteen-year-old girl might say of a friend, "He is shy—but not anxious." In order to make such a statement, she had to consider other people's possible misinterpretation of her descriptions—

indicating reflective thought. Adolescents also show their understanding that a person's feeling or actions differ depending upon the situation — indicating an advanced ability to take another's position.

Understanding What Others See

When Piaget said that young children believe others see exactly as they do, he meant it literally. Not even a blindfold or the removal of the person to another location interferes with the mutual perception. For example, when a three-year-old talks on the phone the child assumes the person on the line can see everything the child does and cannot understand why that person asks about something that is in plain sight.

A well-known demonstration of the young child's supposed inability to realize that others do not perceive the world in precisely the same way involves a three-dimensional model of a landscape. Three cardboard cones of varying sizes (one red, one blue, and one yellow) stand on a piece of green cardboard, and a little clay man is placed beside them. The experimenter tells the child that the man is going to walk around the mountains and take pictures of them with his camera. As the little man moves around the model, the experimenter shows the child cards that illustrate the display from various perspectives. The child's job is to pick the card that shows the display as the little man would see it. In a second section of the study, the child looks at a card and places the little man where he would have to stand in order to see the scene on the card.

Using this display, Monique Laurendeau and Adrian Pinard (1970), who have been closely associated with Piaget, found that children are very slow in developing the ability to choose the correct picture or in placing the little man in the right position. Four-year-olds are often "pre-egocentric": they completely fail to understand the task and may choose a picture because "it's the prettiest." Among children who seem to understand the task, those in the first stage of egocentrism consistently choose the picture that represents the mountains from their own position. Those in the transitional stage show an awareness that the scene would look different to the little man, but they either cannot select the right picture or cannot explain their choice. Those who can successfully complete both tasks are considered to have freed themselves from egocentrism. But only 28 percent of the twelve-year-olds tested by Laurendeau and Pinard were not egocentric — in terms of this test.

As the results from study after study appear, realization has dawned that children have a greater understanding of what other people can see than Piaget and some of his followers supposed. Martin Hughes (1975) found that when the mountaintop display is changed to a "hide-from-the-policeman" game, for example, almost all four-year-olds and more than 60 percent of three-year-olds succeed at the task. Hughes built two small walls that intersected to form a cross and placed them on a table. Then he added two dolls, a policeman doll and a boy doll, to the display. Moving the boy doll from one area of the display to another, Hughes asked children if the policeman could see the boy in that position. Next, Hughes placed the policeman where he could see two of the areas and asked the child to "hide the doll so that the policeman can't see him." Preschoolers had no trouble with either task. (See Figure 19.1.) In the next step, Hughes added another policeman doll to the display. Now three of the four sections were visible to at least one of the policemen, and the child's job was to hide the boy so that neither policeman could see him. If children were indeed egocentric, they would tend to hide the boy where they could not see him but the policeman could. But even when the single area that was hidden from the policemen was in the child's full view, young children solved the problem. And when Hughes added more walls and a third policeman, preschoolers still found it easy to keep the boy out of the policemen's sight. In light of

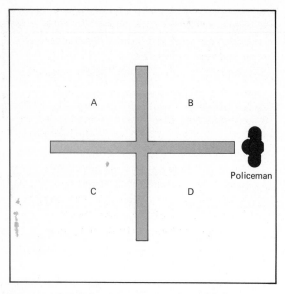

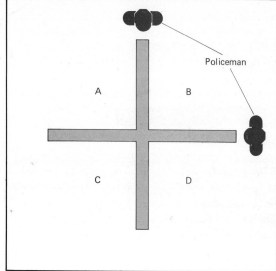

Figure 19.1 Although preschoolers are considered egocentric, they have little trouble hiding a doll in this display so that it is invisible to a policeman doll, even when there are two policemen and the only area out of a policeman's sight (Area C) is in full view of the child.

SOURCE: Reproduced from *Children's Minds* by Margaret Donaldson, by permission of W. W. Norton & Company, Inc. Copyright © 1978 by Margaret Donaldson.

these results, Margaret Donaldson (1979) suggests that the mountaintop display is not so much a test of egocentrism, as of the child's understanding of left-right reversals — the realization, for example, that what is on their right is on the little man's left — and that a child who makes egocentric responses to the mountaintop problem does not fully understand what he or she is to do.

In a study by John Flavell and his associates (1978), even two-and-a-half-year-olds were able to hide a Snoopy doll behind a tabletop screen so that the experimenter could not see Snoopy from where she was sitting. Flavell's group is convinced that the young children it studied could distinguish what they saw from what another person might see, could think about what the other person saw, and could both produce and recognize some physical situations in which the other person could not see some object.

However, when Lynn Liben (1978) used a display similar to the mountaintop problem but constructed of colored blocks, preschoolers even had trouble picking the card that showed the way the display looked to them. They sometimes chose cards showing all the blocks, in spite of the fact that some were hidden from their view; and they were likely to choose the card that correctly depicted the experimenter's view when she could see all the blocks but they could not. In a second test, either the child, the experimenter, or both wore colored glasses, as together they looked at a white card. The child's glasses had yellow lenses; lenses in the experimenter's glasses were green. Six-year-olds always predicted the appearance of the card correctly, but about half the three-year-olds gave an egocentric response, indicating that the experimenter saw the card as they did.

Why, if two-and-a-half-year-olds can hide a doll from another person and if nearly half of the three-year-olds can correctly predict the appearance of the card, do children often fail to allow for other viewpoints in tests such as the mountaintop display?

Janellen Huttenlocher and Clark Presson (1979) suggest that much of the child's failure has to do with the way he or she codes information about space. In their studies, they asked eight-year-olds two different types of questions. In *appearance* questions, children had to point to the picture that showed how the display would look from another position. This is the problem set by Piaget and by Laurendeau and Pinard. In *item* questions, children had to point to the part of the display that would be in a particular position from another viewpoint (in back, in front, on the red side [right], or on the green side [left]). That is, if the display were rotated instead of the viewer. Children found the first question extremely difficult; the eight-year-olds were wrong 56 percent of the time, and 80 percent of

their errors were egocentric. The second question was much easier; this time only 20 percent of the answers were wrong and 49 percent of the wrong answers egocentric.

Huttenlocher and Presson believe that children as old as ten may make egocentric errors in Piaget's problem because of the way they code the mountaintop display. In Chapter 10, we noted that toddlers often use landmarks to remember where an object is hidden. With the mountaintop display, children apparently use the surrounding room in the same manner (as depicted in Figure 19.2). They do not code the display as a unit, with the three mountains in relation to one another; instead, they code each

Figure 19.2 Children's errors in the mountaintop display problem may occur because they code each mountain in reference to the room *(right)*, so that visualizing the display from another's viewpoint requires them to recode each mountain. Adults code the display as a unit, with the mountains in relation to one another *(left)*.

SOURCE: From J. Huttenlocher and C. C. Presson, "The Coding and Transformation of Spatial Information," *Cognitive Psychology*, 11 (1979), 375-394. Reprinted by permission.

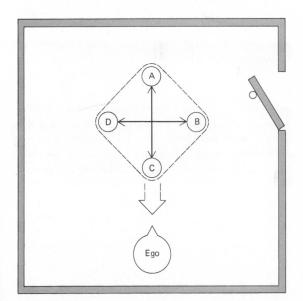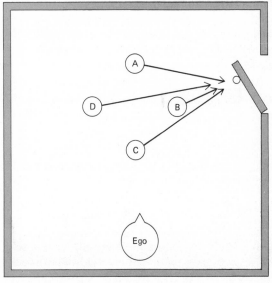

of the three mountains in relation to the larger room. When they are asked to visualize where a particular item would be if they stood in a different position, they have to recode the position of only one object. But when they are asked to visualize the appearance of the entire display from another perspective, they must recode the viewer's position in respect to both the array and its framework, a much more difficult task. The researchers suggest that an increase in information-processing abilities, such as the ability to hold the original coding of the entire display and the viewer's position in working memory while examining possible solutions, may help explain why children get better at the task as they get older.

Understanding How Others Feel

Learning to infer the motivations and reactions of people is a gradual process that goes on throughout childhood, a process that builds on the toddler's rudimentary empathy with the needs of others. Preschoolers can show an appreciation for the abilities and limitations of other people. When Marilyn Shatz (1973) asked four- and five-year-olds to help her select presents for two-year-olds and for children their own age, the children selected toys appropriate to the recipients' ages. As one five-year-old put it, "I didn't pick this [a number-letter board] because he [the two-year-old] can't read."

In another study, Ellen Markman (1973) asked five-year-olds about their memory and motor skills and about those of two-year-olds and of teen-agers, putting such questions to them as how many pictures they could remember or how far they could jump. The children's predictions showed they realized that two-year-olds cannot do as well as four-year-olds, but that teen-agers can do much better. In addition, the children indicated that although they thought two-year-olds had a fair degree of motor skill, they doubted that two-year-olds could remem-

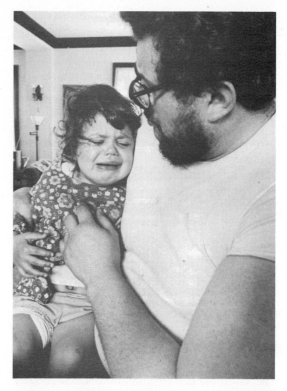

Because young children cannot conceive of individual reactions to a situation, they believe others react exactly as they do—a misunderstanding that can lead to tears and complications. (© Bohdan Hrynewych/Stock, Boston)

ber much, if anything. The five-year-olds were correct; the motor skills of two-year-olds are more advanced than their cognitive skills.

Despite such indications of understanding, studies consistently show improvements with age, and some indicate that young children infer emotional reactions from the situation itself rather than interpreting individual reactions to it. In other words, they assume that all people react the same way to the same situation. Frederick Gove and Daniel Keating (1979) gave four- to six-year-olds pictures and asked them to describe the feelings of the children involved. There were two pictures for each story, and the emotions in each picture were radically different. In one picture, for example, a little boy was delighted to have a new puppy; in the other, a little boy with a new puppy was obviously frightened. Preschoolers tended either to interpret the emotions as the same in both pictures (and invariably the emotion selected was one typical of the situation), or else they changed the situation so that it was different for the two characters. These young children seemed to have difficulty in imagining that people could feel differently unless the situation itself was different. Some of the six-year-olds made similar errors, but many of them were able to understand the different reactions. On the basis of their findings, Gove and Keating suggest that the level of role-taking skills among four-year-olds is a precursor of true role-taking.

A similar shift in role-taking ability between the ages of four and six appeared in a study by Melda Brandt (1978), who told children stories accompanied by pictures and asked them to answer questions from the perspective of a character who lacked some of the information she had given the children. In one story, after a boy had been warned to confine his finger painting to the kitchen, the family dog blundered unseen into the paint and, still unobserved, wagged his paint-covered tail against the living-room door. Four-year-olds had great trouble in predicting the response of the boy's "ignorant" parent to the appearance of paint in the living room or in selecting the parent's response from two alternatives: the logical response dictated by the parent's lack of knowledge and their own response, since they had heard the entire story. First graders showed a sharp improvement; nearly 63 percent could predict the response of an ignorant other. Among third graders, 90 percent were adept at the task. Brandt suggests that younger children may be unable to store the information they have been given and then retrieve it to answer questions about the story.

It may be that young children can empathize with others when the assumption that both self and other react in the same way is correct, but not when reactions are different. Other studies have indicated that it is not until a child is about nine that he or she can manage to coordinate different viewpoints of the same social situation (Kurdek, 1977).

In an attempt to develop role-taking abilities among six- and nine-year-olds, Ronald Iannotti (1978) had children assume the roles of characters in a story, acting out, for example, the behavior of children who have found a billfold bulging with money. The trainer asked questions that encouraged role-taking ("Why did you do what you did?" "Why do you feel that way?") and emphasized facial expression, tone of voice, conversation, and behavior, as well as the children's role-taking skills and reasoning. Some of the children had to role-switch, changing the character they played every five minutes. When these children subsequently were given tests of role-taking ability, both groups showed improvement compared with children in a control group. The ability to take another's role, however, did not affect the children's empathy. When asked to describe the feelings of characters in a story or the way they would respond in situations involving aggression, they were no more empathic or no less aggressive than children without role-taking experience. But role-taking did increase altruistic behavior among the six-year-olds, as indicated by the number of raisins or M&Ms they voluntarily shared with a "poor boy."

Understanding and Communication

Much evidence for the young child's egocentrism comes from tasks in which the child has to describe abstract forms or the rules of a game to someone who is blindfolded or from whom a display is hidden. When John Flavell and his associates (1968) asked children to tell a blindfolded person how to play a game that involved rolling a cube that had sides of various colors, then moving a man along a board to a square of the appropriate color, most second graders made

Understanding Television

If young children only gradually acquire role-taking abilities, how well do they understand what goes on in television dramas? If a seven-year-old watches *The Incredible Hulk,* for example, does he or she understand why the main character periodically turns green and goes berserk? And judging from the popularity of Hulk dolls, one would assume that avid viewers of the program include children younger than seven.

Understanding *The Incredible Hulk,* or any other television program, is not limited to role-taking ability; it involves several processing tasks. Andrew Collins (1979) has indicated that before children can understand a television program they must select essential pieces of information from the drama, order them according to some scheme, then make inferences that go beyond what has been explicitly presented. He points out that in most programs, motives and consequences are portrayed subtly, never made explicit, and they may be separated from each other and from the act they surround by several commercial breaks. In a series of studies (Collins, 1973; Collins, Berndt, and Hess, 1974; Collins *et al.,* 1978; Newcomb and Collins, 1979), Collins has examined the abilities of second-, fifth-, and eighth-grade children to understand the plots of television dramas and to infer the motives, causes, and consequences of the actions.

One study (Collins *et al.,* 1978) used an epi-sode from an action-adventure program. The plot revolves around the theft of a check protector from a repair shop and the murder of an elderly panhandler who stumbles upon the robbery in progress. The murderer is caught when the police trace back to him checks that were forged on the stolen machine. One finding that emerged might have been predicted from research in the development of focused attention: from second to eighth grade, children increasingly remembered more information that was vital to the plot and less that was extraneous to it. When children described the plot afterward, second graders strung together incidents in no particular order, whereas older children related the plot in a way that made the causes of the action clear. Asked about material that was presented explicitly in the program, second graders could remember only 66 percent of the scenes, fifth graders 84 percent of them, eighth graders 92 percent of them.

As expected, the older the children, the more likely they were to make correct inferences about the behavior and the motives of the actors, whether on a subsequent test that required them to choose one of three motives or when they were interrupted during the program and asked to predict what would happen next. In the latter case, most fifth and eighth graders made logical predictions, which followed from what they had seen. Second graders' predictions, on the other hand, were either arbitrary or stereotypical. Complex inferences, those requiring inter-

no effort to adjust their descriptions of the game for people who could not see. Flavell's group also asked children to read or to tell a fable, first to an adult and then to a four-year-old. Only about a quarter of the third graders made an effort to simplify the language or to substitute words in order to make sure that the four-year-old would understand the story, but almost every seventh and eleventh grader took great pains to adjust the story to the level of the audience.

Children of these ages were also asked to describe geometric designs so that they could be reproduced by someone who had never seen

mediate inferential steps, turned out to be overwhelmingly difficult for second graders, and they were less bothered by the kind of inference (motive, action, goal, or consequence) or the kind of cause (psychological or physical).

Collins (1979) concludes that a second grader's difficulties in comprehending television programs involves both poor memory and a failure to integrate what he or she remembers. He suggests that there is a pronounced change in information-processing skills between the second and fifth grades. Second graders are not very good at selecting information for storage or at retrieving needed information for inference. When older children were wrong in their predictions of actions or motives, it was generally because they had made a wrong inference from the material they recalled.

A store of knowledge derived from previous experience can help young children to interpret what they see on television. Andrew Newcomb and Collins (1979) showed edited episodes from network comedies to middle- and lower-class black and white children. One episode centered around a white, middle-class family; the father was a supervisor and the family of four lived in the suburbs. The other featured a black, working-class family; the father worked at a loading dock and the family of four lived in a housing project. After the children, who were again second, fifth, and eighth graders, had seen one of the episodes, they were asked questions about the

plot, the actors, the actors' feelings, and the reasons for their behavior. As in the earlier study, recall, understanding, and inference all got progressively better with age. Ethnic background made no difference to comprehension at any age. Among fifth and eighth graders, social class also had no effect on their understanding of either program; but among second graders, social class had a strong influence. Middle-class second graders understood the program about the middle-class family much better than did lower-class second graders, doing significantly better at comprehending the story and on inferring an actor's feelings and the cause for his or her behavior. But the picture was reversed when it came to second graders' understanding of the working-class program; those from the lower socioeconomic class did significantly better at both comprehension and inference.

Despite the age-related differences in cognitive processing, point out Newcomb and Collins, when younger children's previous social experiences bear some relation to the dramatic content of programs, their understanding of all aspects of those programs is improved. Children's experiences give them a context within which to interpret new information. Michelene Chi (1978), for example, has found that eight- to twelve-year-olds who are skilled chess players can recall chess positions much better than adults who are indifferent chess players. The youngsters also predict good moves more accurately (a measure of inference).

them. Third graders gave the least information in their descriptions, eleventh graders the most. When the task was changed so that the children were to give just enough information to enable a listener who was looking at four designs to select the correct one, both third and seventh graders gave as much information as they had

when the task was to reproduce the entire design. Most eleventh graders, on the other hand, sharply curtailed the information they gave, some of them giving only the single fact needed to make the selection (e.g., "The design with the blue triangle").

Flavell's group suggests that once the seventh

graders had generated the exhaustive information required for the reproduction of the design, they found it difficult to keep from repeating it on the next task, the simpler one of identifying the figure. As for the third graders, although egocentrism may have been a part of their problem, their own smaller store of skills and knowledge could also have figured in both the fable task and the geometric design task. Simply reading and comprehending the fable may have occupied all the third graders' processing abilities, leaving them unable to handle the additional task of adjusting the retelling to the audience. As for the designs, there was always a simple way to distinguish among them ("It's the one with only three things in it" or "It's the one with the tiniest circle"). However, even a cursory examination of Figure 19.3, which shows the four designs used, indicates that the ability to use such terms as "diamond" and "triangle" and to distinguish between left and right greatly facilitates communication in this task.

It appears that the way children judge communications changes as they grow older. E. J. Robinson and W. P. Robinson (1977) had children listen to a communication game in which Mickey Mouse and Donald Duck dolls sat at opposite ends of a table. The dolls were separated by a screen and each had a set of six identical cards. The object of the game was for a doll to send a message that would enable the other doll to select the correct card. Conditions varied: the message was either precise or ambiguous, and the doll who heard the messages answered half of them correctly and half of them incorrectly. The job of the five- to eight-year-old observers was to decide whether the success or failure of each message was the fault of the sender or the receiver. When messages failed, five-year-olds generally blamed the receiver. Most said that all the messages were adequate, including those that did not contain essential information. Eight-year-olds, on the other hand, tended to judge good messages as adequate and bad ones as inadequate. Robinson and Robinson

Figure 19.3 When egocentrism is tested by asking children to describe the designs in this display, third graders do not do very well. Some of their problems may not come from their inability to consider another's viewpoint, however, but from a lack of language skills.

SOURCE: From J. H. Flavell *et al., The Development of Role-Taking and Communication Skills in Children.* Huntington, NY: Krieger, 1975. (Originally published 1968.) Reprinted by permission of John Wiley & Sons, Inc.

suggest that young children assume that all messages are good and that it is some time before they discover that some are better than others at getting across one's meaning.

The inadequate messages sent in the above experiment were ambiguous. That is, the Mickey Mouse doll would say, for example, that the correct card was a flower when two flower cards, one red and the other blue, were in the pack. Other studies have shown that young children have difficulty dealing with ambiguous material. Marsha Ironsmith and Grover Whitehurst (1978a) had children select which of four pictures was being described by an experimenter who was sometimes deliberately ambiguous. Children were told to ask questions if they did not have enough information. Kindergartners seemed to have difficulty detecting that messages were ambiguous. Second graders could tell when a message did not have enough information, but they tended to ask general questions, as if they could not isolate the information they needed to know. Even sixth graders asked appropriate questions only about half the time.

Young schoolchildren are fluent speakers, but their ability to communicate is still developing; only in the past year or so has this girl learned that ambiguous communications from adults are often the fault of the adult speaker and not her own inability to understand the message. (© Ellis Herwig/Stock, Boston)

However, other investigators (Patterson, Cosgrove, and O'Brien, 1980) have found that much younger children do realize, at some level, when messages are ambiguous and indicate their realization by nonverbal behavior. When a message lacks essential information, preschoolers seek eye contact, move their hands, and are slow to respond. Kindergartners and second graders are also slow to respond to ambiguous messages, and they move their bodies as well as their hands.

Ironsmith and Whitehurst suggest that if a message is ambiguous, competent listeners must have the same skills as competent speakers in order to realize the ambiguity. Young children may not compare the information in the message with the information in the display but instead make impulsive choices. It is also possible, say these researchers, that young children do not understand the value of giving feedback when information is inadequate. When children first watched an adult play the guessing game with the four pictures (selecting which of the four was being described by the experimenter), children tended to ask more questions during the game than when there had been no adult model (Ironsmith and Whitehurst, 1978b). Second graders profited more than kindergartners from watching the adult model, indicating that the effectiveness of modeling interacts with the child's skill in making perceptual discriminations.

Training can also improve a child's skill in producing informative messages. In another study (Lefebvre-Pinard and Reid, 1980), some six- to eight-year-olds watched models take part in exercises designed to enhance communication skills. Other children took part in the exercises themselves, and a third group did both. Two months later, all these groups were still better at communicating than children in a control group.

Taken together, these studies indicate that communication abilities improve throughout childhood and that both egocentrism and level of skill appear to affect a child's ability to communicate. In appropriate circumstances, however, young children are less egocentric than has been assumed. When children are given tasks that fit their cognitive skills, their level of egocentrism appears to drop sharply. As noted in Chapter 7, four-year-olds adapt their speech when describing the workings of a toy to two-year-olds (Gelman and Shatz, 1977) and even take into account the apparent individual abilities of their two-year-old pupils (Masur, 1978). Children can also profit to a certain degree from instruction in the skills of communication.

Children's understanding of others develops gradually, as does their ability to communicate. Preschoolers see others in terms of concrete attributes. They understand that others have different visual experiences but seem to lack any understanding of how those differences manifest themselves. They infer emotions from a situation, assuming that all people react the same way to the same event. By middle childhood, children are seeing people in terms of inner qualities. They understand how a scene may appear to another person, and they can understand differing reactions to the same event. The adolescent has become proficient at all these skills and sees subtleties and complexities that are absent from the view of children. The adolescent not only infers another's reactions but attempts to explain them. As we move on to a discussion of understanding society, we shall see that views of the larger group are built upon the child's understanding of individuals.

UNDERSTANDING SOCIETY

Children's understanding of the way society works and the role of law and convention develops slowly. Both areas have recently been analyzed by developmental psychologists, who have proposed that children go through regular, predictable stages in the development of their understanding.

How Society Works

The way children gradually sort out such aspects of the social system as money and work showed in a series of lengthy interviews that Hans Furth (1980) conducted with almost 200 British schoolchildren. Furth found that these children, whose ages ranged from five to eleven, went through four different stages in their concepts of society (see Figure 19.4). He points out, however, that ways of thinking from one stage tend to continue into later stages and on into adulthood, just as adults use sensorimotor thought in playing the piano or riding a bicycle.

Each child constructs society, says Furth, by the same process of equilibration (discussed in Chapter 2) that produces all knowledge and all development, so that each succeeding generation, although it is influenced by previous generations, shapes its own knowledge and its own society. The process of equilibration is an open-ended spiral, in which a child uses assimilation and accommodation to achieve a temporary equilibrium. This equilibrium will eventually be upset by new information that is difficult to assimilate or by cognitive advances that leave the child open to further accommodation, leading to a new, still temporary, equilibrium at a higher level. Children progress through the stages at their own individual pace, as Figure 19.5 (p. 500) indicates.

Although both assimilation and accommodation are part of every mental act, thinking in Stage I is dominated by accommodation, in which the child submissively accepts the results of social actions as an end in themselves. Since Furth's five- and six-year-olds saw no need to explain the workings of the social system they observed, they showed no evidence of an interpretive system. Five-year-olds believed that money was freely available. They noticed that money accompanies transactions in a store, but they believed that merchants give the goods to the purchasers and also present them with money (change). Almost uniformly, five- and six-year-olds said that change from purchases is

	Approximate Age	Dominant Mode of Thought	General Criteria
Stage I Absence of Interpretive System	5–6	*Accommodation* Submissive acceptance of social events	Confusion of personal and social roles Failure to recognize basic function of money
Stage II Understanding First-Order Functions	7–8	*Assimilation* Playful elaboration of social events beyond experience Events in own experience taken seriously	Distinction made between personal and social roles Understanding of money as instrument of exchange
Stage III Part-Systems in Conflict	9–10	*Disequilibrium* Incomplete functional systems leading to cognitive conflict Either reluctant thinking or compromise solutions	Understanding of buying, selling, paid employment
Stage IV Concrete-Systematic Framework	10–11	*Equilibrium* Reversible thinking; consistent, concrete, logical	Understanding of differences in social role Appreciation of differences in scale between personal and social events Understanding of mechanism of profit

Figure 19.4 FURTH'S STAGES OF SOCIETAL UNDERSTANDING According to Hans Furth, children go through four stages in their understanding of society, moving to a new stage each time new information or cognitive advance upsets the understanding established in the previous stage.

SOURCE: Based on data from H. G. Furth, *The World of Grown-Ups: Children's Conceptions of Society*. New York: Elsevier North Holland, Inc. 1980.

the source of money, although one boy added that a shopkeeper bought a store by finding money in the mud. Other children in this stage indicated that garbage men live on the presents they get at Christmas and that telephones are free, generally a gift from friends who have more than they need.

For children in this first stage, there is no difference between personal and social roles. Five-year-old Sally, asked if a mother can be a teacher, replied, "No. If teachers are teachers, they can't be mothers, or if big ladies go to school, that means they're teachers." When the researcher pursued the question by asking who

could be a mother, Sally replied, "Not the teachers, but only the people who stay at home and do work, not at school, but everywhere." She also denied that a woman who works in a shop could be a mother.

In Stage II, children's thinking is characterized primarily by assimilation, in which children elaborate playfully on social actions, creating a childish form of social reality in which play and actuality are not easily distinguished. Children in Stage II understood many of the social functions they observed or experienced directly. These seven- and eight-year-olds understood the difference between paying for an item in a store and giving money as change. Although they understood the function of change, they might believe that merchandise is free to the shopkeeper and that the money paid for various items is then given to the blind or the poor.

Children in this stage could distinguish between personal and social roles, and knew that teachers and merchants could also be parents. When asked about parts of society with which they had no contact, however, they resorted to

Thinking About Society:

Percentage of Children in Each Age Group That Adhered
to the Thinking of a Particular Stage

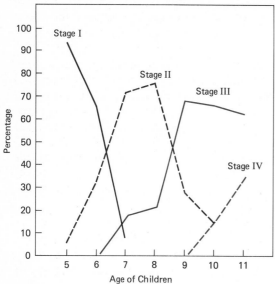

Figure 19.5 Children progress steadily through
the stages of understanding society, from the
submissive acceptance of Stage I to the concrete understanding of Stage IV, with most
primary-school children in one of the transitional stages.

SOURCE: Reprinted by permission of the publisher
from *The World of Grown-Ups: Children's Conceptions
of Society,* by H. G. Furth. Copyright 1980 by Elsevier
North Holland, Inc.

playful elaborations. Jeannie, nearly seven,
suggested that "The mayor decides a lot of
things, like if you just wanted to climb Mount
Everest, you couldn't just go and do it without
permission, could you? . . . If you don't know
where it is and you want to, because there's
some treasure up there, you could go and ask
the mayor, but if he didn't know, you wouldn't
go at all." Children at this age, says Furth, indicate a need for rules and the approval of superiors. They are also preoccupied with bad people
and fear them. One girl suggested that a robber
might pose as a teacher in order to rob the
school.

Most nine- and ten-year-olds had reached
Stage III, in which children begin to interpret
parts of society with which they have no contact. This is a transitional stage, when children
search for logical and factual consistency but
construct incomplete explanations for aspects of
society that conflict, which throws them into a
state of disequilibrium. Many children were
aware of this cognitive gap and handled the conflict in one of two ways. Either they refused to

This child's concept of society is still in a rudimentary form; for example, he sees no difference between personal and social roles. In his
view of the world, teachers and doctors cannot
also be parents. (© Elizabeth Hamlin/Stock,
Boston)

push their interpretations beyond the immediate situation (which Furth calls reluctant thinking), or else they made compromise solutions, in which they came up with a logically possible, but incorrect, explanation. One young reluctant thinker said that libraries ran on the fines they got from overdue books. Asked if fine money would pay for all the books in the library, he replied, "Yes. You can tell if they do, because if they didn't, you wouldn't have all the books." A compromise solution to the workings of society was advanced by Nick, who indicated that the government gets all the money paid into the system in economic transactions and in turn pays all wages, builds all schools, and provides goods for all stores.

Children who had found real solutions to the conflicts of the third stage had achieved a temporary equilibrium and moved into Stage IV. At this level, boys and girls make sense out of the system, and their ideas of society begin to approximate an adult viewpoint. The understanding of these ten- and eleven-year-olds was concrete and, for the first time, logical — corresponding to Piaget's concrete operational thought. Although a knowledge of the abstract system escaped them, these children understood the way profit functions and knew that shopkeepers sell goods for more than they pay for them. Children in the fourth stage are aware of personal motivations and individual differences. Asked if any particular job required a certain kind of person, for example, one ten-year-old boy said that being a good clown at a circus called for a "jolly, jumpy person," and being a teacher of small children required "patience." He also said that one needed training to become a policeman, and that teachers could also be students. Another child advanced five reasons for working: money, national need, keeping fit, satisfying ambitions, and controlling anger.

Children's thinking about government itself was studied by Robert Hess (1969) and his associates, who collected information from 12,000 American schoolchildren. Since the data were collected in the early 1960s, before Americans went through the assassination of one President and the resignation of another, they must be interpreted cautiously. During the sixties, however, elementary school children held an idealized view of government and an extremely high estimate of the power of the individual voter. One primary school child said, "If it wasn't for the United States, there probably would be a lot of wars and regular Dark Ages." Second graders had an emotional attachment to the President, who, they believed, protected them and would talk to them if they visited the White House. These children would probably be in Furth's second stage, in which rules and the approval of superiors are important.

The idealization of government and law declined as children went through school, but 76 percent of eighth graders believed that what goes on in government is all for the best. Although 57 percent of the second graders believed that punishment generally follows crime, only 16 percent of eighth graders believed this. Understanding of the way various interest groups operate developed slowly. Even second graders had heard of unions and knew that they have some influence on the passage of laws, but these seven-year-olds also said that policemen have as powerful an effect. Eighth graders believed that corporations have less influence on law than do unions or the average citizen, and they continued to believe that the President has the most power of all.

Hess views the child's understanding of politics from the behavioral-learning perspective, seeing the child as socialized by parents, schools, churches, authority figures, and peers, with the process largely complete by early adolescence (Gallatin, 1980). After interviewing a thousand adolescents over the period of a decade, Joseph Adelson (1975), who uses a cognitive-developmental approach, concluded that the understanding of government and politics on an abstract adult level emerges slowly during adolescence. Most eleven- to thirteen-year-olds he

The understanding of government emerges slowly during adolescence; eleven-year-olds can understand concrete acts of governmental figures and thirteen-year-olds can consider the social consequences of political acts, but not until children are fifteen can they handle easily abstract concepts of government and politics. (© Peter Southwick/Stock, Boston)

interviewed saw society as did the children in Furth's State IV — in a highly concrete way.

> The young adolescent can imagine a church but not the church, the teacher and the school but not education, the policeman and the judge and the jail but not law, the public official but not government (Adelson, 1975).

In the political realm, eleven-year-olds are still functioning at the concrete operational level (Adelson and O'Neill, 1966). By the time they are thirteen, they are just entering the formal operational stage. They can reason about the political system and envision long-range social consequences of political acts, but not in any consistent way, often sliding back into the concrete, present-bound view of the concrete operational child. Fifteen-year-olds seem solidly into the formal operational stage and deal easily with the abstract concepts of government and politics. Adelson and his colleagues found few qualitative differences between fifteen- and eighteen-year-olds. Eighteen-year-olds have a greater store of knowledge and are more fluent in expressing their ideas, but their basic understanding is similar to that of fifteen-year-olds.

Understanding Law and Social Convention

With Robert Hess and Leigh Minturn, June Tapp (1970) examined the way children in different countries think about law, studying 5,000 schoolchildren in Greece, Denmark, India, Japan, and the United States. The children studied were between ten and fourteen years old, so presumably they would understand the general workings of the social system on a concrete level. No matter where these children lived, they regarded laws as either prescriptive (neutral guidelines), prohibitive (guidelines forbidding behavior), or beneficial (rational, positive guidelines). In every culture studied, children said that if there were no laws at all, chaos would prevail. Children in Greece, Japan, and the United States also believed that greed, violence, and crime would rise sharply. As one American ten-year-old put it, "Well, it would be a lot of disorganizing in the world. You know, people would go around killing each other."

Most children could distinguish between "rules" and "unfair rules." Only Indian children believed that all rules were fair. In other cultures studied, children tended to say that fair rules were those that everyone agreed were good and that everyone must follow, regardless of wealth or position. Americans, however, added another quality. Rules, they said, must also be reasonable and useful. In most cultures children believed that it was all right to break rules. American children were inclined to break rules according to the situation. One eighth grader said, "If it's a matter of life and death or you know something pretty important, then it's all right. But the rules should be followed as much as possible." Italian children, on the other hand, believed that it was right to break any rule that was intrinsically unfair. As Piaget would have predicted, the older the children, the more likely they were to agree that it was sometimes all right to break a rule.

The striking result of this study is the similarity of children's attitudes across the five nations. In the United States, the results also divided into black and white groups. Although fewer blacks than whites saw rules as beneficial, in most respects their answers were similar to those of whites. No matter what culture the

researchers studied, by the time children were ten years old, they realized the need for law in ordering human affairs.

Social convention, as distinguished from law, is the focus of Elliot Turiel's (1978) interest. He separates social convention (which structures children's thinking about family patterns, forms of address, dress codes, and national order) from morality (which covers concepts of justice, trust, responsibility, and physical or psychological harm to others). After interviewing 125 children and young adults, Turiel suggests that children's thinking about social convention goes through seven different age-related phases from Level 1, where six- and seven-year-olds believe that convention describes perceived and necessary uniformities in behavior, to Level 7, where the young adult sees convention as uniform behavior that coordinates and facilitates social interaction, making the social system run smoothly. Throughout this development, children switch back and forth between upholding and rejecting convention, but each new affirmation or rejection is based on a different level of understanding. Turiel sees this development as the result of a dialectical process, in which each level the child enters is a negation of the previous level. During each phase of negation, children reevaluate the concept of social structure they held during the previous phase. Their reevaluation forms the basis for their construction of a new level, in which they affirm the value of convention. At each level, however, children realize that conventions are arbitrary social constructions.

The six- and seven-year-olds of Level 1 see conventional behavior as necessary and as enforced by the social sanction of ridicule. Men should not be nurses, say children at this level, because they "just wouldn't look right." A male nurse would "just look funny." At the second level, where most eight- and nine-year-olds are found, there is no need to follow conventions, because they are arbitrary. If a woman wants to be a fireman, says an eight-year-old, it's all right "if she really wants to and feels she can handle the job." Ten- and eleven-year-olds, who tend to be at the third level, have gone back to upholding convention. Now they begin to see social convention as affirming a system of rules, and "there's no sense in making a rule if no one's going to pay any attention to it."

At the fourth level, twelve- and thirteen-year-olds again reject convention, indicating that the rules are nothing but the expectations of others. Such expectations, they say, are insufficient to keep people from following their own wishes. These children believe that as long as breaking convention does not actually hurt anyone else, the violation is a matter of individual preference. Asked about a boy who wanted to eat with his hands in public, the child at Level 4 says, "It's up to him if he wants to. . . . I think he should keep on doing this if this is what he wants, if there's no health hazard." Level-5 fourteen- and fifteen-year-olds again uphold convention, but on the basis that the individual is subordinate to the social system. It is wrong to eat with one's hands because, "Society says it's wrong." If one wants to participate in the system, one must follow the conventions. As they get slightly older, children at Level 5 believe that unless conventions are maintained, the system will fall apart: "If nobody ever followed the rules of what they were supposed to do, we'd have chaos."

At the sixth level (seventeen- to eighteen-year-olds), conventions are again nothing but social expectations. Conventions may provide uniform behavior in a group, but breaking them will not destroy the system. Finally, sometime between eighteen and twenty-five, young adults see social convention as shared norms. A man who learns to abide by social codes "will be measurably better off." Each person follows arbitrary social conventions because they facilitate social interaction. They "make things move along smoothly and also—are most consistently understandable communication." In Turiel's view, it is not the acceptance or rejection of the importance of convention that reveals an individual's

level of thinking, but the reasons given for that acceptance or rejection.

No matter what aspect of understanding we have considered, whether understanding the self, others, or the workings of society, the same developmental process has appeared—progressing from the self to the wider world, from the concrete to the abstract. The baby who could not distinguish between self and world has become, through the interaction of genetic inheritance, cognitive development, and individual experiences, the adolescent who sees the complexities inherent in a world of unique individuals.

SUMMARY

1. Throughout early childhood, children perceive themselves in terms of concrete attributes, reflecting their present-oriented view of the world. In middle childhood, they add personal qualities to their descriptions, and by adolescence, the self-descriptions include ambitions, aspirations, values, and beliefs.

2. Adolescents generally reexamine their self-concepts, incorporating their new sexual and physical attributes and opportunities. If the integration is not successful, the adolescent may fall into totalism.

3. Children's understanding of others develops gradually, generally following the same path as the development of self-concept. Preschoolers understand that others have different visual experiences but seem to lack any understanding of how the differences manifest themselves. By middle childhood, children can understand how a scene may appear to another person. The ability to understand how others feel develops from the preschooler's assumption that all people react the same way to the same event, to the child's realization that people can have different reactions to the same event, to the

adolescent's attempt to explain the reactions of others.

4. Communication abilities improve throughout childhood, and both egocentrism and skill appear to affect a child's ability to communicate. When children are given tasks that fit their cognitive skills, their level of egocentrism appears to drop sharply.

5. In Hans Furth's view, children go through four stages in their understanding of society, beginning at age five with a submissive acceptance that makes no attempt to explain what they see, and developing, by age eleven, into a good understanding of the concrete workings of the system. During adolescence, as formal thought becomes established, an abstract understanding of the nature and function of government and politics appears.

6. All during childhood and adolescence, children switch back and forth between accepting and rejecting social convention. The process is a dialectical one, proposes Elliot Turiel, with each new affirmation or rejection based on different reasons, which reveal the child's level of understanding.

References

Abrahams, B., S. S. Feldman, and S. C. Nash. "Sex-Role Self-Concept and Sex-Role Attitudes: Enduring Personality Characteristics or Adaptations to Changing Life Situations?" *Developmental Psychology*, 14 (1978), 393–400.

Abramovitch, R., C. Corter, and B. Lando. "Sibling Interaction in the Home," *Child Development*, 50 (1979), 997–1003.

———, and J. E. Grusec. "Peer Imitation in a Natural Setting," *Child Development*, 49 (1978), 60–65.

Abravanel, E. "The Development of Intersensory Patterning With Regard to Selected Spatial Dimensions," *Monographs of the Society for Research in Child Development*, 33 (1968), whole no. 118.

Acheson, R. M. "Effects of Nutrition and Disease on Human Growth," in J. M. Tanner (ed.), *Human Growth*. New York: Pergamon Press, 1960, pp. 73–92.

———. "Maturation of the Skeleton," in F. Falkner (ed.), *Human Development*. Philadelphia: Saunders, 1966, pp. 465–502.

Acredolo, C., and L. P. Acredolo. "Identity, Compensation, and Conservation," *Child Development*, 50 (1979), 524–535.

Acredolo, L. P. "Developmental Changes in the Ability to Coordinate Perspectives of a Large-Scale Space," *Developmental Psychology*, 13 (1977), 1–8.

———. "Development of Spatial Orientation in Infancy," *Developmental Psychology*, 14 (1978), 224–234.

———. "Laboratory Versus Home: The Effect of Environment on the 9-Month-Old Infant's Choice of Spatial Reference System," *Developmental Psychology*, 15 (1979), 666–667.

———, H. L. Pick, Jr., and M. G. Olsen, "Environmental Differentiation and Familiarity as Determinants of Children's Memory for Spatial Location," *Developmental Psychology*, 11 (1975), 495–501.

Adams, G. R., and R. M. Jones. "Imaginary Audience Behavior: A Validation Study," *Journal of Early Adolescence*, 1 (1981), 1–10.

Adamsons, K., Jr. "The Role of Thermal Factors in Fetal and Neonatal Life," *Pediatric Clinics of North America*, 13 (1966), 599–619.

Adelson, J. "The Development of Ideology in Adolescence," in S. Dragastin and G. H. Elder (eds.), *Adolescence in the Life Cycle*. Washington, D. C.: Hemisphere, 1975, pp. 63–78.

———, and R. P. O'Neill. "Growth of Political Ideas in Adolescence: The Sense of Community," *Journal of Personality and Social Psychology*, 4 (1966), 295–306.

Ahr, P. R., and J. Youniss. "Reasons for Failure on the Class Inclusion Problem," *Child Development*, 41 (1970), 131–143.

Ainsworth, M. D. S. *Infancy in Uganda: Infant Care and the Growth of Love*. Baltimore: Johns Hopkins University Press, 1967.

———, S. M. Bell, and D. J. Stayton. "Infant-Mother Attachment and Social Development: Socialisation as a Product of Reciprocal Responsiveness to

Signals," in M. P. M. Richards (ed.), *The Integration of the Child Into a Social World*. London: Cambridge University Press, 1974, pp. 99–135.

———, M. C. Blehar, E. Waters, and S. Wall. *Patterns of Attachment: A Psychological Study of the Strange Situation*. Hillsdale. N. J.: Lawrence Erlbaum, 1978.

———, and B. A. Wittig. "Attachment and Exploratory Behavior of One-Year-Olds in a Strange Situation," in B. M. Foss (ed.), *Determinants of Infant Behaviour*. Vol. 4. London: Methuen, 1969, pp. 111–136.

Aldrich, C. A., and E. S. Hewitt. "A Self-Regulating Feeding Program for Infants," *Journal of the American Medical Association*, 135 (1947), 340–342.

Aleksandrowicz, M. M., and D. R. Aleksandrowicz. "Obstetrical Pain-Relieving Drugs as Predictors of Infant Behavioral Variability," *Child Development*, 45 (1974), 935–945.

Allen, G. L., K. C. Kirasic, A. W. Siegel, and J. F. Herman. "Developmental Issues in Cognitive Mapping: The Selection and Utilization of Environmental Landmarks," *Child Development*, 50 (1979), 1062–1070.

Allen, K. E., B. Hart, J. S. Buell, F. R. Harris, and M. M. Wolf. "Effects of Social Reinforcement on Isolate Behavior of a Nursery School Child," *Child Development*, 35 (1964), 511–518.

Allinsmith, W. "The Learning of Moral Standards," in D. R. Miller and G. E. Swanson (eds.), *Inner Conflict and Defense*. New York: Holt, Rinehart and Winston, 1960, pp. 141–176.

Als, H., E. Tronick, B. M. Lester, and T. B. Brazelton. "Specific Neonatal Measures: The Brazelton Neonatal Behavior Assessment Scale," in J. D. Osofsky (ed.), *Handbook of Infant Development*. New York: Wiley-Interscience, 1979, pp. 185–215.

American Psychiatric Association. *Diagnostic and Statistical Manual of Mental Disorders*. 3rd ed. Washington, D. C.: American Psychiatric Association, 1980.

American Psychological Association. "Ethical Standards for Research with Human Subjects," *APA Monitor* (May 1972), I–XIX.

Anderson, D. R. "Active and Passive Processes in Children's Television Viewing." Paper presented at the Annual Meeting of the American Psychological Association. New York, September 1979.

———, L. F. Alwitt, E. P. Lorch, and S. R. Levin. "Watching Children Watch Television," in G.

Hale and M. Lewis (eds.), *Attention and Cognitive Development*. New York: Plenum Press, 1980, pp. 331–361.

Anderson, R. B., and J. F. Rosenblith. "Sudden Unexpected Death Syndrome: Early Indicators," *Biology of the Neonate*, 18 (1971), 395–406.

Anglin, J. M. "Introduction," in J. S. Bruner, *Beyond the Information Given*. New York: Norton, 1973, pp. xiii–xxiv.

———. *Word, Object, and Concept Development*. New York: Norton, 1977.

Apgar, V., and L. S. James. "Further Observations on the Newborn Scoring System," *American Journal of Diseases of Children*, 104 (1962), 419–428.

Ariès, P. *Centuries of Childhood: A Social History of Family Life*. New York: Vintage, 1962.

Aronfreed, J. "The Concept of Internalization," in D. A. Goslin (ed.), *Handbook of Socialization Theory and Research*. Chicago: Rand McNally, 1969, pp. 263–323.

———. "Moral Development From the Standpoint of a General Psychological Theory," in T. Lickona (ed.), *Moral Development and Behavior: Theory, Research, and Social Issues*. New York: Holt, Rinehart and Winston, 1976, pp. 54–69.

———, and V. Pascal. "The Development of Sympathetic Behavior in Children: An Experimental Test of a Two-Phase Hypothesis." Unpublished manuscript. University of Pennsylvania, 1966.

Asher, S. R. "Children's Peer Relations," in M. E. Lamb (ed.), *Social and Personality Development*. New York: Holt, Rinehart and Winston, 1978, pp. 91–113.

Ashmead, D. H., and M. Perlmutter. "Infant Memory in Everyday Life," in M. Perlmutter (ed.), *New Directions in Child Development*. No. 10. *Children's Memory*. San Francisco: Jossey-Bass, 1980, pp. 1–16.

Atkin, C., B. Reeves, and J. Hocking. "Children's Responses to Television Food Advertising: Survey Evidence." Paper presented at the Annual Meeting of the American Psychological Association. New York, September 1979.

Atkinson, R. D., and R. M. Shiffrin. "Human Memory: A Proposed System and Its Control Processes," in K. W. Spence and J. T. Spence (eds.), *The Psychology of Learning and Motivation*. Vol. 2. New York: Academic Press, 1968.

Ault, R. L. *Children's Cognitive Development*. New York: Oxford University Press, 1977.

Ausubel, D. P. *Theory and Problems of Child Develop-*

ment. New York: Grune & Stratton, 1958.

Babson, S. G., M. L. Pernoll, G. I. Benda, and K. Simpson. *Diagnosis and Management of the Fetus and Neonate at Risk: A Guide for Team Care.* 4th ed. St. Louis: C. V. Mosby, 1980.

Bacharach, V. R., and M. A. Luszcz. "Communicative Competence in Young Children: The Use of Implicit Linguistic Information," *Child Development,* 50 (1979), 260–263.

Bacon, M., and M. B. Jones. *Teenage Drinking.* New York: Crowell, 1968.

Bahrick, L., A. Walker, and U. Neisser. "Infants' Perception of Multimodal Information in Novel Events." Paper presented at the meeting of the Eastern Psychological Association. Washington, D. C., March 1978.

Ball, S., and G. A. Bogatz. "Summative Research of *Sesame Street:* Implications for the Study of Preschool Children," in A. D. Pick (ed.), *Minnesota Symposia on Child Psychology.* Vol. 6. Minneapolis: University of Minnesota, 1972, pp. 3–17.

Baltes, P. B., and K. W. Schaie. "Aging and IQ: The Myth of the Twilight Years," *Psychology Today,* 7 (March 1974), 35–40.

Bandura, A. "Social-Learning Theory of Identificatory Processes," in D. A. Goslin (ed.), *Handbook of Socialization Theory and Research.* Chicago: Rand McNally, 1969, pp. 213–262.

———. *Aggression: A Social Learning Analysis.* Englewood Cliffs, N. J.: Prentice-Hall, 1973.

———. *Social Learning Theory.* Englewood Cliffs, N. J.: Prentice-Hall, 1977.

———, and A. C. Huston. "Identification as a Process of Incidental Learning," *Journal of Abnormal and Social Psychology,* 63 (1961), 311–318.

———, and R. H. Walters. *Social Learning and Personality Development.* New York: Holt, Rinehart and Winston, 1963.

Barron, F. "The Dream of Art and Poetry," *Psychology Today,* 2 (December 1968), 18–23+.

Barry, H., I. L. Child, and M. K. Bacon. "Relation of Child Training to Subsistence Economy," *American Anthropologist,* 61 (1959), 51–63.

———, M. K. Bacon, and I. L. Child. "A Cross-Cultural Survey of Some Sex Differences in Socialization," *Journal of Abnormal and Social Psychology,* 55 (1957), 327–332.

Bartel, H. W., N. R. Bartel, and J. J. Grill. "A Sociometric View of Some Integrated Open Class-rooms," *Journal of Social Issues,* 29 (1973), 159–173.

Bates, E. *The Emergence of Symbols: Cognition and Communication in Infancy.* New York: Academic Press, 1979.

Bates, J. F., P. M. Bentler, and S. K. Thompson. "Measurements of Deviant Gender Development in Boys," *Child Development,* 44 (1973), 591–598.

Baumrind, D. "Authoritarian vs. Authoritative Parental Control," *Adolescence,* 3 (1968), 255–272.

———. "An Exploration of Socialization Effects on Black Children: Some Black-White Comparisons," *Child Development,* 43 (1972a), 261–267.

———. "Socialization and Instrumental Competence in Young Children," in W. W. Hartup (ed.), *The Young Child: Reviews of Research,* Vol. 2. Washington, D. C.: National Association for the Education of Young Children, 1972b, pp. 202–224.

———. "The Contribution of the Family to the Development of Competence in Children," *Schizophrenia Bulletin,* 14 (1975), 12–37.

Bay, E. "Ontogeny of Stable Speech Areas in the Human Brain," in E. H. Lenneberg and E. Lenneberg (eds.), *Foundations of Language Development: A Multidisciplinary Approach.* Vol. 2. New York: Academic Press, 1975.

Bayley, N. "Consistency and Variability in the Growth of Intelligence From Birth to Eighteen Years," *Journal of Genetic Psychology,* 75 (1949), 165–196.

———. "On the Growth of Intelligence," *American Psychologist,* 10 (1955), 805–818.

———. "Individual Patterns of Development," *Child Development,* 27 (1956), 45–74.

———. *Manual for the Bayley Scales of Infant Development.* New York: Psychological Corporation, 1969.

Beatty, R. A., and S. Gluecksohn-Waelsch. *Edinburgh Symposium on the Genetics of the Spermatozoan.* Edinburgh/New York, 1972.

Beauchamp, G. K., and O. Maller. "The Development of Flavor Preferences in Humans: A Review," in M. R. Kare and O. Maller (eds.), *The Chemical Senses and Nutrition.* New York: Academic Press, 1977, pp. 291–310.

Becker, J. M. "A Learning Analysis of the Development of Peer-Oriented Behavior in Nine-Month-Old Infants," *Developmental Psychology,* 13 (1977), 481–491.

Beckwith, J. B. "The Sudden Infant Death Syndrome," *Current Problems in Pediatrics,* 3 (1973), 1–36.

Beit Hallahmi, B., and A. I. Rabin. "The Kibbutz as a Social Experiment and a Child-Rearing Laboratory," *American Psychologist*, 32 (1977), 532–541.

Bell, S. M. "The Development of the Concept of Object as Related to Infant-Mother Attachment," *Child Development*, 41 (1970), 291–311.

Bellugi, U. "Learning the Language," *Psychology Today*, 4 (December 1970), 32–35+.

Belmont, L., and F. A. Marolla. "Birth Order, Family Size, and Intelligence," *Science*, 182 (1973), 1096–1101.

Belsky, J., and L. D. Steinberg. "The Effects of Day Care: A Critical Review," *Child Development*, 49 (1978), 929–949.

Bem, S. L. "The Measurement of Psychological Androgyny," *Journal of Consulting and Clinical Psychology*, 42 (1974), 155–162.

――――. "Theory and Measurement of Androgyny: A Reply to the Pedazur-Tetenbaum and Locksley-Colten Critiques," *Journal of Personality and Social Psychology*, 37 (1979), 1047–1054.

Bereiter, C. *et al.* "An Academically Oriented Preschool for Culturally Deprived Children," in F. M. Hechinger (ed.), *Pre-School Education Today*. New York: Doubleday, 1966, pp. 105–137.

――――, and S. Engelmann. *Teaching Disadvantaged Children in the Preschool*. Englewood Cliffs, N. J.: Prentice-Hall, 1966.

Berg, W. K., and K. M. Berg. "Psychophysiological Development in Infancy: State, Sensory Function, and Attention," in J. D. Osofsky (ed.), *Handbook of Infant Development*. New York: Wiley-Interscience, 1979, pp. 283–343.

Berg-Cross, L. G. "Intentionality, Degree of Damage, and Moral Judgments," *Child Development*, 46 (1975), 970–974.

Berko, J. "The Child's Learning of English Morphology," *Word*, 14 (1958), 150–177.

Bernal, J. F. "Crying During the First Ten Days of Life and Maternal Response," *Developmental Medicine and Child Neurology*, 14 (1972), 367–372.

Berndt, T. J. "Developmental Changes in Conformity to Peers and Parents," *Developmental Psychology*, 15 (1979), 608–616.

Bernstein, B. "Linguistic Codes, Hesitation Phenomena and Intelligence," *Language and Speech*, 5 (1962), 31–47.

――――. "Elaborated and Restricted Codes: Their Social Origins and Some Consequences," in A. G. Smith (ed.), *Communication and Culture*. New York:

Holt, Rinehart and Winston, 1966, pp. 427–442.

Bertenthal, B. I., and K. W. Fischer. "Development of Self-Recognition in the Infant," *Developmental Psychology*, 14 (1978), 44–50.

Berzonsky, M. "The Role of Familiarity in Children's Explanations of Physical Causality," *Child Development*, 42 (1971), 705–715.

Bever, T. G. "The Cognitive Basis for Linguistic Structures," in J. R. Hayes (ed.), *Cognition and the Development of Language*. New York: Wiley, 1970, pp. 279–362.

Bijou, S. W. *Child Development: The Basic Stage of Early Childhood*. Englewood Cliffs, N. J.: Prentice-Hall, 1976.

――――, and D. M. Baer. *Child Development*. Vol. 1. *A Systematic and Empirical Theory*. New York: Appleton-Century-Crofts, 1961.

――――, and ――――. *Child Development*. Vol. 2. *Universal Stage of Infancy*. New York: Appleton-Century-Crofts, 1965.

Biller, H. B. "The Father and Personality Development: Paternal Deprivation and Sex-Role Development," in M. E. Lamb (ed.), *The Role of the Father in Child Development*. New York: Wiley, 1976, pp. 89–156.

Bingham, M. T. "Beyond Psychology," in *Homo sapiens auduboniensis: A Tribute to Walter Van Dyke Bingham*. New York: National Audubon Society, 1953, pp. 5–29.

Birch, H. G. "Field Measurement in Nutrition, Learning, and Behavior," in N. S. Scrimshaw and J. E. Gordon (eds.), *Malnutrition, Learning, and Behavior*. Cambridge, Mass.: MIT Press, 1968.

Birren, J. E. "A Brief History of the Psychology of Aging, Part II," *Gerontologist*, 1 (1961), 127–134.

Blaney, N. T., C. Stephan, D. Rosenfield, E. Aronson, and J. Sikes. "Interdependence in the Classroom: A Field Study," *Journal of Educational Psychology*, 69 (1977), 121–128.

Blank, M., and W. H. Bridger. "Cross-Modal Transfer in Nursery-School Children," *Journal of Comparative and Physiological Psychology*, 58 (1964), 277–282.

Blau, Z. S. "Maternal Aspirations, Socialization, and Achievement of Boys and Girls in the White Working Class," *Journal of Youth and Adolescence*, 1 (1972), 35–37.

Block, J. H. "Issues, Problems, and Pitfalls in Assessing Sex Differences: A Critical Review of the Psychology of Sex Differences," *Merrill-Palmer Quarterly*, 22 (1976), 283–308.

Bloom, K. "Eye Contact as a Setting Event for Infant Learning," *Journal of Experimental Child Psychology*, 17 (1974), 250–263.

Bloom, L., P. Lightbown, and L. Hood. "Structure and Variation in Child Language," *Monographs of the Society for Research in Child Development*, 40 (1975), whole no. 160.

Blurton-Jones, N. "Rough-and-Tumble Play Among Nursery School Children," in J. S. Bruner, A. Jolly, and K. Sylva (eds.), *Play—Its Role in Development and Evolution*. New York: Basic Books, 1976, pp. 352–363.

Boden, M. *Jean Piaget*. New York: Viking, 1979.

Boismier, J. D. "Visual Stimulation and Wake-Sleep Behavior in Human Neonates," *Developmental Psychobiology*, 10 (1977), 219–227.

Bond, E. A. *Tenth-Grade Abilities and Achievements*. New York: Columbia University Teachers College, 1940.

Bonney, M. E. "Values of Sociometric Studies in the Classroom," *Sociometry*, 6 (1943), 251–254.

Bornstein, M. H., W. Kessen, and S. Weiskopf. "The Categories of Hue in Infancy," *Science*, 191 (1976), 201–202.

Botvin, G. J., and F. B. Murray. "The Efficacy of Peer Modeling and Social Conflict in the Acquisition of Conservation," *Child Development*, 46 (1975), 796–799.

Bower, T. G. R. "Slant Perception and Shape Constancy in Infants," *Science*, 151 (1966a), 832–834.

———. "The Visual World of Infants," *Scientific American*, 215 (December 1966b), 80–92.

———. *The Perceptual World of Children*. Cambridge, Mass.: Harvard University Press, 1977.

Bowerman, M. "Systematizing Semantic Knowledge: Changes Over Time in the Child's Organization of Word Meaning," *Child Development*, 49 (1978), 977–987.

Bowes, W. A., Y. Brackbill, E. Conway, and A. Steinschneider. "The Effects of Obstetrical Medication on Fetus and Infant," *Monographs of the Society for Research in Child Development*, 35 (1970), whole no. 137.

Bowlby, J. "Some Pathological Processes Set in Train by Early Mother-Child Separation," *Journal of Mental Sciences*, 99 (1953), 265–272.

———. *Attachment*. New York: Basic Books, 1969.

———, M. D. Ainsworth, M. Boston, and D. Rosenbluth. "The Effects of Mother-Child Separation: A Follow-Up Study," *British Journal of Medical Psychology*, 29 (1956), 211–247.

Brackbill, Y. "Obstetrical Medication and Infant Behavior," in J. D. Osofsky (ed.), *Handbook of Infant Development*. New York: Wiley-Interscience, 1979, pp. 76–125.

Bradley, R. H., and B. M. Caldwell. "The Relation of Infants' Home Environments to Mental Test Performance at Fifty-four Months: A Follow-up Study," *Child Development*, 47 (1976), 1172–1174.

Braine, M. D. S. "Children's First Word Combinations," *Monographs of the Society for Research in Child Development*, 41 (1976), whole no. 164.

Brainerd, C. J. "Feedback, Rule Knowledge, and Conservation Learning," *Child Development*, 48 (1977), 404–411.

———. *Piaget's Theory of Intelligence*. Englewood Cliffs, N. J.: Prentice-Hall, 1978.

Brandt, M. M. "Relations Between Cognitive Role-Taking Performance and Age, Task Presentation, and Response Requirements," *Developmental Psychology*, 14 (1978), 206–213.

Brazelton, T. B. *Neonatal Behavioral Assessment Scale*. Philadelphia: Lippincott, 1973.

Bremner, J. G., and P. E. Bryant. "Place Versus Response as the Basis of Spatial Errors Made by Young Infants," *Journal of Experimental Child Psychology*, 23 (1977), 162–171.

Bridger, W. H. "Sensory Habituation and Discrimination in the Human Neonate," *American Journal of Psychiatry*, 117 (1961), 991–996.

Brill, R. G. "Total Communication as a Basis of Educating Deaf Children," in P. J. Fine (ed.), *Deafness in Infancy and Early Childhood*. New York: Medcome, 1974, pp. 132–150.

Brittain, C. V. "Adolescent Choices and Parent-Peer Cross Pressures," *American Sociological Review*, 28 (1963), 385–391.

Brodzinsky, D. M. "Cognitive Style Differences in Children's Spatial Perspective Taking," *Developmental Psychology*, 16 (1980), 151–152.

Bronfenbrenner, U. *Two Worlds of Childhood: U.S. and U.S.S.R.* New York: Russell Sage Foundation, 1970.

———. *The Ecology of Human Development*. Cambridge, Mass.: Harvard University Press, 1979.

Bronson, G. "Aversive Reactions to Strangers: A Dual Process Interpretation," *Child Development*, 49 (1978), 495–499.

Bronstein, I. P., S. Wexler, A. W. Brown, and L. J. Halpern. "Obesity in Childhood: Psychologic

Studies," *American Journal of the Disturbed Child*, 63 (1942), 238–251.

Brooks, J., and M. Lewis. "Infant's Response to Strangers: Midget, Adult, and Child," *Child Development*, 47 (1976), 323–332.

Brown, A. L. "The Development of Memory: Knowing, Knowing About Knowing, and Knowing How to Know," in H. W. Reese (ed.), *Advances in Child Development and Behavior*. Vol. 10. New York: Academic Press, 1975, pp. 104–152.

Brown, R. *Words and Things*. New York: Free Press, 1958.

———. *A First Language: The Early Stages.* Cambridge, Mass.: Harvard University Press, 1973.

———. "Introduction," in C. Snow and C. Ferguson (eds.), *Talking to Children: Language Input and Acquisition*. New York: Cambridge University Press, 1977, pp. 1–27.

———. "The Maintenance of Conversation," in D. R. Olson (ed.), *The Social Foundations of Language and Thought*. New York: Norton, 1980, pp. 187–210.

———, C. Cazden, and U. Bellugi-Klima. "The Child's Grammar From I to III," in J. P. Hill (ed.), *Minnesota Symposia on Child Psychology*. Vol. 2. Minneapolis: University of Minnesota Press, 1968, pp. 28–73.

Brozoski, T. J., R. M. Brown, H. E. Rosvold, and P. S. Goldman. "Cognitive Deficit Caused by Regional Depletion of Dopamine in Prefrontal Cortex of Rhesus Monkey," *Science*, 205 (1979), 929–932.

Bruch, H. *The Importance of Overweight*. New York: Norton, 1957.

Bruck, K. "Temperature Regulation in the Newborn Infant," *Biologia neonatorum*, 3 (1961), 65–119.

Bruner, J. S. "The Course of Cognitive Growth," *American Psychologist*, 19 (1964), 1–15.

———. "Nature and Uses of Immaturity," *American Psychologist*, 27 (1972), 687–708.

———. *Beyond the Information Given*. New York: Norton, 1973.

———. "Berlyne Memorial Lecture: Acquiring the Uses of Language," *Canadian Journal of Psychology*, 32 (1978a), 204–218.

———. "Learning the Mother Tongue," *Human Nature*, 1 (September 1978b), 42–49.

———. "The Social Context of Language Acquisition," The Witkin Memorial Lecture. Presented at Educational Testing Service. Princeton, N. J., May 1980a.

———. *Under Five in Britain*. London: Grant McIntyre, 1980b.

———, R. R. Olver, and P. M. Greenfield. *Studies in Cognitive Growth*. New York: Wiley, 1966.

Bryan, J. H. "Children's Cooperation and Helping Behaviors," in E. M. Hetherington (ed.), *Review of Child Development Research*. Vol. 5. Chicago: University of Chicago Press, 1975, pp. 127–182.

Bryant, P. E. *Perception and Understanding in Young Children*. New York: Basic Books, 1974.

———, P. Jones, V. C. Claxton, and G. M. Perkins. "Recognition of Shapes Across Modalities by Infants," *Nature*, 240 (1972), 303–304.

———, and T. Trabasso. "Transitive Inferences and Memory in Young Children," *Nature*, 232 (1971), 456–458.

Bullock, T. H., R. Orkland, and A. Grinnell. *Introduction to Nervous Systems*. San Francisco: Freeman, 1977.

Burgess, A. *Language Made Plain*. Rev. ed. Glasgow: Fontana/Collins, 1975.

Burgess, R. L., and R. D. Conger. "Family Interaction in Abusive, Neglectful, and Normal Families," *Child Development*, 49 (1978), 1163–1173.

Burton, R. V. "Honesty and Dishonesty," in T. Lickona (ed.), *Moral Development and Behavior: Theory, Research, and Social Issues*. New York: Holt, Rinehart and Winston, 1976, pp. 173–197.

Butler, N. "Late Postnatal Consequences of Fetal Malnutrition," in M. Winick (ed.), *Nutrition and Fetal Development*. Vol. 2: *Current Concepts of Nutrition*. New York: Wiley-Interscience, 1974.

Butterfield, E. C., and G. N. Siperstein. "Influence of Contingent Auditory Stimulation upon Non-Nutritional Suckle," in *Proceedings of Third Symposium on Oral Sensation and Perception: The Mouth of the Infant*. Springfield, Ill.: Charles C Thomas, 1974.

Butterworth, G. "Object Disappearance and Error in Piaget's Stage IV Task," *Journal of Experimental Child Psychology*, 23 (1977), 391–401.

Byrne, D. *The Attraction Paradigm*. New York: Academic Press, 1971.

Caldwell, B. M. "The Rationale for Early Intervention," *Exceptional Children*, 36 (1970), 717.

Callard, E. "Achievement Motive in the Four-Year-Old and Its Relationship to Achievement Expectations of the Mother." Doctoral dissertation, University of Michigan, 1964.

Campbell, J. D., and M. R. Yarrow. "Perceptual and Behavioral Correlates of Social Effectiveness,"

Sociometry, 24 (1961), 1–20.

Campione, J. C., and A. L. Brown. "Memory and Metamemory Development in Educable Retarded Children," in R. V. Kail, Jr., and J. W. Hagen (eds.), *Perspectives on the Development of Memory and Cognition.* Hillsdale, N. J.: Lawrence Erlbaum, 1977, pp. 367–406.

Campos, J. J. "Heart Rates: A Sensitive Tool for the Study of Emotional Development," in L. Lipsitt (ed.), *Developmental Psychobiology: The Significance of Infancy.* Hillsdale, N. J.: Lawrence Erlbaum, 1976.

————, S. Hiatt, D. Ramsay, C. Henderson, and M. Svejda. "The Emergence of Fear on the Visual Cliff," in M. Lewis and L. Rosenblum (eds.), *The Origins of Affect.* New York: Plenum Press, 1978.

Cantor, J. H., and C. C. Spiker. "The Effects of Introtacts on Hypothesis Testing in Kindergarten and First-Grade Children," *Child Development*, 50 (1979), 1110–1120.

Carey, S. "Are Children Little Scientists with False Theories of Amounts?" Doctoral dissertation. Harvard University, 1972.

————. "Cognitive Competence," in K. Connolly and J. S. Bruner (eds.), *The Growth of Competence.* New York: Academic Press, 1974, pp. 169–193.

Carlsmith, L. "Effect of Early Father Absence on Scholastic Aptitude," *Harvard Educational Review*, 34, Winter (1964), 3–21.

Caron, A. J., R. F. Caron, and V. R. Carlson. "Do Infants See Objects or Retinal Images? Shape Constancy Revisited," *Infant Behavior and Development*, 1 (1978), 229–243.

Carpenter, C. J., and A. Huston-Stein. "Activity Structure and Sex-Typed Behavior in Preschool Children," *Child Development*, 51 (1980), 862–872.

Carroll, J. "Psychometric Tests as Cognitive Tasks: A New 'Structure of Intellect,' " in L. B. Resnick (ed.), *The Nature of Intelligence.* Hillsdale, N. J.: Lawrence Erlbaum, 1976, pp. 27–56.

Carter, G. L., and M. Kinsbourne. "The Ontogeny of Right Cerebral Lateralization of Spatial Mental Set," *Developmental Psychology*, 15 (1979), 241–245.

Cattell, P. *The Measurements of Intelligence of Infants and Young Children.* New York: Psychological Corporation, 1940.

Cattell, R. B. "Are IQ Tests Intelligent?" *Psychology Today*, 1 (March 1968), 56–62.

Cavanaugh, J. C., and M. Perlmutter. "Metamemory: A Critical Examination," *Child Development* (in press).

Cermak, L. S., and F. I. M. Craik (eds.), *Levels of Processing in Human Memory.* Hillsdale, N. J.: Lawrence Erlbaum, 1979.

Chabon, I. *Awake and Aware: Participating in Childbirth Through Psychoprophylaxis.* New York: Delacorte, 1966.

Chall, J. S. *Learning to Read: The Great Debate.* New York: McGraw-Hill, 1967.

Chandler, M. J. "Egocentrism and Antisocial Behavior: The Assessment and Training of Social Perspective-Taking Skills," *Developmental Psychology*, 9 (1973), 326–332.

————, S. Greenspan, and C. Barenboim. "Assessment and Training of Role-Taking and Referential Communication Skills in Institutionalized Emotionally Disturbed Children," *Developmental Psychology*, 10 (1974), 546–553.

Chaplin, J. P., and T. S. Krawiec. *Systems and Theories of Psychology.* 3rd ed. New York: Holt, Rinehart and Winston, 1974.

Charles, D. C. "Historical Antecedents of Life-Span Developmental Psychology," in L. R. Goulet and P. B. Baltes (eds.), *Life-Span Developmental Psychology: Research and Theory.* New York: Academic Press, 1970, pp. 24–52.

Charlesworth, R., and W. W. Hartup. "Positive Social Reinforcement in the Nursery School Peer Group," *Child Development*, 38 (1967), 993–1002.

Charlesworth, W. R. "Human Intelligence as Adaptation: An Ethological Approach," in L. B. Resnick (ed.), *The Nature of Intelligence.* Hillsdale, N. J.: Lawrence Erlbaum, 1976, pp. 147–168.

Chernoff, G. "The Fetal Alcohol Syndrome in Mice: An Animal Model," *Teratology*, 15 (1977), 223–230.

Chi, M. T. H. "Knowledge Structure and Memory Development," in R. S. Siegler (ed.), *Children's Thinking: What Develops?* Hillsdale, N. J.: Lawrence Erlbaum, 1978, pp. 73–96.

Chomsky, C. *Acquisition of Syntax in Children from 5 to 10.* Cambridge, Mass.: MIT Press, 1969.

Chomsky, N. *Language and Mind.* Enl. ed. New York: Harcourt Brace Jovanovich, 1972.

————. *Reflections on Language.* New York: Pantheon, 1975.

————. *Language and Responsibility.* New York: Pantheon, 1979.

Churchill, J. A., and H. W. Berendes. "Intelligence of Children Whose Mothers Had Acetonuria During Pregnancy," in *Perinatal Factors Affecting Human Development, Proceedings.* Pan American Health Organization. Scientific Publication No. 185, 1969.

Cicirelli, V. G. "Sibling Influence Throughout the

Life Span." Paper presented at the Annual Meeting of the American Psychological Association. New York, September, 1979.

Cioffi, J., and G. L. Kandel. "Laterality of Stereognostic Accuracy of Children for Words, Shapes, and Bigrams: A Sex Difference for Bigrams," *Science*, 204 (1979), 1432–1434.

Clark, E. V. "What's in a Word? On the Child's Acquisition of Semantics in His First Language," in T. E. Moore (ed.), *Cognitive Development and the Acquisition of Language.* New York: Academic Press, 1973, pp. 65–110.

––––––. "Awareness of Language: Some Evidence From What Children Say and Do," in A. Sinclair, R. J. Jarvella, and W. J. M. Levelt (eds.), *The Child's Conception of Language.* New York: Springer-Verlag, 1978, pp. 17–44.

Clark, H. H., and E. V. Clark. *Psychology and Language.* New York: Harcourt Brace Jovanovich, 1977.

Clarke-Stewart, K. A. "Recasting the Lone Stranger," in J. Glick and K. A. Clarke-Stewart (eds.), *The Development of Social Understanding.* New York: Gardner Press, 1978, pp. 109–176.

Coates, B., and W. W. Hartup. "Age and Verbalization in Observational Learning," *Developmental Psychology*, 1 (1969), 556–562.

Cohen, E., M. Perlmutter, and N. A. Myers. "Memory for Location of Multiple Stimuli by 2- to 4-Year-Olds." Unpublished manuscript. University of Massachusetts, 1977.

Cohen, L. B. "Habituation of Infant Visual Attention," in T. J. Tighe and R. N. Leaton (eds.), *Habituation: Perspectives From Child Development, Animal Behavior, and Neurophysiology.* Hillsdale, N. J.: Lawrence Erlbaum, 1976, pp. 207–238.

––––––. "Concept Acquisition in the Human Infant." Paper presented at the Biennial Meeting of the Society for Research in Child Development. New Orleans, March 1977.

––––––, J. S. DeLoache, and M. S. Strauss. "Infant Visual Perception," in J. D. Osofsky (ed.), *Handbook of Infant Development.* New York: Wiley-Interscience, 1979, pp. 393–438.

Cohen, R., L. M. Baldwin, and R. G. Sherman. "Cognitive Maps of a Naturalistic Setting," *Child Development*, 49 (1978), 1216–1218.

Cohen, S., D. C. Glass, and J. E. Singer. "Apartment Noise, Auditory Discrimination, and Reading Ability," *Journal of Experimental Social Psychology*, 9 (1973), 407–422.

Colby, A. "Evolution of a Moral-Developmental Theory," in W. Damon (ed.), *New Directions for Child Development.* No. 2. *Moral Development.* San Francisco: Jossey-Bass, 1978, pp. 89–104.

Cole, M. "How Education Affects the Mind," *Human Nature*, 1 (April 1978), 50–58.

Cole, M., and S. Scribner. *Culture and Thought.* New York: Wiley, 1974.

––––––, and ––––––. "Cross-Cultural Studies of Memory and Cognition," in R. V. Kail, Jr., and J. W. Hagen (eds.), *Perspectives on the Development of Memory and Cognition.* Hillsdale, N. J.: Lawrence Erlbaum, 1977, pp. 239–271.

––––––, and ––––––. "Introduction," in L. S. Vygotsky, *Mind in Society.* Cambridge, Mass.: Harvard University Press, 1978, pp. 1–14.

Collins, W. A., "Effect of Temporal Separation Between Motivation, Aggression, and Consequences: A Developmental Study," *Developmental Psychology*, 8 (1973), 215–221.

––––––. "Children's Comprehension of Television Content," in E. Wartella (ed.), *Children Communicating.* Beverly Hills, Calif.: Sage, 1979, pp. 21–52.

––––––, T. Berndt, and V. Hess. "Observational Learning of Motives and Consequences for Television Aggression: A Developmental Study," *Child Development*, 45 (1974), 799–802.

––––––, H. Wellman, A. Keniston, and S. Westby. "Age-related Aspects of Comprehension and Inferences From a Televised Dramatic Narrative," *Child Development*, 49 (1978), 389–399.

Columbia Broadcasting System. *A Study of Messages Received by Children Who Viewed an Episode of Fat Albert and the Cosby Kids.* New York: CBS, 1974.

Condry, J. C., and S. L. Dyer. "Fear of Success: Attribution of Cause to the Victim," *Journal of Social Issues*, 32, no. 3 (1976), 63–83.

––––––, and ––––––. "Behavioral and Fantasy Measures of Fear of Success in Children," *Child Development*, 48 (1977), 1417–1425.

Conel, J. L. R. *The Postnatal Development of the Human Cerebral Cortex.* 7 vols. Cambridge, Mass.: Harvard University Press, 1939–1963.

Connell, D. B., J. I. Layzer, and B. D. Goodson, "National Study of Day Care Centers for Infants: Findings and Implications." Paper presented at the Annual Meeting of the American Psychological Association. New York, September 1979.

Connor, J. M., L. A. Serbin, and M. Schackman. "Sex Differences in Children's Response to Training on a Visual-Spatial Task," *Developmental Psychology,* 13 (1977), 293–294.

Cook, M., J. Field, and K. Griffiths. "The Perception of Solid Form in Early Infancy," *Child Development,* 49 (1978), 866–869.

Coopersmith, S. *The Antecedents of Self-Esteem.* San Francisco: Freeman, 1967.

Coren, S. "Development of Ocular Dominance," *Developmental Psychology,* 10 (1974), 302.

Cornell, E. H. "Infants' Visual Attention to Pattern Arrangement and Orientation," *Child Development,* 46 (1975), 229–232.

Costanzo, P. R., and M. E. Shaw. "Conformity as a Function of Age Level," *Child Development,* 37 (1966), 967–975.

Cowan, P. "Cognitive Egocentrism and Social Interaction in Children," *American Psychologist,* 21 (1966), 623.

Cowan, W. M. "The Development of the Brain," *Scientific American,* 241 (September 1979), 88–133.

Cowen, E. L., A Pederson, H. Babijian, L. D. Izzo, and M. A. Trost. "Long-term Follow-up of Early Detected Vulnerable Children," *Journal of Clinical and Consulting Psychology,* 41 (1973), 438–446.

Cravioto, J., and E. Delicardie. "Mental Performance in School Age Children," *American Journal of Diseases of Children,* 120 (1970), 404.

———, and B. Robles. "Evolution of Adaptive and Motor Behavior during Rehabilitation from Kwashiorkor," *American Journal of Orthopsychiatry,* 35 (1965), 449.

Crook, C. K. "The Organization and Control of Infant Sucking," in H. W. Reese and L. P. Lipsitt (eds.), *Advances in Child Development and Behavior.* Vol. 14. New York: Academic Press, 1979, pp. 209–253.

———, and L. P. Lipsitt. "Neonatal Nutritive Sucking: Effects of Taste Stimulation Upon Sucking Rhythm and Heart Rate," *Child Development,* 47 (1976), 518–522.

Cruise, M. G. "A Longitudinal Study of the Growth of Low Birth Weight Infants: 1. Velocity and Distance Growth, Birth to 3 Years," *Pediatrics,* 51 (1973), 620–628.

Csikszentmihalyi, M. *Beyond Boredom and Anxiety.* San Francisco: Jossey-Bass, 1976.

Cummins, R. A., P. J. Livesey, J. G. M. Evans, and R. N. Walsh. "Mechanism of Brain Growth by Environmental Stimulation," *Science,* 205 (1979), 522.

Curtiss, S. R. *Genie: A Psycholinguistic Study of a* Modern-Day 'Wild Child.' New York: Academic Press, 1977.

Darley, J. M., E. C. Klosson, and M. P. Zanna. "Intentions and Their Contexts in the Moral Judgment of Children," *Child Development,* 49 (1978), 66–74.

Darlington, R. B., J. M. Royce, A. S. Snipper, H. W. Murray, and I. Lazar. "Preschool Programs and Later School Competence of Children from Low-Income Families," *Science,* 208 (1980), 202–204.

Darwin, C. *The Expression of the Emotions in Man and Animals.* New York: The Philosophical Library, 1955 (orig. pub. 1872).

Dawe, H. C. "An Analysis of Two Hundred Quarrels of Preschool Children," *Child Development,* 5 (1934), 139–157.

Day, M. C. "Developmental Trends in Visual Scanning," in H. W. Reese (ed.), *Advances in Child Development and Behavior.* Vol. 10. New York: Academic Press, 1975, pp. 154–193.

Deaux, K. "Ahhhh, She Was Just Lucky," *Psychology Today,* 10 (March 1976), 70–75.

Debakan, A. *Neurology of Infancy.* Baltimore: Williams & Wilkins, 1959.

DeCasper, A. J., and W. P. Fifer. "Of Human Bonding: Newborns Prefer Their Mothers' Voices," *Science,* 208 (1980), 1174–1176.

Delia, J. G., and B. J. O'Keefe. "Constructivism: The Development of Communication in Children," in E. Wartella (ed.), *Children Communicating.* Beverly Hills, Calif.: Sage, 1979, pp. 157–185.

DeLoache, J. S., M. W. Rissman, and L. B. Cohen. "An Investigation of the Attention-Getting Process in Infants," *Infant Behavior and Development,* 1 (1978), 11–25.

———, M. S. Strauss, and J. Maynard. "Picture Perception in Infancy," *Infant Behavior and Development,* 2 (1979), 77–89.

deMause, L. (ed.). *The History of Childhood.* New York: Harper & Row, 1974.

Dement, W. "The Effect of Dream Deprivation," *Science,* 131 (1960), 1705–1707.

Denenberg, V. H. "Animal Studies on Developmental Determinants of Behavioral Adaptability," in O. J. Harvey (ed.), *Experience, Structure, and Adaptability.* New York: Springer, 1966.

Dennis, W. "Infant Development Under Conditions of Restricted Practice and of Minimum Social

Stimulation," *Genetic Psychology Monographs*, 23 (1941), 143–191.

———. "Causes of Retardation Among Institutional Children: Iran," *Journal of Genetic Psychology*, 96 (1960), 47–59.

———, and M. G. Dennis. "The Effect of Cradling Practices Upon the Onset of Walking in Hopi Children," *Journal of Genetic Psychology*, 56 (1940), 77–86.

———, and P. Najarian. "Infant Development Under Environmental Handicap," *Psychological Monographs*, 71 (1957), 436.

———, and Y. Sayegh. "The Effect of Supplementary Experiences Upon the Behavioral Development of Infants in Institutions," *Child Development*, 36 (1965), 81–90.

Desor, J. A. "Taste Preferences in Children During the First Six Months." Paper presented at the Meeting of the Eastern Psychological Association. New York, 1975.

———, O. Maller, and L. S. Greene. "Preference for Sweet in Humans: Infants, Children, and Adults," in J. M. Weiffenbach (ed.), *Taste and Development: The Genesis of Sweet Preference*. Bethesda, Md.: U. S. Department of Health, Education, and Welfare, 1977, pp. 161–172.

Deutsch, M., and H. G. Gerard. "A Study of Normative and Informational Social Influence Upon Individual Judgment," *Journal of Abnormal and Social Psychology*, 51 (1955), 629–636.

deVilliers, J. G., and P. A. deVilliers. "Development of the Use of Word Order in Comprehension," *Journal of Psycholinguistic Research*, 2 (1973), 331–341.

——— and ———. *Language Acquisition*. Cambridge, Mass.: Harvard University Press, 1978.

DeVries, R. "Constancy of Generic Identity in the Years Three to Six." *Monographs of the Society for Research in Child Development*, 34 (1969), whole no. 127.

Dick-Read, G. *Childbirth Without Fear: The Principles and Practice of Natural Childbirth*. New York: Harper & Bros., 1944.

Dion, K. K. "Young Children's Stereotyping of Facial Attractiveness," *Developmental Psychology*, 9 (1973), 183–188.

Dobbing, J. "Effects of Experimental Undernutrition on Development of the Nervous System," in N. S. Scrimshaw and J. E. Gordan (eds.), *Malnutrition, Learning, and Behavior*. Cambridge, Mass.: MIT Press, 1968, pp. 181–202.

———, and J. L. Smart. "Vulnerability of the Developing Brain and Behavior," *British Medical Bulletin*, 30 (1974), 164–168.

Dodd, B. "Lip Reading in Infants: Attention to Speech Presented in and out of Synchrony," *Cognitive Psychology*, 11 (1979), 478–484.

Dollard, J., L. W. Doob, N. E. Miller, O. H. Mowrer, and R. R. Sears. *Frustration and Aggression*. New Haven, Conn.: Yale University Press, 1939.

———, and N. E. Miller. *Personality and Psychotherapy*. New York: McGraw-Hill, 1950.

Donaldson, M. *Children's Minds*. New York: Norton, 1979.

———, and G. Balfour. "Less Is More: A Study of Language Comprehension in Children," *British Journal of Psychology*, 59 (1968), 461–472.

Douglas, J. W. B. "The Age at Which Premature Children Walk," *Medical Officer*, 95 (1956), 33–35.

Douglas, V. I., and K. G. Peters. "Toward a Clearer Definition of the Attentional Deficit of Hyperactive Children," in G. A. Hale and M. Lewis (eds.), *Attention and Cognitive Development*. New York: Plenum Press, 1979, pp. 173–248.

Douvan, E. "Social Status and Success Strivings," *Journal of Abnormal and Social Psychology*, 52 (1956), 219–223.

———, and J. Adelson. *The Adolescent Experience*. New York: Wiley, 1966.

———, and M. Gold. "Modal Patterns in American Adolescence," in L. W. Hoffman and M. L. Hoffman (eds.), *Review of Child Development Research*. Vol. 2. New York: Russell Sage Foundation, 1966.

Doyle, A., J. Connolly, and L. Rivest. "The Effect of Playmate Familiarity on the Social Interactions of Young Children," *Child Development*, 51 (1980), 217–223.

Duck, S. W. *Personal Relationships and Personal Constructs: A Study of Friendship Formation*. New York: Wiley-Interscience, 1973.

———. *Theory and Practice in Interpersonal Attraction*. New York: Academic Press, 1977.

Dulit, E. "Adolescent Thinking à la Piaget: The Formal Stage," *Journal of Youth and Adolescence*, 1 (1972), 281–301.

Dunn, J. *Distress and Comfort*. Cambridge, Mass.: Harvard University Press, 1977.

Dunphy, D. C. "The Social Structure of Urban Adolescent Peer Groups," *Sociometry*, 26 (1963), 230–246.

Dustman, R. E., and E. C. Beck. "Visually Evoked

Potentials: Amplitude Changes With Age," *Science*, 151 (1966), 1013–1015.

Dweck, C. S. "Achievement," in M. E. Lamb (ed.), *Social and Personality Development*. New York: Holt, Rinehart and Winston, 1978, pp. 114–130.

———, W. Davidson, S. Nelson, and B. Enna. "Sex Differences in Learned Helplessness: II. The Contingencies of Evaluative Feedback in the Classroom, and III. An Experimental Analysis," *Developmental Psychology*, 14 (1978), 268–276.

———, and T. E. Goetz. "Attributions and Learned Helplessness," in J. W. Harvery, W. Ickes, and R. F. Kidd (eds.), *New Directions in Attribution Research*. Vol. 2. Hillsdale, N. J.: Lawrence Erlbaum, 1977.

Dwyer, J., and J. Mayer. "Psychological Effects of Variations in Physical Appearance During Adolescence," *Adolescence*, 3 (Winter 1968–1969), 353–380.

———, and ———. "Overfeeding and Obesity in Infants and Children," *Bibliotheca Nutritio et Dieta*, no. 18 (1973), 123–152.

Dziadosz, G. M., and M. J. Schaller. "Acuity and Sighting Dominance in Children and Adults," *Developmental Psychology*, 13 (1977), 288.

Easterbrooks, M. A., and M. E. Lamb. "Relationship between Infant-Mother Attachment and Infant Competence in Initial Encounters with Peers," *Child Development*, 50 (1979), 380–387.

Eckerman, C. O., and H. L. Rheingold. "Infants' Exploratory Responses to Toys and People," *Developmental Psychology*, 10 (1974), 225–259.

Edelbrock, C., and A. I. Sugawara. "Acquisition of Sex-Typed Preferences in Preschool-Aged Children," *Developmental Psychology*, 14 (1978), 614–623.

Ehrhardt, A. A., and S. W. Baker. "Hormonal Aberrations and Their Implications for the Understanding of Normal Sex Differentiation," in P. H. Mussen, J. J. Conger, and J. Kagan (eds.), *Basic and Contemporary Issues in Developmental Psychology*. New York: Harper & Row, 1975, pp. 113–121.

Eichenwald, H. F., and P. C. Fry. "Nutrition and Learning," *Science*, 163 (1969), 644–648.

Eichorn, D. *Biological Correlates of Behavior*. Chicago: National Society for the Study of Education, 1963.

Eiduson, B. T. "Emergent Families of the 1970s: Values, Practices, and Impacts Upon Children," in D. Reiss and H. A. Hoffman (eds.), *The American Family: Dying or Developing*. New York: Plenum Press, 1979, pp. 157–201.

Eilers, R. E., W. R. Wilson, and J. M Moore. "Devel-

opmental Changes in Speech Discrimination in Three-, Six-, and Twelve-Month-Old Infants," *Journal of Speech and Hearing Research*, 20 (1977), 766–780.

Eimas, P. D. "Speech Perception in Early Infancy," in L. B. Cohen and P. Salapatek, *Infant Perception: From Sensation to Cognition*. Vol. 2: *Perception of Space, Speech, and Sound*. New York: Academic Press, 1975, pp. 193–231.

———, and V. C. Tartter. "On the Development of Speech Perception: Mechanisms and Analogies," in H. W. Reese and L. P. Lipsitt (eds.), *Advances in Child Development and Behavior*. Vol. 13. New York: Academic Press, 1979, pp. 155–193.

Eisenberg, R. B. "The Development of Hearing in Man: An Assessment of Current Status," *Journal of the American Speech and Hearing Association*, 12 (1970), 119–123.

———, E. J. Griffin, D. B. Coursin, and M. A. Hunter. "Auditory Behavior in the Human Neonate: A Preliminary Report," *Journal of Speech and Hearing Research*, 7 (1964), 245–269.

Elkind, D. "Perceptual Development in Children," in I. Janis (ed.), *Current Trends in Psychology*. Los Altos, Calif.: Kaufmann, 1977, pp. 121–129.

———. "Strategic Interactions in Early Adolescence," in J. Adelson (ed.), *Handbook of Adolescent Psychology*. New York: Wiley-Interscience, 1980, pp. 432–446.

———, and R. Bown. "Imaginary Audience Behavior in Children and Adolescents," *Developmental Psychology*, 15 (1979), 38–44.

———, and R. F. Dabek. "Personal Injury and Property Damage in Moral Judgments of Children," *Child Development*, 48 (1977), 518–522.

Elliott, V. "Impact of Day Care on Economic Status of the Family," in D. Peters (ed.), *A Summary of the Pennsylvania Day Care Study*. University Park: Pennsylvania State University, 1973.

Elmer, N. P., and J. P. Rushton. "Cognitive-Developmental Factors in Children's Generosity," *British Journal of Social and Clinical Psychology*, 13 (1974), 277–281.

Emde, R. N., and C. Brown. "Adaptation to the Birth of a Down's Syndrome Infant," *Journal of the American Academy of Child Psychiatry*, 17 (1978), 299–323.

———, T. J. Gaensbauer, and R. J. Harmon. *Emotional Expression in Infancy: A Biobehavioral Study*. New York: International Universities Press, 1976.

Emmerich, W. "Continuity and Stability in Early Social Development: II. Teacher Ratings," *Child Development*, 37 (1966), 17–27.

Engen, T., and L. P. Lipsitt. "Decrement and Recovery of Responses to Olfactory Stimuli in the Human Neonate," *Journal of Comparative and Physiological Psychology*, 59 (1965), 312–316.

Entingh, D., A. Dunn, E. Glassman, J. E. Wilson, E. Hogan, and T. Damstra. "Biochemical Approaches to the Biological Basis of Memory," in M. S. Gazzaniga and C. Blakemore (eds.), *Handbook of Psychobiology*. New York: Academic Press, 1975, pp. 201–240.

Entwisle, D. R., and L. A. Hayduk. *Too Great Expectations*. Baltimore: Johns Hopkins University Press, 1978.

Epstein, R., R. P. Lanza, and B. F. Skinner. "Symbolic Communication Between Two Pigeons (Columbia livia domestica)," *Science*, 207 (1980), 543–545.

Erikson, E. H. *Childhood and Society*. 2nd rev. ed. New York: Norton, 1963.

———. *Identity, Youth, and Crisis*. New York: Norton, 1968.

Eron, L. D., L. R. Huesmann, M. M. Lefkowitz, and L. O. Walder. "Does Television Cause Aggression?" *American Psychologist*, 27 (1972), 253–263.

Ervin-Tripp, S. "Language Development," in *Master Lecture Series*, American Psychological Association, 1976.

Estes, W. K. "Is Human Memory Obsolete?" *American Scientist*, 68 (1980), 62–69.

Evans, R. I. "Smoking in Children: Developing a Social Psychological Strategy of Deterrence," *Journal of Preventive Medicine*, 5 (1976), 122–127.

Evans, W. F., and G. Gratch. "The Stage IV Error in Piaget's Theory of Object Concept Development: Difficulties in Object Conceptualization or Spatial Localization?" *Child Development*, 43 (1972), 682–688.

Evers, W. L., and J. C. Schwartz. "Modifying Social Withdrawal in Pre-Schoolers: The Effects of Filmed Modeling and Teacher Praise," *Journal of Abnormal Child Psychology*, 1 (1973), 248–256.

Fagan, J. F., III. "Infants' Recognition Memory for a Series of Visual Stimuli," *Journal of Experimental Child Psychology*, 11 (1971), 244–250.

———. "Infants' Recognition of Invariant Features of Faces," *Child Development*, 47 (1976), 627–638.

———, R. L. Fantz, and S. B. Miranda. "Infants' Attention to Novel Stimuli as a Function of Postnatal and Conceptual Age." Paper presented at the Biennial Meeting of the Society for Research in Child Development. Minneapolis, 1971.

———, and L. T. Singer. "The Role of Simple Feature Differences in Infants' Recognition of Faces," *Infant Behavior and Development*, 2 (1979), 39–46.

Fagot, B. I. "Sex Differences in Toddlers' Behavior and Parental Reaction," *Developmental Psychology*, 10 (1974), 554–558.

———. "Consequences of Moderate Cross-Gender Behavior in Preschool Children," *Child Development*, 48 (1977), 902–907.

———. "The Influence of Sex of Child on Parental Reactions to Toddler Children," *Child Development*, 49 (1978a), 459–465.

———. "Reinforcing Contingencies for Sex-Role Behaviors: Effect of Experience With Children," *Child Development*, 48 (1978b), 30–36.

Falbo, T. "Achievement Attributions of Kindergartners," *Developmental Psychology*, 11 (1975), 529–530.

Falkner, F. T. (ed.), *Human Development*. Philadelphia: Saunders, 1966.

Fantz, R. L. "Visual Perception From Birth as Shown by Pattern Selectivity," *Annals of the New York Academy of Sciences*, 118 (1965), 793–814.

———. "Pattern Discrimination and Selective Attention as Determinants of Perceptual Development From Birth," in A. H. Kidd and J. E. Rivoire (eds.), *Perceptual Development in Children*. New York: International Universities Press, 1966, pp. 181–224.

———, J. F. Fagan III, and S. B. Miranda. "Early Visual Selectivity," in L. B. Cohen and P. Salapatek (eds.), *Infant Perception: From Sensation to Cognition*. Vol. 1: *Basic Visual Processes*. New York: Academic Press, 1975, pp. 249–345.

———, and S. B. Miranda. "Newborn Infant Attraction to Form of Contour," *Child Development*, 46 (1975), 224–228.

Faulkender, P. J., J. C. Wright, and A. Waldron. "Generalized Habituation of Conceptual Stimuli in Toddlers," *Child Development*, 45 (1974), 351–356.

Faust, M. S. "Developmental Maturity as a Determinant in Prestige of Adolescent Girls," *Child Development*, 31 (1960), 173–184.

Fein, D. "Just World Responding in 6- and 9-Year-

Old Children," *Developmental Psychology*, 12 (1976), 79–80.

Feldman, S. S., and S. C. Nash. "Interest in Babies During Young Adulthood," *Child Development*, 31 (1960), 173–184.

———, and ———. "Sex Differences in Responsiveness to Babies Among Mature Adults," *Developmental Psychology*, 15 (1979), 430–436.

———, ———, and C. Cutrona. "The Influence of Age and Sex on Responsiveness to Babies," *Developmental Psychology*, 13 (1977), 675–676.

Ferguson, C. A. "Baby Talk as a Simplified Register," in C. E. Snow and C. A. Ferguson (eds.), *Talking to Children: Language Input and Acquisition*. New York: Cambridge University Press, 1977, pp. 219–236.

———, and C. Farwell. "Words and Sounds in Early Language Acquisition: English Consonants in the First 50 Words," *Language*, 51 (1975), 419–439.

Feshbach, S. "The Function of Aggression and the Regulation of Aggressive Drive," *Psychological Review*, 71 (1964), 257–272.

———. "Aggression," in P. H. Mussen (ed.), *Carmichael's Manual of Child Psychology*. Vol. 2. New York: Wiley, 1970, pp. 159–259.

———, and R. D. Singer. *Television and Aggression*. San Francisco: Jossey-Bass, 1971.

Field, J., D. DiFranco, P. Dodwell, and D. Muir. "Auditory-Visual Coordination in 2½-Month-Old Infants," *Infant Behavior and Development*, 2 (1979), 113–122.

Field, T. "Interaction Behaviors of Primary Versus Secondary Caretaker Fathers," *Developmental Psychology*, 14 (1978), 183–184.

Fishbein, H. D. *Evolution, Development, and Children's Learning*. Santa Monica, Calif.: Goodyear, 1976.

Fitzgerald, H., and Y. Brackbill. "Classical Conditioning in Infancy: Development and Constraints," *Psychological Bulletin*, 83 (1976), 353–376.

Flanery, R. C., and J. D. Balling. "Developmental Changes in Hemispheric Specialization for Tactile Spatial Ability, *Developmental Psychology*, 15 (1979), 364–372.

Flavell, J. H. *The Developmental Psychology of Jean Piaget*. Princeton, N. J.: Van Nostrand, 1963.

———. "Developmental Studies of Mediated Memory," in H. W. Reese and L. P. Lipsitt (eds.), *Advances in Child Development and Behavior*. Vol. 5. New York: Academic Press, 1970, pp. 182–211.

———. *Cognitive Development*. Englewood Cliffs,

New Jersey: Prentice-Hall, 1977.

———, D. R. Beach, and J. M. Chinsky. "Spontaneous Verbal Rehearsal in a Memory Task as a Function of Age," *Child Development*, 37 (1966), 283–299.

———, P. T. Botkin, C. L. Fry, Jr., J. W. Wright, and P. E. Jarvis. *The Development of Role-Taking and Communication Skills in Children*. Huntington, N. Y.: Krieger, 1975 (orig. pub. 1968).

———, S. G. Shipstead, and K. Croft. "Young Children's Knowledge About Visual Perception: Hiding Objects From Others," *Child Development*, 49 (1978), 1208–1211.

———, and H. M. Wellman. "Metamemory," in R. V. Kail, Jr., and J. W. Hagen (eds.), *Perspectives on the Development of Memory and Cognition*. Hillsdale, N. J.: Lawrence Erlbaum, 1977, pp. 3–33.

Floyd, J. M. "Effects of Amount of Reward and Friendship Status of the Other on the Frequency of Sharing in Children," *Dissertation Abstracts*, 25 (1965), 5396–5397.

Forgus, R. H. "The Effects of Early Perceptual Learning on the Behavioral Organization of Adult Rats," *Journal of Comparative Physiological Psychology*, 47 (1954), 331–336.

Fortes, M. "Social and Psychological Aspects of Education in Taleland," in J. S. Bruner, A. Jolly, and K. Sylva (eds.), *Play—Its Role in Development and Education*. New York: Basic Books, 1976, pp. 474–483 (orig. pub. 1938).

Fowler, W., and N. Kahn. "The Development of a Prototype Infant and Child Day Care Center in Metropolitan Toronto. Ontario Institute for Studies in Education, Year III Progress Report, December 1974; Year IV Progress Report, December 1975.

Fox, G. L. "The Family's Role in Adolescent Sexual Behavior." Paper presented to the Family Impact Seminar, Washington, D. C., October 1978.

Fox, N. "Attachment of Kibbutz Infants to Mother and Metapelet," *Child Development*, 48 (1977), 1228–1239.

Fox, R., R. N. Aslin, S. L. Shea, and S. T. Dumais. "Steropsis in Human Infants," *Science*, 207 (1980), 323–324.

Fraiberg, S., and E. Adelson. "Self-Representation in Language and Play: Observations of Blind Children," *Psychoanalytic Quarterly*, 42 (1973), 539.

———, and N. Bayley. "Gross Motor Development in Infants Blind From Birth," *Child Development*, 45 (1974), 114–126.

Frank, F. "Perception and Language in Conservation," in J. S. Bruner, R. R. Olver, P. M. Greenfield *et al.*, *Studies in Cognitive Growth.* New York: Wiley, 1966.

Frank, L. K. *On the Importance of Infancy.* New York: Random House, 1966.

Freda, V. J., J. G. Gorman, W. Pollack, and E. Howe. "Prevention of Rh Hemolytic Disease — Ten Years' Clinical Experience With Rh Immune Globulin," *New England Journal of Medicine*, 282 (1975), 19.

Freedman, D. G. "Constitutional and Environmental Interactions in Rearing of Four Breeds of Dogs," *Science*, 127 (1958), 585–586.

———. *Human Infancy, an Evolutionary Perspective.* Hillsdale, N. J.: Lawrence Erlbaum, 1974.

Freud, S. "Three Essays on the Theory of Sexuality," in *The Standard Edition of the Complete Psychological Works of Sigmund Freud.* Vol. 7. London: Hogarth, 1953, pp. 125–245 (orig. pub. 1905).

———. *Psychopathology of Everyday Life.* New York: Macmillan, 1917.

Frias, J. L. "Prenatal Diagnosis of Genetic Abnormalities," *Clinical Obstetrics and Gynecology*, 18 (1975), 221–236.

Friedl, E. "Society and Sex Roles," *Human Nature*, 1 (April 1978), 68–75.

Friedman, S. "Habituation and Recovery of Visual Response in the Alert Human Newborn," *Journal of Experimental Child Psychology*, 13 (1972), 339–349.

———, L. A. Bruno, and P. Vietze. "Newborn Habituation to Visual Stimuli: A Sex Difference in Novelty Detection," *Journal of Experimental Child Psychology*, 18 (1974), 242–251.

Fries, M. E. "Some Hypotheses on the Role of the Congenital Activity Type in Personality Development," *International Journal of Psychoanalysis*, 35 (1954), 206–207.

Frisch, H. L., "Sex Stereotypes in Adult-Infant Play," *Child Development*, 48 (1977), 1671–1675.

Frodi, A. M., and M. E. Lamb. "Sex Differences in Responsiveness to Infants: A Developmental Study of Psychophysiological and Behavioral Responses," *Child Development*, 49 (1978), 1182–1188.

——— and ———."Child Abusers' Responses to Infant Smiles and Cries," *Child Development*, 51 (1980), 238–241.

———, ———. L. A. Leavitt, and W. L. Donovan. "Fathers' and Mothers' Responses to Infant Smiles and Cries," *Infant Behavior and Development*, 1 (1978a), 187–198.

———, ———, ———, ———, C. Neff, and D.

Sherry. "Fathers' and Mothers' Responses to the Faces and Cries of Normal and Premature Infants," *Developmental Psychology*, 14 (1978b), 490–498.

Frodi, A.M., J. Macaulay, and P.R. Thome. "Are Woman Always Less Aggressive Than Men? A Review of the Experimental Literature, *Psychological Bulletin*, 84 (1977), 634–660.

Froggatt, P., M. A. Lynas, and G. MacKenzie. "Epidemiology of Sudden Unexpected Death in Infants ('Cot Death') in Northern Ireland," *British Journal of Preventive and Social Medicine*, 25 (1971), 119–134.

Frueh, T., and P. E. McGhee. "Traditional Sex Role Development and Amount of Time Spent Watching Television," *Developmental Psychology*, 11 (1975), 109.

Fry, D. *Homo Loquens: Man as a Talking Animal.* New York: Cambridge University Press, 1977.

Fryer, J. G., and J. R. Ashford. "Trends in Perinatal and Neonatal Mortality in England and Wales, 1960–69," *British Journal of Preventive and Social Medicine*, 26 (1972), 1–9.

Furth, H. G. "The Influence of Language on the Development of Concept Formation in Deaf Children," *Journal of Abnormal and Social Psychology*, 63 (1961), 386–389.

———. *The World of Grown-Ups: Children's Conceptions of Society.* New York: Elsevier, 1980.

———, and N. A. Milgram. "Labeling and Grouping Effects in the Recall of Pictures by Children," *Child Development*, 44 (1973), 511–518.

———, B. M. Ross, and J. Youniss. "Operative Understanding in Reproductions of Drawings," *Child Development*, 45 (1974), 63–70.

Gagné, R. M. "Contributions of Learning to Human Development," *Psychological Review*, 75 (1968), 177–191.

Gagnon, J. H. *Human Sexualities.* Glenview, Ill.: Scott, Foresman, 1977.

Gaitonde, M. K. "Report on Meeting of Neurochemical Group of the Biochemical Society," *Nature*, 221 (1969), 808.

Galin, D., J. Johnstone, L. Nakell, and J. Herron. "Development of the Capacity for Tactile Information Transfer Between Hemispheres in Normal Children," *Science*, 204 (1979), 1330–1332.

Gallatin, J. "Political Thinking in Adolescence," in J. Adelson (ed.), *Handbook of Adolescent Psychology.* New York: Wiley-Interscience, 1980, pp. 344–382.

Garbarino, J. "A Preliminary Study of Some Ecological Correlates of Child Abuse: The Impact of
Socioeconomic Stress on Mothers," *Child Development*, 47 (1976), 178–185.

_____, and A. Crouter. "Defining the Community
Context for Parent-Child Relations: The Correlates of Child Maltreatment," *Child Development*,
49 (1978), 604–616.

_____, and D. Sherman. "High-Risk Neighborhoods
and High-Risk Families: The Human Ecology of
Child Maltreatment," *Child Development*, 51 (1980),
188–198.

Gardner, H. *The Shattered Mind*. New York: Knopf,
1975.

_____. "The Loss of Language," *Human Nature*, 1
(March 1978), 76–84.

Gardner, L. "Deprivation Dwarfism," *Scientific American*, 227 (1972), 76–82.

Gardner, R. A., and B. T. Gardner. "Teaching Sign
Language to a Chimpanzee," *Science*, 165 (1969),
664–672.

Garnica, O. K. "The Development of Phonemic
Speech Perception," in T. E. Moore (ed.), *Cognitive
Development and the Acquisition of Language*. New
York: Academic Press, 1973, pp. 215–222.

Garvey, C. "Requests and Responses in Children's
Speech," *Journal of Child Language*, 2 (1975), 41–60.

_____. *Play*. Cambridge, Mass.: Harvard University
Press, 1977a.

_____. "Play With Language," in B. Tizard and D.
Harvey (eds.), *Biology of Play*. Philadelphia: Lippincott, 1977b, pp. 74–99.

Garwood, S. G. "First-Name Stereotypes as a Factor
in Self-Concept and School Achievement," *Journal
of Educational Psychology*, 68 (1976), 482–487.

Gazzaniga, M. S. "Brain Mechanism and Behavior,"
in M. S. Gazzaniga and C. Blakemore (eds.), *Handbook of Psychobiology*. New York: Academic Press,
1975, pp. 565–590.

_____. "One Brain–Two Minds?" in I. L. Janis
(ed.), *Current Trends in Psychology*. Los Altos, Calif.:
Kaufmann, 1977, pp. 7–13.

Geffen, G. "Development of Hemispheric Specialization for Speech Perception," *Cortex*, 12 (1976),
337–346.

Gelles, R. J. "Violence Toward Children in the
United States," *American Journal of Orthopsychiatry*,
48 (1978), 580–592.

Gelman, R. "How Young Children Reason About
Small Numbers," in N. J. Castellan, D. P. Pisoni,

and G. R. Potts (eds.), *Cognitive Theory*. Hillsdale,
N. J.: Lawrence Erlbaum, 1977, pp. 219–238.

_____. "Cognitive Development," in M. R. Rosen-
zweig and L. W. Porter (eds.), *Annual Review of
Psychology*. Vol. 29. Palo Alto, Calif.: Annual Reviews, 1978, pp. 297–332.

_____, and C. R. Gallistel. *The Child's Understanding
of Number*. Cambridge, Mass.: Harvard University
Press, 1978.

_____, and M. Shatz. "Appropriate Speech Adjust-
ments: The Operation of Conversational Constraints to Talk to Two-Year-Olds," in M. Lewis
and L. A. Rosenblum (eds.), *Interaction, Conversation, and the Development of Language*. New York:
Wiley, 1977, pp. 27–61.

Gentner, D. "On Relational Meaning: The Acquisition of Verb Meaning," *Child Development*, 49 (1978),
988–998.

George, C., and M. Main. "Social Interaction of
Young Abused Children: Approach, Avoidance,
and Aggression," *Child Development*, 50 (1979),
306–318.

Gerbner, G. "The Violence Profiles: Some Indicators
of the Trends in and the Symbolic Structure of
Network Television Drama, 1967–1970." Unpublished manuscript. Annenberg School of Communications, University of Pennsylvania, 1972.

_____, and L. Gross. "Living With Television: The
Violence Profile," *Journal of Communication*, 26
(1976a), 173–199.

_____, and _____. "The Scary World of TV's
Heavy Viewer," *Psychology Today*, 9 (April 1976b),
41–45.

Geschwind, N. "Specialization of the Human Brain,"
Scientific American, 241 (September 1979), 180–201.

Gesell, A. L. *The Mental Growth of the Pre-School Child:
A Psychological Outline of Normal Development From
Birth to the Sixth Year, Including a System of Develop-
mental Diagnosis*. New York: Macmillan, 1925.

Gewirtz, J. L. "The Course of Infant Smiling in Four
Child-Rearing Environments in Israel," in B. M.
Foss (ed.), *Determinants of Infant Behavior*. Vol. 3.
London: Methuen, 1965, pp. 205–260.

Gibbs, F. A., and E. L. Gibbs. *Atlas of Electroenceph-
alography*. Vol. 3. Reading, Mass.: Addison-Wesley,
1964.

Gibson, E. J. "Development of Perception: Discrimination of Depth Compared With Discrimination of
Graphic Symbols," in J. C. Wright and J. Kagan
(eds.), "Basic Cognitive Processes in Children,"

Monographs of the Society for Research in Child Development, 28 (1963), whole no. 85.

————. *Principles of Perceptual Learning and Development*. Englewood Cliffs, N. J.: Prentice-Hall, 1969.

————, C. J. Owsley, and J. Johnston. "Perception of Invariants by Five-Month-Old Infants: Differentiation of Two Types of Motion," *Developmental Psychology*, 14 (1978), 407–415.

————, and R. D. Walk. "The Visual Cliff," *Scientific American*, 202 (April 1960), 64–71.

Gilligan, C. "In a Different Voice: Women's Conceptions of Self and of Morality," *Harvard Educational Review*, 47 (1977), 481–517.

Gleason, J. B. "Do Children Imitate?" *Proceedings of the International Conference on Oral Education of the Deaf*, 2 (1967), 1441–1448.

————, and S. Weintraub. "Input Language and the Acquisition of Communicative Competence," in K. E. Nelson (ed.), *Children's Language*. Vol. 1. New York: Gardner Press, 1978, pp. 171–222.

Gluck, L., and M. V. Kulovich. "Fetal Lung Development: Current Concepts," *Pediatric Clinic of North America*, 20 (1973), 367–379.

Gold, D., and D. Andreas. "Developmental Comparisons Between Ten-Year-Old Children With Employed and Unemployed Mothers," *Child Development*, 49 (1978), 75–84.

Goldberg, S. "Social Competence in Infancy: A Model of Parent-Infant Interaction," *Merrill-Palmer Quarterly*, 23 (1977), 163–177.

————, and M. Lewis. "Play Behavior in the Year-Old Infant: Early Sex Differences," *Child Development*, 40 (1969), 21–31.

Golden, M., and B. Birns. "Social Class and Infant Intelligence," in M. Lewis (ed.), *Origins of Intelligence: Infancy and Early Childhood*. New York: Plenum Press, 1976, pp. 299–352.

————, W. H. Bridger, and A. Montare. "Social-Class Differences in the Ability of Young Children to Use Verbal Information to Facilitate Learning," *American Journal of Orthopsychiatry*, 44 (1974), 86.

Goleman, D. "A New Computer Test of the Brain," *Psychology Today*, 9 (May 1976), 44–48.

Goodenough, F. L. *Anger in Young Children*. Minneapolis: University of Minnesota Press, 1931.

Gordon, I. J., and B. J. Guinagh. "A Home Learning Center Approach to Early Stimulation." Final Report to the National Institute of Mental Health, Project No. R01 MH 16037-01. Gainesville: Institute for Development of Human Resources, University of Florida, 1974.

Gottlieb, D. E., S. E. Taylor, and A. Ruderman. "Cognitive Bases of Children's Moral Judgments," *Developmental Psychology*, 13 (1977), 547–556.

Gottman, J. M. "Toward a Definition of Social Isolation in Children," *Child Development*, 48 (1977), 513–517.

————, J. Gonso, and B. Rasmussen. "Social Interaction, Social Competence and Friendship in Children," *Child Development*, 46 (1975), 709–718.

Govatos, L. A. "Relationships and Age Differences in Growth Measures and Motor Skills," *Child Development*, 30 (1959), 333–340.

Gove, F. L., and D. P. Keating. "Empathic Role-Taking Precursors," *Developmental Psychology*, 14 (1979), 594–600.

Graham, D. *Moral Learning and Development: Theory and Research*. New York: Wiley, 1972.

Gratch, G. "Recent Studies Based on Piaget's View of Object Concept Development," in L. B. Cohen and P. Salapatek (eds.), *Infant Perception: From Sensation to Cognition*. Vol. 2: *Perception of Space, Speech, and Sound*. New York: Academic Press, 1975, pp. 51–99.

————, K. J. Appel, W. F. Evans, G. K. LeCompte, and N. A. Wright. "Piaget's Stage IV Object Concept Error: Evidence of Forgetting or Object Conception?" *Child Development*, 45 (1974), 71–77.

Green, R. "Children's Quest for Sexual Identity," *Psychology Today*, 7 (February 1974), 44–51.

Greenfield, P. M. "Informativeness, Presupposition, and Semantic Choice in Single-Word Utterances," in E. Ochs and B. B. Schieffelin (eds.), *Developmental Pragmatics*. New York: Academic Press, 1979, pp. 159–166.

————, and J. S. Bruner. "Culture and Cognitive Growth," *International Journal of Psychology*, 1 (1966), 89–107.

Griffin, D. R. *The Question of Animal Awareness*. New York: Rockefeller University Press, 1976.

Griffiths, R. *The Abilities of Babies*. New York: McGraw-Hill, 1954.

Grinker, J. "Effects of Metabolic State on Taste Parameters and Intake: Comparisons of Human and Animal Obesity," in J. M. Weiffenbach (ed.), *Taste and Development: The Genesis of Sweet Preference*. Bethesda, Md.: U. S. Department of Health, Education, and Welfare, 1977, pp. 309–327.

Gronlund, N. E. *Sociometry in the Classroom*. New York: Harper, 1959.

Grosser, D., N. Polansky, and R. Lippitt. "A Laboratory Study of Behavioral Contagion," *Human Relations*, 4 (1951), 115–142.

Gruendel, J. M. "Referential Overextension in Early Language Development," *Child Development*, 48 (1977), 1567–1576.

Grusec, J. E., L. Kuczynski, J. P. Rushton, and Z. M. Simutis. "Learning Resistance to Temptation Through Observation," *Developmental Psychology*, 15 (1979), 233–240.

———, and S. L. Skubiski. "Model Nurturance, Demand Characteristics of the Modeling Experiment, and Altruism," *Journal of Personality and Social Psychology*, 14 (1970), 352–359.

Guerrero, R. "Type and Time of Insemination Within the Menstrual Cycle and the Human Sex Ratio at Birth," *Studies of Family Planning*, 6 (1975), 367–371.

Guilford, J. P. "Theories of Intelligence," in B. B. Wolman (ed.), *Handbook of General Psychology*. Englewood Cliffs, N. J.: Prentice-Hall, 1973, pp. 630–643.

Guinagh, B. J., and I. J. Gordon. "School Performance as a Function of Early Stimulation," Final Report to the Office of Child Development, 1976.

Gump, P. V. "School Environments," in I. Altman and J. F. Wohlwill (eds.), *Children and the Environment*. New York: Plenum Press, 1978, pp. 131–174.

Gutteridge, M. V. "A Study of Motor Achievements of Young Children," *Archives of Psychology*, no. 244 (1939).

Guttman, D. "Parenthood: A Key to the Comparative Study of the Life Cycle," in N. Datan and L. H. Ginsberg (eds.), *Life-Span Developmental Psychology: Normative Life Crises*. New York: Academic Press, 1975, pp. 167–184.

Haaf, R. A. "Visual Response to Complex Facelike Patterns by 15- and 20-Week-Old Infants," *Developmental Psychology*, 13 (1977), 77–78.

Haan, N., M. B. Smith, and J. Block. "Moral Reasoning of Young Adults: Political-Social Behavior, Family Background, and Personality Correlates," *Journal of Personality and Social Psychology*, 10 (1968), 183–201.

Haber, R. N. "Visual Perception," in M. R. Rosenzweig and L. W. Porter (eds.), *Annual Review of Psychology*. Vol. 29. Palo Alto, Calif.: Annual Reviews, 1978, pp. 31–60.

———, and M. Hershenson. *The Psychology of Visual Perception*. New York: Holt, Rinehart and Winston, 1973.

Hagen, J. W., and G. H. Hale. "The Development of Attention in Children," in A. D. Pick (ed.), *Minnesota Symposia on Child Psychology*. Vol. 7. Minneapolis: University of Minnesota Press, 1973, pp. 117–140.

———, and N. Huntsman. "Selective Attention in Mental Retardates," *Developmental Psychology*, 5 (1971), 151–160.

———, and K. G. Stanovich. "Memory: Strategies of Acquisition," in R. V. Kail, Jr., and J. W. Hagen, *Perspectives on the Development of Memory and Cognition*. Hillsdale, N. J.: Lawrence Erlbaum, 1977, pp. 89–111.

Hainline, L. "Developmental Changes in the Visual Scanning of Face and Nonface Patterns by Infants," *Journal of Experimental Psychology*, 25 (1978), 90–115.

———, and E. Feig. "The Correlates of Father Absence in College-Aged Women," *Child Development*, 49 (1978), 37–42.

Haith, M. M. "The Responses of the Human Newborn to Visual Movement," *Journal of Experimental Child Psychology*, 3 (1966), 235–243.

———. *Rules That Babies Look By: The Organization of Newborn Visual Activity*. Hillsdale, N. J.: Lawrence Erlbaum, 1980.

———, T. Bergman, and M. J. Moore. "Eye Contact and Face Scanning in Early Infancy," *Science*, 198 (1977), 853–855.

Hall, E. "Will Success Spoil B. F. Skinner?" *Psychology Today*, 6 (November 1972), 65–72+.

———. "Acting One's Age: New Rules for Old," *Psychology Today*, 13 (April 1980), 66–81.

Hall, G. S. "Notes on the Study of Infants," *The Pedagogical Seminary*, 1 (1891), 127–138.

———. *Adolescence*. 2 vols. New York: Appleton, 1904.

Hamill, P. V., F. E. Johnston, and S. Lemeshow. *Height and Weight of Children: Socio-economic Status: United States*. Rockville, Md.: U. S. Department of Health, Education, and Welfare. Pub. No. HRA 73–1601, 1972.

Hammer, E. F. "Creativity and Feminine Ingredients in Young Male Artists," *Perceptual and Motor Skills*, 19 (1964), 414.

Harari, H., and J. W. McDavid. "Situational Influence on Moral Justice: A Study of 'Finking,'" *Journal of Personality and Social Psychology*, 3 (1969), 240–244.

———, and ———. "Teachers' Expectations and Name Stereotypes," *Journal of Educational Psychology*, 65 (1973), 222–225.

Hardyck, C., and F. Petrinovich. "Left-Handedness," *Psychological Bulletin*, 84 (1977), 385–404.

Harkness, S. "The Cultural Context of Child Development," in C. M. Super and S. Harkness (eds.), *New Directions for Child Development*. No. 8: *Anthropological Perspectives on Child Development*. San Francisco: Jossey-Bass, 1980, pp. 7–13.

Harlap, S. "Gender of Infants Conceived on Different Days of the Menstrual Cycle," *The New England Journal of Medicine*, 300 (1979), 1445–1448.

Harlow, H. F., and M. K. Harlow. "Learning to Love," *American Scientist*, 54 (1966), 244–272.

———, and ———. "Effects of Various Mother-Infant Relationships on Rhesus Monkey Behaviors," in B. M. Foss (ed.), *Determinants of Infant Behavior*. Vol. 4. London: Methuen, 1969, pp. 15–36.

Harrell, T. W., and M. S. Harrell. "Army General Classification Test Scores for Civilian Occupations," *Educational and Psychological Measurement*, 5 (1945), 229–239.

Harrison, C. W., J. R. Rawls, and D. J. Rawls. "Difference Between Leaders and Nonleaders in Six- to Eleven-Year-Old Children," *Journal of Social Psychology*, 84 (1971), 262–272.

Hartshorne, H., and M. A. May. *Studies in Deceit*. New York: Macmillan, 1928.

Hartup, W. W. "Friendship Status and the Effectiveness of Peers as Reinforcing Agents," *Journal of Experimental Child Psychology*, 1 (1964a), 154–162.

———. "Patterns of Imitative Behavior in Young Children," *Child Development*, 35 (1964b), 183–191.

———. "Peer Interaction and Social Organization," in P. H. Mussen (ed.), *Carmichael's Manual of Child Psychology*. Vol. 2. New York: Wiley, 1970, pp. 361–456.

———. "Aggression in Childhood: Developmental Perspectives," *American Psychologist*, 29 (1974), 336–341.

———. "The Social Worlds of Childhood," *American Psychologist*, 34 (1979), 944–950.

———, and B. Coates. "Imitation of a Peer as a Function of Reinforcement From the Peer Group and Rewardingness of the Model," *Child Development*, 38 (1967), 1003–1016.

———, J. A. Glazer, and R. Charlesworth. "Peer Reinforcement and Sociometric Status," *Child Development*, 38 (1967), 1017–1024.

Haynes, H., B. L. White, and R. Held. "Visual Accommodation in Human Infants," *Science*, 148 (1965), 528–530.

Hebb, D. O. *Organization of Behavior*. New York: Wiley, 1949.

Hecox, K. "Electrophysiological Correlates of Human Auditory Development," in L. B. Cohen and P. Salapatek (eds.), *Infant Perception: From Sensation to Cognition*. Vol. 2: *Perception of Space, Speech, and Sound*. New York: Academic Press, 1975, pp. 151–191.

Heider, E. R. "Universals in Color Naming and Memory," *Journal of Experimental Child Psychology*, 93 (1972), 10–20.

Helson, R. "Personality of Women with Imaginative and Artistic Interests: The Role of Masculinity, Originality, and Other Characteristics in Their Creativity," *Journal of Personality*, 34 (1966), 1–25.

———, and R. S. Crutchfield. "Mathematicians: The Creative Researcher and the Average Ph.D.," *Journal of Consulting and Clinical Psychology*, 34 (1970), 250–257.

Hermelin, B., and N. O'Connor. "Functional Asymmetry in the Reading of Braille," *Neuropsychologia*, 9 (1971), 431–435.

Hershenson, M. "Visual Discrimination in the Human Newborn," *Journal of Comparative and Physiological Psychology*, 58 (1964), 270–276.

Herzog, E., and C. E. Sudia. "Children in Fatherless Families," in B. M. Caldwell and H. N. Ricciuti (eds.), *Review of Child Development Research*. Vol. 3. Chicago: University of Chicago Press, 1973, pp. 141–232.

Hess, E. H. "Imprinting in Birds," *Science*, 146 (1964), 1128–1139.

———. "Imprinting in a Natural Laboratory," *Scientific American*, 227 (1972), 24–31.

Hess, R. D. "Political Attitudes in Children," *Psychology Today*, 2 (January 1969), 24–28.

———. "Social Class and Ethnic Influences on Socialization," in P. H. Mussen (ed.), *Carmichael's Manual of Child Psychology*. Vol. 2. 3rd ed. New York: Wiley, 1970, pp 457–557.

Hetherington, E. M. "Effects of Paternal Absence on Sex-Typed Behaviors in Negro and White Preadolescent Males," *Journal of Personality and Social Psychology*, 4 (1966), 87–91.

———. "Effects of Father Absence on Personality Development in Adolescent Daughters," *Developmental Psychology*, 7 (1972), 313–326.

———, M. Cox, and R. Cox. "Family Interaction and the Social, Emotional, and Cognitive Development of Children Following Divorce." Paper presented at the Symposium on the Family: Setting Priorities. Washington, D. C.: May 1978.

————, and J. Deur. "The Effects of Father Absence on Child Development," in W. W. Hartup and N. L. Smothergill (eds.), *The Young Child: Reviews of Research*. Vol. 2. Washington, D.C.: National Association for the Education of Young Children, 1972, pp. 303–319.

Hicks, D. J. "Imitation and Retention of Film-Mediated Aggressive Peer and Adult Models." *Journal of Personality and Social Psychology*, 2 (1965), 97–100.

————. "Girls' Attitudes Toward Modeled Behaviors and the Content of Imitative Private Play," *Child Development*, 42 (1971), 139–147.

Hicks, R. E., and M. Kinsbourne. "Human Handedness: A Partial Cross-Fostering Study," *Science*, 192 (1976), 908–910.

Higgins, E. T. "Social Class Differences in Verbal Communication Accuracy: A Question of 'Which Question'?" *Psychological Bulletin*, 83 (1976), 695–714.

Hill, R. B. *Strengths of Black Families*. New York: Emerson Hall, 1971.

Hirsch, H. V. B., and M. Jacobson. "The Perfectible Brain: Principles of Neuronal Development," in M. S. Gazzaniga and C. Blakemore (eds.), *Handbook of Psychology*. New York: Academic Press, 1975, pp. 107–140.

Hiscock, M., and M. Kinsbourne. "Selective Listening Asymmetry in Preschool Children," *Developmental Psychology*, 13 (1977), 217–224.

Hochberg, J. E., and V. Brooks. "Pictorial Recognition as an Unlearned Ability: A Study of One Child's Performance," *American Journal of Psychology*, 75 (1962), 625–628.

Hoffman, M. L. "Altruistic Behavior and the Parent-Child Relationship," *Journal of Personality and Social Psychology*, 31 (1975), 937–943.

————. "Empathy, Role Taking, Guilt, and the Development of Altruistic Motives," in T. Lickona (ed.), *Moral Development and Behavior: Theory, Research, and Social Issues*. New York: Holt, Rinehart and Winston, 1976, pp. 124–143.

————. "Moral Internalization: Current Theory and Research," in L. Berkowitz (ed.), *Advances in Experimental Social Psychology*. Vol. 10. New York: Academic Press, 1977a, pp. 85–133.

————. "Sex Differences in Empathy and Related Behaviors," *Psychological Bulletin*, 84 (1977b), 712–722.

————. "Development of Moral Thought, Feeling, and Behavior," *American Psychologist*, 34 (1979), 958–966.

————, and H. D. Saltzstein. "Parent Discipline and the Child's Moral Development," *Journal of Personality and Social Psychology*, 5 (1967), 45–57.

Hoffman, R. F. "Developmental Changes in Human Infant Visual-Evoked Potentials to Patterned Stimuli Recorded at Different Scalp Locations," *Child Development*, 49 (1978), 110–118.

Hogan, R. "Moral Conduct and Moral Character: A Psychological Perspective," *Psychological Bulletin*, 79 (1973), 217–232.

————. "Moral Development and the Structure of Personality," in D. J. DePalma and J. M. Foley (eds.), *Moral Development: Current Theory and Research*. Hillsdale, N. J.: Lawrence Erlbaum, 1975, pp. 153–167.

————, and N. P. Emler. "Moral Development," in M. E. Lamb (ed.), *Social and Personality Development*. New York: Holt, Rinehart and Winston, 1978, pp. 200–223.

Hollos, M., and P. A. Cowan. "Social Isolation and Cognitive Development: Logical Operations and Role-Taking Abilities in Three Norwegian Social Settings," *Child Development*, 44 (1973), 630–641.

Holmes, L. "How Fathers Can Cause the Down Syndrome," *Human Nature*, 1 (October 1978), 70–72.

Holstein, C. B. "Irreversible, Stepwise Sequences in the Development of Moral Judgment: A Longitudinal Study of Males and Females," *Child Development*, 47 (1976), 51–61.

Honess, T. "Self-Reference in Children's Descriptions of Peers: Egocentricity or Collaboration?" *Child Development*, 51 (1980), 476–480.

Honzik, M. P. "Developmental Studies of Parent-Child Resemblance in Intelligence," *Child Development*, 28 (1957), 215–228.

Hooker, D. *The Prenatal Origins of Behavior*. Lawrence: The University of Kansas Press, 1952.

Horn, J. L. "Organization of Data on Life-Span Development of Human Abilities," in L. R. Goulet and P. B. Baltes (eds.), *Life-Span Developmental Psychology: Research and Theory*. New York: Academic Press, 1970, pp. 423–466.

Horner, M. "Fail: Bright Women," *Psychology Today*, 3 (November 1969), 36–38.

Horowitz, F. D., J. Ashton, R. Culp, E. Gaddis, S. Levin, and B. Reichmann. "The Effects of Obstetrical Medication on the Behavior of Israeli Newborn Infants and Some Comparisons with

Uruguayan and American Infants," *Child Development*, 48 (1977), 1607–1623.

————, and L. Y. Paden. "The Effectiveness of Environmental Intervention Programs," in B. M. Caldwell and H. N. Ricciuti (eds.), *Review of Child Development Research*. Vol. 3. Chicago: University of Chicago Press, 1973, pp. 331–402.

Hubel, D. H. "The Brain," *Scientific American*, 241 (September 1979), 44–53.

————, and T. N. Wiesel. "Receptive Fields of Cells in Striate Cortex of Very Young, Visually Inexperienced Kittens," *Journal of Neurophysiology*, 26 (1963), 994–1002.

Hughes, M. "Egocentrism in Pre-School Children." Doctoral dissertation. Edinburgh University, 1975.

Humphrey, T. "The Development of Human Fetal Activity and Its Relation to Postnatal Behavior," in H. W. Reese and L. P. Lipsitt (eds.), *Advances in Child Development and Behavior*. Vol. 5. New York: Academic Press, 1970, pp. 2–59.

Hunt, E. "What Kind of Computer Is Man?" *Cognitive Psychology*, 2 (1971), 57–98.

————. "Varieties of Cognitive Power," in L. B. Resnick (ed.), *The Nature of Intelligence*. Hillsdale, N. J.: Lawrence Erlbaum, 1976, pp. 237–260.

Hutt, C. J. *Males and Females*. Baltimore: Penguin, 1972.

Huttenlocher, J., and C. C. Presson. "The Coding and Transformation of Spatial Information," *Cognitive Psychology*, 11 (1979), 375–394.

Hyman, I. A. "Psychology, Education, and Schooling," *American Psychologist*, 34 (1979), 1024–1029.

Hymel, S., and S. R. Asher. "Assessment and Training of Isolated Children's Social Skills." Paper presented at the Biennial Meeting of the Society for Research in Child Development. New Orleans, March 1977.

Iannotti, R. J. "Effect of Role-Taking Experiences on Role-Taking, Empathy, Altruism, and Aggression," *Developmental Psychology*, 14 (1978), 119–124.

Ingram, D. "Motor Asymmetries in Young Children," *Neuropsychologia*, 13 (1975a), 95–102.

————. "Cerebral Speech Lateralization in Young Children," *Neuropsychologia*, 13 (1975b), 103–105.

Inhelder, B. "Memory and Intelligence in the Child," in B. Inhelder and H. H. Chipman (eds.), *Piaget and His School*. New York: Springer-Verlag, 1976, pp. 100–120.

————, and J. Piaget. *The Growth of Logical Thinking From Childhood to Adolescence*. New York: Basic Books, 1958.

Interprofessional Task Force on Health Care of Women and Children. *The Development of Family-Centered Maternity/Newborn Care in Hospitals*. Chicago: International Task Force, 1978.

Ironsmith, M., and G. J. Whitehurst. "The Development of Listener Abilities in Communication: How Children Deal With Ambiguous Information," *Child Development*, 49 (1978a), 348–352.

————, and ————. "How Children Learn to Listen: The Effects of Modeling Feedback Styles on Children's Performance in Referential Communication," *Developmental Psychology*, 14 (1978b), 546–554.

Iverson, L. I. "The Chemistry of the Brain," *Scientific American*, 241 (September 1979), 134–149.

Jackson, E., J. J. Campos, and K. W. Fischer. "The Question of Decalage Between Object Permanence and Person Permanence," *Developmental Psychology*, 14 (1978), 1–10.

James, W. *The Principles of Psychology*. Vol. 1. New York: Dover, 1950 (orig. pub. 1890).

Jarvik, L. F., and D. Cohen. "A Biobehavioral Approach to Intellectual Changes With Aging," in C. Eisdorfer and M. P. Lawton (eds.), *The Psychology of Adult Development and Aging*. Washington, D. C.: American Psychological Association, 1973, pp. 220–280.

Jensen, A. R. "How Much Can We Boost IQ and Scholastic Achievement?" *Harvard Education Review*, 39 (1969), 1–123.

————. "Another Look at Culture Fair Testing," in J. Hellmuth (ed.), *The Disadvantaged Child (Compensatory Education: A National Debate*. Vol. 3). New York: Bruner-Mazel, 1970.

————, and W. D. Rohwer, Jr. "Syntactical Mediation of Serial and Paired-Associate Learning as a Function of Age," *Child Development*, 36 (1965), 601–608.

Jerison, H. J. *Evolution of the Brain and Intelligence*. New York: Academic Press, 1973.

Jersild, A. *In Search of Self: An Exploration of the Role of the School in Promoting Self-Understanding*. New York: Columbia University Press, 1952.

————, and F. B. Holmes. *Children's Fears*. New York: Columbia University Press, 1935.

Joffe, J. M. "Genotype and Prenatal and Premating

Stress Interact to Affect Adult Behavior in Rats," *Science*, 150 (1965), 1844–1845.

John, E. R. "How the Brain Works – A New Theory," *Psychology Today*, 9 (May 1976), 48–52.

Johnson, J. E., J. Ershler, and C. Bell. "Play Behavior in a Discovery-based and a Formal-Education Preschool Program," *Child Development*, 51 (1980), 275–278.

Johnson, P., and D. M. Salisbury. "Breathing and Sucking During Feeding in the Newborn," in *Parent-Infant Interaction*. Amsterdam: CIBA Foundation Symposium 33, new series, ASP, 1975.

Jones, K. L., D. W. Smith, A. P. Streissguth, and N. C. Myrianthopoulos. "Outcome in Offspring of Chronic Alcoholic Women," *Lancet*, 1 (1974), 1076–1078.

Jones, M. C. "The Later Careers of Boys Who Were Early- or Late-Maturing," *Child Development*, 28 (1957), 113–128.

———. "Psychological Correlates of Somatic Development," *Child Development*, 36 (1965), 899–911.

———, and N. Bayley. "Physical Maturing Among Boys as Related to Behavior," *Journal of Educational Psychology*, 41 (1950), 129–248.

Julesz, B. *Foundations of Cyclopean Perception*. Chicago: University of Chicago Press, 1971.

Jusczyk, P. W. "Perception of Syllable-Final Stop Consonants by 2-Month-Old Infants," *Perception and Psychophysics*, 21 (1977), 450–454.

Kagan, J. "The Concept of Identification," *Psychological Review*, 65 (1958), 296–305.

———. *Change and Continuity in Infancy*. New York: Wiley, 1971.

———. "Cognitive Development," in *Master Lecture Series*, American Psychological Association, 1976.

———. *The Growth of the Child*. New York: Norton, 1978.

———, R. B. Kearsley, and P. R. Zelazo. *Infancy: Its Place in Human Development*. Cambridge, Mass.: Harvard University Press, 1978.

———, and H. A. Moss. *Birth to Maturity: A Study in Psychological Development*. New York: Wiley, 1962.

———, and S. R. Tulkin. "Social Class Difference in Child Rearing During the First Year," in H. R. Schaffer (ed.), *The Origins of Human Social Relations: Proceedings, Centre for Advanced Study in the Developmental Sciences Study Group*. New York: Academic Press, 1971, pp. 165–186.

Kail, R. V., Jr., and J. W. Hagen. "Introduction," in R. V. Kail, Jr., and J. W. Hagen (eds.), *Perspectives on the Development of Memory and Cognition*. Hillsdale, N. J.: Lawrence Erlbaum, 1977, pp. xi–xiii.

Kamin, L. J. "Heredity, Intelligence, Politics, and Psychology." Invited address, Eastern Psychological Association. Washington, D. C., March 1973.

Kandel, D. B., and G. S. Lesser. *Youth in Two Worlds*. San Francisco: Jossey-Bass, 1972.

Kandel, E. R. "Small Systems of Neurons," *Scientific American*, 241 (September 1979), 66–87.

Kare, M. R. "Changes in Taste with Age – Infancy to Senescence," *Food Technology*, 29 (1975), 78–79.

Karmel, B. Z., H. Kaye, and E. R. John. "Developmental Neurometrics: The Use of Quantitative Analysis of Brain Electrical Activity to Probe Mental Function Throughout the Life Span," in W. A. Collins (ed.), *Minnesota Symposia on Child Psychology*. Vol. 11. Hillsdale, N. J.: Lawrence Erlbaum, 1978, pp. 141–198.

Karniol, R. "Children's Use of Intention Cues in Evaluating Behavior," *Psychological Bulletin*, 85 (1978), 76–85.

Kaye, K., and A. J. Wells. "Mothers' Jiggling and the Burst-Pause Pattern in Neonatal Feeding," *Infant Behavior and Development*, 3 (1980), 29–46.

Kearsley, R. B. "The Newborn's Response to Auditory Stimulation: A Demonstration of Orienting and Reflexive Behavior," *Child Development*, 44 (1973), 582–590.

———, P. R. Zelazo, J. Kagan, and R. Hartmann. "Separation Protest in Day-Care and Home-Reared Infants," *Pediatrics*, 55 (1975), 171–175.

Keeney, T. J., S. R. Cannizzo, and J. H. Flavell. "Spontaneous and Induced Verbal Rehearsal in a Recall Task," *Child Development*, 38 (1967), 953–966.

Keller, A., L. H. Ford, Jr., and J. A. Meacham. "Dimensions of Self-Concept in Preschool Children," *Developmental Psychology*, 14 (1978), 483–489.

Keller, B. B., and R. Q. Bell. "Child Effects on Adult's Method of Eliciting Altruistic Behavior," *Child Development*, 50 (1979), 1004–1009.

Kempe, R. S., and H. C. Kempe. *Child Abuse*. Cambridge, Mass.: Harvard University Press, 1978.

Kendler, H. H., and T. S. Kendler. "From Discrimination Learning to Cognitive Development: A Neobehavioristic Odyssey," in W. K. Estes (ed.), *Handbook of Learning and Cognitive Processes*. Vol. 1. Hillsdale, N. J.: Lawrence Erlbaum, 1975, pp. 191–247.

Kendler, T. S. "The Development of Discrimination Learning: A Levels-of-Functioning Explanation," in H. W. Reese and L. P. Lipsitt (eds.), *Advances in Child Development and Behavior*. Vol. 13. New York: Academic Press, 1979, pp. 83–117.

Kershner, J. R. "Ocular-Manual Laterality and Dual Hemisphere Specialization," *Cortex*, 10 (1974), 293–302.

Kessen, W., M. M. Haith, and P. H. Salapatek. "Human Infancy: Bibliography and Guide," in P. H. Mussen (ed.), *Carmichael's Manual of Child Psychology*. Vol. 1. 3rd ed. New York: Wiley, 1970, pp. 287–445.

———, J. Levine, and K. A. Wendich. "The Imitation of Pitch in Infants," *Infant Behavior and Development*, 2 (1979), 93–100.

Keyserling, M. D. *Windows on Day Care*. New York: National Council of Jewish Women, 1972.

Kimura, D. "The Asymmetry of the Human Brain," *Scientific American* (1975), 70–78.

Kinsbourne, M., and J. M. Swanson. "Developmental Aspects of Selective Orientation," in G. A. Hale and M. Lewis (eds.), *Attention and Cognitive Development*. New York: Plenum Press, 1979, pp. 119–134.

Kinsey, A. C., W. B. Pomeroy, and C. E. Martin. *Sexual Behavior in the Human Male*. Philadelphia: Saunders, 1948.

———, ———, ———, and P. H. Beghard. *Sexual Behavior in the Human Female*. Philadelphia: Saunders, 1953.

Kirkpatrick M., K. V. R. Smith, and R. Roy. "Adjustment and Sexual Identity of Children of Lesbian and Heterosexual Single Mothers," Paper presented at the Annual Meeting of the American Psychological Association. New York, September 1979.

Kirschenblatt-Gimblett, B. "Speech Play and Verbal Art," in B. Sutton-Smith (ed.), *Play and Learning*. New York: Gardner Press, 1979, pp. 219–238.

Klahr, D., and J. G. Wallace. *Cognitive Development: An Information-Processing View*. Hillsdale, N. J.: Lawrence Erlbaum, 1976.

Klima, E. S., and U. Bellugi. "Teaching Apes to Communicate," in G. A. Miller (ed.), *Communication, Language, and Meaning: Psychological Perspectives*. New York: Basic Books, 1973, pp. 95–106.

Kobasigawa, A. "Utilization of Retrieval Cues by Children in Recall," *Child Development*, 45 (1974), 127–134.

———. "Retrieval Strategies in the Development of Memory," in R. V. Kail, Jr., and J. W. Hagen (eds.), *Perspectives on the Development of Memory and Cognition*. Hillsdale, N. J.: Lawrence Erlbaum, 1977, pp. 177–201.

Koch, H. L. *Twins and Twin Relations*. Chicago: University of Chicago Press, 1966.

Koffka, K. *The Growth of the Mind*. 2nd ed. New York: Harcourt, 1931.

Kohlberg, L. "The Development of Children's Orientation Toward a Moral Order: I. Sequence in the Development of Moral Thought," *Vita Humana*, 6 (1963), 11–33.

———. "A Cognitive-Developmental Analysis of Children's Sex Role Concepts and Attitudes," in E. E. Maccoby (ed.), *The Development of Sex Differences*. Stanford, Calif.: Stanford University Press, 1966, pp. 82–173.

———. "Stage and Sequence: The Cognitive-Developmental Approach to Socialization," in D. A. Goslin (ed.), *Handbook of Socialization Theory and Research*. Chicago: Rand McNally, 1969, pp. 347–480.

———. "Education for Justice: A Modern Statement of the Platonic View," in N. F. and T. R. Sizer (eds.), *Moral Education: Five Lectures*. Cambridge, Mass.: Harvard University Press, 1970, pp. 56–83.

———. "Moral Stages and Moralization: The Cognitive-Developmental Approach," in T. Lickona (ed.), *Moral Development and Behavior*. New York: Holt, Rinehart and Winston, 1976, pp. 31–53.

———. "Revisions in the Theory and Practice of Moral Development," in W. Damon (ed.), *New Directions for Child Development*. No. 2: *Moral Development*. San Francisco: Jossey-Bass, 1978, pp. 83–87.

———, and C. Gilligan. "The Adolescent as a Philosopher: The Discovery of the Self in a Post-Conventional World," *Daedalus*, 100 (1971), 1051–1086.

Kohn, M. "The Effects of Social Class on Parental Values and Practices," in D. Reiss and H. A. Hoffman (eds.), *The American Family: Dying or Developing*. New York: Plenum Press, 1979, pp. 45–68.

Kolata, G. B. "Developmental Biology: Where Is It Going?" *Science*, 206 (1979), 315–316.

Konner, M. "Infancy Among the Kalahari San," in P. H. Leiderman, S. R. Tulkin, and A. Rosenfeld (eds.), *Culture and Infancy: Variations in the Human Experience*. New York: Academic Press, 1977, pp. 287–328.

Kopp, C. B., and A. H. Parmelee. "Prenatal and Peri-natal Influences on Infant Behavior," in J. D. Osof-sky (ed.), *Handbook of Infant Development*. New York: Wiley-Interscience, 1979, pp. 29–75.

―――, and J. Shaperman. "Cognitive Development in the Absence of Object Manipulation During In-fancy," *Developmental Psychology*, 9 (1973), 430.

Kornfeld, J. R. "Theoretical Issues in Child Phonol-ogy," *Proceedings of the Seventh Annual Meeting of the Chicago Linguistic Society* (CLS 7), University of Chicago, 1971, pp. 454–468.

Kosslyn, S. M. "The Representational-Development Hypothesis," in P. A. Ornstein, *Memory Develop-ment in Children*. Hillsdale, N. J.: Lawrence Erl-baum, 1978, pp. 157–190.

Krebs, D., and A. A. Adinolfi. "Physical Attractive-ness, Social Relations, and Personality Style," *Jour-nal of Personality and Social Psychology*, 31 (1975), 245–253.

Krebs, R. L. "Some Relationships Between Moral Judgment, Attention, and Resistance to Tempta-tion." Doctoral dissertation, University of Chicago, 1968.

Kremenitzer, J. P., H. G. Vaughan, Jr., D. Kurtzberg, and K. Dowling. "Smooth-Pursuit Eye Movements in the Newborn Infant," *Child Development*, 50 (1979), 442–448.

Kreutzer, M. A., C. Leonard, and J. H. Flavell. "An Interview Study of Children's Knowledge About Memory," *Monographs of the Society for Research in Child Development*, 40 (1975), whole no. 159.

Kuczaj, S. A., II. "Children's Judgments of Gram-matical and Ungrammatical Irregular Past-Tense Verbs," *Child Development*, 49 (1978), 319–326.

―――. "Evidence of a Language Learning Strategy: On the Relative Ease of Acquisition of Prefixes and Suffixes," *Child Development*, 50 (1979), 1–13.

Kumaresan, P., G. S. Han, P. B. Anandarangam, and A. Vasicka. "Oxytocin and Maternal and Fetal Blood," *Journal of Obstetrics and Gynecology*, Vol. 46, no. 3 (1975), 272–274.

Kun, A. "Evidence for Preschoolers' Understanding of Causal Direction in Extended Causal Se-quences," *Child Development*, 49 (1978), 218–222.

Kurdek, L. R. "Structural Components and Intellec-tual Correlates of Cognitive Perspective Taking in First- Through Fourth-Grade Children," *Child De-velopment*, 48 (1977), 1503–1511.

Kurtines, W., and E. B. Greif. "The Development of Moral Thought: Review and Evaluation of Kohl-berg's Approach," *Psychological Bulletin*, 8 (1974), 453–470.

Labov, W. "Contraction, Deletion and Inherent Vari-ability of the English Copula," *Language*, 45 (1969a), 715–762.

―――. "The Logic of Nonstandard English," *George-town Monographs on Languages and Linguistics*, Vol. 22 (1969b), pp. 1–31.

―――. *Language in the Inner City: Studies in the Black English Vernacular*. Philadelphia: University of Pennsylvania Press, 1973.

Ladd, G. W., and S. L. Oden. "The Relationship Be-tween Children's Ideas About Helpfulness and Peer Acceptance," *Child Development*, 50 (1979), 402–408.

Lamb, M. E. "Effects of Stress and Cohort on Mother- and Father-Infant Interaction," *Developmental Psy-chology*, 12 (1976a), 435–443.

―――. "Interactions Between Eight-Month-Old Children and Their Fathers and Mothers," in M. E. Lamb (ed.), *The Role of the Father in Child Develop-ment*. New York: Wiley, 1976b, pp. 307–328.

―――. "Twelve-Month-Olds and Their Parents: In-teraction in a Laboratory Playroom," *Developmental Psychology*, 12 (1976c), 237–244.

―――. "Father-Infant and Mother-Infant Interac-tion in the First Year of Life," *Child Development*, 48 (1977), 167–181.

―――. "Interactions Between Eighteen-Month-Olds and Their Preschool-Aged Siblings," *Child Devel-opment*, 49 (1978a), 51–59.

―――. "The Development of Sibling Relationships in Infants: A Short-Term Longitudinal Study," *Child Development*, 49 (1978b), 1189–1196.

―――. "Social Interaction in Infancy and the De-velopment of Personality," in M. E. Lamb (ed.), *Social and Personality Development*. New York: Holt, Rinehart and Winston, 1978c, pp. 26–49.

―――. "What Can 'Research Experts' Tell Parents About Effective Socialization?" in M. D. Fantini and R. Cardenas (eds.), *Parenting in a Multicultural Society*. London: Longmans, 1980.

―――. "The Development of Social Expectations in the First Year of Life," in M. E. Lamb and L. R. Sherrod (eds.), *Infant Social Cognition: Theoretical and Empirical Considerations*. Hillsdale, N. J.: Law-rence Erlbaum, 1981, pp. 155–175.

―――, and D. Baumrind. "Socialization and Personality Development in the Preschool Years," in M. E. Lamb (ed.), *Social and Personality Development*. New York: Holt, Rinehart and Winston, 1978.

———, and S. K. Bronson. "Fathers in the Context of Family Influences: Past, Present, and Future," *School Psychology Review*, 9 (1980), 336–353.

———, M. A. Easterbrooks, and G. W. Holden. "Reinforcement and Punishment Among Preschoolers: Characteristics, Effects, and Correlates," *Child Development*, 51 (1980), 1230–1236.

———, A. Frodi, C. P. Hwang, and M. Frodi. "Varying Degrees of Paternal Involvement in Infant Care: Additudinal and Behavioral Correlates," in M. E. Lamb (ed.), *Nontraditional Families: Parenting and Childrearing*. Hillsdale, N. J.: Lawrence Erlbaum, 1982.

———, and J. L. Roopnarine. "Peer Influences on Sex-Role Development in Preschoolers," *Child Development*, 50 (1979), 1219–1222.

———, and K. A. Urberg. "The Development of Gender Role and Gender Identity," in M. E. Lamb (ed.), *Social and Personality Development*. New York: Holt, Rinehart and Winston, 1978, pp. 178–199.

Lange, G. "Organization-Related Processes in Children's Recall," in P. A. Ornstein (ed.), *Memory Development in Children*. Hillsdale, N. J.: Lawrence Erlbaum, 1978, pp. 101–128.

Langlois, J. H., and C. F. Stephan. "The Effects of Physical Attractiveness and Ethnicity on Children's Behavioral Attributions and Peer Preferences," *Child Development*, 48 (1977), 1694–1698.

Laurendeau, M., and A. Pinard. *The Development of the Concept of Space in the Child*. New York: International Universities Press, 1970.

Leboyer, F. *Birth Without Violence*. New York: Knopf, 1975.

Lefebvre-Pinard, M., and L. Reid. "A Comparison of Three Methods of Training Communication Skills: Social Conflict, Modeling, and Conflict-Modeling," *Child Development*, 51 (1980), 179–187.

Leifer, A., and D. F. Roberts. "Children's Responses to Television Violence," in J. P. Murray, E. A. Rubenstein, and G. A. Comstock (eds.), *Television and Social Behavior*. Vol. 2: *Television and Social Learning*. Washington, D. C.: U. S. Government Printing Office, 1972, pp. 43–180.

Leiter, M. P. "A Study of Reciprocity in Preschool Play Groups," *Child Development*, 48 (1977), 1288–1295.

Lemoine, P., H. Haronsseau, P.-P. Borteryu, and J.-C. Menuet. "Les Infants de parents alcooliques: anomalies observées à propos de 127 cas," *Ouest Medical*, 25 (1968), 476–482.

Lempert, H. "Extrasyntactic Factors Affecting Passive Sentence Comprehension by Young Children," *Child Development*, 49 (1978), 694–699.

Lenneberg, E. H. "Speech as a Motor Skill With Special Reference to Nonaphasic Disorders," in U. Bellugi and R. Brown (eds.), "The Acquisition of Language," *Monographs of the Society for Research in Child Development*, Vol. 29 (1964), whole no. 92.

———. *Biological Foundations of Language*. New York: Wiley, 1967.

———. "Biological Aspects of Language," in G. A. Miller (ed.), *Communication, Language and Meaning*. New York: Basic Books, 1973, pp. 49–60.

Leopold, W. F. *Grammar and General Problems in the First Two Years*. Vol. 3: *Speech Development of a Bilingual Child: A Linguist's Record, 1939–49*. Evanston, Ill.: Northwestern University Press, 1949.

Lesser, G. S. *Children and Television: Lessons From Sesame Street*. New York: Random House, 1974.

Lester, B. M., M. Kotechuck, E. Spelke, M. J. Sellers, and R. E. Klein. "Separation Protest in Guatemalan Infants: Cross Cultural and Cognitive Findings," *Developmental Psychology*, 10 (1974), 79–84.

Leventhal, A. S., and L. P. Lipsitt. "Adaptation, Pitch Discrimination, and Sound Localization in the Neonate," *Child Development*, 35 (1964), 756–767.

Levitin, T. E., and J. D. Chananie. "Responses of Female Primary School Teachers to Sex-Typed Behaviors in Male and Female Children," *Child Development*, 43 (1972), 1309–1316.

Lewis, M. "A Developmental Study of Information Processing Within the First Three Years of Life: Response Decrement to a Redundant Signal," *Monographs of the Society for Research in Child Development*, Vol. 34 (1969), whole no. 133.

———, and J. Brooks. "Self, Other, and Fear: Infants' Reactions to People," in M. Lewis and L. Rosenblum (eds.), *The Origins of Fear. (The Origins of Behavior*. Vol. 2.) New York: Wiley, 1974.

———, and ———. "Infants' Social Perception: A Constructivist View," in L. B. Cohen and P. Salapatek (eds.), *Infant Perception: from Sensation to Cognition*. Vol. 2: *Perception of Space, Speech, and Sound*. New York: Academic Press, 1975, pp. 102–148.

Lewis, M., and R. Freedle. "The Mother-Infant Dyad,"

in P. Pliner, L. Kranes, and T. Alloway (eds.), *Communication and Affect: Language and Thought.* New York: Academic Press, 1973.

Liben, L. S. "Memory in the Context of Cognitive Development: The Piagetian Approach," in R. V. Kail, Jr., and J. W. Hagen (eds.), *Perspectives on the Development of Memory and Cognition.* Hillsdale, N. J.: Lawrence Erlbaum, 1977, pp. 297–332.

————. "Perspective-Taking Skills in Young Children: Seeing the World Through Rose-Colored Glasses," *Developmental Psychology,* 14 (1978), 87–92.

Lickona, T. "Research on Piaget's Theory of Moral Development," in T. Lickona (ed.), *Moral Development and Behavior.* New York: Holt, Rinehart and Winston, 1976, pp. 219–240.

Lieberman, A. F. "Preschoolers' Competence with a Peer: Relations with Attachment and Peer Experience," *Child Development,* 48 (1977), 1277–1287.

Liebert, R. M., and R. A. Baron. "Some Immediate Effects of Televised Violence on Children's Behavior," *Developmental Psychology,* 6 (1972), 467–475.

————, R. B. McCall, and M. A. Hanratty. "Effects of Sex-Typed Information on Children's Toy Preferences," *Journal of Genetic Psychology,* 119 (1971), 133–136.

Lind, J. "The Infant Cry," *Proceedings of the Royal Society of Medicine,* 64 (1971), 468.

Lindgren, G. "Height, Weight, and Menarche in Swedish Urban Schoolchildren in Relation to Socioeconomic and Regional Factors," *Annals of Human Biology,* 3 (1976), 510–528.

Lipsitt, L. P. "Learning in the Human Infant," in H. W. Stevenson, E. H. Hess, and H. L. Rheingold (eds.), *Early Behavior: Comparative and Developmental Approaches.* New York: Wiley, 1967, pp. 225–247.

————. "Critical Conditions in Infancy," *American Psychologist,* 34 (1979), 973–980.

————, W. Q. Sturner, and B. Burke. "Perinatal Indicators and Subsequent Crib Death," *Infant Behavior and Development,* 2 (1979), 325–328.

Livesley, W. J., and D. B. Bromley. *Person Perception in Childhood and Adolescence.* New York: Wiley, 1973.

Locke, J. *An Essay Concerning Human Understanding.* Oxford: Clarendon Press, 1894 (orig. pub. 1690).

Locke, J. L. "Phonemic Effects in the Silent Reading of Hearing and Deaf Children," *Cognition,* 6 (1978), 175–187.

————. "The Child's Processing of Phonology," in W. A. Collins (ed.), *Minnesota Symposia on Child Psychology.* Vol. 12: *Children's Language and Communication.* Hillsdale, N. J.: Lawrence Erlbaum, 1979, pp. 83–120.

————, and K. J. Kurz. "Memory for Speech and Speech for Memory," *Journal of Speech and Hearing Research,* 18 (1975), 176–191.

Loftus, E. F., and J. C. Palmer. "Reconstruction of Automobile Destruction: An Example of the Interaction Between Language and Memory," *Journal of Verbal Learning and Verbal Behavior,* 13 (1974), 585–589.

Lomas, J., and D. Kimura. "Intrahemispheric Interaction Between Speaking and Sequential Manual Activity," *Neuropsychologia,* 14 (1976), 23–33.

Lorch, E. P., D. R. Anderson, and S. R. Levin. "The Relation of Visual Attention to Children's Comprehension of Television," *Child Development,* 50 (1979), 722–727.

Lorenz, K. "Die Angeborenen formen möglicher Erfahrung," *Zeitschrift für Tierpsychologie,* 5 (1942–1943), 235–409.

————. *Evolution and Modification of Behavior.* Chicago: University of Chicago Press, 1965.

————. *On Aggression.* New York: Harcourt, Brace and World, 1966.

Lovell, K., and E. Ogilvie. "A Study of the Conservation of Weight in the Junior School Child," *British Journal of Educational Psychology,* 31 (1961), 138–144.

Lynch, A. M. "Ill-Health and Child Abuse," *Lancet,* 16 August 1975, p. 317.

Maccoby, E. E. "Sex Differentiation During Childhood Development," in *Master Lecture Series.* American Psychological Association, 1976.

————, and C. Jacklin. *The Psychology of Sex Differences.* Stanford, Calif.: Stanford University Press, 1974.

————, and ————. "Sex Differences in Aggression: A Rejoinder and Reprise," *Child Development,* 51 (1980), 964–980.

Macfarlane, A. *The Psychology of Childbirth.* Cambridge, Mass.: Harvard University Press, 1977.

————, P. Harris, and I. Barnes. "Central and Peripheral Vision in Early Infancy," *Journal of Experimental Child Psychology,* 21 (1976), 532–538.

MacKinnon, D. W. "The Nature and Nurture of Creative Talent," *American Psychologist,* 17 (1962), 484–495.

MacLean, P. D. "The Triune Brain, Emotion, and

Scientific Bias," in F. O. Schmitt (ed.), *The Neurosciences: Second Study Program*. New York: Rockefeller University Press, 1970.

Magoun, H. W., L. Darling, and J. Prost. "The Evolution of Man's Brain," in J. F. Lubar (ed.), *A First Reader in Physiological Psychology*. New York: Harper & Row, 1972, pp. 35–47.

Mahan, A., and T. Mahan. "Changes in Cognitive Style: An Analysis of the Impact of White Suburban Schools on Inner-City Children," *Integrated Education*, 8 (1970), 58–61.

Maller, O., and J. A. Desor. "Effect of Taste on Ingestion by Human Infants," in J. Bosma (ed.), *Oral Sensation and Perception: Development in the Fetus and Infant*. Washington, D. C.: U. S. Government Printing Office, 1974, pp. 279–291.

Mans, L., D. Cicchetti, and L. A. Sroufe. "Mirror Reaction of Down's Syndrome Infants and Toddlers: Cognitive Underpinnings of Self-Recognition," *Child Development*, 49 (1978), 1247–1250.

Maratsos, M., S. A. Kuczaj, II, D. E. C. Fox, and M. A. Chalkley. "Some Empirical Studies in the Acquisition of Transformational Relations: Passives, Negatives, and the Past Tense," in W. A. Collins (ed.), *Minnesota Symposia on Child Psychology*. Vol. 12. Hillsdale, N. J.: Lawrence Erlbaum, 1979, pp. 1–46.

Marcus, D. E., and W. F. Overton. "The Development of Cognitive Gender-Constancy and Sex Role Preference," *Child Development*, 49 (1978), 434–444.

Marcus, T. L., and D. A. Corsini. "Parental Expectations of Preschool Children as Related to Child Gender and Socioeconomic Status," *Child Development*, 49 (1978), 243–246.

Markman, E. M. "Factors Affecting the Young Child's Ability to Monitor His Memory." Doctoral dissertation. University of Pennsylvania, Philadelphia, 1973a.

––––––. "The Facilitation of Part-Whole Comparisons by Use of the Collective Noun 'Family'," *Child Development*, 44 (1973b), 837–840.

––––––. "Classes and Collections: Conceptual Organization and Numerical Abilities," *Cognitive Psychology*, 11 (1979), 395–411.

––––––, and J. Siebert. "Classes and Collections: Internal Organization and Resulting Holistic Properties," *Cognitive Psychology*, 8 (1976), 561–577.

Martin, M. F., D. M. Gelfand, and D. P. Hartmann. "Effects of Adult and Peer Observers on Boys' and Girls' Responses to an Aggressive Model," *Child Development*, 42 (1971), 1271–1275.

Martin, R. M. "Effects of Familiar and Complex Stimuli on Infant Attention," *Developmental Psychology*, 11 (1975), 178–185.

Mason, W. A., and M. D. Kenney. "Redirection of Filial Attachments in Rhesus Monkeys: Dogs as Mother Surrogates," *Science*, 183 (1974), 1209–1211.

Masur, E. F. "Preschool Boys' Speech Modifications: The Effect of Listeners' Linguistic Levels and Conversational Responses," *Child Development*, 49 (1978), 924–927.

Matas, L., R. A. Arend, and L. A. Sroufe. "Continuity of Adaptation in the Second Year: The Relationship Between Quality of Attachment and Later Competence," *Child Development*, 49 (1978), 547–556.

Maurer, D. "Infant Visual Perception: Methods of Study," in L. B. Cohen and P. Salapatek (eds.), *Infant Perception: From Sensation to Cognition*. Vol. 1: *Basic Visual Processes*. New York: Academic Press, 1975, pp. 1–76.

––––––, and T. L. Lewis. "Peripheral Discrimination by Three-Month-Old Infants," *Child Development*, 50 (1979), 276–279.

––––––, and P. Salapatek. "Developmental Changes in the Scanning of Faces by Infants," *Child Development*, 47 (1976), 523–527.

McCall, R. B. "Attention in the Infant: Avenue to the Study of Cognitive Development," in D. N. Walcher and D. L. Peters (eds.), *Early Childhood: The Development of Self-Regulatory Mechanisms*. New York: Academic Press, 1971, pp. 107–140.

––––––. "Childhood IQ's as Predictors of Adult Educational and Occupational Status," *Science*, 197 (1977), 482–483.

––––––. "The Development of Intellectual Functioning in Infancy and the Prediction of Later IQ," in J. D. Osofsky (ed.), *Handbook of Infant Development*. New York: Wiley-Interscience, 1979a, pp. 707–741.

––––––. "Stages in Play Development Between Zero and Two Years of Age," in B. Sutton-Smith (ed.), *Play and Learning*. New York: Gardner Press, 1979b, pp. 35–44.

––––––, M. I. Appelbaum, and P. S. Hogarty. "Developmental Changes in Mental Performance," *Monographs of the Society for Research in Child Development*, 38 (1973), whole no. 150.

McCallum, C. "The Contingent Negative Variation

as a Cortical Sign of Attention in Man," in C. R. Evans and T. B. Mulholland (eds.), *Attention in Neurophysiology*. London: Butterworth, 1969, pp. 40–54.

McCarthy, D. "Language Development in Children," in L. Carmichael (ed.), *Manual of Child Psychology*. 2nd ed. New York: Wiley, 1954, pp. 492–630.

McClearn, G. E. "Genetic Influences on Behavior and Development," in P. H. Mussen (ed.), *Carmichael's Manual of Child Psychology*. Vol. 1. 3rd ed. New York: Wiley, 1970, pp. 39–76.

McClelland, D. C. "Testing for Competence Rather Than for Intelligence," *American Psychologist*, 28 (1973), 1–14.

McDavid, J. W., and H. Harari. "Stereotyping of Names and Popularity in Grade School Children," *Child Development*, 37 (1966), 453–459.

McGraw, M. B. *Growth: A Study of Johnny and Jimmy*. New York: Appleton-Century-Crofts, 1935.

————. "Later Development of Children Specially Trained During Infancy: Johnny and Jimmy at School Age," *Child Development*, 10 (1939), 1–19.

McGuinness, D. "How Schools Discriminate Against Boys," *Human Nature*, 2 (February 1979), 82–88.

McMichael, R. E., and R. E. Grinder. "Children's Guilt After Transgression: Combined Effect of Exposure to American Culture and Ethnic Background," *Child Development*, 37 (1966), 425–431.

McNeill, D. *The Acquisition of Language*. New York: Harper & Row, 1970.

McQueen, A. J. "The Adaptation of Urban Black Families: Trends, Problems, and Issues," in D. Reiss and H. A. Hoffman (eds.), *The American Family: Dying or Developing*. New York: Plenum Press, 1979, pp. 79–101.

Meacham, J. A. "Soviet Investigations of Memory Development," in R. V. Kail, Jr., and J. W. Hagen (eds.), *Perspectives on the Development of Memory and Cognition*. Hillsdale, N. J.: Lawrence Erlbaum, 1977, pp. 273–295.

Mead, M. *Coming of Age in Samoa: A Psychological Study in Primitive Youth for Western Civilization*. New York: Dell, 1968.

————, and N. Newton. "Cultural Patterning of Perinatal Behavior," in S. A. Richardson and A. F. Guttmacher (eds.), *Childbearing: Its Social and Psychological Factors*. Baltimore: Williams & Wilkins, 1967.

Means, B. M., and W. D. Rohwer, Jr. "A Develop-

mental Study of the Effects of Adding Verbal Analogs to Pictured Paired Associates." Unpublished paper. University of California, Berkeley, 1974.

Meichenbaum, D. H., and J. Goodman. "Training Impulsive Children to Talk to Themselves: A Means of Developing Self-Control," *Journal of Abnormal Psychology*, 77 (1971), 115–126.

Mendelson, M. J., and M. M. Haith. "The Relation Between Audition and Vision in the Human Newborn," *Monographs of the Society for Research in Child Development*, 41 (1976), whole no. 167.

Menyuk, P. *The Acquisition and Development of Language*. Englewood Cliffs, N. J.: Prentice-Hall, 1971.

————, and N. Bernholtz. "Prosodic Features and Children's Language Production," *M.I.T. Research Laboratory of Electronics Quarterly Progress Reports*, no. 93 (1969), 216–219.

Menzel, E. W., Jr., R. K. Davenport, Jr., and C. M. Rogers. "The Effect of Environmental Restriction Upon the Chimpanzee's Responsiveness to Objects," *Journal of Comparative and Physiological Psychology*, 56 (1963), 78–85.

Mercer, J. R. "IQ: The Lethal Label," *Psychology Today*, 6 (September 1972), 44–47+.

Meredith, H. V. "Change in the Stature and Body Weight of North American Boys During the Last 80 Years," in L. P. Lipsitt and C. C. Spiker (eds.), *Advances in Child Development and Behavior*. Vol. 1. New York: Academic Press, 1963, pp. 69–114.

————. "A Synopsis of Pubertal Changes in Youth," *Journal of School Health*, 37 (1967), 171–176.

Meyers, L. "The Relationship Between Substitute Child Care, Maternal Employment, and Female Marital Satisfaction," in D. Peters (ed.), *A Summary of the Pennsylvania Day Care Study*. University Park: Pennsylvania State University, 1973.

Michaels, R. H., and G. W. Mellin. "Prospective Experience With Maternal Rubella and the Associated Congenital Malformations," *Pediatrics*, 26 (1960), 200–209.

Midlarsky, E., and J. H. Bryan. "Training Charity in Children," *Journal of Personality and Social Psychology*, 5 (1967), 408–415.

Milewski, A. E. "Visual Discrimination and Detection of Configural Invariance in 3-Month Infants," *Developmental Psychology*, 15 (1979), 357–363.

Milgram, S. "Behavioral Study of Obedience," *Journal of Abnormal and Social Psychology*, 67 (1963), 371–378.

————. *Obedience to Authority*. New York: Harper & Row, 1974.

Millar, W. S. "A Study of Operant Conditioning Under Delayed Reinforcement in Early Infancy," *Monographs of the Society for Research in Child Development*, 37 (1972), whole no. 147.

Miller, D. R., and G. E. Swanson. *Inner Conflict and Defense*. New York: Holt, Rinehart and Winston, 1966.

Miller, G. A. "The Magical Number Seven, Plus or Minus Two: Some Limits on Our Capacity for Processing Information," *Psychological Review*, 63 (1956), 81–96.

————. *Spontaneous Apprentices*. New York: Seabury Press, 1977.

————. "The Acquisition of Word Meaning," *Child Development*, 49 (1978a), 999–1004.

————. "Reconsiderations: *Language, Thought, and Reality*," *Human Nature*, 1 (June 1978b), 92–96.

Miller, N. E., and J. Dollard. *Social Learning and Imitation*. New Haven, Conn.: Yale University Press, 1941.

Miller, W. R. "The Acquisition of Formal Features of Language," *American Journal of Orthopsychiatry*, 34 (1964), 862–867.

————, and S. Ervin. "The Development of Grammar in Child Language," in *Cognitive Development in Children*. Chicago: University of Chicago Press, 1970, pp. 309–334.

Milner, B. "CNS Maturation and Language Acquisition," in H. Whitaker and H. A. Whitaker (eds.), *Studies in Neurolinguistics*. Vol. 1, New York: Academic Press, 1976.

Minkowski, A. (ed.), *Regional Development of the Brain in Early Life*. Oxford: Blackwell, 1967.

Mirabile, P. J., R. J. Porter, Jr., L. F. Hughes, and C. I. Berlin. "Dichotic Lag Effect in Children 7 to 15," *Developmental Psychology*, 14 (1978), 277–285.

Mischel, W. "Theory and Research on the Antecedents of Self-Imposed Delay of Reward," in B. A. Maher (ed.), *Progress in Experimental Personality Research*. Vol. 3. New York: Academic Press, 1966, pp. 85–132.

————, and N. Baker. "Cognitive Appraisals and Transformations in Delay Behavior," *Journal of Personality and Social Psychology*, 31 (1975), 254–261.

————, and H. Mischel. "A Cognitive Social-Learning Approach to Morality and Self-Regulation," in T. Lickona (ed.), *Moral Development and Behavior*.

New York: Holt, Rinehart and Winston, 1976, pp. 84–107.

Miscione, J. L., R. S. Marvin, R. G. O'Brien, and M. T. Greenberg. "A Developmental Study of Preschool Children's Understanding of the Words 'Know' and 'Guess'," *Child Development*, 49 (1978), 1107–1113.

Moely, B. E. "Organizational Factors in the Development of Memory," in R. V. Kail, Jr., and J. W. Hagen (eds.), *Perspectives on the Development of Memory and Cognition*. Hillsdale, N. J.: Lawrence Erlbaum, 1977, pp. 203–236.

Mogford, K. "The Play of Handicapped Children," in B. Tizard and D. Harvey (eds.), *Biology of Play*. Philadelphia: Lippincott, 1977, pp. 170–184.

Mohr, D. M. "Development of Attributes of Personal Identity," *Developmental Psychology*, 14 (1978), 427–428.

Molfese, D. L., R. B. Freeman, Jr., and D. S. Palermo. "The Ontogeny of Brain Lateralization for Speech and Nonspeech Stimuli," *Brain and Language*, 2 (1975), 356–368.

————, and V. J. Molfese. "Hemisphere and Stimulus Differences as Reflected in the Cortical Responses of Newborn Infants to Speech Stimuli," *Developmental Psychology*, 15 (1979), 505–511.

Money, J., and A. A. Ehrhardt. *Man and Woman, Boy and Girl*. Baltimore: Johns Hopkins University Press, 1972.

Montemayor, R., and M. Eisen. "The Development of Self-Conceptions From Childhood to Adolescence," *Developmental Psychology*, 13 (1977), 314–319.

Moore, B. S., S. Clyburn, and B. Underwood. "The Role of Affect in Delay of Gratification," *Child Development*, 47 (1976), 273–276.

Moore, M. J., J. Kagan, and M. M. Haith. "Memory and Motives," *Developmental Psychology*, 14 (1978), 563–564.

Moore, S. G. "Correlates of Peer Acceptance in Nursery School Children," in W. W. Hartup and N. L. Smothergill (eds.), *The Young Child*. Washington, D. C.: National Association for the Education of Young Children, 1967.

Moore, T. "Exclusive Early Mothering and Its Alternatives: The Outcome to Adolescence," *Scandinavian Journal of Psychology*, 16 (1975), 255–272.

Morgan, G. A., and H. N. Ricciuti. "Infants' Responses to Strangers During the First Year," in

B. M. Foss (ed.), *Determinants of Infant Behavior*. Vol. 4. London: Methuen, 1969, pp. 253–272.

Moro, E. "Das Erste Timenon," *Münchener Medizinische Wochenschrift*, 65 (1918), 1147–1150.

Moss, H. A. "Early Sex Differences and Mother-Infant Interaction," in R. C. Friedman, R. N. Richard and R. L. Van de Wiele (eds.), *Sex Differences in Behavior*. New York: Wiley, 1974.

Moyer, K. E. *The Physiology of Hostility*. Chicago: Markham, 1971.

Muir, D., and J. Field. "Newborn Infants Orient to Sounds," *Child Development*, 50 (1979), 431–436.

Mundy-Castle, A. C., and J. Anglin. "The Development of Looking in Infancy." Paper presented at the Biennial Meeting of the Society for Research in Child Development. Santa Monica, Calif., 1969.

Murray, A. D., R. M. Dolby, R. L. Nation, and D. P. Thomas. "The Effects of Epidural Anesthesia on Newborns and Their Mothers," *Child Development*, 52 (1981), 71–82.

Murray, F. S., and J. M. Szymczyk. "Effects of Distinctive Features on Recognition of Incomplete Pictures," *Developmental Psychology*, 14 (1978), 356–362.

Murray, J. P., and S. Kippax. "From the Early Window to the Late Night Show: International Trends in the Study of Television's Impact on Children and Adults," in L. Berkowitz (ed.), *Advances in Experimental Social Psychology*. Vol. 12. New York: Academic Press, 1979, pp. 322–352.

Muson, H. "Moral Thinking: Can It Be Taught?" *Psychology Today*, 12 (February 1979), 48–68+.

Mussen, P., and N. Eisenberg-Berg. *Roots of Caring, Sharing, and Helping: The Development of Prosocial Behavior in Children*. San Francisco: Freeman, 1977.

———, and M. C. Jones. "Self-Conceptions, Motivations, and Interpersonal Attitudes of Late- and Early-Maturing Boys," *Child Development*, 28 (1957), 243–256.

Muuss, R. E. "Adolescent Development and the Secular Trend," *Adolescence*, 5 (1970), 267–284.

Myers, N. A., and M. Perlmutter. "Memory in the Years From Two to Five," in P. A. Ornstein (ed.), *Memory Development in Children*. Hillsdale, N. J.: Lawrence Erlbaum, 1978, pp. 191–218.

Nagy, M. "The Child's View of Death," *Journal of Genetic Psychology*, 73 (1948), 2–27.

National Childcare Consumer Study (contract 105-74-1107). Washington, D. C.: Office of Child Development, Department of Health, Education, and Welfare, 1975.

Naus, M. J., P. A. Ornstein, and S. Aivano. "Developmental Changes in Memory: The Effects of Processing Time and Rehearsal Instructions," *Journal of Experimental Child Psychology*, 23 (1977), 237–251.

———, ———, and K. L. Hoving. "Developmental mental Implications of Multistore and Depth-of-Processing Models of Memory," in P. A. Ornstein (ed.), *Memory Development in Children*. Hillsdale, N. J.: Lawrence Erlbaum, 1978, pp. 219–232.

Neimark, E. D. "Intellectual Development During Adolescence," in F. D. Horowitz (ed.), *Review of Child Development Research*. Vol. 4. Chicago: University of Chicago Press, 1975, pp. 541–594.

Neisser, U. "Academic and Artificial Intelligence," in L. B. Resnick (ed.), *The Nature of Intelligence*. Hillsdale, N. J.: Lawrence Erlbaum, 1976, pp. 135–144.

Nelson, K. "Structure and Strategy in Learning to Talk," *Monographs of the Society for Research in Child Development*, 38 (1973), whole no. 149.

———. "Semantic Development and the Development of Semantic Memory," in K. E. Nelson (ed.), *Children's Language*. Vol. 1. New York: Gardner Press, 1978, pp. 39–80.

———. "Explorations in the Development of a Functional Semantic System," in W. A. Collins (ed.), *Minnesota Symposia on Child Psychology*. Vol. 12. Hillsdale, N. J.: Lawrence Erlbaum, 1979, pp. 47–82.

———, L. Rescorla, J. Gruendel, and H. Benedict. "Early Lexicons: What Do They Mean?" *Child Development*, 49 (1978), 960–968.

Nelson, K. E., and S. M. Kosslyn. "Recognition of Previously Labeled or Unlabeled Pictures by 5-Year-Olds and Adults," *Journal of Experimental Child Psychology*, 21 (1976), 40–45.

———, and K. Nelson. "Cognitive Pendulums and Their Linguistic Realization," in K. E. Nelson (ed.), *Children's Language*. Vol. 1. New York: Gardner Press, 1978, pp. 223–286.

Newcomb, A. F., and W. A. Collins. "Children's Comprehension of Family Role Portrayals in Televised Dramas: Effects of Socioeconomic Status, Ethnicity, and Age," *Developmental Psychology*, 15 (1979), 417–423.

Newman, L. "Two Children: A Study in Contrasts,"

in P. J. Fine (ed.), *Deafness in Infancy and Early Childhood*. New York: Medcom, 1974, pp. 162–186.

Newton, N. "Putting the Child Back in Childbirth," *Psychology Today*, 9 (August 1975), 24–25.

———. "Key Psychological Issues in Human Lactation," in L. R. Waletzky (ed.), *Symposium on Human Lactation*. No. HSA 79-5107. Rockville, Md.: Department of Health, Education, and Welfare, 1979, pp. 25–37.

Ochs, E. "Introduction: What Child Language Can Contribute to Pragmatics," in E. Ochs and B. B. Schieffelin (eds.), *Developmental Pragmatics*. New York: Academic Press, 1979, pp. 1–17.

Oden, M. H. "The Fulfillment of Promise: 40-Year Follow-Up of the Terman Gifted Group," *Genetic Psychology Monographs*, 77 (1968), 3–93.

Oden, S., and S. R. Asher. "Coaching Children in Social Skills for Friendship Making," *Child Development*, 48 (1977), 495–506.

Office of the Surgeon General. *Television and Growing Up: The Impact of Televised Violence*. Washington, D. C.: U. S. Government Printing Office, 1972.

Oller, D. K., L. A. Wieman, W. J. Doyle, and C. Ross. "Infant Babbling and Speech," *Journal of Child Language*, 3 (1976), 1–12.

Olsho, L. W. "Frequency Discrimination in Young Infants." Paper presented at the Annual Meeting of the American Psychological Association. New York, September 1979.

Olson, D. R. "Some Social Aspects of Meaning in Oral and Written Language," in D. R. Olson (ed.), *The Social Foundations of Language and Thought*. New York: Norton, 1980, pp. 90–108.

Olweus, D. "Aggression and Peer Acceptance in Adolescent Boys: Two Short-Term Longitudinal Studies of Ratings," *Child Development*, 48 (1977), 1301–1313.

Ornstein, P. A. (ed.). *Memory Development in Children*. Hillsdale, N. J.: Lawrence Erlbaum, 1978.

———, and M. J. Naus. "Rehearsal Processes in Children's Memory," in P. A. Ornstein (ed.), *Memory Development in Children*. Hillsdale, N. J.: Lawrence Erlbaum, 1978, pp. 69–99.

———, ———, and C. Liberty. "Rehearsal and Organizational Processes in Children's Memory," *Child Development*, 26 (1975), 818–830.

Ornstein, R. E. "The Split and Whole Brain," *Human Nature*, 1 (May 1978), 76–83.

Osborn, D. K., and R. C. Endsley. "Emotional Reactions of Young Children to TV Violence," *Child Development*, 41 (1971), 321–331.

Osler, S. F., and E. Kofsky. "Stimulus Uncertainty as a Variable in the Development of a Conceptual Ability," *Journal of Experimental Child Psychology*, 2 (1965), 264–279.

Osofsky, J. D., and K. Connors. "Mother-Infant Interaction: An Integrative View of a Complex System," in J. D. Osofsky (ed.), *Handbook of Infant Development*. New York: Wiley-Interscience, 1979, pp. 519–548.

Overton, D. "High Education," *Psychology Today*, 3 (November 1969), 48–51.

Overton, W. F., and H. W. Reese. "Models of Development: Methodological Implications," in J. R. Nesselroade and H. W. Reese (eds.), *Life-Span Developmental Psychology: Methodological Issues*. New York: Academic Press, 1973, pp. 65–86.

Palermo, D. S., and D. L. Molfese. "Language Acquisition From Age Five Onward," *Psychological Bulletin*, 78 (1972), 409–428.

Papousek, H., and M. Papousek. "Interdisciplinary Parallels in Studies of Early Human Behavior: From Physical to Cognitive Needs, From Attachment to Dyadic Education," *International Journal of Behavioral Development*, 1 (1978), 37–49.

Parke, R. D. "Children's Home Environments: Social and Cognitive Effects," in I. Altman and J. F. Wohlwill (eds.), *Children and the Environment*. New York: Plenum Press, 1978, pp. 33–81.

———, and C. W. Collmer. "Child Abuse: An Interdisciplinary Analysis," in E. M. Hetherington (ed.), *Review of Child Development Research*. Vol. 5. Chicago: University of Chicago Press, 1975, pp. 509–590.

———, and D. B. Sawin. "The Father's Role in Infancy: A Re-evaluation," *The Family Coordinator*, 25 (1976), 365–371.

Parmalee, A. H., W. H. Wenner, and H. R. Schulz. "Infant Sleep Patterns: From Birth to 16 Weeks of Age," *Journal of Pediatrics*, 65 (1964), 576–582.

Patterson, C. J., J. M. Cosgrove, and R. G. O'Brien. "Nonverbal Indicants of Comprehension and Noncomprehension in Children," *Developmental Psychology*, 16 (1980), 38–48.

Patterson, G. R., and J. A. Cobb. "Stimulus Control for Classes of Noxious Behaviors," in J. F. Knutson (ed.), *The Control of Aggression*. Chicago: Aldine, 1973, pp. 145–200.

———, R. A. Littman, and W. Bricker. "Assertive Behavior in Children: A Step Toward a Theory of Aggression," *Monographs of the Society for Research in Child Development*, 32 (1967), whole no. 113.

Pavlov, I. P. *Conditioned Reflexes: An Investigation of the Physiological Activity of the Cerebral Cortex*. London: Oxford University Press, 1927.

Peel, E. A. *The Nature of Adolescent Judgment*. New York: Wiley-Interscience, 1971.

Peeples, D. R., and D. Y. Teller. "Color Vision and Brightness Discrimination in Two-Month-Old Infants," *Science*, 189 (1975), 1102–1103.

Perlmutter, M. "Development of Memory in the Pre-school Years," in R. Greene and T. D. Yawkey (eds.), *Childhood Development*. Westport, Conn.: Technemic Publishing, 1980.

———, and G. Lange. "A Developmental Analysis of Recall-Recognition Distinctions," in P. A. Ornstein (ed.), *Memory Development in Children*. Hillsdale, N. J.: Lawrence Erlbaum, 1978, pp. 243–258.

———, and N. A. Myers. "Development of Recall in 2- to 4-Year-Old Children," *Developmental Psychology*, 15 (1979), 73–83.

Perry, D. G., and K. Bussey. "The Social Learning Theory of Sex Differences: Imitation Is Alive and Well," *Journal of Personality and Social Psychology*, 37 (1979), 1699–1712.

Peskin, H. "Pubertal Onset and Ego Functioning," *Journal of Abnormal Psychology*, 72 (1967), 1–15.

Phillips, S., S. King, and L. DuBois. "Spontaneous Activities of Female Versus Male Newborns," *Child Development*, 49 (1978), 590–597.

Piaget, J. *The Language and Thought of the Child*. New York: Harcourt, Brace, 1926.

———. *The Child's Conception of Physical Causality*. London: Kegan-Paul, 1930.

———. *The Moral Judgment of the Child*. New York: Free Press, 1965 (orig. pub. 1932).

———. *Play, Dreams and Imitation in Childhood*. New York: Norton, 1951.

———. *The Child's Conception of Number*. New York: Humanities Press, 1952a.

———. *The Origins of Intelligence in Children*. New York: International Universities Press, 1952b.

———. *Logic and Psychology*. Manchester: Manchester University Press, 1953.

———. *The Construction of Reality in the Child*. New York: Basic Books, 1954.

———. *On the Development of Memory and Identity*. Barre, Mass.: Clark University Press, 1968.

———. *The Mechanisms of Perception*. New York: Basic Books, 1969.

———. *Genetic Epistemology*. New York: Columbia University Press, 1970a.

———. "Piaget's Theory," in P. H. Mussen (ed.), *Carmichael's Manual of Child Psychology*. Vol. 1. 3rd ed. New York: Wiley, 1970b, pp. 703–732.

———. *Biology and Knowledge*. Chicago: University of Chicago Press, 1971a.

———. *The Child's Concept of Time*. New York: Basic Books, 1971b.

———. *The Grasp of Consciousness: Action and Concept in the Young Child*. Cambridge, Mass.: Harvard University Press, 1976a.

———. "Need and Significance of Cross-Cultural Research in Genetic Psychology," in B. Inhelder and H. H. Chipman (eds.), *Piaget and His School*. New York: Springer-Verlag, 1976b, pp. 259–268.

Piaget, J., and B. Inhelder. *Le Développement des quantités chez l'enfant; conservation et atomisme*. Neuchâtel: Delachaux et Niestle, 1941.

———, and ———. *The Psychology of the Child*. New York: Basic Books, 1969.

———, and ———. *Memory and Intelligence*. New York: Basic Books, 1973.

Piazza, D. S. "Cerebral Lateralization in Young Children as Measured by Dichotic Listening and Finger Tapping Tasks," *Neuropsychologia*, 15 (1977), 417–425.

Pitkin, R. M. "Nutritional Support in Obstetrics and Gynecology," *Clinical Obstetrics and Gynecology*, 19 (1976), 489.

Pollio, H. R. *The Psychology of Symbolic Activity*. Reading, Mass.: Addison-Wesley, 1974.

Pollitt, E., and D. Granoff. "Mental and Motor Development of Peruvian Children Treated for Severe Malnutrition," *Review of Interamericana Psicologia*, 1 (1967), 93.

Powell, G. F., J. A. Brasel, and R. M. Blizzard. "Emotional Deprivation and Growth Retardation Simulating Idiopathic Hypopituitarism. I. Clinical Evaluation of the Syndrome." *New England Journal of Medicine*, 276 (1967), 1271–1278.

Pratt, K. C. "The Neonate," in L. Carmichael (ed.), *Manual of Child Psychology*. 2nd ed. New York: Wiley, 1954, pp. 215–291.

Prechtl, H. F. R. "Problems of Behavioral Studies in the Newborn Infant," in D. S. Lehrman, R. A.

REFERENCES

Hinde, and E. Shaw (eds.), *Advances in the Study of Behavior.* Vol. 1. New York: Academic Press, 1965, pp. 75–98.

———, and D. Beintema. "The Neurological Examination of the Full Term Newborn Infant," *Clinics in Developmental Medicine.* No. 12. London: Spastic Society with Heinemann Medical, 1964.

Premack, A. J. *Why Chimps Can Read.* New York: Harper & Row, 1976.

Premack, D. "Discussion," in S. R. Harnad, H. D. Steklis, and J. Lancaster (eds.), *Origins and Evolution of Language and Speech.* New York: New York Academy of Sciences, 1976.

Pritchard, J. A., and P. C. MacDonald. *Obstetrics.* 15th ed. New York: Appleton-Century-Crofts, 1976.

Ramey, C., and F. Campbell. "The Prevention of Developmental Retardation in High-Risk Children," in P. Mittler (ed.), *Research to Practice in Mental Retardation.* Vol. 1: *Care and Intervention.* Baltimore: University Park Press, 1977.

Ramsay, D. S. "Manual Preference for Tapping in Infants," *Developmental Psychology*, 15 (1979), 437–441.

———. "Beginnings of Bimanual Handedness and Speech in Infants," *Infant Behavior and Development*, 3 (1980), 67–78.

———, J. J. Campos, and L. Fenson. "Onset of Bimanual Handedness in Children," *Infant Behavior and Development*, 2 (1979), 69–76.

Reese, H. W. "Imagery and Associative Memory," in R. V. Kail, Jr., and J. W. Hagen (eds.), *Perspectives on the Development of Memory and Cognition.* Hillsdale, N. J.: Lawrence Erlbaum, 1977, pp. 113–175.

———, and W. F. Overton. "Models of Development and Theories of Development," in L. R. Goulet and P. B. Baltes (eds.), *Life-Span Developmental Psychology: Research and Theory.* New York: Academic Press, 1970, pp. 116–145.

Reinisch, J. M., N. G. Simon, W. G. Karow, and R. Gandelman. "Prednisone Therapy and Birth Weight," *Science*, 206 (1979), 97.

Reisman, J. M., and S. I. Shorr. "Friendship Claims and Expectations among Children and Adults," *Child Development*, 49 (1978), 913–916.

Reiss, I. L. *Heterosexual Relationships Inside and Outside Marriage.* Morristown, N. J.: General Learning Press, 1973.

Resnick, L. B. "Introduction: Changing Conceptions of Intelligence," in L. B. Resnick (ed.), *The Nature of Intelligence.* Hillsdale, N. J.: Lawrence Erlbaum, 1976, pp. 1–10.

Rest, J. "The Hierarchical Nature of Moral Judgment: A Study of Patterns of Comprehension and Preference of Moral Stages," *Journal of Personality*, 41 (1973), 86–109.

———. "New Approaches in the Assessment of Moral Judgment," in T. Lickona (ed.), *Moral Development and Behavior.* New York: Holt, Rinehart and Winston, 1976, pp. 198–218.

———, M. L. Davison, and S. Robbins. "Age Trends in Judging Moral Issues: A Review of Cross-Sectional, Longitudinal, and Sequential Studies of the Defining Issues Test," *Child Development*, 49 (1978), 263–279.

———, E. Turiel, and L. Kohlberg. "Levels of Moral Development as a Determinant of Preference and Comprehension of Moral Judgments Made by Others," *Journal of Personality*, 37 (1969), 225–252.

Rheingold, H. L. "The Social and Socializing Agent," in D. A. Goslin (ed.), *Handbook of Socialization Theory and Research.* Chicago: Rand McNally, 1969, pp. 779–791.

———, and C. O. Eckerman. "The Infant Separates Himself From His Mother," *Science*, 168 (1970), 78–83.

———, J. L. Gewirtz, and H. W. Ross. "Social Conditioning of Vocalizations in the Infant," *Journal of Comparative and Physiological Psychology*, 52 (1959), 68–73.

Richards, M. "Early Separation," in R. Lewin (ed.), *Child Alive!* Garden City, N. Y.: Anchor Press/Doubleday, 1975, pp. 13–21.

Riegel, K. F. "Adult Life Crises: A Dialectic Interpretation of Development," in N. Datan and L. H. Ginsberg (eds.), *Life-Span Developmental Psychology: Normative Life Crises.* New York: Academic Press, 1975a, pp. 99–128.

———. "Toward a Dialectical Theory of Development," *Human Development*, 18 (1975b), 50–64.

———. "The Dialectics of Human Development," *American Psychologist*, 31 (1976), 689–699.

Rieser, J. J. "Spatial Orientation of Six-Month-Old Infants," *Child Development*, 50 (1979), 1078–1087.

Ritter, K., B. H. Kaprove, J. P. Fitch, and J. H. Flavell. "The Development of Retrieval Strategies in Young Children," *Cognitive Psychology*, 5 (1973), 310–321.

Roberts, D. F., C. Herold, M. Hornby, S. King, D. Sterne, S. Whiteley, and T. Silver. "Earth's a Big Blue Marble: A Report of the Impact of a Television Series on Children's Opinions." Unpublished manuscript. Stanford University, 1974.

Robinson, E. J., and W. P. Robinson. "Development in the Understanding of Causes of Success and Failure in Verbal Communication," *Cognition*, 5 (1977), 363–378.

Robinson, H. B., and N. M. Robinson. *The Mentally Retarded Child: A Psychological Approach.* New York: McGraw-Hill, 1965.

Rock, I. *An Introduction to Perception.* New York: Macmillan, 1975.

Roeper, T. "Connecting Children's Language and Linguistic Theory," in T. E. Moore (ed.), *Cognitive Development and the Acquisition of Language.* New York: Academic Press, 1973, pp. 187–196.

Roff, N., S. B. Sells, and M. M. Golden. *Social Adjustment and Personality Development in Children.* Minneapolis: University of Minnesota Press, 1972.

Roffwarg, H. P., J. N. Muzio, and W. C. Dement. "Ontogenic Development of the Human Dream Cycle," *Science*, 152 (1966), 604–619.

Rohwer, W. D., Jr. "Learning, Race, and School Success," *Review of Educational Research*, 41 (1971), 191–210.

Rosch, E. M. "On the Internal Structure of Perceptual and Semantic Categories," in T. E. Moore (ed.), *Cognitive Development and the Acquisition of Language.* New York: Academic Press, 1973, pp. 111–144.

Rose, S. *The Conscious Brain.* New York: Knopf, 1973.

Rose, S. A., and M. Blank. "The Potency of Context in Children's Cognition: An Illustration Through Conservation," *Child Development*, 45 (1974), 499–502.

———, A. W. Gottfried, and W. H. Bridger. "Cross-Modal Transfer in Infants: Relation to Prematurity and Socioeconomic Background," *Developmental Psychology*, 14 (1978), 643–652.

Rosen, B. C. "Socialization and Achievement Motivation in Brazil," *Sociological Review*, 27 (1962), 612–624.

———, and R. D'Andrade. "The Psychological Origins of Achievement Motivation," *Sociometry*, 22 (1959), 185–218.

Rosenthal, R. "The Pygmalion Effect Lives," *Psychology Today*, 7 (September 1973), 56–63.

Rosenthal, T. L., and B. J. Zimmerman. *Social Learning and Cognition.* New York: Academic Press, 1978.

Rosenzweig, M. R., E. L. Bennett, and M. C. Diamond. "Brain Changes in Response to Experience," *Scientific American*, 226 (February 1972), 22–29.

Rosett, H. L., and L. W. Sander. "Effects of Maternal Drinking on Neonatal Morphology and State Regulation," in J. D. Osofsky (ed.), *Handbook of Infant Development.* New York: Wiley-Interscience, 1979, pp. 809–836.

Rossman, E., M. Golden, B. Birns, A. Moss, and A. Montare. "Mother-Child Interaction, IQ, and Social Class." Paper presented at the Biennial Meeting of the Society for Research in Child Development. Philadelphia, March 1973.

Rovee-Collier, C. K., M. W. Sullivan, M. Enright, D. Lucan, and J. W. Fagen. "Reactivation of Infant Memory," *Science*, 208 (1980), 1159–1161.

Rozin, P. "The Evolution of Intelligence and Access to the Cognitive Unconscious," in J. M. Sprague and A. N. Epstein (eds.), *Progress in Psychobiology and Physiological Psychology.* Vol. 6. New York: Academic Press, 1976, pp. 245–280.

Rubenstein, E. A., R. M. Liebert, J. M. Neale, and R. W. Poulos. *Assessing Television's Influence on Children's Prosocial Behavior.* Stony Brook, N. Y.: Brookdale International Institute, 1974.

Rubenstein, J., and C. Howes. "The Effects of Peers on Toddler Interaction With Mothers and Toys," *Child Development*, 47 (1976), 990–997.

Rubin, K. H., and F. W. Schneider. "The Relationship Between Moral Judgment, Egocentrism, and Altruistic Behavior," *Child Development*, 44 (1973), 661–665.

Ruble, D. N., A. K. Boggiano, N. S. Feldman, and J. H. Loebl. "Developmental Analysis of the Role of Social Comparison in Self-Evaluation," *Developmental Psychology*, 16 (1980), 105–115.

———, J. E. Parsons, and J. Ross. "Self-Evaluative Responses of Children in an Achievement Setting," *Child Development*, 47 (1976), 990–997.

Ruff, H. A. "Infant Recognition of the Invariant Form of Objects," *Child Development*, 49 (1978), 293–306.

Rumbaugh, D. M. (ed.). *Language Learning by a Chimpanzee: The Lana Project.* New York: Academic Press, 1977.

———, and T. V. Gill. "The Mastery of Language-Type Skills by the Chimpanzee (*Pan*)," in S. R. Harnad, H. D. Steklis, and J. Lancaster (eds.), *Origins and Evolution of Language and Speech.* New York: New York Academy of Sciences, 1976.

Rushton, J. P. "Generosity in Children: Immediate and Long Term Effects of Modeling, Preaching, and Moral Judgments," *Journal of Personality and Social Psychology*, 31 (1975), 755–765.

Rutter, M. "Parent-Child Separation: Psychological Effects on the Children," *Journal of Child Psychology and Psychiatry and Allied Disciplines*, 12 (1971), 233–260.

———. "Maternal Deprivation, 1972–1978: New Findings, New Concepts, New Approaches," *Child Development*, 50 (1979), 283–305.

Sachs, J. S., and M. Johnson. "Language Development in a Hearing Child of Deaf Parents," in W. von Raffler Engel and Y. Le Brun (eds.), *Baby Talk and Infant Speech*. Amsterdam: Swets and Zweitlinger, 1976, pp. 246–252.

Saegert, S., and R. Hart. "The Development of Sex Differences in the Environmental Competence of Children," in P. Burnett (ed.), *Women in Society*. Chicago: Maaroufa Press, 1976.

Sagi, A., and M. L. Hoffman. "Empathic Distress in Newborns," *Developmental Psychology*, 12 (1976), 175–176.

St. James-Roberts, I. "Neurological Plasticity, Recovery From Brain Insult, and Child Development," in H. W. Reese and L. P. Lipsitt (eds.), *Advances in Child Development and Behavior*. Vol. 14. New York: Academic Press, 1979, pp. 254–320.

Salapatek, P. "Pattern Perception in Early Infancy," in L. B. Cohen and P. Salapatek (eds.), *Infant Perception: From Sensation to Cognition*. Vol. 1: *Basic Visual Processes*. New York: Academic Press, 1975, pp. 133–248.

———, and W. Kessen. "Visual Scanning of Triangles by the Human Newborn," *Journal of Experimental Child Psychology*, 3 (1966), 155–167.

Salatas, H., and J. H. Flavell. "Retrieval of Recently Learned Information: Development of Strategies and Control Skills," *Child Development*, 47 (1976), 941–948.

Sameroff, A. J. "The Components of Sucking in the Human Newborn," *Journal of Experimental Child Psychology*, 6 (1968), 607–623.

———. "Infant Risk Factors in Developmental Deviancy," in E. J. Anthony, C. Koupernik, and C. Chiland (eds.), *The Child in His Family: Vulnerable Children*. New York: Wiley-Interscience, 1978, pp. 173–184.

Sander, L. W. "The Regulation of Exchange in the Infant-Caretaker System and Some Aspects of the Context-Content Relationship," in M. Lewis and L. Rosenblum (eds.), *Interaction, Conversation, and the Development of Language*. New York: Wiley, 1977, pp. 133–156.

Savage-Rumbaugh, E. S., D. M. Rumbaugh, and S. Boysen. "Do Apes Use Language?" *American Scientist*, 68 (1980), 49–61.

Savin-Williams, R. C. "Dominance Hierarchies in Groups of Early Adolescents," *Child Development*, 50 (1979), 923–935.

Scaife, M., and J. S. Bruner. "The Capacity for Joint Visual Attention in the Infant," *Nature*, 253 (1975), 265–266.

Scarr, S., and P. Salapatek. "Patterns of Fear Development During Infancy," *Merrill-Palmer Quarterly*, 16 (1970), 53–90.

———, and R. A. Weinberg, "Attitudes, Interests, and IQ," *Human Nature*, 1 (April 1978), 29–36.

Scarr-Salapatek, S. "Unknowns in the IQ Equation," *Science*, 174 (1971), 1223–1228.

———. "Genetics and the Development of Intelligence," in F. D. Horowitz *et al.* (eds.), *Review of Child Development Research*. Vol. 4. Chicago: University of Chicago Press, 1975.

———. "An Evolutionary Perspective on Infant Intelligence: Species Patterns and Individual Variations," in M. Lewis (ed.), *Origins of Intelligence: Infancy and Early Childhood*. New York: Plenum Press, 1976, pp. 165–198.

Schaffer, H. R. *The Growth of Sociability*. Baltimore: Penguin, 1971.

———. *Mothering*. Cambridge, Mass.: Harvard University Press, 1977.

Schaffer, H. R., and P. E. Emerson. "The Development of Social Attachments in Infancy." *Monographs of the Society for Research in Child Development*, 29 (1964a), whole no. 94.

———, and ———. "Patterns of Response to Physical Contact in Early Human Development," *Journal of Child Psychology and Psychiatry*, 5 (1964b), 1–13.

Schaie, K. W. "A General Model for the Study of Developmental Problems," *Psychological Bulletin*, 64 (1965), 92–107.

Schneider, B., S. E. Trehub, and D. Bull, "High-Frequency Sensitivity in Infants," *Science*, 207 (1980), 1003–1004.

Schonfeld, W. A. "Body-Image in Adolescents: A Psychiatric Concept for the Pediatrician," *Pediatrics*, 31 (1963), 845–855.

———. "Body-Image Disturbances in Adolescents

With Inappropriate Sexual Development," *American Journal of Orthopsychiatry*, 34 (1964), 493–502.

Schrag, P., and D. Divoky. *The Myth of the Hyperactive Child*. New York: Pantheon, 1975.

Schwartz, G., and D. Merten. "The Language of Adolescence: An Anthropological Approach to the Youth Culture," *American Journal of Sociology*, 72 (1967), 453–468.

Schwartz, J. C., R. G. Strickland, and G. Krolick. "Infant Day Care: Behavioral Effects at Preschool Age," *Developmental Psychology*, 10 (1974), 502–506.

Schwartz, J., and P. Tallal. "Rate of Acoustic Change May Underlie Hemispheric Specialization for Speech Perception," *Science*, 207 (1980), 1380–1381.

Schwartz, M., and J. Schwartz. "Evidence Against a Genetical Component to Performance on IQ Tests," *Nature*, 248 (March 1974), 84–85.

Scollan, R. "A Real Early Stage: An Unzippered Condensation of a Dissertation on Child Language," in E. Ochs and B. B. Schieffelin (eds.), *Developmental Pragmatics*. New York: Academic Press, 1979, pp. 215–227.

Scott, E. M., R. Illsby, and A. M. Thompson. "A Psychological Investigation of Primigravidae. II. Maternal Social Class, Age, Physique, and Intelligence," *Journal of Obstetrics and Gynaecology of the British Empire*, 63 (1956), 338–343.

Scott, J. P. "Genetics and the Development of Social Behavior in Mammals," *American Journal of Orthopsychiatry*, 32 (1962), 878–893.

———. "The Development of Social Motivation," *Nebraska Symposium on Motivation*, 15 (1967), 111–132.

Scribner, S., and M. Cole. "Effects of Constrained Recall Training on Children's Performance in a Verbal Memory Task," *Child Development*, 43 (1972), 845–857.

Scrimshaw, N. S. "Early Malnutrition and Central Nervous System Function," *Merrill-Palmer Quarterly*, 15 (1969), 375–388.

———, and J. E. Gordon (eds.), *Malnutrition, Learning, and Behavior*. Cambridge, Mass.: MIT Press, 1968.

Searleman, A. "A Review of Right Hemisphere Linguistic Capabilities," *Psychological Bulletin*, 84 (1977), 503–528.

Sears, R. R. "Relation of Early Socialization Experiences to Self-Concepts and Gender Role in Middle Childhood," *Child Development*, 41 (1970), 267–290.

———. "Your Ancients Revisited: A History of Child Development," in E. M. Hetherington (ed.), *Review of Child Development Research*. Vol. 5. Chicago: University of Chicago Press, 1975, pp. 1–73.

———. "Sources of Life Satisfaction of the Terman Gifted Men," *American Psychologist*, 32 (1977), 119–128.

———, E. E. Maccoby, and H. Levin. *Patterns of Child Rearing*. Stanford, Calif.: Stanford University Press, 1976 (orig. pub. 1957).

———, L. Rau, and R. Alpert. *Identification and Child Rearing*. Stanford, Calif.: Stanford University Press, 1965.

Seligman, M. E. P. *Helplessness: On Depression, Development, and Death*. San Francisco: Freeman, 1975.

Selye, H. *The Stress of Life*. New York: McGraw-Hill, 1976.

Semb, G. (ed.). *Behavior Analysis and Education*. Lawrence: University of Kansas Press, 1972.

Serbin, L. A., K. D. O'Leary, R. N. Kent, and I. J. Tonick. "A Comparison of Teacher Response to the Pre-academic and Problem Behavior of Boys and Girls." *Child Development*, 33 (1973), 796–804.

Shanab, M. E., and K. A. Yahya. "A Behavioral Study of Obedience," *Journal of Personality and Social Psychology*, 35 (1977), 550–586.

Shantz, C. U. "The Development of Social Cognition," in E. M. Hetherington (ed.), *Review of Child Development Research*. Vol. 5. Chicago: University of Chicago Press, 1975.

Shatz, M. "Preschoolers' Ability to Take Account of Others in a Toy Selection Task." M.A. thesis. University of Pennsylvania, Philadelphia, 1973.

———. "The Comprehension of Indirect Directives: Can 2 Year Olds Shut the Door?" Paper presented at a meeting of the Linguistic Society of America, 1974.

———. "On the Development of Communicative Understandings: An Early Strategy for Interpreting and Responding to Messages," *Cognitive Psychology*, 10 (1978), 271–301.

Shaw, E. B. "Sudden Unexpected Death in Infancy Syndrome," *American Journal of Diseases of Children*, 119 (1970), 416–418.

———. "Nasal Obstruction Theories as Related to the Sudden Infant Death Syndrome." Paper presented at the Research Planning Workshops on the Sudden Infant Death Syndrome: 7. Recognition of Infants at Risk for Sudden Infant Death: An Approach to Prevention. Bethesda, Md.: NICHHD, February 1974.

Shelton, L. A. "A Comparative Study of Educational

Achievement in One-Parent and Two-Parent Families," *Dissertation Abstracts*, 29 (8-A) (1969), 2535–2536.

Sherif, M., O. J. Harvey, B. J. White, W. R. Hood, and C. W. Sherif. *Intergroup Conflict and Cooperation. The Robbers Cave Experiment*. Norman, Okla.: Institute of Group Relations, 1961.

————, and C. W. S. Sherif. *Groups in Harmony and Tension: An Integration of Studies on Intergroup Relations*. New York: Harper & Row, 1953.

————, and ————. *Reference Groups: Explorations Into Conformity and Deviation of Adolescents*. New York: Harper & Row, 1964.

Sherman, J. A. *On the Psychology of Women: A Survey of Empirical Studies*. Springfield, Ill.: Charles C Thomas, 1973.

Shultz, T. R. "Development of the Appreciation of Riddles," *Child Development*, 45 (1974), 100–105.

Siegel, A. W., K. C. Kirasic, and R. V. Kail, Jr. "Stalking the Elusive Cognitive Map: The Development of Children's Representations of Geographical Space," in I. Altman and J. F. Wohlwill (eds.), *Children and the Environment*. New York: Plenum Press, 1978, pp. 223–258.

Siegel, L. S., A. E. McCabe, J. Brand, and J. Matthews. "Evidence for the Understanding of Class Inclusion in Preschool Children: Linguistic Factors and Training Effects," *Child Development*, 49 (1978), 688–693.

Siegler, R. S. "The Origins of Scientific Reasoning," in R. S. Siegler (ed.), *Children's Thinking: What Develops?* Hillsdale, N. J.: Lawrence Erlbaum, 1978, pp. 109–149.

————, D. E. Liebert, and R. M. Liebert. "Inhelder and Piaget's Pendulum Problem: Teaching Preadolescents to Act as Scientists," *Developmental Psychology*, 9 (1973), 97–101.

————, and D. D. Richards. "Development of Time, Speed, and Distance Concepts," *Developmental Psychology*, 15 (1979), 288–298.

Sigel, I. E., and E. Mermelstein. "Effects of Nonschooling on Piagetian Tasks of Conservation." Unpublished paper. (Cited in J. H. Flavell, "Concept Development," in P. H. Mussen [ed.], *Carmichael's Manual of Child Psychology*. 3rd ed. New York: Wiley, 1970.)

Simner, M. L. "Newborn's Response to the Cry of Another Infant," *Developmental Psychology*, 5 (1971), 136–150.

Simon, H. A. "An Information Processing Theory of Intellectual Development," in *Cognitive Develop-ment in Children*. Chicago: University of Chicago Press, 1970, pp. 126–131.

Simon, W., and J. H. Gagnon. "On Psychological Development," in D. A. Goslin (ed.), *Handbook of Socialization Theory and Research*. Chicago: Rand McNally, 1969, pp. 733–752.

Simpson, E. L. "Moral Development Research: A Case Study of Scientific Cultural Bias," *Human Development*, 17 (1974), 81–106.

Sinclair, C. B. *Movement of the Young Child: Ages Two to Six*. Columbus, Ohio: Merrill, 1973.

Singleton, L. C., and S. R. Asher. "Racial Integration and Children's Peer Preferences: An Investigation of Developmental and Cohort Differences," *Child Development*, 50 (1979), 936–941.

Skinner, B. F. *The Behavior of Organisms: An Experimental Analysis*. New York: Appleton-Century-Crofts, 1938.

————. *Verbal Behavior*. New York: Appleton-Century-Crofts, 1957.

————. "Pigeons in a Pelican," *American Psychologist*, 15 (1960), 28–37.

————. *Cumulative Record: A Selection of Papers*. 3rd ed. New York: Appleton-Century-Crofts, 1972.

————. *The Shaping of a Behaviorist*. New York: Knopf, 1979.

Skodak, M., and H. M. Skeels. "A Final Follow-up Study of One Hundred Adopted Children," *Journal of Genetic Psychology*, 75 (1949), 85–125.

Slaby, R. G., and K. S. Frey. "Development of Gender Constancy and Selective Attention to Same-Sex Models," *Child Development*, 46 (1975), 849–856.

Slobin, D. I. "Children and Language: They Learn the Same All Around the World," *Psychology Today*, 6 (July 1972), 71–74+.

————. "Cognitive Prerequisites for the Development of Grammar," in C. A. Ferguson and D. I. Slobin (eds.), *Studies of Child Language Development*. New York: Holt, Rinehart and Winston, 1973, pp. 175–208.

————. "On the Nature of Talk to Children," in E. H. Lenneberg and E. Lenneberg (eds.), *Foundations of Language Development: A Multidisciplinary Approach*. UNESCO-IBRO, 1975.

————. "A Case Study of Early Language Awareness," in A. Sinclair, R. J. Jarvella, and W. J. M. Levelt (eds.), *The Child's Conception of Language*. New York: Springer-Verlag, 1978, pp. 45–54.

Smith, A. "Lenneberg, Locke, Zangwill, and the Neuropsychology of Language and Language Disorders," in G. A. Miller and E. Lenneberg (eds.), *Psychology and Biology of Language and Thought*. New York: Academic Press, 1978, pp. 133–150.

Smith, C. "Effects of Maternal Undernutrition Upon the Newborn Infant in Holland (1944–1945)," *Journal of Pediatrics*, 30 (1947), 229–243.

———, and B. Lloyd. "Maternal Behavior and Perceived Sex of Infant: Revisited," *Child Development*, 49 (1978), 1263–1265.

Smith, P. K. "Aspects of the Playgroup Environment," in D. Canter and T. Lee (eds.), *Psychology and the Built Environment*. London: Architectural Press, 1974, pp. 56–64.

———. "Social and Fantasy Play in Young Children," in B. Tizard and D. Harvey (eds.), *Biology and Play*. Philadelphia: Lippincott, 1977, pp. 123–145.

———. "A Longitudinal Study of Social Participation in Preschool Children: Solitary and Parallel Play Reexamined," *Developmental Psychology*, 14 (1978), 517–523.

———, and L. Daglish. "Sex Differences in Parent and Infant Behavior in the Home," *Child Development*, 48 (1977), 1250–1254.

———, and S. Dutton. "Play and Training in Direct and Innovative Problem Solving," *Child Development*, 50 (1979), 830–836.

Snow, C. E. "The Development of Conversation Between Mothers and Babies," *Journal of Child Language*, 4 (1977a), 1–22.

———. "Mothers' Speech Research: From Input to Interaction," in C. E. Snow and C. A. Ferguson (eds.), *Talking to Children*. New York: Cambridge University Press, 1977b, pp. 31–50.

———, A. Arlman-Rupp, Y. Hassing, J. Jobse, J. Jootsen, and J. Vorster, "Mothers' Speech in Three Social Classes," *Journal of Psycholinguistic Research*, 5 (1976), 1–20.

———, and M. Hoefnagel-Höhle. "The Critical Period for Language Acquisition: Evidence From Second Language Learning," *Child Development*, 49 (1978), 1114–1128.

Sontag, L. W. "Implications of Fetal Behavior and Environment for Adult Personalities," *Annals of the New York Academy of Sciences*, 134 (1966), 782.

———, and H. Newbery. "Normal Variations of Fetal Heart Rate During Pregnancy," *American Journal of Obstetrics and Gynecology*, 40 (1940), 449–452.

Soroka, S. M., C. M. Corter, and R. Abramovitch. "Infants' Tactual Discrimination of Novel and Familiar Stimuli," *Child Development*, 50 (1979), 1251–1253.

Spearman, C. *The Abilities of Man*. New York: Macmillan, 1927.

Spelke, E. S. "Perceiving Bimodally Specified Events in Infancy," *Developmental Psychology*, 15 (1979), 626–636.

———, and C. J. Owsley. "Intermodal Exploration and Knowledge in Infancy," *Infant Behavior and Development*, 2 (1979), 13–27.

Spelt, D. K. "The Conditioning of the Human Fetus in utera," *Journal of Experimental Psychology*, 38 (1948), 338–346.

Spence, J. T. "Traits, Roles, and the Concept of Androgyny," in J. E. Gullahorn (ed.), *Psychology and Women: In Transition*. New York: Wiley, 1979, pp. 167–187.

Spinetta, J. J., and D. Rigler. "The Child-Abusing Parent: A Psychological Review," *Psychological Bulletin*, 77 (1972), 296–304.

Stroufe, L. A. "Wariness of Strangers and the Study of Infant Development," *Child Development*, 48 (1977), 731–746.

———, and J. P. Wunsch. "The Development of Laughter in the First Year of Life," *Child Development*, 43 (1972), 1326–1344.

Staffieri, J. R. "A Study of Social Stereotype of Body Image in Children," *Journal of Personality and Social Psychology*, 7 (1967), 101–104.

Starr, R. H., Jr. "Child Abuse," *American Psychologist*, 34 (1979), 872–878.

Staub, E. "A Child in Distress: The Influence of Age and Number of Witnesses on Children's Attempts to Help," *Journal of Personality and Social Psychology*, 14 (1970), 130–140.

———. "A Child in Distress: The Influence of Nurturance and Modeling on Children's Attempts to Help," *Developmental Psychology*, 5 (1971), 124–132.

———. *The Development of Prosocial Behavior in Children*. New York: General Learning Press, 1975.

Stayton, D., R. Hogan, and M. D. S. Ainsworth. "Infant Obedience and Maternal Behavior: The Origins of Socialization Reconsidered," *Child Development*, 42 (1971), 1057–1069.

Steele, B. F., and D. Pollock. "A Psychiatric Study of Parents Who Abuse Infants and Small Children," in R. E. Helfer and C. H. Kempe (eds.), *The Battered Child*. Chicago: University of Chicago Press, 1968.

Stein, A. H., and M. M. Bailey. "The Socialization of Achievement Orientation in Females," *Psychological Bulletin*, 80 (1973), 345–366.

————, and L. K. Friedrich. "The Effect of Television Content on Young Children," in A. D. Pick (ed.), *Minnesota Symposia on Child Psychology*. Vol. 9. Minneapolis: University of Minnesota Press, 1975, pp. 78–105.

Stein, Z. "Strategies for the Prevention of Mental Retardation," *Bulletin of New York Academy of Medicine*, 51 (1975), 130–142.

Steiner, J. E. "Facial Expressions in Response to Taste and Smell Stimulation," in H. W. Reese and L. P. Lipsitt (eds.), *Advances in Child Development and Behavior*. Vol. 13. New York: Academic Press, 1979, pp. 257–296.

Steinschneider, A. "Implications of the Sudden Infant Death Syndrome for the Study of Sleep in Infancy," in A. D. Pick (ed.), *Minnesota Symposia on Child Psychology*. Vol. 9. Minneapolis: University of Minnesota Press, 1975, pp. 106–134.

Stendler, C., D. Damrin, and A. C. Haines. "Studies in Cooperation and Competition: I. The Effects of Working for Group and Individual Rewards on the Social Climate of Children's Groups," *Journal of Genetic Psychology*, 79 (1951), 173–197.

Stephan, H., R. Bauchot, and O. J. Andy. "Data on Size of the Brain and of Various Brain Parts in Insectivores and Primates," in C. R. Noback and W. Montagna (eds.), *The Primate Brain*. New York: Appleton-Century-Crofts, 1970.

Stephens, M. W., and P. Delys. "External Control Expectancies Among Disadvantaged Children at Preschool Age," *Child Development*, 44 (1973), 670–674.

Stern, C. *Principles of Human Genetics*. 2nd ed. San Francisco: Jossey-Bass, 1960.

Stern, D. N. *The First Relationship: Infant and Mother*. Cambridge, Mass.: Harvard University Press, 1977.

Sternberg, R. J. *Intelligence, Information Processing, and Analogical Reasoning: The Componential Analysis of Human Abilities*. Hillsdale, N. J.: Lawrence Erlbaum, 1977.

————. "Stalking the IQ Quark," *Psychology Today*, 13 (September 1979), 42–54.

————, and G. Nigro. "Developmental Patterns in the Solution of Verbal Analogies," *Child Development*, 51 (1980), 27–38.

Sternglanz, S. H., and L. A. Serbin. "Sex Role Stereotyping in Children's Television Programs," *Developmental Psychology*, 10 (1974), 710–715.

Stevenson, H. W. *Children's Learning*. New York: Appleton-Century-Crofts, 1972.

Stirnimann, F. "Uber das Farbempfinden Neugeborener," *Annales Paediatrici*, 163 (1944), 1–25.

Stolz, H. R., and L. H. Stolz. *Somatic Development of Adolescent Boys: A Study of the Growth of Boys During the Second Decade of Life*. New York: Macmillan, 1951.

Stolz, L. M. *et al. Father Relations of War-Born Children*. Stanford, Calif.: Stanford University Press, 1954.

Strayer, F. D., and J. Strayer. "An Ethological Analysis of Social Agonism and Dominance Relations Among Preschool Children," *Child Development*, 47 (1976), 980–989.

Strayer, J. "Social Conflict and Peer-Group Status." Paper presented at the Biennial Meeting of the Society for Research in Child Development. New Orleans, March 1977.

Streissguth, A. P. "Psychologic Handicaps in Children With Fetal Alcohol Syndrome. Work in Progress on Alcoholism," *Annals of the New York Academy of Science*, 273 (1976), 140–145.

————, S. Landesman-Dwyer, J. C. Martin, and D. W. Smith. "Teratogenic Effects of Alcohol in Humans and Laboratory Animals," *Science*, 209 (1980), 353–361.

Studdert-Kennedy, M., and D. Shankweiler. "Hemispheric Specialization for Speech Perception," *Journal of the Acoustical Society of America*, 48 (1970), 579–594.

Sullivan, H. S. *The Interpersonal Theory of Psychiatry*. New York: Norton, 1953.

Sulloway, F. S. "The Role of Cognitive Flexibility in Science." Unpublished paper. Harvard University, 1972.

Suls, J., and R. J. Kalle. "Children's Moral Judgments as a Function of Intention, Damage, and an Actor's Physical Harm," *Developmental Psychology*, 15 (1979), 93–94.

Suomi, S. J. "Adult Male-Infant Interactions Among Monkeys Living in Nuclear Families," *Child Development*, 48 (1977), 1255–1270.

————, and H. Harlow. "Social Rehabilitation of Isolate-Reared Monkeys," *Developmental Psychology*, 6 (1972), 487–496.

————, and ————. "The Role and Reason of Peer Relationships in Rhesus Monkeys," in M. Lewis and L. A. Rosenblum (eds.), *Friendship and Peer Relations*. New York: Wiley, 1975, pp. 153–185.

Surber, C. F. "Developmental Processes in Social Inference: Averaging of Intentions and Consequences in Moral Judgment," *Developmental Psychology*, 13 (1977), 654–665.

Susman, E. J. "Visual and Verbal Attributes of Television and Selective-Attention in Preschool Children," *Developmental Psychology*, 14 (1978), 565–566.

Sutton-Smith, B., and B. G. Rosenberg. *The Sibling*. Holt, Rinehart and Winston, 1970.

Swanson, J. M., and M. Kinsbourne. "The Cognitive Effect of Stimulant Drugs on Hyperactive Children," in G. A. Hale and M. Lewis (eds.), *Attention and Cognitive Development*. New York: Plenum Press, 1979, pp. 249–296.

Sylva, K., J. S. Bruner, and P. Genova. "The Role of Play in the Problem-Solving of Children 3 to 5 Years Old," in J. S. Bruner, A. Jolly, and K. Sylva (eds.), *Play—Its Role in Development and Evolution*. New York: Basic Books, 1976, pp. 244–257.

Tanner, J. M. *Growth of Adolescence, With a General Consideration of the Effects of Hereditary and Environmental Factors Upon Growth and Maturation From Birth to Maturity*. 2nd ed. Oxford: Blackwell, 1962.

———. *Fetus Into Man: Physical Growth From Conception to Maturity*. Cambridge, Mass.: Harvard University Press, 1978.

———, R. H. Whitehouse, and M. J. R. Healy. *A New System for Estimating Skeletal Maturity From the Hand and Wrist, With Standards Derived From a Study of 2,600 Healthy British Children*. Parts I and II. Paris: Centre International de l'Enfance, 1962.

Tapp, J. L. "A Child's Garden of Law and Order," *Psychology Today*, 4 (December 1970), 29–31+.

Tavris, C., and C. Offir. *The Longest War: Sex Differences in Perspective*. New York: Harcourt Brace Jovanovich, 1977.

Taylor, D. C. "Differential Rates of Cerebral Maturation Between Hemispheres," *Lancet*, 2 (1969), 140–142.

Terman, L. M. (ed.). *Genetic Studies of Genius*. Vol. 5. Stanford, Calif.: Stanford University Press, 1959.

Terrace, H. S. *Nim: A Chimpanzee Who Learned Sign Language*. New York: Knopf, 1979.

Thomas, A., S. Chess, and H. G. Birch. *Temperament and Behavior Disorders in Children*. New York: New York University Press, 1968.

———, ———, and ———. "The Origin of Personality, *Scientific American*, 223 (August 1970), 102–109.

———, ———, ———, M. E. Hertzig, and S. Korn. *Behavioral Individuality in Early Childhood*. New York: New York University Press, 1963.

Thompson, S. K. "Gender Labels and Early Sex Role Development," *Child Development*, 46 (1975), 339–347.

Thompson, W. P. "Influences of Prenatal Maternal Anxiety on Emotionality in Young Rats," *Science*, 125 (1957), 698–699.

Thorndike, E. L. *Educational Psychology*. Vol. 1. New York: Columbia University, 1913. Vols. 2 and 3. New York: Teachers College, 1913.

Thurstone, L. L. *Multiple-Factor Analysis*. Chicago: University of Chicago Press, 1947.

Tinbergen, N. *The Study of Instinct*. Oxford: Clarendon Press, 1951.

Todd, C. M., and M. Perlmutter. "Reality Recalled by Preschool Children," in M. Perlmutter (ed.), *New Directions in Child Development*. No. 10. *Children's Memory*. San Francisco: Jossey-Bass, 1980, pp. 69–86.

Trabasso, T. "Representation, Memory, and Reasoning: How Do We Make Transitive Inferences?" in A. D. Pick (ed.), *Minnesota Symposia on Child Psychology*. Vol. 9. Minneapolis: University of Minnesota Press, 1975, pp. 135–172.

———. "The Role of Memory as a System in Making Transitive Inferences," in R. V. Kail, Jr., and J. W. Hagen (eds.), *Perspectives on the Development of Memory and Cognition*. Hillsdale, N. J.: Lawrence Erlbaum, 1977, pp. 333–366.

———, and G. H. Bower. *Attention in Learning Theory and Research*. New York: Wiley, 1968.

———, A. G. McLanahan, A. M. Isen, C. A. Riley, P. Dolecki, and T. Tucker. "How Do Children Solve Class Inclusion Problems?" in R. S. Siegler (ed.), *Children's Thinking: What Develops?* Hillsdale, N. J.: Lawrence Erlbaum, 1978, pp. 151–180.

Tracy, R. L., M. E. Lamb, and M. D. Ainsworth. "Infant Approach Behavior as Related to Attachment," *Child Development*, 47 (1976), 571–578.

Trause, M. A. "Stranger Responses: Effects of Familiarity, Strangers' Approach, and Sex of Infant," *Child Development*, 48 (1977), 1657–1661.

Tresemer, D. "Fear of Success: Popular but Unproven," *Psychology Today*, 7 (March 1974), 82–85.

Tryon, R. C. "Genetic Differences in Maze Learning in Rats," *Thirty-Ninth Yearbook, National Society for the Study of Education*. Part 1. Bloomington, Ill.: Public School Publishing Co., 1940, pp. 111–119.

Tuchman-Duplessis, H. *Drug Effects on the Fetus*. Sydney: ADIS Press, 1975.

Tulkin, S. R., and J. Kagan. "Mother-Child Interaction in the First Year of Life," *Child Development*, 43 (1972), 31–41.

Tumolo, P. J., P. L. Mason, and A. Kobasigawa. "Presenting Category Size Information to Facilitate Children's Recall." Paper presented at the Annual Meeting of the Canadian Psychological Association. Windsor, Ontario, 1974.

Turiel, E. "The Development of Concepts of Social Structure: Social Convention," in J. Glick and K. A. Clarke-Stewart (eds.), *The Development of Social Understanding*. New York: Gardner Press, 1978, pp. 25–107.

Turing, A. M. "Computing Machinery and Intelligence," *Mind*, 59 (1950), 433–460.

Tyler, L. E. "The Intelligence We Test — An Evolving Concept," in L. B. Resnick (ed.), *The Nature of Intelligence*. Hillsdale, N. J.: Lawrence Erlbaum, 1976, pp. 13–26.

Ulian, D. Z. "The Development of Conceptions of Masculinity and Femininity," in B. Lloyd and J. Ascher (eds.), *Exploring Sex Differences*. London: Academic Press, 1976.

Ullman, C. A. "Teachers, Peers, and Tests as Predictors of Adjustment," *Journal of Educational Psychology*, 48 (1957), 257–267.

Urberg, K. A. "Sex Role Conceptualizations in Adolescents and Adults," *Developmental Psychology*, 15 (1979), 90–92.

Uzgiris, I. C. "Situational Generality of Conservation," *Child Development*, 35 (1964), 831–841.

Van Lawick-Goodall, J. *In the Shadow of Man*. Boston: Houghton Mifflin, 1971.

Vlietstra, A. G., and J. C. Wright. "Sensory Modality and Transmodal Stimulus Properties in Children's Discrimination Learning and Transfer," *Annual Report, Kansas Center for Research in Early Childhood Education*. Lawrence: University of Kansas, 1971.

Von Frisch, K. *The Dance Language and Orientation of Bees*. Cambridge, Mass.: Belknap/Harvard University Press, 1967.

Vurpillot, E. "The Development of Scanning Strategies and Their Relation to Visual Differentiation," *Journal of Experimental Child Psychology*, 6 (1968), 622–650.

Vygotsky, L. S. *Thought and Language*. Cambridge, Mass.: MIT Press, 1962.

_____. *Mind in Society*. Cambridge, Mass.: Harvard University Press, 1978.

Waber, D. P. "Sex Differences in Cognition: A Func-

tion of Maturation Rates?" *Science*, 192 (1976), 572–573.

_____. "Sex Differences in Mental Abilities, Hemisphere Lateralization, and Rate of Physical Growth at Adolescence," *Developmental Psychology*, 13 (1977), 29–38.

Wachs, T. "Utilization of a Piagetian Approach in the Investigation of Early Experience Effects: A Research Strategy and Some Illustrative Data," *Merrill-Palmer Quarterly*, 22 (1976), 11–30.

Wahler, R. G. "Child-Child Interactions in Free Field Settings: Some Experimental Analyses," *Journal of Experimental Child Psychology*, 5 (1967), 278–293.

Walk, R. D., and S. H. Dodge. "Visual Depth Perception of a 10-Month-Old Monocular Human Infant," *Science*, 137 (1962), 529–530.

Walters, C. E. "Prediction of Postnatal Development From Fetal Activity," *Child Development*, 36 (1965), 801–806.

Walters, R. H., M. Leat, and L. Mezei. "Response Inhibition and Disinhibition Through Empathetic Learning," *Canadian Journal of Psychology*, 17 (1968), 235–243.

_____, and R. D. Parke. "Influence of Response Consequences to a Social Model on Resistance to Deviation," *Journal of Experimental Child Psychology*, 1 (1964), 260–280.

_____, _____, and V. Cane. "Timing of Punishment and the Observation of Consequences to Others as Determinants of Response Inhibition," *Journal of Experimental Child Psychology*, 2 (1965), 10–30.

Waterlow, J. C. "Note on the Assessment and Classification of Protein-Energy Malnutrition in Children," *Lancet*, 2 (1973), 87–89.

_____, and P. R. Payne. "The Protein Gap," *Nature*, 258 (1975), 113–117.

Waters, E., J. Wippman, and L. A. Sroufe. "Attachment, Positive Effect, and Competence in the Peer Group: Two Studies in Construct," *Child Development*, 50 (1979), 821–829.

Watson, J. B. "Psychology as the Behaviorist Views It," *Psychological Review*, 20 (1913), 158–177.

_____. *Behaviorism*. New York: Norton, 1970 (orig. pub. 1924).

Watson, J. S. "The Development and Generalization of 'Contingency Awareness' in Early Infancy: Some Hypotheses," *Merrill-Palmer Quarterly*, 12 (1966), 123–135.

Webb, P. A., and A. A. Abrahamson. "Stages of Egocentrism in Children's Use of 'This' and 'That': A Different Point of View," *Journal of Child Language*, 3 (1976), 349–367.

Wechsler, D. "Intelligence Defined and Undefined," *American Psychologist*, 30 (1975), 135–139.

Weinrott, M. R., J. A. Corson, and M. Wilchesky. "Teacher-Mediated Treatment of Social Withdrawal," *Behavior Therapy*, 10 (1979), 280–294.

Weiss, G., and L. Hechtman. "The Hyperactive Child Syndrome," *Science*, 205 (1979), 1348–1354.

Wellman, H. M. "Preschoolers' Understanding of Memory-Relevant Variables," *Child Development*, 48 (1977), 1720–1723.

———, K. Ritter, and J. H. Flavell. "Deliberate Memory Behavior in the Delayed Reactions of Very Young Children," *Developmental Psychology*, 11 (1975), 780–787.

Werner, E. E., J. M. Bierman, and F. E. French. *The Children of Kauai*. Honolulu: University of Hawaii Press, 1971.

Werner, H. *Comparative Psychology of Mental Development*. New York: International Universities Press, 1948.

———. "The Concept of Development From a Comparative and Organismic Point of View," in D. B. Harris (ed.), *The Concept of Development: An Issue in the Study of Human Behavior*. Minneapolis: University of Minnesota Press, 1957, pp. 125–148.

Werner, J. S., and M. Perlmutter. "Development of Visual Memory in Infants," in H. W. Reese and L. P. Lipsitt (eds.), *Advances in Child Development and Behavior*. Vol. 14. New York: Academic Press, 1979, pp. 1–56.

Whalen, C. K., B. Henker, B. E. Collins, S. McAuliffe, and A. Vaux. "Peer Interactions in a Structured Communication Task: Comparisons of Normal and Hyperactive Boys and of Methylphenidate (Ritalin) and Placebo Effects," *Child Development*, 50 (1979), 388–401.

White, B. L. "An Experimental Approach to the Effects of Experience on Early Human Behavior," in J. P. Hill (ed.), *Minnesota Symposia on Child Psychology*. Vol. 1. Minneapolis: University of Minnesota Press, 1967, pp. 201–226.

———. *Human Infants: Experience and Psychological Development*. Englewood Cliffs, N.J.: Prentice-Hall, 1971.

———, and R. Held. "Plasticity of Sensorimotor Development in the Human Infant," in J. F. Rosenblith and W. Allinsmith (eds.), *The Causes of Be-*

havior. II: Readings in Child Development and Educational Psychology. 2nd ed. Boston: Allyn & Bacon, 1966, pp. 60–70.

White, C. B., N. Bushnell, and J. L. Regnemer. "Moral Development in Bahamian School Children: A 3-Year Examination of Kohlberg's Stages of Moral Development," *Developmental Psychology*, 14 (1978), 58–65.

White, D. G. "Effects of Sex-Typed Labels and Their Source on the Imitative Performance of Young Children," *Child Development*, 49 (1978), 1266–1269.

White, E., B. Elson, and R. Prawat. "Children's Conceptions of Death," *Child Development*, 49 (1978), 307–310.

Whitehurst, G. J. "The Role of Comprehension Training in the Generative Production of Direct-Indirect Object Sentences by Preschool Children." Unpublished paper. State University of New York, Stony Brook, 1974.

———, and R. Vasta. "Is Language Acquired Through Imitation?" *Journal of Psycholinguistic Research*, 4 (1975), 37–59.

Whiting, B. B. *Six Cultures: Studies of Child Rearing*. New York: Wiley, 1963.

Whiting, J. W. M. "Resource Mediation and Learning by Identification," in I. Iscoe and H. W. Stevenson (eds.), *Personality Development in Children*. Austin: University of Texas Press, 1960, pp. 112–126.

———, and I. L. Child. *Child Training and Personality: A Cross-Cultural Study*. New Haven: Yale University Press, 1953.

Whorf, B. L. *Language, Thought, and Reality*. Cambridge, Mass.: MIT Press, 1956.

Wickelgren, L. W. "Convergence in the Human Newborn," *Journal of Experimental Child Psychology*, 5 (1967), 74–85.

Widdowson, E. M. "Mental Contentment and Physical Growth," *Lancet*, 260 (1951), 1316–1318.

Winer, G. A. "Class-Inclusion Reasoning in Children: A Review of the Empirical Literature," *Child Development*, 51 (1980), 309–328.

Winterbottom, M. "The Relation of Need for Achievement to Learning Experiences in Independence and Mastery," in J. Atkinson (ed.), *Motives in Fantasy, Action, and Society*. Princeton, N.J.: Van Nostrand, 1958, pp. 453–478.

Witelson, S. F. "Sex and the Single Hemisphere: Specialization of the Right Hemisphere for Spatial Processing," *Science*, 193 (1976), 425–427.

———. "Developmental Dyslexia: Research Methods and Interferences," *Science*, 203 (1979), 201–203.

Witkin, H. A., S. A. Mednick, F. Schulsinger, E. Bakkestrom, K. O. Christiansen, D. R. Goodenough, K. Hirchhorn, C. Lundsteen, D. R. Owen, J. Philip, D. B. Ruben, and M. Stocking. "Criminality in XYY and XXY Men," *Science*, 193 (1976), 547–555.

Wittig, M. A., and A. C. Peterson (eds.). *Sex Differences in Cognitive Performance*. New York: Academic Press, 1979.

Wolf, T. M. "A Developmental Investigation of Televised Modeled Verbalizations on Resistance to Temptation," *Developmental Psychology*, 6 (1972), 537.

Wolff, G. "Increased Bodily Growth of School-Children Since the War," *Lancet*, 228 (1935), 1006–1011.

Wolff, P. H. "Observations on the Development of Smiling," in B. M. Foss (ed.), *Determinants of Infant Behaviour*. Vol. 2. London: Methuen, 1963.

————. "The Role of Biological Rhythms in Early Psychological Development," *Bulletin of the Menninger Clinic*, 31 (1967), 197–218.

————. "The Natural History of Crying and Other Vocalizations in Early Infancy," in B. M. Foss (ed.), *Determinants of Infant Behaviour*. Vol. 4. London: Methuen, 1969, pp. 81–109.

————, and I. Hurwitz. "Sex Differences in Finger Tapping: A Developmental Study," *Neuropsychologia*, 14 (1976), 35–41.

Women on Words and Images. *Dick and Jane as Victims: Sex Stereotyping in Children's Readers*. Princeton, N.J.: Women on Words and Images, 1972.

Wozniak, R. H. "A Dialectical Paradigm for Psychological Research: Implications Drawn From the History of Psychology in the Soviet Union," *Human Development*, 18 (1975), 50–64.

Yakovlev, P. I., and A. R. Lecours. "The Mylogenetic Cycles of Regional Maturation of the Brain," in A. Minkowski (ed.), *Regional Development of the Brain in Early Life*. Oxford: Blackwell, 1967.

Yalisove, D. "The Effect of Riddle Structure on Children's Comprehension of Riddles," *Developmental Psychology*, 14 (1978), 173–180.

Yang, R. K., and H. A. Moss. "Neonatal Precursors of Infant Behavior," *Developmental Psychology*, 14 (1978), 607–613.

Yarrow, M. R., P. M. Scott, and C. Z. Waxler. "Learning Concern for Others," *Development Psychology*, 8 (1973), 240–260.

Yates, B. T., and W. Mischel. "Young Children's Preferred Attentional Strategies for Delaying Gratification," *Journal of Personality and Social Psychology*, 37 (1979), 286–300.

Yendovitskaya, T. V. "Development of Memory," in A. V. Zaporozhets and D. Elkonin (eds.), *The Psychology of Preschool Children*. Cambridge, Mass.: MIT Press, 1971.

Yonas, A., C. Oberg, and A. Norcia. "Development of Sensitivity to Binocular Information for the Approach of an Object," *Developmental Psychology*, 14 (1978), 147–152.

————, and H. L. Pick, Jr. "An Approach to the Study of Infant Space Perception," in L. B. Cohen and P. Salapatek (eds.), *Infant Perception: From Sensation to Cognition*. Vol. 2: *Perception of Space, Speech, and Sound*. New York: Academic Press, 1975, pp. 3–31.

Young, L. *Wednesday's Children: A Study of Child Neglect and Abuse*. New York: McGraw-Hill, 1964.

Zaporozhets, A. V. "The Development of Perception in the Preschool Child," in P. H. Mussen (ed.), "European Research in Cognitive Development," *Monographs of the Society for Research in Child Development*, 30 (1965), 82–101.

Zelazo, N. A., P. R. Zelazo, and S. Kolb. "Walking in the Newborn," *Science*, 176 (1972), 314–315.

Zeskind, P. S., and B. M. Lester. "Acoustic Features and Auditory Perceptions of the Cries of Newborns With Prenatal and Perinatal Complications," *Child Development*, 49 (1978), 580–589.

Zucker, K. J., R. W. Doering, S. J. Bradley, and J. K. Finegan. "Sex-Typed Play in Gender-Disturbed Children and Their Siblings." Paper presented at the Annual Meeting of the American Psychological Association. New York, September 1979.

Glossary

accommodation. In Piaget's theory, the modification of schemes to incorporate new knowledge that did not fit them. In terms of visual perception, the change in the lens of the eye to keep an image in sharp focus.

achievement motivation. The need to accomplish something of value, to overcome obstacles, or to meet standards of excellence.

acuity. The ability to see objects clearly and to resolve detail.

adaptation. A key principle in ethological theories, referring to the way that behavior changes or develops to meet environmental demands and to ensure survival and reproduction.

affiliative behavioral system. According to Bowlby, a behavioral system that encourages babies to interact with people outside the immediate family, promoting social development.

afterbirth. The placenta, its membranes, and the remainder of the umbilical cord, delivered in the final stage of labor.

aggressiveness. Verbal or physical behavior that is inappropriate or that harms someone.

alleles. The alternative forms of a gene found at a given site on a chromosome.

altruism. An unselfish concern for the welfare of others.

amniocentesis. A way to detect fetal abnormalities by drawing out a sample of amniotic fluid and performing chromosomal analyses.

amnion. The inner membrane of the sac that surrounds and protects the developing fertilized ovum.

anal stage. The second of Freud's stages of psychosexual development, covering the second and third years of life. During this period, a child's primary sensual pleasure is in expelling and retaining feces.

androgens. Male hormones.

androgyny. A development characterized by a self-concept that incorporates characteristics considered typical of both sexes.

animism. The belief that inanimate objects have thoughts, feelings, and life.

Apgar score. A common scoring system, developed in 1962 by Apgar and James; it assesses the newborn's physiological condition, rating color, heart rate, reflex irritability, activity, muscle tone, and respiratory effort.

aphasia. A speech disorder due to brain injury. Aphasia takes many forms; the most common are Broca's aphasia and Wernicke's aphasia, named to indicate the site of the brain damage.

artificialism. A kind of precausal thinking that refers to explanations involving either God or man as the artisan of all natural things.

assertiveness. Verbal or physical behavior that is appropriate and that injures no one.

assimilation. In Piaget's theory, the incorporating of new knowledge into existing schemes.

association areas. Regions in the human cortex that have neither motor nor sensory function and no direct connections outside the cortex.

asynchrony. The maturation of different body parts at different rates, a growth characteristic typical of adolescence.

attachment. The primary social bond that develops between infant and caregiver.

attachment behavioral system. According to Bowlby, a behavioral system of infancy. It develops in three stages: indiscriminate social responsiveness, discriminate social responsiveness, and specific attachments.

authoritarian. A disciplinary style of child rearing in which unquestioning obedience, respect for authority, work, and the preservation of order are paramount.

authoritative. A disciplinary style of child rearing in which parents exert firm control, but use reason as well as power to achieve it.

autonomy. A feeling of self-control and self-determination; also called executive independence.

babbling. Sound sequences of alternating vowels and consonants, such as "bababababa," which the infant produces and which may be a form of motor practice that facilitates language development.

baby talk. The simplified speech adults typically use with infants who are acquiring language.

basal metabolism. The rate of energy required to maintain body functions while resting.

behavior. An observable act that can be described or measured reliably. Many psychologists include everything an individual experiences (dreams, thoughts, sensations) in the category of behavior, although these experiences can be measured only indirectly, for example, by recording brain waves or eye movements.

binocular disparity. The separate images seen by the left and right eye that fuse to form a single three-dimensional image.

body ideal. The body type defined by a culture as ideally attractive and sex-appropriate.

canalization. The temporary deviation from and subsequent return to a child's normal growth curve.

catch-up growth. A period of rapid growth found in most children after a condition that has been retarding growth has been eliminated.

central nervous system. The brain and the spinal cord.

cephalocaudal development. The progression of physical and motor growth from head to foot. For example, a baby's head develops and grows before the torso, arms, and legs.

cerebral dominance. The greater proficiency of one hemisphere of the brain over the other in the control of body movements, as in handedness.

cervix. The pinhead-sized opening that separates the vagina from the uterus.

chorion. The outer membrane of the sac that surrounds and protects the developing fertilized ovum.

chromosomes. Beadlike strings of genes present in every cell of the body. Except in the gametes, they occur in pairs that reproduce and split during cell formation.

chronological approach. Studying all aspects of growth simultaneously, proceeding from infancy and progressing through adulthood.

circular reaction. Any behavior the baby tends to repeat because of the stimulation it provides. There are three levels of circular reactions (primary, secondary, tertiary), each more sophisticated than the last.

classical conditioning. The association of one stimulus with another, so that the first evokes the response that normally follows the second stimulus. It is a simple form of learning, sometimes called respondent conditioning.

class inclusion. The knowledge that a superordinate class (fruit) is always larger than any of its subordinate classes (apples).

clinical study. A study consisting of in-depth interviews and observations, sometimes supplemented by questionnaires and tests.

closure. In Gestalt psychology, the innate perceptual tendency to supply any broken or missing lines in a figure.

co-dominant genes. Genes that are not recessive but that require the existence of another like themselves before a trait can be expressed.

cognition. All intellectual processes, including sensing, perceiving, remembering, using symbols, thinking, and imagining.

cognitive theorists. Theorists who describe intellectual development, and who see the thought of children as being different from adult thought but no less effective.

cohort. The members of a certain age group; a group of people of the same age.

common fate. In Gestalt psychology, the innate perceptual tendency to see objects that move or change together as a unit.

componential analysis. An approach to intelligence that analyzes both the mental steps required to solve a problem and the higher-order processes that are used to decide how to solve the problem.

concept. A symbol with many examples. "Jennifer" is a symbol, but "girl" is a concept.

concrete operational stage. The third stage in Piaget's theory; it begins when children are about age six or seven and lasts until around age eleven. In this stage, thought is logical, but only in regard to concrete objects and situations.

conditioned reflex. A response to a formerly neutral stimulus that has been transformed by association with an unconditioned stimulus so that the formerly neutral stimulus evokes the same response as the unconditioned stimulus.

conditioning. A form of learning in which a person comes to respond in a specific manner to a specific object, action, or situation.

conservation. The understanding that irrelevant changes in the physical appearance of objects do not affect their quantity, mass, weight, or volume. Conservation is one of Piaget's concrete operations.

constructionism. The view that the world cannot be known objectively but is actively constructed by the perceiver.

constructionist. Piaget's term that describes the child's understanding of reality. By acting on objects, the child discovers the effects of his or her actions and the properties of the objects; this knowledge leads to a construction of an understanding of the world.

continuity. In Gestalt psychology, the innate tendency to expect the next element in a group (such as dots forming a curve) to follow the line taken by the rest.

control. The intentional modification of any condition of a study, including the selection of subjects, the experiences they have in the study, and the responses they can give to that experience.

conventional level. The level of moral reasoning in which value is placed in maintaining the social order and the expectations of others.

convergence. The mechanism by which the slightly different objects seen by each eye come together to form a single image.

corpus callosum. A wide band of myelinated fibers that connects the two halves of the brain, ensuring the exchange of information.

correlation. A numerical expression of how closely two sets of measurements correspond. Correlations range from $+1.00$ (perfect positive correlation) to -1.00 (perfect negative correlation).

cortex. A mantle of neural cells that covers the brain and comprises 99 percent of the cerebral hemispheres. The cortex is the seat of language, attention, memory, spatial under-standing, and motor skills.

cross-sectional study. A study that compares the performance of different age groups.

decoding. Retrieving information from memory.

deictic words. Words whose meaning changes because they locate things in reference to the speaker. Among common deictic words are "I" and "you," "this" and "that," "right" and "left."

deoxyribonucleic acid (DNA). The complex chemical containing the genetic code that guides development.

dependence. Reliance on others for comfort, nurturance, or assistance in accomplishing a task. In executive dependence, the parent acts as an executive arm, instrumental to the baby's needs.

dependent variable. A factor that changes as the result of the introduction of an inde-pendent variable.

dialectical psychology. An approach that sees human development as proceeding in a dia-lectic between the individual and society, with each new interaction leading to a higher level of functioning.

dichotic listening technique. A method of re-search in which two stimuli are presented at the same time, one to each ear.

differentiation. The developmental trend in which an infant's abilities become increasingly distinct and specific.

discrimination learning. A type of study in which a person sees two stimuli, chooses between them, and is rewarded for a correct choice. Discrimination studies are used to discover how people learn and whether they form hypotheses to guide their choices.

displacement. The ability to communicate in-formation about objects in another place or another time; one of language's three formal properties.

dominant gene. The gene whose correspond-ing trait appears in an individual when the gene is paired with a different gene for the same trait.

Down's syndrome. A condition that results when an extra Chromosome 21 is present in the fertilized egg; or when extra material from Chromosome 21 becomes attached to another chromosome. Formerly called mon-golism, it produces various physical abnor-malities and mental retardation in the afflicted child.

ecological approach. A view of human devel-opment that sees the growing individual as influenced not only by genes and the imme-diate physical and social settings, but also by the relationships among the settings and by the influence of the entire society.

ectoderm. The layer of cells in the embryo from which the skin, sense organs, and ner-vous system will develop.

ego. The conscious self, which in Freudian theory guides behavior and mediates the per-petual conflict between id and superego.

egocentric. Among babies, the inability to dis-tinguish between the self and the external world; among older infants and young chil-dren, the belief that everyone sees the world and responds to it exactly as the child does.

embryo. The individual from the second to the eighth week of development within the uterus.

embryonic period. The six weeks after the ger-minal period; during this period the organism begins to take shape, and organ systems begin to form.

empathy. The vicarious identification with an-other's emotions.

enactive representation. Motor responses that serve as models for information in memory. They are the only form of representation during most of the first year of life.

encoding. Putting information into memory.

endoderm. The layer of cells in the embryo from which the visceral organs and digestive tract develop.

environment. The physical and social surround-ings of any organism or part of an organism;

this includes the prenatal environment of the individual before birth and the internal environment of cells within the body.

equilibration. Piaget's developmental principle stating that the organism always tends toward biological and psychological balance, and that development consists of progressive approximations to an ideal state of balance between assimilation and accommodation that is never fully achieved.

erythroblastosis. An abnormal condition that can develop in an Rh-positive fetus if substances from the mother's Rh-negative blood cross the placenta.

estrogens. Female hormones.

ethology. The scientific study of animal behavior in evolutionary terms.

evoked potential. A characteristic electrical response in the brain that is evoked by a new stimulus, such as a sight or a sound.

experiment. A type of study designed to control the arrangement and manipulation of conditions in order to systematically observe particular phenomena.

exploratory behavioral system. According to Bowlby, a behavioral system that allows the child to explore the surrounding world; this promotes competency.

extinction. The elimination of a response that is not reinforced.

factor analysis. A system of analyzing experimental results by correlating scores on a variety of tests, in the belief that strong correlations among scores indicates a common factor.

Fallopian tube. The passage leading from an ovary to the uterus.

fear of success. The purported tendency of women to withdraw from competition with men or to avoid it because of social reprisal.

fear-wariness system. According to Bowlby, a behavioral system that helps a baby avoid potentially dangerous situations; often called wariness of strangers.

fetus. The developing organism from eight weeks after conception to birth.

field study. A study in which the investigator introduces some factor into a natural setting that changes the setting.

fixated. In Freudian theory, to become stalled emotionally at an immature level of personality development, so that in adulthood the characteristic traits of that immature level dominate behavior.

formal operational stage. The final stage in Piaget's theory; it begins when children are about age eleven, and represents the culmination of cognitive development. Thought is logical and fully abstract and can be applied to hypothetical situations.

frustration-aggression hypothesis. The belief that aggression results when someone or something interferes with the activity toward a goal.

gametes. Mature reproductive cells: the sperm and the egg.

gender constancy. The understanding that gender will never change, that boys always become men and girls always become women.

gender identity. The inner experience of gender; the unchanging sense of self as male or female.

genes. Microscopic particles that are carried by the chromosomes. Genes contain instructions that guide the development of physical traits and behavioral dispositions.

genetic epistemology. Piaget's basic approach to development, focusing on the development of intelligence (genetic = developmental; epistemology = how we know the world).

genetics. The scientific study of the effects of heredity.

genital stage. The final stage in Freud's theory of psychosexual development; it begins at puberty. Primary sensual pleasure transfers to mature sexual relationships with members of the opposite sex.

genotype. The specific combination of alleles

that make up an individual's genetic inheritance.

germinal period. The first two weeks after conception; during this period the fertilized ovum is primarily engaged in cell division.

gestation period. The period of prenatal development, calculated from fertilization (thirty-eight weeks) or from the date of last menstruation (forty weeks).

gestational age. The age of the fetus calculated from the date of conception.

glial cells. Supporting and connecting cells in the brain that play an essential role in the nourishment of neurons.

gonococcus. The bacterium that produces gonorrhea.

gonorrhea. A venereal disease.

grammar. The structural principles of a language made up of phonology and syntax.

grasping reflex. A reflex that is strong during the first month of life; it consists of the baby's tendency to clutch any small object placed in his or her hand.

guilt. A negative feeling that arises when a person deviates from his or her own internalized moral standards.

habituation. Reduced response to a stimulus after repeated or continuous encounters with it; analogous to becoming bored with the stimulus.

hardware. In information-processing terms, the basic storage system of human memory; it consists of such elements as circuits of neurons in the brain.

heritability. An estimate, based upon a sample of individuals, of the relative contribution of genetics to any trait in that group.

herpes simplex. An acute viral infection, often transmitted through intercourse.

heterozygous. The condition in which the alleles at a given chromosome site are different. In such cases, the dominant gene generally determines the appearance of the affected trait.

hierarchic integration. The tendency, in Werner's view, for the child's developing responses and skills to become increasingly organized into hierarchies.

homozygous. The condition in which the alleles at a given chromosome site are identical.

hostile aggression. Aggression aimed at hurting another person. (See instrumental aggression.)

iconic representation. Visual images that serve as models for information in memory. They begin to develop toward the end of the first year of life.

id. That aspect of the personality that, in Freudian theory, contains all the unconscious impulses or drives.

identification. A developmental process through which a child tries to resemble specific people whom the child respects, admires, or loves.

identity. In Piaget's theory, the understanding that objects and people remain the same even if irrelevant properties are changed. In Erikson's psychosocial theory, a combination of self-esteem and the relation between self-concept and the description of the self by significant others; its achievement is the crucial developmental task of adolescence.

imagery. An encoding strategy in which a person uses visual images to associate two or more things that must be remembered.

imitation. Copying or reproducing observed behavior.

imprinting. The phenomenon occurring during a sensitive period of an animal's infancy; the young animal follows a moving object (generally the mother) and forms a strong, enduring attachment to it.

independent variable. In a study, a factor that is selected or changed in some way by the investigator.

induced abortion. The premature removal of a fetus by deliberate interference.

inflection. A grammatical marker, such as the past tense "-ed," that is added to words to change their meaning.

instrumental aggression. Aggression aimed at retrieving or acquiring an object, territory, or privilege. (See hostile aggression.)

instrumental competence. A combination of independence and social responsibility; instrumentally competent children are self-assertive, friendly with peers, and not intrusive with adults.

instrumental conditioning. (See operant conditioning.)

instrumental dependence. Dependence that involves seeking assistance as a means of accomplishing some task.

Klinefelter's syndrome. A condition resulting from the presence in boys of an extra female sex chromosome (XXY). The boys are sterile, have rounded bodies, and may be somewhat retarded.

kwashiorkor. A severe, often fatal disease caused by prolonged protein deficiency.

labor. The birth process. It begins with the first contractions of the uterus, and does not end until both the infant and the placenta have been delivered.

lanugo. Fine hair appearing on some newborns' bodies; it disappears within a few weeks.

latency period. In Freudian theory, the fourth period of psychosexual development; it lasts from about age six until puberty. Libidinal pleasures become less important, and children discover moral and esthetic interests.

lateralization. The establishment of functions in one hemisphere of the brain, such as the establishment of language in the left hemisphere of most right-handed people.

learned helplessness. A condition in which repeated failure in situations over which a person has no control leads to a refusal to try.

levels-of-processing view. An approach to memory that rejects the idea of structures (sensory register, short-term store, long-term store) and maintains that information is processed at increasingly deeper levels of analysis, with retention depending upon the depth of the analysis.

libido. The life force, including all mental energy.

locus of control. The perceived location of control over an individual's life. If the locus is internal, individuals believe they control their own lives; if the locus is external, individuals believe their lives are controlled by forces outside themselves.

longitudinal study. A study that follows the same subjects over time, comparing their performance at different ages.

long-term store. Permanent memory; where information is held indefinitely.

maternal deprivation. The loss or lack of mothering.

meiosis. The form of cell division followed by gametes, in which four daughter cells, each containing twenty-three single chromosomes, are produced.

menarche. The first incidence of menstruation.

menstrual age. The age of the fetus when calculated from the beginning of the mother's last menstrual period.

menstrual cycle. The discharge of blood and tissue from the uterus; it occurs monthly from puberty to menopause, except during pregnancy and lactation.

mesoderm. The layer of cells in the embryo from which the muscular, circulatory, and skeletal systems will develop.

metamemory. An understanding of the workings of the memory system.

minimal brain damage (MBD). A term applied to hyperactive children when it was thought the condition was the result of structural damage to the central nervous system.

miscarriage. A spontaneous abortion; the expulsion from the uterus of a fetus less than twenty-eight weeks old.

mitosis. The form of cell division followed by all body cells except gametes, in which two daughter cells, each with forty-six chromosomes (twenty-three pairs), are produced.

modeling. Learning by observing the behavior of others.

Moro reflex. A reflex present during the first three months of life; it consists of the baby's tendency to thrust out the arms and curl the the hands when support for the neck and head is removed.

motion parallax. The changing separation between images of objects located at different distances from the eye.

myelin. A fatty substance that keeps nerve impulses channeled along neural fibers and reduces the random spread of impulses from one fiber to another.

näive realism. The view that our perceptions are true copies of the world, which exists independently of the perceiver.

naturalistic observation. A form of study in which behavior is observed in natural settings with no interference from the investigator.

nature. The genetic-biological determinants used to explain developmental change.

negative reinforcer. Anything that, when removed, makes it more likely that the response that removed it will be repeated, such as pressing a lever to end electric shock.

neonate. A baby during the first month of independent life.

neurometrics. Mental testing with computers. Evoked potentials and brain waves are analyzed by computers in order to assess cognitive functioning and to identify specific disorders.

neuron. One of the neural cells in the central nervous system.

neurotransmitter. One of the thirty or more chemicals that act as messengers in the brain. Neurotransmitters can cause neurons to fire or keep them from firing. Among the neurotransmitters are norepinephrine, serotonin, and dopamine.

nonconformist. A disciplinary style of child rearing in which parents tend to be permissive but may demand high performance in some areas.

non-REM sleep. Sleep during which there is no movement of the eyes, when respiration is slowed, and brain waves show an uneven pattern; also called quiet sleep.

norm. A pattern of growth or achievement that describes the way in which important attributes and skills develop and the approximate ages at which they appear.

nurture. The environmental determinants used to explain developmental changes.

object concept. The understanding that objects remain the same although they may move from one place to another (object identity) and that they continue to exist when out of sight (object permanence).

operant conditioning. A form of learning in which a response is strengthened or changed as a result of rewards or punishments (the consequences of the response); sometimes called instrumental conditioning.

operations. Flexible and rigorous cognitive processes that first appear during the concrete operational stage.

operative representation. A stored representation in memory that changes as the result of mental operations.

oral stage. The earliest stage in psychosexual development, according to Freud. It consists of the first year of life when the lips and mouth are the focus of sensual pleasure.

organization. An encoding strategy in which a person groups items to be remembered around a common element.

orthogenetic principle. The major theme of Werner's developmental theory; it holds that the child moves from a global, undifferentiated state to one of high differentiation and integration.

ovaries. The female reproductive glands, which release ova.

overextension. A generalization in the child's meaning for a word so that it includes a number of dissimilar objects or events.

overregularization. A temporary error in language acquisition in which the child makes the language more regular than it actually is. In English, a common form of overregularization appears in the past tense of verbs ("breaked") or in the plural form of nouns ("foots").

ovum. The female reproductive cell; this egg cell is the largest cell in the human body.

oxytocin. A hormone produced by the pituitary glands of both mother and fetus, stimulating labor.

perception. An important cognitive process involving the transformation of sensations into information.

permissive. A disciplinary style of child rearing in which parents are nonpunitive, accepting, and affirmative. It allows children to regulate their own activities and encourages them to develop their own standards.

perspective. The effect that makes a two-dimensional drawing appear to have depth.

perspectivism. A sense of the self as separate from the world and the realization that one's perceptions, feelings, and reactions are not identical with those of others.

phallic stage. The third, highly critical stage in Freud's theory of psychosexual development; it spans the years from three to six. During this period the genitals are the focus of sensual pleasure.

phenotype. Physical or behavioral traits as they appear in the individual, reflecting the influence of both genetic and environmental factors.

phenylketonuria (PKU). An inherited inability to metabolize phenylalanine, a component of some foods.

phonemes. The basic sound elements of a language.

phonology. The study of the production and comprehension of speech sounds.

placenta. A pliable structure of tissue and blood vessels that transmits nourishment and waste between mother and fetus.

placing response. A reflex present during the first few months of life. It consists of the in-fant's lifting up the foot and placing it on top of a surface.

polygenic. Indicates that several genes have an equal and cumulative effect in producing a trait.

positive reinforcer. Any consequence, whether tangible (such as money) or intangible (such as praise), that follows a response and makes it more likely that the response will be repeated.

pragmatics. The study of a language's social purposes.

precausal thinking. A type of thinking found in young children who do not believe in accidents and who do believe that inanimate objects have thoughts and feelings.

premature delivery. The spontaneous termination of a pregnancy when the fetus is older than twenty weeks but younger than thirty-eight weeks.

premoral level. The level of moral reasoning in which value is placed on physical acts and needs, not on persons or social standards.

preoperational stage. The second stage in Piaget's theory; it covers the preschool period and may extend until children are age seven. Although children record experiences symbolically and use language, their thought is intuitive—not logical.

principled level. The level of moral reasoning in which value resides in self-chosen principles and standards that have a universal logical validity and can therefore be shared.

probability. A numerical expression that indicates the likelihood that experimental findings are simply the result of chance.

production deficiency. The failure to use a skill or capacity that a person possesses.

productivity. The ability to combine a finite number of words into an infinite number of sentences; one of language's three formal properties.

prosocial behavior. Action intended to benefit another person; it is taken without the anticipation of external reward and often at some risk to the actor.

proximal development. Vygotsky's term for the area in which children, with the help of adults or more capable peers, can solve problems they are unable to handle by themselves.

proximity. In Gestalt psychology, the innate perceptual tendency to see as a group elements that are physically close together.

proximodistal development. The progression of physical and motor growth from the center of the body to the periphery. For example, a baby learns to control shoulder movements before arm or finger movements.

psychoanalysis. A type of psychotherapy devised by Sigmund Freud; it attempts to give a patient insights into his or her unconscious conflicts.

psychodynamic theories. Theories of human personality that view behavior as resulting from the interplay of active mental and biological forces with the environment.

psychometrics. Mental testing; the branch of psychology that has developed intelligence tests.

psychosexual theory. A psychodynamic theory of personality development proposed by Freud; it focuses on the changing seat of libidinal pleasures in the individual.

psychosocial theory. A psychodynamic theory of personality development proposed by Erikson; it focuses on the individual's interactions with society.

puberty. The attainment of biological sexual maturity.

punishment. Any consequence, whether physical pain, harsh words, isolation, or withdrawal of affection, that makes it less likely that a response will be repeated.

reaction range. The range of possible responses within which a genetic trait can express itself.

reaction time. The interval of time between the instant a stimulus is presented and the individual's reaction to it.

recall. The most complex form of memory, in which information is remembered in its absence.

recessive gene. The subordinate member of a pair of genes, whose corresponding trait fails to appear in an individual who carries the gene.

recognition. The simplest form of memory, in which an object is perceived as something that has been perceived in the past.

reconstruction. An intermediate form of memory, in which a person constructs a three-dimensional reproduction of an object previously seen.

reflex. An unlearned or naturally occurring reaction to a stimulus.

rehearsal. An encoding strategy in which a person repeats information that is to be remembered.

reinforcement. The presentation or withdrawal of an event following a response; it increases the likelihood of that response occurring again.

reinforcement theory. The view that behavior can be explained by the consequences of an organism's actions; that is, by reinforcement and punishment.

reinforcer. Anything that makes the repetition of a response more likely.

releasing stimuli. Events that regularly evoke certain behavior in all members of a species and help to explain regularities in typical behavior.

reliability. The dependability and consistency of a measure, observation, or finding.

REM sleep. Sleep that is accompanied by rapid eye movements (REM), rapid respiration, diminished muscular activity, and a more even pattern of brain waves; also called active sleep.

replication. The repetition of an investigation's essential features and its findings.

representation. A model that represents information in memory so that it can be retrieved.

respiratory distress syndrome. A lung condition (formerly called hyaline membrane disease) in which the premature infant cannot maintain necessary surfactin levels.

respondent conditioning. (See classical conditioning.)

response. Any reaction to a stimulus — whether word, deed, or bodily change — such as glandular secretion, brain wave, and variation in heart rate, blood pressure, or the electrical resistance of the skin.

retrieval. Removing information from long-term store to short-term store where it can be used; also called decoding.

reversibility. The understanding that irrelevant changes in appearance can be reversed and that such changes tend to compensate one another; reversibility is one of Piaget's concrete operations.

rickets. A condition caused by calcium deficiency during infancy and childhood; characterized by softening and malformation of the bones.

role-taking. The ability to assume the role or point of view of another person.

rooting reflex. A reflex present during the first two or three months of life; it consists of the tendency to turn the head and mouth in the direction of any object that gently stimulates the mouth.

sample. Individuals selected for study in any investigation; a good sample accurately reflects the nature of the larger group from which it is drawn.

schedules of reinforcement. Timetables for reinforcing behavior, based either on intervals of time or on the number of responses.

schemes. Piaget's term for patterns of action (banging, sucking) or mental structures (classification of objects) that are involved in the acquisition and structuring of knowledge. In infants, schemes are like concepts without words.

secondary sex characteristics. Genetically based characteristics — such as breast development, facial hair, and voice quality — that accompany puberty; these characteristics differentiate the genders but have no direct reproductive function.

self-concept. The sum of ideas each person has about him- or herself.

self-demand feeding. A feeding schedule in which babies are fed whenever they are hungry instead of when an imposed schedule calls for meals.

self-esteem. The way a person evaluates him- or herself.

self-regulation. The regulation of one's own conduct.

semanticity. The ability to transmit meaning; one of language's three formal properties.

semantics. The study of meaning in language.

sensation. The reception through the sense organs of stimulation from the external world.

sensitive period. A period of development during which an organism is most likely to be susceptible to a particular influence.

sensitivity. An empathic understanding of a child's needs, so that babies' signals are interpreted and responded to effectively and older children are encouraged to be autonomous.

sensorimotor stage. The first major stage in Piaget's theory; it lasts through most of the first two years of life. During this stage knowledge derives from the infant's sensations (sensori) and physical actions (motor).

sensory register. The first form of storage in the memory system, which holds a fleeting record of all stimuli received by the sense organs.

separation distress. A baby's negative reaction to being parted from an attachment figure.

seriation. The ordering of objects by size or weight.

sex role. The socially prescribed pattern of behavior and attitudes considered characteristic of each gender.

sex-role stereotype. A simplified, fixed concept concerning the behavior and traits typical of each gender.

shame. A negative feeling that results from the disapproval of others.

short-term store. Temporary, working memory; holds active information in a person's awareness.

sickle-cell anemia. A hereditary condition caused by co-dominant alleles, in which red blood cells sickle at high altitudes, sometimes leading to severe anemia or even death.

similarity. In Gestalt psychology, the innate perceptual tendency to see as a group elements that are generally alike in form.

sleep apnea. A temporary halt in breathing during sleep.

social-contract family. A family in which the parents cohabit but are not married.

socialization. The process by which an individual acquires the behavior, attitudes, values, and roles expected from its members by a society.

social-learning theory. A view of development in which behavioral change results from conditioning, observation, and imitation. Cognitive social-learning theorists believe that cognition also plays an important role, since a person's interpretation of the stimulus—not the stimulus itself—regulates behavior.

sociometric analysis. A method for charting how often a child is chosen by peers as a friend or preferred companion.

software. In information-processing terms, the programs—or methods—used to code, analyze, and retrieve information and to make decisions.

sonogram. A picture produced by bouncing soundwaves off an object. Sonograms are used to detect the presence of twins, fetal abnormalities, and other visible complications of pregnancy.

spermatozoon. The male reproductive cell; a sperm.

stage. A concept used to explain the orderly relationship among developmental changes in behavior and to indicate that the organization of behavior is qualitatively different from one stage to the next.

stepping response. A reflex present during the first few months of life; it consists of the baby's tendency to straighten out the legs at knee and hip as if to stand when the infant is held with feet touching a surface.

stimulus. Anything within the body or in the world outside that evokes a response.

strabismus. Lack of coordination between the muscles of the eyeballs so that the two eyes fail to focus on exactly the same point.

sublimation. Handling the conflict between social demands and instincts by altering behavior in socially acceptable ways.

successive approximations. Behavior that resembles more and more closely a desired response.

sudden infant death syndrome (SIDS). An affliction, commonly called crib death, in which apparently healthy infants between two and four months old suddenly die in their sleep.

superego. The conscience, in Freudian theory. It develops in early childhood as a child internalizes parental values and standards.

surfactin. A liquid that coats the air sacs of the lung, enabling infants to transmit oxygen from the air to the blood.

symbolic play. Play involving imagination and pretense, in which objects or people stand for something they are not.

symbolic representation. Words and symbols that serve as models for information in memory; the last and most sophisticated form of representation to develop.

synapse. The space between neurons in the central nervous system, across which electrical and chemical signals pass.

syntax. The structural principles that determine the form of sentences. (See grammar.)

Tay-Sachs disease. A hereditary condition caused by recessive alleles, in which the lack of an enzyme renders the individual unable to metabolize certain fatty substances. It results in blindness, paralysis, and death within seven years.

teratogen. Any influence that can disrupt fetal growth or cause malformation in the developing organism.

term. The gestational age of 266 days from conception. Babies born before term were once considered premature.

testes. The male reproductive glands, which release sperm.

theory. A set of logically related statements that explain the nature of related phenomena.

topical approach. Studying the processes of growth and development separately, exploring each single process from birth to adulthood.

totalism. An organization of self-concept that has rigid, absolute, and arbitrary boundaries.

transfer. A process in which learning one task results in improvement of performance on a related, but different task.

transitivity. The making of logical inferences based on separate observations; it requires the joining of two or more abstract relations.

transsexual. A person whose gender identity does not correspond with his or her anatomical gender.

trimester. A period of approximately three months, often used when discussing pregnancy.

Turner's syndrome. A condition resulting from the absence in girls of one female sex chromosome (XO). The girls are generally short, lack secondary sex characteristics, and have mild to moderate mental retardation.

umbilical cord. The flexible cord, containing two arteries and one vein, that connects the developing organism to the placenta.

unconditioned reflex. A response to a stimulus that occurs naturally, without any learning.

unconscious impulses. In Freud's theory, the irrational urges that reside in the id and that the individual lacks any awareness of.

underextension. A temporary period in which the child's meaning for a word fails to include the entire meaning adults attribute to it, as when a child fails to include "lollipops" in the meaning of "food."

variable. A factor that can vary in size or strength and that may or may not affect the result of a study.

vernix. The white greasy material that lubricates the fetus for passage through the birth canal.

visual accommodation. The ability to alternate focus for objects at different distances.

vital capacity. The capacity of the lungs to hold air.

wariness of strangers. (See fear-wariness system.)

Name Index

Beck, E. C., 160
Becker, Jacqueline, 396
Beckwith, J. B., 142
Beit-Hallahmi, B., 356
Bell, Coleen, 72
Bell, Richard, 456
Bell, Silvia, 349, 353
Bellugi-Klima, Ursula, 184, 194, 222
Belmont, L., 61
Belsky, Jay, 19, 336, 358, 376, 378
Bem, Sandra, 445–446
Bentler, P. M., 429
Bereiter, C., 198
Berendes, H. W., 333
Berg-Cross, L. G., 462
Berg, K. M., 109
Bergman, T., 258
Bergson, Henri, 42
Berg, W. K., 109
Berkeley Growth Study, 323
Berko, Jean, 224
Bernal, Judith, 126
Berndt, Thomas, 410, 494
Bernholtz, Nancy, 220
Bernstein, Basil, 198
Bertenthal, Bennett, 484
Berzonsky, Michael, 309
Bever, Thomas, 225
Bierman, J. M., 334
Big Blue Marble, 474
Bijou, Sidney, 25, 27, 205, 351
Biller, Henry, 379
Binet, Alfred, 42, 315–316, 319
Bingham, M. T., 330
Bionic Woman, 439
Birch, Herbet, 122, 374
Birns, B., 334–335
Birren, James, 12
Blaney, N. T., 403
Blank, Marion, 254, 294
Blau, Z. S., 382
Blizzard, R. M., 144
Block, Jeanne, 432, 467
Bloom, K., 221, 397
Blurton-Jones, Nicholas, 398
Boden, Margaret, 319
Bogatz, Gerry Ann, 336
Boismier, J. D., 109
Bond, E. A., 326

Bonney, M. E., 412
Botvin, Gilbert, 295
Bowen, Robert, 486
Bowerman, Melissa, 215–216
Bower, Thomas, 240, 243, 288
Bowes, W. A., 99
Bowlby, John, 34, 39, 344, 350–351, 358
Boy Scouts, 389
Boysen, S., 185
Brackbill, Yvonne, 99, 121–122
Bradley, R. H., 334
Brady Bunch, The, 474
Braine, Martin, 221
Brainerd, Charles, 292, 294, 296
Brandt, Melda, 493
Brasel, J. A., 144
Brazelton, T. B., 90
Bremner, J. G., 291–292
Bricker, William, 399
Bridger, W. H., 114, 254
Brill, R. G., 241
Bromley, D. B., 484–485, 488
Bronfenbrenner, Urie, 64, 359, 412
Bronson, Susan, 352, 386
Bronstein, I. P., 141
Brooks, J., 360, 484
Brooks, V., 250
Brown, Craig, 194, 346–347
Brown, Roger, 182–183, 194, 198, 222, 277
Brown University, 143
Brozoski, Thomas, 159
Bruch, H., 141
Brück, K., 107
Bruner, Jerome, 40, 50, 186–187, 192–194, 207, 216, 264–265, 274, 290, 300, 376, 398
Bruno, L. A., 119
Bryan, James, 470–471
Bryant, Peter, 244, 253, 291–292, 296
Bull, D., 234
Bullock, Merry, 157, 309
Bunker, Archie, 466
Burgess, R. L., 182, 390
Burke, Patrick, 143
Burton, Roger, 453
Bushnell, N., 466
Bussey, Kay, 436

Butler, N., 98, 333
Butterfield, Earl, 207
Butterworth, G., 291
Byrne, D., 407

Caldwell, Bettye, 334, 337
Callard, E., 433
Campbell, Frances, 19
Campbell, J. D., 402
Campos, J. J., 167, 241, 349
Cane, Valerie, 457, 459
Cannizzo, S. R., 278
Cantor, Joan, 288
Carey, Susan, 215, 219, 295
Carlsmith, L., 379
Caron, Albert, 243
Carpenter, Jan, 66, 72
Carroll, John, 320
Carter, G. L., 166, 205
Cattell, Raymond, 135, 317
Cavanaugh, J. C., 282
Cazden, Courtney, 194, 222
Cermak, L. S., 271
Chabon, I., 92
Chall, J. S., 17
Chananie, J. D., 478
Chandler, Michael, 468
Chaplin, J. P., 316
Charcot, Jean Martin, 33
Charles, D. C., 10–12
Charlesworth, Rosalind, 397, 405
Charlesworth, William, 318
Charlie's Angels, 439
Chernoff, G., 98
Chess, S., 122, 374
Child, Irvin, 382, 424, 455
Chi, Michelene, 495
Chinsky, Jack, 277
Chomsky, C., 226
Chomsky, N., 183, 204, 207
Churchill, J. A., 333
Cicchetti, D., 360
Cicirelli, V. G., 375
Cioffi, Joseph, 169
Clarke-Stewart, Alison, 352
Clark, Eve, 213–214, 222
Clark, H. H., 213
Clyburn, Andrea, 473
Coates, Brian, 188–189, 401

Subject Index

altruism (*continued*)
    generosity as, 471–472
    giving aid as, 471, 474
ambivalent attachment bonds, 351,
    353–354, 363
American dialectical psychology,
    49–50
American Indians, 35, 142, 145
amino acids, 159
amniocentesis, 97, 100–101, 103
amniotic fluid, 100
amphetamines, 176
analogies, 320–321
anal stage, 32–33
androgens, 149
    fetal exposure to, 429–431
androgyny, 444–447
anemia, 143
animal studies:
    of attachment, 345–348
    of brain functions, 160, 171–172
    of early deprivation effects, 358,
        364
    experimental, 71–72
    genetic, 54–56, 75
    of intelligence, 313–315
    of language and communication,
        184–185
    of malnutrition effects, 140
    of peer contact, 393–396, 398,
        420
    of sensitive periods, 364
animism, 308, 311
anthropology, 15–16, 35, 92
antisocial behavior, 474–481
Apgar scores, 90, 98, 143
aphasias, 162, 172
appearance:
    abuse and, 388
    peer relationships and, 403
    socialization and, 370
apprenticeship, 6–8
aspirin, 98
assimilation, 42–46, 51
    social cognition and, 498–499
association areas, cortical, 156, 158
asynchrony, 150–151
attachment, 50
    day care experience and, 376
    differences in, 353–354

Down's syndrome and, 346–347
to fathers, 354–357
function of, 349–350
to multiple caregivers, 354–359
parental sensitivity and, 373
personality and, 362–364
separation distress and, 350–351,
    367
in single-mother households, 385
social skill development and,
    359–362, 394
sociocultural influences on, 359
specific, 348–349
stages of, 344–349
theories of, 350–351
wariness of strangers and, 349,
    351–353, 367
attention, 325
    auditory, 117–119, 127
    development of, 258–264
    selective, 259–264, 277, 283
    visual, 116–117, 127
attentional inertia, 261
attractiveness, 405–406; *see also* appearance
auditory attention, 117–119, 127
auditory discrimination, 60
authoritative parents, 371–373, 383,
    391, 460
autonomy, 15, 36, 361–362, 367,
    460
    social class and, 380–381

babbling, 208–210
    in deaf children, 240
    as social responsiveness, 344
babysitters, 376
baby talk, 193–194, 207
    by primary and secondary caregivers, 356
barbiturates, 412
basal metabolism, 148–149, 153
behavioral geneticists, 332
behavior-learning theories, 25–30,
    50–51
    aggression as viewed by, 475
    attachment as viewed by, 351
    social cognition as viewed by,
        501

behavior modification, 176
    social skills taught by, 412–414
binocular disparity, 242
biological factors, 6, 11, 15–16, 46
    in aggression, 475, 478, 481
    intelligence and, 317–318, 339
    language acquisition and, 204–
        205, 228
    organismic theories and, 41–47
    prenatal period and, 79
    sex roles and, 429–431
    in sexual maturation, 148–151,
        440–442
    in transsexuality, 428–429
birth, *see* childbirth
birth defects, 7
birthing rooms, 92
birth order:
    height and, 143
    intelligence and, 61
    personality and, 374, 391
Black English, 198–200
blacks:
    sickle cell anemia and, 95
    socialization and, 382–383, 391
    sudden infant death syndrome
        and, 142
blind children, 167, 240–241
body ideal, 440
body proportions, 133, 150–151
body temperature, *see* temperature
bonding:
    adaptation theory of, 39–40
    developmental and birth complications and, 93, 103
    early separation and, 125
    lack of, 144
    prematurity and, 388
    sensitive periods and, 364–367;
        see also attachment
books, 335
    sex-role stereotypes in, 439, 446
boys:
    achievement motivation in, 415–
        416
    aggression in, 477–478
    early school curriculum and, 438
    fear of success in, 416
    teachers' criticisms of, 419–420,
        438

ABOUT THE AUTHORS

ELIZABETH HALL is the co-author of *Developmental Psychology Today* (3rd ed.). Before she turned to college textbooks, she was Editor-in-Chief of *Human Nature*, a magazine about the human sciences. From 1967 to 1976, she was with *Psychology Today*, and was Managing Editor of that magazine at the time she left to start *Human Nature*. As a science writer, Hall has interviewed many prominent psychologists, including Jean Piaget, Bärbel Inhelder, Jerome Bruner, B. F. Skinner, D. O. Hebb, George A. Miller, Bruno Bettelheim, Joseph Adelson, and Bernice Neugarten. She has also written a number of books for children; two of them, *Why Do We Do What We Do: A Look at Psychology* and *From Pigeons to People: A Look at Behavior Shaping*, received Honorable Mention in the American Psychological Foundation's National Media Awards. Hall was graduated with highest honors from California State University, Fresno, in 1962.

MICHAEL E. LAMB is Professor of Psychology, Psychiatry, and Pediatrics at the University of Utah in Salt Lake City. A developmental psychologist by training, his research is concerned with social and emotional development, especially in infancy and early childhood, the determinants and consequences of adaptive and maladaptive parental behavior, and the interface of psychology and biology. Dr. Lamb was, at age twenty-one, one of the youngest persons to complete a Ph.D. at Yale University, and was later, at age twenty-six, one of the youngest academics to become a full professor in an American university. He has written and edited several books, including *The Role of the Father in Child Development*, *Social and Personality Development*, *Social Interaction Analysis*, *Infant Social Cognition*, *Nontraditional Families*, *Sibling Relationships*, and another Random House text, *Development in Infancy*. He has also published widely in all the major psychology journals. In recognition of his contribution to developmental psychology, Dr. Lamb has received two national awards: The Young Psychologist Award (1976) and the Boyd McCandless Young Scientist Award (1978).

MARION PERLMUTTER is an Associate Professor of Child Development at the University of Minnesota's Institute of Child Development. A developmental psychologist, her major research interests concern cognitive development across the life span. Perlmutter has been at the University of Minnesota since receiving her Ph.D. in Developmental Psychology at the University of Massachusetts at Amherst in 1976. Prior to that, she studied at the State University of New York at Albany, where she received a M.S. in Educational Psychology in 1971, and at Syracuse University, where she received a B.A. in Psychology in 1970. She has published numerous articles on memory development in preschool children, and memory aging in adults, and also contributed many chapters to several books. In 1980 she edited *New Directions in Child Development: Children's Memory*, and in 1981 she assumed the editorship of the *Minnesota Symposia on Child Psychology*. Perlmutter recently received the Division of Developmental Psychology of the American Psychological Association's Boyd McCandless Young Scientist Award for Early Contributions to Developmental Psychology.